Mechanics of User Identification and Authentication

Mechanics of User Identification and Authentication

Fundamentals of Identity Management

DOBROMIR TODOROV

Auerbach Publications
Taylor & Francis Group
Boca Raton New York

Auerbach Publications is an imprint of the Taylor & Francis Group, an **informa** business

Auerbach Publications
Taylor & Francis Group
6000 Broken Sound Parkway NW, Suite 300
Boca Raton, FL 33487-2742

Printed in Canada on acid-free paper
10 9 8 7 6 5 4 3 2 1

International Standard Book Number-13: 978-1-4200-5219-0 (Hardcover)

Library of Congress Cataloging-in-Publication Data

Todorov, Dobromir.
Mechanics of user identificatlion and authentication : fundamentals of identity management / Dobromir Todorov.
p. cm.
Includes bibliographical references and index.
ISBN 978-1-4200-5219-0 (alk. paper)
1. Computer networks--Security measures. 2. Computers--Access control. 3. Computer security. I. Title.

TK5105.59T575 2007
005.8--dc22 2007060355

Visit the Taylor & Francis Web site at
http://www.taylorandfrancis.com

and the Auerbach Web site at
http://www.auerbach-publications.com

Disclaimer

The names of all companies, individuals, groups of individuals, computers, domains, sites, etc., in this book are fictitious and are not related to any actual existing companies, individuals or groups of individuals, computers, domains, or sites.

The ideas and opinions expressed in this book, unless explicitly noted, belong to the author and do not necessarily coincide with the ideas, opinions, and approaches taken by the author's employer, affiliate or partner organizations, or third parties.

Although the author and Auerbach Publications have made every possible effort to provide the best information to the readers, and have tried to ensure the correctness of information, they accept no liabilities — expressed or implied — for any damage, loss, missed profits, and other business impact to any business caused by the use or the failure to use information provided in this book.

Trademarks

I invent nothing. I rediscover.

—Auguste Rodin

Contents

Acknowledgments

First and foremost, I want to thank my wife Marina and my kids Andrey and Yana for their love, understanding, and support despite all the time I stole from them while I was working on this book. I love you too, and I owe you a lot!

I want to thank my parents, in-laws, and all my friends who have always supported me in my endeavors. Nothing would have been possible without them.

I would especially like to thank Justin Bannister of INS UK and Marin Marinov of Microsoft Canada for their time and efforts in reviewing the manuscript and providing invaluable input.

I want to thank my teachers at the Technology Education and Training Centre (also known as UKTC) in Pravetz, Bulgaria, who introduced me to the inner workings of Information Technologies many years ago. I have learned only a few new things since then.

The content of this book has been influenced indirectly by all the individuals with whom I have worked, from whom I have learned, and with whom I have discussed technical concepts at IT Consulting & Education (ITCE), Hewlett Packard, INS, Accenture, and Visa Europe — thank you!

Last but not least, I would like to give special thanks to Richard O'Hanley, Ray O'Connell, Andrea Demby, Catherine Giacari, and Jonathan Pennell, and the entire team from Auerbach Publications for their time and effort in making this book a quality product.

To all of you I have somehow forgotten here — thanks!

Dobromir Todorov, M.Sc.

About the Author

Dobromir Todorov has 14 years of professional experience in IT, ranging from systems development in assembly language to systems and infrastructure architecture. He has worked with large customers in the telecommunications, financial, healthcare, manufacturing, and government sectors on projects ranging from Voice-over-IP and call centers to public key infrastructure and SSL termination. Primarily based in the United Kingdom, Dobromir has worked with large enterprises in Europe, the United States, India, the Philippines, and China.

Dobromir received his M.Sc. degree in computer engineering from the Technical University of Sofia, Bulgaria, Faculty of Computer Systems and Management in 2000. He became a Microsoft Certified Systems Engineer on Windows NT 3.51 in 1997, and achieved the Microsoft MCSE: Security and MCSE: Messaging specializations in 2002. In the same year, Dobromir worked as a subject matter expert to provide content for the CompTIA Security+ exam, and became one of the exam "grandfathers." He achieved Cisco CCNA in 2001, and CCIE Routing and Switching in 2003. In 2005, reflecting his extensive exposure to security architecture and management, he also achieved ISC^2 CISSP certification.

In addition to IT infrastructure architecture and delivery experience, Dobromir has considerable experience delivering technical training. He became a Microsoft Certified Trainer (MCT) in 1996 and has delivered many Microsoft official curriculum courses and presentations, as well as custom training on security, networking, and project management.

Dobromir lives near Reading, United Kingdom, with his wife and two children. In addition to spending time with his family, he enjoys philosophy, foreign languages, sports, and good food.

About This Book

User identification and authentication are essential parts of information security. Users authenticate as they access their computer systems at work or at home every day. Yet there seems to be ignorance in regard to why and how they are actually being authenticated, what the security level of the authentication mechanism that they are using is, and what the potential impacts are of selecting one authentication mechanism or another.

There are very few printed or online resources that discuss authentication technologies per se. The few out there concentrate on either authentication mechanisms provided by specific products or services, or on the theory behind user authentication with complete detachment from industry solutions. Neither the Internet nor enterprise infrastructures are comprised of just one product or service. Authentication services are very often based on standards and support heterogeneous infrastructures, systems, and user access.

The lack of structured information has often led to misunderstandings and myths about specific products, services, or technologies. This certainly does not help the end user, or the security professional, and may pose threats to a business and the overall protection of information resources.

There is a lot of information on the Internet on how to attack information systems, and there are hacker tools as well. However unsystematic this information may be, and however unprofessional the tools, there is still more information that can benefit the attackers than the enterprise infrastructure architect, consultant, or engineer. Security and network infrastructure professionals deserve to have at least as much information as is available to the potential attackers of his information system.

Finally, if an IT (information technology) professional wants to understand how to design a secure authentication strategy, or whether a specific authentication mechanism presents specific risks, the only option seems to be to try and read a large amount of books, online resources, and

RFCs, and even then the answer may still be missing, either because the information sources do not provide a systematic view of the subject, or because there is too much information.

This book is meant to provide structured and in-depth information on user identification and authentication. The structure of the book is as follows.

Chapter 1 provides background on a number of topics that are essential to user authentication. First, it presents an overview of today's security landscape and the specific threats to user authentication. Then the chapter outlines the process of controlled access to resources by means of identification, authentication, authorization, and accounting. This chapter discusses the types of user credentials that can be presented as proof of identity prior to accessing a computer system. Finally, the first chapter contains a crash course on cryptography with the essential approaches and terms required to understand how user authentication works.

Chapters 2 and 3 relate to specific implementations and provide information on the mechanisms of the user authentication process in the two most popular operating systems today: (1) UNIX (and derivatives) and (2) Windows NT/2000/2003. These chapters are meant to provide a consistent level of technical knowledge on all aspects of user authentication in both operating systems. The content is technical and provides screenshots and configuration files so that the reader can relate the content to knowledge that he already has and the things he has already seen to the philosophy and the authentication concepts discussed in the book.

Chapter 2 provides in-depth information about the user authentication model used in UNIX systems. Along with credential stores, technologies such as process creation, impersonation, and delegation are discussed in this chapter.

Chapter 3 provides detailed information on the user authentication architecture of Windows NT, Windows 2000, and Windows 2003. This chapter covers local authentication, credential stores, and protection, as well as the Windows Domain Model. Both Windows NT directory services and Active Directory are discussed.

Chapters 4 and 5 are more standards oriented and provide a level of abstraction from specific products and technologies. The reader will become familiar with the design and implementation fundamentals of different user authentication protocols and technologies that are independent of specific products and can easily be applied to every product that follows the standards.

Chapter 4 is dedicated to upper-level applications and services. First, it presents common security and user authentication models, such as GSS-API, SSPI, and SASL. Then, it provides information about authentication mechanisms and includes generic authentication protocols, such as Kerberos, NTLM, and SSL/TLS, that can be used for authentication to any type of service or application. Information that becomes specific to applications and then user authentication for access to files, e-mail, and databases are explained in detail.

Chapter 5 discusses user authentication for access to the infrastructure, and covers user authentication architecture on Cisco routers and switches, Remote Access Authentication protocols, as well as IPSec and VPN authentication. Past and current wireless authentication mechanisms are also discussed. Finally, Chapter 5 discusses how user authentication can be centralized using security protocols such as RADIUS and TACACS+.

The book includes a number of case studies, diagrams, snapshots, and network traffic captures that demonstrate the inner workings of different authentication mechanisms and technologies. A technical lab was built to reproduce authentication scenarios for the purposes of this book. A description of the lab configuration and diagram can be found in Appendix B.

All traffic captures were made using Ethereal version 0.10.13. An excerpt from most capture files is included inline with text as the authentication mechanism or technology is discussed. Finally, the companion and resource Web site for this book (http://www.iamechanics.com) provides additional reading, the lab diagram, all Ethereal capture files in .CAP and .TXT format, as well as other information that may be useful to the reader.

We hope that the book will provide the reader with the knowledge and skills to analyze, design, implement, and support user authentication and identification solutions. We also hope that the readers will enjoy reading this book as much as we enjoyed creating it.

Happy reading!

Chapter 1

User Identification and Authentication Concepts

> The modern world needs people with a complex identity who are intellectually autonomous and prepared to cope with uncertainty; who are able to tolerate ambiguity and not be driven by fear into a rigid, single-solution approach to problems, who are rational, foresightful and who look for facts; who can draw inferences and can control their behavior in the light of foreseen consequences, who are altruistic and enjoy doing for others, and who understand social forces and trends.
>
> — **Robert Havighurst**

This chapter introduces the main concepts of user identification and authentication. It also provides the terms used throughout this book.

1.1 Security Landscape

Information is an asset for today's organizations and individuals. Information may be less or more important and very often has a monetary value. The disclosure, improper modification, or unavailability of information may incur expenses (loss) or missed profits for the organization or the individual. Therefore, most organizations and individuals protect information to a certain extent. IT security is the science of protecting information assets from threats.

An information asset is an atomic piece of information that has meaning to the organization or the individual. Information assets have an owner. The information assets of a business organization are owned by a business owner, and those of an individual are owned by the actual individual. Organizations delegate the responsibility of protecting information assets to the IT department, the Information Security department, or the Information Risk Management department; individuals typically protect their own resources, but they may interact with other individuals and organizations, and may seek advice or transfer protection responsibilities to other individuals and organizations.

Whoever is managing protection is considered a custodian of the information asset; however, the owner is still responsible for valuating information, posing requirements for information protection, ensuring that information is protected by following defined procedures for information protection and auditing the protection mechanisms in place. The custodian is responsible for defining security protection mechanisms that meet the requirements of the information owner.

Both organizations and individuals typically have three main requirements to information asset protection:

1. *Confidentiality: information protection from disclosure to unauthorized individuals and other organizations.* Information that represents a patent, a trade secret, most types of military information, or financial information are examples of information that typically needs protection from disclosure. The company payroll information is normally a resource that requires protection from unauthorized disclosure.
2. *Integrity: information protection from accidental or intentional modification that may affect data validity.* Financial transactions are a typical example of an information asset that requires integrity protection. If an individual wants to transfer $1000 and someone modifies the amount to $20,000, it does make a difference.
3. *Availability: information and services that expose information to organizations and individual users must be available when users need them.* If an online Web banking application uses very secure technologies for user authentication, information encryption, and signing but the site is down and not available to users who need it, then it will hardly meet protection requirements.

In an ideal world, a custodian will apply the best technologies in terms of countermeasures to protect confidentiality, integrity, and availability of information assets. However, IT costs money in terms of hardware, software, training, labor, and other resources required to provide protection, confidentiality, integrity, and availability. Targets may be set accordingly so that protection is cost effective in relation to the information asset being protected.

Regardless of the level of protection, and mainly due to unclear requirements set by the information asset owners, by failing to implement protection for properly defined requirements, as well as due to hardware, software, and configurations thereof that may have security flaws, information assets may be vulnerable to one or more security threats that will typically compromise information asset confidentiality, integrity, or availability. Threat agents such as malicious individuals (or attackers) may give rise to threats and exploit vulnerabilities.

If vulnerabilities exist in the protection scheme — and they are very likely to exist regardless of the time and effort spent to protect the information asset — the possibility exists that a threat agent will exploit a vulnerability and compromise information asset protection. This is referred to as *risk*. The level of risk can sometimes be quantified and is often represented by the product of the value of a potential damage to asset protection multiplied by the probability of this occurring. Risk is not a problem but rather the likelihood of a problem happening, so risk probability is less than 100 percent. A risk that is 100 percent likely to occur is a problem — such as a risk that has materialized — and should be treated as such.

A typical approach to information security management is to analyze risks to information assets and mitigate these risks by imposing countermeasures. Furthermore, information security protection will also devise reactive (contingency) plans to minimize damage if for some reason a risk materializes and turns into a problem.

It is very important for a security professional to understand the requirements of business for information asset protection, to understand the risks for the particular information asset, as well as to devise and understand the countermeasures for information asset protection from threats.

To protect information, security professionals must implement security controls. User identification and authentication play a vital role in security controls by providing user identity and assurance before user access to resources is granted to an individual.

This book provides insight into how user identification and authentication mechanisms work, and provides security professionals with information on when to use specific mechanisms and what the implications of doing so would be.

1.2 Authentication, Authorization, and Accounting

Whether a security system serves the purposes of information asset protection or provides for general security outside the scope of IT, it is common to have three main security processes working together to provide access to assets in a controlled manner. These processes are:

1. *Authentication:* often referred to as Identification and Authentication, determining and validating user identity.
2. *Authorization:* providing users with the access to resources that they are allowed to have and preventing users from accessing resources that they are not allowed to access.
3. *Accounting:* providing an audit trail of user actions. This is sometimes referred to as auditing.

The following sections discuss these three processes and the relationship between them.

1.2.1 Identification and Authentication

A computer system comprised of hardware, software, and processes is very often an abstraction of an actual business model that exists in the real world outside the computer system. A financial application, for example, can be considered a model of actual financial relationships between actual organizations and individuals. Every element of the actual financial relationship can be projected onto the computer model (financial application), and then the computer model can be used to determine the outcomes of financial interactions between components of the actual system projected into the computer model.

Actual individuals using a computer system are typically humans (and sometimes applications or services) that exist outside the system. The user ID is a projection of an actual individual (or application or service) into the computer system. The computer system typically uses an abstract object, called a user account, that contains a set of attributes for each actual individual. The object has a name (user ID or logon ID) that is used to represent the abstract object to the system. Additional attributes of the object may include the full name of the actual user, the department for which he is working, his manager and direct reports, extension number, etc. Objects may or may not have credentials as their attributes. Apart from the user ID or logon ID, a security system will typically assign users an internal number (Security Identifier) that is used by the system to refer to the abstract object.

Establishing a unique abstract object in the form of a user account for each individual who will access resources in a computer system is very important. This object is used to identify the user in the system; this object is referred to by the system when user access to information assets is defined, and the system will also trace user actions and record an audit trail referring to the actual user by his abstract object ID. The user ID is therefore the basis for access control and it also helps to implement accountability. Hence, it is essential to have a separate user ID for each user, because each individual has specific access requirements and should be individually kept accountable for his actions.

The process of Authentication is often considered to consist of two distinct phases: (1) identification and (2) (actual) authentication.

Identification provides user identity to the security system. This identity is typically provided in the form of a user ID. The security system will typically search through all the abstract objects that it knows about and find the specific one for the privileges of which the actual user is currently applying. Once this is complete, the user has been identified.

Authentication is the process of validating user identity. The fact that the user claims to be represented by a specific abstract object (identified by its user ID) does not necessarily mean that this is true. To ascertain that an actual user can be mapped to a specific abstract user object in the system, and therefore be granted user rights and permissions specific to the abstract user object, the user must provide evidence to prove his identity to the system. Authentication is the process of ascertaining claimed user identity by verifying user-provided evidence.

The evidence provided by a user in the process of user authentication is called a *credential*. Different systems may require different types of credentials to ascertain user identity, and may even require more than one credential. In computer systems, the credential very often takes the form of a user password, which is a secret known only to the individual and the system. Credentials may take other forms, however, including PIN numbers, certificates, tickets, etc.

Once the individual has been authenticated, the system will associate an initial process to the user (a user shell), and the user will be able to launch other processes. All the processes launched by the user access resources (information assets) using the identity of the user, which has already been ascertained by the system.

User identification and authentication are typically the responsibility of the operating system. Before being allowed to create even a single process on a computer, the individual must authenticate to the operating system. Applications and services may or may not honor authentication provided by the operating system, and may or may not require additional authentication upon access to them.

There are typically three components involved in the process of user authentication (Figure 1.1):

1. *Supplicant:* the party in the authentication process that will provide its identity, and evidence for it, and as a result will be authenticated. This party may also be referred to as the authenticating user, or the client.

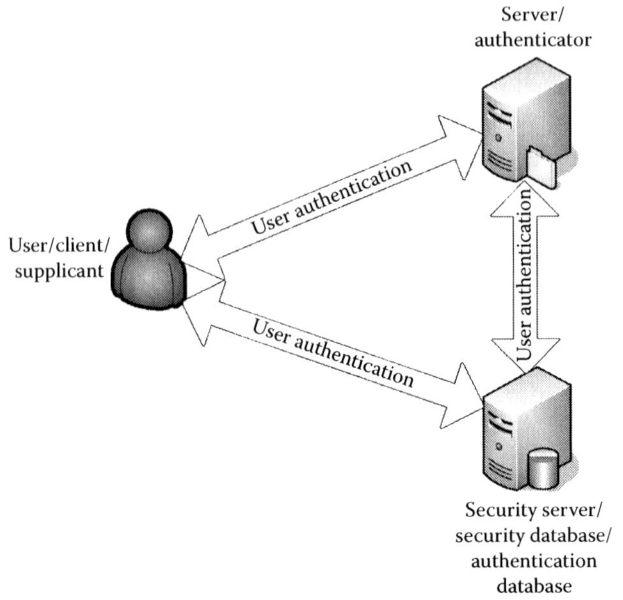

Figure 1.1 Components of a user authentication system.

2. *Authenticator:* the party in the authentication process that is providing resources to the client (the supplicant) and needs to ascertain user identity to authorize and audit user access to resources. The authenticator can also be referred to as the server.
3. *Security authority/database:* storage or mechanism to check user credentials. This can be as simple as a flat file, or a server on the network providing for centralized user authentication, or a set of distributed authentication servers that provide for user authentication within the enterprise or on the Internet.

In a simple scenario, the supplicant, authenticator, and security database may reside on the same computer. It is also possible and somewhat common for network applications to have the supplicant on one computer and the authenticator and security database collocated on another computer. It is also possible to have the three components geographically distributed on multiple computers.

It is important to understand that the three parties can communicate independently with one another. Depending on the authentication mechanism used, some of the communication channels might not be used — at least not by an actual dialogue over the network. The type of communication and whether or not it is used depends on the authentication mechanism and the model of trust that it implements.

For example, authentication protocols such as Kerberos will typically involve direct communication between the supplicant and the security server and the supplicant and the authenticator; but with regard to user authentication, there is no direct communication between the authenticator and the security server. Still, messages from the supplicant to the authenticator contain information sent by the security server to the authenticator.

1.2.2 Authorization

Authorization is the process of determining whether an already identified and authenticated user is allowed to access information resources in a specific way. Authorization is often the responsibility of the service providing access to a resource.

For example, if a user tries to access a file that resides on a file server, it will be the responsibility of the file service to determine whether the user will be allowed this type of access. Authorization can provide for granular control and may distinguish between operations such as reading or writing to a file, deleting a file, launching an executable file, etc.

Before authorization takes place, the user must be identified and authenticated. Authorization relies on identification information to maintain access control lists for each service.

Operating systems typically facilitate the process of authorization by providing authorization tools to applications. The operating system will typically provide for a *security kernel* (or an operating system Security Reference Monitor) that can be used to mediate access to resources by making sure that the operation is authorized. Alternatively, applications can implement their own authorization model, and Security Reference Monitor.

A user can be authenticated using a certain identity but he can request to be authorized to access a resource under a different identity. When the user explicitly requests this upon access to an application or resource, this is typically referred to as *authorization identity*. When this is performed by an application or service acting on behalf of the user, this is referred to as *impersonation*. In the case of impersonation, a user may posses an authentication identity that has been ascertained by the authentication process. In addition, the user may temporarily or permanently use an authorization identity, if the user is authorized by the operating system or application to impersonate another user by assuming the other user's identity. Impersonation is very useful in client/server computing where a server application running under a server account can access resources on behalf of users connecting to that server. Impersonation also allows a user to connect to a server using somebody else's broader or more restricted access permissions.

1.2.3 User Logon Process

Authentication and authorization work very closely together, and it is often difficult to distinguish where authentication finishes and where authorization starts. In theory, authentication is only supposed to ascertain the identity of the user. Authorization, on the other hand, is only responsible for determining whether or not the user should be allowed access.

To provide for the logical interdependence between authentication and authorization, operating systems and applications typically implement the so-called *user logon process* (or *login process*, also *sign-in process*). The logon process provides for user identification; it initiates an authentication dialogue between the user and the system, and generates an operating system or application-specific structure for the user, referred to as an *access token*. This access token is then attached to every process launched by the user, and is used in the process of authorization to determine whether the user has or has not been granted access. The access token structure sits in between user authentication and authorization. The access token contains user authorization information but this information is typically provided as part of the user identification and authentication process.

The logon process can also perform non-security-related tasks. For example, the process can set up the user work environment by applying specific settings and user preferences at the time of logon.

1.2.4 Accounting

Users are responsible for their actions in a computer system. Users can be authorized to access a resource; and if they access it, the operating system or application needs to provide an audit trail that gives historical data on when and how a user accessed a resource. On the other hand, if a user tries to access a resource and is not allowed to do so, an audit trail is still required to determine an attempt to violate system authorization and, in some cases, authentication policies.

Accounting is the process of maintaining an audit trail for user actions on the system. Accounting may be useful from a security perspective to determine authorized or unauthorized actions; it may also provide information for successful and unsuccessful authentication to the system.

Accounting should be provided, regardless of whether or not successful authentication or authorization has already taken place. A user may or may not have been able to authenticate to the system, and accounting should provide an audit trail of both successful and unsuccessful attempts. Furthermore, if a user has managed to authenticate successfully and tries to access a resource, both successful and unsuccessful attempts should be monitored by the system, and access attempts and their status should appear in the audit trail files. If authorization to access a resource was successful, the user ID of the user who accessed the resource should be provided in the audit trail to allow system administrators to track access.

1.3 Threats to User Identification and Authentication

The main goal of user identification and authentication is to validate the identity of the user. Computer systems typically require authentication. At the same time, attackers try to penetrate information systems and often their goal is to compromise the authentication mechanism protecting the system from unauthorized access.

Attackers can take different approaches when they attempt to compromise the user identification and authentication mechanisms of a system, some of which are described in this section.

1.3.1 Bypassing Authentication

If an attacker does not have a username and a password or other credentials, and is not able to authenticate to a system, he may try to bypass the authentication process. This can be accomplished in a number of ways, depending on the application, and the type of access that attackers have to the computer where the application is running.

If an application is running locally on a computer, and an attacker has physical access to this computer, then the attacker can potentially obtain administrative privileges, which may well be already available or may be obtained by privilege escalation. Once the attacker has administrative access, he can typically access all files and processes on the local computer, which allows him to debug running applications or swap files on the file system. The attacker can therefore debug an application that requires authentication, and potentially modify the application to replace the command or statement that compares the user password with commands that do nothing or return successful authentication. The user can then access the application. The modification can be performed for either code that is already in memory or for executable files on the file system, and take effect the next time the executable is launched. To protect against such attacks, the operating system can implement tools that detect and potentially alert the administrator or the user if they determine that the content of the file has been changed. This includes software that scans files on the file system and saves their hashes in a hash database, as well as signed executables.

The above authentication bypassing technique is more difficult to implement for network servers — unless the server is vulnerable to some attack over the network, where techniques such as smashing the application stack can be used to launch arbitrary code, or obtain administrative or local access. However, there are other approaches for bypassing authentication to network servers. One common approach is authentication to Web resources. Very often, these resources are published with anonymous authentication. Later on, system administrators may decide that they want to protect resources. A simple login form may exist on the home page, and it may require the user to enter a username and password, which may be statically configured in the code behind HTML/HTTP, or reside in a user database. Once the user has authenticated to that Web page, he can access resources. This approach is easy to implement but apparently there are problems associated with it. One of them is that if a user knows (or manages to guess) the URL behind the authentication page, he may be able to access resources without authentication. To resolve this problem, one of the best possible methods is to have the Web server impersonate requests from users using their actual user accounts, and access resources on behalf of the user; at the same time, Web pages and other files should be protected with permissions for actual users or groups of users. In this case, even if an application login page is bypassed, when a user tries to access the actual resource (a file), the operating system will request user authentication for the user, and will not allow access to the file. If the user refuses or fails to authenticate, the operating system will return a failure result. The Web server can therefore rely on the operating system to determine access to the specific file.

1.3.2 Default Passwords

One of the major challenges of secure user authentication is represented by default passwords. Many software and hardware vendors assign default passwords for built-in users in their operating systems, software, and hardware. Very often, system architects and engineers implementing a solution are too busy concentrating on the business functionality and features of the system or application, and security is often left in the second place. If the system designer or implementer fails to change the default passwords, someone else knowing or guessing what the device may be, might happen to have network access to the device and authentication accordingly.

System designers and engineers should always change the default passwords on all devices.

1.3.3 Privilege Escalation

During the logon process, a user authenticates using a set of credentials. When a user tries to access resources, this request is actually performed by processes running on behalf of the user, that use the user access token to be authorized by resource servers. In some cases, users may be able to find a security hole in an application or an operating system.

Very often, a service or an application may be running with its own account on a server. This account may have limited or unrestricted access privileges. By providing invalid input, an attacker can change the authentication logic of the service or application and assume the credentials of this application. A popular attack of this type is represented by the stack overflow attack. By providing invalid parameters (typically strings longer than the buffer reserved for user input by the application), an attacker can inject code and an incorrect return address pointing to the injected code into the application stack. This may force the application to execute arbitrary code using its own privileges.

The risk of privilege escalation attacks can be mitigated by strict checking of input parameters and other secure code writing techniques. Once the code has been fixed, it is important that it be applied to all affected servers and workstations in a timely fashion.

1.3.4 Obtaining Physical Access

Security is not only a matter of strong authentication mechanisms, secure code, and cryptography. There are multiple other factors that affect the security of a system, and physical security is one of them.

If an attacker has physical access to a computer, he may be able to bypass or alter authentication mechanisms and easily get to the resources needed to access even without authenticating.

For example, if an attacker is able to steal or temporarily be in possession of a laptop with confidential files, this attacker can boot into an operating system of his choice, such as a live Linux operating system available on a CD, and access files on the file system of the laptop while completely bypassing local authentication mechanisms imposed by the operating system installed on the laptop.

Alternatively or in addition, an attacker can steal the password database from the laptop and launch offline attacks against it to crack usernames and passwords. The attacker can then use cracked usernames and passwords to authenticate and access resources, which may even leave an audit trail as if a valid user authenticated to the system and accessed resources.

Another physical access attack method would be to modify the password of a user in the local security database on the laptop. Many operating systems and products store passwords in a nonreversible (one-way) format, so that they cannot be easily decrypted. However, the attacker can select a cleartext password of his choice, encrypt it using the one-way function used by the operating system, and store it in an encrypted format in the security database. The attacker can then boot into the local operating system and authenticate using the user account for which he has just changed the password. To cover his tracks, the attacker can then just restore the original password database, or just the one-way hash of the original password.

Another approach that an attacker can take is to replace an executable on the local file system that runs with administrator or system privileges with a crafted executable that performs operations on behalf of the attacker. The attacker can then start the local operating system and wait to have the crafted executable launched by the operating system with specific access rights, and then obtain access to whatever information he needs.

There is not much that user authentication can do against attacks that compromise the physical security of a computer. Cryptography may be able to help mitigate the risks of such attacks by encrypting partially or fully the file system of computers that should be protected. Encryption mechanisms typically require that a key be provided, and this key or derivatives of the key can be used to encrypt data. As long as the key is not stored on the same computer, this may prevent an attacker from accessing information.

1.3.5 Password Guessing: Dictionary, Brute Force, and Rainbow Attacks

One of the oldest types of attacks is *password guessing*. User authentication using a username and password has been available since the dawn of IT, and password guessing attacks have always been relatively easy to implement. They have also had surprising success every so often.

If a system requires the user to authenticate with a username and password, an attacker can try to guess the username and the password, and then authenticate as the actual user. Information about usernames can be easily obtained by an attacker. In many cases, the username of a user is the same as the first portion of the user's e-mail address. An attacker may also know the naming convention used by the organization to create user IDs for new users. Alternatively, the attacker may even have access to a directory with all the users in the system — which is very likely for attackers internal to the organization. To launch the attack, the attacker will try one or more passwords that are likely to be used by the actual user as the password.

If the attacker has no clue what the password is, he can use a brute force attack. Brute forcing is also known as exhaustive search. A password cracking tool will generate every possible combination of the user password and try to authenticate to the system with the same username and with each different combination of the password. Such a brute force attack may be able to succeed given enough time, and provided the user does not change his password in the meantime. The problem with brute force attacks is that the number of possible combinations for the user password may be huge, and may therefore require years, and in some cases hundreds or thousands of years to complete. The total number of combinations depends on the range of characters, digits, and special symbols included in the password, as well as on the length of the password. For example, a password that consists of exactly four digits (such as a PIN code) provides for $10^4 = 10,000$ possible combinations, which an automated cracking tool will be able to generate and check for a couple of seconds. However, if the password also includes capital and small letters, as well as special characters, or international characters, the number of combinations can be astronomical. In a security system with established password management policies, a user may be required to change his password long before a brute force attack has managed to check all the possible combinations, which would render the brute force attack ineffective. Therefore, password brute force attacks only make sense for relatively short passwords with a restricted range of characters. To mitigate the risk of brute force attacks, administrators should require users to change their passwords more often, and may also impose other countermeasures such as complexity requirements for user passwords.

Another popular and very successful approach to password guessing is the dictionary attack. It is based on the fact that users (unlike computers) select memorable words for their passwords. This may include names of relatives, pets, towns, dates of birth, or simply English or other human language words (such as the word "password"). The number of possible combinations can be considerably reduced when only meaningful words are used as the password. An attacker can obtain a list of English words and names either online or from a paper book such as a dictionary. This list of words can then be compiled into a dictionary. The attacker can then launch a search against the system by trying the same user account and words from the dictionary file as the password. To mitigate the risk from such attacks, password complexity requirements and regular password changes can be implemented.

Brute force attacks take a lot of system resources and time to complete. To decrease the time required to crack user passwords, brute force attacks can utilize Rainbow tables with precomputed values. Because precomputed values are readily available, the cracker tool does not need to calculate all the permutations or combinations, which saves time.

To mitigate the risk of Rainbow table attacks, the authentication system can use challenge-response authentication schemes, as well as password salting. By adding a random factor (such as the challenge) in a password authentication scheme, Rainbow tables cannot be efficiently used as precomputed information. If during every authentication attempt a new challenge is generated by the server, then Rainbow tables need to either include all the salt combinations as well (which would make them unmanageably large), or recalculate the table every time, which makes them similar in terms of efficiency to brute force attacks.

1.3.6 Sniffing Credentials off the Network

An easy way to obtain user passwords or other credentials might be sniffing traffic off the network. Many older operating systems, applications, and services transfer user identification information and credentials across the network in unencrypted form. Typical examples include FTP, HTTP, and Telnet. In their most simple and default configuration, all these popular protocols do not encrypt the user authentication dialogue; and if someone wants to sniff traffic on the network, he can get hold of plaintext usernames and passwords.

To protect from password sniffing attacks, user authentication must be properly encrypted.

1.3.7 Replaying Authentication

Authentication replay is another popular attack method against user authentication mechanisms. It still requires that the user performing the attack has access to the network between the client and the server, or has other means for interfering with the authentication process. Authentication replay is a mechanism whereby the attacker may not be able to obtain the plaintext password but will use the encrypted password text to authenticate. If a client always sends an encrypted string to the server that provides for user authentication, this encrypted string (which may well be irreversibly encrypted) can be captured by the attacker and presented to the server by the attacker.

Authentication schemes that use static authentication parameters are susceptible to password replay attacks. Many authentication protocols use challenge-response mechanisms for user authentication.

In a typical challenge-response scheme, the authenticator will generate a random (and therefore different every time) string and will present it as a challenge to the supplicant. The supplicant will typically manipulate the server challenge in some way and will typically encrypt it using the user password or a derivative as the key, or generate a hash based on the challenge and the user password. In any case, the user plaintext password will be used by the client to generate a response to the server challenge. If an attacker manages to capture a challenge-response authentication session, he may be able to see encrypted supplicant responses that depend on the server-provided challenge. If the attacker tries to authenticate to a server, he will receive a new challenge from the server. Unless the attacker knows the user password, he will not be able to authenticate.

The strength of challenge-response authentication mechanisms depends heavily on the randomness of the challenge. If a server reuses the same challenge, an attacker collecting traffic on the network that has already seen the challenge, and a response, can reuse the response to authenticate to the server. To provide for further protection even if a challenge is reused, some authentication schemes make the response dependent on other parameters as well, such as the current time.

1.3.8 Downgrading Authentication Strength

This attack is typically launched against authentication negotiation protocols. If a client and a server support more than one authentication mechanism, they may wish to negotiate and select the best mechanism. Some of the authentication mechanisms may be strong but some may be weak. The client can specify an ordered list of authentication mechanisms, and the server can choose one specific mechanism from the those provided by the client. This can also work vice versa, such that the client may be presented with a choice of mechanisms and select one.

If a malicious attacker ("man-in-the-middle") somewhere on the network between the supplicant and the authenticator is able to capture and modify traffic, he may be able to alter client and server proposals for authentication mechanisms in such a way that a weak authentication mechanism is selected as the preferred one, or as the only one supported by both ends. This may force the client and the server to use a weak algorithm as the only resort. This weak authentication mechanism may provide plaintext user passwords or other usable credentials, so the attacker may be able to collect the required information off the wire.

To protect against such attacks, the client and the server may need to protect the communication channel between them before negotiating authentication mechanisms. Alternatively, the client and the server may be configured to only use strong authentication mechanisms and reject weak authentication mechanism, so that the attacker cannot force them to use a weak authentication mechanism.

1.3.9 Imposter Servers

Another possible attack on user authentication occurs when a user wants to access resources on the network and an attacker introduces an imposter server into the network (instead of the real server). The user will try to authenticate to the imposter, thinking that this is the real server. The user may be misled to provide his credentials (such as a plaintext password) to the imposter, and may even submit confidential data.

To avoid such attacks on user authentication, many authentication mechanisms provide for mutual authentication, whereby not only does the client authenticate to the server, but the server also authenticates to the client. In this way, if a server fails to authenticate to the client, the client knows that the server is an imposter and can terminate the authentication process. The client also will not send data to the server.

1.3.10 Man-in-the-Middle Attacks

"Man-in-the-middle" is a name for an entire set of attacks where the attacker sits somewhere between the client and the server, or between two communicating peers on the network, or as a process between them. The attacker is able to receive messages from both parties and send messages to both parties. The attacker can therefore either relay a message from one party to the other in its original form, or alter it deliberately before forwarding.

Man-in-the-middle attacks can be effective against both user authentication and actual user data traffic. To protect against such attacks, systems typically implement peer authentication (mutual authentication), channel encryption, and integrity protection.

1.3.11 Session Hijacking

Session hijacking is a variant of man-in-the-middle attacks. An attacker performing session hijacking has control over the communication channel between the client and the server. The attacker may wait for a user to establish a new session and authenticate successfully to the server. Once authentication has completed successfully, the attacker can interfere with the established session and assume the identity of one of the parties, not relaying any more traffic to the other party, or relaying it selectively.

Protection against session hijacking requires the same countermeasures as protection against man-in-the-middle attacks.

1.3.12 Shoulder Surfing

A non-IT and potentially nontechnical but still somewhat effective attack is the shoulder surfing attack. As the name implies, the attacker can look over the user's shoulder as the user types in his password to authenticate to the system.

Users can protect against this type of attack by making sure that no one is looking at them when they are typing in their passwords. One-time passwords can be very useful here as well.

1.3.13 Keyboard Loggers, Trojans, and Viruses

If an attacker wants to obtain a user password, it may be possible for him to alter software on the user workstation and install a key-logging facility. This will typically be a resident program that will collect information about all the keystrokes that the user has made. Information is logged into a log file.

A Trojan or a virus can also intercept communication between the client and the server, and store the obtained information in a database that can later be used for offline analysis.

1.3.14 Offline Attacks

Attackers often try to obtain offline access to the user credentials database. This database is typically stored in a single file, which may be copied from the authentication server to a location where the attacker has access and can analyze the database file. Stealing the password file (credentials database) may be possible if the attacker has administrative permissions on the computer where the authentication server resides, or if the attacker has physical access to the authentication server and can reboot the machine into another operating system with full access to the file system.

There is considerable risk that an offline attack will succeed, even if the password file is encrypted, and the password is stored in a different, secure location. Therefore, to avoid offline attacks, there must be careful planning of physical and administrative access to the authentication servers.

1.3.15 Social Engineering

Social engineering is a powerful approach to attacking user authentication. Social engineering techniques may involve carrying out a rich set of personal and interpersonal skills. A lot of information on social engineering is available in [III].

Social engineering techniques involve the attacker tricking the user into believing that he (the user) needs to provide specific information or perform a specific action. For example, an attacker might pose as a system administrator, call a user, and request him to provide his password because the central authentication database has been lost and user authentication must be reinstated. Alternatively, an attacker might request a user to change his password to one that is known to the attacker. In both cases, an uneducated user, or even a security professional, might believe that this was a genuine request.

The best countermeasures against social engineering, which is a nontechnical approach, are security policies and procedures, and user awareness training.

1.3.16 Dumpster Diving and Identity Theft

Another nontechnical method for attacking user authentication is dumpster diving. In today's world of information, users can release confidential information to the public without even realizing it. For example, an individual can dispose of his bank statements and drop them in a trash bin. An attacker can, however, search through the trash and find those bank statements. Using the information provided there, in combination with nontechnical methods (such as social engineering) and technical methods, an attacker might be able to authenticate to the bank's Web portal and submit transactions on behalf of the actual user. The attacker can, in general, assume the identity of the victim and carry out other attacks apart from transferring funds.

1.4 Authentication Credentials

Authentication is the process of ascertaining user identity. To ascertain that users are who they say they are, the operating system or the application requiring authentication will request evidence from the user. This evidence is known as user credentials.

A bank can authenticate one of its customers by requiring proof of ID, which may include a photo ID, such as an ID card; a driver's license or a passport; or other proof, such as a credit card, a bank statement, a utility bill, etc.

A computer security system may allow for one or more types of credentials as proof of the user's identity. This section discusses the types of credentials that can typically be used in the process of user authentication.

The process of authentication is based on characteristics or unique information that is available to the authenticating parties in the process of user authentication. Authentication credentials fall into one or more of the following categories:

- *"Something you know."* This authentication factor is based on a secret shared between the authenticating parties (the authenticator and the supplicant). Static password authentication schemes are based on the "something you know" factor.

- *"Something you are."* This authentication factor requires the authenticator to authenticate the supplicant based on biometric information, such as fingerprints, retina scan, facial scan, etc. This method relatively closely mimics identification and authentication in legacy security systems, whereby a customer is authenticated by his bank by walking into a branch and showing a photo ID. The client is identified based on his biometric parameters — facial recognition and matching against the photo ID in this instance.
- *"Something you have."* This authentication factor requires the possession of an authentication token, which is an actual object. The authentication token might be a smart card, a key-fob type device, a USB stick, a serial tap, or other object. If a supplicant possesses a token, he is probably who he says he is, so his identity can be ascertained; and as a result, the user can be authenticated.

The use of a single factor to ascertain user identity is very common but not always very secure. Therefore, many systems that require strong user authentication policies implement multiple-factor authentication schemes, whereby the supplicant may be required to provide more than one type of evidence in order to be authenticated. For example, a supplicant may need to provide biometric evidence ("something you are") and a password ("something you know"), or even a password ("something you know"), biometric evidence ("something you are"), and a security token ("something you have").

The use of multiple authentication factors considerably increases the security of a system from a user authentication perspective. If the risk exists that a single-factor authentication system will be compromised, then when a second factor of authentication is taken into consideration, this risk is significantly mitigated.

At the same time, it is important to understand that multiple-factor authentication is very likely to increase the time it takes for users to log in. Therefore, users may be resistant to using multiple-factor authentication mechanisms.

User authentication sometimes extends to peer authentication. The server (authenticator) needs to ascertain the identity of the client (supplicant) by means of client authentication, but the client may need to ascertain the identity of the server as well, and make sure that it is talking to the right server and not to an imposter. If the client needs to submit confidential information to the server, or if the client needs to obtain information from the server that is sensitive and must not be tampered with, the client needs to make sure that the server is genuine. When both the client and the server must be authenticated, the process is known as mutual authentication. Some authentication mechanisms support mutual authentication by default; other mechanisms may support mutual authentication using two separate authentication dialogues in both directions. Some authentication mechanisms do not support mutual authentication at all.

1.4.1 Password Authentication

Authentication based on passwords requires the supplicant and the security server to share a common secret. No one else should know the secret; so if the supplicant provides identification information and the correct shared secret during authentication, the security server can safely consider that the supplicant is genuine and client authentication should succeed. If the supplicant and the authenticator have agreed to use mutual authentication, the client can in the same way ensure that the server knows the password.

Two types of password credentials can be used by today's authentication solutions: (1) static and (2) one-time passwords. These two types of credentials are discussed in the following subsections.

1.4.1.1 Static Passwords

Static passwords are the oldest and most widespread form of user credentials. Static passwords are secrets shared between the client and the authentication server, and these secrets do not change very often. Security administrators apply security policies for an organization or departments within the organization, and define how often users need to change their passwords, and this may happen, for example, every week or every month. The model of trust for static passwords is that only the supplicant and the authentication server know the secret password; and even when it changes, still only the two of them are going to know it.

The authentication server stores the static password in its authentication database, where it should be securely protected. Very often, the supplicant will not store the password anywhere and will ask the user to provide the password just before authentication. In some cases, applications running on the supplicant computer can store the password in a file or an in-memory password cache, and use it every time the user tries to access resources to authenticate automatically.

Static passwords are convenient and do not require special configuration on the supplicant, the authentication server, or the authenticator. Virtually any application, platform, or operating system supports authentication with static passwords. On the client computer, no special hardware or software is required to authenticate using static passwords. This means that a user may be able to access a specific resource from the office or from a shared computer in a coffee shop with public Internet access.

Static passwords are therefore very convenient for users and provide flexibility in terms of client capability and location.

The major disadvantage of static passwords is that they may be an easy target for attackers. The strength of user authentication primarily depends on the strength of the authentication mechanism but, in general, authentication mechanisms that provide for static passwords may potentially be vulnerable to many types of attacks. Default passwords, password guessing, sniffing off the network, replaying, man-in-the-middle, shoulder surfing, social engineering, and dumpster diving are all attacks primarily meant to attack static user passwords.

For most of the above attacks, the password can be successfully attacked if it is weak. Many authentication mechanisms based on static passwords use the actual password or a derivative of the password to encrypt authentication messages, or to authenticate the integrity of these messages. As a result, the strength of a user password must be the same as the strength of a cryptographic key, and all requirements for symmetric cryptographic keys must be met by user passwords (see subsection 1.8.2.1). If the password does not meet some of the requirements for symmetric keys, it can be considered weak.

Humans are not good at generating passwords. Most of the time, humans use readable passwords, comprised of letters (very often part of a meaningful word) and digits, and rarely special characters. Therefore, a password generated by a human can be relatively easy to remember but it considerably reduces the keyspace for the password (which is a symmetric key as well). Machine-generated passwords are typically generated in such a way that the entire keyspace can be used. Unfortunately, this makes the password difficult to remember for humans, which may render it unusable, or even easier to crack — in case the user who is not able to memorize it writes it down on a sticky note on the side of the computer display. Another problem with machine passwords is that they are generated using pseudo-random functions. Unfortunately, unlike humans who have feelings, emotions, senses, and many other factors that influence the decision-making process, machines always behave in exactly the same predictable way, and there is hardly any random material they can use to generate random passwords. Computers may use the current date and time, the time since the last reboot, the content of a specific memory cell, the number of running processes on the computer, etc. to generate a random password. However, none of these is necessarily random, and someone with enough knowledge of the environment may be able to guess the pseudo-random password.

Static passwords are a common authentication method that is widespread, widely supported, and convenient, but at the same level provides for moderate to low levels of security.

1.4.1.2 One-Time Passwords

One-time passwords are secrets that can be used for authentication only once, or a few times. Technically, this means that the user must have a new password every time he needs to authenticate. One-time passwords require special software or hardware on both the user authentication server and the supplicant.

List of One-Time Passwords

One of the possible approaches to one-time passwords is to have a list of passwords and the stipulation that each of them will be used only once. The authentication server ticks off each password once it has been used by the user, and it cannot be used again. When all the passwords have been used, the supplicant and the authentication server must generate a new list of passwords to use.

This mechanism would be simple enough but it has not found much support and is therefore not used in the real world in this very form. Still, the one-time password mechanisms described below follow a similar concept.

S/KEY and OPIE

S/KEY is a one-time password scheme, and at the same time an authentication mechanism, invented by Bellcore for UNIX systems. With S/KEY, the supplicant and the authentication server must choose an initial password. This password is never used by itself for user authentication, but is used to generate one-time passwords so it can be considered a master secret. The client and server will never use the same password generated from the initial password for user authentication. Every time the supplicant authenticates, it is required to compute a new password.

An S/KEY initial password can be used to generate a one-time password a limited number of times (**N**) and then can be changed. To compute the password for the particular authentication attempt, the supplicant and the authentication server maintain an index (**i**) of authentication attempts. The index is increased after each attempt.

The one-time password $\mathbf{p_i}$ is a function of the index **i**, the total number of one-time passwords **N**, and the initial password $\mathbf{p_0}$. The one-time password is the (**i**–1)-time hash of the initial password $\mathbf{p_0}$ — the hash function **H( )** is applied (**N**–i) times on the initial password $\mathbf{p_0}$. The hash function can be MD4 or MD5.

$$\mathbf{P_i = H^{N-i}(p_0)}$$

For the first password, the hash function is applied **N** times; for the second, **N–1** times. For the (**N–1**) authentication attempt, the hash function will be applied only once.

It is important to understand that one-time passwords that come first in the list have been generated using passwords that come next in the list. If an attacker manages to capture a password (e.g., the one with index **m**), the attacker still cannot calculate the next password without first breaking the one-way hash function; this is because a one-time password with index **m** is the one-way hash of a one-time password with index **m+1**, and **m+1** will still be used in the future.

Technically, when a user authenticates to the S/KEY system, the login prompt will indicate the index for the current authentication attempt for this user. The user then needs to calculate the S/KEY one-time password from the initial password and the index, and provide it to the server. In some implementations, a salt may be provided as well.

```
% telnet linus
Trying 10.0.2.102...
Connected to linus
Escape character is '^]'.

Fedora Core 4/i386 (linus.ins.com)

login: PeterB
s/key 97 fw13894
Password: *********
```

The user needs to calculate the one-time password from the initial password, the index, and potentially the salt. This is typically performed using another system — which may be a laptop or a handheld PC — that is a local trusted system. The user feeds the authentication parameters from the S/KEY server into the local trusted system (the program **key** is typically used) and as a result is provided with a one-time password, that he then submits as his S/KEY authentication reply.

The model of protection provided by S/KEY is based on the fact that it is easy to calculate the **N**-time hash of a secret initial password; but due to the fact that the hash is a nonreversible function, it is not possible to calculate the initial password, nor is it possible to calculate any forthcoming one-time password without the knowledge of the initial password. More information on S/KEY is provided in [133].

The S/KEY algorithm was originally open source but was later protected by a trademark, and Bellcore started selling it as a product. The open source community came up with a separate standard, known as OPIE (One-time Passwords In Everything), that was being developed in software and hardware.

The S/KEY authentication mechanism is not susceptible to replay attacks. However, considering the fact that the initial password is selected by a user, S/KEY may be susceptible to a whole spectrum of password guessing attacks; if as a result of network traffic sniffing or shoulder surfing an attacker manages to obtain the one-time password, dictionary, brute force, and potentially rainbow techniques for password guessing can be used. Selecting a strong password is still important for S/KEY OTP.

RSA SecurID

RSA SecurID is a one-time password scheme and an associated authentication mechanism developed by RSA Security. SecurID requires hardware that requires the use of tokens for user authentication, as well as a user PIN, and is therefore a two-factor authentication mechanism. RSA SecurID is a very popular authentication scheme used by many infrastructure solutions.

The SecurID supplicant has a security token that is a key-fob type device. This device has a quartz clock and generates a new passcode (a six-digit number) every minute. The user also has a four-digit static PIN number. The PIN code is a secret number known to the user and the SecurID authentication server. This PIN can be changed if forgotten. The one-time password (or passphrase) is the concatenation of the four-digit user PIN code and the six-digit passcode. Some devices generate the passphrase after the user has provided a PIN code, which makes them marginally more secure. When the user is prompted for authentication, the user enters his username as usual but uses his one-time password (passphrase) in the Password field instead of a static password.

The passcode is generated every 60 seconds by the SecurID token. When the token is manufactured, a seed is encoded into the specific token; and from that time until the time when the access token stops working (two or three years after being manufactured), the same seed is used, as the client token is not programmable or configurable. The initial seed for every access token is shipped on a floppy disk or by some other means to the customer. This initial seed is specific for the access token and must be provided to the authentication server. The RSA authentication server serves user authentication requests, and is available using industry-standard protocols such as RADIUS, and may also use integration modules and work with file services, Web services, etc.

The algorithm used by the client and the server to calculate a new passcode from the initial seed and the current time every 60 seconds is not known, but is believed to be a complex one-way hash function. Due to the algorithm being secret and only known to a limited number of individuals, attacks against the process of generating new passcodes are less likely to succeed, unless information about it leaks to the public or attackers deliberately reverse-engineer the hardware tokens and the authentication server.

RSA SecurID is not susceptible or has limited exposure to some of the attacks specific to static passwords, and is not susceptible to some of the attacks that are specific to one-time password mechanisms.

The passcode is valid for only 60 seconds. As the passcode is a machine (token)-generated password, and the initial seed is secret, the passcode cannot be easily guessed. It is not susceptible to dictionary attacks, and may be susceptible to brute force attacks. However, considering the six-digit passcode, an attacker attempting brute force attacks may need to try 10^6 passcodes within the 60-second period of validity of the passphrase if the PIN code is known; this will require that more than 16,666 passcodes be tested every single second. If the PIN is not known, the number of combinations would be 10^{10}, so the attacker will need to verify 166,666,600 passphrases (PIN and passcode) per second. If an attacker does not manage to guess the passcode within a single 60-second interval, the calculation will need to start again from the very beginning for the next passcode. As a result, brute forcing the RSA SecurID algorithm possibly does not represent a viable attack method at the time of this writing.

Other attacks, such as network traffic sniffing, shoulder surfing, keyboard logging, and social engineering, may have limited success. If by one of these methods an attacker manages to obtain a passcode and knows the user PIN number, the attacker can only use this passphrase to authenticate within a limited period of time — up to 60 seconds after the passcode was initially generated on the SecurID token. Furthermore, the user must not have used this pincode to authenticate, or the passphrase will be rejected as already used.

If the attacker does not try authentication within the 60-second period after having obtained actual credentials, the chance is lost and the attacker needs to find another passphrase. However, if an attacker manages to capture a valid passphrase for a user, the attacker already has the PIN code for the user as the first four digits of the captured passphrase. The PIN code can be used for brute force attacks, decreasing the unknown keyspace from 10^{10} to 10^6 (see above) but this is still not likely to lead to success due to the limited time that the attacker has. Beyond the 60-second validity period of the passcode, other attacks such as password guessing, sniffing, man-in-the-middle, etc. are not possible because the passcode has already changed (pretty much like a changed static password). Some third-party devices implement challenge-response authentication schemes using one-time passwords. Unfortunately, these authentication schemes are harder to integrate with existing authentication solutions.

RSA SecurID authentication is a very secure authentication mechanism when combined with other security techniques and secure authentication approaches. Using unsecure authentication mechanisms such as Telnet clear-text authentication or plain FTP authentication may still expose user credentials to an attacker, although for a limited period of time. Hence, RSA SecurID authentication must be planned carefully.

1.4.2 Asymmetric Keys and Certificate-Based Credentials

Asymmetric cryptography presents a powerful approach to protecting information. Users who want to use asymmetric cryptographic mechanisms need to possess an asymmetric keypair that can be used for encryption and data signing. The private key is secret and can be considered equivalent to a user password; the public key can be made available to all users on the Internet and is not secret.

An asymmetric keypair — be it an RSA or a DSA keypair — by itself does not contain information about the user to whom it belongs. However, in many cases, it is useful to be able to identify the user to whom an asymmetric keypair belongs. It is also important to have assurance that a particular public key belongs to a specific user, rather than to an imposter.

One of the approaches used by some applications, such as SSH, is to use the public key as a means to identify the user and the private key as a means to authenticate the user. The public key, which is known to everyone, can be mapped to the user's identity. The private key is secret and the individual uses it to ascertain his identity. Because the public and the private key are mathematically bound to one another, the identity of the user (the public key) is bound to the secret key (the private key).

However, using only keys does not provide for much flexibility. For example, there is no information as to when the keys were created and for how long will they be valid; nor is there information on the purposes for which these keys can be used. Certificates provide for such information. A certificate is a collection of publicly available user attributes (metadata about the user) and a public key, all signed by a trusted third party that guarantees that it has verified the information in the certificate as correct. The trusted third party is called certification authority (CA).

Because each certificate contains the identity of the user, along with the user's public key, certificates can be used for user authentication. The private key is not part of the certificate but every certificate has a corresponding private key that is mathematically bound to the public key contained in that certificate.

The X.509 standard was defined by ITU-T in 1988 (X.509 version 1) and then revisited in 1993 (X.509 version 2) and 1995 (X.509 version 3). It defines digital certificates as an authentication method and describes how asymmetric keys can be bound to user identity using such certificates. More details on the actual standards can be found in [134, 135].

X.509 version 1 of the standard defines the basic certificate format, and X.509 version 3 defines the extended certificate format. Table 1.1 shows the X.509 certificate fields and their usage.

Table 1.1 X.509 Certificate Fields

Field Name	*X.509 Version*	*Description*
Subject	1	Name of the certificate holder. This name can virtually take any format but commonly used are X.500 distinguished name, e-mail address, DNS name, and LDAP name.
Serial Number	1	A unique identifier of the certificate
Issuer	1	The name of the party that issued the certificate. This is typically a certificate authority. The format can be X.500, LDAP, or DNS.
Valid From	1	Date and time when the certificate became (or will become) valid
Valid To	1	Date and time until when the certificate will be (or was) valid
Public Key	1	The public key portion of the asymmetric keypair for the certificate holder
Version	3	X.509 version on which this certificate is based (1, 2, or 3)
Subject Alternative Name	3	Another name by which the holder of the certificate is known Provided that the Subject field is an LDAP name, the Subject Alternative Name may contain the user logon name for users, or the computer account name for computers
CRL Distribution Points (CRL-DP)	3	URL of the Certificate Revocation list of the Certification Authority
Authority Information Access (AIA)	3	URL with information about the Certification Authority
Enhanced Key Usage	3	Purposes of the certificate — what will it be used for This is a collection of ISO-defined object identifiers (OIDs), one for each purpose of use for the certificate
Application Policies	3	Defines applications and services that can use the certificate by specifying OIDs

Table 1.1 X.509 Certificate Fields (continued)

Field Name	*X.509 Version*	*Description*
Certificate Policies	3	Specifies the assurance policies and mechanisms that the Certification Authority observes in order to receive requests for, handle, authorize, issue, and manage certificates.
Signature Algorithm	1	The algorithm used by the Certification Authority to sign the certificate This is typically RSA or DSA, with SHA-1 or MD5 hash
Signature Value	1	The actual signature using RSA or DSA (or potentially other signature algorithm) on the certificate

The following example shows the content of an actual certificate:

```
C:\> openssl x509 -text -in dt.pem
Certificate:
  Data:
    Version: 3 (0x2)
    Serial Number:
      11:9f:5e:a8:00:00:00:00:00:05
    Signature Algorithm: sha1WithRSAEncryption
    Issuer: DC=com, DC=ins, CN=INS CA
    Validity
      Not Before: Jul 13 00:22:30 2005 GMT
      Not After : Jul 13 00:32:30 2006 GMT
    Subject: CN=Dobromir Todorov/emailAddress=Test@test.com
    Subject Public Key Info:
      Public Key Algorithm: rsaEncryption
      RSA Public Key: (2048 bit)
        Modulus (2048 bit):
          00:d4:5a:48:86:cd:50:b2:49:c8:cd:12:ec:12:ab:
          b7:84:97:c4:0f:7f:16:48:c9:0a:6e:c9:1b:cc:c1:
          61:c5:fb:cb:ce:72:30:46:f6:cb:10:fa:ab:75:ce:
          bd:cc:0d:e0:ce:73:6d:be:fa:b3:89:b3:14:d6:0a:
          d1:eb:7f:fd:18:c2:c2:b2:59:a9:ba:09:99:34:03:
          f3:63:8d:71:78:04:9b:36:aa:8a:76:3d:26:a7:4b:
          01:0c:a1:00:8f:95:0b:9a:49:1d:09:9f:9e:5a:50:
          3f:e3:3f:57:e9:72:dc:9b:91:36:52:b3:23:d2:e9:
          16:fe:7a:97:63:51:ca:b9:a4:55:b0:6f:00:cf:2c:
          14:76:80:81:c3:ed:74:fa:cd:89:53:c2:c6:15:e6:
          87:11:e3:46:6b:89:74:18:d6:e0:7f:81:dc:cd:77:
          96:4e:d8:f7:10:14:39:91:f5:1f:cd:b1:d3:53:e5:
          08:88:38:97:ae:45:ba:b1:f7:c3:dc:50:23:a8:b7:
```

```
          26:5a:25:4a:55:01:ee:d9:6c:7d:53:47:9d:4f:de:
          00:f3:9b:8d:6f:66:8b:fa:ad:8b:fc:9d:01:ba:59:
          86:15:fb:85:b4:32:15:5f:ec:04:a2:5f:60:70:57:
          b5:a4:bc:a5:8e:67:26:d2:1c:9d:b9:94:64:39:e6:
          72:07
        Exponent: 65537 (0x10001)
    X509v3 extensions:
      X509v3 Key Usage: critical
        Digital Signature, Non Repudiation, Key Encipherment,
Data Encipherment
      S/MIME Capabilities:
      X509v3 Subject Key Identifier:
        2C:3E:29:D3:C5:56:D3:8D:6A:E5:45:97:96:C6:9A:3F:A5:29:9A:4C
      X509v3 Extended Key Usage:
        TLS Web Client Authentication
      X509v3 Authority Key Identifier:
        keyid:18:FB:CB:95:2D:59:AC:16:4F:B0:02:4D:1D:6D:92:AC:FE:29:
         8B:4C

      X509v3 CRL Distribution Points:
        URI:ldap:///CN=INS%20CA,CN=BILL,CN=CDP,CN=Public%20Key%20
         Services,CN=Services,CN=Configuration,DC=ins,DC=com?
         certificateRevocationList?base?objectClass=cRLDistribution
         Point
        URI:http://bill.ins.com/CertEnroll/INS%20CA.crl

      Authority Information Access:
        CA Issuers - URI:ldap:///CN=INS%20CA,CN=AIA,CN=Public%20Key%
         20Services,CN=Services,CN=Configuration,DC=ins,DC=com?cA
         Certificate?base?objectClass=certificationAuthority
        CA Issuers - URI:http://bill.ins.com/CertEnroll/BILL.ins.com_
         INS%20CA.crt

  Signature Algorithm: sha1WithRSAEncryption
    91:08:78:be:95:f3:26:60:53:dc:31:3d:2b:66:c5:48:3a:65:
    78:d6:34:e9:46:47:04:37:ca:26:f3:ab:3f:d1:25:6a:31:47:
    57:76:aa:60:4a:e8:e0:20:f7:dc:be:2c:aa:65:5d:f7:9d:6c:
    95:4f:4a:fc:2f:3c:1a:cb:7a:27:35:7c:2e:0d:59:e8:08:c0:
    06:46:d1:a2:8b:a6:30:17:57:cb:4f:41:33:87:7a:d8:14:07:
    8b:d8:b8:ad:c4:8c:11:c1:53:39:a8:75:63:b3:31:de:2a:7a:
    f9:58:7c:2a:a3:0e:e5:5e:87:39:fb:7c:94:00:e1:20:3a:5f:
    a3:90:18:78:05:32:b0:92:bd:e4:9a:50:ce:9d:c6:db:6f:2c:
    0b:e5:ae:0e:6c:5f:2f:49:a2:12:b0:fb:3c:4f:b8:5e:0c:5e:
    a8:ec:8f:0b:48:12:f3:70:16:06:61:2d:1e:71:d9:13:75:07:
    cd:cf:e0:24:54:f1:96:f2:8a:24:9c:14:02:1e:4c:48:0e:d3:
    44:bf:af:ca:0a:4c:c3:8d:0c:5d:25:2d:8e:a0:74:dd:6f:d5:
    7a:ac:2a:68:c6:01:52:2b:28:b3:ee:2c:59:fe:71:31:59:42:
    0e:7f:b5:73:6e:eb:a8:ed:a7:ef:ea:9e:d3:ba:9c:4d:d4:7b:
    47:35:c9:38
```


```
-----BEGIN CERTIFICATE-----
MIIFlzCCBH+gAwIBAgIKEZ9eqAAAAAAABTANBgkqhkiG9w0BAQUFADA7MRMwEQYK
CZImiZPyLGQBGRYDY29tMRMwEQYKCZImiZPyLGQBGRYDaW5zMQ8wDQYDVQQDEwZJ
TlMgQ0EwHhcNMDUwNzEzMDAyMjMwWhcNMDYwNzEzMDAzMjMwWjA5MRkwFwYDVQQD
```

```
ExBEb2Jyb21pciBUb2Rvcm92MRwwGgYJKoZIhvcNAQkBFg1UZXN0QHRlc3QuY29t
MIIBIjANBgkqhkiG9w0BAQEFAAOCAQ8AMIIBCgKCAQEA1FpIhs1QsknIzRLsEqu3
hJfED38WSMkKbskbzMFhxfvLznIwRvbLEPqrdc69zA3gznNtvvqzibMU1grR63/9
GMLCslmpugmZNAPzY41xeASbNqqKdj0mp0sBDKEAj5ULmkkdCZ+eWlA/4z9X6XLc
m5E2UrMj0ukW/nqXY1HKuaRVsG8AzywUdoCBw+10+s2JU8LGFeaHEeNGa410GNbg
f4HczXeWTtj3EBQ5kfUfzbHTU+UIiDiXrkW6sffD3FAjqLcmWiVKVQHu2Wx9U0ed
T94A85uNb2aL+q2L/J0BulmGFfuFtDIVX+wEol9gcFe1pLyljmcm0hyduZRkOeZy
BwIDAQABo4ICnTCCApkwDgYDVR0PAQH/BAQDAgTwMEQGCSqGSIb3DQEJDwQ3MDUw
DgYIKoZIhvcNAwICAgCAMA4GCCqGSIb3DQMEAgIAgDAHBgUrDgMCBzAKBggqhkiG
9w0DBzAdBgNVHQ4EFgQULD4p08VW041q5UWXlsaaP6UpmkwwEwYDVR0lBAwwCgYI
KwYBBQUHAwIwHwYDVR0jBBgwFoAUGPvLlS1ZrBZPsAJNHW2SrP4pi0wwgewGA1Ud
HwSB5DCB4TCB3qCB26CB2IaBqGxkYXA6Ly8vQ049SU5TJTIwQ0EsQ049QklMTCxD
Tj1DRFAsQ049UHVibGljJTIwS2V5JTIwU2VydmljZXMsQ049U2VydmljZXMsQ049
Q29uZmlndXJhdGlvbixEQz1pbnMsREM9Y29tP2NlcnRpZmljYXRlUmV2b2NhdGlv
bkxpc3Q/YmFzZT9vYmplY3RDbGFzcz1jUkxEaXN0cmlidXRpb25Qb2ludIYraHR0
cDovL2JpbGwuaW5zLmNvbS9DZXJ0RW5yb2xsL0lOUyUyMENBLmNybDCB/AYIKwYB
BQUHAQEEge8wgewwgaMGCCsGAQUFBzAChoGWbGRhcDovLy9DTj1JTlMlMjBDQSxD
Tj1BSUEsQ049UHVibGljJTIwS2V5JTIwU2VydmljZXMsQ049U2VydmljZXMsQ049
Q29uZmlndXJhdGlvbixEQz1pbnMsREM9Y29tP2NBQ2VydGlmaWNhdGU/YmFzZT9v
YmplY3RDbGFzcz1jZXJ0aWZpY2F0aW9uQXV0aG9yaXR5MEQGCCsGAQUFBzAChjho
dHRwOi8vYmlsbC5pbnMuY29tL0NlcnRFbnJvbGwvQklMTC5pbnMuY29tX0lOUyUy
MENBLmNydDANBgkqhkiG9w0BAQUFAAOCAQEAkQh4vpXzJmBT3DE9K2bFSDpleNY0
6UZHBDfKJvOrP9ElajFHV3aqYEro4CD33L4sqmVd951slU9K/C88Gst6JzV8Lg1Z
6AjABkbRooumMBdXy09BM4d62BQHi9i4rcSMEcFTOah1Y7Mx3ip6+Vh8KqMO5V6H
Oft81ADhIDpfo5AYeAUysJK95JpQzp3G228sC+WuDmxfL0miErD7PE+4XgxeqOyP
C0gS83AWBmEtHnHZE3UHzc/gJFTxlvKKJJwUAh5MSA7TRL+vygpMw40MXSUtjqB0
3W/VeqwqaMYBUisos+4sWf5xMVlCDn+1c27rqO2n7+qe07qcTdR7RzXJOA==
-----END CERTIFICATE-----
C:\>
```


All users and services within a single domain of administration trust one or more certification authorities (CAs). Each CA is responsible for receiving, verifying, and issuing certificates, as well as managing certificate revocation information. Typically within an organization, there is one top-level CA; there may be zero or more levels of subordinate CAs. Any certificate issued by any of the CAs within the CA hierarchy is trusted by each other CA and all the users and services in the same CA hierarchy.

The X.509 PKI model defines hierarchical relationships between certificates that correspond to the model of trust. Top-level CAs are known as root CAs. Because there is no CA above them, these CAs sign their own certificates. Due to the fact that these CAs are well known and have strong identity and assurance policies, users trust them to be the ultimate verifier of information stored in certificates throughout the organization. CAs below the top-level CA have their certificates signed by the root CA. Because users trust the root CA, they also trust each certificate of subordinate CAs, as they have been signed by the root CA that has verified the identity of the subordinate CA.

Cross certification provides for trust with certificates issued by other domains (PKI Hierarchies). If a trusted CA signs the certificate of an untrusted CA, the untrusted CA becomes trusted along with all the certificates issued to its subordinate CAs and user/service certificates. Such cross certification may become the model for authentication between organizations.

Users, services, and CAs choose which CAs to trust. The CA must provide for strong identity assurance mechanisms to be trusted by other parties. Before a CA issues a certificate to a requestor, the CA needs to ensure that the information that the user has requested in the certificate request is genuine and truthful. To validate this information, a CA (more precisely, an issuing committee that manages the CA) may request a user to bring a photo ID, or the CA may use other means to ensure that the information is correct. The X.509 model of trust is based on the fact that if information has been included in a certificate, this information is correct and a trusted CA has verified it. In some cases, before issuing a certificate to a user, a committee of individuals may need to consider the request and decide whether to issue a certificate or reject the request. Using hardware security modules, it is possible that the CA private key will be spread to a number of smart cards, so that all (or a qualified quorum of) committee members need to provide their cards so that that CA private key can be retrieved from them, and the request can be signed.

To obtain a certificate and have it signed by a CA, users generate an asymmetric keypair and submit a certificate request. Once the CA has verified the information requested by a user or a service, the CA must sign it. Signature is performed by first generating a hash of the certificate fields, and then signing the hash using some signature algorithm such as RSA Signature or DSA. The CA signs the hash using its own private key. Because this private key is secret, no one but the signing CA can generate this signature. The signature can be verified using the CA's public key, which is included in the CA certificate.

Each user or service can trust one or more root certification authorities (root CAs). Each certificate issued directly or indirectly (following the model of trust of subordinate certificate authorities) by a trusted CA is automatically trusted. A user or service that needs to verify whether a certificate is valid only needs to verify the signature on the certificate, which is an offline process and does not require any connectivity to the issuing CA. The verifying user or service has both the peer certificate that must be verified and the trusted CA certificate. To verify the peer certificate, the verifying user or service needs to decrypt the Signature field in the peer certificate using the signing CA's public key, and compare it with a locally calculated hash for the certificate. If the two match, the certificate is genuine and has a valid signature from a trusted CA. As a result, the certificate and the information contained within it may be considered valid, because it has been verified by a trusted party.

Each user, application or computer, or other entity may request and potentially obtain a certificate. The typical process of obtaining a certificate involves the following steps:

1. A user or a service generates an asymmetric key pair (RSA or DSA).
2. The user or computer generates a certificate request to a CA. The request includes only the public key from the asymmetric keypair and additional attributes that the user or service wants to add to the certificate, such as a Subject Name (the user directory name), the Subject Alternative Name (such as the user logon name), and potentially key usage information. The request is typically signed with the user's newly generated private key, and the signature can be verified using the newly generated public key, which is included in the certificate request.
3. A CA receives the request either online (through a Web page or through a certificate enrollment protocol) or offline (a file containing the request from the user or service).
4. The CA starts a process to verify that the information provided by the requestor in the certificate request is correct. For example, the CA may need to verify that the user who requested the certificate can really use the Subject Name and the Subject Alternative Name in the request. The user or service may therefore be required to provide identification information, or an internal organizational process may be used to verify the information.
5. After verifying that the request from the user or service is genuine and that requested attributes correspond and properly identify the user or service, the CA adds attributes such as validity period (Valid From/Valid To), CRL, and AIA URLs, and potentially other attributes, and generates an SHA-1 or MD5 hash for all the fields.
6. The CA signs the hash using its own private key.
7. The CA constructs a certificate with all the signed fields and the actual signature added to them.
8. The CA returns the certificate to the requestor.
9. The requesting user or service stores the certificate in its local certificate store and associates it with its secretly stored private key that corresponds to the certificate's public key.
10. Either the CA or the user (or service) can optionally publish the certificate into a directory where other users can find it.

Certificates used as credentials by themselves can be considered a single-factor authentication mechanism ("something you know"). However, certificates are very often used along with smart cards. When the user first generates a keypair, a smart card can be used for the actual calculation. The user private key can therefore be generated and stored on the smart card and protected by a PIN code. The user private key is typically not saved in the file system in this case. If the user needs to use his private key — for example, to authenticate, to decrypt data it has received from a peer, or to sign data that he wants to send to a peer — the smart card must be provided along with the protecting PIN code and the private key will be read from the card. The use of smart cards to store private keys corresponding to X.509 certificates makes certificate-based authentication a two-factor authentication method. Smart card authentication is a relatively popular authentication method that provides for very good security.

The model of trust for certificates used as authentication credentials is that user identification information is contained within the certificate (verified by a trusted third party — a CA), and that only the trusted third party can generate a verifiable signature for the certificate in question. If an attacker is able to steal the identity of a CA (i.e., steal the private key), the attacker can sign and issue new certificates compromising the model of trust.

To protect against and mitigate the effects of compromise, certificates use two mechanisms: (1) validity period and (2) certificate revocation checking (CRC). Each certificate is valid for a limited period of time, specified in the certificate itself. If a certificate is not within its validity period when a user or service checks it, this certificate is invalid. Parties that have expired certificates must renew them before they can successfully use them.

On the other hand, if a certificate is compromised (e.g., its private key is stolen), then this certificate can no longer be trusted and therefore should be revoked. The user or service to which this certificate belongs is responsible for notifying the CA that their certificate has been compromised. The CA can then add the certificate to a list of revoked certificates, known as a certificate revocation list (CRL). Users and services that use certificates may choose to verify every certificate against the CRL before using it. In this way, even if a certificate is compromised before its validity period has ended, this certificate can be immediately invalidated and the party to which it belongs can request a new certificate.

The security of X.509 certificates as user credentials depends on a number of factors. First, X.509 certificates are considered strong due to the fact that cryptographic signing algorithms (RSA Signature and DSA) cannot be easily compromised at the time of this writing. Second, it is vitally important that all levels of CAs and the actual certificate owner keep their private keys secret. If even one private key in the certificate chain is compromised, the entire chain from the point of compromise downward can be considered compromised and certificates must be revoked and reissued. Third, CAs must have a reliable way of checking information in certificate request before actually signing and issuing certificates to individuals.

X.509 certificates and corresponding private keys can be used as very secure authentication credentials, especially if the private key is stored on a smart card, as this provides for two-factor authentication.

PGP (Pretty Good Privacy) is a public key system similar in many respects to X.509. The major difference is that instead of relying on a hierarchical trust, PGP relies on the so-called "web of trust." With PGP, anyone can play the role of a CA and can generate a signed PGP certificate for another user. PGP parties that sign other parties' public keys are known as introducers. Each introducer can be trusted by a party (such as a user or a service), which means that certificates that he has signed will be trusted as well by that party. For example, if Bob trusts Alice as a trusted introducer, and Alice has signed a public key for another user, then Bob trusts the public key signed by Alice.

Enterprise trust is typically easier to model using the hierarchical and centralized X.509 model based on trusted root and subordinate certificate authorities. PGP, on the other hand, sometimes appears to be more convenient for open user communities exchanging information over the Internet. Both X.509 and PGP certificates can be used as credentials for user authentication, depending on the requirements and the environment.

1.4.3 Biometric Credentials

Biometric credentials represent the "something you are" factor of authentication. They are based on the physical or behavioral characteristics of the user. The idea behind biometric credentials is that measurable characteristics such as the user fingerprint or the dynamics of user handwriting do not or hardly ever change, and can therefore be used to authenticate the identity of a user.

Biometric credentials can be used for either authentication only (verification) or both identification and authentication (recognition). In either case, the authentication database must be populated with the biometric profiles of all the individuals who will be identified or authenticated. The process of population is known as enrollment; each user must provide specific biometric patterns to the system. Typically, the user will present the same pattern (such as a fingerprint) a number of times for calibration and to store a more accurate profile.

Measurements of biometric device accuracy and effectiveness are the false acceptance rate (FAR) and the false rejection rate (FRR) parameters, which are specific for each and every type of biometric credential, and potentially for different implementations. The FAR is an expression of the number of times a user was recognized by the system as a valid user while at the same time he was not a valid user. The FRR is an expression of the number of times a user was rejected by the authentication process while in fact he was a valid user. The goal of biometric authentication systems is to keep FAR and FRR low, and at the same time provide for convenient and quick authentication.

When biometric credentials are used for authentication (verification), the user must present his identity to the system in the form of a user ID. Biometric authentication will then capture the user's biometric credentials and compare them against the patterns stored for the user in the authentication database, so there will be a one-to-one comparison with the existing enrollment credentials. This process typically takes less than a couple of seconds.

When biometric credentials are used for user identification (recognition), the user does not need to present a user ID to the system. The biometric credentials will be analyzed and then a search will be carried out against the authentication database to determine whether there is a known user with the specific biometric profile. If a match is found, the user is both identified and authenticated. In this case, the biometric profile is compared against many entries in the authentication database; thus, the process can take considerable time for large databases of users. This approach is typically used at airports or by the police to identify individuals, but it is not widely adopted for user authentication in IT systems.

There are two main types of biometric credentials:

1. *Static (pattern-based).* These credentials are based on a static pattern of a biometric characteristic, such as a fingerprint, a retina pattern, or an iris pattern. The pattern is typically stored as a raster or vector image in an authentication database. At the time of user authentication, recognition is based on the number of matching points between the stored image and the authentication image. More matching points mean better accuracy.
2. *Dynamic (behavior-based).* Authentication using dynamic biometric credentials is based on the recognition of user-specific behavior, such as the dynamics of user handwriting or the way the user types in a specific text, such as his password.

Some of the most popular biometric authentication methods include:

- *Fingerprint authentication.* This pattern-based authentication method is, by far, the most popular. It is based on the fact that user fingerprints are virtually unique. The user needs to place his finger on a fingertip reader device that may use optical or semiconductor-generated electric field to scan the fingerprint. This type of credential is used for user identification at U.S. airports, and the technology is quickly evolving. Fingerprint readers are currently available with keyboard and mouse devices, as well as on PDAs.

- *Retina scan.* This is a pattern-based authentication method and is based on the uniqueness of the formation of blood vessels in the back of the eye. To authenticate, the user needs to look into a special receptacle in a specific way and the system will scan the individual's retina by optical means.
- *Iris scan.* Similar to a retina scan, this method is based on the uniqueness of the colored ring of tissue around the pupil (the iris). This authentication method can use a relatively simple camera for the scan, and is based on optical scanning. Due to the relatively simple equipment required, some airports are currently experimenting with this type of credential for individual identification.
- *Hand geometry.* This method is based on the uniqueness of dimensions and proportions of the hand and fingers of the individual. The image is three-dimensional and taken by optical means, and can use conventional cameras.
- *Face geometry.* This mechanism was developed to mimic the natural, human way of identifying individuals based on their faces. The authentication process relies on the recognition of specific facial patterns, such as the dimensions and proportions of the face, the distance between face elements, as well as the shape and proportion of the nose, eyes, chin, etc. The image is taken by optical means and can use conventional cameras.
- *Skin pattern.* Based on the uniqueness of the texture of the skin, this method creates a "skinprint." Unlike hand and face recognition, this method can distinguish between individuals who are physically similar, such as twins. The image is taken by optical means and can use conventional cameras.
- *Voice pattern.* This method is based on the uniqueness of the human voice. A conventional microphone can be used to enroll and authenticate users. Background noise can have a negative impact on the authentication process, so this method is not appropriate in noisy environments.
- *Handwriting.* This method is a behavioral approach based on user handwriting. Sensors detect the speed, direction, and pressure of individual handwriting for a predefined pattern, such as the individual's signature. The accuracy of this method can vary.

Biometric authentication methods remain rarely used. One of the reasons why they have not been widely adopted is cost. Most biometric solutions are relatively expensive (at least much more expensive than user passwords, or even certificates stored on smart cards), and are not suitable for authentication at each and every user workstation, unless very high security requirements must be met. User reluctance to use biometric authentication is another factor. This may be a due to fear (a retina scan requires the user to look into a receptacle, which may be considered intrusive), inconvenience, or privacy concerns. Another important factor is accuracy. Despite the fact that biometric devices use natural user characteristics to identify and authenticate users, the technologies used are not perfect, so recognition or authentication may require a number of attempts. The placement of the finger on the fingerprint reader, the clarity of the image which may be affected by an unclean optical surface on the fingertip reader, whether the finger is dry or wet — these are all factors that affect the effectiveness of fingerprint authentication. A user may be required to provide credentials a number of times; and due to human nature, the chances of obtaining a good pattern when the user is under pressure are likely to decrease.

Biometric authentication technologies present more potential rather than actual effectiveness and wide implementation. As the technologies evolve, the accuracy and the convenience for users are likely to increase, and biometric devices may take the natural and well-deserved lead as user authentication credentials.

1.4.4 Ticket-Based Hybrid Authentication Methods

The ticket authentication approach combines legacy authentication methods, such as static passwords, with encryption-based methods, similar to certificates (Figure 1.2). Ticket-based systems rely on a trusted third party (the security server) that authenticates the user (supplicant) and issues a ticket. This ticket can then be presented upon access to resources.

The ticket-based approach has two phases:

- *User authentication by a security server.* The user who needs to obtain access to resources connects to a trusted third party (security server) and provides authentication credentials, such as a username and a password. The server verifies the credentials and issues a ticket to the user. The ticket is signed and may be potentially encrypted by the security server so that the user cannot modify the content and may potentially not be able to read the content of the ticket.
- *Authentication to a resource server.* Once the user has obtained a ticket, he can try to access a resource on the network. The user needs to present the ticket to the resource server. The resource server trusts the security server who issued the ticket to the user.

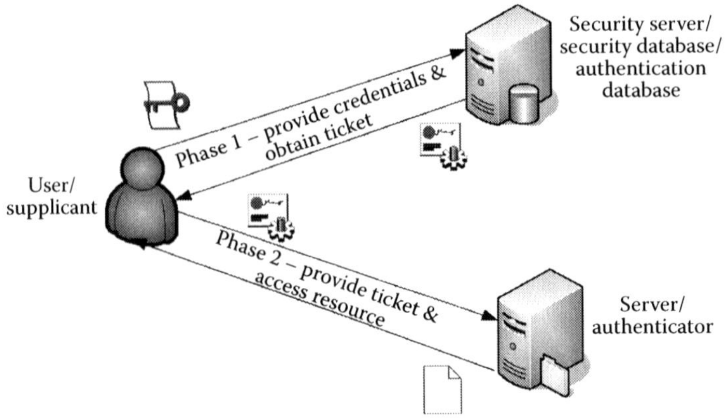

Figure 1.2 Hybrid user authentication using tickets.

> The resource server must check the signature of the ticket, and potentially decrypt the ticket in order to extract user identification and authorization information (such as group membership). The resource server then allows or denies access for the user, based on authorization.

The user can use any supported set of credentials in the dialogue with the security server. This includes passwords, certificates, biometric devices, etc. The ticket issued by the server is proof that the user has provided a valid set of credentials. At the same time, the resource server (authenticator) does not need to understand the authentication method used by the client to authenticate to the security server. For example, the resource server does not need to understand biometric authentication methods if the user can present a valid ticket.

The ticket issued by the security server is a proof of the user's identity and contains identification and authorization information. The security server puts all the required attributes in the ticket and then signs the ticket. Potentially, the ticket can also be encrypted. The ticket is returned to the user, and now the user can present it when he tries to access resources over the network. The user cannot modify the ticket (and cannot change his group membership, for example) because the ticket is signed. The user cannot generate a forged ticket, because he does not have the security server's key used for ticket signing. If the user needs to access resources, the user must present the original ticket.

The resource server (authenticator) can verify the signature of the ticket presented by the user. If the signature is correct, then the ticket is genuine. If not, the ticket has been tampered with and the resource server will reject the access request. The resource server does not need to connect to the security server to verify the signature. The signature verification process is local and is based on calculations.

The security server and the resource server can use different signing and encryption methods. Some authentication schemes (Kerberos) use symmetric keys (passwords) that are shared between the security server and the resource server. Other authentication methods also support asymmetric keys (certificates and private keys) (e.g., SESAME and SAML).

1.5 Enterprise User Identification and Authentication Challenges

During the time of centralized computing when users had to use terminals connected by means of serial links to a mainframe or central computer, authentication was centralized and there was only one place where it could be performed — the only intelligent component was the central host. Later on, when minicomputers were connected to the first networks and started communicating with one another using protocols such as TCP/IP, the authentication model started to change and became relatively decentralized. Users now needed an account on every host that they wanted to connect to. Apart from interactive sessions, however, because of the small number of networked hosts (and therefore authentication databases), accessing resources that resided on one host from another host was a matter of a simple model of trust where authentication was not really vital. The model of trust at that time was based on the UNIX r* commands (such as **rsh** and **rlogin**) that provide for an authorization file with a list of remote users who are allowed equivalent access to the one a local user has on a particular host. Authentication was not really involved; it was simple identification, wherein the user ID of the requesting user, as well as the name or IP address of the requesting host, could be deduced by the r* request.

In the early 1980s, the IBM Personal Computer and Apple Macintosh started the personal computer (PC) revolution, and now every user had a microcomputer on his desk. UNIX workstations also became popular and now even UNIX users could have their own dedicated host on their desks. Personal computers meant (somewhat) decentralized computing; and in order to be able to share resources in a decentralized world, networking advances were required by the industry. Among the main requirements from the network infrastructure was the ability to authenticate in a network of micro-hosts.

As a result, many authentication systems were developed, and this book presents many of commercial and industry systems that have survived for the past 20 years. However different these systems might be, they fall

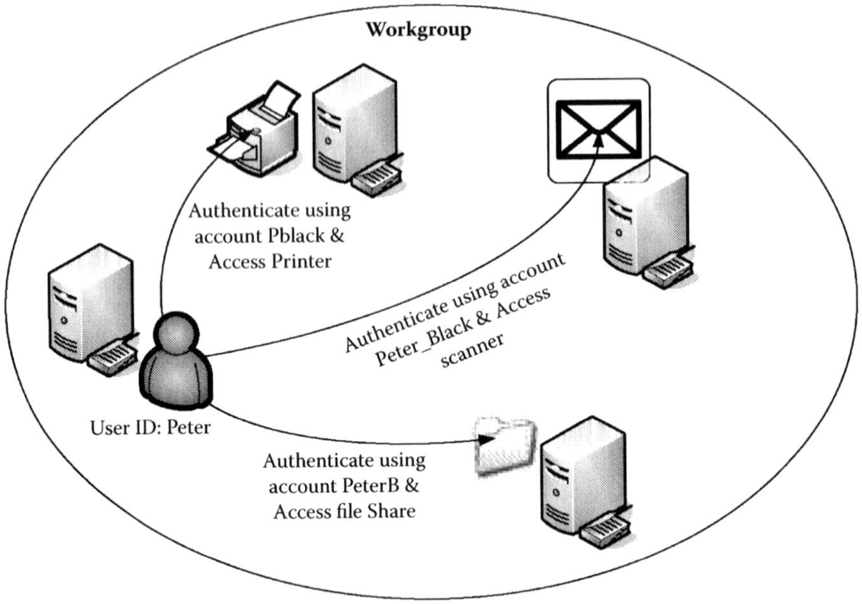

Figure 1.3 Decentralized authentication: Workgroup model.

into two main categories: (1) centralized and (2) decentralized authentication systems.

The decentralized authentication approach (Figure 1.3) allows each network host to maintain its own user authentication database and policies. UNIX hosts have their own and are independent from other hosts' **/etc/passwd** file and may potentially use PAM but will still maintain an independent database of users. Windows hosts maintain their own local security accounts manager (SAM) database and authenticate users against this database.

The centralized authentication approach (Figure 1.4) requires hosts to trust and follow the policies defined by a central authentication authority. This may be just one host, or it may be a set of hosts that form a logical authentication authority. The authentication authority has an authentication database that can be used by all the hosts participating in the centralized authentication system.

An advantage of the decentralized approach is that it allows for user authentication autonomy. In systems that require a very high level of security, designated hosts may be hardened and configured in a secure way to allow access to highly sensitive information assets. Such high security hosts or workstations are not likely to trust other parts of an information system which have a lower level of security. Another advantage of the decentralized approach is that there is no dedicated hardware

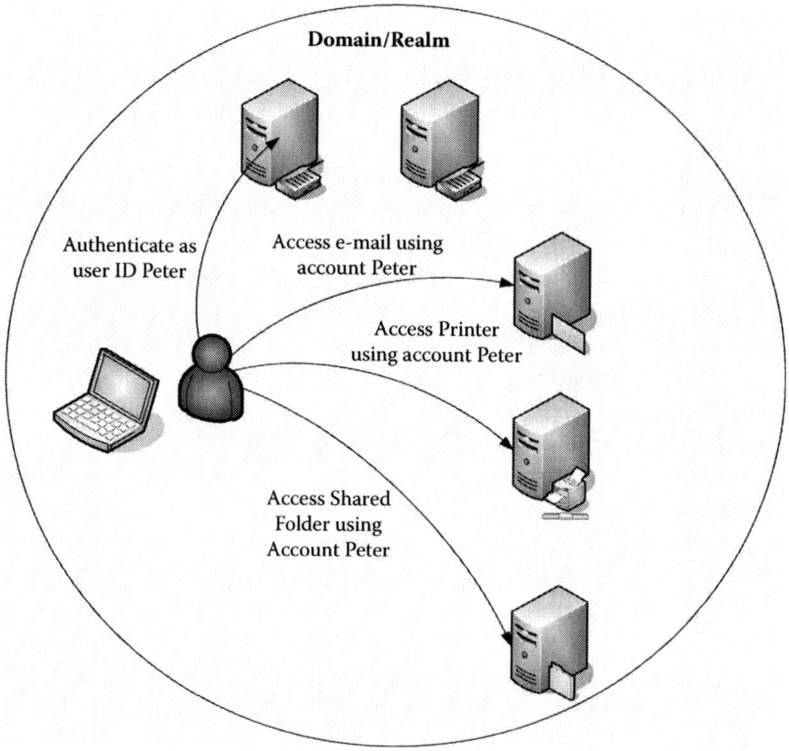

Figure 1.4 Centralized authentication — domain/realm model.

required for centralized authentication authority servers, so this makes this model appropriate for home networking and small organizations of a couple of networked computers.

The disadvantage of the decentralized approach is that it requires authentication every time a user from one host needs to access resources on another host. Every user needs to have an account and associated credentials (such as a password) on every host on which there are resources that this user may need to access. A separate account should be created on every host. Unfortunately, this does not scale well for more than a few computers. In a network of ten computers where each user has his own computer, and administers his own authentication database, for a complete trust between all the users so that every user can access resources on every other computer, 10 × 10 = 100 accounts will be required (every user has an account on his own host, and a separate local account on every of the other nine hosts). Every time a user needs to access a resource on a remote host, he might potentially need to use a different username (assigned by the administrator of the remote host). Potentially, he may also need a different password. If the user wants to maintain the same password on all hosts, then every time the password is changed on one host, it should also be changed on all other hosts. The whole maintenance of this otherwise simple model takes a lot of user and administrative time and effort.

The advantage of centralized authentication is that authentication information is stored in a central authentication database and one or more servers play the role of an authentication authority. If a supplicant trusts the centralized authentication authority, it can become part of the centralized authentication system. Because the centralized authentication authority is trusted to provide authentication information, all participating hosts can authenticate any user who has an account in the central authentication database. Therefore, each user only needs to have one account, stored in the central authentication store, and he can log in from any host in the centralized authentication system, and then access resources (to which he has been granted access) on any host in the centralized authentication system without the need to re-authenticate. This approach gives significant advantages to enterprise information systems in terms of user account management, and centralized security.

A disadvantage of the centralized approach is that if a user account is compromised, the attacker has access to any resource to which the user account has access. For some information systems, this model may be unacceptable.

An example of decentralized authentication is the Windows Workgroup authentication model (Figure 1.3). In this model, each computer stores authentication information locally, in a portion of the machine registry called the Security Accounts Manager (SAM). Each computer in a workgroup defines its own local authentication policies and user accounts. To log on interactively from such a workstation or to access resources on this workstation over the network, users must have a user account defined locally in the SAM for this workstation.

Examples of centralized authentication are Windows NT and Active Directory domains (see Figure 1.4). In both cases, information is stored centrally in a user database, which is made available by set of authentication servers known as domain controllers. In the case of Windows NT, authentication information resides in the SAM. For Windows 2000 and later, user authentication information is a subset of the information stored in Active Directory.

Centralized authentication is a generic term for Single Sign-On (SSO). In today's information systems, organizations invest money and effort to make sure that users are authenticated only once (sign-on only once) but then are able to access resources anywhere on the network. SSO implies unified authentication for access to both the infrastructure (using port access control technologies, or remote access, such as dial-up or VPN), as well as services (e-mail, file services, Web portals, management information systems, etc.). Unfortunately, at the time of this writing, true SSO is rarely possible.

In an ideal world, all the applications and services in an organization will use a single centralized authentication database to provide for user authentication. Unfortunately, services at the infrastructure layer, as well as applications and services at upper layers, have their own authentication methods and databases.

One of the approaches to SSO is identity management. Organizations — especially those with legacy applications and information systems — may have a multitude of directory services with information about users. For example, many organizations have a human resources database, a phone directory, and legacy plaintext files in the file system for user authentication. Users in the phone directory may be listed by their full names, and plaintext authentication files may use user IDs. The human resources database may use employee IDs as the primary way of identifying users. Identity management solutions typically provide for directory replication or synchronization so that system designers can create relationships and effectively use information from all the directories. This is often achieved using a metadirectory — a centralized, consolidated directory with information from all potential sources. Once data has been consolidated in the metadirectory, it can then be replicated to each and every directory, and updated as necessary or on a regular basis.

1.6 Authenticating Access to Services and the Infrastructure

Users should be required to authenticate access to both services and the infrastructure if they are trying to access business applications, or if they are attempting to establish a VPN (virtual private network) connection from home to the corporate network. Users may even need to use the same username and password or other credentials for both access to the business application and for the VPN connection. However, these two types of access require two independent authentication processes.

1.6.1 Authenticating Access to the Infrastructure

Infrastructure access is meant to provide users with network connectivity to where the desired resources reside. In case the client resides on a local area network (LAN) connection, the user will typically be provided with network access to the LAN and to the corporate WAN (wide area network), as well as to the Internet. The fact that the user has physical access to the building where the corporate wired LAN resides, and that security has checked the user's badge as he entered the building, is often enough as an authentication means to provide the user with LAN network access as well. In some special cases, the user workstation may be required to authenticate to the network switch where the client computer is connected before it is allowed to transfer and receive traffic from the network. This is typically performed using the IEEE 802.1x protocol.

When a user resides outside the corporate network, where he has no physical access to the building, the user needs to be authenticated before being provided with network access. Such access includes dial-up remote access over asynchronous links (telephone lines) or ISDN lines to corporate remote access servers (RASs), as well as VPN links over the Internet to the corporate VPN concentrators.

Another case when infrastructure access may need to be authenticated are Wi-Fi connections. Due to the nature of wireless links, which are based on communication using radio waves, the user may or may not have physical access to the building where wireless access is provided. A user may be well outside a building (e.g., in a car parked in front of the building) and still be able to communicate with the Wi-Fi network using radio waves. Due to the fact that an organization cannot be sure whether users trying access to the Wi-Fi network are physically in the building (and have therefore been authenticated by showing their badges when they entered the building), authentication will most likely be required for such type of access.

1.6.2 Authenticating Access to Applications and Services

While the network infrastructure is just a communication layer, applications and services are the actual resources that users need to perform their daily jobs. These include management information systems, financial applications, e-mail, file and print services, corporate Web portals, the Internet, etc. These services rely on the network infrastructure to provide connectivity in a secure way. These services typically have no knowledge of whether the user has been authenticated for access to the infrastructure, or whether he has been granted access based on the fact that he is physically in the building. Applications and services typically require their own authentication, regardless of whether or not infrastructure authentication has been performed.

As a result, user authentication is considered to consist of at least an infrastructure and an application authentication layer. A user trying to connect to applications may therefore need to authenticate twice: to the infrastructure and then to applications.

1.7 Delegation and Impersonation

When a user logs into a system, he typically does so using his user account. The process performing user logon launches a user shell using the identity of the logged-on user. From that point on, processes launched by the user will assume the identity and the privileges of the user as they access resources.

Network services and applications work in the same way: they typically have dedicated user accounts (or use the machine account — as is the case for many services in Windows).

If a user tries to access a network service, the user needs to authenticate. The service will typically take one of the following approaches:

- *Allow anonymous access.* The service does not need to know the identity of the user and provides the same access to all users.
- *Identify the user.* The service will determine the identity of the user. The service will then perform its own authorization and check its own access control lists on what access to provide for this user.
- *Impersonate the user.* The service will assume the identity of the network user and will typically spawn a new process or thread with this identity and privileges. The service will then try to access local resources on behalf of the user. It will be the responsibility of the operating system or platform to perform authorization for the operations performed by the service on behalf of the user. If access is successful, the user will be provided with the results. If the access attempt fails, the user is not authorized to access the specific resource. In any case, the service will only be able to access local resources on the same computer where it is running. The service cannot connect to a remote server on behalf of the user.
- *Use delegated credentials.* The user may provide the service with a password (rarely) or a ticket, or other credentials, that the service can use to impersonate the user on the computer where the service is running. In addition to that, the service can access other services on the network on behalf of the user, passing on the credentials provided by the user.

Different applications can choose different impersonation and delegation approaches, depending on their architecture and security requirements.

1.8 Cryptology, Cryptography, and Cryptanalysis

Cryptography is the science of protecting information, while cryptanalysis is the science of breaking protection, provided by cryptography. Cryptography and cryptanalysis together make cryptology.

1.8.1 The Goal of Cryptography

The goal of cryptography is to protect information using a mathematical approach. Cryptography is often expected to provide for the following types of protection:

- *Nondisclosure.* Cryptography allows for encryption of information and therefore protection of that information against disclosure to unauthorized individuals. For example, if Alice needs to send a secret message to Bob and no one else should be able to read this message, Alice can encrypt the message before sending it and Bob will decrypt the message to read it.
- *Signatures and data integrity.* Cryptography can be used to add a signed integrity control structure to messages so that the recipient of a message can determine if the message is genuine or has been modified. If Alice needs to send a message to Bob and wants to make sure that no one else will be able modify the contents of the message, then she needs to sign the message to protect its integrity.
- *Signatures and non-repudiation.* Cryptographic signatures can be used to determine whether a message has really been sent by a particular individual or is fake. If Alice enters into an agreement with Bob and digitally signs a contract, this certifies that Alice has agreed with all the requirements and benefits of that contract. The digital signature is proof of her identity and consent, similar to the signature on a piece of paper.
- *Identification and authentication.* Cryptography can be used to determine the identity and to authenticate users and services. In fact, most authentication methods are based on some cryptographic transformations. If Bob needs to make sure that Alice is who she says she is, he can use cryptographic algorithms to validate her identity.
- *Timestamping.* Cryptography can be used to add a timestamp to messages sent by a user or service. The timestamp is typically added by an independent party (a notary) to certify that a message has been sent at a certain time and date. If Alice sends a message to Bob at a specific date and time, a time notary service can add a signed timestamp to Alice's message to validate the time when the message was sent.

Cryptography achieves the above goals by two main cryptographic mechanisms: encryption and signing.

Protection provided by cryptography is not unbreakable. Cryptography is not impossible to overcome by a determined and skilful attacker that has unlimited time and resources at his disposal. Virtually every protection method is susceptible to compromise. The goal of cryptography is to make potential attacks computationally, and as a result — financially and timewise — infeasible. For example, information about patents is worth protecting for a limited period of time. Once the patent protection period has ended, information can be considered public. If breaking the protection of a document containing information about a patent will take 30 years, then it is not computationally feasible to try and break it. Furthermore, if protected information can be worth $100,000, and computing resources to break it will cost $500,000, then it is not financially acceptable to look at breaking the protection. In a similar fashion, if breaking the encryption of an encrypted user password will take two months, and a password policy forces users to change passwords every 14 days, then decrypting the password will not be worth the effort. Similarly, if a user account has access to information that may cost $10,000, and the resources needed to break the authentication mechanism are worth $50,000, then it is not cost effective to even attempt to break the protection.

1.8.2 Protection Keys

Cryptographic technologies take two main protection approaches:

1. *Secret algorithm.* Keep the algorithm used to protect messages secret so that only parties who need to be able to encrypt, decrypt, and sign messages know how to do that. For example, if an encryption algorithm defines a specific transformation of the plaintext in order to encrypt it, this transformation should be kept secret. The problem with this approach is that it does not work efficiently in commercially available systems. If a software company takes this protection approach for the products it is selling, a user with sufficient knowledge who already has the software product can reverse-engineer it and determine the encryption algorithm, and then even make it public by publishing it on the Internet, which will render the protection useless. This also applies in a similar fashion to hardware.
2. *Secret key(s).* Use a special password (a key or a number of keys) as input to the protection mechanism to protect messages. Keep the key (or keys) used to protect messages secret, although the protection algorithm may be well known and publicly available. The key is only known to the parties that need to be able to encrypt or decrypt the messages, and potentially generate or check the signature. For example, if communication between two computers needs to be encrypted, and encryption/decryption agents

on both computers are the only two that know the encryption key, even if a computer running the same encryption product in between the two peers is trying to decrypt the communication, it will fail to do so until it obtains the correct key.

For commercial systems, the approach using secret keys and publicly available algorithms has proven much more successful and provides much better protection than the approach using secret algorithms. Some of the most important reasons for this include:

- *Open encryption algorithms are available to the IT community, including cryptologists.* The strength of these algorithms can be analyzed; and if problems are found with the specific algorithm, cryptologists may be able to propose workarounds for these problems. This may include changes in the algorithm itself, the advice to not use specific keys (weak keys) with this algorithm, or other forms of advice that may be able to identify and contribute to the development of the specific algorithm, as well as other existing and future algorithms.
- *Secret keys scale better.* If two users need to communicate in a secure fashion, all they need is a shared secret (a password). It is not necessary to invent a new encryption algorithm for each secret conversation between two or more users, services, or applications.
- *Secret keys may change,* so that if two users no longer need to communicate with each other or do not trust each other anymore, they just need to use a different set of keys and they can start communicating with other users.
- *Keys may provide variable-strength protection.* Some cryptographic algorithms allow for the use of keys of variable size, so that if two parties communicate using messages that do not require the strongest possible protection, they can spare some CPU cycles using an algorithm that provides weaker protection and consumes less resources; if at some point in time the two users need to start communicating on a very secure matter, all they need to do is generate a longer key, which will consume more CPU resources but will provide for better protection.

When keys are used to encrypt information, there are two main approaches related to the types of keys being used:

1. *Symmetric approach.* The same key (called shared or symmetric key) is used by both the party encrypting the messages and the party decrypting the messages. An administrator may be able to

distribute the key in a secure fashion to only the parties that require this key. Key management is a problem with this approach, and often requires manual intervention. It is not easy to change keys very often due to the fact that there is typically manual intervention involved. A key compromise may lead to a third party being able to encrypt and decrypt messages. The size of the key is typically 56/64/128/168/256-bits, so encryption is not too resource consuming with regard to CPU cycles.
2. *Asymmetric approach.* A set of keys — private and public — is used to encrypt and, respectively, decrypt messages between the communicating parties. If the sender encrypts a message with the receiver's public key, the receiver can only use his own private key to decrypt the message. If the sender encrypts a message with his own private key, then the message can only be decrypted using the sender's public key, which is known to the recipient. Each party should make every effort possible to hide (protect) its private key, and should make its public key widely available by sending e-mails with the public key, or publishing the public key in the directory. Encryption in the long public key is very resource consuming and is typically avoided for bulk data encryption operations. Public key sizes vary but typically are 768/1028/2048 bits in size.

A hybrid approach is available as well: communicating parties can generate a secret symmetric key for actual encryption. The parties then use asymmetric encryption and protect the messages between them, and exchange the symmetric key that they have generated. Once this has been done, both parties have a copy of the symmetric key and they can switch to symmetric encryption for bulk user data.

1.8.2.1 Symmetric Encryption

Symmetric encryption mechanisms use one key or set of keys to encrypt messages, and exactly the same key or set of keys to decrypt messages. They are symmetric with regard to the encryption keys being used on the encrypting and decrypting end.

With symmetric encryption, the strength of protection strongly depends on the selection of a suitable secret key. Important factors to consider when using secret keys include:

- *Random/predictable keys.* If a key is to be secret, it must only be known to the parties that want to communicate. A third party that wants to interfere with the communication process must not be able to predict what the key will be. A key should therefore not be based on publicly available information. The best keys would be those that are completely random. Unfortunately, there is nothing random in the way computers operate, so machine-generated keys are pseudo-random. Human-generated keys are likely to be even less random. A combination of the two — such as having the user generate some random input, such as mouse movements or a sequence of keystrokes, that can then be fed as input into the machine pseudo-random function — is likely to provide the best results.

- *Keyspace.* If an attacker tries to guess a key, he will try to determine combinations that are more likely to be used and will try those first. For example, if a key is 4 bytes long, the possible key space would be $2^{8*4} = 2^{32} = 4{,}294{,}967{,}296$ possible combinations. However, if the key only consists of digits (such as a PIN code), then the possible combinations are only $10^4 = 10{,}000$. It is important for keys to use the entire keyspace, and not just portions of it.
- *Key length.* In general, the longer the key, the more difficult it is to guess the key and — as a result — to decrypt a message. If the key is generated in a random (or pseudo-random) fashion, all the attacker can do is try to guess the key by trying all the possible keys, or at least the most likely keys. A key that is 2 bytes (16-bits) long will result in 65,536 possible combinations, which a modern computer will be able to generate and check in less than one second. A key that is 32 bits in length will result in more than 4,294,967,296 possible combinations, which appears to be a minor challenge. Keys of length 64 bits are virtually 4,294,967,296 times stronger than 32-bit keys, and even these keys are considered week nowadays. 128- and 256-bit keys are considered secure at the time of this writing.
- *Key protection.* Communicating parties must provide appropriate protection for the secret keys. It is important not only to generate such a key, but also to store it in a secure fashion. Possible locations include files on the hard drive of a computer, floppy disks, and smart cards. The secret key can also be entered by a human when required, and not stored anywhere. Unfortunately, this can only be the case for weak keys, such as human-readable and memorable words, and is unlikely to be the case for random, 128-bit keys, especially if they are changed on a regular basis.
- *Key exchange.* After generating the key, it must be delivered to the communicating parties in a secure manner. The key can be configured by an administrator for all the communicating devices and services. Alternatively, the key can be transported on physical

media, such as a USB drive or memory stick, floppy disk, or smart card. Finally and most often, there may be a special key management protocol responsible for generating keys and distributing them across the network.

1.8.2.2 Asymmetric Keys

Asymmetric keys are pairs of keys such that if one of the keys is used to encrypt a message, only the other key from the pair can decrypt the message, and vice versa. Unlike symmetric cryptographic algorithms, if a key is used to encrypt a message, this same key cannot be used to decrypt the message. Therefore, asymmetric algorithms are asymmetric with regard to the protection keys being used.

The pair of keys typically consists of a public key and a private key. The public key for a party is publicly known and everyone who will communicate with this party needs to know its public key. Every party is responsible for distributing its public key to other peers by publishing it in a directory, sending it in an e-mail message, or exchanging it with them in some other way. When such a party distributes its public key, there is no need to protect it by means of encryption because it is not secret. However, the party can sign the key to make sure that it is authentic and not replaced by a malicious third party that may do so to launch a man-in-the-middle attack. Public key signing is available in some key distribution approaches, such as X.509 certificates.

There are different algorithms that can be used to generate asymmetric keys for data protection. All of these algorithms are based on mathematical problems that are difficult to solve. All the algorithms rely on a keypair, consisting of a public key, which is publicly known and typically made available in user directories, and a corresponding private key, which needs to be kept secret by its holder and not disclosed to any party, however trusted. There is a strong mathematical relation between the private and public keys, and each public key has one corresponding private key.

The most popular asymmetric key scheme is RSA. It was inspired by the Diffie-Hellman Key Agreement algorithm, invented in the 1970s. The three researchers who invented RSA were Ron Rivest, Adi Shamir, and Leonard Adelman, and the algorithm was named after the first letters of their surnames. Rivest, Shamir, and Adelman later established their own security company — RSA Security.

The RSA algorithm is based on the assumption that factoring is difficult. The RSA algorithm generates keypairs in the following way:

1. Find two large primes **p** and **q**.
2. Calculate **n** = **p*q** (**n** is called the modulus).

3. Find another number **e** < **n**; **(n, e)** is called the public key.
4. Find another number **d** such that **(e*d**–1) is divisible by (**p**–1) * (**q**–1). (**n, d)** is the private key.

It is straightforward to compute **e** by following the algorithm above. However, given only **e**, it is not easy to compute **d**. As a result, if someone only knows the public key for a user, he cannot decrypt messages sent to that user.

There are other asymmetric key algorithms in use today. For example, elliptic curve problems are the basis of Elliptic Curves Cryptosystems (ECCs). The mathematical problem behind ECC is known as the elliptic curve discrete logarithm problem. Elliptic curves are an important and growing area of asymmetric cryptography, primarily due to the fact that unlike RSA keys, ECC key lengths can be considerably shorter than RSA public/private keys, and yet provide for the same level of security. The actual ECC calculation is also very simple, so this makes ECC very useful for embedded devices and other devices that have limited processing power.

Another asymmetric key generation approach is the ElGamal algorithm, which is based on the discrete logarithm problem and is similar to the Diffie-Hellman algorithm (see below). Although the mathematical problem is different, key sizes and protection are similar to those provided by RSA. The ElGamal algorithm provides for both data encryption and signing. More details are available from the IEEE (see [132]).

The ElGamal algorithm for asymmetric keys has been implemented by the FIPS Digital Signature Standard (DSS), and keys are sometimes referred to as DSA keys. The DSS Digital Signature Algorithm is used for signing purposes only, and not for encryption (see subsection 1.8.4.2).

Asymmetric keys can be used by themselves or in combination with X.509 or PGP certificates to implement a trust model or to tie additional attributes to the actual keys.

1.8.2.3 Hybrid Approaches: Diffie-Hellman Key Exchange Algorithm

When two parties want to communicate in a secure fashion over an insecure medium, they must first establish protection keys. If the two parties know each other, they may want to use a secret key. If the two parties do not know each other, they may want to use certificates issued by trusted third parties. There are cases, however, where neither of the two parties knows each other and can therefore share a secret key, nor have both parties certificates they can use.

Diffie-Hellman is a key agreement protocol wherein the two communicating parties can establish protection keys for their conversation over an insecure medium, without having prior knowledge of each other. Whitfield Diffie and Martin Hellman invented the protocol in the 1970s. Along with Ralph Merkle, they are considered the inventors of public key cryptography.

Before trying to establish a connection, the communicating parties (say, Alice and Bob) need to negotiate, or have set to use a specific cyclic group known as a Diffie-Hellman group. The cyclic groups are well-known arrays of numbers. Each group has a generator **g**. Within this group, Alice and Bob can choose a prime number **p** such that **b** < **p**. The prime number **p** is such that for every number $\mathbf{1 <= n <= p-1}$, the following is true: $\mathbf{n = g^k}$ mod **p**. The numbers **p** and **g** are publicly known and are available to Alice, Bob, and potential attackers who may be eavesdropping on the insecure channel between Alice and Bob.

After selecting the numbers **g** and **p**, the Diffie-Hellman key algorithm is the following:

1. Alice generates a secret random number **a** and sends Bob ($\mathbf{g^a}$ mod **p**), which is Alice's public value. **a** is Alice's private value, known only to Alice.
2. Bob generates a secret random number **b** and sends Alice ($\mathbf{g^b}$ mod **p**), which is Bob's public value. **b** is Bob's private value, known only to Bob.
3. Alice calculates ($\mathbf{g^a}$ mod $\mathbf{p})^{\mathbf{b}}$ mod **p**.
4. Bob calculates ($\mathbf{g^b}$ mod $\mathbf{p})^{\mathbf{a}}$ mod **p**.
5. From the above calculation, both Alice and Bob deduce that **k** = $\mathbf{g^{ab}}$ mod **p**. And **k** is the secret key that Alice and Bob will use.

The protection provided by the Diffie-Hellman key agreement protocol is based on the fact that both Alice and Bob can easily calculate the key **k** = $\mathbf{g^{ab}}$ mod **p** using the above algorithm, despite the fact that Alice does not know **b** and Bob does not know **a**. A potential attacker on the insecure channel, however, will not be able to calculate **k**, as this attacker knows neither **a** nor **b**.

It is important to note that as a result of the Diffie-Hellman key agreement, a single encryption key is generated. This key will typically be used by secret key (symmetric) encryption algorithms.

A problem with Diffie-Hellman is that it is susceptible to man-in-the-middle attacks. A third party can sit on the communications channel between Alice and Bob, intercept their messages, and replace the ($\mathbf{g^a}$ mod **p**) and ($\mathbf{g^b}$ mod **p**) values from Alice and Bob, respectively, with his own values. The man-in-the-middle can then intercept the communication channel between Alice and Bob, decrypt messages sent from one to another, and potentially relay and re-encrypt the messages if it does not want to be noticed. To avoid man-in-the-middle attacks, Diffie-Hellman typically involves peer authentication schemes.

1.8.3 Encryption

Encryption is the art of reversibly transforming data so that it can only be available to authorized users. Encryption takes a plaintext message, which can be human readable or structured in some way, applies an encryption algorithm to it, and converts the message into cryptotext. Decryption is the reverse process, whereby an encrypted message is transformed into plaintext. If someone wants to read the message, he must decrypt it.

The fact that encryption provides a reversible transformation between a cleartext message and a cryptotext means that there is correspondence between the cleartext and the cryptotext. The cryptotext will always be restored to the same cleartext, provided that the algorithm, the encryption key, and other encryption parameters are the same.

Historically, there have been many types of encryption algorithms. The two types of encryption algorithms with regard to the way they process the plaintext message are (1) block ciphers and (2) stream ciphers.

Block ciphers process messages in portions, typically 64 bytes in size. Block ciphers break messages into smaller chunks and then encrypt each piece separately. Then all the encrypted blocks are concatenated together, and this results in the final encrypted message.

Stream ciphers do not process information in blocks. They receive information as a stream (byte by byte). Protection keys can be generated as a virtually endless, binary stream of 0's and 1's. The user message is then combined with the keystream, typically using XOR.

A consideration with both block and stream ciphers is that they are reversible — there is a two-way correspondence between the ciphertext and the cleartext, and someone who knows the key can easily generate either the cryptotext from the ciphertext, or vice versa. If the processes of encryption and decryption only depend on the key, the same cleartext will always produce the same ciphertext. If the key is rarely changed, an attacker may be able to deduce the correspondence between ciphertext and cleartext, especially if the attacker has some knowledge of what the cleartext might contain. An attacker can therefore build a dictionary and even come up with a list of encrypted messages and their cleartext equivalent without knowing the actual key.

To avoid such attacks, most of today's encryption protocols allow for the so-called *salt* or *initial vector*. The salt is a random octet string generated by the sender of the message and is provided to the receiver in cleartext. The salt is not encrypted and is therefore also known to the attacker. The salt is used by the encryption algorithm to either modify the cleartext before the actual encryption, or to generate an encryption key from the shared key. A new salt can be generated either for every message or for a specific session, or at predetermined intervals. As a result of using a salt, encrypted messages are no longer a function of the shared key only — they are a function of the shared key (which is only known to the communicating peers) *and* the salt (which is publicly known). This means that even if the same cleartext is encrypted twice with the same shared key, the cryptotext will be different, subject to the salt being different and randomly generated for every message or session.

More details on encryption algorithms can be found in the RSA FAQ (see [123]), as well as Bruce Schneier's *Applied Cryptography* (see [I]).

Some of the most popular encryption algorithms, which are also used in user authentication, are DES/3DES, RC4, RC5, and AES. The following sub-sections provide a brief overview of how these algorithms operate.

1.8.3.1 Data Encryption Standard (DES/3DES)

The Data Encryption Standard (DES) is a U.S. Federal Information Processing (FIPS) Standard that defines the Data Encryption Algorithm (DEA) that was invented by IBM in the 1970s. The DEA was based on the Lucifer encryption algorithm. The DES was originally a U.S. federal standard but it is widely used all over the world and has been adopted as standard by other countries as well.

DES supports both block and stream encryption mechanisms. The key used by DES is 56 bits in size (7 octets). The DES algorithm expands the 56-bit key to 64 bits by distributing the 56 bits of the key in 8 octets, adding a parity bit to each octet.

The actual DES encryption process is a combination of permutations, substitutions, and rotations based on the DES key and precalculated substitution tables. The details are available in [124].

Many block cipher algorithms, including DES, support two block modes and two stream modes of operation, as described below.

- *ECB (electronic code book)— block mode.* This is the simplest form of operation. Data is divided into 64-bit blocks and encryption is performed independently for every block. There is no feedback between the blocks. The final result is the concatenation of all the encrypted blocks. This easy-to-implement mode of operation has one disadvantage: unlike other modes of operation, it does not use a salt to modify the plaintext, so every time ECB is used on a plaintext with the same key, it will generate the same result. Furthermore, because there is no feedback between the 64-bit blocks, and each is encrypted independently, they can also be attacked independently. Compromising the key used to encrypt one block can lead to a full compromise of all the available blocks, regardless of whether the message is available in full.

- *CBC (cipher block chaining)— block mode.* This mode of operation provides for a feedback function. The algorithm uses a DES key and an initial vector to encrypt cleartext data using block mode. The first cleartext block is XORed with the initial vector, and then encrypted using ECB, as described above. Every next cleartext block is first XORed with the previous ciphertext block. This provides for feedback (chaining) between the blocks, so blocks cannot be attacked separately. This makes it more difficult for a cryptanalyst to successfully decrypt the ciphertext.
- *CFB (cipher feedback) — stream mode.* In this mode, the plaintext is not encrypted using the DES algorithm. For the first block, the initial vector is fed into a 64-bit shift register and encrypted using DES; then the result is XORed with the first block from the cleartext message to produce the cipher block. This cipher block is then XORed with the contents of the shift register. The shift register is then encrypted using DES, and the result is XORed with the next cleartext block, etc.
- *OFB (output feedback) — stream mode.* This mode is similar to CFB. However, instead of XORing the shift register with the actual ciphertext block, it is XORed with the previous DES encrypted shift register value. The cleartext therefore does not provide feedback into the key for the next block. As a result, a ciphertext block can be decrypted if the initial vector and the key are known, even without having the complete message.

In the 1990s, several researchers came to the conclusion that DES has some inherent weaknesses and thus cannot be considered secure. Furthermore, using distributed applications such as Distributed Net that allows the consolidated computing power of tens of thousands computers on the Internet to be used in parallel, it was proven that DES messages can be decrypted in as little as a couple of hours. Therefore, for most applications, standard 56-bit DES is now considered insufficient in terms of the protection that it can provide.

3DES (TripleDES) is a popular update of the DES standard that provides considerably better protection. In essence, the 3DES encryption process is a combination of three DES encryption and decryption operations, and is not a separate encryption algorithm per se.

3DES can use one, two, or three 56-bit keys (K1, K2, or K3) to perform encryption, depending on the selected mode of operation. 3DES has two popular modes of operation:

1. *3DES-EDE (Encrypt-Decrypt-Encrypt).* In this mode of operation, encryption of the cleartext block is performed by applying DES encryption in key K1, DES decryption in key K2, and then DES encryption in key K3, in this order. The message can be decrypted using the original three keys and applying the encryption and decryption operations above in reverse order.
2. *3DES-EEE (Encrypt-Encrypt-Encrypt).* In this mode of operation, the message is DES encrypted three times in the keys K1, K2, and K3 in this order. Decryption requires the same three keys and decryption in them is applied in reverse order.

It is commonly accepted that due to the use of three 56-bit encryption keys, the key strength of 3DES is 168 bits. In some implementations, however, the keys K1, K2, and K3 are not independent. Some implementations may use K1=K3, and some may even use K1=K2=K3 (which is equivalent to DES when applied in EDE mode).

1.8.3.2 Advanced Encryption Standard (AES)

AES was developed by the Belgian cryptographers Joan Daemen and Vincent Rijmen in response to an initiative of the U.S. NIST to develop a replacement for DES back in 1997. The name of the algorithm at the time of submission was Rijndael but it was later renamed AES. The AES standard was published by NIST at the end of 2001 and is now considered a *de jure* standard for strong encryption. In fact, NIST's intention is to use AES for the next couple of decades — so strong is this encryption mechanism considered.

AES is a byte-oriented iterated block cipher. It consists of four steps:

1. *Byte stub:* a step to ensure that encryption is nonlinear.
2. *Shift row:* diffusion between columns.
3. *Mix column:* diffusion within each column.
4. *Round key addition:* final transformation.

The algorithm is believed to be very efficient and requires moderate processing power, despite its strength. It can be easily parallelized on today's multiprocessor computers.

AES supports three key sizes: 128-bit keys, 192-bit keys, and 256-bit keys. Apparently, with longer keys, encryption is expected to be virtually unbreakable for today's computers.

1.8.3.3 RC4 (ARCFOUR)

RC4 (Rivest Cipher 4) is a symmetric keystream cipher, invented by Ronald Rivest, one of the founders of RSA Security. RC4 was a trade secret but leaked into the public in 1994, and since then it has been used on the Internet. However, the name RC4 was protected by a trademark. Hence, some RC4 implementations refer to the algorithms as ARCFOUR.

RC4 is surprisingly simple. It uses a pseudo-random function and the substitution table to generate a keystream. The pseudo-random function is run as many times as required to generate a keystream of the same size as the message to be encrypted. Each time the pseudo-random function is invoked, the substitution table is modified, which presents feedback into the encryption process. The substitution table also provides for an encryption state for the RC4 algorithm. To decrypt a message, the recipient must perform operations similar to the ones performed by the sender to reach the specific encryption state (substitution table). The use of an encryption state plays the role of a salt and makes the RC4 encryption algorithm stronger. Some applications ignore the state of the RC4 protocol and reinitialize the substitution table every time they need to send a new message but this considerably weakens the strength of RC4.

RC4 works as follows. First, RC4 initializes a substitution table that is 256 bytes in size, and assigns two pointers to it. Then RC4 uses the encryption key to modify the contents of the substitution table. As a final step in the encryption process, the keystream generated by a pseudo-random function is XORed with the cleartext message to produce the ciphertext. RC4 supports different key lengths. Most implementations use 40-, 128-, or 256-bit keys.

There are a number of attacks against the RC4 protocol. Some of them are based on the fact that RC4-generated keystreams are not truly random, and some are based on the fact that weak RC4 implementations reset the substitution table before each encryption. Technically, RC4 is considered an encryption algorithm providing for moderate data protection.

In addition to RC4, Rivest created some other encryption algorithms, including RC2, RC5, and RC6, which are block encryption algorithms and are not as widely used as RC4.

1.8.3.4 RSA Encryption Algorithm (Asymmetric Encryption)

The RSA encryption algorithm uses RSA asymmetric keypairs. To encrypt a message, the sender must obtain the public key of the recipient. The public key can be stored in a directory, or can be provided by the recipient to the sender by some other means (e.g., e-mail) or stored in a file in a shared access location. The public key is not secret.

The public key is typically 1024 or 2048 bits long, although this size can vary. The public key is a function of the numbers **n** and **e.**

The sender performs encryption of a message **m** using the recipient public key (**n, e**) and obtaining the crypto message **c** using the following formula:

$$\mathbf{c} = \mathbf{m}^{\mathbf{e}} \bmod \mathbf{n}$$

The message **c** cannot be easily decrypted using the public key (**n, e**). The reason for this is that it is too difficult to factor the values **p** and **q** from **n**. To decrypt the message **c**, the recipient must use his private key (**n, d**) and the following formula:

$$\mathbf{m} = \mathbf{c}^{\mathbf{d}} \bmod \mathbf{n}$$

Due to the fact that the private key **(n, d)** is secret and no one except the recipient knows it, the message cannot be decrypted by anyone else — unless they solve the factoring problem.

It is important to understand the interdependency between the private key **(n, d)** and the public key **(n, e).** If a message is encrypted using the public key **(n, e)**, it can only be decrypted using the private key **(n, d)**, and no other key. If the message is encrypted using the private key **(n, d)**, it can only be decrypted using the public key **(n, e).** The latter is the basis of the RSA Signing algorithm.

The RSA encryption algorithm is considered very secure but it is impractical for the encryption of bulk data. Due to the large key sizes used by asymmetric encryption methods, the encryption process is very CPU intensive. In most cases, communicating parties will select a random or pseudo-random encryption key and will exchange it using RSA encryption. The key will be encrypted using RSA but the actual data encryption will typically use symmetric encryption in the exchanged key.

1.8.4 Data Integrity

An important aspect of cryptography is protecting data integrity from accidental or intentional modification. Accidental data integrity violations include transmission errors, media errors, and noise. Intentional modification generally refers to hacker attacks trying to modify data content while stored on media or in transit.

To provide for data integrity, today's cryptography typically suggests the use of message integrity codes (MICs) that can then be protected with a symmetric or asymmetric key to become message authentication codes (MACs).

Although they are often confused, MACs differ from user authentication. MACs are meant to use cryptographic mechanisms to ascertain that user data is not modified improperly. The process of ascertaining the integrity of user data is often referred to as data integrity authentication, or message authentication, or data authentication, or even just authentication, which makes it even more confusing.

User authentication is the process of ascertaining the identity of a user and typically takes place before user data is transferred on the network. User authentication is also sometimes referred to as just authentication. Apparently, there is difference between the two, and they should not be confused.

1.8.4.1 Message Integrity Code (MIC)

Message integrity code (MIC) is a one-way function of the message that must be protected. The MIC provides a hash (digest) of the entire message and can use a linear or nonlinear algorithm. It can be considered a checksum for the message. It is important to understand that the actual message cannot be restored from the MIC, and hence the statement that the MIC is a one-way function.

If a sender needs to guarantee the integrity of a message, he can send the message followed by a MIC code, calculated for that specific message. If the message is modified in transit, the recipient will calculate the MIC for the received message and compare it with the MIC sent with the original message. If the two do not match, the message has been altered.

Because the MIC represents a one-way function, there is more than one cleartext message that corresponds to a specific MIC. Technically, this means that if a sender generates a message and an MIC for it, and the message gets modified in transit, then a recipient might receive a completely different message with the same MIC. The recipient can therefore be convinced that the message has not been modified. The fact that each MIC has more than one corresponding cleartext message is referred to as collision. MIC algorithms should provide for as few collisions as possible. Apparently, it is not possible to eliminate all collisions due to the one-way nature of the hash function.

There are a number of algorithms that can be used to calculate MICs. Some of the popular algorithms that are also used in user authentication mechanisms include the following.

- *CRC32.* CRC32 is a linear MIC that generates a 32-bit hash from the cleartext message. CRC32 represents the message to be protected as a polynomial, and uses polynominal division to generate the MIC. CRC32 is capable of detecting specific changes in the message, but not all. For example, the addition or deletion of a string of 0's cannot be detected. Furthermore, it is easy to modify data without changing the MIC for that data. Therefore, CRC32 is primarily used in hardware for error detection and is not recommended for data integrity protection.

- *MD2, MD4, and MD5.* MD2 (Message Digest 2), MD4 (Message Digest 4), and MD5 (Message Digest 5) are MIC functions invented by Roland Rivest (see [5], [125], [126]). All these functions generate a 128-bit hash from a cleartext message.

  MD2 is now considered old, and collisions have been found in this algorithm. It is virtually not used anymore.

  MD4 was designed for implementation in software on 32-bit computers. The original cleartext message is processed in three rounds. Not long after its release, however, it became clear that there are collisions in the MD4 algorithm, and that the one-way function is not really irreversible. Therefore, MD4 is currently considered weak and should be avoided.

  MD5 was designed as a strengthened version of MD4. MD5 uses four rounds of processing. Compared to MD4, round 4 is a new function and the function in round 2 has been altered. Furthermore, MD5 uses additive constants and feedback between processing steps. Still, collisions have been found in the MD5 compression function.

  The MD4 and MD5 algorithms are widely used and are very similar. Despite the fact that they have collisions, MD5 is considered reasonably secure and is the most popular data integrity algorithm on the Internet.

- *SHA-1.* SHA-1 is the U.S. National Security Agency (NSA) standard for message integrity. SHA-1 generates a 160-bit output hash. SHA-1 uses an algorithm very similar to MD5 but is generally considered stronger than MD5, and unlike MD5 is a government agency published standard rather than an Internet standard.

  Despite the fact that SHA-1 is not collision-free either (see [129]), it is currently considered very secure and is widely used in the Internet.

1.8.4.2 Message Authentication Code (MAC)

Message integrity codes (MICs) provide for error detection but are not suitable by themselves for message authentication or digital signatures. This is primarily due to the fact that the MIC might protect a message from modification but there is nothing that can protect the MIC itself. If an attacker is able to modify the message and the attached MIC, then data integrity is no longer guaranteed. Therefore, the industry has come up with MACs that involve symmetric or public key cryptography to protect the integrity of messages.

HMAC

HMAC (Hashed Message Authentication Code) is a NIST standard, defined in [130]. HMAC specifies how a key can be used to protect MIC functions. HMAC defines the protection of the MIC function by a stream cipher function in the secret key.

HMAC is very simple to implement. If the cleartext message to be protected is **b** bytes long, then the HMAC specification defines the so-called inner and outer pads in the following way:

ipad = the byte 0x36 repeated **b** times

opad = the byte 0x5C repeated **b** times

There can virtually be HMAC equivalents for all MIC functions. If **H** is the MIC function for which the HMAC equivalent is being calculated, and **K** is the secret **K** to protect the MAC, then:

MAC(**text**) = HMAC(**K**, **text**)
= H((**K** XOR **opad**) || H((**K** XOR **ipad**) || **text**))

Similar to MICs, HMACs always have a fixed size, which is the same as the corresponding MIC. If the result from the above calculation is longer than the standard hash size, only the leftmost part of it is used so that the HMAC size is adjusted accordingly.

To denote the use of a particular MIC, HMACs are typically referred to as HMAC-MD5 (denoting the use of MD5) or HMAC-SHA1 (denoting the use of SHA-1).

MD2.5

RFC 1964 (see [51]) defines a keyed MD5 variant referred to as MD2.5. This MAC algorithm only uses half (i.e., 8 bytes) of the MIC generated by MD5. Before generating the MD5 hash, the MD2.5 algorithm also prepends the cleartext to be hashed with the result from the DES-CBC encryption of a message consisting of all 0's with a zero initial vector and the protection key in reverse order as the key. The MD2.5 algorithm is considered a MAC because the string prepended to the cleartext depends on the protection key.

DES-CBC MAC

As already discussed, block ciphers in cipher block chaining (CBC) mode are capable of using feedback between blocks, so that the encryption of each block, as well as the cryptotext for the block, depend on all previous blocks of the message. This has led researchers to use DES-CBC as a message authentication code. The last encrypted block from a message will be generated with feedback from all previous blocks, and the DES algorithm uses a key to perform encryption. Therefore, if only the last block of a message is taken, the entire message cannot be restored (so the algorithm is irreversible, which is a requirement), the block depends on all previous blocks of the message and is protected with a key (the DES key).

DES-CBC MACs are not as widely used as HMAC functions but are a secure way for protecting message integrity.

A variant of DES-CBC MAC is DES-CBC MD5, whereby as a final round, a 16-byte MD5 hash is calculated for the DES-CBC MAC.

RSA Signature (Asymmetric Algorithm)

The RSA Signature algorithm is based on the RSA encryption algorithm. If a message **m** needs to be signed, RSA Signature requires the sender of the message to sign it using his own private key **(n, d)** and the following formula:

$$\mathbf{s} = \mathbf{m}^{d} \bmod \mathbf{n}$$

Essentially, the above formula represents RSA Encryption using the sender's private key. Because only the sender possesses his public key, no one else can generate the signature **s** from the message **m**. A recipient can verify the signature of the message **s** by decrypting **s** using the sender's public key **(n, e).**

The signature algorithm described above is based on encryption and provides for assurance that the sender and the message are genuine. In RSA implementations, however, the algorithm used to generate an RSA signature is a bit different.

The signature of a message in RSA implementations is not represented by the actual message, encrypted in the sender's private key. To generate a signature, the sender first generates a hash of the message, using an MIC algorithm supported by both the sender and the recipient, such as MD5. The hash itself is then encrypted in the sender's private key and attached to the actual message. Therefore, the message is not encrypted but it has an encrypted hash (called signature) attached to it that can validate both the sender and the message. Upon receipt of the message, the recipient needs to calculate the same hash for the cleartext message, and then decrypt the signature using the sender's public key. If the calculated and the decrypted hash for this message match, the message and the sender are genuine. If they do not match, either the sender does not possess the private key (and therefore may be an attacker claiming to be the real sender of the message) or the message has been tampered with (an attacker has maliciously modified the message).

DSA/DSS (Asymmetric Algorithm)

The Digital Signature Algorithm (DSA) is another public key cryptographic technique used for data signing. The use of the DSA for data signing is defined as the NIST Digital Signature Standard (DSS) in [131].

DSA is very similar to RSA but does not provide for message encryption — only for message signing. Key sizes for DSA are 512 or 1024 bits. DSA uses SHA-1 as the hashing algorithm.

It is important to note that RSA signature generation is a relatively slow process, whereas RSA signature verification is a fast process. With DSA, signature generation is a fast process while signature verification is a slow, processor-intensive process. Due to the fact that the signature is generated only once and then verified many times, RSA supporters claim that the RSA signature is more efficient than DSS because it consumes less cycles. Considering the processing power of today's computers, however, this is becoming less important.

DSA is currently considered a secure algorithm and is used in a number of applications and authentication schemes.

Chapter 2

UNIX User Authentication Architecture

UNIX is basically a simple operating system, but you have to be a genius to understand the simplicity.

— **Dennis Ritchie**

This chapter discusses the general mechanics of user authentication in UNIX. It begins with the legacy concepts and plain user authentication files, and then shows how user authentication works in large network environments.

2.1 Users and Groups

Before a user can access resources on a UNIX computer, he needs to have an account and typically a password for this account. Authentication methods other than a password are being relatively widely adopted as well.

2.1.1 Overview

The user account in UNIX has at least the following three important attributes:

1. Username: a unique name by which the user is identified to the system.
2. UID (User ID): a number (integer) that uniquely identifies the user on the system.
3. GID (Group ID): a number (integer) that specifies the user's primary group.

When a user logs in to the system interactively or accesses resources from the network, these three attributes must be made available to the server system, and they are used to authorize the user to access resources and potentially to reflect this access in system log and audit files. As discussed, these three attributes are the result of the authentication process, and are typically called privileges, or access token (in addition, some UNIX documentation sources call these simply IDs, others call them persona).

User IDs (or UIDs) are unique numbers assigned to users. Actually, the UNIX system expects that these numbers are unique but does not enforce uniqueness. Most system programs as well as applications will typically use the UID to provide or deny access (authorize access), while the username is typically used only during the authentication process as a human readable equivalent of the UID/GID.

The user **root** is a superuser in UNIX. This user can potentially access and modify everything on a UNIX system, and security restrictions are typically not enforced for this user. The operating system distinguishes the superuser by its UID, which must always be zero. The root user account may have a different name but will still have administrative privileges if the UID for that account is zero. Therefore, the superuser can be (and sometimes due to security reasons is) renamed to something different than root.

On a typical UNIX system, in addition to the superuser system account (**root**), there are also other system accounts and they are used by various daemons. As a convention — which is again not being enforced by the operating system — system accounts should use the lowest 100 user IDs (or 500, as is the case with Fedora; see the configuration file **/etc/login.defs**) to distinguish them from regular users.

To simplify administration and authorization for resource access and sometimes for non-security-related purposes, UNIX provides group accounts, simply called groups. Groups are collections of user accounts. Each group can have zero or more members. Each user can be a member of one or more groups.

When a user logs in, he is assigned a list of group IDs (GIDs) for groups of which the user is a member by default, and this membership is reflected in his access token. From that point on, the user's privileges are such that they provide access to any resource for which either the user individually, or any of the group accounts of which this user is effectively a member, has access.

One and only one group is defined as the user's primary group. This is the only group specified by its GID as a user attribute in the **/etc/passwd** file (membership to non-primary groups is specified in the **/etc/group** file and is an attribute of the group). The primary group has a simple purpose: it is used as the group owner for objects (mostly files, as everything in UNIX, but these might be database records or other objects, too) that the user creates. When the user logs in to the system, the effective group set as the owner of newly created objects by that user is the primary group. However, the user can use the **newgrp** command to change the effective group to another group, of which the user may or may not be a member.

In addition to the primary group, each user can be assigned or log in to supplementary groups. In fact, the user access permissions to resources are determined based on the cumulative permissions, granted to the user individually, to the user's primary group, and to all user's supplementary groups.

In UNIX, groups have passwords that allow access to them by non-members. Users who are not explicitly listed as members of a group but know the password for the group can log in to that group, which will add this group's privileges to their current effective privileges (i.e., will add another GID to their list of effective GIDs), and users can then access all the resources to which this new group has access.

2.1.2 Case Study: Duplicate UIDs

Fedora allows the administrator to create user entries with duplicate UIDs. An administrator that wants to create accounts with duplicate UIDs can do so by either modifying directly the **/etc/passwd** and **/etc/shadow** files, or use the **useradd** command with the **–o** switch.

As a result, the administrator may have the following entries in the **/etc/passwd** file:

```
[root@Dennis ~]# cat /etc/passwd | grep 9111
user1:x:9111:500:User1:/home/user1:/bin/bash
user2:x:9111:500:User2:/home/user2:/bin/bash
[root@Dennis ~]#
```

It is important to note that the UID for both **user1** and **user2** is the same — **9111**. If a user tries to log in using each of these two accounts, he would likely see the following results:

```
login as: user1
user1@10.0.2.101's password:
Last login: Sun Sep  4 00:20:30 2005 from 10.0.2.1
-bash-3.00$ id
uid=9111(user1) gid=500(admin) groups=500(admin)
-bash-3.00$
-bash-3.00$ exit
$ ssh 10.0.2.101
login as: user2
user2@10.0.2.101's password:
Last login: Sun Sep  4 00:44:45 2005 from 10.0.2.1
-bash-3.00$
-bash-3.00$ id
uid=9111(user1) gid=500(admin) groups=500(admin)
-bash-3.00$
```

Apparently, although the user authenticates as **user2**, sshd resolves the username to the UID — **9111** in this instance — and from that point on uses the UID exclusively. When the user tries to determine his effective user and group IDs (UIDs and GIDs), it turns out that effectively he is using the identity of **user1** in both cases, despite the fact that he has been successfully authenticated as **user2** using **user2**'s password in the second part of this example.

A possible scenario where an administrator might want to use duplicate IDs is when he wants to have different usernames and passwords that result in the exact same set of privileges — multiple root-level access accounts, for example. It is arguable whether this is a good approach because, to a certain extent, it limits the ability to track and audit user activities on the system, and this is a severe problem from a security perspective. To avoid such confusion, duplicate UIDs should be avoided whenever possible.

2.1.3 Case Study: Group Login and Supplementary Groups

The following sample session shows how users can manipulate the list of effective groups of which they are a member:

```
login as: user1
user1@10.0.2.101's password:
Last login: Sun Sep  4 01:16:12 2005 from 10.0.2.1
-bash-3.00$
-bash-3.00$ groups user1
user1 : group1 group2
-bash-3.00$ id
```

```
uid=9111(user1) gid=9201(group1) groups=9201(group1),9202(group2)
-bash-3.00$ newgrp group3
Password:
bash-3.00$ id
uid=9111(user1) gid=9203(group3) groups=9201(group1),9202(group2),920
3(group3)
bash-3.00$ newgrp group4
Password:
bash-3.00$ id
uid=9111(user1) gid=9204(group4) groups=9201(group1),9202(group2),920
3(group3),    9204(group4)
bash-3.00$
```

When **user1** logs into the system, he is only assigned membership to the two groups for which he is listed as a member: **group1** and **group2** (see the output from the **groups user1** command, which basically returns information based on the content of the **/etc/passwd** and **/etc/groups** files).

Using the command **newgrp**, **user1** logs in to **group3**. Apparently, the user now has **group3** as part of his effective access token. Furthermore, the effective group has been changed to **group3;** the **newgrp** command not only allows the user to authenticate to the new group; but also sets this group as the effective group to be used as the owner of newly created objects by that user.

As **user1** uses **newgrp** to log in to **group4** as well, this new group is also added to his access token, while membership to the rest of the groups is still retained. When the user creates new files and other objects, **group4** will be specified as the owner of these objects but the user will be able to access resources to which either he (**user1**) or any of the groups **group1**, **group2**, **group3,** and **group4** have been allowed access (effective permissions).

The concept of user authentication to groups is different from Windows NT/2000/2003, where user membership to groups is defined by the system administrator or an individual with appropriate permissions for the group, and users cannot utilize the group and its assigned permissions unless they are explicitly added to the group.

2.2 Simple User Credential Stores

To authenticate to the operating system, the UNIX user must provide proof of identity (credentials). Depending on the factors of user authentication, and the configuration of the operating system or service, there may be a combination of credential authorities and databases used to validate user credentials. The following sections discuss some of the common user authentication databases and authorities.

2.2.1 UNIX Password Encryption

UNIX stores user passwords in an encrypted form. Despite the popular misconception, encrypted passwords cannot be decrypted easily. Nevertheless, it is a good idea to move these passwords to the root-only accessible **/etc/shadow** file and keep them away from malicious users. In addition to decryption, there are other effective password attacks, such as dictionary attacks, brute force, etc.

Historically, UNIX has used the **crypt( )** function to encrypt user passwords. The crypt function accepts two parameters: key and salt. The key parameter is the user's password. The salt parameter is a randomly generated two-character string, used to perturb the DES algorithm. Only the first 12 bits from this parameter are used, which allows for 4096 different variations of the DES algorithm. The result from **crypt( )** is the encrypted user password.

The legacy **crypt( )** function is based on DES encryption. To encrypt the password, this function would typically do the following:

1. Create an empty string, one that contains the NUL character only.
2. Select the first 7 bits from the first 8 characters of the key (user password).
3. Using the bits selected above, create a 56-bit key to be used for DES encryption.
4. Encrypt the empty string using the 56-bit key; use the salt parameter to perturb the DES algorithm in one of 4096 possible ways.
5. Repeat the previous step 25 times.

The result from the legacy **crypt( )** function is an encrypted fixed-length string, which consists of the following characters: [a-z][A-Z][0-9]./. This password is then stored in either the **/etc/passwd** file or the **/etc/group** file (later implementations would use **/etc/shadow** and **/etc/gshadow** instead).

The first two characters of the encrypted password contain the original salt, so that it is available later during authentication to provide the specific way in which DES was used to generate the encrypted password. The salt can therefore be publicly or widely known. The remaining characters contain the encrypted password, as returned by crypt. The crypt password format is shown in Figure 2.1.

It is important to note that regardless of the length of the password, the legacy algorithm only uses the first eight characters. The use of a salt will ensure that even when two passwords that are exactly the same need to be encrypted, the result will be different, as the passwords — although used to encrypt an empty string — will use a different set of encryption functions as part of the DES transforms.

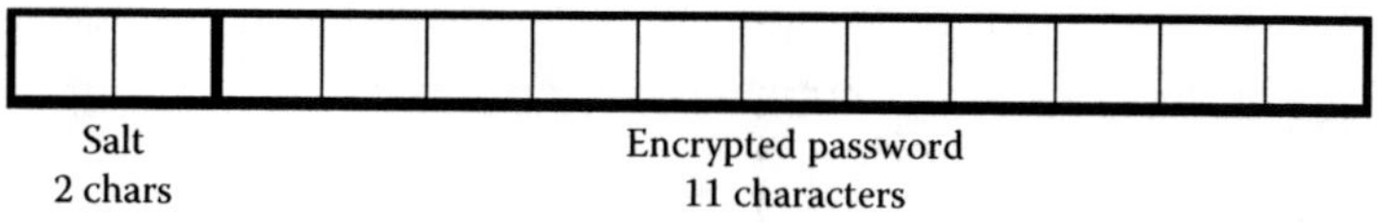

Figure 2.1 Crypt password format.

For example, if both **user1** and **user2** want to use the same password "password123" and invoke the **passwd** command to change their passwords, the result in the **/etc/shadow** file is likely similar to the following:

```
user1:r/2WTCYrcT6Eg:13030:0:99999:7:::
user2:40EQinNC6Or/.:13030:0:99999:7:::
```

Due to the salt (the random string '**r/**' in the first instance, and '**40**' in the second), the encrypted passwords do not match.

Apparently, the use of a password that is eight characters or less in length is a security limitation; therefore, modern GNU and other implementations of the **crypt( )** function allow for other protection methods in addition to the legacy modified DES. Most of today's implementations support MD5 in addition to legacy **crypt( )** with DES.

It is important to note that unlike DES, MD5 is not an encryption algorithm; MD5 is a message digest algorithm and it is meant to provide a one-way function (virtually irreversible transformation) that can transform a user password into a password hash but the hash cannot be used to easily recover the original password. The GNU **crypt( )** function implements MD5 digest transformations in addition to DES encryption — if the invoking application (such as the **passwd** command) generates a random eight-character salt (used to initialize the MD5 algorithm and produce different results even with the same password) and provides the salt parameter to the crypt command using the following format: **1<string>[$],** where **<string>** is the eight-character salt, then the **crypt( )** function will use MD5 instead of DES to generate an encrypted password.

The way MD5 works to encrypt UNIX user passwords in Fedora is as follows.

1. The password is padded to a length congruent to 448 modulo 512. At least one "1" bit is added, then zero or more "0" bits.
2. A 64-bit word that represents the original password length is appended to the password.
3. A password digest is generated using MD5 on the salt and the key (the user's password).

The result from the MD5 transformation is a string that consists of the fields shown in Figure 2.2.

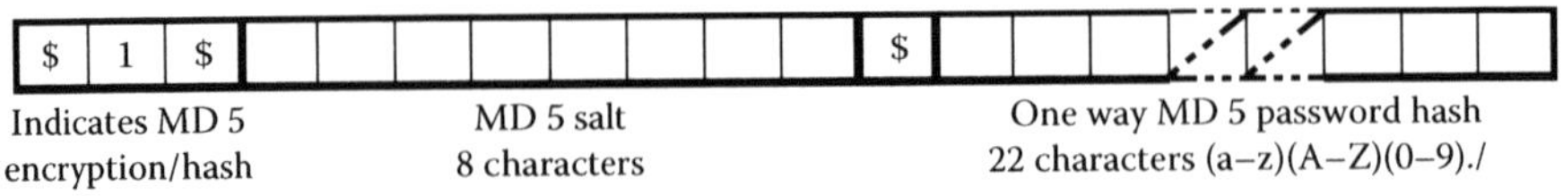

Figure 2.2 UNIX MD5 encrypted password format.

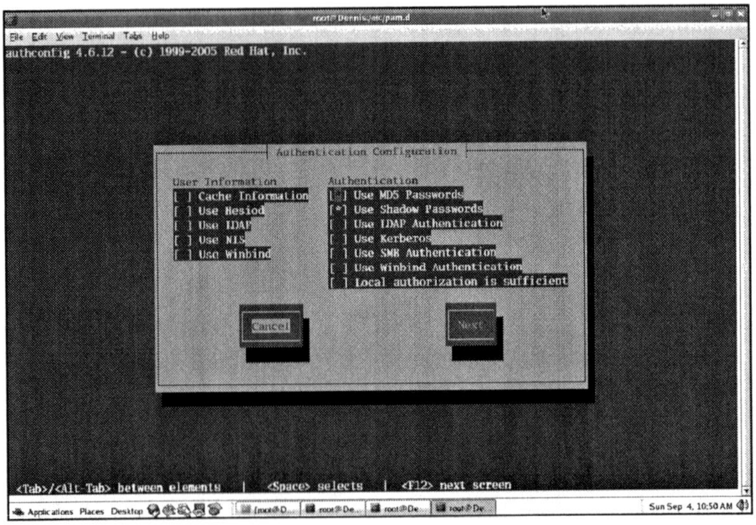

Figure 2.3 Configuring user authentication in Fedora.

On a system that has MD5 passwords enabled, if two users set their passwords to the same password string — for example, "password123" — one is likely to see the following lines in the shadow file:

```
user1:$1$/uTQhcV4$2ESsIGLLDrbeV9Jl7v5IW/:13030:0:99999:7:::
user2:$1$s/87S1PW$bEVunThZyMGA0QsKlAXSD1:13030:0:99999:7:::
```

Although the two users have used the same password, the MD5 strings stored in the shadow file are completely different from one another due to the different salt.

It is important to note that MD5 transformed passwords can be more than eight characters long, and that the entire password length is used. Therefore, MD5 allows for stronger passwords.

Some implementations allow the use of other encryption algorithms, such as Blowfish, to encrypt user passwords.

In Fedora, the **authconfig** application can be used to switch between DES and MD5 encrypted passwords. Either the command line interface or the menu interface can be used (Figure 2.3).

authconfig will configure PAM with the md5 parameter for the passwd component: details regarding PAM are provided in Chapter 2.4.

authconfig does not convert existing passwords in the newly configured format; cleartext passwords are not known to the operating system, and they are required to perform the transformation to either a DES encrypted password or an MD5 digest. The password conversion will take place the next time the user tries to change his password.

2.2.2 The /etc/passwd File

In the early days of UNIX, user authentication was a relatively simple process. User information, such as usernames, passwords, as well as user, were stored in a single flat text file — **/etc/passwd**. Each user's attributes were specified in a single line of the **/etc/passwd** file.

To create a new user, the system administrator would typically use a text editor and add a new line to the file. User attributes' modification and user account deletion were basically operations on the text file. Different UNIX flavors use slightly different **/etc/passwd** file formats. Some UNIX flavors, such as NetBSD, use template files for **/etc/passwd**.

The following is an example of a typical **/etc/passwd** file on a Fedora system:

```
root:x:0:0:root:/root:/bin/bash
bin:x:1:1:bin:/bin:/sbin/nologin
daemon:x:2:2:daemon:/sbin:/sbin/nologin
adm:x:3:4:adm:/var/adm:/sbin/nologin
lp:x:4:7:lp:/var/spool/lpd:/sbin/nologin
sync:x:5:0:sync:/sbin:/bin/sync
shutdown:x:6:0:shutdown:/sbin:/sbin/shutdown
halt:x:7:0:halt:/sbin:/sbin/halt
mail:x:8:12:mail:/var/spool/mail:/sbin/nologin
news:x:9:13:news:/etc/news:
uucp:x:10:14:uucp:/var/spool/uucp:/sbin/nologin
operator:x:11:0:operator:/root:/sbin/nologin
games:x:12:100:games:/usr/games:/sbin/nologin
gopher:x:13:30:gopher:/var/gopher:/sbin/nologin
ftp:x:14:50:FTP User:/var/ftp:/sbin/nologin
nobody:x:99:99:Nobody:/:/sbin/nologin
dbus:x:81:81:System message bus:/:/sbin/nologin
vcsa:x:69:69:virtual console memory owner:/dev:/sbin/nologin
rpm:x:37:37::/var/lib/rpm:/sbin/nologin
haldaemon:x:68:68:HAL daemon:/:/sbin/nologin
pcap:x:77:77::/var/arpwatch:/sbin/nologin
nscd:x:28:28:NSCD Daemon:/:/sbin/nologin
named:x:25:25:Named:/var/named:/sbin/nologin
netdump:x:34:34:Network Crash Dump user:/var/crash:/bin/bash
sshd:x:74:74:Privilege-separated SSH:/var/empty/sshd:/sbin/nologin
rpc:x:32:32:Portmapper RPC user:/:/sbin/nologin
mailnull:x:47:47::/var/spool/mqueue:/sbin/nologin
smmsp:x:51:51::/var/spool/mqueue:/sbin/nologin
```

```
rpcuser:x:29:29:RPC Service User:/var/lib/nfs:/sbin/nologin
nfsnobody:x:65534:65534:Anonymous NFS User:/var/lib/nfs:/sbin/nologin
apache:x:48:48:Apache:/var/www:/sbin/nologin
squid:x:23:23::/var/spool/squid:/sbin/nologin
webalizer:x:67:67:Webalizer:/var/www/usage:/sbin/nologin
xfs:x:43:43:X Font Server:/etc/X11/fs:/sbin/nologin
ntp:x:38:38::/etc/ntp:/sbin/nologin
gdm:x:42:42::/var/gdm:/sbin/nologin
dovecot:x:97:97:dovecot:/usr/libexec/dovecot:/sbin/nologin
ldap:x:55:55:LDAP User:/var/lib/ldap:/bin/false
admin:x:500:500:Linux Administrator:/home/admin:/bin/bash
user1:x:9111:9201:User1:/home/user1:/bin/bash
user2:x:9112:9201:User2:/home/user2:/bin/bash
```

The /**etc/passwd** file uses the colon ('**:**') symbol to separate attributes and has the fixed structure shown in Table 2.1.

Table 2.1 User Attributes in UNIX

Field	*Format*	*Description*
Username	String, typically eight characters or less; case sensitive; usually only lowercase letters	This is the name that represents the user to the system, aka user ID, user name, or account name
Password	String	In case of password authentication, this field contains the password that the system uses to validate user identity The "x" character in this field denotes that the password is stored in the **/etc/shadow** file Typically, when a new user account is created, the password is set to star ("*"), which denotes an invalid password; then the **passwd** tool is used to set the user password Some implementations use this field to store additional account information, such as account expiration information
User ID (uid)	Number — typically integer (2 bytes); avoid negative values	This must be a unique number identifying the user to the system; this ID is used internally by the system to authorize access to resources

Table 2.1 User Attributes in UNIX (continued)

Field	*Format*	*Description*
Group ID (gid)	Number — typically integer (2 bytes); avoid negative values	This number must identify the primary group of which the user is a member; the group should exist This ID is used internally by the system to authorize access to resources along with other groups (and therefore group IDs) of which the user is a member
Full Name (or gecos)	String	This field contains the actual name of the user, such as the name on the user's drivers license, or the name by which the user is known to colleagues and friends It may contain other information, such as the user phone number
Home directory	String	This field contains the path to the home directory of the user When the user logs on to the system interactively, he will typically start working in his own home directory This field is not required, and the home directory may not exist
User shell	String	This field defines the program that will be run to provide the user with a command shell to use during interactive logon to the system This field is not required if the user is not expected to log on interactively (e.g., users who will only require file services on the system using SMB do not require a user shell on that system)

Typically, the **/etc/passwd** file is readable for all users of the system, so that they can obtain information about other users. However, most often, the only user allowed to modify the **/etc/passwd** file is the system administrator (the **root** user).

The concept of having all user information (including passwords) in a single file and readable by everyone poses some problems. First, any user with a valid login ID on a system will be able to enumerate all the users on that system and obtain their login IDs and user (or group) IDs. Second, any user with a valid login ID on a system will be able to acquire the encrypted user password for every other user on the system. Although the encrypted password is not plaintext, an attacker can potentially try to crack the password by popular means such as dictionary or brute force attacks.

2.2.3 The /etc/group File

The **/etc/group** file is the database of user groups on the system. This file is similar to the **/etc/passwd** file in terms of structure except that instead of users it actually contains group accounts. Below is a typical example of the **/etc/group** file:

```
root:x:0:root
bin:x:1:root,bin,daemon
daemon:x:2:root,bin,daemon
sys:x:3:root,bin,adm
adm:x:4:root,adm,daemon
ldap:x:55:
screen:x:84:
admin:x:500:
testgrp:x:501:ldap,ntp
group1:x:9201:user1
group2:x:9202:user1
group3:x:9203:user2
group4:x:9204:user2
```

Although it might differ between different UNIX flavors, the **/etc/group** file typically contains the fields shown in Table 2.2.

An interesting fact about group passwords is that if they are left blank ("::"), only users explicitly specified as group members can log in to the group. Users not specified as group members cannot log in to the group and therefore cannot use the group privileges.

2.2.4 The /etc/shadow File

As discussed, a problem with the **/etc/passwd** file is that it is required by applications to look up user information while at the same time, due to being readable by all users on the system, it does not provide for strong password and other credentials protection techniques.

```
[root@Dennis ~]# ls -al /etc/passwd
-rw-r--r--  1 root root 1799 Jul  9 01:59 /etc/passwd
[root@Dennis ~]#
```

To split the functions of providing information about users and authenticating users in a secure manner, the **/etc/shadow** file was created as a

Table 2.2 Group Attributes

Field	*Format*	*Description*
Group Name	String, typically eight characters or less; case sensitive; usually only lowercase letters	This is the name that represents the group to the system, aka group ID or group name
Password	String	This field contains the password that the system uses to validate user identity for users trying to join a group for which they have not been enlisted as members
Group ID (gid)	Number — typically integer (2 bytes); avoid negative values	This number must be a unique number of the group on the system This ID is used internally by the system to authorize access to resources along with other groups
User List	String, comma delimited entries	This field contains a list of all the user names that belong to users, members of the group

secure place where passwords and other user information can be stored. The **/etc/shadow** file is typically readable by the user root only. No other user can access this file.

```
[root@Dennis ~]# ls -al /etc/shadow
-r--------  1 root root 1141 Jul  9 01:59 /etc/shadow
[root@Dennis ~]#
```

When the **/etc/shadow** file is used to store passwords and other system and administrative information about the users, the **/etc/passwd** file is used just as a simple flat directory containing user information, and it is still readable by all users, so that legacy applications can use it without changes.

When the **/etc/shadow** file is used, the password field in the **/etc/passwd** file is marked with the 'x' character. While trying to authenticate a user, the operating system will find the 'x' character in the **/etc/passwd** file and will therefore look into the **/etc/shadow** file. The password will be found in that file, in an encrypted format.

The **/etc/shadow** file typically contains the fields shown in Table 2.3.

Table 2.3 Shadow File Attributes

Field	*Format*	*Description*
User name	String, typically eight characters or less; case sensitive; usually only lowercase letters	This is the name that represents the user to the system Note that this name is used to match the password and other account information to the information stored for this users in the /etc/passwd file - uid and gid
Password	String, 13 or 34 characters Contains upper- and lowercaseletters, as well as digits, and the characters "." and "/"	The password is encoded using either DES or MD5 If this field is blank, then the user's password is blank. Under some circumstances, this might mean that the user account has been disabled If this field contains an asterisk "*" character, then the user account is disabled — this is typically the case right after a new account has been created
Password Last Changed	Long integer (4 bytes) Days	Indicates the date when the password was last changed This field is the number of days since January 1, 1970
Password May Be Changed	Long integer (4 bytes) Days	Indicates the number of days since the last change (see above) before a password change is allowed Apparently, a value of 0 in this field indicates that the password can be changed immediately
Password Must Be Changed	Long integer (4 bytes) Days	Indicates the maximum password age in days; after this number of days, the user will be required to change his password A value of 14, for example, indicates that the user will be required to change his password every other week
Password Change Warning	Long integer (4 bytes) Days	Indicates the number of days before the password expires to warn the user that he is required to change his password

Table 2.3 Shadow File Attributes (continued)

Field	*Format*	*Description*
Disable Account	Long integer (4 bytes) Days	This field allows the administrator to specify account validity, depending on password age After the user password expires, the system will wait for the specified number of dates and then consider the account disabled
Disabled Since	Long integer (4 bytes) Days	This field represents the time period since the account has been disabled, starting January 1, 1970
Reserved	String	Reserved for future use

Table 2.4 Group Shadow File Attributes

Field	*Format*	*Description*
Group name	String, typically eight characters or less; case sensitive; usually only small letters	This field is the group name and it must match the name specified in the **/etc/group** file.
Password	String, 13 or 34 characters Contains small and capital letters, as well as digits, and the characters "." and "/"	The password is encoded either using DES or using MD5
Group administrators	String, comma delimited entries	A list of users who can administer the group; for example these users can modify group membership
Group members	String, comma delimited entries	A list of all the group members — usually the same as the one found in the **/etc/group** file

2.2.5 The /etc/gshadow File

The **/etc/gshadow** file is used to store the encrypted group passwords in a manner similar to the **/etc/shadow** file. In addition to that, the **/etc/gshadow** file contains information about the group administrators, as well group members (Table 2.4).

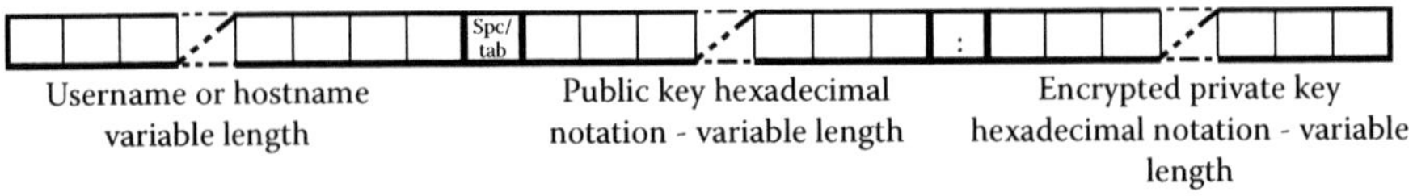

Figure 2.4 /etc/publickey entry format.

2.2.6 The /etc/publickey file

Users can use credentials other than passwords to authenticate to the operating system and to services. Asymmetric keys are also a possible authentication option. Asymmetric key authentication is often used by the SecureRPC Protocol, and can be used by SSH.

The **/etc/publickey** file is used to store asymmetric keys for user authentication. The file consists of multiple entries, each on separate line. The entries have the format depicted in Figure 2.4.

The username or hostname is used to identify the user or host to whom the specific keypair belongs. The public key is the public key from the asymmetric keypair in hexadecimal.

The private key is stored in encrypted form. It is encrypted using DES based on the user password. Because only the user (and not even the operating system) knows the user password, the private key is considered protected. Apparently, the protection of the private key depends on the selection of a strong password. If the user selects a weak password, the protection scheme may be subject to brute force, dictionary, or rainbow attacks.

Systems that use SecureRPC provide for a private key caching mechanism, which resembles single sign-on technologies. The **keyserv** daemon is an operating system service that can decrypt user private keys in memory and provide them automatically every time the user needs to authenticate. The user uses the **keylogin** command to provide his password to the **keyserv** daemon. The **keyserv** daemon then obtains the encrypted private key for this user from the **/etc/publickey** file, decrypts it in the provided password, and stores it in memory. If a process running with the same effective ID as the user requests the private key, the **keyserv** daemon will provide the decrypted private key to this process.

Although SecureRPC uses asymmetric keys for direct user authentication, the approach of storing the private key in the **/etc/publickey** file makes the credentials dependent on the user password, so indirectly user authentication and the model of trust depend on the login password.

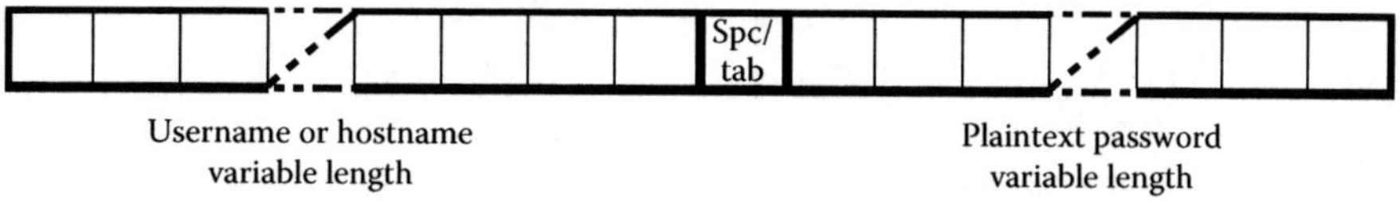

Figure 2.5 /etc/cram-md5.pwd entry format.

2.2.7 The /etc/cram-md5.pwd File

The **/etc/cram-md5.pwd** file stores user plaintext passwords. This is sometimes required by authentication mechanisms that require the security server to have a plaintext password of the user. Such mechanisms include SASL CRAM-MD5 (see Chapter 4) and PPP CHAP.

The format of the file is simple: it consists of entries, each on a separate line, and the format of each entry is given in Figure 2.5.

There is no requirement that the password be the same as the password in **/etc/passwd** or NSS. Potentially, there may be no requirement that the username be the same as in **/etc/passwd** but technically this is often required. Because authentication mechanisms, such as CRAM-MD5, are often used by e-mail protocols (POP3/IMAP), the mail daemon needs to determine the location of the mailbox and to do so it will look up the user information database, potentially using NSS. The mail daemon will not be able to find where user mail must be delivered unless the username from the **/etc/cram-md5.pwd** file corresponds to a name in the user information database, which may either be the local **/etc/passwd** file, or LDAP, or other NSS-supported source.

Below is a typical **cram-md5.pwd** file. The username is typically the same as the username from the **/etc/passwd**. The password is provided in plaintext, using the {PLAIN} prefix:

```
[root@linus etc]# cat /etc/cram-md5.pwd
hemmingway:{PLAIN}hPASSWORDy
faulkner:{PLAIN}fPASSWORDr
steinbeck:{PLAIN}sPASSWORDs

[root@linus etc]# cat /etc/passwd
root:x:0:0:root:/root:/bin/bash
bin:x:1:1:bin:/bin:/sbin/nologin

---- OUTPUT TRUNCATED FOR BREVITY ----

hemmingway:x:503:503::/home/hemmingway:/bin/bash
faulkner:x:504:504::/home/faulkner:/bin/bash
steinbeck:x:505:505::/home/steinbeck:/bin/bash
```

The **/etc/cram-md5.pwd** file should be owned by root and should only be available for reading and writing (0600) or even only for reading (0400) to root. If the security of the file is compromised, the attacker has the plaintext passwords for the users. If user passwords are the same as in the NSS database or **/etc/passwd**, this may seriously compromise the security of the system.

2.2.8 The SASL User Database

Many products use SASL as their authentication layer. Although SASL can utilize the **/etc/passwd** file, PAM, or NSS for user authentication, very often it has its own database with user authentication information. Similar to the **/etc/cram-md5.pwd** file, the SASL database can be used in case the user needs to use an authentication method that requires the server to have the plaintext password for the user.

The SASL database is typically stored in the **/etc/sasldb** or **/etc/sasldb2** file. Depending on the SASL configuration, the file format might be db, ndbm, or gdbm. The SASL database contains a row for each user with entries for the username, the plaintext user password, and the allowed authentication mechanisms for this user (CRAM-MD5, DIGEST-MD5, PLAIN, etc.). The tools **saslpasswd/saslpasswd2** and **sasldblistusers** can be used to manage the SASL database.

It is important to note that user passwords are not encrypted in the SASL database. Therefore, access to the password database file must be configured appropriately, because a compromise of the password database will compromise user passwords, which may well match user passwords for the operating system or for access to sensitive resources.

SASL is described in more detail in Chapter 4.

2.2.9 The htpasswd File

The Apache Web server allows the system administrator to configure a separate user authentication file for use in each Web site. This provides for better security than using the **/etc/passwd** file because the **htpasswd** file only provides the user with access to resources provided by Apache; and even if the username and password are compromised, this still does not provide the attacker with access to other resources.

The **htpasswd** file is typically located in the **/etc/httpd/conf.d/htpasswd** file but technically can reside anywhere and have any name as long as Apache is configured with the full path to the file.

The **/etc/httpd/conf.d/htpasswd** file contains a separate line for each user, and the format is shown in Figure 2.6.

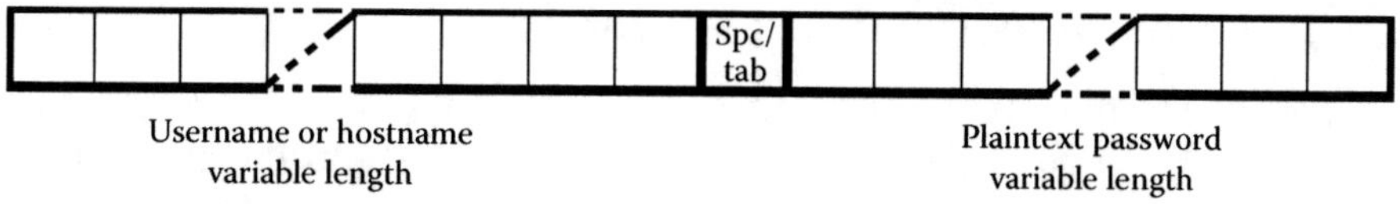

Figure 2.6 htpasswd entry format.

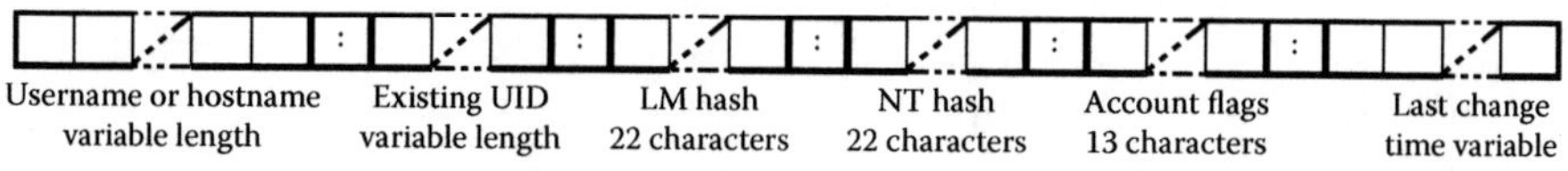

Figure 2.7 smbpasswd entry format.

The username is stored in plaintext. The password can be stored in plaintext, as an MD5 or SHA-1 hash, or encrypted with **crypt( )**. While HTTP basic authentication can use any of these encryption algorithms, other mechanisms such as HTTP digest authentication would require a plaintext password. The systems administrator needs to consider the HTTP authentication mechanism that will be used as he plans whether passwords should be stored in plaintext or cryptographically protected with one of the above mechanisms.

2.2.10 Samba Credentials

The SMB daemon (Samba) can use different authentication databases, including Winbind and LDAP, to authenticate users. However, the native security database for Samba consists of local password and machine secrets files that mimic the **/etc/passwd** file but provide for Windows NT LM and NT Hashes (see Chapter 3).

The **/etc/smb.d/smbpasswd** file is used as the user account database by the Samba suite. The format of the file is as in Figure 2.7.

The UID must match an existing ID in the NSS database or **/etc/passwd** file. The LM Hash and NT Hash fields contain Windows NT password hashes, as discussed in Chapter 3. The account flags specify whether the account is a user, workstation, or interdomain trust account, and whether the account is disabled or has a blank password.

Samba also stores plaintext password information in the **/etc/samba/secrets.tdb** file. This file is similar to the Windows NT SAM Secrets database but is not encrypted. If the UNIX box running Samba is a domain member, an entry in the **/etc/samba/secrets.tdb** file will store the machine password for the domain.

2.2.11 The Kerberos Principal Database

When the MIT Kerberos V KDC is installed on a server, a user principal file is created that contains information about users and their credentials (typically passwords). When users authenticate against this KDC, user credentials are validated against the Kerberos principal database. The Kerberos V principal database is typically located in the **/var/kerberos/krb5kdc/principal** file.

The Kerberos database contains a separate entry for each user (principal). Furthermore, each principal can potentially have a different password stored for every supported encryption method. The password must be available in plaintext.

All password fields, and only password fields in the Kerberos database, are encrypted using DES in the master password. The master password is provided by the database administrator when the database is initially created. The master password can be stored in a separate file (a stash file) or can be provided by the administrator every time Kerberos services need to be restarted.

It is more convenient to be able to restart Kerberos services automatically, so many Kerberos administrators choose to create a stash file for every Kerberos database they have. Apparently, the stash file must be stored in a secure location, because a compromise to the contents of the stash file might expose user plaintext passwords to an attacker who has online or offline access to the Kerberos principal database.

2.3 Name Services Switch (NSS)

Password, group, and shadow files provide for a simple approach to authenticate UNIX users. They are relatively easy to set up and manage on a single host but are not scalable in large environments with multiple hosts. The problem is that these files must be maintained separately on a per-host basis. In addition to the files used for authentication, other files, such as **/etc/hosts** and **/etc/networks** used for name resolution, should be managed centrally in enterprise environments.

Sun Microsystems came up with an extension to the legacy **/etc** files with a technology known as Name Services Switch (NSS). This technology, along with its name, was later adopted by many other vendors, as well as by GNU.

In essence, the NSS allows administrators to specify a list of sources where authentication files, host name mappings, and other information will be stored and searched for. The local files in the **/etc** directory are just one of the possible sources of information for NSS. Other sources include Network Information System (NIS — aka YellowPages) and

Network Information System Plus (NIS+), DNS (Hesiod authentication), LDAP (Lightweight Directory Access Protocol), and others. NSS is therefore responsible for creating a virtual and consolidated information database, which is distributed in nature and can be pulled together from multiple sources.

When an NSS request is submitted by an application, appropriate information sources will be queried, and the information returned from each source will be merged with information returned from other sources. This does not necessarily mean that NSS modules will generate network traffic or waste CPU cycles and memory each time — most of the information can be cached in a local NSS cache.

The sources from which NSS collects information may differ in their format, representation, access methods, etc. The role of the NSS module is to virtualize access to information from the particular source; although the module has all the inside knowledge about the information source, the result from NSS in the case of the password database is formatted as the **/etc/passwd** file and NSS system calls return information to the caller in this format.

The Fedora NSS implementation modifies the GNU C libraries and changes the behavior of legacy functions, such as **getpwent( )** and **getpwnam( )**, which have traditionally been used to access the **/etc/passwd** and **/etc/shadow** files. Thus, all existing applications, as well as new applications that may use these system calls will still function properly, and they do not need to be recompiled in order to use NSS. This makes NSS a very simple, but at the same time an elegant and flexible approach for providing information about users and groups, and potentially for user and group authentication in enterprise environments.

NSS uses a simple configuration file that specifies a list of sources that the system will use instead of each legacy flat file.

```
#
# /etc/nsswitch.conf
#
# An example Name Service Switch config file. This file should be
# sorted with the most-used services at the beginning.
#
# Legal entries are:
#
#    nisplus or nis+     Use NIS+ (NIS version 3)
#    nis or yp           Use NIS (NIS version 2), also called YP
#    dns                 Use DNS (Domain Name Service)
#    files               Use the local files
#    db                  Use the local database (.db) files
#    compat              Use NIS on compat mode
#    hesiod              Use Hesiod for user lookups
#    [NOTFOUND=return]   Stop searching if not found so far
#
```

```
passwd:     files ldap
shadow:     files ldap
group:      files ldap

hosts:      files dns

bootparams: nisplus [NOTFOUND=return] files
ethers:     files
netmasks:   files
networks:   files
protocols:  files ldap
rpc:        files
services:   files ldap

netgroup:   files ldap

publickey:  nisplus

automount:  files ldap
aliases:    files nisplus
```

In this example, there is a list of legacy UNIX databases. For example, the **passwd** database is now extended to include both the **/etc/passwd** (denoted as **files**) file and LDAP (denoted as **ldap**) to provide information about users and their attributes (user directory). In a similar fashion, group information is provided using two information sources: the local file **/etc/group** (denoted as **files**) as well as LDAP (denoted as **ldap**).

Each of the NSS information sources is implemented by means of an NSS module file, which is a shared object library file. This file typically resides in the **/lib** directory, and its name uses the following format: **libnss_*module*.so.*x***, where ***module*** represents the name of the information source (as specified in the **/etc/nsswitch.conf** file), and ***x*** represents the NSS version.

NSS modules use configuration files that typically reside in **/etc** and are module specific. A popular NSS module for LDAP, for example, is the PADL implementation that uses the library **lib_nss_ldap.so.2,** and it utilizes **/etc/ldap.conf** as its configuration file.

The system administrator can specify the appropriate list of sources to be used for user and other system information using the **/etc/nsswitch.conf** file, and then configure each module using its own configuration file. In addition, the **/etc/nsswitch.conf** configuration file provides the administrator with the ability to take appropriate actions in case the specific information source is unavailable, or returns an error. If the administrator fails to specify the action for each possible module status, NSS uses default values, as specified in Table 2.5. Using these default values is common practice.

Table 2.5 NSS Authentication Status and Actions

NSS Module Status (return code)	*Description*	*Default Action*
Success	The module has successfully accessed the information source and found a matching entry	Return (do not try other information sources)
Notfound	The information source was available but an entry with the specified attributes has not been found	Continue (try the next information source)
Unavail	The information source is unavailable (e.g., due to a network problem)	Continue (try the next information source)
Tryagain	The information source is temporarily unavailable, typically due to a recoverable error	Continue (try the next information source)

NSS allows the administrator to obtain consolidated information from all the specified information sources using the **getent** GNU tool:

```
login as: root
root@10.0.2.101's password:
Last login: Sat Sep  3 11:18:19 2005 from 10.0.2.1
[root@Dennis ~]#
[root@Dennis ~]# getent passwd
root:x:0:0:root:/root:/bin/bash
bin:x:1:1:bin:/bin:/sbin/nologin
daemon:x:2:2:daemon:/sbin:/sbin/nologin
adm:x:3:4:adm:/var/adm:/sbin/nologin
admin:x:500:500:Linux Administrator:/home/admin:/bin/bash
John:lFeuV/Q78Swvk:10004:20003:John White:/home/John:/bin/sh
Peter:x:10007:20005:Peter Black:/home/Peter:/bin/sh
David:$1$1IewI/..$mHdJxdGzdbNkmQEIb.Usg1:10001:20002:David Green:
 /home/David:/bin/sh
George:LAoCMgjzUreJo:10002:20001:George Blue:/home/George:/bin/sh
Susan:sv/CcsNDDKHSE:10008:20003:Susan Red:/home/Susan:/bin/sh
Jane:y/d6sWyZXc5NU:10003:20004:Jane Brown:/home/Jane:/bin/sh
Kate:70FsGbn7KrNb6:10005:20003:Kate Green:/home/Kate:/bin/sh
Laura:7cn8jGfWhqTy2:10006:20005:Laura Purple:/home/Laura:/bin/sh
[root@Dennis ~]#
```

In similar fashion, the **getent** tool can be used to obtain information on group accounts (**getent group**) or shadow files (**getent shadow**).

2.4 Pluggable Authentication Modules (PAM)

The legacy authentication technologies described in the preceding sections are still very widely used. However, there are some shortcomings in using plain authentication files or even NSS, including

- The authentication mechanism is hard-coded in the application. When the application needs to be deployed in a particular infrastructure, it might need to be modified and recompiled before it integrates with the existing information sources
- Applications are responsible for performing user authentication themselves. The operating system only provides information, such as usernames, encrypted (or plaintext) passwords, and user Ids.
- Application developers need to implement and use security specific functions, such as encryption and password management.
- There is no universal approach to user password management. NSS provides user information that is very often read-only from an application point of view. Users might need to use different utilities to change their passwords, depending where their user accounts reside.
- NSS does not easily provide for multiple-factor authentication or required authentication by more than one authentication source.

PAM (Pluggable Authentication Modules) is a mechanism that provides for separation between user authentication and user information. PAM was meant to resolve some of the above problems. It was developed by SunSoft (Sun Microsystems' software sales division, which was an independent subsidiary at that time) in the early 1990s and then published as Open Software Foundation RFC 86 (see [8]). Many commercial UNIX products have adopted the PAM concept, and Linux also has its own PAM implementation. PAM is an accepted standard for the Common Desktop Environment (CDE) group.

PAM is a set of libraries that provide a configurable authentication platform for applications and the underlying operating system. PAM is a universal and configurable approach toward user authentication and can be used to provide the following services:

- *User credentials validation (authentication).* PAM provides modules that can utilize the **/etc/passwd** and **/etc/shadow** files, as well as LDAP, NTLM, SMB, RADIUS, and many others. This is the authentication **(auth)** service of PAM.
- *User account verification.* Verify whether the user is already logged in to the system from a different location, whether the password has expired, or whether there are time restrictions for access with this account. This is the accounting **(account)** service of PAM.

- *Track user activities as the user accesses the system.* PAM can be configured to log user access to the event log. This is the session (**session)** service.
- *Allows users to change their passwords, as well as administrators to reset passwords for other users.* This is the password (**passwd)** service.

The current implementation of PAM does not provide for user information services; thus, PAM does not necessarily recognize UIDs and GIDs, nor does it necessarily have access to the user Full Name attribute. Therefore, PAM still requires the services of NSS as a user information virtual database, which in the simplest possible scenario includes only the local **/etc/passwd** file.

It is important to note that not every PAM module supports every service type. Some modules — such as the **pam_cracklib** module, used to check for password complexity — only provide for the **passwd** service (invoked when the user changes his password or when an administrator changes the password for a user) and are never used for user authentication. Other modules (such as **pam_access**) used to check whether the user is trying to log in from a valid location only implement an **account** service (invoked to check user attributes and restrictions).

To use PAM, applications such as **login, su**, and **sshd** should be specifically designed (or patched) to use the PAM dynamic link libraries and then they can virtually use any authentication method provided by the PAM libraries.

The best way to check whether a specific application supports PAM is to look in the product documentation. If documentation is not available, it is still possible to speculate by means of checking the library dependencies for the application. For example, to check whether the version of **su** on a UNIX system supports PAM, the **ldd** tool can be used to obtain a list of library dependencies:

```
[root@Dennis ~]# ldd /bin/su
  linux-gate.so.1 =>  (0x00a5a000)
  libpam.so.0 => /lib/libpam.so.0 (0x003a8000)
  libpam_misc.so.0 => /lib/libpam_misc.so.0 (0x00507000)
  libcrypt.so.1 => /lib/libcrypt.so.1 (0x00ccf000)
  libdl.so.2 => /lib/libdl.so.2 (0x00e37000)
  libc.so.6 => /lib/libc.so.6 (0x00111000)
  libaudit.so.0 => /lib/libaudit.so.0 (0x00d96000)
  /lib/ld-linux.so.2 (0x006f9000)
[root@Dennis ~]#
```

In this example, the **su** tool depends on the **libpam.so.0** and **libpam_misc.so.0** libraries, which is a good indication that it probably utilizes PAM for user authentication.

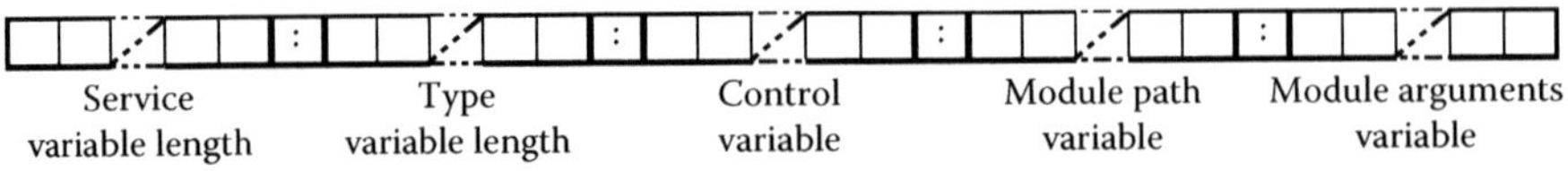

Figure 2.8 pam.conf entry format — old style.

The PAM libraries use one or more configuration files that reside under the **/etc** directory.

In some implementations, PAM utilizes a single configuration file — **/etc/pam.conf**. The format of entries in this file is depicted in Figure 2.8. Table 2.6 outlines the **/etc/pam.conf** configuration fields.

Starting with version 0.56, PAM allows for dedicated configuration files for each service, as well as system-wide configuration files. Instead of using the **/etc/pam.conf** file, this and later versions of PAM endorse the use of the **/etc/pam.d** directory and configuration files for every application that requires specific settings. Basically, this means that the **service** field of the **/etc/pam.conf** file now becomes the file name of the configuration file, while all other fields retain their names and functions; thus, the format of the service-specific configuration files is that shown in Figure 2.9.

Table 2.6 PAM Configuration Options

Field	*Format*	*Description*
Service	String	When a single monolith configuration file is used, this field denotes the application or daemon to which the specific line of the configuration file relates (e.g., specific configuration for the login utility will contain the string 'login' in this field, and configuration settings related to the SSH daemon will contain the string 'sshd' in this field) The default catch-all service is 'other'; it relates to all the applications for which there are no specific PAM settings
Type	String	Denotes the service for which the specific line provides configuration settings; this can be: **auth** (for authentication) **account** (for user account checking) **session** (for session logging and settings) **passwd** (user password settings)

Table 2.6 PAM Configuration Options (continued)

Field	*Format*	*Description*
Control	String	This field controls the behavior of the PAM module in case there are multiple modules that must be executed for a single service This field can contain one of the following values: **required** — this module will always be invoked, regardless of whether other modules for the same service and type have returned success or failure; the application has no visibility of which services have returned success and which have returned failure. All modules of this service and type must succeed for the service to return "success" to the application **requisite** — the module will always be invoked but if it returns failure, no further modules for the service and type will be checked and control will be returned to the application; this is very similar to **required** — the only difference is that failure is considered ultimate and not all modules will be invoked **sufficient** — if this module succeeds, control is returned to the application and the result is success regardless of whether other modules for this service and type have succeeded or failed. If the service using this module fails, other modules will be invoked and the success or failure of the service will depend on them **optional** — the result of the authentication using this module will be ignored, unless there is no module of other type that can determine the success or the failure of the service **include** — this is a control statement that allows the inclusion of other configuration files and specifically the lines for the specified service and type. This is useful when system-wide configuration files must be maintained separately Note: There is new syntax for this field that allows for even more granular configuration and module interdependencies (details can be found in [6])
Module-path	String	This is the path to the module that implements the PAM service (e.g., such as **/lib/security/pam_ldap.so**)

Table 2.6 PAM Configuration Options (continued)

Field	*Format*	*Description*
Module-arguments	String	Each module (executable) accepts configuration parameters, which can either be PAM universal or module specific Some of the PAM universal parameters are: **debug** — write debugging information to system log files **try_first_pass** — do not prompt the user for a password if another module has already done that — reuse the password from the previous module in the stack. If authentication does not succeed, ask the user for a password **use_first_pass** — same as try_first_pass but never ask the user for a password **expose_account** — instructs the module that extended user information, such as full name, or home directory can be exposed to the application

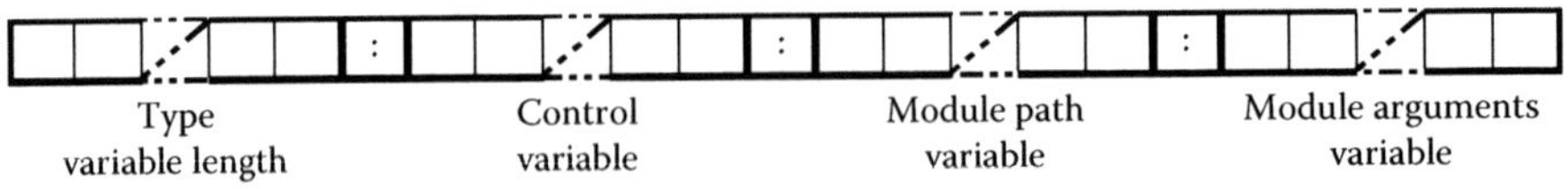

Figure 2.9 pam.conf entry format — new style.

Apart from this change, field syntax and designation remain unchanged. However, there are some important advantages in the new approach:

- When new applications are installed, it is easy to add a new PAM configuration file for this application only, without modifying existing configuration files.
- By means of file system permissions, access to PAM configuration files can be restricted so that some users and applications have access to them, while others do not.

The **authconfig** tool can be used to configure a Fedora system to provide user authentication using LDAP and SMB authentication, in addition to legacy UNIX authentication (Name Services Switch — NSS, including **/etc/passwd** and **/etc/shadow** databases).

The **/etc/pam.d/system-auth** file is a system-wide configuration file used by most services. Below is the typical configuration used on a Fedora system:

```
#%PAM-1.0
# This file is auto-generated.
# User changes will be destroyed the next time authconfig is run.
auth       required      /lib/security/$ISA/pam_env.so
auth       sufficient    /lib/security/$ISA/pam_unix.so likeauth nullok
auth       sufficient    /lib/security/$ISA/pam_ldap.so use_first_pass
auth       sufficient    /lib/security/$ISA/pam_smb_auth.so use_first_
                          pass nolocal
auth       required      /lib/security/$ISA/pam_deny.so

account    required      /lib/security/$ISA/pam_unix.so broken_shadow
account    sufficient    /lib/security/$ISA/pam_succeed_if.so uid < 100
                          quiet
account    [default=bad success=ok user_unknown=ignore] /lib/security/
            $ISA/pam_ldap.so
account    required      /lib/security/$ISA/pam_permit.so

password   requisite     /lib/security/$ISA/pam_cracklib.so retry=3
password   sufficient    /lib/security/$ISA/pam_unix.so nullok use_
                          authtok md5 shadow
password   sufficient    /lib/security/$ISA/pam_ldap.so use_authtok
password   required      /lib/security/$ISA/pam_deny.so
session    required      /lib/security/$ISA/pam_limits.so
session    required      /lib/security/$ISA/pam_unix.so
session    optional      /lib/security/$ISA/pam_ldap.so
```

An analysis of the above PAM configuration file reveals that:

- The **pam_env.so** module (set user environment variables using **/etc/security/pam_env.conf**) is required and will always be invoked. This module is not likely to fail.
- The **pam_unix.so** module (revert to NSS authentication) will always be invoked as well. The **use_authtok** parameter specifies that the new password should be used as submitted by the previous module in the stack; the user will not be asked to enter the new password again as control is transferred to the next PAM module. Because it is denoted as **sufficient**, if it succeeds, the next three lines will not be invoked.
- If **pam_unix.so** (NSS) does not work, try **pam_ldap.so** (authentication against LDAP) using the same password that the user entered when he was challenged by the **pam_unix.so** module. If this succeeds, this is considered sufficient and the user will be authenticated.
- If authentication using **pam_ldap.so** does not work, try **pam_smb_auth.so** (authentication against SMB server). If this succeeds, this is considered sufficient and the user will be authenticated.
- If **pam_smb_auth.so** fails also, the user will be denied access after the **pam_deny.so** module is invoked.

It is interesting to explore the system-wide **passwd** service configuration settings, from which it is visible that:

- When a user enters a password, the **pam_cracklib.so** module will be invoked; this module will check the password that the user wants to use for complexity. If the user password is not sufficiently complex, this module will warn the user.
- Then the **passwd** program will invoke the **passwd** service of the **pam_unix.so** module, which in essence will try to use NSS functions to change the password; the password will be hashed using MD5 and will be kept in the **/etc/shadow** file, not in the **/etc/passwd** file
- If NSS password change fails, the **passwd** tool will try to change the password for the user using the **pam_ldap.so** module, which basically invokes LDAP modification procedures.
- If none of these works, the user will not be allowed to change his password.

The **account**, **passwd**, and **session** services are configured in a similar manner.

The **system-auth** file is used by default by most of the application-specific PAM configuration files. An example would be the default SSH Daemon configuration file:

```
#%PAM-1.0

auth        required     pam_stack.so service=system-auth use_first_
                          pass debug
auth        required     pam_nologin.so
account     required     pam_stack.so service=system-auth
password    required     pam_stack.so service=system-auth
session     required     pam_stack.so service=system-auth
```

This module performs authentication by invoking the **pam_stack.so** module passing the parameters **service**, **use_first_pass**, and **debug**. The **pam_stack.so** module allows stacking of PAM configuration files and in this particular case invokes the **system-auth** configuration file. That is, the current default **/etc/pam.d/sshd** configuration file redirects the request for user authentication and other PAM services to the system-wide PAM configuration file **system-auth** — and this is essentially what most PAM-aware applications do by default. However, the flexibility exists to add SSH-specific configuration settings to the **/etc/pam.d/sshd** configuration file, if required. For example, to configure SSHD, try RADIUS-based authentication first, and then try the system-wide configuration; the **/etc/pam.d/sshd** configuration file might look like this:

```
#%PAM-1.0

auth      sufficient  pam_radius.so
auth      required    pam_stack.so service=system-auth use_first_
                       pass debug
auth      required    pam_nologin.so
account   required    pam_stack.so service=system-auth
password  required    pam_stack.so service=system-auth
session   required    pam_stack.so service=system-auth
```

The **control** field of the PAM configuration files allows for multiple-factor authentication, or for authentication against multiple sources. For example, if an administrator wants to authenticate SSH users by means of a username and password, as well as with a one-way password, he can add two lines to the **/etc/pam.d/sshd** configuration files and specify both the password checking module (for example, **pam_unix.so**) and a one-time-password module (for example, **pam_otp.so**) as **requisite** (or even **required**). If the administrator wants to authenticate users only if they have an account on a RADIUS server, which resides in LDAP as well (resides in both, not in either), he can use two lines with either the **requisite** or the **required** statement, specifying the appropriate PAM authentication modules. If the user account does not exist in either of the sources, the module will fail and hence user authentication will fail.

2.5 The UNIX Authentication Process

Different user authentication methods might be used under different circumstances. Applications are free to utilize either legacy password files/NSS system calls or the newer PAM approach for user authentication. User information (including user and group IDs) is typically provided using NSS, although applications may directly access information sources (such as LDAP) to access user information.

In general, applications that use functions such as **getpwent( )** and **getpwuid( )** are legacy applications and will result in queries against the Name Services Switch (NSS) virtual database; NSS can use the local **/etc/passwd** and **/etc/shadow** files but it can also use LDAP and NIS+. Applications will not be able to tell what the actual source of user information is — the NSS libraries will make all the sources look like a large, consolidated **/etc/passwd** file.

Applications that are compiled with PAM support will typically use the PAM-specific functions **pam_start( )**, **pam_authenticate( )**, **pam_end( )**, and **pam_setcred( )**. These functions will use the PAM configuration files to determine which PAM modules to invoke and in what order. It is important to note that the default PAM configuration results in the use of the **pam_unix.so** module as the system default authentication scheme,

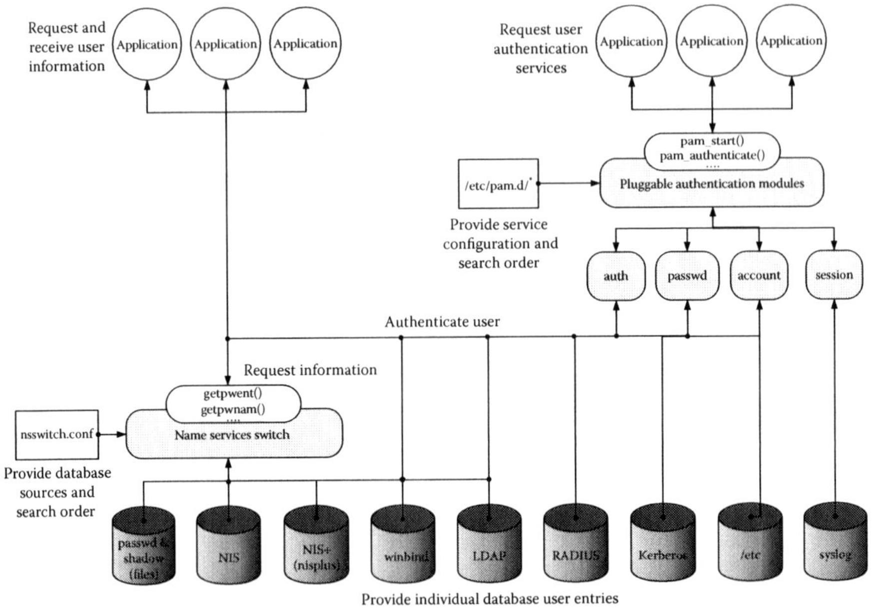

Figure 2.10 UNIX user authentication overview.

and this module basically uses the legacy NSS approach to authenticate the user; therefore, functions **getpwent( )** and **getpwuid( )** are very likely to be invoked here.

Furthermore, the **/etc/pam.d/system-auth** file specifies **pam_unix.so** authentication as **sufficient**, and this is the first PAM rule in the above file to try authentication with (**pam_env.so** is only there to set environment variables). Hence, by default, if the NSS source being used — be it either the local /**etc/passwd** and potentially **/etc/shadow** file, or any other source — contains information about the user trying to authenticate, including the username, UID, GID, and password, and provided that the user specifies the correct password, no other authentication methods will be tried. This means that the local **/etc/passwd** and **/etc/shadow** files take precedence over other sources, which may contain the same or even conflicting user entries. Figure 2.10 provides an overview of UNIX user authentication.

2.6 User Impersonation

Typically, when a user launches an executable, it uses the privileges of the user as it accesses resources. However, under certain circumstances it may be desirable to have an application executed with a specific set of privileges (user and group IDs) to impersonate another user and obtain a different set of privileges (user and group IDs). This process is called impersonation.

Very often, impersonation is required by daemon applications, which initially are launched using one set of privileges, and later on, as users connect to the daemon over the network, the user may need to be impersonated so the daemon may need to assume the privileges of the connected user.

UNIX implementations slightly differ in the way they implement impersonation but they all provide for the POSIX standard **setuid( )** system call, which allows a process to assume a different set of privileges. In the case of the superuser (a user with UID zero), **setuid( )** allows the calling process to impersonate any user on the system. In the case of regular system users, **setuid( )** allows the caller to switch between effective, saved, and real user IDs, as described below. The system call **setgid( )** is similar to **setuid( )** but as the name implies, it allows a process to impersonate a group. The differences between **setuid( )** implementations, some pitfalls and a state model for **setuid( )** are provided in [136].

In general, when a user starts the executable, the user ID (UID) and the group ID (GID) of that user are assigned to the Real User ID (RUID) and Real Group ID (RGID) attributes of the invoked process. Under normal circumstances, these are the only UIDs and GIDs used by the user and the invoked process.

It is sometimes possible for a process to acquire a new set of user and group IDs if it launches an executable. **setuid** and **setgid** are two special permissions on every executable and indicate whether the operating system should execute the file using the current user ID and group IDs, or switch to the user ID and group ID of the executable file owner. The privileges under which the executable will be run might be lower, higher, or equal to the current privileges of the user invoking the executable. The operating system is responsible for switching user and group IDs, depending on the file permissions and the **setuid** or **setgid** permissions.

If a user launches an executable that has the **setuid** or **setgid** permissions set, the RUID and RGID are still made equal to the UID and GID of the invoking user. However, the process launched by the user (and only this process) now uses a new set of privileges, known as Effective User ID (EUID) and Effective Group ID (EGID). The EUID and EGID are initially set the same as the executable user owner (if the **setuid** attribute has been set) and the executable group owner (if the **setgid** attribute has been set). As a result, the process running under **setuid/setgid** privileges now may have access to resources to which EUID/EGID have access, which may (and typically will) differ from those to which the launching user (RUID/RGID) has access. The user has launched an application that uses a different set of privileges.

The EUID and EGID are used even with executables, for which **setuid** and **setgid** are not set. In this case, EUID and EGID are equal to the RUID and RGID.

Most modern UNIX implementations use an additional set of IDs to increase the flexibility of **setuid/setgid** executables. The Saved User ID (SUID) and the Saved Group ID (SGID) are used to allow the **setuid/setgid** process to temporarily switch to a different set of IDs but still save the current effective IDs for later use. Some implementations may require special privileges in order to use SUID and SGID.

By default, when a process is started, SUID and SGID are set to the EUID and EGID. Later, if the process needs to temporarily drop the current Effective IDs (EUID and EGID) and switch to another (lower or higher in terms of permissions) set of IDs, the process can save the current EUID and/or EGID to SUID/SGID and perform the switching. Later, the process may revert to the saved SUID and SGID, setting EUID or EGID to SUID or SGID.

Now having three different sets of IDs, a process executed by a regular user can manipulate IDs using the **setuid( )/setgid( )** families of system calls following these rules:

- EUID or EGID can be set to SUID or SGID (if a process has saved IDs, it can revert to the saved IDs and drop the current effective IDs).
- EUID or EGID can be set to RUID or RGID (a process can drop its effective IDs by reverting to the invoking user and group IDs).
- RUID or RGID can be set to EUID or EUID (a process can drop its real user and group IDs).

The above rules are effective even in case the **setuid/setgid** process launches another **setuid/setgid** process.

Linux allows for yet another set of user and group IDs; File System User ID (FSUID) and File System Group ID (FSGID) are only used when the process is trying to access file system objects. This mechanism is very useful for daemons that share files across the network — such as NFS. In essence, the NFS daemon is able to impersonate the user access files across the network for file system operations only, instead setting effective user IDs of the user worker process to such having higher privileges, which can be used to compromise the NFS daemon.

FSUID and FSGID are always set to EUID and EGID when the effective IDs are changed. However, the application can then change FSUID and FSGID using the **setfsuid( )/setfsgid( )** system calls. Unless the user invoking the **setfsuid( )/setfsgid( )** is the superuser, the following operations are permitted:

- FSUID and/or FSGID can be set to SUID or SGID (if a process has saved IDs, it can set the File System IDs to the saved IDs).
- FSUID and/or FSGID can be set to EUID and/or EGID (this is the case by default, so this only makes sense if the FSUID has already been changed to a different ID).
- FSUID or FSGID can be set to RUID/RGID (thus reverting to the original file permissions of the user that invoked the process).

The **id** utility can be used to display both the effective and the real user IDs. By default, **id** shows effective user IDs.

It is important to note that **setuid( )** and **setgid( )** calls manipulate IDs that are process attributes, rather than user attributes. The user still has his original User ID and group ID, but the specific process that the user invokes (and potentially children and grandchildren of this process) may run using different privileges, which results in the user effectively having new permissions to access resources for the time during which the invoked process is running.

Let us assume that user Peter has his own version of the **bc** program and wants this program to execute with his own privileges every time another user on that system tries to launch it. Peter has configured **bc** to log an entry to a log file every time it starts, and the log file resides in Peter's home directory, to which only Peter has access.

To allow for **setuid**, the **bc** file permissions are configured as follows:

```
-bash-3.00$ ls -al bc
-rwsr-xr-x  1 Peter domain users 63272 Sep 16 23:55 bc
-bash-3.00$
```

User **David** logs in to the system and wants to use the **bc** application:

```
login as: David
David@10.0.2.101's password:
Last login: Fri Sep 16 23:58:42 2005 from 10.0.2.1
-bash-3.00$
```

At the same time, the superuser **root** logs in and can obtain information about the users on the system and the processes they have launched using the **ps** program, specifying the columns he wants to see and the terminal line for which he wants to see information:

```
[root@Dennis ~]# who
root     :0          Sep 16 22:47
root     pts/1       Sep 16 22:48 (:0.0)
root     pts/2       Sep 16 22:49 (:0.0)
David    pts/3       Sep 17 01:18 (10.0.2.1)
root     pts/4       Sep 16 23:49 (10.0.2.1)
[root@Dennis ~]#
```

```
[root@Dennis ~]# ps -o euid,ruid,suid,fsuid,f,comm,pid -t pts/3
 EUID   RUID   SUID FSUID F COMMAND              PID
16777224 16777224 16777224 16777224 0 bash 27741
[root@Dennis ~]#
[root@Dennis ~]# ps -o euser,ruser,suser,fuser,f,comm,pid -t pts/3
EUSER     RUSER     SUSER     FUSER     F COMMAND            PID
David     David     David     David     0 bash             27741
[root@Dennis ~]#
```

David has logged into the system and the only process he has running is his shell. His Effective User ID (EUID) is David, and so are his Real User ID (RUID), Saved user ID (SUID), and File System ID (FSID).

Now assume that David launches the **setuid** program **bc**, which belongs to user Peter:

```
-bash-3.00$ id
uid=16777224(David) gid=16777216(domain users) groups=16777216(domain
 users)
-bash-3.00$
-bash-3.00$ ./bc
bc 1.06
Copyright 1991-1994, 1997, 1998, 2000 Free Software Foundation, Inc.
This is free software with ABSOLUTELY NO WARRANTY.
For details type `warranty'.
123+321
444
```

David currently is using the superuser console:

```
[root@Dennis ~]# ps -o euid,ruid,suid,fsuid,f,comm,pid -t pts/3
 EUID   RUID   SUID FSUID F COMMAND              PID
16777224 16777224 16777224 16777224 0 bash 27741
16777223 16777224 16777223 16777223 0 bc   27874
[root@Dennis ~]#
[root@Dennis ~]# ps -o euser,ruser,suser,fuser,f,comm,pid -t pts/3
EUSER     RUSER     SUSER     FUSER     F COMMAND            PID
David     David     David     David     0 bash             27741
Peter     David     Peter     Peter     0 bc               27874
[root@Dennis ~]#
```

Apparently, the **bc** program has been started by David (RUSER David). However, the EID/EUSER, SID/SUSER, and FSUID/FUSER IDs are now set to the executable's owner (Peter) so the application is now running using Peter's privileges. The **bc** application will now be able to access Peter's home directory and write to the log file there, although the launching user David has no permissions to Peter's home directory where this file resides.

An executable file with **setuid** permissions and root as its owner (aka **setuid-root**) will run using superuser privileges. Such a process can use the **setuid( )** family of system calls to set its EUID/EGID to those of any other user on the system. In the case of the **setuid( )/setgid( )** system call invoked by the superuser, all IDs of the current process are effectively set to the new user or group, and the superuser ID and privileges are lost. This is used to switch to a new security context by some system utilities, such as **su** (see below). In security terms, the mechanism used to switch to another user's privileges is known as impersonation.

Linux does not support **setuid/setgid** on scripts, and simply ignores these attributes. Some script languages, such as Perl, have a special approach to implement and handle this behavior in a secure manner; it is called Taint mode.

A typical program that uses the **setuid** approach to run using a different set of privileges is the **passwd** tool that allows users to change their passwords. Because both the **/etc/passwd** file and the **/etc/shadow** file cannot be modified by regular users, the **passwd** tool, which is often invoked by regular users that want to change their passwords, needs to use a different set of privileges to be able to access these files. Hence, in most UNIX implementations, the **passwd** tool is owned by root and is configured as setuid-root.

Another application that uses the **setuid( )** system call is **passwd**, which is used by users to change their passwords:

```
[root@Dennis ~]# ls -al /usr/bin/passwd
-r-s--x--x  1 root root 18852 Mar  7 10:06 /usr/bin/passwd
[root@Dennis ~]#
```

It is important to note the '**s**'-permission, which indicates that the program is **setuid**. As the file owner is **root**, the **passwd** program is said to be setuid-root.

If user Peter logs in to the system using SSH and tries to change his password, the likely result from that operation is:

```
login as: Peter
Peter@10.0.2.101's password:
Last login: Fri Sep 16 23:57:43 2005 from 10.0.2.1
-bash-3.00$
-bash-3.00$ id
uid=16777223(Peter) gid=16777216(domain users) groups=16777216
 (domain users)
-bash-3.00$
-bash-3.00$ passwd
Changing password for user Peter.
Enter login(LDAP) password:
```

While the user is using the **passwd** tool to accomplish this, and the tool is still running, a superuser connected to another session can see the following results if he tries to display running processes and their privileges:

```
[root@Dennis ~]# who
root      :0           Sep 16 22:47
root      pts/1        Sep 16 22:48 (:0.0)
root      pts/2        Sep 16 22:49 (:0.0)
Peter     pts/3        Sep 17 01:46 (10.0.2.1)
root      pts/4        Sep 16 23:49 (10.0.2.1)
[root@Dennis ~]#
[root@Dennis ~]# ps -o euid,ruid,suid,fsuid,f,comm,pid -t pts/3
 EUID    RUID     SUID     FSUID    F COMMAND         PID
16777223 16777223 16777223 16777223 0 bash            28009
   0     16777223  0        0       0 passwd          28030
[root@Dennis ~]#
[root@Dennis ~]# ps -o euser,ruser,suser,fuser,f,comm,pid -t pts/3
EUSER    RUSER    SUSER    FUSER    F COMMAND         PID
Peter    Peter    Peter    Peter    0 bash          28009
root     Peter    root     root     0 passwd        28030
```

From the output above, the user shell (**bash**) is running using the privileges of user Peter. At the same time, the **passwd** tool on the same TTY is running using the privileges of user root — this has not been requested explicitly; this is a clear indication that the **passwd** program has been **setuid**-root.

As most UNIX implementations, Fedora provides a utility that allows the system administrator, as well as daemons running using superuser privileges, to impersonate other users. This tool is **su**.

Fedora uses **setuid**-root permissions on the **su** executable to set the effective user ID of the user process to 0 (superuser). Then, the **su** utility, using the **setuid( )** family of system calls, can easily impersonate any user on the system.

The **su** executable typically has the '**s**' flag set and is owned by root, and as a result it needs to be **setuid**-root.

```
[root@Dennis ~]# whereis su
su: /bin/su /usr/share/man/man1/su.1.gz
[root@Dennis ~]# ls -al /bin/su
-rwsr-xr-x  1 root root 59740 May 25 10:49 /bin/su
[root@Dennis ~]#
```

The **su** tool can be used by either the superuser or a regular user who does not possess superuser privileges. When the superuser launches the **su** command, he is only required to provide the name of the user to whose identity he wants to switch. The sample **su** session below shows this.

```
[root@Dennis ~]# id
uid=0(root) gid=0(root) groups=0(root),1(bin),2(daemon),3(sys),
 4(adm),6(disk),10(wheel)
[root@Dennis ~]#
```

```
[root@Dennis ~]# su David
bash-3.00$
bash-3.00$ id
uid=16777224(David) gid=16777216(domain users) groups=16777216
 (domain users)
bash-3.00$
bash-3.00$ id -rnu
David
bash-3.00$ id -rnG
domain users
bash-3.00$
bash-3.00$ ps -o euser,ruser,suser,fuser,f,comm,pid -T
EUSER    RUSER    SUSER    FUSER    F COMMAND          PID
David    David    David    David    4 bash           28343
David    David    David    David    0 ps             28351
bash-3.00$
bash-3.00$ who am i
root     pts/4        Sep 16 23:49 (10.0.2.1)
bash-3.00$
bash-3.00$
```

The user root can easily switch to the identity of user David (impersonate David) without having to know David's password. Now, the user root is effectively known as David and has David's UID and David's group membership. The current EUID, RUID, SUID, and FSUID have been set to David's. The **who** command can be used to determine the name of the user that initially connected to this TTY. However, this user's privileges are not in effect anymore.

Logically, switching from one set of privileges to another is not so straightforward if the originally logged-in user is different from the superuser. For example, if user Peter is logged in to the system and needs to temporarily acquire superuser privileges, this user needs to provide the superuser password, as shown below:.

```
-bash-3.00$ id
uid=16777223(Peter) gid=16777216(domain users) groups=16777216
 (domain users)
-bash-3.00$
-bash-3.00$ su root
Password:
[root@Dennis /]#
[root@Dennis /]# id
uid=0(root) gid=0(root) groups=0(root),1(bin),2(daemon),3(sys),
 4(adm),6(disk),10(wheel)
[root@Dennis /]#
[root@Dennis /]# id -rnu
root
[root@Dennis /]#
[root@Dennis /]# id -rnG
root bin daemon sys adm disk wheel
```

```
[root@Dennis /]#
[root@Dennis /]# who am i
Peter    pts/3        Sep 17 01:46 (10.0.2.1)
[root@Dennis /]#
[root@Dennis /]# exit
-bash-3.00$
-bash-3.00$ id
uid=16777223(Peter) gid=16777216(domain users) groups=16777216
 (domain users)
-bash-3.00$
```

In the example above, it is seen that both the effective and real (**id –rnu** and **id –rnG**) user IDs are now set to user root. Peter has successfully acquired superuser privileges and therefore is logged in as the superuser.

The **su** command from the **coreutils** 5.2.1 package of Fedora Core 4 (FC4) supports PAM, and by default uses the system-wide **/etc/pam.d/system-auth** PAM settings file.

If PAM is in use on a system where the **passwd** command is invoked, the PAM **passwd** service will be used in an attempt to change the user password, rather than the **/etc/passwd** and **/etc/shadow** files directly. If the user happens to be a local user, defined in the local **/etc/passwd** file, the PAM **passwd** service will perform the update rather than the **passwd** tool. However, if the user is defined, for example, in LDAP, and the LDAP server resides on a remote host, then setting the **passwd** tool effective user ID to root is useless. If all the users reside in LDAP or other security database, it may be worth considering alternative means of changing their passwords and disabling the **setuid** behavior for the **passwd** tool.

2.7 Case Study: User Authentication against LDAP

It is becoming increasingly popular to use LDAP for user authentication on UNIX systems. LDAP provides for a centralized hierarchical data store for user and other object information, and can be used by UNIX hosts to provide for single sign-on. User and group account information and passwords or other credential information can be stored in a centralized LDAP database, which can be replicated between all the LDAP servers within the enterprise.

There are a number of LDAP NSS and PAM implementations for UNIX. PADL LDAP [3] is among the most popular and will be used for the purposes of this case study.

This section covers user authentication against LDAP from a UNIX perspective. The details of LDAP user authentication from an LDAP protocol perspective are discussed in Chapter 4.

2.7.1 Preparing Active Directory

Since 2000 when Windows 2000 introduced Active Directory, UNIX LDAP user authentication has turned into a cornerstone for interoperability with Windows operating systems. Information in Active Directory — including information about users and groups — can be accessed using LDAP. This case study utilizes Windows 2003 as the domain controller and LDAP server against which UNIX users will authenticate.

The default Windows 2003 Active Directory schema does not provide attributes such as the UNIX **uid** or **gid**. Windows 2003 Active Directory objects have a user SID, stored in the **objectSid** attribute, which is the Windows NT equivalent of the UNIX **uid**. However, due to the different formats used, as well as to the different allocation disciplines, **objectSid** cannot be mapped directly to a UNIX **uid** field. This mapping is usually performed manually when the account is created, or later when the account is enabled for use from UNIX hosts. Some tools might be able to automatically generate the **uid** field using predefined criteria and UNIX **uid** ranges; apparently, if this is performed for existing UNIX accounts, the mapping must consider their **uid** attributes in UNIX. The same applies to group accounts — being that Windows NT security principals group accounts have an SID attribute as well, which cannot be directly translated to a UNIX **gid** attribute.

Microsoft has developed an integration suite for UNIX called Microsoft Services for UNIX (MS SFU). Apart from providing client and server software for NFS, NIS/Yellow Pages, and a password synchronization service, MS SFU extends the Active Directory schema to include specific UNIX attributes, such as user UID, group GID, and others. Installing the free Microsoft Services for UNIX on a domain controller using Enterprise Administrator privileges is the easiest way to prepare the Windows Active Directory infrastructure for LDAP user authentication from UNIX hosts.

Without using Microsoft Services for UNIX 3.5, one can still utilize LDAP as an authentication method by:

- Manually extending the Active Directory Schema to include the attributes for UNIX user and group accounts
- Manually assigning specific values for user and group accounts by means of **ldp.exe**, ADSI Editor, scripting, or other tools, capable of modifying Active Directory or extending the user and group property forms in Active Directory Users and Computers with AD Display Specifiers [5]

2.7.2 PADL LDAP Configuration

The PADL LDAP modules can be configured using the **/etc/ldap.conf** file. This file provides the following information:

- LDAP server connectivity information: where is the LDAP server and how to connect to it.
- Secure transport (TLS/SSL) configuration: whether TLS/SSL should be used to protect the communication channel to the LDAP server and what protection scheme to apply. In real life, TLS/SSL will almost certainly be used by the system authentication designer. In this case study, TLS/SSL is disabled to allow packet captures to expose the actual content of authentication traffic, while in real implementations this is undesirable.
- NSS/PAM objects and attribute mappings: establishes mapping between user specific attributes and attributes used by the LDAP server that will be used for user authentication.

The following is a sample **/etc/ldap.conf** file that can be used by PADL LDAP to query Microsoft Active Directory for user and group information:

```
#
# /etc/ldap.conf
#
# LDAP Connectivity
host bill.ins.com
base ou=Employees,dc=ins,dc=com
ldap_version 3
binddn cn=LDAPSearch,ou=ServiceAccounts,dc=ins,dc=com
bindpw password1!
nss_base_passwd ou=Employees,dc=ins,dc=com?sub
nss_base_shadow ou=Employees,dc=ins,dc=com?sub
nss_base_group ou=Employees,dc=ins,dc=com?sub

# SSL Configuration
ssl no
#ssl start_tls
tls_checkpeer yes
tls_cacertfile /tmp/certs/ca.pem
tls_cert /tmp/certs/ldapsearch.cer
tls_key /tmp/certs/ldapsearch.key

# Services for UNIX 3.5 mappings - translate NSS LDAP terms to
 AD+SFU terms

# NSS Configuration
nss_map_objectclass posixAccount User
nss_map_objectclass shadowAccount User
nss_map_objectclass posixGroup Group

nss_map_attribute uid msSFU30Name
nss_map_attribute uniqueMember msSFU30PosixMember
```

```
nss_map_attribute userPassword msSFU30Password
nss_map_attribute homeDirectory msSFU30HomeDirectory
nss_map_attribute loginShell msSFU30LoginShell
nss_map_attribute uidNumber msSFU30UidNumber
nss_map_attribute gidNumber msSFU30GidNumber

# PAM Configuration
pam_login_attribute sAMAccountName
pam_filter objectclass=User
pam_password ad
pam_member_attribute msSFU30PosixMember
```

In the Connectivity section, the PADL LDAP module is configured to connect to server **BILL.ins.com** (Windows 2003 domain controller) and use **OU=Employees,DC=ins,DC=com** as its search base; user and group accounts will reside at or under this level of the LDAP tree. A special user — LDAPSearch — has been created, and this user's password is provided in cleartext in the configuration file as well. User, group and shadow LDAP records reside within the same LDAP OU as the initial search base (**OU=Employees,DC=ins,DC=com**). The statement "**?sub**" specifies that LDAP search requests for security principals within LDAP will take place within the LDAP subfolders (sub-OUs) as well.

To be able to monitor network traffic, SSL is disabled at this time within the configuration file.

The last section provides for mapping between PADL LDAP UNIX specific classes and object attributes to the names of these attributes used by the Active Directory LDAP server. In this example, a Windows 2003 Domain Controller that runs Microsoft Services for UNIX 3.5 (SFU 3.5) will be used, and therefore the mappings in Table 2.7 will be required.

For the Active Directory User class, the attributes in Table 2.8 will be used and mapped to PADL LDAP parameters:

Specifically for the PAM LDAP module, the configuration file defines that user login will be performed using Active Directory objects of type User, the username will be matched against the Active Directory **sAMAccountName** attribute, and the password will follow Active Directory conventions.

The above mappings can be different for different LDAP servers, and depend on the LDAP schema and available options. Furthermore, not all the above parameters are required to exist in order to use user or group objects for authentication purposes. User objects only require having the NSS LDAP **uid** attribute (UNIX user ID), NSS LDAP **uidNumber** attribute (UNIX uid), and NSS LDAP **gidNumber** attribute (UNIX gid) to be used (and enumerated) as part of the NSS user database. Group objects only require NSS LDAP **gidNumber** (UNIX gid) as a mandatory attribute.

Table 2.7 PADL LDAP to MS SFU 3.5 Object Class Mappings

PADL LDAP Object Class	*Windows 2003 + MS SFU 3.5 Object Class*	*Description*
posixAccount	User	Represents user objects within LDAP. To supplement the **passwd** user database from an LDAP source, the NSS LDAP module will search for objects of this class.
ShadowAccount	User	Represents user objects and their passwords within LDAP. To supplement the **shadow** user and password database from an LDAP source, the NSS LDAP module will search for objects of this class. Note: As Windows 2003 AD, similar to other LDAP servers, typically bundles general user attributes with the password, the shadow class basically represents the user class.
posixGroup	Group	Represents group objects within LDAP. To supplement the **group** database from an LDAP source, the NSS LDAP module will search for objects of this class.

2.7.3 User Authentication Using NSS LDAP

As for every other NSS module, PADL NSS LDAP is meant to extend authentication and name resolution information in the **/etc** directory by providing access to other information sources over the network. Technically speaking, NSS LDAP can obtain other information from LDAP, including service or network names, but this case study only concentrates on the way NSS LDAP is applied to authenticate users.

NSS LDAP is configured using the **/etc/nsswitch.conf** file:

```
#
# /etc/nsswitch.conf
#

passwd:      files ldap
shadow:      files ldap
group:       files ldap

hosts:       files dns
```

Table 2.8 PADL LDAP to MS SFU 3.5 Object Attributes Mappings

PADL LDAP Object Attribute	*Windows 2003 + MS SFU 3.5 Object Attribute*	*Description*
Uid	msSFU30Name	Represents the user name aka login name, or just login. This attribute is equivalent to the AD sAMAccountName attribute and must be unique.
uniqueMember	msSFU30PosixMember	Multivalued attribute containing all the users that are members of a specific group.
userPassword	msSFU30Password	The MD5 hash of the user's password. Encoding can be different, depending on the LDAP server.
homeDirectory	msSFU30HomeDirectory	The path to the local home directory.
LoginShell	msSFU30LoginShell	The path to the user shell to be invoked upon interactive login.
uidNumber	msSFU30UidNumber	The UNIX **uid** attribute.
gidNumber	msSFU30GidNumber	The UNIX **gid** attribute.

```
bootparams: nisplus [NOTFOUND=return] files

ethers:     files
netmasks:   files
networks:   files
protocols:  files
rpc:        files
services:   files

netgroup:   files

publickey:  nisplus

automount:  files
aliases:    files nisplus
```

The **/etc/nsswitch.conf** file above will use the local **/etc/passwd**, **/etc/group** and **/etc/shadow** files for user and group authentication; but in addition to that, it will query a preconfigured LDAP server for additional records that might represent additional users and groups.

To validate the NSS LDAP configuration, the **getent passwd** command can be used to enumerate user accounts using NSS functions. The following is a sample result:.

```
[root@Dennis ~]# getent passwd
root:x:0:0:root:/root:/bin/bash
bin:x:1:1:bin:/bin:/sbin/nologin
daemon:x:2:2:daemon:/sbin:/sbin/nologin

<…output truncated for brevity…>

admin:x:500:500:Linux Administrator:/home/admin:/bin/bash
John:lFeuV/Q78Swvk:10004:20003:John White:/home/John:/bin/sh
Peter:8UvwBSxtf3JXQ:10007:20005:Peter Black:/home/Peter:/bin/sh
David:SZ7GVibjHWy9U:10001:20002:David Green:/home/David:/bin/sh
George:LAoCMgjzUreJo:10002:20001:George Blue:/home/George:/bin/sh
Susan:sv/CcsNDDKHSE:10008:20003:Susan Red:/home/Susan:/bin/sh
Jane:y/d6sWyZXc5NU:10003:20004:Jane Brown:/home/Jane:/bin/sh
Kate:70FsGbn7KrNb6:10005:20003:Kate Green:/home/Kate:/bin/sh
Laura:7cn8jGfWhqTy2:10006:20005:Laura Purple:/home/Laura:/bin/sh
[root@Dennis ~]#
```

The network traffic generated by that command can be found in the NSS-LDAP-getent.Cap packet capture.

Frame 4 shows the NSS LDAP client performing an LDAP Bind (user authentication) using the provided service account. The user password is being transferred in cleartext (LDAP Simple authentication), as well as the username (the LDAP Distinguished Name — DN in this instance). Frame 6 shows a confirmation from the LDAP server that the Bind request has been performed successfully.

In Frame 8, the client requests a list of all the objects under the search base (**Base DN**) and specifies that it is interested in **objectClass=User**. A list of user attributes expected from the search is also provided. The reply containing the search results can be found in Frames 9 to 11 (Figure 2.11).

If user Peter tries to log in to the Linux host, here is the network traffic that will be generated (NSS-LDAP-login.Cap).

Frames 4 and 5 show the NSS LDAP module logging into Active Directory, using the LDAPSearch service accounts.

Frames 7 and 8 show the NSS LDAP module performing an LDAP search against Active Directory within the **OU=Employees,DC=ins, DC=com** search base, and searching for objects of class **User** and username (attribute **msSFU30Name**) **Peter**. Frame 8 contains the reply and all the attributes that the object possesses including the

```
Frame 4 (136 bytes on wire, 136 bytes captured)
Ethernet II, Src: 02:00:4c:4f:4f:50, Dst: 00:03:ff:57:ab:2a
Internet Protocol, Src Addr: Dennis.ins.com (10.0.2.101), Dst Addr: bill.ins.com (10.0.1.101)
Transmission Control Protocol, Src Port: 44053 (44053), Dst Port: ldap (389), Seq: 2896238502,
Ack: 2708038115, Len: 70
Lightweight Directory Access Protocol
    LDAP Message, Bind Request
        Message Id: 1
        Message Type: Bind Request (0x00)
        Message Length: 63
        Response In: 6
        Version: 3
        DN: cn=LDAPSearch,ou=ServiceAccounts,dc=ins,dc=com
        Auth Type: Simple (0x00)
        Password: password1!

Frame 6 (88 bytes on wire, 88 bytes captured)
Ethernet II, Src: 00:03:ff:57:ab:2a, Dst: 02:00:4c:4f:4f:50
Internet Protocol, Src Addr: bill.ins.com (10.0.1.101), Dst Addr: Dennis.ins.com (10.0.2.101)
Transmission Control Protocol, Src Port: ldap (389), Dst Port: 44053 (44053), Seq: 2708038115,
Ack: 2896238572, Len: 22
Lightweight Directory Access Protocol
    LDAP Message, Bind Result
        Message Id: 1
        Message Type: Bind Result (0x01)
        Message Length: 7
        Response To: 4
        Time: 0.177456000 seconds
        Result Code: success (0x00)
        Matched DN: (null)
        Error Message: (null)

Frame 8 (286 bytes on wire, 286 bytes captured)
Ethernet II, Src: 02:00:4c:4f:4f:50, Dst: 00:03:ff:57:ab:2a
Internet Protocol, Src Addr: Dennis.ins.com (10.0.2.101), Dst Addr: bill.ins.com (10.0.1.101)
```

Figure 2.11 NSS-LDAP-getent.Cap: User enumeration against LDAP using NSS.

```
Transmission Control Protocol, Src Port: 44053 (44053), Dst Port: ldap (389), Seq: 2896238572,
Ack: 2708038137, Len: 220
Lightweight Directory Access Protocol
    LDAP Message, Search Request
        Message Id: 2
        Message Type: Search Request (0x03)
        Message Length: 211
        Response In: 9
        Base DN: ou=Employees,dc=ins,dc=com
        Scope: Subtree (0x02)
        Dereference: Never (0x00)
        Size Limit: 0
        Time Limit: 0
        Attributes Only: False
        Filter: (objectclass=User)
        Attribute: msSFU30Name
        Attribute: msSFU30Password
        Attribute: msSFU30UidNumber
        Attribute: msSFU30GidNumber
        Attribute: cn
        Attribute: msSFU30HomeDirectory
        Attribute: msSFU30LoginShell
        Attribute: gecos
        Attribute: description
        Attribute: objectClass

Frame 9 (1514 bytes on wire, 1514 bytes captured)
Ethernet II, Src: 00:03:ff:57:ab:2a, Dst: 02:00:4c:4f:4f:50
Internet Protocol, Src Addr: bill.ins.com (10.0.1.101), Dst Addr: Dennis.ins.com (10.0.2.101)
Transmission Control Protocol, Src Port: ldap (389), Dst Port: 44053 (44053), Seq: 2708038137,
Ack: 2896238792, Len: 1448
Lightweight Directory Access Protocol
    LDAP Message, Search Entry
        Message Id: 2
        Message Type: Search Entry (0x04)
        Message Length: 377
```

Figure 2.11 (continued)

```
    Response To: 8
    Time: 0.055386000 seconds
    Distinguished Name: CN=John White,OU=Employees,DC=ins,DC=com
    Attribute: objectClass
        Value: top
        Value: person
        Value: organizationalPerson
        Value: user
    Attribute: cn
        Value: John White
    Attribute: msSFU30Name
        Value: John
    Attribute: msSFU30UidNumber
        Value: 10004
    Attribute: msSFU30GidNumber
        Value: 20003
    Attribute: msSFU30LoginShell
        Value: /bin/sh
    Attribute: msSFU30Password
        Value: lFeuV/Q78Swvk
    Attribute: msSFU30HomeDirectory
        Value: /home/John
LDAP Message, Search Entry
    Message Id: 2
    Message Type: Search Entry (0x04)
    Message Length: 381
    Response To: 8
    Time: 0.055386000 seconds
    Distinguished Name: CN=Peter Black,OU=Employees,DC=ins,DC=com
    Attribute: objectClass
        Value: top
        Value: person
        Value: organizationalPerson
        Value: user
    Attribute: cn
        Value: Peter Black
```

Figure 2.11 (continued)

```
    Attribute: msSFU30Name

        Value: Peter

    Attribute: msSFU30UidNumber

        Value: 10007

    Attribute: msSFU30GidNumber

        Value: 20005

    Attribute: msSFU30LoginShell

        Value: /bin/sh

    Attribute: msSFU30Password

        Value: 8UvwBSxtf3JXQ

    Attribute: msSFU30HomeDirectory

        Value: /home/Peter

<…output truncated for brevity…>
```

Figure 2.11 (continued)

MD5 hash of the password. This will repeat a couple of times as the login process performs searches against the NSS database.

Frames 29 and 30 show the search request and reply for all the properties that Active Directory has for the specific user.

Frames 33 and 34 show the search request and reply for user membership to groups.

Frame 41 the search the UNIX **gid (msSFU30GidNumber)** of any group that contains the user's login name or the user's DN in its member list. Frame 42 shows the result and the group ID 20004. A series of searches in the next couple of frames discovers membership in other groups as well (Figure 2.12).

Finally, the user is authenticated and the output below shows that the current user access token that can then be used to authorize user access to resources:

```
-sh-3.00$ who am i
Peter    pts/3          Jul 26 07:33 (10.0.2.1)
-sh-3.00$ id
uid=10007(Peter) gid=20005(Sales) groups=20004(Marketing),20005(Sales)
-sh-3.00$
```

The problem with LDAP NSS is that traffic between the UNIX server and the LDAP server is not protected. This poses many security threats, some of which include:

```
Frame 4 (136 bytes on wire, 136 bytes captured)
Ethernet II, Src: 02:00:4c:4f:4f:50, Dst: 00:03:ff:57:ab:2a
Internet Protocol, Src Addr: Dennis.ins.com (10.0.2.101), Dst Addr: bill.ins.com (10.0.1.101)
Transmission Control Protocol, Src Port: 44805 (44805), Dst Port: ldap (389), Seq: 618486271,
Ack: 2970090254, Len: 70
Lightweight Directory Access Protocol
    LDAP Message, Bind Request
        Message Id: 1
        Message Type: Bind Request (0x00)
        Message Length: 63
        Response In: 5
        Version: 3
        DN: cn=LDAPSearch,ou=ServiceAccounts,dc=ins,dc=com
        Auth Type: Simple (0x00)
        Password: password1!

Frame 5 (88 bytes on wire, 88 bytes captured)
Ethernet II, Src: 00:03:ff:57:ab:2a, Dst: 02:00:4c:4f:4f:50
Internet Protocol, Src Addr: bill.ins.com (10.0.1.101), Dst Addr: Dennis.ins.com (10.0.2.101)
Transmission Control Protocol, Src Port: ldap (389), Dst Port: 44805 (44805), Seq: 2970090254,
Ack: 618486341, Len: 22
Lightweight Directory Access Protocol
    LDAP Message, Bind Result
        Message Id: 1
        Message Type: Bind Result (0x01)
        Message Length: 7
        Response To: 4
        Time: 0.070742000 seconds
        Result Code: success (0x00)
        Matched DN: (null)
        Error Message: (null)

Frame 7 (310 bytes on wire, 310 bytes captured)
Ethernet II, Src: 02:00:4c:4f:4f:50, Dst: 00:03:ff:57:ab:2a
Internet Protocol, Src Addr: Dennis.ins.com (10.0.2.101), Dst Addr: bill.ins.com (10.0.1.101)
```

Figure 2.12 NSS-LDAP-login.Cap: User Peter logs in using NSS-LDAP authentication.

```
Transmission Control Protocol, Src Port: 44805 (44805), Dst Port: ldap (389), Seq: 618486341,
Ack: 2970090276, Len: 244
Lightweight Directory Access Protocol
    LDAP Message, Search Request
        Message Id: 2
        Message Type: Search Request (0x03)
        Message Length: 235
        Response In: 8
        Base DN: ou=Employees,dc=ins,dc=com
        Scope: Subtree (0x02)
        Dereference: Never (0x00)
        Size Limit: 1
      Time Limit: 0
        Attributes Only: False
        Filter: (&(objectclass=User)(msSFU30Name=Peter))
        Attribute: msSFU30Name
        Attribute: msSFU30Password
        Attribute: msSFU30UidNumber
        Attribute: msSFU30GidNumber
        Attribute: cn
        Attribute: msSFU30HomeDirectory
        Attribute: msSFU30LoginShell
        Attribute: gecos
        Attribute: description
        Attribute: objectClass

Frame 8 (484 bytes on wire, 484 bytes captured)
Ethernet II, Src: 00:03:ff:57:ab:2a, Dst: 02:00:4c:4f:4f:50
Internet Protocol, Src Addr: bill.ins.com (10.0.1.101), Dst Addr: Dennis.ins.com (10.0.2.101)
Transmission Control Protocol, Src Port: ldap (389), Dst Port: 44805 (44805), Seq: 2970090276,
Ack: 618486585, Len: 418
Lightweight Directory Access Protocol
    LDAP Message, Search Entry
        Message Id: 2
        Message Type: Search Entry (0x04)
        Message Length: 381
```

Figure 2.12 (continued)

```
    Response To: 7
    Time: 0.017154000 seconds
    Distinguished Name: CN=Peter Black,OU=Employees,DC=ins,DC=com
    Attribute: objectClass
        Value: top
        Value: person
        Value: organizationalPerson
        Value: user
    Attribute: cn
        Value: Peter Black
    Attribute: msSFU30Name
        Value: Peter
    Attribute: msSFU30UidNumber
        Value: 10007
    Attribute: msSFU30GidNumber
        Value: 20005
    Attribute: msSFU30LoginShell
        Value: /bin/sh
    Attribute: msSFU30Password
        Value: 8UvwBSxtf3JXQ
    Attribute: msSFU30HomeDirectory
        Value: /home/Peter
  LDAP Message, Search Result
    Message Id: 2
    Message Type: Search Result (0x05)
    Message Length: 7
    Response To: 7
    Time: 0.017154000 seconds
    Result Code: success (0x00)
    Matched DN: (null)
    Error Message: (null)

Frame 29 (163 bytes on wire, 163 bytes captured)
Ethernet II, Src: 02:00:4c:4f:4f:50, Dst: 00:03:ff:57:ab:2a
Internet Protocol, Src Addr: Dennis.ins.com (10.0.2.101), Dst Addr: bill.ins.com (10.0.1.101)
```

Figure 2.12 (continued)

```
Transmission Control Protocol, Src Port: 44806 (44806), Dst Port: ldap (389), Seq: 612541058,
Ack: 2233327288, Len: 97
Lightweight Directory Access Protocol
    LDAP Message, Search Request
        Message Id: 2
        Message Type: Search Request (0x03)
        Message Length: 90
        Response In: 30
        Base DN: ou=Employees,dc=ins,dc=com
        Scope: Subtree (0x02)
        Dereference: Never (0x00)
        Size Limit: 1
        Time Limit: 0
        Attributes Only: False
        Filter: (&(objectclass=User)(msSFU30Name=Peter))

Frame 30 (1514 bytes on wire, 1514 bytes captured)
Ethernet II, Src: 00:03:ff:57:ab:2a, Dst: 02:00:4c:4f:4f:50
Internet Protocol, Src Addr: bill.ins.com (10.0.1.101), Dst Addr: Dennis.ins.com (10.0.2.101)
Transmission Control Protocol, Src Port: ldap (389), Dst Port: 44806 (44806), Seq: 2233327288, Ack: 612541155, Len: 1448
Lightweight Directory Access Protocol
    LDAP Message, Search Entry
        Message Id: 2
        Message Type: Search Entry (0x04)
        Message Length: 1647
        Response To: 29
        Time: 0.002575000 seconds
        Distinguished Name: CN=Peter Black,OU=Employees,DC=ins,DC=com
        Attribute: objectClass
            Value: top
            Value: person
            Value: organizationalPerson
            Value: user
        Attribute: cn
            Value: Peter Black
        Attribute: sn
```

Figure 2.12 (continued)

```
        Value: Black
    Attribute: givenName
        Value: Peter
    Attribute: distinguishedName
        Value: CN=Peter Black,OU=Employees,DC=ins,DC=com
    Attribute: instanceType
        Value: 4
    Attribute: whenCreated
        Value: 20050723115216.0Z
    Attribute: whenChanged
        Value: 20050723124135.0Z
    Attribute: displayName
        Value: Peter Black
    Attribute: uSNCreated
        Value: 16496
    Attribute: uSNChanged
        Value: 16700
    Attribute: name
        Value: Peter Black
    Attribute: objectGUID
        Value: \232\030!@\243H\263J\230\024*3\345\225\324\004
    Attribute: userAccountControl
        Value: 66048
    Attribute: badPwdCount
        Value: 5
    Attribute: codePage
        Value: 0
    Attribute: countryCode
        Value: 0
    Attribute: badPasswordTime
        Value: 127668127639895296
    Attribute: lastLogoff
        Value: 0
    Attribute: lastLogon
        Value: 0
    Attribute: pwdLastSet
```

Figure 2.12 (continued)

```
        Value: 127665960953656912
    Attribute: primaryGroupID
        Value: 513
    Attribute: objectSid
        Value: \001\005
    Attribute: accountExpires
        Value: 9223372036854775807
    Attribute: logonCount
        Value: 0
    Attribute: sAMAccountName
        Value: Peter
    Attribute: sAMAccountType
        Value: 805306368
    Attribute: userPrincipalName
        Value: Peter@ins.com
    Attribute: objectCategory
        Value: CN=Person,CN=Schema,CN=Configuration,DC=ins,DC=com
    Attribute: dSCorePropagationData
        Value: 20050723115649.0Z
        Value: 20050723115649.0Z
        Value: 20050723115649.0Z
        Value: 16010108151056.0Z
    Attribute: msSFU30Name
        Value: Peter
    Attribute: msSFU30UidNumber
        Value: 10007
    Attribute: msSFU30GidNumber
        Value: 20005
    Attribute: msSFU30LoginShell

<...output truncated for brevity...>

Frame 33 (249 bytes on wire, 249 bytes captured)
Ethernet II, Src: 02:00:4c:4f:4f:50, Dst: 00:03:ff:57:ab:2a
Internet Protocol, Src Addr: Dennis.ins.com (10.0.2.101), Dst Addr: bill.ins.com (10.0.1.101)
```

Figure 2.12 (continued)

```
Transmission Control Protocol, Src Port: 44806 (44806), Dst Port: ldap (389), Seq: 612541155,
Ack: 2233328972, Len: 183
Lightweight Directory Access Protocol
    LDAP Message, Search Request
        Message Id: 3
        Message Type: Search Request (0x03)
        Message Length: 174
        Response In: 34
        Base DN: ou=Employees,dc=ins,dc=com
        Scope: Subtree (0x02)
        Dereference: Never (0x00)
        Size Limit: 0
        Time Limit: 0
        Attributes Only: False
        Filter: (&(objectclass=Group)(|(memberUid=Peter)(msSFU30PosixMember=CN=Peter
Black,OU=Employees,DC=ins,DC=com)))
        Attribute: msSFU30GidNumber

Frame 34 (187 bytes on wire, 187 bytes captured)
Ethernet II, Src: 00:03:ff:57:ab:2a, Dst: 02:00:4c:4f:4f:50
Internet Protocol, Src Addr: bill.ins.com (10.0.1.101), Dst Addr: Dennis.ins.com (10.0.2.101)
Transmission Control Protocol, Src Port: ldap (389), Dst Port: 44806 (44806), Seq: 2233328972,
Ack: 612541338, Len: 121
Lightweight Directory Access Protocol
    LDAP Message, Search Entry
        Message Id: 3
        Message Type: Search Entry (0x04)
        Message Length: 84
        Response To: 33
        Time: 0.011800000 seconds
        Distinguished Name: CN=Marketing,OU=Employees,DC=ins,DC=com
        Attribute: msSFU30GidNumber
            Value: 20004
    LDAP Message, Search Result
        Message Id: 3
        Message Type: Search Result (0x05)
```

Figure 2.12 (continued)

```
        Message Length: 7
        Response To: 33
        Time: 0.011800000 seconds
        Result Code: success (0x00)
        Matched DN: (null)
        Error Message: (null)

Frame 41 (249 bytes on wire, 249 bytes captured)
Ethernet II, Src: 02:00:4c:4f:4f:50, Dst: 00:03:ff:57:ab:2a
Internet Protocol, Src Addr: Dennis.ins.com (10.0.2.101), Dst Addr: bill.ins.com (10.0.1.101)
Transmission Control Protocol, Src Port: 44806 (44806), Dst Port: ldap (389), Seq: 612541594,
Ack: 2233330799, Len: 183
Lightweight Directory Access Protocol
    LDAP Message, Search Request
        Message Id: 6
        Message Type: Search Request (0x03)
        Message Length: 174
        Response In: 42
        Base DN: ou=Employees,dc=ins,dc=com
        Scope: Subtree (0x02)
        Dereference: Never (0x00)
        Size Limit: 0
        Time Limit: 0
        Attributes Only: False
        Filter: (&(objectclass=Group)(|(memberUid=Peter)(msSFU30PosixMember=CN=Peter
Black,OU=Employees,DC=ins,DC=com)))
        Attribute: msSFU30GidNumber

Frame 42 (187 bytes on wire, 187 bytes captured)
Ethernet II, Src: 00:03:ff:57:ab:2a, Dst: 02:00:4c:4f:4f:50
Internet Protocol, Src Addr: bill.ins.com (10.0.1.101), Dst Addr: Dennis.ins.com (10.0.2.101)
Transmission Control Protocol, Src Port: ldap (389), Dst Port: 44806 (44806), Seq: 2233330799, Ack: 612541777, Len: 121
Lightweight Directory Access Protocol
    LDAP Message, Search Entry
        Message Id: 6
        Message Type: Search Entry (0x04)
```

Figure 2.12 (continued)

```
     Message Length: 84
     Response To: 41
     Time: 0.007561000 seconds
     Distinguished Name: CN=Marketing,OU=Employees,DC=ins,DC=com
     Attribute: msSFU30GidNumber
        Value: 20004
LDAP Message, Search Result
     Message Id: 6
     Message Type: Search Result (0x05)
     Message Length: 7
     Response To: 41
     Time: 0.007561000 seconds
     Result Code: success (0x00)
     Matched DN: (null)
     Error Message: (null)
```

Figure 2.12 (continued)

- An attacker can intercept LDAP communication between the client and the server and can use the service username (LDAPSearch) and password found there to connect to resources throughout the organization. This might include resources other than the LDAP server itself.
- An attacker assumes the identity of the LDAP server and provides false authentication information to LDAP requests from the NSS LDAP client. The attacker may, for example, falsify authentication information and allow an illegitimate user to authenticate, or may deny a legitimate user to authenticate.
- An attacker can modify LDAP Bind and Search requests from the client to the server and back, and cause them to fail. This can result in users being denied access to the system or applications due to the inability to authenticate.
- An attacker can modify user attributes in search replies, such as the user **uid** or group membership, in order to elevate his own privileges.
- An attacker can intercept communication between the client and the server, and obtain sensitive or personal information, such as the user phone number, last login time, or other information stored in the directory.

There are at least two approaches to resolve the problems outlined above and make sure that data is protected, as well as that authenticating parties are able to validate each other's identity. First, there is the approach to encrypt and authenticate information and communicating parties at the application level using SSL/TLS; and second, exactly the same can be done at the network level by means of IPSec.

SSL/TLS is discussed in Chapter 4, and IPSec in Chapter 5.

2.7.4 User Authentication Using PAM LDAP

As already discussed, unlike NSS, PAM is not a user information source. Users cannot search against PAM to find other users' UIDs or GIDs; other sources (such as NSS) can be used for user information, and are required even when PAM is used for user authentication. It is possible, for example, to have NSS LDAP provide user information but no password information, and PAM LDAP can then be used to authenticate the user.

Different PAM implementations can differ in the way they provide for user authentication. PADL LDAP allows for PAM user authentication against LDAP. Unlike PADL NSS LDAP, the authentication process for PAM attempts to authenticate to the LDAP server with the username and credentials supplied by the actual authenticating user. If the authentication attempt is successful, then the user has supplied valid credentials and will be let into the system. If LDAP authentication using the user supplied credentials fails, then the user has not provided the correct credentials.

It is important to note that, due to its behavior, PAM will provide for correct auditing information on the LDAP server. Unlike NSS, where the LDAP server will only see search requests from one user (the LDAP access system account used by NSS), with PAM, authentication requests take place with the actual username, and that is what the LDAP logs will reflect. Therefore, if there is a hacker attack or attempts to brute force (or dictionary attack) a user password, the LDAP server will be able to provide this information if the logs of PAM LDAP are used, and this will go completely unnoticed if NSS LDAP is used.

Computer **DENNIS.ins.com** is configured for PAM authentication against LDAP server **BILL.ins.com**. If user Peter tries to authenticate to server DENNIS, the following output represents the successful user SSH session:

```
login as: Peter
Sent username "Peter"
Peter@10.0.2.101's password:
Last login: Sat Mar 11 15:24:09 2006 from xp-client.ins.com
-bash-3.00$ id
uid=9115(Peter) gid=9115 groups=9115
-bash-3.00$
```

```
Frame 4 (133 bytes on wire, 133 bytes captured)
Ethernet II, Src: 02:00:4c:4f:4f:50 (02:00:4c:4f:4f:50), Dst: Microsof_57:ab:2a
(00:03:ff:57:ab:2a)
Internet Protocol, Src: 10.0.2.101 (10.0.2.101), Dst: 10.0.1.101 (10.0.1.101)
Transmission Control Protocol, Src Port: 39960 (39960), Dst Port: ldap (389), Seq: 956310945,
Ack: 3817033950, Len: 67
Lightweight Directory Access Protocol
    LDAP Message, Bind Request
        Message Id: 1
        Message Type: Bind Request (0x00)
        Message Length: 60
        Response In: 5
        Version: 3
        DN: cn=LDAPMgr,ou=ServiceAccounts,dc=ins,dc=com
        Auth Type: Simple (0x00)
        Password: password1!

Frame 5 (88 bytes on wire, 88 bytes captured)
Ethernet II, Src: Microsof_57:ab:2a (00:03:ff:57:ab:2a), Dst: 02:00:4c:4f:4f:50
(02:00:4c:4f:4f:50)
Internet Protocol, Src: 10.0.1.101 (10.0.1.101), Dst: 10.0.2.101 (10.0.2.101)
Transmission Control Protocol, Src Port: ldap (389), Dst Port: 39960 (39960), Seq: 3817033950,
Ack: 956311012, Len: 22
Lightweight Directory Access Protocol
    LDAP Message, Bind Result
        Message Id: 1
        Message Type: Bind Result (0x01)
        Message Length: 7
        Response To: 4
        Time: 0.025824000 seconds
        Result Code: success (0x00)
        Matched DN: (null)
        Error Message: (null)

Frame 7 (166 bytes on wire, 166 bytes captured)
```

Figure 2.13 PAM-LDAP-login.Cap: User Peter authenticated on server DENNIS using PAM LDAP.

Figure 2.13 shows user Peter logging in to server **DENNIS.ins.com** using SSH. First, the PAM LDAP module carries out a search against Active Directory using the LDAP service account and tries to determine whether a user by the name of Peter exists on the LDAP server. Frames 4 and 5

```
Ethernet II, Src: 02:00:4c:4f:4f:50 (02:00:4c:4f:4f:50), Dst: Microsof_57:ab:2a
(00:03:ff:57:ab:2a)
Internet Protocol, Src: 10.0.2.101 (10.0.2.101), Dst: 10.0.1.101 (10.0.1.101)
Transmission Control Protocol, Src Port: 39960 (39960), Dst Port: ldap (389), Seq: 956311012,
Ack: 3817033972, Len: 100
Lightweight Directory Access Protocol
    LDAP Message, Search Request
        Message Id: 2
        Message Type: Search Request (0x03)
        Message Length: 93
        Response In: 8
        Base DN: ou=Employees,dc=ins,dc=com
        Scope: Subtree (0x02)
        Dereference: Never (0x00)
        Size Limit: 1
        Time Limit: 0
        Attributes Only: False
      Filter: (&(objectclass=User)(sAMAccountName=Peter))

Frame 8 (1514 bytes on wire, 1514 bytes captured)
Ethernet II, Src: Microsof_57:ab:2a (00:03:ff:57:ab:2a), Dst: 02:00:4c:4f:4f:50
(02:00:4c:4f:4f:50)
Internet Protocol, Src: 10.0.1.101 (10.0.1.101), Dst: 10.0.2.101 (10.0.2.101)
Transmission Control Protocol, Src Port: ldap (389), Dst Port: 39960 (39960), Seq: 3817033972,
Ack: 956311112, Len: 1448
Lightweight Directory Access Protocol
    LDAP Message, Search Entry
        Message Id: 2
        Message Type: Search Entry (0x04)
        Message Length: 1887
        Response To: 7
        Time: 0.010816000 seconds
        Distinguished Name: CN=Peter Black,OU=Employees,DC=ins,DC=com
        Attribute: objectClass
            Value: top
            Value: person
```

Figure 2.13 (continued)

show the service account logging into LDAP, and frames 7 and 8 show the search and the results for user Peter.

Frames 11 and 12 in Figure 2.13 show the actual user authentication process. In this example, LDAP Simple authentication is used and the user

```
      Value: organizationalPerson
      Value: user
  Attribute: cn
      Value: Peter Black
  Attribute: sn
      Value: Black
  Attribute: givenName
      Value: Peter
  Attribute: distinguishedName
      Value: CN=Peter Black,OU=Employees,DC=ins,DC=com
  Attribute: instanceType
      Value: 4
  Attribute: whenCreated
      Value: 20050723115216.0Z
  Attribute: whenChanged
      Value: 20060616233917.0Z
  Attribute: displayName
      Value: Peter Black
  Attribute: uSNCreated
      Value: 16496
  Attribute: uSNChanged
      Value: 103737
  Attribute: name
      Value: Peter Black
  Attribute: objectGUID
      Value: \232\030!@\243H\263J\230\024*3\345\225\324\004
  Attribute: userAccountControl
      Value: 66176
  Attribute: badPwdCount
      Value: 0
  Attribute: codePage
      Value: 0
  Attribute: countryCode
      Value: 0
  Attribute: badPasswordTime
      Value: 127949748377245872
```

Figure 2.13 (continued)

provides a username and a cleartext password to the LDAP server. The server validates the credentials and replies with success or failure result to the authentication request.

```
        Attribute: lastLogoff
            Value: 0
        Attribute: lastLogon
            Value: 127949750632288464
        Attribute: pwdLastSet
            Value: 127774947808256320
        Attribute: primaryGroupID
            Value: 513
        Attribute: userParameters
            Value: m:                    d\t                    P
        Attribute: objectSid
            Value: \001\005
        Attribute: accountExpires
            Value: 9223372036854775807
        Attribute: logonCount
            Value: 14
        Attribute: sAMAccountName
            Value: Peter
        Attribute: sAMAccountType
            Value: 805306368
        Attribute: userPrincipalName
            Value: Peter@ins.com
        Attribute: objectCategory
            Value: CN=Person,CN=Schema,CN=Configuration,DC=ins,DC=com
        Attribute: msNPAllowDialin
            Value: TRUE
        Attribute: dSCorePropagationData
            Value: 20050723115649.0Z
            Value: 20050723115649.0Z
            Value: 20050723115649.0Z
[Packet size limited during capture: LDAP truncated]

Frame 11 (162 bytes on wire, 162 bytes captured)
Ethernet II, Src: 02:00:4c:4f:4f:50 (02:00:4c:4f:4f:50), Dst: Microsof_57:ab:2a
(00:03:ff:57:ab:2a)
Internet Protocol, Src: 10.0.2.101 (10.0.2.101), Dst: 10.0.1.101 (10.0.1.101)
```

Figure 2.13 (continued)

Similar to LDAP NSS, if the authentication channel between the server and the LDAP server is not protected, this can give rise to various threats. Therefore, the channel between the resource server and the LDAP server must be protected either by using TLS/SSL or IPSec.

```
Transmission Control Protocol, Src Port: 39960 (39960), Dst Port: ldap (389), Seq: 956311112,
Ack: 3817035896, Len: 96
Lightweight Directory Access Protocol
    LDAP Message, Bind Request
        Message Id: 3
        Message Type: Bind Request (0x00)
        Message Length: 58
        Response In: 12
        Version: 3
        DN: CN=Peter Black,OU=Employees,DC=ins,DC=com
        Auth Type: Simple (0x00)
        Password: password1!
        LDAP Controls
            LDAP Control
                Control OID: 1.3.6.1.4.1.42.2.27.8.5.1

Frame 12 (88 bytes on wire, 88 bytes captured)
Ethernet II, Src: Microsof_57:ab:2a (00:03:ff:57:ab:2a), Dst: 02:00:4c:4f:4f:50
(02:00:4c:4f:4f:50)
Internet Protocol, Src: 10.0.1.101 (10.0.1.101), Dst: 10.0.2.101 (10.0.2.101)
Transmission Control Protocol, Src Port: ldap (389), Dst Port: 39960 (39960), Seq: 3817035896,
Ack: 956311208, Len: 22
Lightweight Directory Access Protocol
    LDAP Message, Bind Result
        Message Id: 3
        Message Type: Bind Result (0x01)
        Message Length: 7
        Response To: 11
        Time: 0.014545000 seconds
        Result Code: success (0x00)
        Matched DN: (null)
        Error Message: (null)
```

Figure 2.13 (continued)

2.8 Case Study: Using Hesiod for User Authentication in Linux

Hesiod was developed as part of the MIT Athena Project (see [1]). It is not widely used and currently works only as part of academic infrastructure solutions. The reason for discussing it here is more to show how flexible user authentication technologies can be, rather than present it as a widespread and well designed authentication mechanism.

Hesiod represents an interesting approach to user authentication; it uses existing DNS zones as an administrative database with authentication information for user and group accounts. Hesiod is typically implemented by means of an NSS module, and apparently can be used to provide other NSS information, such as hosts' files or services mappings. This section concentrates on the importance of Hesiod for user authentication.

To use Hesiod for user authentication, the system administrator configures the authentication services using the **/etc/hesiod.conf** configuration file. Furthermore, the NSS configuration file **/etc/nsswitch.conf** should be modified as well to include Hesiod as a valid user and group information source. An NSS configuration file that provides for Hesiod authentication is:

```
#
# /etc/nsswitch.conf
#

passwd:      files hesiod
shadow:      files hesiod
group:       files hesiod

hosts:       files dns

bootparams: nisplus [NOTFOUND=return] files
ethers:      files
netmasks:    files
networks:    files
protocols:   files
rpc:         files
services:    files

netgroup:    files

publickey:   nisplus

automount:   files
aliases:     files nisplus
```

Hesiod stores information in the DNS hierarchical structures. Provided that a DNS server is configured to serve requests for a particular DNS zone, such as **ins.com**, a sub-domain that will contain the Hesiod records would typically be created. Most implementations use **ns** as the name of the sub-domain for Hesiod, but virtually any sub-domain name can be used for this. The sub-domain name for Hesiod records is known as Left Hand Side domain (LHS), while the upper-level domain is known as Right Hand Side (RHS) domain. For example, if Hesiod records will be stored in the **ns.ins.com** domain, the LHS domain would be **ns**, and the RHS domain would be **ins.com**.

The Hesiod NSS module configuration file usually contains the following information:

```
#
# /etc/hesiod.conf
#

# Left Hand Side Domain
lhs=.ns

# Right Hand Side Domain
rhs=.ins.com

# Record Classes - the default is 'IN,HS'
classes=IN
```

All the Hesiod directory information is stored in standard records of class **IN** (Internet). There is a special class **HS** dedicated to Hesiod records but this class is not widely used.

The Hesiod authentication database that needs to be created in DNS should contain records of type TXT (DNS Text Records), and each of the TXT records should provide information for a single user or group. The format used to describe the user or group is the same used in the **/etc/passwd** and **/etc/group** files. The TXT record name must be either the username with the suffix **.passwd** or the group name with the suffix **.group**; technically, this means that two sub-domains of the Hesiod domain (**ns.ins.com**) are required with the names **passwd.ns.ins.com** and **group.ns.ins.com**, respectively (Figure 2.14 and Figure 2.15).

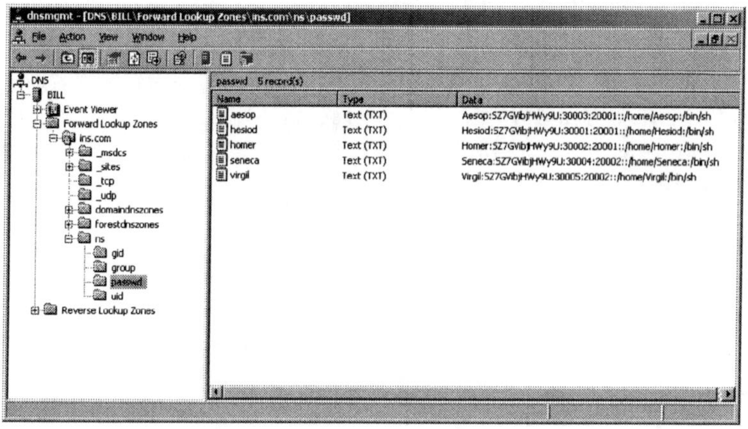

Figure 2.14 Hesiod DNS configuration: DNS as a passwd database.

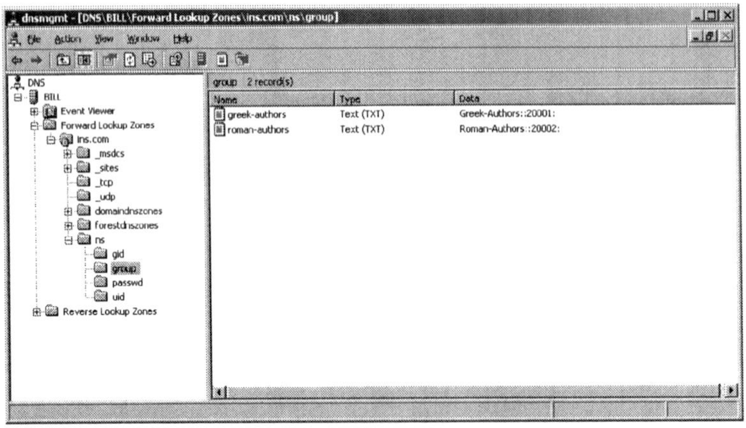

Figure 2.15 Hesiod DNS configuration: group database.

To perform lookups based on user and group IDs (**uid** and **gid**), Hesiod requires that CNAME (Canonical Name = Alias) records be created as well. These records should be created in the Hesiod domain. The CNAME records' names must be composed of two parts: (1) the user or group ID, followed by (2) the suffix **.uid** if the CNAME record refers to a **user** or the suffix **.gid** if the CNAME record refers to a group. This means that two more subdomains will be created under the Hesiod domain: (1) **uid.ns.ins.com**, which will store the user ID CNAME records; and (2) **gid.ns.ins.com**, which will store the group ID CNAME records. Each CNAME record created must be configured as an alias to the **TXT** record, describing the user or the group. Refer to Figure 2.16 and Figure 2.17.

Because Hesiod uses standard DNS queries and receives standard DNS replies from the server that stores the database, the above configuration can be performed using a BIND DNS server, or any other DNS server capable of supporting **TXT** and **CNAME** DNS records.

We can now try and authenticate to the Linux computer (**DENNIS.ins.com**) using SSH:

```
login as: Homer
Homer@10.0.2.101's password:
Last login: Sat Jul 23 05:53:39 2005 from 10.0.2.1
-sh-3.00$ id
uid=30002(Homer) gid=20001(Greek-Authors) groups=20001(Greek-Authors)
-sh-3.00$ cd /home
-sh-3.00$ ls -al
total 32
drwxr-xr-x   6 root   root          4096 Jul 23 03:56 .
drwxr-xr-x  23 root   root          4096 Jul 21 20:39 ..
drwxr-xr-x   2 admin  admin         4096 Jul  9 01:59 admin
drwxr-xr-x   2 Hesiod Greek-Authors 4096 Jul 23 03:54 Hesiod
```

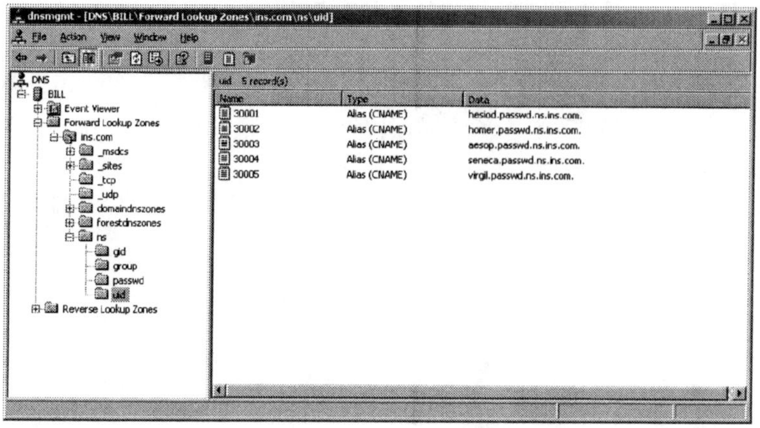

Figure 2.16 Hesiod DNS configuration: user ID pointers.

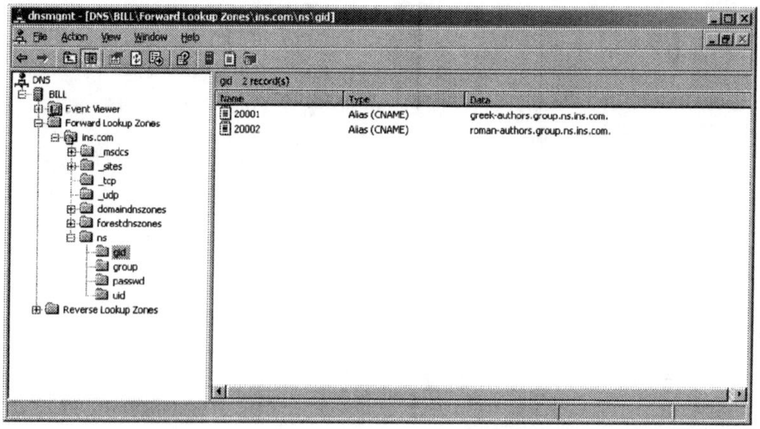

Figure 2.17 Hesiod DNS configuration: group ID pointers.

```
drwxr-xr-x   2 Homer  Greek-Authors 4096 Jul 23 03:57 Homer
drwxr-xr-x   2 Seneca Roman-Authors 4096 Jul 23 03:56 Seneca
-sh-3.00$
```

User authentication and the invocation of the **id** command above will generate the following traffic (Figure 2.18; NSS-Hesiod.Cap).

Frame 1 in Figure 2.18 represents a DNS query for record with name **Homer.passwd.ns.ins.com**, and the reply in Frame 2 provides all the passwd-format attributes for user Homer using the DNS Answer Text field. These requests are repeated multiple times as SSHD performs various search operations against NSS.

```
Frame 1 (83 bytes on wire, 83 bytes captured)
Ethernet II, Src: 02:00:4c:4f:4f:50, Dst: 00:03:ff:57:ab:2a
Internet Protocol, Src Addr: 10.0.2.101 (10.0.2.101), Dst Addr: 10.0.1.101 (10.0.1.101)
User Datagram Protocol, Src Port: 32817 (32817), Dst Port: domain (53)
Domain Name System (query)
    Transaction ID: 0x1fcc
    Flags: 0x0100 (Standard query)
    Questions: 1
    Answer RRs: 0
    Authority RRs: 0
    Additional RRs: 0
    Queries
        Homer.passwd.ns.ins.com: type TXT, class IN
            Name: Homer.passwd.ns.ins.com
            Type: TXT (Text strings)
            Class: IN (0x0001)

Frame 2 (148 bytes on wire, 148 bytes captured)
Ethernet II, Src: 00:03:ff:57:ab:2a, Dst: 02:00:4c:4f:4f:50
Internet Protocol, Src Addr: 10.0.1.101 (10.0.1.101), Dst Addr: 10.0.2.101 (10.0.2.101)
User Datagram Protocol, Src Port: domain (53), Dst Port: 32817 (32817)
Domain Name System (response)
    Transaction ID: 0x1fcc
    Flags: 0x8580 (Standard query response, No error)
    Questions: 1
    Answer RRs: 1
    Authority RRs: 0
    Additional RRs: 0
    Queries
        Homer.passwd.ns.ins.com: type TXT, class IN
            Name: Homer.passwd.ns.ins.com
            Type: TXT (Text strings)
            Class: IN (0x0001)
    Answers
        Homer.passwd.ns.ins.com: type TXT, class IN
            Name: Homer.passwd.ns.ins.com
```

Figure 2.18 NSS-Hesiod.Cap: User Homer authenticates using Hesiod.

```
        Type: TXT (Text strings)
        Class: IN (0x0001)
        Time to live: 1 hour
        Data length: 53
        Text: Homer:SZ7GVibjHWy9U:30002:20001::/home/Homer:/bin/sh

Frame 34 (80 bytes on wire, 80 bytes captured)
Ethernet II, Src: 02:00:4c:4f:4f:50, Dst: 00:03:ff:57:ab:2a
Internet Protocol, Src Addr: 10.0.2.101 (10.0.2.101), Dst Addr: 10.0.1.101 (10.0.1.101)
User Datagram Protocol, Src Port: 32820 (32820), Dst Port: domain (53)
Domain Name System (query)
    Transaction ID: 0x1cdb
    Flags: 0x0100 (Standard query)
    Questions: 1
    Answer RRs: 0
    Authority RRs: 0
    Additional RRs: 0
    Queries
        20001.gid.ns.ins.com: type TXT, class IN
            Name: 20001.gid.ns.ins.com
            Type: TXT (Text strings)
            Class: IN (0x0001)

Frame 35 (148 bytes on wire, 148 bytes captured)
Ethernet II, Src: 00:03:ff:57:ab:2a, Dst: 02:00:4c:4f:4f:50
Internet Protocol, Src Addr: 10.0.1.101 (10.0.1.101), Dst Addr: 10.0.2.101 (10.0.2.101)
User Datagram Protocol, Src Port: domain (53), Dst Port: 32820 (32820)
    Source port: domain (53)
    Destination port: 32820 (32820)
    Length: 114
    Checksum: 0xea3f (correct)
Domain Name System (response)
    Transaction ID: 0x1cdb
    Flags: 0x8580 (Standard query response, No error)
    Questions: 1
    Answer RRs: 2
```

Figure 2.18 (continued)

```
Authority RRs: 0
Additional RRs: 0
Queries
    20001.gid.ns.ins.com: type TXT, class IN
        Name: 20001.gid.ns.ins.com
        Type: TXT (Text strings)
        Class: IN (0x0001)
Answers
    20001.gid.ns.ins.com: type CNAME, class IN, cname greek-authors.group.ns.ins.com
        Name: 20001.gid.ns.ins.com
        Type: CNAME (Canonical name for an alias)
        Class: IN (0x0001)
        Time to live: 1 hour
        Data length: 22
        Primary name: greek-authors.group.ns.ins.com
    greek-authors.group.ns.ins.com: type TXT, class IN
        Name: greek-authors.group.ns.ins.com
        Type: TXT (Text strings)
        Class: IN (0x0001)
        Time to live: 1 hour
        Data length: 22
        Text: Greek-Authors::20001:
```

Figure 2.18 (continued)

Frames 34 and 35 represent the search for the user primary group with **gid** 20001.

Frames 36 through 45 represent DNS queries and replies as a result of the **ls –al** command as the shell is trying to visualize information about directory ownership (user and group) under the **/home** directory.

There are at least two security concerns relevant to the configuration in Figure 2.18:

1. User passwords hashes are visible on the network. Although the MD5 hash is not a plaintext password, it can be susceptible to brute force attacks. By default, most DNS servers will allow queries for all the records that they store, which means that users can potentially send queries to the DNS server and obtain the entire password database. To avoid this, restricted access to DNS records must be used and only trusted hosts should be allowed to read

Hesiod records from DNS. DNS Secure Updates/access in Windows 2000 and restrict access from hosts in BIND provide for this functionality.

2. DNS information can be maliciously modified in transit over the network — attackers can modify either the password for a specific user account, or the user or group IDs, which can result in privilege escalation. To prevent this from happening, traffic encryption using IPSec can be implemented or, alternatively, DNS transaction signing (DNS SIG) can be used.

Chapter 3

Windows User Authentication Architecture

> Security is, I would say, our top priority because for all the exciting things you will be able to do with computers — organizing your lives, staying in touch with people, being creative — if we don't solve these security problems, then people will hold back. Businesses will be afraid to put their critical information on it because it will be exposed.
>
> — **Bill Gates**

This chapter presents the mechanics of user authentication in Windows NT, Windows 2000, Windows 2003, and Windows XP. First, it looks at local user and group accounts, then at the domain model, and finally it explores user impersonation technologies.

Windows NT was designed with security in mind. Unlike its notorious distant relatives — Windows for Workgroups, Windows 95, Windows 98, and Windows ME — Windows NT has always been an operating system providing users and system administrators with powerful and flexible security features. In recent years, these features have evolved into a mature, large-enterprise authentication and security management architecture. These features are discussed in detail in the following sections.

For brevity, Windows NT, Windows 2000, Windows 2003, and Windows XP are simply referred to as Windows. Apparently, there are essential differences between these operating systems, especially regarding authentication, and therefore their specific names and versions will be used when the specifics and differences among them are discussed.

3.1 Security Principals

Windows uses the term "security principal" to denote a security subject that is in a position to access resources (security objects). The security principal is active from a security perspective and typically takes the initiative to access resources, whereas the security object is being accessed. Windows considers users and groups (and computers — they are a special case) to be security principals. Files, printers, Web pages, and other resources are being accessed, and therefore they are objects.

3.1.1 Security Identifiers (SIDs)

Every security principal in Windows must have a Security Identifier (SID). SIDs are a fundamental concept in Windows authentication, authorization, and accounting, as they uniquely identify security principals. SIDs can have numeric and string format. The latter is more popular and uses the form in Figure 3.1 and Table 3.1.

The SID authority identifier can take one of the values in Table 3.2.

Most system security principals have well-known SIDs that are exactly the same across all Windows installations. These SIDs are local to the computer where they were created and never traverse the network. As these security principals have local importance to the computer where they have been created, and due to the fact that they are added to the access token of local processes, this does not represent a conflict with SID uniqueness. In fact, system SIDs can be regarded as flags that specify the authentication status of the user, and not as unique identifiers. Well-known SIDs never change; they are the same every time a new Windows installation is performed. This is different from user and group SIDs, which require uniqueness.

3.1.2 Users and Groups

Windows is an operating system that requires mandatory logon. With a few notable exceptions, every process running on the Windows platform uses the privileges of a specific security principal (subject).

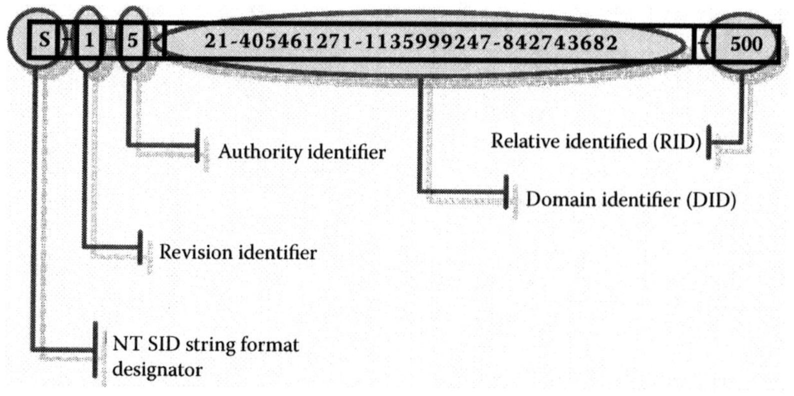

Figure 3.1 String format of Windows NT SIDs.

Table 3.1 String Format of Windows SIDs

Field	*Format*	*Description*
SID Designator	One character, always the same	Designates that this is a SID This field only contains the 'S'-character
Revision Identifier	1 byte	This number has been the revision number since the NT days: the current revision number is 1
Authority Identifier	6 bytes	For user objects, this is typically 5 (NT Authority)
Domain Identifier:		
Subauthority 1	Number — variable length	Identifies the security domain or unit that has issued this SID
Subauthority 2		
Subauthority 3		
…		
Subauthority n		
Relative Identifier (RID)	4 bytes	Identifies the security principal within the domain

Table 3.2 SID Authority Values

SID Authority	*Value*	*Description*
SECURITY_NULL_SID_AUTHORITY	0	This authority does not contain any members
SECURITY_WORLD_SID_AUTHORITY	1	This authority contains all users
SECURITY_LOCAL_SID_AUTHORITY	2	This authority contains security principals on the local computer only
SECURITY_CREATOR_SID_AUTHORITY	3	This authority contains the creators and owners of objects
SECURITY_NT_AUTHORITY	5	Regular Windows NT user and group accounts are created by the NT Authority

Windows provides for two types of user accounts:

1. *Built-in user accounts.* These are created automatically by the operating system and cannot be deleted. The two main accounts that belong to this category are the Administrator account that is given a full set of privileges to perform any task on the operating system, and the Guest user that has very limited privileges and is typically disabled in Windows 2000 and later operating systems.
2. *Regular (or user defined) user accounts.* These are created by system administrators for every user that needs to access the system.

Group types in Windows are the following:

1. *System groups.* These groups are created automatically by the operating system, and membership in these groups is automatic and dynamic, dependent on the actions the user is performing on the operating system (OS). The OS is responsible for adding and removing users from system groups automatically, depending on their activities. An example of such a group is the interactive system group. Every user who is currently logged in to the stand-alone or member server on its console is automatically added to the Interactive System Group. Thus, the user has all the permissions that have been granted to the interactive system group.

2. *Built-in groups*. These groups are automatically created by the operating system during installation. They contain group accounts that are important for the operation of the default security model of the system. An example is the local administrators group, which can be used to grant administrative privileges to local users. Built-in groups are not much different in terms of their usage to user defined groups — they exist to provide the system administrator with a set of groups with predefined privileges, and help the administrator to quickly start using the system. All rights and permissions granted to built-in groups can be granted also to user-defined groups.
3. *User-defined groups*. These groups are created by the administrator of the system and contain regular operating system users, and potentially other groups.

Groups can also have different scopes. Domain members only have local groups, while Windows domain controllers can have domain local and global scopes, as well as universal scope in Active Directory. Domain group accounts are discussed in subsections 3.3.14.2 and 3.3.15.12.

System groups (Table 3.3) are an example of system security principals, and as already mentioned, membership in these groups is automatic and dynamic; if users and groups are currently performing actions specific to the given system group, they automatically become members of this group for the time that they are performing this action. Once they stop performing the action which defines their system group membership, they are no longer considered members of the specific system group.

Table 3.3 System Groups and Their SIDs in Windows

SID	*System User or Group Name*	*Description*
S-1-0-0	Null SID	Empty group that has no members
S-1-1-0	World (Everyone)	Every user belongs to this group (Windows XP and Windows 2000/2003 can control whether anonymous users are members of this group)
S-1-2-0	Local	Users logged on to the system from its console
S-1-3-0	Creator Owner ID	Represents the owner of an object In Windows, this is most often the user who created the object or took ownership of the object after its creation

Table 3.3 System Groups and Their SIDs in Windows (continued)

S-1-3-1	Creator Group ID	Represents the primary group of which the user who created or took ownership of an object belongs Mainly supported for POSIX compliance and rarely used
S-1-5-10	Principal Self	Represents a right of a security principal, which is at the same time an object within the directory services, to access its own properties
S-1-5-1	Dial-up	When a user connects to a Windows RAS server, he is automatically made a member of this system group
S-1-5-2	Network	When a user accesses resources on a given computer from another computer (across the network), he is automatically made a member of the network system group on the computer where the accessed resources reside Note that this system group only exists in the local access token for the user on the resource computer, and not in the local access token on the computer from which resources are being accessed.
S-1-5-3	Batch	Includes all users logged in as batch jobs — most often the result of task scheduler jobs
S-1-5-4	Interactive	On a given computer, users who log on locally to that computer are considered members of the interactive system group Initially, this included users logged on from the local console; however, as the operating system evolved, this included users logged on using Terminal Services (RDP) as well as other applications that use user-provided usernames and passwords (e.g., IIS with Basic Authentication, Telnet server, etc.)

Table 3.3 System Groups and Their SIDs in Windows (continued)

S-1-5-5-X-Y	Logon Session	This SID is actually used as a unique session identifier, and not as a security principal ID Each time a user logs in to the system, the user session is assigned a unique ID (the X and Y fields) The logon session ID is added to the user access token; if the user logs off and then on again, a new logon session ID will be created The logon session ID can be visualized using the **whoami/logonid** command Session ID is used by Windows XP computers for fast user switching Applications can use this SID to protect temporary files that should be used within a particular logon session only, rather than on a per-user basis
S-1-5-6	Service	In Windows NT, both users and services can create processes and access resources, and in both cases they use a user account to do so However, only services have the service system group SID in their local access token
S-1-5-7	Anonymous Logon	A user who is accessing resources without providing a username and password across the network Typical examples are the so-called Null sessions (see subsection 3.3.15.14), used by some older operating system components and some hacker tools Note: There is a principal difference between Windows NT, Windows 2000, and Windows 2003/XP with regard to Null sessions. (See below for more details)
S-1-5-8	Proxy	Not currently used
S-1-5-9	Enterprise Domain Controllers	(Windows 2000/2003 only) Includes all the domain controllers of the forest

Table 3.3 System Groups and Their SIDs in Windows (continued)

S-1-5-10	Self	This SID is used as a reference to the user from his own account in Active Directory (e.g., granting the self system group access to the telephone number field of every user in Active Directory allows every user to change their own telephone number only)
S-1-5-11	Authenticated Users	This system group contains all users from any domain who have been authenticated to the system, except the Guest account
S-1-5-12	Restricted	(Windows 2003 and XP) Windows 2003 and Windows XP software restriction policies may control the security token of the running process If specific restriction policies have been applied to the running process, its access token will include membership to the restricted system group
S-1-5-13	Terminal Server User	Users accessing resources from a remote computer using terminal services (RDP) are members of this system group
S-1-5-14	Remote Interactive Logon	Users accessing resources from a remote computer using Terminal Services (RDP) are members of this system group This type of logon is considered interactive as well
S-1-5-18	System (or LocalSystem)	This account/system group is used by the operating system itself This account is an implicit and hidden member of the administrator's local group
S-1-5-19	LocalService	(Windows XP and Windows 2003) This is a special user account with restricted privileges on the local system This account is typically used to run services on a computer when these services require limited or no access to resources on the computer

Table 3.3 System Groups and Their SIDs in Windows (continued)

		Note: Unlike the system (local system) account used on Windows 2000 and earlier operating systems, the local service account has very limited privileges
S-1-5-20	NetworkService	Very similar to the local service account, however, it is used only for services that will be accessed from the network
S-1-5-15	This Organization	Added to the access token of users from the same forest, or from external domains and forests for which full authentication is allowed
S-1-5-1000	Other Organization	Added to the access token of users from other domains and forests for which only selective authentication is allowed across the trust
S-1-5-64-10	NTLM Authentication	Indicates that the user used the NTLM Protocol to authenticate
S-1-5-64-21	Digest Authentication	Indicates that the user used the IIS Digest Authentication Protocol to authenticate
S-1-5-64-14	SChannel Authentication	Indicates that the user has used SSL authentication

The built-in security principals are created automatically by the operating system and they exist on all Windows installations. Some of the built-in accounts (primarily user and global group accounts) have unique SIDs (they contain a unique domain portion), although most of them have well-known RIDs (Table 3.4). Built-in local groups have well-known SIDs (both authority/domain ID and RID) but due to the fact that these groups are local, they are still unique within the security database where they exist.

Built-in groups in Windows are created during operating system installation. They exist on all Windows systems (there are some differences on domain controllers — see the following sections).

Table 3.4 Built-In Accounts and Groups and Their SIDs in Windows

SID	*System User or Group Name*	*Description*
S-1-5-*domainID*-500	Administrator	The first user account on every system; cannot be deleted or disabled but can be renamed. The well-known RID of this account and its inevitably broad rights and permissions have been targeted by some hacker tools.
S-1-5-*domainID*-501	Guest	Exists on all Windows platforms and can be used to provide users with guest (restricted and temporary) access to the system. By default, this account is not a member of the Authenticated Users group, and is only a member of the Everyone and Guest groups. The domain Guest account is also a member of the Domain Guests and Domain Users groups. This account is typically disabled on servers.
S-1-5-*domainID*-502	Krbtgt	This account only exists in Active Directory and is used by the Kerberos Protocol. This account is always disabled. The Kerberos Distribution Center (KDC) AS and TGS services use this account to store the KDC password from which they derive an encryption key for the KDC.
S-1-5-*domainID*-512	Domain Admins	Only exists in Active Directory. This global group is a member of the local Administrators group on every domain controller, as well as on every domain member. This grants its members administrative privileges across the domain.
S-1-5-*domainID*-513	Domain Users	Only exists in Active Directory. This global group is member of the local Users group on every domain controller, as well as on every domain member. This grants its members user privileges across the domain.

Table 3.4 Built-In Accounts and Groups and Their SIDs in Windows (continued)

SID	*System User or Group Name*	*Description*
S-1-5-*domainID*-514	Domain Guests	Only exists in Active Directory. This global group is a member of the local Guests group on every domain controller, as well as on every domain member. This grants its members guest privileges across the domain.
S-1-5-*domainID*-515	Domain Computers	All computers of the domain that are not Domain Controllers.
S-1-5-*domainID*-516	Domain Controllers	All domain controllers of a domain. New domain controllers will automatically obtain membership to this group.
S-1-5-*domainID*-517	Cert Publishers	This global group contains the computer accounts of all enterprise certificate authorities. This group is typically permitted to edit some user properties in Active Directory, such as the user certificate field; therefore, certification authorities can automatically publish issued user certificates in the directory.
S-1-5-*root domainID*-518	Schema Admins	Only exists in Active Directory. This group is granted privileges to update the AD schema. By default, this can be performed by the Administrator of the forest root domain only.
S-1-5-*root domainID*-519	Enterprise Admins	This group only exists in the forest root domain of a Windows 2000/Windows 2003 forest. By default, it is granted permissions to administer almost any aspect of the Active Directory domain model. This is the forest-level equivalent of the Domain Admins group.
S-1-5-*domainID*-520	Group Policy Creator Owners	Members of this group are allowed to create Group Policy Objects within Active Directory and modify their own group policy objects.

Table 3.4 Built-In Accounts and Groups and Their SIDs in Windows (continued)

SID	*System User or Group Name*	*Description*
S-1-5-*domainID*-533	RAS and IAS Servers	This domain local group contains the computer accounts of Windows 2000/2003 RAS and IAS servers, and provides them with access to some user properties (such as the dial-in permission) within Active Directory.
S-1-5-32-544	Administrators	This Windows NT built-in group exists on workstations, servers, and domain controllers. The permissions assigned to this group are enough to transform its members into full administrators of the system. By default, the Administrator user is the only member of the local Administrators group. Every other user or group added to the local Administrators group will have administrative privileges on the computer where the Administrators group is created.
S-1-5-32-545	Users	This built-in group exists on workstations, servers, and domain controllers. This group is meant to provide regular users with basic access to the system and its resources.
S-1-5-32-546	Guests	This built-in group exists on workstations, servers, and domain controllers. It is meant to provide its members with limited access to resources on the computer where this group is created.
S-1-5-32-547	Power Users	This built-in group only exists on workstations and member servers. This group is used to grant some users more privileges than would typically be granted to other users on the system. A typical right granted to this group by default is to share files and folders on the network.

Table 3.4 Built-In Accounts and Groups and Their SIDs in Windows (continued)

SID	*System User or Group Name*	*Description*
S-1-5-32-548	Account Operators	Only exists on Windows NT/2000/2003 domain controllers. This group allows users to create user accounts and user information for existing accounts, created by the same user.
S-1-5-32-549	Server Operators	This group has default permissions that allow its members to start or stop the server, to review event logs, or reboot the computer.
S-1-5-32-550	Print Operators	This built-in group exists on workstations, servers, and domain controllers. It provides users with basic access to printers and privileges to manage printer queues.
S-1-5-32-551	Backup Operators	This built-in group exists on workstations, servers, and domain controllers. Basically, members of this group are granted the "Backup files and directories" user right, which permits the user performing the backup to do so even if this user does not have permission to access the specific file.
S-1-5-32-552	Replicators	This group was used in Windows NT 4.0 to support the directory replication process.

For all the other accounts, the Windows security model requires that regular user and group SIDs be universally unique. There should be no two users or groups that have the same SIDs. To guarantee uniqueness, Windows enforces the following SID generation rules:

- For user and group accounts, the Domain portion of the SID is randomly generated during the installation of the operating system. The randomness of generation is meant to provide uniqueness of the Domain Identifier portion.

- All the user and group accounts within a domain or computer security database share the same Domain Identifier portion. However, they have relative identifiers (RIDs) that are allocated in a sequential fashion to be unique within the domain.
- RIDs are never reused; even if a user account is deleted, its RID is never reused, to avoid information leakage as a result of old permissions on user objects; technically speaking, if the RIDs get depleted, the operating system should refuse to create new security principals. Due to the large number of RIDs, however, this is not likely to happen.

Because the domain portion of the SID is unique to the particular domain or computer within the universe, and the RID portion is unique within the domain or computer account database, the SID is also unique within the universe. Assuming that every user has a unique SID, despite their physical location or the time of the creation of their account, the operating system can provide universal access to resources in any domain without the risk of having duplicate SIDs and therefore duplicate access permissions.

There is just one type of user-defined group on a Windows NT standalone or member server, or a Windows NT workstation — Local Groups. They are collections of users who can be granted user rights or permissions to access resources. Local groups are local in the sense that they are not visible and cannot be granted access on other computers. They can only live within the security context of the computer where they were created. Another limitation is that local groups on a member server or a standalone computer cannot be nested.

3.1.3 Case Study: Group SIDs

Because groups are considered security principals, they have SIDs that look exactly the same as user SIDs. In fact, if one looks at an SID, one cannot tell whether it is a user SID or a group SID.

User Mozart is a local user on stand-alone server STEVE. He is a member of a local group by the name of Composers. When user Mozart logs in, here is what his access token would potentially look like:

```
C:\Documents and Settings\Mozart> whoami /user /groups

USER INFORMATION
----------------

User Name     SID
============ ============================================
steve\mozart S-1-5-21-405461271-1135999247-842743682-1008
```

```
GROUP INFORMATION
-----------------

Group Name         Type        SID                   Attributes
================== ========== ===================== ===========================
Everyone           Well-known S-1-1-0               Mandatory group, Enabled
                    group                            by default, Enabled group
STEVE\Composers    Alias       S-1-5-21-405461271-   Mandatory group, Enabled
                               1135999247-           by default, Enabled group
                               842743682-1012
BUILTIN\Users      Alias       S-1-5-32-545          Mandatory group, Enabled
                                                     by default, Enabled group
NT AUTHORITY\      Well-known  S-1-5-4               Mandatory group, Enabled
 INTERACTIVE        group                            by default, Enabled group
NT AUTHORITY\      Well-known  S-1-5-11              Mandatory group, Enabled
 Authenticated      group                            by default, Enabled group
 Users
NT AUTHORITY\This  Well-known  S-1-5-15              Mandatory group, Enabled
 Organization       group                            by default, Enabled group
LOCAL              Well-known  S-1-2-0               Mandatory group, Enabled
                    group                            by default, Enabled group
NT AUTHORITY\NTLM  Well-known  S-1-5-64-10           Mandatory group, Enabled
 Authentication     group                            by default, Enabled group

C:\Documents and Settings\Mozart>
```

Now compare Mozart's user SID and group Composers' group SID:

User Mozart:	**S-1-5-21-405461271-1135999247-842743682-1008**
Group Composers:	**S-1-5-21-405461271-1135999247-842743682-1012**

The only difference between the two SIDs is the last part, which is the RID. Whenever a new RID is created, the operating system assigns the next available value. The Domain ID part of the SID for both objects is the same, because these objects reside in the same security database. The Domain ID uniquely identifies the security database.

3.1.4 Access Tokens

When a user authenticates, he is assigned the so-called access token that consists of a structure containing the user SID, all the group SIDs that the user is a member of (including system groups, built-in groups, and user-defined groups), as well as the user rights of that user. The access token is initially assigned to the user shell (**EXPLORER.EXE** by default) for interactive logon, and to the server application in the case of network logon. When the interactive user starts a new process, the user access token is used to create an access token for the process. All child processes by default inherit the access token of the parent process.

The access token has the structure shown in Table 3.5.

Table 3.5 Access Token Structure

Field	*Description*
Logon Session ID	Before the user is authenticated, Windows creates an internal structure known as Logon Session. This session has a locally unique ID (a 64-bit number) that is part of the user's access token. It is just an object identifier and not used in relation to actual user authentication or authorization.
User SID	This is the SID of the user.
Group SIDs	The user is usually a member of one or more systems, built-in, and regular user groups, so the list of SIDs for these groups is stored in the user's access token.
User rights	This is a list of all the user rights, assigned either directly to the user or to some of the groups in which the user is a member. Windows 2000/2003 allow for negative user rights, whereby some user rights cannot only be granted but can also be explicitly revoked.
Owner SID	The SID that will be used as the owner of newly created objects by the user. This is typically equal to the user SID but can be different; for example, when users from the Administrators group create objects, the owner of these objects is the Administrators group rather than the user.
SID for the primary group	Mainly for POSIX compatibility, this field contains the SID of the group that is specified as the primary for the user.
Default DACL	The access control list that will be applied by default for objects created by this user.
Access Token Source	A string describing the source of the access token. This is typically the application or network service that requested it.
Logon Type	Specifies the type of logon that generated this access token: Interactive — the security principal is logging on interactively Network — the security principal is logging on using a network Batch — the logon is for a batch process Service — the logon is for a service account Proxy — not supported Unlock — the logon is an attempt to unlock a workstation

Table 3.5 Access Token Structure (continued)

Field	*Description*
Primary or impersonation	Specifies whether this token is a result of direct user authentication, or from impersonation (typically used by server processes — see subsection 3.5.2)
An optional list of restricting SIDs	A process that has appropriate access to an access token can restrict the usage of the access token by removing user rights (privileges) from the token, denying some of the SIDs during access checks, or providing a restricted set of SIDs. This field is typically used by server-side applications that limit the privileges of the server process running on behalf of an authenticated user.
Current impersonation level	This can be one of the following impersonation levels: Anonymous Identify Impersonate Delegate Impersonation is discussed in detail later in this chapter.

3.1.5 Case Study: SIDs in the User Access Token

When a user logs in to a Windows system, he is provided with an access token that contains all the user and group memberships for that user. The access token for a user can be visualized using the **WHOAMI.EXE** Resource Kit tool. A user with administrative privileges logs on to a stand-alone Windows NT computer using the local Administrator account. Using the **WHOAMI.EXE** Resource Kit tool, the following information can be collected about this user:

```
C:\PROGRA~1\Windows Resource Kits> whoami /user /groups

USER INFORMATION
----------------

User Name           SID
=================== ==========================================
steve\administrator S-1-5-21-405461271-1135999247-842743682-500

GROUP INFORMATION
-----------------

Group Name                 Type        SID          Attributes
========================== =========== ============ ===========================
Everyone                   Well-known  S-1-1-0      Mandatory group, Enabled
                            group                    by default, Enabled group
BUILTIN\Administrators     Alias       S-1-5-32-544 Mandatory  group, Enabled
                                                     by default, Enabled group,
                                                     Group owner
```

```
BUILTIN\Users                 Alias        S-1-5-32-545 Mandatory group, Enabled
                                                          by default, Enabled group
NT AUTHORITY\INTERACTIVE      Well-known   S-1-5-4      Mandatory group, Enabled
                               group                      by default, Enabled group
NT AUTHORITY\Authenticated    Well-known   S-1-5-11     Mandatory  group, Enabled
 Users                         group                      by default, Enabled group
NT AUTHORITY\This             Well-known   S-1-5-15     Mandatory group, Enabled
 Organization                  group                      by default, Enabled group
LOCAL                         Well-known   S-1-2-0      Mandatory  group, Enabled
                               group                      by default, Enabled group
NT AUTHORITY\NTLM             Well-known   S-1-5-64-10  Mandatory group, Enabled
 Authentication                group                      by default, Enabled group

C:\PROGRA~1\Windows Resource Kits>
```

An analysis shows that the user is logged into computer STEVE using the Administrator local account (**STEVE\Administrator**). The user SID is **S-1-5-21-405461271-1135999247-842743682-500**, from which the following can be deduced:

- This is an SID issue by the NT Authority (**S-1-5**).
- The computer STEVE local accounts use the following Domain ID: **21-405461271-1135999247-842743682**.
- Every SID in the local user database on computer STEVE will have an SID starting with **S-1-5-21-405461271-1135999247-842743682**.
- User Administrator has a RID of **500** (this is a well-known SID for the default Administrator user — see above).

In addition, user Administrator is a member of a couple of groups:

- He is a member of the system Everyone group (well-known SID **S-1-1-0**).
- He is a member of the built-in Administrators group (built in; well-known **SID S-1-5-32-544**).
- He is a member of the built-in Users group (built in, well-known SID **S-1-5-32-545**).
- Because the user has logged in from the console, he is considered an interactive user and is automatically assigned as a member of the system Interactive group (well-known SID **S-1-5-4**).
- As the user has logged in using his own credentials (and therefore has been authenticated), he is automatically added as a member of the Authenticated Users group (well-known SID **S-1-5-11**). This distinguishes the user session from Null sessions, which are unauthenticated and anonymous.
- **S-1-5-15** indicates that this account belongs to a domain in the same organization (forest); see subsection 3.3.15.20 for more information.

- Because this is a local User account, the user is automatically added as a member of the system group Local (well-known SID **S-1-2-0**).
- The user authenticated using NTLM authentication and therefore he is automatically made a member of the system group NTLM Authentication (well-known SID **S-1-5-64-10**).

3.1.6 User Rights

Windows uses resource permissions to authorize user access to resources. Typically, resources have Access Control Lists (ACLs) that are comprised of Access Control Entries (ACEs), and each ACE provides discrete permissions to allow or explicitly deny a user or group to perform a specific discrete task on the resource.

There are specific tasks for which users can be granted permissions, and these tasks are not necessarily related to specific resources, such as files or registry entries. Tasks such as changing the system time or rebooting the operating system require permissions at the operating system level. Such permissions are known as user rights.

Unlike resource permissions that are stored where the resource resides (e.g., NTFS file permissions are stored in security descriptor blocks in the file system itself), user rights are stored as part of the access token created for the user when he logs in.

If user rights for a particular user change while the user is logged into the system, the user will not be able to experience the effect of the new user rights. This is because the security access token for the user has already been created during logon, and will not change until next logon. Therefore, if components of the user access token change — such as user rights, or group membership for example — the user will need to log out and log on again for the changes to take effect.

User rights and permissions together are the mechanisms used by Windows to provide both the default permissions for access to the operating system, as well as user-defined permissions and user rights.

The operating system built-in groups as well as the system groups are granted specific permissions to resources, as well as user rights to manage the operating system. Some built-in groups, such as the Administrators built-in local group, have been granted almost all possible permissions on operating system files and user rights. Therefore, users of this group — by default the Administrator local user only — will inherit these permissions and user rights, and as a result will possess significant privileges to use and manage the operating system. Other built-in local groups, such as the Users local group, have been granted basic permission to operating system files and limited user rights, such as **Log on locally** (allows the user to log on to the system using the computer console), and will therefore have basic but limited privileges to utilize the operating system, and almost no permissions to manage its behavior.

Users with appropriate permissions — such as the Administrators local group — have permissions that allow them to create new user-defined groups, and grant these groups specific permissions to resources as well as user rights. Technically, users can be granted permissions to access resources, as well as user rights directly, without first being made a member of local groups. However, this is not the recommended approach (see subsections 3.3.14.2 and 3.3.15.12).

The Windows 2003 documentation distinguishes between two types of user rights: (1) privileges, which are meant to provide the user with access to perform management tasks on the operating system, and (2) logon rights, which are used to allow the user the right to log on to the operating system. This chapter concentrates on the logon rights, as they are more relevant to the user authentication process.

Table 3.6 outlines some of the most important logon rights. For more information on privileges, see [14].

Table 3.6 User Logon Rights

User Logon Right	*Description*	*By Default Granted To:*
Access this computer from a network	Provides users with access to this computer from remote computers. This user right primarily provides access to Microsoft file services on this computer (CIFS/SMB); but because these services are used by many processes (including MS RPC /DCE communication, and therefore user logon), this user right is typically required on servers. Most non-file access related communication will ignore this user right – applications such as the SMTP Server and IIS FTP server do not use this user right.	On workstations and member servers: Administrators Backup operators Power users Users Everyone On domain controllers: Administrators Authenticated users Everyone

Table 3.6 User Logon Rights (continued)

User Logon Right	*Description*	*By Default Granted To:*
Allow logon locally	Provides the user with the right to sit in front of the user console and log in to the system using his user credentials. This is appropriate for user workstations but not very appropriate for all servers. Therefore, by default, users are not allowed to log in locally to domain controllers.	On workstations and servers: Administrators Backup operators Power users Users Guest On domain controllers: Account operators Administrators Backup operators Print operators Server operators
Allow logon through Terminal Services	As the name implies, this user right is meant to provide users with the right to connect to a remote computer using the RDP protocol.	On workstation and servers: Administrators Remote desktop users On domain controllers: Administrators
Deny access to this computer from network (Windows 2000/2003/XP)	Similar to the "Access this computer from the network" user right but explicitly denies such access. Explicit denial always takes precedence over other rights and permissions.	None
Deny logon as a batch job (Windows 2000/2003/XP)	Similar to the "Logon as a batch job" user right but explicitly denies such access. Explicit denial always takes precedence over other rights and permissions.	None
Deny logon as a service (Windows 2000/2003/XP)	Similar to the "Logon as a service" user right but explicitly denies such access. Explicit denial always takes precedence over other rights and permissions.	None

Table 3.6 User Logon Rights (continued)

User Logon Right	*Description*	*By Default Granted To:*
Deny logon locally (Windows 2000/2003/XP)	Similar to the "Logon locally" user right but explicitly denies such access. Explicit denial always takes precedence over other rights and permissions. Note that denying the "Log on locally" user right to a specific group of users will prevent them from using the computer locally. Denying this user right for the Everyone group is dangerous and might require one to reinstall the computer.	None
Deny logon through Terminal Services (Windows 2000/2003/XP)	Similar to the "Logon through the terminal services" user right but explicitly denies such access. Explicit denial always takes precedence over other rights and permissions.	None
Log on as a batch job	This user right allows a user account to be used to start batch jobs.	Local system
Log on as a service	To be managed by the Service Control Manager (SCM), services need to be provided with a user account, under the context of which they will run. The user account that will be used to start the service must be granted the "Log on as a service" user right.	None

3.2 Stand-Alone Authentication

Windows users can be authenticated using their local credentials on a computer or by means of their domain user credentials and domain accounts across the network. This section examines local authentication.

3.2.1 Interactive and Network Authentication

There are two main authentication scenarios in Windows: (1) interactive user logon and (2) network user login.

When a user logs interactively in to a Windows NT workstation, the following will occur:

1. The **WinLogon.EXE** process will provide the user with a login prompt to enter his username, password and domain, or smart card PIN number, or other credentials to log into the system.
   Note: When the user selects to use username/password authentication the user must specify the name of the authentication authority – this is either a domain name, or the local computer.
2. **WinLogon.EXE** will pass the information that the user has entered to the local security authority (LSA) subsystem.
3. The local security subsystem will try to negotiate an authentication mechanism. By default, a domain member will use the following authentication mechanisms:
   - Local computer (always and only used when the user specifies the local computer as the authentication authority)
   - Domain authentication (either the domain for which the workstation from which the user is logging on is a member, or a trusted domain)
4. If the user authenticates successfully, the authentication authority will return a user access token to the **WinLogon.EXE** process. If the user fails to authenticate against the selected authentication authority, he will be asked to provide authentication credentials again, up to the maximum number of allowed wrong passwords. After that, the user account can be locked out.
5. The Winlogon process will invoke the user shell (typically **EXPLORER.EXE**) and will copy the access token providing the shell with the same privileges as the user.
6. The shell can then be used to create new processes, and will in turn copy (or sometimes modify) the user access token for every new process that it creates.

If a user tries to access resources over the network, the following will typically occur:

1. The server application to which the user is connecting will use an application-specific mechanism to request the user to authenticate. Some client applications, such as the Microsoft SMB/CIFS protocol, will try to authenticate without waiting for the server to request

authentication; other applications such as Web servers may try to connect anonymously first.
2. The server process will pass user credentials to the local security system (LSA). The LSA will, in turn, try to select an authentication method, such as local authentication or domain authentication.
3. The LSA process will provide the server application with the access token for the user.
4. The server application can now choose between one of two typical approaches:
   - Impersonate the user using the provided user access token. From that point on, the server process will try to access resources on behalf of the user, and the local operating system will be responsible for authorizing such access as if the user were a local user. The Security Reference Monitor (SRM) of the operating system is responsible for performing this authorization.
   - Parse the Access token and obtain user SIDs, etc; when the user needs to access a specific file or other object provided by the server process, compare user and group SIDs, and potentially user rights against a server application specific authorization list or other mechanism. The application is responsible for granting access to the resources that it provides

More information on network authentication and impersonation is provided later in this chapter.

3.2.2 Interactive Authentication on Windows Computers

Local authentication on Windows computers typically takes place when either there is a user on the console or when a remote user is using terminal services (Remote Desktop Protocol) to authenticate to the computer. As a result of the interactive logon, the user is presented with a shell on the computer that he can use to start new processes and access resources.

Figure 3.2 provides an overview of the interactive authentication process.

Interactive user authentication starts with the **WinLogon.EXE** process that interacts with the Graphical Identification and Authentication DLL (GINA) to detect that either Security Authentication Sequence (SAS) Ctrl-Alt-Del has been used, or a smart card has been inserted in the reader. The user is then presented with an appropriate authentication dialogue that will either request that the user provides a username, password and domain (not required if the user provides UPN for username), or smart card PIN (smart card authentication is not natively supported on Windows

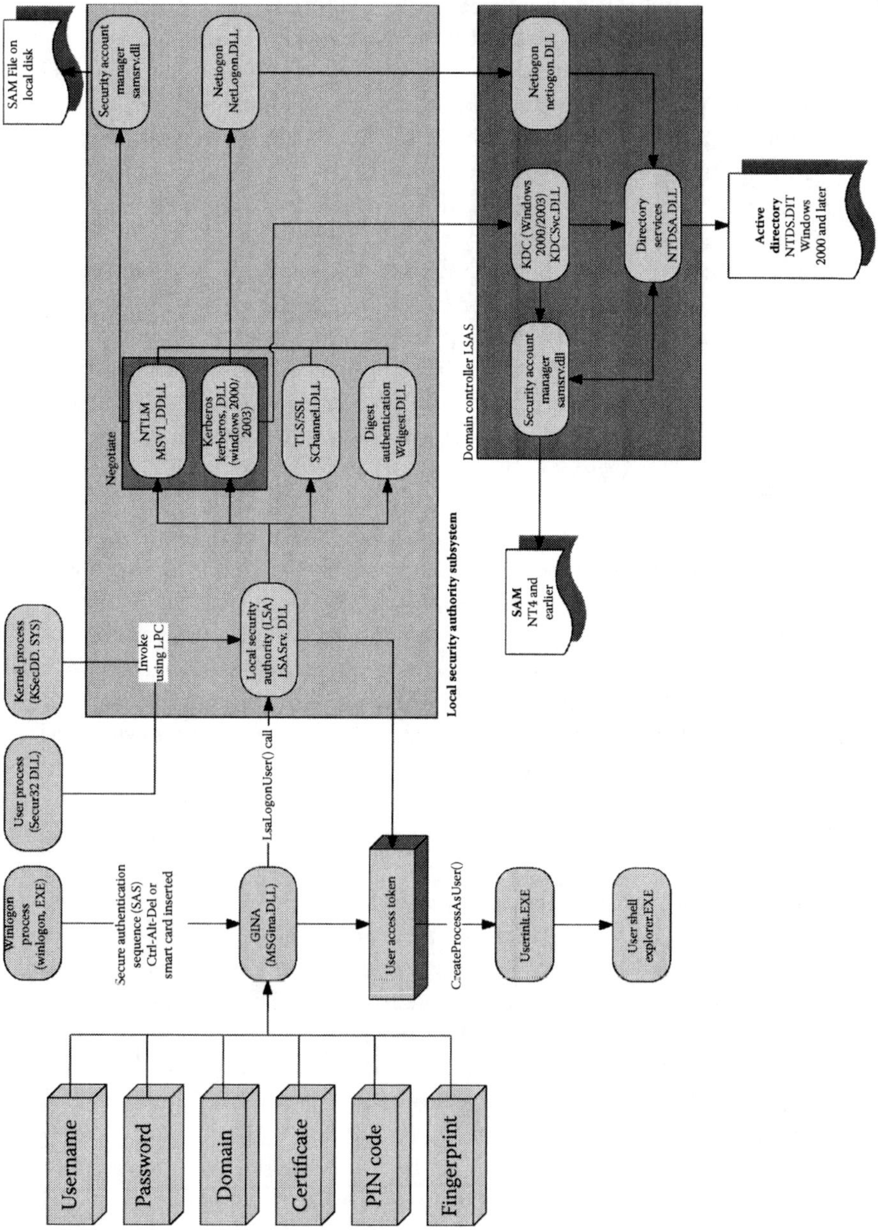

Figure 3.2 Interactive logon in Windows NT.

NT 4.0 computers). The GINA is responsible for collecting all the information and passing it appropriately to the local security authority subsystem (LSASS).

Windows operating systems come with a standard GINA component that is suitable in most scenarios. However, if required, the GINA component can be either partially or fully replaced by a custom GINA component that can use alternative authentication methods and add its own custom authentication handling. More information on how to substitute the standard GINA can be found in [15].

The LSASS has multiple authentication components running within its address space and using its privileges. The security support providers (SSPs), also known as authentication packages, are the components responsible for user authentication. Depending on the type of logon, the LSASS can use one or more of the authentication packages.

On Windows NT 4.0 computers, NTLM is the only supported authentication method for interactive logons. Once it acquires the authentication parameters from GINA, NTLM will determine whether it should use the local SAM or pass the authentication request to a domain controller using the NetLogon module.

On Windows 2000/XP/2003 computers, the NTLM and Kerberos protocols are presented to the LSASS as a package by the name of Negotiate. Typically, interactive logon attempts using username/password/domain name authentication will be passed on to the Negotiate component and it will determine what authentication to use. If authentication is local, it will always be handled by the NTLM component in the same way as in Windows NT 4.0. If authentication against a domain must be performed, Windows 2000/XP/2003 will prefer the Kerberos protocol (provided that they are members of a Windows 2000 or later domain) and fall back to NTLM if Kerberos authentication is either not supported or not available at the time of logon.

If authentication requires that a domain controller be contacted, either Kerberos or the NTLM authentication protocol will be used across the network to process the request. Windows domain controllers will forward the authentication request against the domain SAM database. Windows 2000 and later domain controllers that do not have a SAM (apart from DS restore mode, which is not used under normal circumstances) will use the Active Directory database. What the authentication source is will not be known to the user workstation.

If the authenticating authority — either the local SAM or a domain controller — confirms user authentication, GINA builds a user access token using the information provided by this authority, impersonates the user using the newly built token, and invokes the **UserInit.EXE** executable using the new user privileges. After **UserInit.EXE** loads and configures the initial user environment, the user shell (typically **EXPLORER.EXE** on

Windows NT 4.0 and later) is invoked and the user is provided with interactive access to the system.

3.2.3 The Security Accounts Manager Database

Local Windows user and group accounts are stored in the Windows registry along with other operating system configuration parameters. The SAM database is stored under the **HKEY_LOCAL_MACHINE\SAM** portion of the registry. There is a separate value for each user or group account in SAM. User and group attributes are stored in the "F" and "V" values for user accounts, as well as in the "C" values for group accounts under the respective security principal's key.

Local Windows user accounts have the attributes shown in Table 3.7

Table 3.7 User Account Attributes

Field	*Format*	*Stored In*	*Description*
Username	String up to 20 Unicode characters (internally, there is support for 104 characters); case insensitive	SAM: User V value	This is the name that represents the user to the system, aka user ID, username, or account name.
Password	String, up to 128 Unicode characters, although the user interface will often limit this to 14 characters; case sensitive	SAM: User V value	This is the password for the user.
User SID	SID format — see above	SAM: Key name contains user RID	The security identified (SID) uniquely identifies the security principal; in theory, this number should uniquely identify the security principal within the universe, not just within the domain, or the organization.

Table 3.7 User Account Attributes (continued)

Field	*Format*	*Stored In*	*Description*
Primary Group ID	SID format — see above	SAM: Group C Value	SID of a group, considered as a primary for the user. Only used for POSIX compliance and has no special meaning in Windows NT. This is only used on Windows NT domain controllers.
Full Name	String, up to 256 Unicode characters; case insensitive but preserves case	SAM: User V value	This is the full name of the user in real life.
Description	String, up to 256 Unicode characters; case insensitive but preserves case	SAM: User V value	User description
User comment	String, up to 256 Unicode characters; case insensitive but preserves case	SAM: User V value	Additional user comment (not displayed in most standard administrative tools).
Home drive	String, typically one character	SAM: User V value	Drive on which the user home directory resides. This path may be either local or network.
Home directory	String, up to 260 Unicode characters; case insensitive but preserves case	SAM: User V value	Not required in Windows. This is typically a folder to which the user will have read/write permissions and be able to store and access his documents.

Table 3.7 User Account Attributes (continued)

Field	*Format*	*Stored In*	*Description*
Profile path	String, up to 260 Unicode characters; case insensitive but preserves case	SAM: User V value	Where the user profile will be stored. The user profile contains the user environment — the user portion of the registry file, user preferences, the user desktop, the My Documents folder, local settings, etc.
Logon script	String, up to 260 Unicode characters; case insensitive but preserves case	SAM: User V value	Execute a specific command (.BAT, .CMD, .EXE, .COM, etc) every time the user logs on.
Logon hours	8 bytes	SAM: User V value	When the user is allowed to log in to the system.
Account active	1 bit	SAM: User F value (part of the Account Control byte)	Indicates whether the user account is enabled or disabled.
Allow empty password	1 bit	SAM: User F value (part of the Account Control byte)	Can the user password be empty?
Password never expires	1 bit	SAM: User F value (part of the Account Control byte)	Indicates that the user is exempt from password expiration policies.
Allow user to change password	1 bit	SAM: User F value (part of the Account Control byte)	Indicates whether the user can change his own password.
User/ workstation/ domain trust account	3 bits	SAM: User F value (part of the Account Control byte)	Type of user account (this is only used on domain controllers).

Table 3.7 User Account Attributes (continued)

Field	*Format*	*Stored In*	*Description*
User account expiration	8 bytes	SAM: User F value	Limits the period of validity of the user account to a specific date and time.
Password Last Set	8 bytes	SAM: User F value	When was the last time that the user password was changed?
Lockout time	8 bytes	SAM: User F value	The time when the user account was locked out.
Creation time	8 bytes	SAM: User F value	The time when the user account was created.
Last login time	8 bytes	SAM: User F value	The time when the user last logged in to the system.

3.2.4 Case Study: User Properties — Windows NT Local User Accounts

Both Local User Manager in Windows NT 4.0 and Local Users and Groups (Computer Management Console) in Windows 2000 only display a limited set of user properties. The **NET.EXE** command line utility can be used to display more (although not all) information about local user accounts.

The following example shows the information available for local user account Mozart on member server STEVE:

```
C:\Documents and Settings\Administrator> net user mozart
User name                    Mozart
Full Name                    Wolfgang Amadeus Mozart
Comment                      Austrian Composer
User's comment
Country code                 000 (System Default)
Account active               Yes
Account expires              12/20/2006 12:00 AM

Password last set            9/23/2005 11:22 PM
Password expires             Never
Password changeable          9/24/2005 11:22 PM
Password required            Yes
User may change password     Yes
```

Table 3.8 Group Account Attributes

Field	*Format*	*Stored In*	*Description*
Group name	String up to 256 Unicode characters (Windows NT supports up to 64 characters through the user interface)	SAM: Group C Value	This is the name that represents the group to the system
Membership	List of SIDs — see format above	SAM: Group C Value	List of users, identified by their SID, that are members of this group **Note:** Membership is a property of the group, not of the user
Description	String, up to 256 Unicode characters, case insensitive but preserves case	SAM: Group C Value	Group description

```
Workstations allowed         All
Logon script
User profile
Home directory
Last logon                   9/23/2005 11:57 PM

Logon hours allowed          All

Local Group Memberships      *Composers             *Users
Global Group memberships     *None
The command completed successfully.
```

Most of the user parameters are defined in Table 3.7. The **NET.EXE** utility can be used to modify some of the user parameters.

Local Windows NT group accounts possess the attributes shown in Table 3.8.

3.2.5 Case Study: Group Properties — Windows Local Group Accounts

The **NET.EXE** command can be used to explore local group accounts as well. The following represents sample output from this command:

```
C:\Documents and Settings\Administrator> net localgroup Composers
Alias name      Composers
Comment         Famous Composers

Members

-------------------------------------------------------------------------------
Chopin
Mozart
Tchaikovsky
The command completed successfully.
```

Similar information is provided by most Windows administrative utilities as well.

3.2.6 SAM Registry Structure

Information about local user and group accounts on stand-alone and domain member Windows computers is stored in the registry file **%SYSTEMROOT%\SYSTEM32\Config\SAM**. As with every other registry file, it has a complex structure that can be explored using standard operating system tools such as **REGEDIT.EXE**. All the user and group account information is stored in the Security Accounts Manager (SAM) file.

The SAM file can be accessed using **REGEDIT.EXE** in Windows NT 4.0 and later, or **REGEDT32.EXE** in Windows NT 4.0 and previous versions. By default, neither users nor administrators have permissions on the SAM tree in the registry (Figure 3.3). Only the operating system is allowed to access SAM content.

However, if logged in as Administrator, one might notice that the Administrators group is actually the owner of the SAM key and its subkeys; and as a result, the user Administrator of a Windows computer can obtain arbitrary permissions on the SAM portion of the registry (Figure 3.4). The easiest way to do that would be to grant the Administrators group full access to the SAM key and its subkeys (in Windows 2000 and later, the permissions from the parent key will automatically be inherited by subkeys).

User information is stored under the SAM | Domains key (Figure 3.5). The Account subkey contains information about user-defined security principals (users and groups) and the Built-in subkey contains the operating system default security principals. Accounts such as the Administrator account and the Guest account are considered user defined, although they are automatically created by the operating system.

There is a key for every user-defined account, and the key name is the user or group RID. For users, the key contains two values of type REG_BINARY. Although their structure is not documented, it is believed

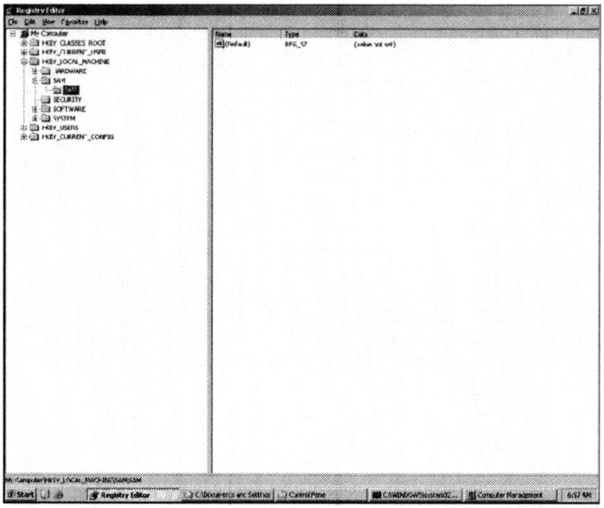

Figure 3.3 Registry SAM structure.

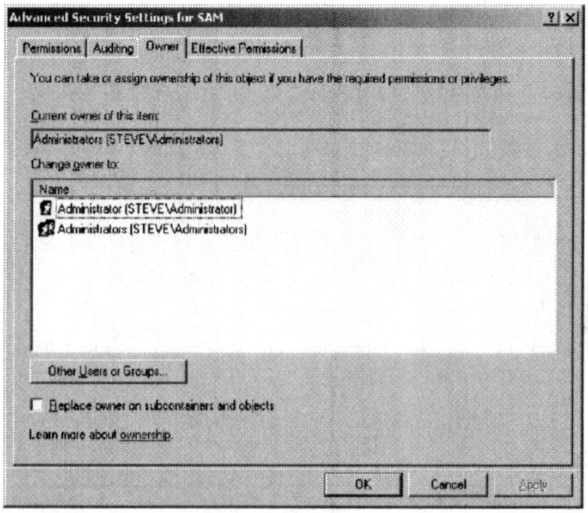

Figure 3.4 User access permissions.

that they contain user account information, including user password hashes. Figure 3.6 shows a typical V field.

Most of the information about users can easily be spotted in the text field. It is important to note that the password is not shown in cleartext here, and neither is the password hash. As is discussed in the following sections, password hashes are obfuscated using simple DES encryption while

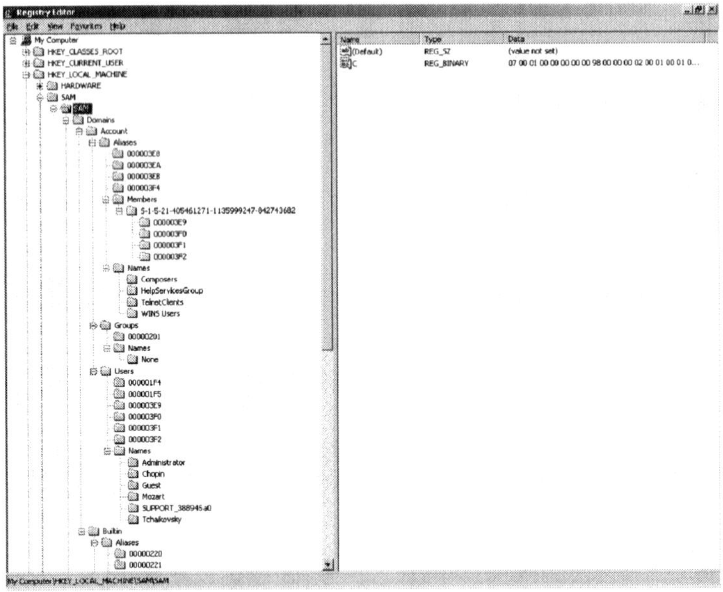

Figure 3.5 SAM structure.

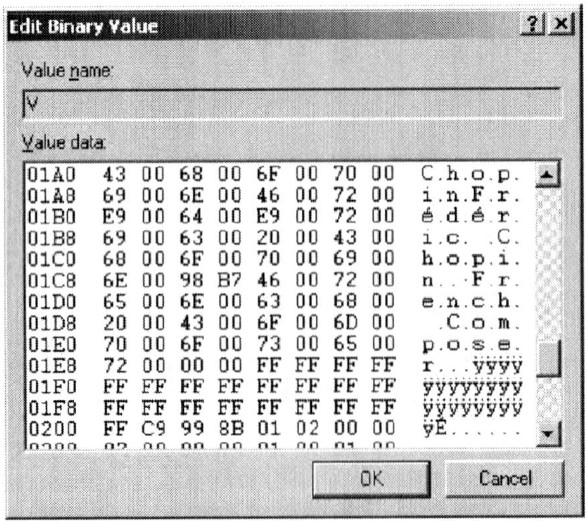

Figure 3.6 SAM registry values.

they are being stored in the registry and operating system functions that access the registry (see subsection 3.2.8.3). Other fields, such as the account name and account description, appear in plaintext and Unicode format.

3.2.7 User Passwords

Windows does not provide the system developer with functions that return the plaintext user password (passwords stored using reversible encryption are an exception — see below). Even Windows administrators do not easily have access to the password hash. In fact, with a few exceptions that will are discussed later in this chapter, the operating system does not store the plaintext password for the user. The SAM file stores a password hash. Although this hash is extensively used for authentication purposes, operating system calls and application functions do not typically need to know what the stored user password hash value is; most often, they will provide the operating system with the password that the user has entered and ask the operating system to perform the comparison (authentication). Alternatively, server-side applications and services typically use impersonation to act on behalf of the user.

Despite the fact that the operating system tries to hide the password hashes, it inevitably needs access to these hashes. There are different approaches to accessing and displaying (and even changing) the password hash. These approaches are employed by numerous third-party tools on the Internet, and are typically meant to help the administrator in auditing user password complexity, or to recover a lost administrator password, although malicious users can use these tools for purposes other than auditing.

Most of the tools used to provide password hashes from online Windows systems require that the invoking user has administrative privileges. Using these privileges, the password hash dumping tools will typically use the **seDebugPrivilege** user right granted to the local Administrators group and inject a crafted piece of code into the Local Security Authority (LSA) address space. Then they will dump portions of the LSA address space, which in turn reveal portions of the SAM file, which appear to be the user password hashes. Note that although this behavior of Windows is not necessarily normal, this is not typically considered a major security breach from a security perspective as the requirement for administrative access to perform this operation still exists. Someone who already has administrative permissions has full access to the system and all the resources anyway.

The SAM file contains two password hashes for each user. The first is the old-style LAN Manager password hash required to authenticate down-level clients such as MS Client for DOS, Windows for Workgroups and Windows 96/98/ME, and under certain circumstances Windows NT and later operating systems. The second is the NT password hash, which is used to authenticate Windows NT/2000/2003/XP. Windows needs to support both password formats for compatibility reasons. As always, compatibility and flexibility require trade-offs in terms of security, and the network architect can choose whether security or compatibility is a priority. It is important to understand what the risks involved in using LM hashes are, and how to minimize these risks.

When the user account is initially created, or as the password is modified later, the user provides just one password. The operating system generates two password hashes from this password using two different hashing algorithms, which result in the so-called LM hash and NT hash. There are some essential differences between the LM password hash and the NT password hash:

- The LM password uses a restricted ASCII set of characters, and it transforms all lowercase letters into uppercase letters (i.e., it is case insensitive); only 142 ASCII characters are supported; NT passwords support UNICODE character set (potentially 65536 characters).
- The LM password length is restricted to 14 characters; the NT password length is 128 Unicode characters — virtually unrestricted (although the user interface of the operating system and system tools might restrict that, especially in Windows NT 3.51 and NT 4.0).
- Different algorithms are used to calculate the hash from potentially the same password; hence, the hash values are different.

The user password is hashed using the LM and NT algorithms and then stored in the SAM file. In both cases, the result is a 128-bit string (hash), regardless of the actual password length. The hash is a one-way function so the original password cannot be (easily) deduced from the hash.

3.2.8 Storing Password Hashes in the Registry SAM File

Although the user password is typically not stored in cleartext or using reversible encryption, Windows still performs a series of cryptographic operations on NT and LM hash values to protect them from being stolen by malicious users who might use dictionary or brute force attacks against the password hash. The cleartext password is first hashed using the LM hash and the NT hash algorithms, and then the two different password hashes undergo specific manipulations, including DES encryption for obfuscation purposes, as well as SYSKEY encryption.

Figure 3.7 provides an overview of the cryptographic manipulations on user passwords before being stored in the SAM file.

3.2.8.1 LM Hash Algorithm

The LM Hash calculation uses the DES-ECB algorithm to encrypt the user password. The DES algorithm is typically used for encryption, and not for generating hashes. However, in this instance, DES is used with a

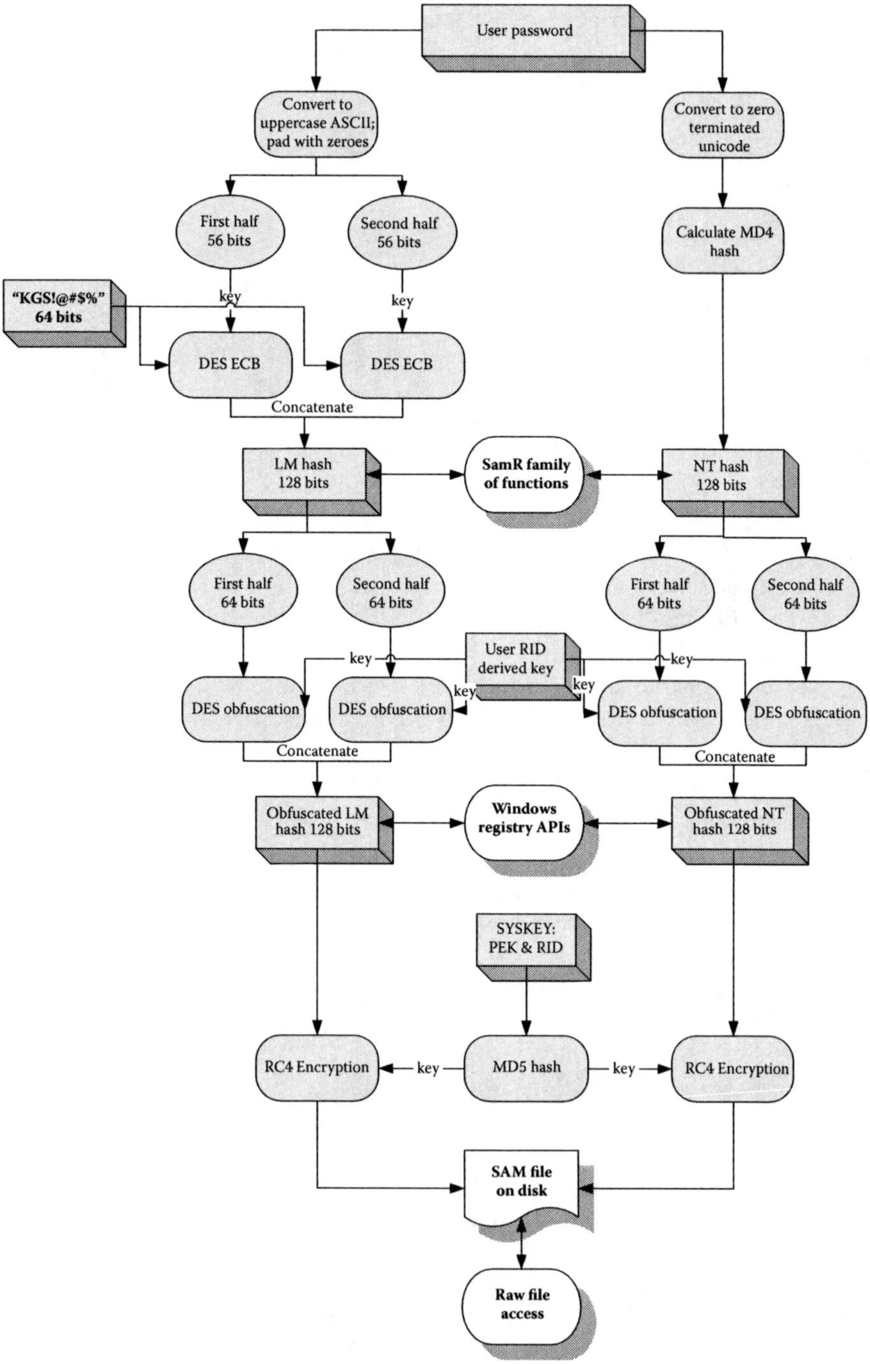

Figure 3.7 Cryptographic operations on user passwords in Windows.

fixed-length string to generate a fixed-length result that depends on the secret user password. Hence, it can be considered similar to hash functions, and both Microsoft and the security community have adopted the name LM Hash.

Microsoft has not published the details of the LM Hash calculation. However, it is believed that the steps to calculate the LM Hash from the plaintext user password are the following:

1. Convert all the lowercase letters to uppercase (all characters are ASCII).
2. If the password length is less than 14 characters (bytes), pad the password to 14 characters using zero (0x00).
3. Split the 14-byte password into two halves, 7 bytes each.
4. From the 7 byte (56-bit) password field, generate a 64-bit key by separating the 56-bit stream into eight 7-bit data chunks and adding a parity bit to each 7-bit data chunk as the eighth bit.
5. Encrypt the following string "**KGS!@#$%**" (it is interesting to find where these symbols reside on the keyboard) with the first half of the password as the key using the DES algorithm in 64-bit blocks (the well-known string).
6. Encrypt the same string "**KGS!@#$%**" with the second half of the password as the key using the DES algorithm in 64-bit blocks (the well-known string).
7. Concatenate the results from Steps 5 and 6 into a single string, 16 characters (128 bits) in length. This is the LM Hash.

There are a couple of problems from a security perspective with regard to the LM Hash calculation. Some of them are the following:

- The password is converted to uppercase, which reduces the number of possible characters.
- The restricted number of characters (142) reduces the number of possible combinations and therefore the keyspace. This makes the LM Hash susceptible to brute force and rainbow attacks.
- The password is used to encrypt a known plaintext; this makes it susceptible to known-plaintext cryptanalysis.
- The plaintext being encrypted with the password is constant; there is neither salt, nor initial vector, nor any other randomness. Two matching plaintext passwords will have matching hashes also. This makes password guessing easier. Blank passwords always give the same hash value so blank passwords can be spotted immediately.
- The password is padded with zeroes to 14 characters. A password shorter than seven characters will have zeroes in its last seven

characters. As the plaintext to be encrypted is known, and the password is padded with zeroes, the ciphertext for the second half of the hash is constant and known. Hence, it is easy to guess if a password is shorter than seven characters
- The password is split into two, and the two halves are used independently of one another — there is no cryptographic feedback between them. This allows the two halves to be attacked separately.

Considering the fact that the LM password hash and the NT password hash are both derived from the plaintext user password, an attacker who is trying to obtain the plaintext password is likely to try to break the weaker hash. Therefore, provided that someone has administrative access to a Windows computer, the resultant protection of user passwords in Windows is equal to the protection provided by the LM Hash, despite the fact that the NT Hash provides for a stronger protection per se.

Due to the inherent weaknesses of the LM password hash, in Windows NT 4.0 and later operating systems, it is possible to disable the generation of LM Hashes for user passwords and considerably increase the protection of the user password by only using the stronger NT Hash. To do that, the administrator should perform one of the following actions:

- When assigning a password to a user (or when the user is changing his own password), use a password that is more than 14 characters in length. As the LM Hash only supports passwords that are 14 characters or less, no LM Hash is generated for non-conforming passwords. Windows NT 4.0 and earlier administrative tools and user interface limit the password length to 14 characters; however, it is possible to enter longer passwords programmatically or by using Windows 2000 and later administrative tools.
- Disable LM Hash generation on a stand-alone computer or domain member (local SAM), or domain controllers by either editing the registry (Windows XP and 2003: **HKEY_LOCAL_MACHINE\SYSTEM\CurrentControlSet\Control\Lsa\NoLMHash: REG_DWORD=1**), or using a GPO (**Network security: Do not store LAN Manager hash value on next password change**). If the setting is applied at the domain level, it should be implemented on each domain controller (either use **REGEDIT.EXE** to configure each individual DC, or apply a GPO on the OU where all domain controllers reside). The users will then need to change their passwords before this setting takes effect.

More information on how to disable LM Hash generation is available in [27].

If an LM Hash is not present for a user account, this account cannot be used to authenticate from computers that only support the LM authentication protocol; this includes the default installations of Windows 95 and Windows 98, as well as earlier operating systems.

3.2.8.2 NT Hash Algorithm

The NT Hash is generated using the publicly available and widely used MD4 algorithm (the MD5 predecessor) (see [9]). The password can be any length up to 128 Unicode characters but the hash is always 128 bits in size (16 bytes).

The NT Hash calculation works in the following way:

1. The password is converted to Unicode, regardless of whether it contains any characters other than ASCII. Each character is therefore represented with 2 bytes (16 bits). The Unicode string will have **NULL (0x00)** as the last character (zero-terminated string).
2. The MD4 algorithm is used to create a hash of the Unicode password; the result is the 128-bit hash value — the NT Hash.

Being a publicly available and a well-known hashing algorithm, MD4 has been analyzed by cryptographic researches and has been proven to have a number of security weaknesses. Although the NT Hash is stronger than the LM Hash, it is still susceptible to various attacks, including dictionary and brute force attacks. MD4 is not collision free (two or more plaintext messages can generate the same hash) and there are some MD4-specific attacks as well (see [10]). The lack of salt contributes to the exposure of the NT Hash algorithm to cryptographic analysis and attacks.

3.2.8.3 Password Hash Obfuscation Using DES

To additionally protect password hashes while being stored in the registry, Windows applies an additional round of encryption, using the DES protocol and keys derived from the user RID. DES-ECB encryption is applied to both the LM Hash and the NT Hash.

The password obfuscation algorithm has not been published by Microsoft. However, security researchers on the Internet have been able to grasp some understanding of the inner workings of the operating system (see [13]).

DES encryption for password hashes requires two 56-bit (7-byte) keys calculated individually for every user. The keys **k1** and **k2** are functions of the user RID (a 4-byte value). The first 4 bytes of **k1** are equivalent to the 4 bytes of the user RID, and the last 3 bytes (5–7) are the same as the first 3 bytes of **k1** (therefore equal to the first 3 bytes of the RID). **k2** is calculated using the fourth, first, second, then third bytes of the user RID, and the last 3 bytes are the same as the first 3 bytes of **k2** (therefore equal to the fourth, first, and second of the user RID) (see Figure 3.8). Both the NT Hash and the LM Hash are 128-bit (16-byte) values. To encrypt the hash values, each 16-byte hash block is separated into two halves, 8 bytes each. Each of these halves is encrypted separately; the first half (8 bytes) is encrypted using DES ECB using **k1** as the key, and the second half is encrypted separately using **k2** as the key. The resulting strings are then concatenated and stored in the registry in the respective password hash fields.

Because the encryption key is known (derivative of the user RID) and the encryption algorithm is known (DES-ECB), the above encryption is for obfuscation purposes only. It does not provide true protection for the password hash in terms of inability to recover the password hash from the ciphertext. An attacker who has access to the SAM file can easily eliminate the obfuscation and obtain the password hash (still not the plaintext password).

With the obfuscation applied to password hashes, even if two users have the same password, the obfuscated hash will appear different for both users because the user RID is used to generate the DES obfuscation key, and the RIDs are different. Apparently, a determined attacker might just decrypt passwords using the well-known RIDs.

3.2.8.4 SYSKEY Encryption for Storing Password Hashes in the SAM

DES obfuscation only adds a few additional steps before an attacker can access user password hash values, and does not really prevent attackers from accessing the hashes. To mitigate the risk of offline attacks (direct access to the SAM file) against password hashes, Microsoft invented the SYSKEY utility in Windows NT 4 SP3. Windows 2000 and later operating systems use SYSKEY encryption by default. The use of SYSKEY does not bypass the DES-ECB obfuscation, as discussed in the previous section; it adds an additional layer of encryption for password hashes and other system secrets, such as LSA Secrets.

The idea behind SYSKEY is simple: password hashes and LSA Secrets can be additionally encrypted, and therefore protected from attackers who may try to copy the SAM file from a computer. To accomplish this protection, SYSKEY uses a system-generated password encryption key (PEK), which is then used to encrypt only the password-related fields in the SAM file — the LM Hash, the NT Hash, and the password history, as well as the LSA Secrets (see subsection 3.2.9). Therefore, an attacker will first need to gain access to the PEK and decrypt the password field, and

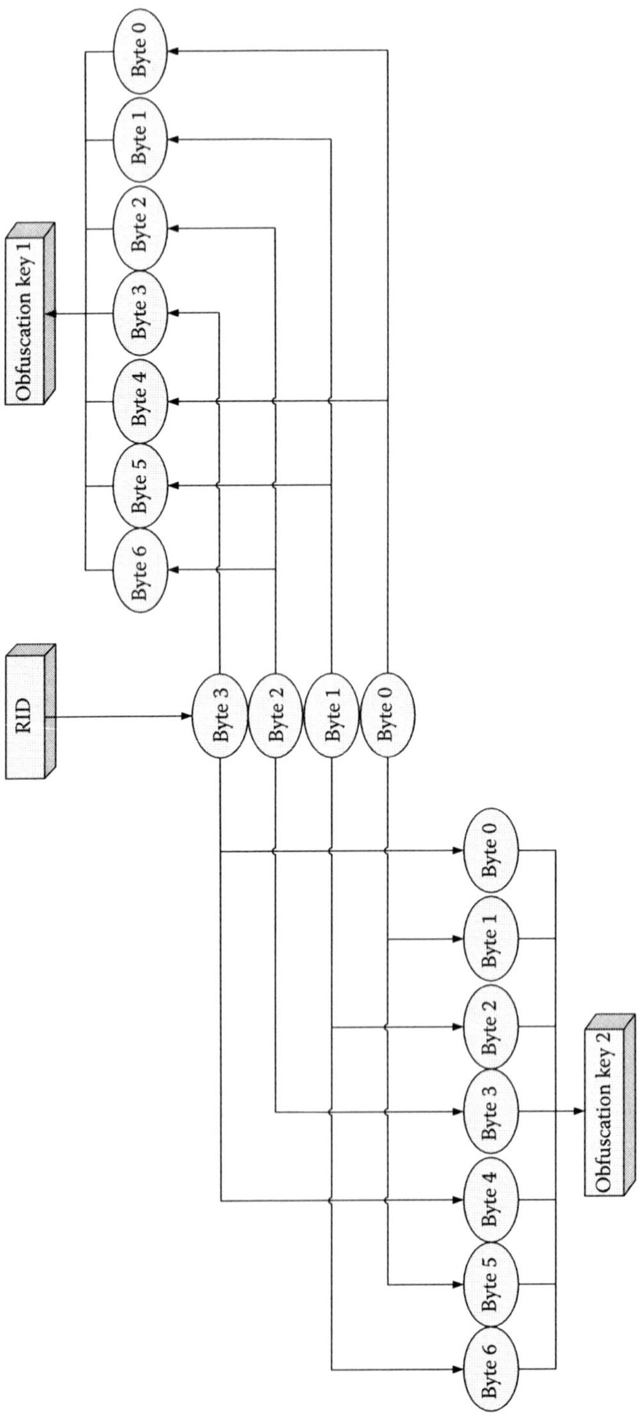

Figure 3.8 Password hash obfuscation: DES keys.

then remove obfuscation (discussed in the previous section) and this will still only provide him with the password hash, not with the password itself.

Key material for the PEK is generated for every single Windows system when SYSKEY is enabled for the first time, regardless of the computer membership in a domain or workgroup. The PEK key material is randomly generated. The PEK is used to protect machine local accounts, or accounts in the local copy of the Active Directory Database. Apparently, the operating system needs to know the PEK material to be able to calculate the PEK, and then decrypt the information in the SAM or the Active Directory database and obtain the password hashes. Therefore, PEK key material is stored in the registry. To protect the PEK from attackers, the operating system generates the PEK using the random key material and the so-called System Key — and hence the name of the SYSKEY utility. Some sources refer to the system key as the boot key, or the startup key.

By default, the system key is stored in the registry. When the operating system boots, it reads the key from the registry. Every time the operating system or authorized applications try to access SYSKEY encrypted data, **LSASS.EXE** will use the system key and the above algorithm to decrypt the data and provide it to the application or service transparently. Therefore, the system key is only effective against offline attacks against the registry, not against online attacks from applications running on the same computer as **LSASS.EXE**, if these applications possess administrative privileges.

3.2.8.5 Case Study: The SYSKEY Utility, the System Key, and Password Encryption Key

Microsoft does not provide the details of the encryption algorithm used by SYSKEY. The official documentation only mentions that a "complex obfuscation algorithm" is used. However, security researchers have come up with the steps used to encrypt and decrypt user password hashes (see [12]).

The information below is believed valid for SAM files, and may or may not be valid for the **NTDS.DIT** files used by Active Directory.

Although this is not documented, it is believed that SYSKEY information is stored in the following location of the registry:

HKEY_LOCAL_MACHINE\System\CurrentControlSet\Control\LSA.

The REG_DWORD value **SecureBoot** under this key determines whether (1) SYSKEY is stored locally in the registry (SYSTEM file), (2) SYSKEY is derived from an administrator selected password, or (3) SYSKEY will be stored on a floppy disk. The keys **JD**, **Skew1**, **GBG**, and **Data** (in this order) each contain 4 bytes of the system key. To obtain the system key, these 4 bytes are concatenated, and the bytes are reordered as follows: [8th, 10th, 3rd, 7th, 2nd, 1st, 9th, 15th, 0th, 5th, 13th, 4th, 11th, 6th, 12th, 14th]. The SYSTEM key is then used by the operating system to calculate the password encryption key (PEK). A second copy of the SYSKEY configuration is stored under the following key:

HKEY_LOCAL_MACHINE\Security\Policy\PolSecretEncryptionKey

The key material for the PEK is stored in the SAM. On stand-alone computers and domain members, key material for the PEK (called for brevity **PEK-KM**) is obtained using the following algorithm: 32 bytes from offset 0x80 of **F** the value under **HKEY_LOCAL_MACHINE\SAM\SAM\Domains\Account** are taken and encrypted with the RC4 algorithm using the following as the key: the MD5 hash of the 16 bytes from offset 0x70 of the F-value concatenated with the constant string "**!@#$%^&*( )qwertyUIOPAzxcvbnmQQQQQQQQQQQQ)(*@&%**" concatenated with the System Key concatenated with the constant string "**0123456789012345678901234567890123456789**".

The PEK used to encrypt the LM Hash, or the LM password history, is obtained by calculating the MD5 hash of the **PEK-KM,** concatenated with the user RID, concatenated with the string "**LMPASSWORD**".

The PEK used to encrypt the NT Hash, or the NT password history, is obtained by calculating the MD5 hash of the **PEK-KM,** concatenated with the user RID, concatenated with the string "**NTPASSWORD**".

The password hash or password history is then encrypted with the RC4 algorithm using the respective PEK as calculated above as the key.

Reference [12] describes an earlier implementation of SYSKEY where both the LM Hash and the NT Hash used to be encrypted using the same PEK, which as a result made the password hashes vulnerable to relatively simple cryptanalysis attacks. Microsoft then released Q248183 to patch this vulnerability and started generating different PEKs, as described above, for the LM hash and the NT hash.

It becomes clear from the information provided above that all the components used to protect the user database are readily available from the registry, including the system key (it is stored in the registry by default). The system key can be moved to a floppy, or a start-up password can be used as key material for the system key. The last two options are highly recommended because only in case one of them is applied can the administrator rest assured that the SYSKEY encryption is likely remain secure.

The operating system now needs to protect the system key, which in turn protects the confidentiality of the PEK, which in turn is used to encrypt user password hashes, which are presumably one-way functions

(OWF) of the user password; and in addition to that, they are encrypted (obfuscated) using the DES algorithm and user RID-derived keys.

With SYSKEY, offline attacks against user password hashes and LSA Secrets become more complicated. Unlike user hashes that are stored in the SAM file, the system key is stored in the SYSTEM file of the registry, so an attacker now needs to have both the SYSTEM and SAM files. On the other hand, if the system key is stored in the registry, all the decryption tasks can be technically performed in a row and the decrypted password hash will be obtained. Because SAM and SECURITY files reside in the same folder, and typically go together, a determined attacker can potentially overcome this countermeasure easily. Storing the SYSKEY in the registry will not prevent determined attackers with physical access from obtaining whatever they need.

To provide for really strong protection against offline attacks, the SYSKEY utility allows for two other options for storing the system key and these options are considered more secure: require an administrator to enter a password during system start-up, or generate a secure password and require an administrator to provide a floppy disk with this password every time the system starts up (Figure 3.9). Both methods require administrator intervention during system start-up and require a trade-off between flexibility/ease of use and security.

The **Password Startup** option requires the administrator to create a password, which is used to derive the system key (using the MD5 algorithm), and is then used to encrypt the PEK. Every time the system starts up, the operating system will stop and require the administrator to

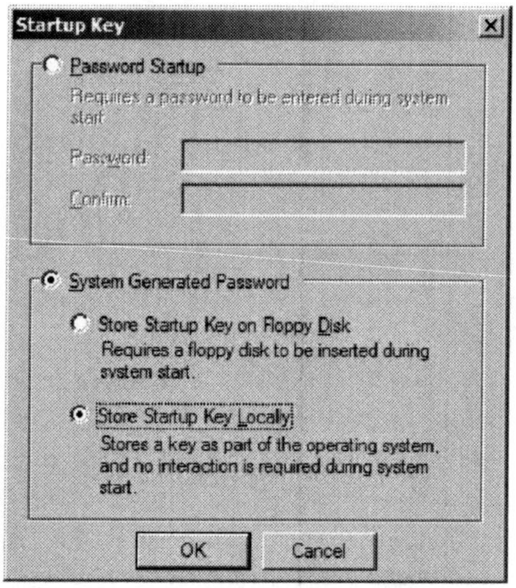

Figure 3.9 SYSKEY options.

enter the password before the boot process continues. The operating system, and the Local Security Authority Subsystem (LSASS) in particular, will use this password to decrypt the PEK in memory, and then decrypt each user's password hash, as required. If the administrator attending the operating system boot fails to provide the correct password, the LSASS will fail to decrypt the PEK and the boot process will be interrupted. This method provides for user authentication using the "something you know" factor — the Startup password.

The **Floppy Disk Startup** option will store the System Key on a floppy disk. Every time the system reboots, an administrator will be required to attend the boot process (subject to available BIOS options) and provide a floppy disk where the start-up key is stored. The failure to provide such a disk will interrupt the boot process. This method provides for user authentication using the "something you have" factor — the floppy disk. Arguably, this can be considered a "something you know" factor because the floppy can be copied.

Both **Password Startup** and **Floppy Disk Startup** will provide for SAM file security and greatly reduce the chances for success of offline SAM file attacks. However, neither of the SYSKEY options protects passwords from online attacks (an Administrator dumping the passwords from a working operating system to a file) or from network sniffing attacks (capturing network traffic). It is important to understand that SYSKEY can only be used to protect user passwords in a limited number of scenarios, and it is not universally applicable when it comes to protecting password hashes.

Some older password hash dumping utilities from the time before SYSKEY was invented will try to access password hashes in SAM directly, instead of trying to decrypt them first using the PEK. Apparently, this will fail and, so to speak, SYSKEY protects from attacks using older tools by means of changing the encryption in use for password hashes. However, newer utilities will be able to compute the PEK (if stored locally or from an online OS) and will use it to decrypt the password field and obtain the hash. Both the new and the old tools are readily available on the Internet, so an effective protection strategy should ensure that hashes are protected from both.

It is important to note that SYSKEY encryption is only effective for passwords as they are stored in the SAM file, or the Windows 2000 directory services information tree (**NTDS.DIT**) — the so-called offline attacks. Applications that are able to dump password hashes from an online Windows NT system will see DES obfuscated NT and LM hashes (provided that they use standard registry access functions), not SYSKEY encrypted hashes. Once the operating system has been brought up, all the Windows functions behave as if there is no SYSKEY encryption.

3.2.8.6 Threats to Windows Password Hashes

Neither LM Hashes nor NT Hashes are considered cryptographically strong. This means that if an attacker gained access to the hashes, he could potentially obtain some or all of the user passwords. Therefore, password hashes must be considered sensitive information and stored as securely as plaintext passwords.

To successfully manage the risk of stolen passwords or password hashes, it is important to understand what the potential threats to these hashes are. Some common threats to passwords and password hash confidentiality in Windows NT are given in Table 3.9.

Table 3.9 Threats to Windows Password Hashes

Threat	*Conditions*	*Description*
Offline access to the registry	Physical access to the computer	An attacker can reboot the computer, boot into another OS, and obtain a copy of the SAM file from the following folder: **%SYSTEMROOT%\SYSTEM32\Config** *Note:* Physical access to the computer can pose risks considerably greater than this. Physical security is the first thing to consider before looking at other security aspects.
	Access to backup tapes	An attacker could obtain a copy of the SAM file from Windows backup media.
	Access to ERD or system state backup	An attacker could obtain a copy of the SAM file from a Windows NT 4.0 or earlier emergency repair disk (ERD) or a Windows 2000 or later system state backup.
	Access to LSA Secrets	An attacker with physical access to the computer can reboot the machine in another OS, reset the Administrator password, and then reboot into Windows, log on as administrator, and dump the LSA Secrets database (provided that SYSKEY is stored in registry).

Table 3.9 Threats to Windows Password Hashes (continued)

Threat	*Conditions*	*Description*
	Access to the local logon cache	An attacker who has access to the LSA Secrets can potentially obtain hashed values of the local logon cache on the computer containing hashed credentials from previous network logon attempts. More details can be found in Chapter 3.2.10.
Online — administrative access to the SAM	Obtain password hashes using Administrator account	At the time of writing this book, all the utilities that can efficiently access the password hashes require that the user executing the application has the Debug applications (**seDebugPrivilige**) user right. By default, this user right is only granted to the local Administrators group on a computer, and not to regular users. Therefore, only members of this group can use utilities that can dump the user hashes from the SAM. Because a user with administrative permissions can virtually access anything on a system, password hashes are just one of the many concerns if this user happens to be malicious or unauthorized.
	User-readable registry files or **%SYSTEMROOT%\REPAIR** directory	By default, Windows will prevent regular users from accessing the SAM file (which is open when the operating system is online) or its offline ERD copy (**%SYSTEMROOT%\REPAIR\SAM**). However, if the administrator changes the access permissions to the file system to allow users access to these files, or if the operating system is installed on a FAT/FAT32 partition, which does not provide for file access permissions, the SAM can be stolen by a regular user. *Note:* By default, Windows NT 4.0 and earlier domain controllers do not create a copy of the SAM file in the ERD unless the /s option is used.

Table 3.9 Threats to Windows Password Hashes (continued)

Threat	*Conditions*	*Description*
	Privilege escalation to an Administrator account	At the time of writing this book, there are known exploits that can provide an attacker having a regular user account with administrative privileges (privilege escalation). However, these exploits only work on old, unpatched Windows NT systems. There are various other methods to obtain Administrative privileges, including Trojans, worms, social engineering, and locally cached credentials. Therefore, even a regular user can potentially obtain administrative privileges and then access the password hashes. Apparently, an attacker who already has the administrative privileges would typically have more than enough access to do whatever he wants; and unless he wants to hide and keep his access for a long time, secretly utilizing other users' credentials, he is not likely to need the hashes of other users.
Access to password hashes on the network (passive — sniffing)	SMB/CIFS (including file access, MS RPC, and RAS/VPN)	Network authentication protocols (including NTLM, NTLM v.2, CHAP, MS-CHAP v.1, and MS-CHAP v.2) will exchange network hashes across the network. Provided that an attacker has access to the communication channel in between, he can collect these hashes and end up with information pretty similar to that which he would get from the SAM file. *Note:* Sniffing may or may not be passive. Some password sniffers will generate fake ARP announcements to hijack another computer's ARP mapping on a router or flood the switch forwarding table and have all the traffic from the VLAN copied to their port.

3.2.8.7 Tools to Access Windows Password Hashes

Despite the fact that Microsoft has not documented the mechanisms used to hash, encrypt, obfuscate, store, and access user passwords, security researchers on the Internet have been able to reverse-engineer the inner workings of the operating system and, as a result, there are many tools on the Internet that will dump Windows NT password hashes and LSA Secrets from either a working computer (locally or across the network) or from an offline copy of the SAM file.

Some of the tools that can be used to dump password hashes are shown in Table 3.10.

In addition to read access to password hashes, some tools allow write access as well. For example, a popular category of utilities is offline password changing utilities and registry editors. Some of these utilities allow a user with physical access to a computer to reboot the machine in another OS, load a simple offline registry editor that accesses the original operating system registry files, and replaces the Administrator (or other user) password with a new one. Note that these utilities may still be unable to decrypt and obtain the Administrator password but they can apparently change it, as they know where user passwords are stored in the registry, as well as how to encrypt a new password and store it where the unknown password resides.

3.2.8.8 Case Study: Accessing Windows Password Hashes with pwdump4

One of the online password hash auditing utilities available on the Internet is the **pwdump4.exe** utility. The following example shows the output from this tool:

```
C:\pwdump4> pwdump4 /l

PWDUMP4.02 dump winnt/2000 user/password hash remote or local for
 crack. by bingle@email.com.cn
This program is free software based on pwpump3 by Phil Staubs
under the GNU General Public License Version 2.

SRV>Version: OS Ver 5.2, Service Pack 1, ServerEnterprise Terminal
Administrator:500:E52CAC67419A9A224A3B108F3FA6CB6D:8846F7EAEE8FB117AD06BDD830B75
86C:::
Chopin:1009:E52CAC67419A9A22CE171273F527391F:5B4C6335673A75F13ED948E848F00840:::

Guest:501:AAD3B435B51404EEAAD3B435B51404EE:31D6CFE0D16AE931B73C59D7E0C089C0:::
Mozart:1008:E52CAC67419A9A22CE171273F527391F:5B4C6335673A75F13ED948E848F00840:::

SUPPORT_388945a0:1001:AAD3B435B51404EEAAD3B435B51404EE:14026EEA11606C051C2253CD6
8B57A1D:::
Tchaikovsky:1010:E52CAC67419A9A22CE171273F527391F:5B4C6335673A75F13ED948E848F008
40:::
LSA>Samr Enumerate 6 Users In Domain STEVE.
```

Table 3.10 Tools that Provide Access to Windows Password Hashes

Tool	*Password Hash Access Method*	*Description*
Pwdump	Online password hash access tool that uses standard registry access functions (**RegConnectRegistry( )** and **RegQueryValueEx( )**)	This is one of the first tools to dump password hashes. Essentially, it accesses the V values in the registry, removes DES obfuscation, and dumps the LM and NT password hashes in hexadecimal format. *Note:* This is an old tool that does not support SYSKEY. Although it provides output data, this data is incorrect.
pwdump2, pwdump3 and pwdump4	Online password hash access tools based on pwdump but use different functions to access the SAM. Essentially, all three tools use Windows internal RPC functions of the Samr family (**SamrQuery InformationUser( )**)	Similar to pwdump and provide similar results. As the functions used by these tools are Windows NT internal, they provide the LM and NT Hash directly, and there is no need to remove SYSKEY encryption or password obfuscation.
Cain & Abel	Online and offline access to SAM files, LSA Secrets, Protected Store, and many others	This a powerful tool meant to access different security databases for auditing purposes.
samdump	Offline access to the SAM file	This requires a copy of the SAM file. This tool is able to find the password hashes in the SAM file, as well as the System Key, of SYSKEY was enabled and configured for local System Key storage.
Lsadump/ lsadump2	Online access to the LSA Secrets database	These utilities will dump the contents of the LSA Secrets database, which contains machine and user secrets.

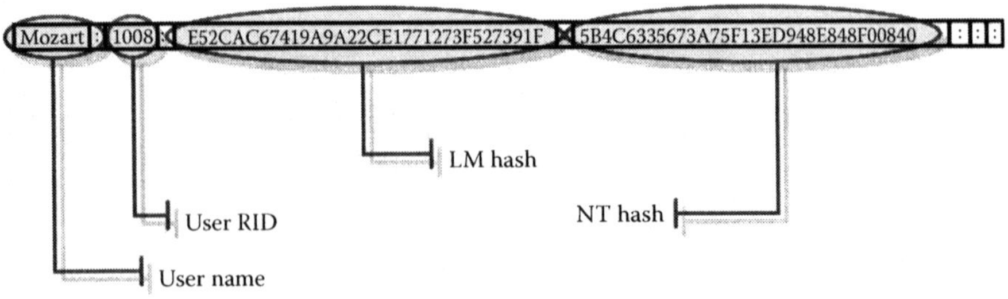

Figure 3.10 pwdump4 password entry format.

The format used by the **pwdump4.exe** utility is given in Figure 3.10. This format is often used by similar utilities. It can be used by the SAMBA product as well, and can be imported into the **smbpasswd** file (see Chapter 2). The LM Hash and NT Hash fields are 128-bit values represented in hexadecimal format.

3.2.9 LSA Secrets

In addition to user data, there is certain system information that the operating systems needs to use and at the same time protect. Such information includes service account passwords (widely used in Windows NT 4 and earlier), cached credentials encryption keys, etc.

For example, if a service needs to run in the context of a specific user account, the operating system needs to know what account to use and, furthermore, needs to know the passwords for this account. Every time the Service Control Manager needs to start a service with a specific user account, it will check the LSA Secrets database and obtain the encrypted password for this account.

LSA Secrets is a shared system store for protected data, primarily passwords. Although it can be used to store user specific secrets as well, this is typically avoided because the LSA Secrets store is available to the machine administrators as well as to the operating system, so applications cannot easily "hide" their own information there, unless they implement an additional layer of application encryption. Applications that need to access the LSA Secrets typically use the **LsaStorePrivateData( )** and **LsaRetrievePrivateData( )** system functions to access LSA Secrets.

Physically, LSA Secrets are stored in the following registry location:

HKEY_LOCAL_MACHINE\SECURITY\Policy\Secrets

There is a key for every secret under the above base, and the value Default under the **CurrVal** key contains the actual secret. Other information kept in LSA Secrets includes the previous value (**OldVal**), the last update of the current value (**CupdTime**), and the time of update of the old value (**OupdTime**).

There are three scopes of security objects that LSA can store:

1. *Local objects* (typically prefixed by L$). These secrets are local to the computer where they are created and should only be read by local computer administrators.
2. *Machine objects* (typically prefixed by M$ or NL$). These secrets are readable by the operating system only.
3. *Global objects* (typically prefixed by G$). These are global secrets used by domain controllers for interdomain trust accounts, and replicated between domain controllers — unlike Local and Machine objects.

Some of the information typically stored in LSA Secrets includes that given in Table 3.11.

Table 3.11 Typical LSA Secrets

Name	*Description*
$MACHINE.ACC	This LSA Secret only exists on computers that are domain members and contains the computer password in the domain.
G$$DomainName	Contains the interdomain trust account password for trusted domain DomainName. This LSA Secret can be found in the trusting (resource) domain, while the trusted (account) domain has an interdomain trust account in the account database, and this account will be of the form DomainName$, where DomainName is the name of the trusting (resource) domain. When a trusting domain controller connects to a trusted domain controller, it will use its own domain name, followed by the dollar sign as the username for the connection, and the password will be the LSA Secret G$$DomainName.
NL$xx	Only exists in Windows NT 4 and earlier. Contains cached logon credentials from users who have successfully logged on from this computer. xx is a sequence number, starting at 0. Windows 2000 and later use a separate store for this type of information — see subsection 3.2.10 for more information.

Table 3.11 Typical LSA Secrets (continued)

Name	*Description*
NL$KM	Contains key material that is used to generate an encryption key for password hashes. This key material is a random string, unique for each computer — see subsection 3.2.10 for more information.
DPAPI_SYSTEM	Used by Windows 2000/XP and later for the purposes of DPAPI. Believed to be used to store the password for machine-level encryption
_SC_ServiceName	Contains the password for a specific service on the local computer that uses a specific user account. When the Service Control Manager (SCM) starts services on a computer, it uses this password to start the service with the specific privileges defined by the computer administrator. It is important to note that LSA Secrets only contains the password, and not the username or SID of the user used by the service. The username of the user used by the service is stored in the service description part of the registry **HKLM\System\CurrentControlSet\Services\ServiceName\Security**, where ServiceName is the specific key for the service.
RasDialParams!UserSID#0	RAS Dial-in account for a specific user with SID UserSID. LSA Secrets stores information about RAS entries on a computer.

3.2.9.1 *Case Study: Exploring LSA Secrets on a Windows NT 4.0 Domain Controller That Is an Exchange 5.5 Server*

A popular tool — **LSADUMP2.EXE** — can be used to explore the LSA Secrets on a Windows NT 4.0 computer running Exchange 5.5. Exchange 5.5 services require special service accounts to be created for them and provided during the installation, and Exchange 5.5 services are configured to start using these accounts.

```
Z:\ lsadump2
$MACHINE.ACC
 52 00 4F 00 64 00 76 00 70 00 74 00 62 00 49 00  R.O.d.v.p.t.b.I.
 34 00 71 00 63 00 51 00 77 00 71 00              4.q.c.Q.w.q.
FTPD_ANONYMOUS_DATA
 66 00 4B 00 45 00 50 00 36 00 67 00 25 00 5A 00  f.K.E.P.6.g.%.Z.
 30 00 75 00 4E 00 44 00 50 00 70 00 00 00        0.u.N.D.P.p...
```

```
FTPD_ROOT_DATA
 66 00 4B 00 45 00 50 00 36 00 67 00 25 00 5A 00  f.K.E.P.6.g.%.Z.
 30 00 75 00 4E 00 44 00 50 00 70 00 00 00        0.u.N.D.P.p...
G$$IMMEDIENT
 C2 EE 39 A7 D7 A3 31 CB 1A 91 CC 90 1A 91 CC 90  ..9...1.........
GOPHERD_ANONYMOUS_DATA
 66 00 4B 00 45 00 50 00 36 00 67 00 25 00 5A 00  f.K.E.P.6.g.%.Z.
 30 00 75 00 4E 00 44 00 50 00 70 00 00 00        0.u.N.D.P.p...
GOPHERD_ROOT_DATA
 66 00 4B 00 45 00 50 00 36 00 67 00 25 00 5A 00  f.K.E.P.6.g.%.Z.
 30 00 75 00 4E 00 44 00 50 00 70 00 00 00        0.u.N.D.P.p...
NL$1
 25 FD 08 FA 89 79 5E D5 42 07 E6 E8 44 2A 6C A0  %....y^.B...D*l.
 1E C1 DC 20 5B 56 57 B3 B8 F4 2A D3 14 6D 90 2F  ... [VW...*..m./
 01 01 00                                         ...
NL$10
NL$2
 60 94 5C 79 1E F2 16 38 42 DA 55 E8 64 6A CC 58  `.\y...8B.U.dj.X
 31 57 BF E0 F2 45 C7 FB 14 D6 1D A3 BE 54 0E 0F  1W...E.......T..
 01 01 00                                         ...
NL$3
NL$4
NL$5
NL$6
NL$7
NL$8
NL$9
W3_ANONYMOUS_DATA
 66 00 4B 00 45 00 50 00 36 00 67 00 25 00 5A 00  f.K.E.P.6.g.%.Z.
 30 00 75 00 4E 00 44 00 50 00 70 00 00 00        0.u.N.D.P.p...
W3_PROXY_USER_SECRET
 66 00 4B 00 45 00 50 00 36 00 67 00 25 00 5A 00  f.K.E.P.6.g.%.Z.
 30 00 75 00 4E 00 44 00 50 00 70 00 00 00        0.u.N.D.P.p...
W3_ROOT_DATA
 66 00 4B 00 45 00 50 00 36 00 67 00 25 00 5A 00  f.K.E.P.6.g.%.Z.
 30 00 75 00 4E 00 44 00 50 00 70 00 00 00        0.u.N.D.P.p...
_SC_MSExchangeDS
 70 00 61 00 73 00 73 00 77 00 6F 00 72 00 64 00  p.a.s.s.w.o.r.d.
_SC_MSExchangeIMC
 70 00 61 00 73 00 73 00 77 00 6F 00 72 00 64 00  p.a.s.s.w.o.r.d.
_SC_MSExchangeIS
 70 00 61 00 73 00 73 00 77 00 6F 00 72 00 64 00  p.a.s.s.w.o.r.d.
_SC_MSExchangeKMS
 70 00 61 00 73 00 73 00 77 00 6F 00 72 00 64 00  p.a.s.s.w.o.r.d.
_SC_MSExchangeMTA
 70 00 61 00 73 00 73 00 77 00 6F 00 72 00 64 00  p.a.s.s.w.o.r.d.
_SC_MSExchangeSA
 70 00 61 00 73 00 73 00 77 00 6F 00 72 00 64 00  p.a.s.s.w.o.r.d.
Z:\>
```

Tools such as **LSADUMP2.EXE** can show all the LSA Secrets in plaintext, as specified in [31]. This includes the machine account password (see **$MACHINE.ACC** above), the password for the anonymous FTP user (see

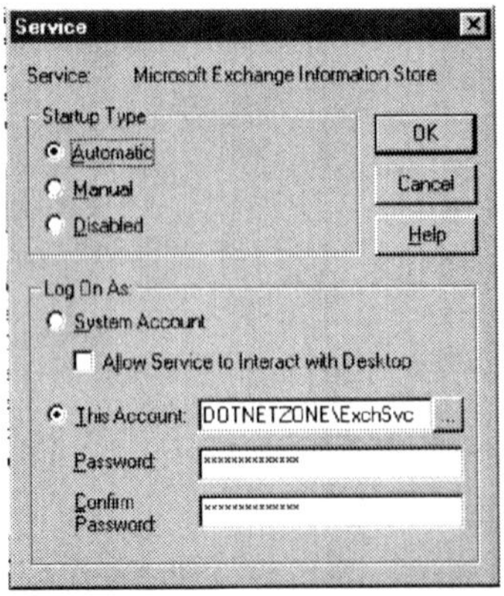

Figure 3.11 Exchange 5.5 service configuration.

FTPD_ANONYMOUS_DATA above), and the password for the interdomain trust account with a domain by the name of IMMEDIENT (see **G$$IMMEDIENT** above). Some information, such as cached user credentials **NL$xx**, is stored in a hashed form so that it cannot be easily decrypted and used. The **_SC_MSExchangexx** entries pertain to Exchange 5.5 services, and **LSADUMP2.EXE** can display information about the password used by the Exchange 5.5 user account in cleartext.

Microsoft Exchange Server 5.5 on this computer uses a service account, as shown in Figure 3.11. **LSADUMP2.EXE** shows the password for this account, used by all Exchange 5.5 services on this computer.

The following example shows a similar dump from a Windows 2003 domain controller for the domain INS:

```
$MACHINE.ACC
 F7 40 FD C0 4E 33 78 D4 AA 99 3B 7A 12 A4 4B AF  .@..N3x...;z..K.
 21 79 98 17 80 A8 FA 01 2A E2 6B 0F              !y......*.k.

D6318AF1-462A-48C7-B6D9-ABB7CCD7975E-SRV
 C9 55 F7 34 CE C3 E2 46 BA 6F 3B F2 04 B7 D1 39  .U.4...F.o;....9

DPAPI_SYSTEM
 01 00 00 00 D1 7F C1 09 71 41 6C 9A 9C 34 E6 CC  ........qAl..4..
 AA 63 D1 C2 A0 AD E8 97 98 30 10 9D 6E BE EF 0E  .c.......0..n...
 23 78 04 4D 51 FF 02 28 AF 81 E3 81              #x.MQ..(....

L$HYDRAENCKEY_28ada6da-d622-11d1-9cb9-00c04fb16e75
 52 53 41 32 48 00 00 00 00 02 00 00 3F 00 00 00  RSA2H.......?...
 01 00 01 00 97 94 A5 12 69 73 5D DC 73 1C 1E 09  ........is].s...
 77 4E 5F AB E2 FB A5 D0 EB 27 2E DC FD 02 EE 5E  wN_......'.....^
 46 AB A8 89 76 D3 59 6B E2 25 86 8C FE D4 B2 9F  F...v.Yk.%......
 A7 FA BE FA BA 81 5A 6F 51 E9 CD BE 33 46 77 29  ......ZoQ...3Fw)
```

```
 9D 25 1B A0 00 00 00 00 00 00 00 00 A1 8F 67 6C  .%...........gl
 53 A8 F0 88 A4 1F 74 53 ED 38 64 41 48 41 F2 2D  S.....tS.8dAHA.-
 BA 50 F7 80 53 6C 56 8C 39 24 98 CA 00 00 00 00  .P..SlV.9$......
 37 19 FF 5A 40 D8 F0 6F 66 61 D5 53 15 40 2F D8  7..Z@..ofa.S.@/.
 07 EE BA B6 41 84 E1 7D 2C BE 4C 9E 1D BB 4F CA  ....A..},.L...O.
 00 00 00 00 A1 23 18 05 49 B7 8E 34 A8 C8 41 7D  .....#..I..4..A}
 63 70 37 7E 0C 55 13 AA 13 8F 7B B0 44 5A 75 49  cp7~.U....{.DZuI
 AD 61 30 66 00 00 00 00 5D 6F 21 8D E3 B0 DF 6E  .a0f....]o!....n
 5F 34 37 6F F6 A3 BE EE 06 4C 0C 29 90 97 78 0A  _47o.....L.)..x.
 C0 2C 83 B5 F3 92 65 2B 00 00 00 00 59 E2 7E 69  .,....e+....Y.~i
 9D 90 28 12 46 21 51 FD 1E 2A D1 9C 6C 0A 67 DB  ..(.F!Q..*..l.g.
 30 7D 36 B8 C4 73 31 14 6E F9 00 A8 00 00 00 00  0}6..s1.n.......
 C1 E9 9F 7B 0B A2 CB 25 1B E7 46 89 16 E1 2C 3C  ...{...%..F...,<
 C7 D8 8A 9E 95 F1 78 2B F5 F1 9E 84 50 B7 F6 1A  ......x+....P...
 5A 4E AC 51 A8 9A 6C CB B7 06 1D B2 AE 6E EA 63  ZN.Q..l......n.c
 8D 37 94 A0 9D 75 02 FA 4B 74 7C 3F 51 AF 78 12  .7...u..Kt|?Q.x.
 00 00 00 00 00 00 00 00 00 00 00 00 00 00 00 00  ................
 00 00 00 00 00 00 00 00 00 00 00 00 00 00 00 00  ................
 00 00 00 00 00 00 00 00 00 00 00 00              ............

L$RTMTIMEBOMB_1320153D-8DA3-4e8e-B27B-0D888223A588
 00 D9 04 BA A6 E0 C5 01                          ........

L$TermServLiceningSignKey-12d4b7c8-77d5-11d1-8c24-00c04fa3080d

L$TermServLicensingExchKey-12d4b7c8-77d5-11d1-8c24-00c04fa3080d

L$TermServLicensingServerId-12d4b7c8-77d5-11d1-8c24-00c04fa3080d

L$TermServLicensingStatus-12d4b7c8-77d5-11d1-8c24-00c04fa3080d

L${6B3E6424-AF3E-4bff-ACB6-DA535F0DDC0A}
 B9 DE 5E 63 02 79 45 A9 87 B3 05 33 88 92 65 60  ..^c.yE....3..e`
 39 42 48 37 43 CE D4 C5 D7 9A 7B A6 94 C7 06 EE  9BH7C.....{.....
 76 3F DA AD 65 AC B8 EF 25 52 F6 B6 11 1E 31 5F  v?..e...%R....1_
 21 64 18 89 23 AD 72 2A                          !d..#.r*

NL$KM
 EE 5B C9 A9 FE 6E 8D 04 40 36 1B 1E 1C 13 1D 0E  .[...n..@6......
 4A 88 54 57 45 0E 6C 0F A1 FA 58 59 4D F5 5E 09  J.TWE.l...XYM.^.
 B5 A7 85 27 1C 7C C1 1A 21 7B BA E8 43 54 AE BF  ...'.|..!{..CT..
 55 B7 91 C3 EB 84 E2 4A 1C F8 53 0D 4B 02 B2 83  U......J..S.K...

RADIUSServer.steve.ins.com
 70 00 61 00 73 00 73 00 77 00 6F 00 72 00 64 00  p.a.s.s.w.o.r.d.

SAC
 02 00 00 00                                      ....

SAI
 02 00 00 00                                      ....

SCM:{148f1a14-53f3-4074-a573-e1ccd344e1d0}
 00 00                                            ..
```

```
SCM:{3D14228D-FBE1-11D0-995D-00C04FD919C1}
 32 00 30 00 31 00 79 00 30 00 31 00 2E 00 3B 00  2.0.1.y.0.1...;.
 73 00 36 00 6C 00 68 00 38 00 4C 00 00 00        s.6.l.h.8.L...

_SC_Alerter

_SC_ALG

_SC_Dhcp

_SC_Dnscache

_SC_LicenseService

_SC_LmHosts

_SC_MSDTC

_SC_RpcLocator

_SC_stisvc

_SC_TlntSvr

_SC_WebClient
```

Most of the services — including DHCP and MSDTC — use either the Local Service account or the Network Service account. As these are system accounts in Windows 2003, their passwords do not need to be stored in LSA Secrets and therefore cannot be compromised.

Another interesting discovery here is the password for RADIUS. As discussed later in this book, RADIUS servers and clients share common secrets used to authenticate the communicating parties, before user authentication, authorization, and accounting take place. The password used by RADIUS clients is also stored as an LSA Secret.

Considering the sensitive information stored in the LSA Secrets database, the operating system provides for cryptographic protection for the LSA store. First, the operating system applies an undocumented encryption mechanism. Apparently, this mechanism is reversible and is only meant to hide LSA Secrets from an attacker who tries casual access to them using registry editing tools only. A determined attacker might be able to obtain all the secrets. Second, since the advent of SYSKEY, LSA Secrets have been additionally encrypted with the SYSKEY of the computer, where they reside (see Chapter 3.2.8.4). By default, SYSKEY information is stored in the registry, and this makes SYSKEY encryption reversible for an attacker who has physical access to the computer. The attacker can make a copy of the SYSTEM and SECURITY files of the registry and take these with him to analyze them on a computer, where he can change the administrator password for the machine from which these accounts were taken, boot into the operating system, and dump the contents of LSA.

When the operating system boots, the **LSASS.EXE** module automatically launches and it starts LSA. The **LSASS.EXE** module then decrypts all the LSA secrets using both SYSKEY (if used) and the Local LSA Secrets encryption (possibly based on DES), and stores LSA Secrets in cleartext in memory. An application that has administrative access to the computer (or one that at least has the **seDebugPrivilege**) can dump the contents of the memory and show all the LSA Secrets, a technique on which most LSA Secret dumping applications rely.

3.2.10 Logon Cache

When users log on to a domain, the workstation or server from which the logon is taking place will try to contact a domain controller for their own domain in an attempt to authenticate the user. However, there might be circumstances when the workstation cannot access the domain controller and should still allow logon to the domain. This may be performed using cached credentials from previous successful logons that the same user has had from this workstation.

For a user to use his previously cached credentials, he must be able to provide the correct username and password. The cached credentials contain a copy of the user NT Hash that is used to authenticate the user locally, when the domain controller is not available. Cached credentials also contain the user access token, with user and group SIDs and other information, so that the workstation can simulate a domain logon and utilize cached group membership even when the domain controller is not available.

Apparently, cached credentials will only cache password hashes when a successful domain logon was performed; and if the user password is changed on a domain controller in the meantime, the user will need to use an old password to log on locally using cached credentials.

In Windows NT 4.0 and earlier, both NT and LM cached entries are generated and stored as LSA Secrets, and are not additionally encrypted (see subsection 3.2.9). The protection of cached password hashes is therefore equivalent to the protection of local account password hashes without SYSKEY.

The process of caching credentials and logon cache protection is different in Windows 2000 and later. Once the user has logged in successfully, the system will add an entry for the user credentials and access token under the following registry location: **HKLM\Security\Cache** (Windows 2000 and later). There is one value of type REG_BINARY for each successful logon attempt, and by default there will be up to ten entries in the logon cache. The names of the entries are of the form **NL$x**, where **x** is a number between 1 and the maximum number of cache entries.

All the information provided by the user during the logon process is stored in the local password cache, including the username, domain name, as well as the NT hash. Login information is stored in a data structure that, in addition to other information, contains a hashed password hash, the username, and the domain name of the user who has successfully logged in. The hashed password hash is an MD4 hash of the NT password hash, salted using bitwise OR (addition) with the lowercase username. The username and domain name are stored in lowercase in the data structure.

In Windows 2000 and later, information is encrypted using the LSA key, and only the NT hash will be stored. The logon cache data structure for the user is encrypted and stored in the registry using the format in Table 3.12.

To encrypt the credentials structure, the following algorithm is used:

1. An LSA encryption key (**L**) is generated, probably by DES-encrypting the LSA secret **NL$KM** using a fixed string.
2. An RC4 encryption key is generated by calculating the HMAC-MD5 of LSA Key **L** using the Key Material field as the HMAC key:
   - A new LSA encryption key (**A**) is generated by means of an XOR operation on the LSA encryption key (**L**) and a well-known string (64 times the symbol "6" — this is the constant HMAC MD5 **ipad** string).
   - A new LSA encryption key (**B**) is generated by means of an XOR operation on the LSA encryption key (**L**) and a well-known string (64 times the symbol "V" — this is the constant HMAC MD5 **opad** string).
   - A new LSA key (**C**) is generated by calculating the MD5 hash of the concatenation of Key **A** and the Key Material field from the registry entry structure (see Table 3.12).
   - A new key (**D**) is generated by calculating the MD5 hash of the concatenation of Key **B** and Key **C.**
3. The Credentials Structure field is encrypted using RC4 and the encryption key from Step 2.

Table 3.12 Registry Entry Structure for Cached Logon Credentials

Metadata (plaintext)	*Key Material (plaintext, random)*	*Miscellaneous (plaintext)*	*Credentials Structure (stored encrypted — Win2K and later)*
64 bytes	16 bytes	16 bytes	Variable

Unlike LM and NT hashes that are a hash of the user password, cached credentials contain a salted (using the username) hash of the password hash (double hashed and salted password). Apparently, because this is a hash and not an encrypted string, it is not an easy task to find the original string (password) that produced the hash, and there might be more than one string that can correspond to the hash. Therefore, potential attackers will find it much more difficult to obtain useful information from cached credentials than from user hashes. At the time of this writing, mainly dictionary attacks can be used against cached credentials hashes, and the success of such attacks will virtually depend on the complexity of the user password and the likelihood that the password is contained in the dictionary file of the attacker.

A popular application used to visualize cached logon credentials is CacheDump [28]. This application requires administrative privileges on the computer where it is started, and it works against a live operating system. Considering the fact that all the information required to extract password hashes is contained in the registry of the local computer, it is also technically possible to obtain cached logon information from an offline copy of the registry.

3.2.11 Protected Storage

While LSA Secrets provide a protected storage area for system secrets, such as machine password and other confidential information, user applications need to store confidential information that belongs to users, applications, and services. Although some applications may choose to store such information in the LSA Secrets database, this is typically not appropriate because LSA Secrets is a single store for the machine, and users with administrative privileges can access LSA Secrets. There is no isolation between secrets that belong to one user or applications from these that belong to other users and applications.

Therefore, with Internet Explorer 4.0, Microsoft introduced the Protected Storage service to allow users to save Web logon and other confidential information in their own dedicated and encrypted space. Access to the Protected Storage was provided by the service running in the context of **PSTORES.EXE**. User confidential information was stored in the user portion of the registry **HKEY_CURRENT_USER\Software\Microsoft\Protected Storage System Provider** (the user portion of the registry is stored in the user profile, in the **NTUser.DAT** file and the associated LOG file). Access to the Protected Storage service was provided by means of CryptoAPI functions.

Protected Storage is used to store the following user information:

- Outlook Express passwords (OE account information itself is stored in **HKEY_CURRENT_USER\Software\Microsoft\Internet Account Manager**)
- Internet Explorer protected sites passwords
- Internet Explorer Autocomplete information, which may include usernames and passwords (form based authentication) and other confidential information
- User private keys (Windows 2000 and earlier)

The approach that Protected Storage uses to protect information is not documented. It is believed that the operating system generates a per-user encryption key, which is then stored in the user profile. The Protected Storage information is encrypted using this encryption key and is stored in the user profile as well (see above). Considering the fact that both are stored in the user profile, it is theoretically possible to decrypt user information, including private keys and Internet Explorer passwords, by having access to the user profile. This is something that administrators have by default, and because roaming user profiles by default have a copy on every computer that the user logged in from, this makes the user profile available to local machine administrators as well.

When a user tries to access information from protected store, the relevant Protected Storage service (**PSTORE.EXE** in Windows NT, **SERVICES.EXE** in Windows 2000 and **LSASS.EXE** in Windows XP and Windows 2003) will retrieve the user encryption key from the registry (the key is stored in registry keys to which the user does not have access by default), and then impersonate the user and access his encrypted data. The Protected Storage service will then decrypt the data and provide it to the user.

Although the Protected Storage service stores usernames and passwords, it is not really an essential component for user authentication; it is just a moderately secure place to store information.

3.2.12 Data Protection API (DPAPI)

Although Internet Explorer and Outlook Express in Windows 2000 and Windows XP still use the Protected Storage service, the operating system and newer applications now rely on a different mechanism for storing secrets — Data Protection API (DPAPI). In fact, DPAPI by itself does not provide for a protected storage; it is just a set of functions provided to user applications and the operating system to protect sensitive data. It is up to the applications and the operating system to decide where they will store this data. Data is encrypted using 3DES and a key that is not stored anywhere on the system, which makes this data protection mechanism very reliable. DPAPI also provides machine-level encryption, which is shared by all users on the computer and does not use a particular user profile.

Typically, DPAPI applications store protected information in the following location:

%USERPROFILE%\Application Data\Microsoft\Protect\<User SID>

This is, however, not necessarily the location for any type of information and, as already discussed, DPAPI does not restrict user applications (e.g., the user shell) in terms of information storage location. For example, unless user certificate keypairs are stored on smart cards or other secure storage devices, they will be encrypted using DPAPI and stored in the following location of the user profile:

%USERPROFILE%\Application Data\Microsoft\Crypto\RSA\<User SID>

for RSA keys, and

%USERPROFILE%\Application Data\Microsoft\Crypto\DSA\<User SID>

for DSA keys. Certificates are not encrypted (they are not confidential) and they are stored in

%USERPROFILE%\Application Data\Microsoft\
SystemCertificates\My\Certificates

DPAPI prepares to encrypt user data by generating a unique Master Key (key material) for each user. Once this key has been generated, DPAPI uses it to encrypt and decrypt user data every time an application requests this.

Microsoft has not documented this process but security researchers on the Internet believe that the following algorithm is used to calculate and store the Master Key for DPAPI for the specific user.

To prepare for encryption, DPAPI performs the following steps to provide a Master Key:

1. A Master Key is generated — 512 random bytes.
2. A password hash is calculated on the user password using the SHA-1 algorithm.
3. The SHA-1 hash of the user password is used in the PBKDF1 algorithm (some sources refer to PBKDF2, although this contradicts with the use of SHA-1), using a random 16-byte salt and an iteration count of 4000 (by default) to generate a Master Key Encryption Key.

- First, the PBKDF1 algorithm performs a bitwise OR of the SHA-1 password hash from the previous step and the salt.
- Second, the PBKDF1 algorithm calculates the SHA-1 hash of the bitwise OR result from the previous step.
- Then, the PBKDF1 algorithm repeats 3999 more times (by default) and calculates the SHA-1 hash of the hash from the previous step.
- The result from the previous step is the Master Key Encryption Key.

4. The Master Key is encrypted using the 3DES encryption algorithm and the Master Key Encryption Key as the key. This is to protect the Master Key from information disclosure. The result is stored in the **CREDHIST** file.
5. The HMAC-SHA1 of the Master Key is calculated using the Master Key Encryption Key as the key, then encrypted using 3DES and the same Master Key Encryption Key. This is meant to protect the Master Key from unauthorized modification. The result is then stored in the **CREDHIST** file.
6. The random 16-byte salt and the iteration count (4000 by default) are stored in cleartext in the **CREDHIST** file.
7. A new 128-bit Globally Unique Identifier (GUID) is generated for the Master Key and saved in the **CREDHIST** file.

More information on the PBKDF1 and PBKDF2 algorithms can be found in [32].

By default, user workstations using DPAPI will try to generate a new Master Key every 90 days. The new master key will be different from the old one because the random salt will be different, and possibly because the user may have changed his password. The new Master Key will be appended to the **CREDHIST** file; it will not overwrite existing keys. Master Keys are kept forever. The **CREDHIST** file is stored in the user profile in the following location:

%USERPROFILE%\Application Data\Microsoft\Protect

DPAPI is another information protection mechanism not published to the security community. Nevertheless, it is believed that the subsequent information is correct. If an application requests DPAPI data encryption, the following will happen:

1. DPAPI extracts the current Master Key from the **CREDHIST** file using the current user password and following the above Master Key encryption process but decrypting instead of encrypting in Step 4.

2. A 16-byte random salt is generated.
3. The Master Key and the salt are combined using SHA-1.
4. The hash from the previous step is then combined with an optional user-defined session password and the user logon password. This results in a session encryption key.
5. The cleartext is encrypted using the 3DES Protocol and the above session key.
6. The cleartext is hashed using HMAC-SHA-1 using the same session key.
7. The function returns an encrypted BLOB to the calling application so that it can store it where appropriate; the BLOB includes the encrypted user data, an HMAC of the user data for integrity validation, the random salt, and a Master Key GUID.

DPAPI decryption works the other way around: the user application just passes the encrypted BLOB and, as a result, receives the plaintext.

When applications require the use of DPAPI, they will typically call the DPAPI functions **CryptProtectData( )** and **CryptUnprotectData( )**. It is interesting to note that starting with Windows 2003, DPAPI provides applications with a function that can be used to protect a portion of the memory of a running process as well — **CryptProtectMemory( )** — so applications can protect cleartext passwords against online attacks.

On a Windows 2000 or Windows XP computer, when a user changes his password using standard operating system tools and APIs on a workstation that he is logged in to, DPAPI will automatically open the **CREDHIST** file, decrypt all the master keys using the old password, and then encrypt all the master keys with the new password. Thus, the user can transparently use DPAPI functions even after changing his password.

On the other hand, if the password of a Windows XP user is changed from a remote location (such as an administrator resetting the user password using administrative tools) or by an application that does not use operating system password changing APIs (e.g., LDAPS modify against the **unicodePwd** attribute), DPAPI will not be able to hook into the password changing process, decrypt and re-encrypt all the master keys in the **CREDHIST** file. When the user logs in to the system next time, DPAPI will not be able to extract the Master Keys and user will not be able to decrypt his secrets using the password that the user used to log in — that is because his **CREDHIST** files still store Master Keys encrypted with the old password. Because the Reset password functionality is an essential part of user account management and for Windows XP domain members, DPAPI will also store a backup copy of the Master Key; it will use the backup copy if the primary copy is lost or inaccessible. If a Windows XP computer is a member of a Windows 2003 or later domain, every time a new Master Key is generated, the client will use RPC to connect to a domain controller and obtain the shared domain controller certificate that has a corresponding private key known to all DCs in the domain. Then the client will extract the public key from the certificate and use it to encrypt a backup copy of the Master Key and store it in the **CREDHIST** file. When a user tries to decrypt his data using DPAPI, if for some reason he cannot access his Master Key in the **CREDHIST** file, his workstation will automatically extract the encrypted Backup Key, initiate an encrypted secured RPC channel to a domain controller, and request that the Backup Key be decrypted by a domain controller. Because all the domain controllers have a copy of the private key for the encrypting certificate, the domain controller will decrypt the Backup Key and provide it to the client that can then use it to access DPAPI encrypted data and potentially re-encrypt the **CREDHIST** file.

Windows 2000 supports a different approach for DPAPI data recovery, which is pretty much a result of Windows 2000 legacy in Windows NT 4.0 and earlier domains, where domain controllers do not have certificates. Windows 2000 can use an LSA secret on the client computer (instead of a domain controller certificate) to encrypt the backup key and store in the **CREDHIST** file. The LSA Secret used for this is believed to be DPAPI_SYSTEM (see subsection 3.2.9). If DPAPI is not able to access data for a specific user, it can obtain the LSA Secret (stored locally), decrypt the Backup Key, and then use it to decrypt confidential data. The problem with this data recovery approach is that someone with physical access to the user workstation can potentially obtain a copy of the user profile and attach the **CREDHIST** and other files to a new local user profile, log in with this profile on the user workstation, and use the backup access mechanism to decrypt all the user secrets because the use of backup secret does not depend on the user password by definition. In this case, due to the fact that user secret protection depends on LSA Secrets protection, it is recommended that they be protected appropriately, and that SYSKEY be used to additionally protect LSA Secrets and, as a result, user passwords.

If the Windows XP computer is not a member of a domain, DPAPI will not store a backup key. This behavior is described in [33] and is by design. It protects against the attacks described above. Windows XP Service Pack 1 and later users can change the behavior of their computers to Windows 2000 mode and have their backup keys encrypted with an LSA Secret instead of a DC public key. To accomplish this, the administrator needs to use the following registry setting:

HKEY_LOCAL_MACHINE\SOFTWARE\Microsoft\Cryptography\Protect\Providers\df9d8cd0-1501-11d1-8c7a-00c04fc297eb\MasterKeyLegacyNt4Domain:DWORD=1.

With either Windows XP or Windows 2000, if the user knows the previous password and can change his current password to be equivalent to the previous password, this will suffice to allow the user to decrypt all the master keys and restore his access to protected secrets. Another option for Windows XP stand-alone computer users is to backup their passwords and keys to password reset disks, which basically creates a floppy disk with all the encrypted user credentials and secrets on it. If for some reason the users lose access to their stored secrets, these can be restored from the floppy.

Windows XP and Windows 2003 can use both Protected Storage and DPAPI to protect user information. Credential Manager information as well as user private keys will be protected by the more secure DPAPI approach. However, Internet Explorer will still use Protected Storage to save Autocomplete information, and Outlook Express will use Protected Storage to store user account information.

It is important to understand that both the Protected Storage and DPAPI were designed to protect confidential information against offline attacks. Protected Storage is possibly not as effective as DPAPI in protecting user secrets against offline attacks because, unlike DPAPI, it does not rely on user-provided entropy, such as the user password. However, both approaches are vulnerable to online attacks, especially those from Trojan horses. Both Protected Storage and DPAPI allow user applications to access protected information transparently and they decrypt it on-the-fly as long as the user has logged on to the system and has his profile loaded. Again, this behavior is by design and it allows any application running with the privileges of the user, and having access to the user profile, to freely access confidential information on behalf of the user; the assumption is that if the user knows the password to log in with the specific set of credentials, and this password has not been modified offline or remotely, then the access is genuine. DPAPI provides for an additional password to be requested by the user when encrypting information but it is rarely used. It is virtually possible for potential attackers to come up with applications that if run by the user can dump the Protected Storage database, or DPAPI stored secrets, and provide them to the potential attacker.

3.2.13 Credential Manager

With Protected Storage and the strong encryption provided by DPAPI in place, the logical evolutionary step that Windows XP and Windows 2003 provides is Credential Manager, a new authentication component considered by some researchers a client-side single sign-on (SSO) solution.

Historically, when a user on a Windows computer tries to access a resource, the request is passed to LSA to handle the authentication, and LSA forwards this request to an authentication package. The typical behavior of authentication packages is to use the current user credentials (either an existing Kerberos ticket, or current username and password for NTLM/LM connections). However, in Windows XP and later, the authentication package will first go to Credential Manager and request credentials to use in order to access the resource. If Credential Manager has an entry for this target (the specific server that the user is trying to access), then it will provide the specific credentials to be used by the authentication package. If there is no entry for the specific server (target), Credential Manager will return the current (primary) credentials, which simulates the behavior of Windows 2000 and earlier operating systems. If the connection succeeds, the user will start using resources on the remote server using his primary credentials. However, if the connection fails, the authentication package will inform LSA, which will pass the details to the requesting application. The application will then prompt the user to specify a different set of credentials to access the resource, and may present the user with the option to save the credentials in the credential store. Depending on the information provided by the user, the connection to the resource may succeed, and if the user has requested so, the credentials will be provided to Credential Manager to store.

To perform these operations, Credential Manager uses a credentials database, stored in the user profile. Credential Manager stores the following information as part of each entry:

- *Target.* This is the name of the server, or DNS domain, for which the specified credentials should be used. This can be a NetBIOS name, a host FQDN, or a domain name. The asterisk ('*') symbol can be used to specify a DNS domain and all its sub-domains. It is important to note that credentials are specified and used on a per-target basis, regardless of the protocol that the application may want to use. Credential Manager cannot handle connections to a server using one set of credentials for the CIFS/SMB protocol and a different set of credentials for HTTP, for example.
- *User credentials.* This will be one of the following (see [32] for more information):
  - *Generic.* The credentials will be stored but will not be provided to a particular authentication package. The requesting application will handle these credentials.
  - *Domain credentials.* These are NTLM/Kerberos credentials that will be passed on to the Negotiate authentication package when

the user attempts a connection to this resource. The credentials will be a username (either using the domainname\username syntax, or a UPN) and a plaintext Unicode password (not a password hash).
- *Certificate.* A certificate can be used to authenticate the user. In this case, the private key that corresponds to this certificate should be used during authentication. If the private key is stored on a smart card, Credential Manager can store the PIN for the smart card.
- *Visible password authentication.* This is used by Microsoft authentication packages such as Microsoft Passport. The credentials stored for this type are a username and a password.

Credential Manager also supports different levels of credential persistence. The following are possible options:

- *Session.* User credentials are only stored in memory for the time of the session. They are removed when the user logs off and will not be available the next time the user logs in.
- *Local.* User credentials are stored in a local portion of the user profile, which does not roam with the user even if the user has a roaming profile. If the user tries to access the target resource from another computer, these credentials will not be available. Local credentials are stored in the

  %USERPROFILE%\Local Settings\Application Data\
  Microsoft\Credentials\<User SID>\Credentials

  file of the user profile.
- *Enterprise.* User credentials are stored in the user profile and available for the user to use on any computer on which the user profile exists. With roaming profiles, the user can use his stored credentials on any computer in the enterprise. Enterprise credentials are stored in the

  %USERPROFILE%\Application Data\Microsoft\Credentials\
  <User SID>\Credentials

  file of the user profile.

Credential Manager stored credentials can be managed by users in several ways:

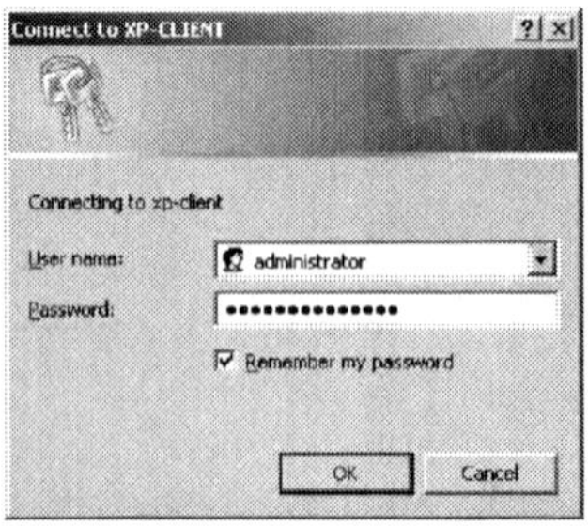

Figure 3.12 Storing credentials when accessing a resource.

- *Windows Explorer.* When a user connects to a resource using Windows Explorer or Internet Explorer, he can select to have his credentials remembered by checking the "Remember my password" checkbox. This effectively creates an entry in the Credential Manager database.
- **NET.EXE**. Windows XP Professional and Windows 2003 have a special switch for the **NET.EXE** command — **/SAVECRED** — which causes the credentials specified for the connection to be stored in the Credential Manager database (see Figure 3.12).
- *Control Panel.* Users can access the Credential Manager entries from Control Panel, using either the Stored User Names and Password applet (Windows 2003 Server) or the User Accounts, Manage my Network Passwords (for a specific account) in Windows XP.
- **CMDKEY.EXE**. Windows 2003 provides a command line interface, **CMDKEY.EXE**, which can be used to manage Credential Manager entries.

Credential Manager can also store credentials for RAS connections. These credentials will only be used when the user is connected using RAS (Client VPN using PPTP/L2TP or Dial-up Networking via a modem or ISDN adapter), and not when the user is connected on the LAN without using a RAS connection. RAS credentials can be used as the primary credentials for the user when connecting to network resources, even if the user has logged on to his remote client computer using a different set of credentials.

3.2.14 Case Study: Exploring Credential Manager

In the following example, user Susan logged on as a user from the **ins.com** domain on computer **STEVE,** which will access resources on computer **BILL**. Susan will specify a different set of credentials to be used by Credential Manager.

Let us assume that Susan Red has logged on interactively as user Administrator from the **ins.com** domain to computer **STEVE** and she is performing some administrative tasks. At the same time, Susan has configured her local profile on computer **STEVE** so that Credential Manager uses Susan's credentials to connect to shared resources on computer **BILL** (**bill.ins.com**) regardless of the fact that she is already logged in using a domain account. Here is what happens when she maps a file share from computer **BILL**:

```
C:\> whoami /user

USER INFORMATION
----------------

User Name          SID
================== =============================================
ins\administrator S-1-5-21-676691431-2304381362-2152039065-500

C:\> cmdkey /list

Currently stored credentials:

    Target: bill.ins.com
    Type: Domain Password
    User: susan@ins.com

C:\>
C:\> net use Y: \\bill.ins.com\Test
The command completed successfully.

C:\> net use
New connections will be remembered.

Status       Local     Remote                    Network
-------------------------------------------------------------------------------
OK           Y:        \\bill.ins.com\Test       Microsoft Windows
                                                  Network
The command completed successfully.

C:\>
```

The currently logged-in user is INS\Administrator, and the Credential Manager cache has an entry requiring access to server **bill.ins.com** to be performed using the credentials of **susan@ins.com** (password is not displayed). When Susan tries to map drive Y: using the **net use** command, she does not need to specify explicitly that she wants to use her own credentials; Credential Manager will handle the credentials for the particular server and provide the authentication package with the username and password for this server.

If a user on computer **BILL** checked user sessions to the server, here is what he would see:

```
C:\> net session

Computer             User name        Client Type          Opens Idle time
------------------------------------------------------------------------------
\\10.0.2.102         SUSAN            Windows Server 20        0 00:00:32

The command completed successfully.
```

Susan has effectively logged on as herself over the network to the file server, despite the fact that she is using another user's credentials on the client computer. One can conclude that Credential Manager credentials effectively override any other implicit credentials that the client may have used to access this particular server.

3.3 Windows Domain Authentication

User workstations running Windows NT are autonomous in terms of security mechanisms. Domain membership is an addition to the stand-alone security model — not a replacement. From an authentication perspective, domains are a trusted third party and authentication authority. This section discusses domain authentication and the additional features that it provides.

3.3.1 Domain Model

It is very important for every workstation and server to run a secure operating system that provides a good authentication foundation. Almost all computers today run in some form of a networked environment, which makes network authentication equally as important as local, interactive authentication.

Being a relatively new operating system, Windows was designed with networking in mind. Windows (more specifically, the Windows NT product family) has always had its network authentication model based on the idea of logical security groups, called domains, which allow for shared security policies and centralized authentication (as well as centralized administration).

In a simple and small network, Windows users can communicate without using a domain model. In such a network, every Windows computer is responsible for managing its own security policies; it has a locally stored (in the SAM file) account database. It is responsible for authenticating both local users who access resources from the computer console and network users who try to access resources across the network to which this computer is connected. This is considered a decentralized authentication (and administration) model, with each SAM database on each computer being a completely separate authority from other computers on the network.

This model has worked and will work for many small networks. However, this model is not scalable and does not support mid-size and large enterprise networks. Some of the problems associated with this model include:

- Provided that every computer shares resources on the network, every user will need to authenticate against every computer on which resources reside. Thus, because every computer has a completely separate database, the user will require a local account (potentially with the same name) on every computer on the network. If the number of computers is 1000, then managing access from each computer to all the other 999 computers will render the model unusable.
- Each SAM database is a separate authentication authority. Even when every user has an account on every computer, this user will require the same password on every computer as well. If the user needs to change his password, he will need to do so on every computer where he has an account (again, doing this for 1000 computers renders the model unusable).
- There is no easy way to enforce user policies for all the users. For example, if an organization wants to configure a minimum password length policy for such a network, the only option is to do so on a computer-by-computer basis.
- The process of adding and removing users from all the local databases when users join and leave the company will be pretty sophisticated and time consuming.

The Windows domain model was created to provide a solution for centralized authentication and administration. It is the preferred authentication approach for most Windows-based networks.

The Windows domain model is a form of single sign-on. It implements the concept of a trusted third party, has a centralized account database, and provides for centralized authentication. Information about users and computers (and potentially other information) is stored in a central database (directory). All computers that want to use this database for user authentication purposes, and agree to comply with the security policies implemented by the administrators of this central database, are said to belong to the same domain and are called domain members. The fact that all domain members agree to trust the domain and comply with common policies establishes a trust between all the domain members, and now users can authenticate to resources within this domain. The domain is considered the main logical security boundary within the Windows infrastructure.

Every domain has a name that should uniquely identify it within the network infrastructure. Windows domains use NetBIOS names, and Windows 2000/2003 support both legacy NetBIOS names and clients, and DNS names.

The central database of the domain, known as the directory services database (or simply, user database, as it is as simple as that in Windows NT 4.0 and earlier), is stored on designated Windows Server computers known as domain controllers. Each domain has at least one domain controller, and it can have a virtually unlimited number of domain controllers. Each domain controller holds exactly the same copy of the directory services database (Active Directory partitions can be considered separate directory services databases in this instance).

Windows domain controllers are responsible for:

- Authenticating users
- Providing access to and managing the directory services database
- Maintaining replicated copies of the directory services database

The reasons for having more than one domain controller include:

- *Availability.* If one domain controller fails, other domain controllers will be able to authenticate users, as all domain controllers virtually use the same database.
- *Fault tolerance.* If the directory database on a particular domain controller fails (but not if its contents are accidentally or deliberately deleted), other domain controllers will have a copy of this database that can then be used to restore the failed copy (by means of replication).
- *Load balancing.* Domain controllers can be configured to balance the load of incoming user authentication requests based on specific rules (different approaches exist to accomplish this in Windows NT and Windows 2000/2003).

Domain controllers do not have a local SAM database (although Windows 2000 and later support a special recovery mode that uses a mini-SAM database for directory services restoration purposes). Instead, they are supposed to maintain a domain directory services database.

The domain directory database stores information about security principals (and potentially about other subjects); and from a user authentication perspective, this information is very similar to the information stored in the SAM file. Security principals have SIDs (just as local accounts) and can be members of groups. They can also be granted permissions and user rights. Because the domain is considered a main authentication boundary and authority, all security principals within the domain have the same Domain ID in their SIDs, and unique (within the domain) Relative Identifiers (RIDs). The uniqueness of the RID implies uniqueness of the entire SID as well.

When logging in to a domain member computer (not domain controller) either interactively or across the network, the user can select whether he wants to use the computer local account database or the domain account database to authenticate. When a computer is a domain member, domain user accounts are likely used in the vast majority of the cases.

Apart from providing a common user database for all the member computers, domain membership does little in terms of changing the security model on the individual Windows computer. It is important to understand that although the domain is considered a security boundary, most security decisions (including such pertaining to user authentication) are made locally on the client computer or on the server computer. When a computer joins a domain, the Domain Admins global group from the domain is automatically added to the joining computer's local Administrators group, and therefore inherits the rights granted to the local Administrators group. This is the only action that provides domain administrators with administrative privileges on domain members. The local administrators on the newly joined domain member will still have full privileges to manage the computer and, technically speaking, they can even remove the Domain Admins group from the local Administrators group, therefore efficiently removing administrator privileges from the domain member for the administrators of the domain. This can be done and, strictly speaking, Windows does not require that the domain administrators be local computer administrators for every computer in the domain. The domain administrator can use a number of techniques to "enforce" a requirement for local administrative access to each domain member, even after the local domain member administrator has denied administrative access to Domain Admins. For example, in Windows 2000/2003, the domain administrator can assign a group policy of type Restricted Groups to the domain members and request that the Domain Admins group be always a member of the local Administrators group on these computers. Another approach would to assign a start-up script to the domain member computer configure the computer start-up script to modify local user groups accordingly.

3.3.2 Joining a Windows NT Domain

For a Windows computer to join a domain, it is required that both sides — computer and domain — agree on domain membership. Technically, the trust is established between the local administrator of the Windows computer and the domain administrator. In general, the two administrators will need to trust each other:

- The Windows computer administrator will trust the domain administrators to maintain the directory services database and implement mutually agreeable security policies at the domain level, which will then apply at the domain member level.
- The domain administrators will trust the Windows computer administrator to join their logical security grouping and potentially share equal or similar access privileges with other domain users.

Although both sides need to undertake actions to establish domain membership, it is believed that the local Windows workstation or server administrator that is joining the domain (which may very often be the Windows NT domain administrator at the same time) needs to trust the domain in terms of user accounts and group membership that this domain provides, as well as in terms of security policies that the domain will provide. The process of adding the workstation to the domain is an act of trust, wherein the local workstation or server administrators demonstrate trust in the domain administrators. Domain administrators will need to check thoroughly each user with whom they provide an account, and carefully assign users to domain groups, as the model of trust by default will provide any domain user with some privileges on every computer in the domain — although limited. Furthermore, when domain administrators assign users to domain groups, they need to understand that these groups might already be granted privileges on computers and resources within the network, and that the act of adding the user to a group will grant this user the privileges that are granted to the group. Again, most of these actions can be performed at the domain level, and the local computer administrator can (and very often will) be unaware of every single administrative task performed at the domain level.

It is important to understand that domain membership does not radically change the security mechanisms used by workstations and servers. Simply speaking, domain members can have an additional source of authentication information, and they will see a broader set of SIDs in user access tokens used in this workstation or server. However, the operating system will continue to authorize access to resources as before, pretty much by means of comparing these domain SIDs against local access control lists and entries (ACLs and ACEs) in DACLs and SACLs. The local operating system will assign domain users privileges to interact with it as specified by the local user rights policies. Another difference from a security perspective is that now domain administrators can apply centralized System Policies (Windows NT 4.0 or earlier) or Group Policies (Windows 2000 and later) that might influence some security mechanisms on the domain member, but these are generally related to modifying registry settings that exist as part of the operating system anyway. Domain policies can potentially run start-up/shutdown or login scripts with system or user privileges, respectively, which apart from the fact that these scripts are run automatically, does not change their nature of being executables that need to comply with the security mechanisms imposed by the operating system.

3.3.3 Computer Accounts in the Domain

Windows computers that are domain members of either a Windows NT 4.0 or an Active Directory domain have computer accounts and passwords that they use to authenticate to the domain at start-up. If a computer fails to authenticate at start-up for reasons such as the account being deleted or the password reset, this computer will not be an effective member of the domain. Windows NT 4.0 Directory Services and Active Directory differ in the way that they create computer accounts and assign passwords to them.

In Windows NT 4.0 and earlier, when an account is created for a computer, the name of the account is set to the computer name (NetBIOS style flat name), followed by the dollar sign ("$"), and the password is set to the lowercase computer name. Thus, every user who knows the name of the account can add his workstation to the domain, provided that the workstation has the same name as the account (without the trailing dollar sign). In Windows NT 4.0 and earlier operating systems, when a workstation or server joins the domain, the user performing the operation may or may not specify the credentials of a domain administrator for the operation. If the computer account has been pre-created by the domain administrator, the user joining the workstation to the domain typically will not provide any credentials, which will result in an anonymous session.

In Active Directory and later, when an administrator creates a new computer account, he can choose whether this account is created for a legacy Windows client (pre-Windows 2000) or a new type of client (Windows 2000 or later). If the account is created for a legacy client, then the computer account and password are set as described above to allow for compatibility with older operating systems. However, if the account is created for a newer operating system, then the computer account name will be set to the computer name, followed by the dollar sign ("$").

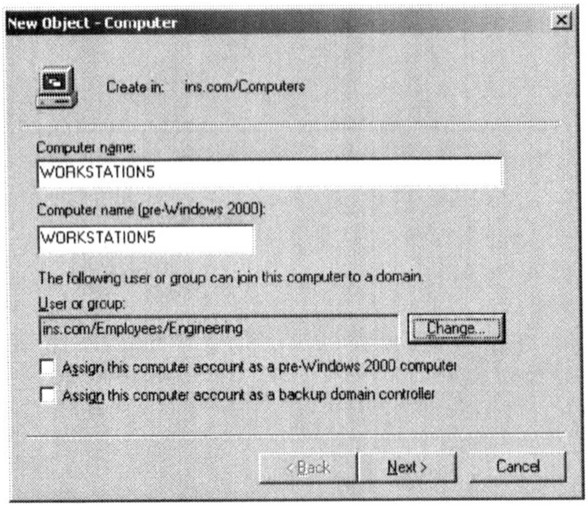

Figure 3.13 Creating a new computer account in Active Directory.

However, unlike legacy clients, the password will be set to a random string longer than 14 characters, so a LM password hash will not be generated for this computer account. When a workstation joins a domain and is running Windows 2000 or later operating systems, it will always request the user to provide an account to be used to join. The Netlogon service on the workstation then will try to log on to the new domain using the provided credentials and, if successful, will try to change the computer account password to a new randomly generated password. Thus, in Windows 2000 and later operating systems, if a computer account has already been created for a computer, the user joining the computer to the domain should be provided with privileges to modify the computer password or have domain administrative privileges. This can be performed while creating the computer account. The options available when creating a new computer account in Active Directory are shown in Figure 3.13. More information on these enhancements to AD is provided in [25].

By default, the NetLogon service on every domain member will try to change the computer account password for its own computer account on a regular basis. Windows NT 4 and earlier domain members will change their passwords every seven days by default, while Windows 2000 and later domain members will change their computer account password every 30 days by default. These password changes are performed to preserve the security of computer accounts and prevent attackers who might have obtained computer account passwords from joining unauthorized computers to the domain. Under some circumstances, the administrator of a particular computer might decide to disable password changes for this domain member only, or domain administrators might decide to implement this at the domain level. It is possible to either disable password change attempts from domain members or configure the domain controllers to reject attempts to change domain member passwords — thus, the setting can be applied on either the client site (domain member) or the server side (domain controller), or both. More information is available in [26].

Domain members store their computer passwords in the **$MACHINE.ACC** LSA secret. For more information, see subsection 3.2.9.

3.3.4 Domains and Trusts

Trusts relationships are a fundamental concept in the Windows user authentication architecture. While the domain is the main administrative unit and security boundary in Windows, the trust relationship is the bridge used to cross this boundary in enterprise environments where more than one domain may exist. Users can be separated from each other in domains created on administrative, geographical, functional, and other principles but this separation should not prevent them from accessing resources across the boundaries in a controlled fashion.

With trust relationships, if Domain B trusts Domain A, a user might have an account created for him in Domain A but at the same time this user can:

- Perform interactive logon from Domain B: log on interactively from a workstation or a server that is a member of Domain B using his user account in Domain A.
- Perform network logon to Domain B: from his workstation that may reside in either domain, access resources in both his own Domain A and the trusting Domain B.

With regard to trust relationships, domains can be either trusting (resource domains) or trusted (account domains). A trusted (account) domain has the following characteristics:

- Contains user, group, and computer accounts that can be used to access resources in the trusting (resource) domain, either by means of interactive logon (not applicable to computer accounts) or across the network
- Contains an interdomain trust account for the trusting domain (similar to user account)

A trusting (resource) domain has the following characteristics:

- Contains workstations and servers that are members of the trusting domain and can be used by users of the trusting domain or any domain trusted by this domain to log on to interactively
- Contains resources (e.g., files, printers, Web servers, database servers, etc.) that can be accessed across the network from accounts residing in one of the domains trusted by the resource domain
- Stores a password for the interdomain trust account in it LSA Secrets database and utilizes this password every time it connects to a trusted domain controller

To form a trust relationship, both the trusting (resource) and trusted (account) domain need to explicitly request this. When a trust relationship is established, the trusting (resource) domain will have a special user account created in the trusted (account) domain. This account is called the interdomain trust account. It is very similar to a user account; the name of the user used for the interdomain trust account is the same as the NetBIOS name of the trusting domain, followed by the dollar ("$") sign. The interdomain trust account has a special flag in the Account Type field that indicates that it is an interdomain trust account. The trusted domain controller stores the interdomain trust account in its directory services database. The trusting domain controller has an entry in its LSA Secrets database that stores the password that trusting domain controllers use when establishing connections to the trusted domain controller. More information on LSA Secrets and interdomain trust account passwords in trusting domains is available in subsection 3.2.9.

The trust relationship has direction. Visually, this is typically expressed using an arrow from the trusting (resource) domain to the trusted (account) domain (Figure 3.14).

If Domain B trusts Domain A, this still does not necessarily mean that Domain A trusts Domain B. Typically, if both domains need to trust each other, the trust relationship from Domain A to domain B also needs to be built (this is automatic for some trust relationships in Active Directory — see below). The relationship being formed as a result of both Domain A trusting Domain B and vice versa is called a two-way trust relationship (Figure 3.15). It is essentially a combination of two one-way trust relationships.

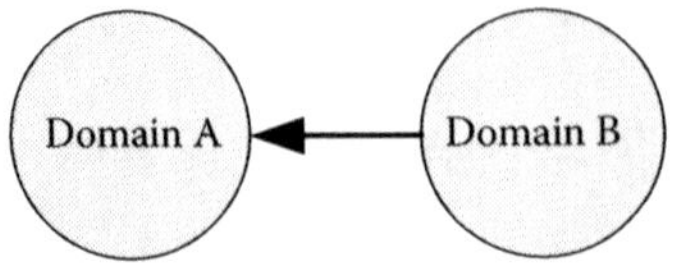

Figure 3.14 Trust relationship: Domain B trusts Domain A.

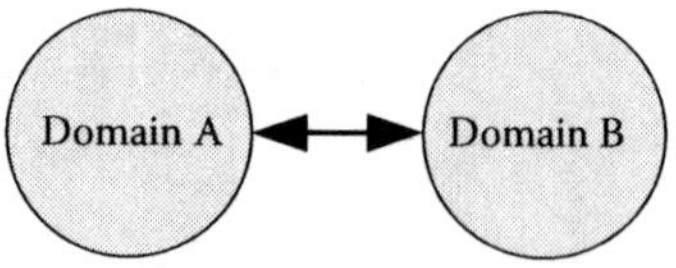

Figure 3.15 Trust relationship: two-way trust.

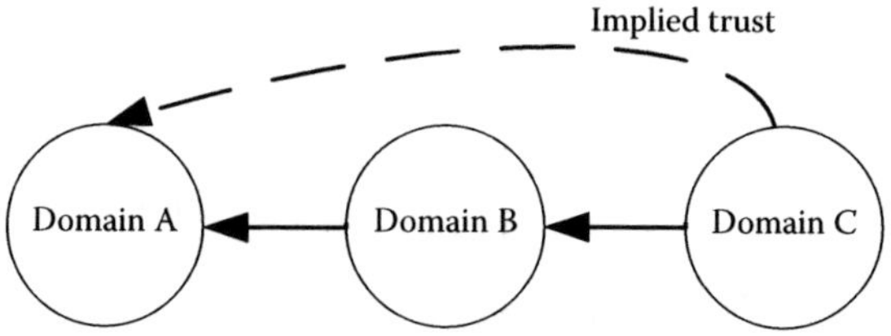

Figure 3.16 One-way transitive trust relationship.

Trust relationships can be transitive or non-transitive. Transitive trust relationships are used where a trusting (resource) domain trusts not only its directly trusted (account) domains, but also their trusted (account) domains, and so on. With a transitive trust relationship, if Domain C trusts Domain B and Domain B trusts domain A, it is implied that Domain C trusts Domain A although no direct trust relationship exists between them. The NTLM authentication protocol does not support transitive trust relationships; therefore, such transitive trusts do not exist in Windows NT 4.0 and earlier domains. The Kerberos authentication protocol supports transitive trust relationships, which allows Windows 2000 and later operating systems to build transitive trust relationships also within the forest and under circumstances with domains in other forests. This is discussed in detail later.

Transitive trust relationships can be one way (Figure 3.16) or two way (Figure 3.17). In a two-way transitive trust relationship, there is complete trust among all participating domains, although they might not trust each other directly.

Non-transitive trust relationships (Figure 3.18) are such that if Domain C trusts Domain B, and Domain B trusts Domain A, then Domain C does not automatically and implicitly trust Domain A. Both the NTLM and Kerberos authentication protocols support non-transitive trust relationships and thus this is available in both Windows NT 4.0 and Active Directory domains.

3.3.5 Case Study: Workstation Trust and Interdomain Trust

The trust relationship wherein a trusting (resource) domain trusts a trusted (account) domain is very similar to the relationship that a Windows NT

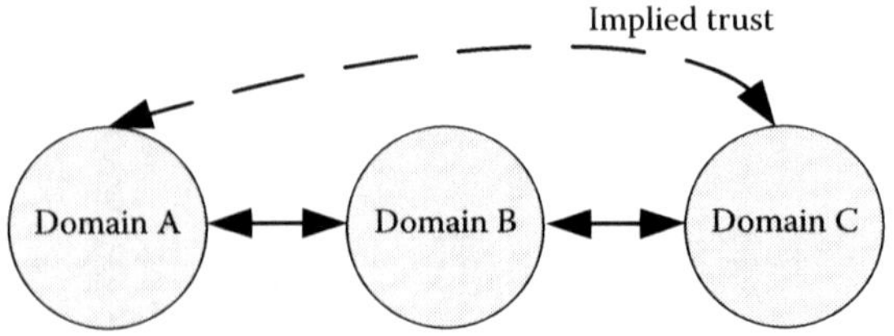

Figure 3.17 Two-way transitive trust relationship.

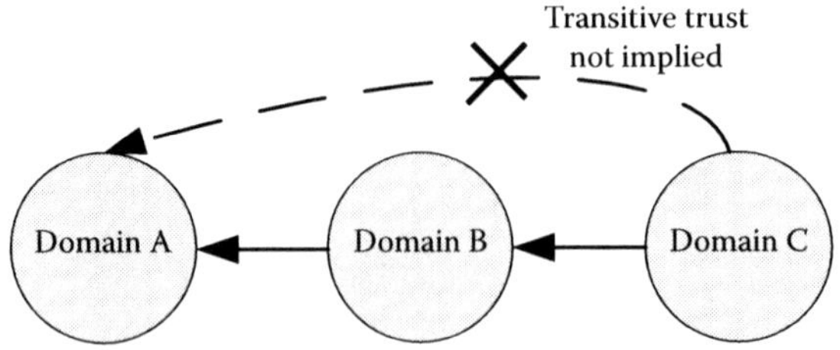

Figure 3.18 Non-transitive trust relationship.

domain member has with its domain controllers. Both the trusting domain and the domain member have their "local" accounts that users can use to authenticate and access resources "locally" (within the trusting domain, or within the computer). However, they trust another authority (a domain) and this authority's administrators, and allow accounts from this other authority to authenticate to the trusting domain computers or the domain member. The trusting (resource) domain has an interdomain trust account created in the trusted (account) domain database; the domain member has a computer account created in the domain database. Both computer accounts and interdomain trust accounts are special cases of user accounts, and they have usernames and passwords as well as other user attributes.

3.3.6 SID Filtering across Trusts

It is important to understand the philosophy of Windows NT trusts to understand the security implications of using trusts. The trusting (resource) domain administrator trusts the trusted (account) domain administrator that the latter will protect the security of the trusted (account) domain and will manage users and groups correctly. If the trusting (resource) domain administrator grants a group from the trusted (account) domain access to resources in his own domain, this is because he trusts the trusted (account) domain administrator with regard to group membership. If the trusting (resource) domain administrator allows users from the account domain to log in on workstations from the trusting (resource) domain, this is again a result of the fact that he trusts the trusted (account) domain administrators.

If the trusted domain administrator (or a malicious user imposing as this administrator, or even an intruder who has physical access to the communication channel between the trusted and trusting domain) wants to do so, he may well compromise the security of the trust. One particular scenario of compromise is where the trusted domain returns the user access token for a user who is trying to authenticate, and includes in the access token SIDs that do not really belong to this user. For example, the trusted (account) domain can return to the trusting (resource) domain a user access token that includes in it the SID of the trusting (resource) domain Domain Admins, effectively setting the privileges of the user to Administrator for the trusting domain. Such a scenario is technically possible due to the fact that user access to resources is determined based on the list of SIDs (user owned SID and group SIDs) that the user has in his access token, and anyone able to modify this list is in a position to raise or lower user privileges.

Such behavior is generally undesirable, and the ability to avoid this is critical in some scenarios; for example, if two companies set up a trust relationship between them, this is typically done to enable them to share information resources and not necessarily because the system administrators of both companies trust each other unconditionally. To help resolve this problem, starting with Windows NT SP 6a and Windows 2000 SP 3, Microsoft provides a feature called SID Filtering. Essentially, this feature allows trusting (resource) domain administrators to selectively impose a "quarantine" on the trust relationship with trusted domains, thus specifying that only SIDs that have their Domain ID equal to the Domain ID of the trusted domain will be allowed in authentication replies (access tokens) through this trust; all non-conforming SIDs in the access tokens will be dropped.

SID Filtering can be very useful from a security perspective. At the same time, it results in the trusting domain filtering all SIDs from domains with which there is no direct trust relationship, as it only allows Domain IDs from directly trusted domains. This is not a problem in Windows NT 4.0 where trusts are based on NTLM authentication and are not transitive by nature; the Windows NT 4.0 trust model requires direct trusts between domains that need to share resources. However, SID Filtering limits the functionality of Windows 2000 and Windows 2003 trust relationships, some of which (based on Kerberos) can be transitive. Using SID Filtering for trust relationships within the same Windows 2000/2003 Active Directory forest is not supported, and applying this setting can result in disruption of authentication services for some domains. Therefore, SID Filtering is effective and primarily used for trust relationships with external organizations.

More information on SID Filtering appears in [16] and [17].

3.3.7 Migration and Restructuring

User SIDs are meant to uniquely identify users but there are certain scenarios where such uniqueness is not desired and therefore Microsoft provides a way to bypass it on a temporary basis. The most notable case for the use of non-unique SIDs is when an organization wants to restructure its internal domain infrastructure. Very often as new domains are being introduced and old domains decommissioned, users from the old domains must be migrated to the new domains. At the same time, as these users are very much likely to have been granted access to various resources throughout the enterprise, their SIDs potentially exist in access controls lists (ACLs) attached to these resources. User access to resources must be retained even though the user may be "copied" or "moved" to a new domain and receives a new SID.

The user SID contains a domain ID that depicts the domain where the account was created, as well as the relative ID (RID) of the user. If a user account for an old user is created in a new domain, even if the account name and other attributes are the same, the new account will have a brand new SID, and will not provide the user with access to the resources to which the old user account has already been granted access. Although not impossible, the effort to change all the ACLs on all resources within an enterprise can be very challenging, especially if accomplished alongside risky operations such as the restructuring itself.

To help resolve this in Windows 2000 and later Native Mode domains, Microsoft supports a user attribute called **sIDHistory**. Migration tools can use this attribute to record previous user and group SIDs for a migrated user, so that the user permissions to resources are not lost after the migration. User and group SIDs can be preserved only when the migration is performed to a Windows 2000 Native Mode domain. If the user account is copied (the original account remains), the target domain needs to reside in a different forest from the original source domain. If the user account is moved (the old account deleted and a new one is created), the move can happen within the forest boundaries as well. The source domain can be a Windows NT 4.0 domain or Windows 2000 and later. The former is commonly used for migration from Windows NT 4.0 directory services to Active Directory; the latter is used for internal restructuring within Active Directory.

As always, there is a trade-off between convenience of use and security, and it is important to understand why and when **sIDHistory** should be used and what the implications of this are.

Migration tools — such as the Microsoft Active Directory Migration Tool (ADMT) or the Clone Principal (**ClonePr.VBS**) script — can be used to clone a user account from one domain to another domain in a different forest. The migration tool will then create a fresh copy of the user account in the target domain and this account will have all the same attributes as the original account, but at the same time it will have a new SID that will have the domain ID portion set to the target domain ID. Then the migration tool will copy the source account user SID, as well as all the SIDs of groups of which the user is a member, into the **sIDHistory** attribute of the newly created account in the target domain.

When a migrated user that has its **sIDHistory** attribute populated as specified above logs from a computer, this user will have the authentication domain controller build an access token for him. Typically, the access token will include the user SID (the SID in the target domain), as well as a list of group SIDs from the target domain of which the user is a member (see subsection 3.1.4). If the **sIDHistory** attribute of the user who is trying to log in is not empty, then the authenticating domain controller will add all the SIDs found in this attribute to the user access token (more specifically, to the group membership field of the access token), and this will effectively grant the user the privileges to resources as they were in the old domain. The **sIDHistory** will typically contain one user SID of the original user and a number of groups SIDs of which the user was a member. As the operating system does not distinguish between user and group SIDs (see subsection 3.1.1), they can all be added to the group membership field of the access token, as if they were all existing groups and the user was member of them all. Typically, a workstation or server performing a local or network logon for a user does not attempt to check whether all the SIDs are valid; and in general, there is no easy and straightforward way that such a check can be performed. When the user tries to access resources, all the SIDs in the access token are simply compared with the SIDs in the access control list of the resources to which the user is attempting access.

Anyone with access to the **sIDHistory** attribute of a user can add arbitrary SIDs to that user's access token and potentially grant or deny access to particular resources, or grant or deny user rights for that given user. For example, a domain administrator who virtually has full access to the directory can add a valid user's SID to his account's **sIDHistory** and therefore obtain access to all the files to which the user has access. It is true that an administrator typically has such broad administrative privileges that he can access any resource — by obtaining ownership of files and other objects, or even by changing the behavior of the operating system or its files. With the advent of **sIDHistory**, an administrator or someone with appropriate privileges now has an even easier way to access files and objects by just modifying a single attribute.

sIDHistory will present a list of SIDs from various domains in the user access token. At the same time, SID filtering is another mechanism that is meant to sanitize the access token and ensure that only expected SIDs exist in this access token. The authentication architect needs to determine the use of these two mechanisms but in general they do not work together.

sIDHistory was not designed for use as a permanent storage of user SIDs. The assumption behind the **sIDHistory** attribute is that it is going to be used only during the migration process to provide users with continuous access to resources as they are being migrated to a new security context, and then the administrators will change the access control lists on all resources to reflect the change in user SIDs, and as a final step will decommission the SID history for all users.

3.3.8 Null Sessions

The Local System (or just System) account has a well-known SID **(S-1-5-18)** and always has administrative privileges on the computer where it resides. Every Windows computer has a Local System account.

In Windows NT 4.0 and earlier, the Local System account, as the name implies, was a local account. It only had meaning on the local computer, and it was not possible to use this account to access resources on the network. This is primarily because only the **S-1-5-18** SID was used by Windows NT 4.0 for this account on every computer; and unless the assumption was that it could only be used on the local computer, there was no way to distinguish between the local account and that residing on another computer in access control lists.

Many Windows NT 4.0 services, platforms, and applications require some way to authenticate and communicate across the network. To provide such network applications with appropriate authentication as they communicate on the network, Windows NT 4.0 and earlier used the concept of service accounts. If a service needed to communicate across the network and authenticate to other services on remote computers, it required the creation of a special user account and provision to the server application for use when accessing network resources. Many network applications (such as Microsoft Exchange Server 5.5 and earlier, and Microsoft SQL Server 7.0 and earlier) still require such accounts.

As an alternative to service accounts, Windows provides another network authentication mechanism for services known as Null Sessions. In essence, a Null Session is a connection to a remote computer where no username and no password are specified.

Null Sessions were extensively used by Windows NT 4.0 computers for many purposes, including:

- Windows NT 4.0 computers connect to Windows NT 4.0 domain controllers to enumerate accounts and groups in the domain to which they belong.
- Windows NT 4.0 trusting (resource) domain controllers connect to Windows NT 4.0 trusted (account) domain controllers using Null Sessions to enumerate the list of users and groups in the account domain in order to grant them permissions or add them to groups in the resource domain.
- Windows NT 4.0 RASs need to check to access user information that resides on domain controllers. To do this, the RAS will establish a Null Session to a domain controller and query the user databases over this session.
- If the LMHOSTS file on a computer uses the "include" statement, which allows portions of the LMHOSTS database to be stored on network servers, these servers will be accessed using a Null Session during computer start-up (when there is no account other than the Local System account available) and after start-up.
- The Browser service that builds a list of computers on the network and provides this list to Windows Explorer to be visualized in Network Neighborhood uses Null Sessions as well.

The problem with Null Sessions is that they are readily available to provide both authenticated and unauthenticated (and potentially malicious) users with information, including a list of user accounts and their properties, shared directories on a computer, etc. Furthermore, in Windows NT 4.0, the Anonymous (Null Session) user is a member of the Network (**S-1-5-2**) and Everyone (**S-1-1-0**) built-in groups. By default, the Everyone built-in group has Full Control privileges on many files and directories, and shared directories by default provide the Everyone group with Full Control access to the share.

Windows NT 4.0 Service Pack 3 (SP3) added the Authenticated Users built-in group (**S-1-5-11**). This group is very similar to the Everyone group; however, it does not include users connected via Null Sessions (Anonymous authentication). It is recommended that the Authenticated Users group be used for providing access to resources, and the Everyone group can still be used for other purposes, such as auditing wherein an administrator needs to track every attempted action to perform a task, even by unauthenticated users. Null Sessions use the Anonymous user SID (**S-1-5-7**) and can be granted permissions, if required.

The use of Null Sessions can be restricted but cannot be disabled in Windows NT 4.0 environments. When Windows NT 4.0 SP3 or later is used, the **RestrictAnonymous** registry setting will restrict user account enumeration over Null Sessions, as well as password policy access over a Null Session. However, workstation NetLogon channel establishment and trust relationship establishment are designed to use Null Sessions in Windows NT 4.0, so this behavior cannot be avoided or disabled.

In Windows 2000 and earlier operating systems, Anonymous users are part of the Everyone group, just as any other user and group, including Authenticated users. By default, in Windows XP and Windows 2003, Anonymous users are no longer members of the Everyone group, and they will have only the Anonymous SID in their access token, not the Everyone SID. As a result, they will only have access to resources to which they have explicitly been granted access, rather than being able to access the various resources to which the Everyone group has access by default. This behavior of Windows XP and Windows 2003 can be modified using the following Group Policy setting:

Network Access: Let Everyone permissions apply to anonymous users

or the registry: **HKLM\SYSTEM\CurrentControlSet\Control\Lsa\Everyone IncludesAnonymous:REG_DWORD**

The use of Anonymous connections can be restricted to a certain extent using the following registry setting in Windows NT 4.0 SP3 and later:

HKEY_LOCAL_MACHINE\SYSTEM\CurrentControlSet\Control\Lsa\
RestrictAnonymous:REG_DWORD

Table 3.13 shows the acceptable values for the **RestrictAnonymous** parameter and their effect.

Running in a mixed mode domain and restricting anonymous sessions can be challenging. To provide for an easy way to configure permissions to directory services objects, required by Windows NT 4.0 and earlier operating systems, Active Directory uses a built-in group by the name of **Pre-Windows 2000 Compatible Access** that has a well-known SID (**S-1-5-32-554**). By default, this group is granted read access to user and group objects in Active Directory to mimic such access in Windows NT directory services. During the installation of Active Directory, the administrator is presented with the choice of whether or not he would like to add the Everyone group to the **Pre-Windows 2000 Compatible Access** group. This can be modified later, after AD installation, by adjusting group membership to this group. Membership in the **Pre-Windows 2000**

Table 3.13 RestrictAnonymous Settings

RestrictAnonymous Value	*Impact*
0	There are no restrictions for anonymous connection; this behavior mimics Windows NT 4 SP2 and earlier.
1 (Windows NT 4 SP3+)	Anonymous users are not allowed to access the SAM and enumerate user and group accounts, and they cannot enumerate shares. However, they can access other resources.
2	Anonymous users require explicit permissions to access resources (in that case, permissions must be granted to the Anonymous built-in group). *Note:* This setting is not supported in Windows NT 4.0 and Windows 2000 mixed environments.

Compatible Access group in conjunction with the **RestrictAnonymous** setting (see Table 3.13) may be used to control access to Active Directory resources from Windows NT computers.

It is important to note that the difference in membership to the Everyone group in Windows 2000 and Windows 2003 results in different membership to the **Pre-Windows 2000 Compatible Access** group as well. If during promotion of a Windows 2000 computer to a domain controller the administrator specifies that access to the domain can be relaxed, then the Everyone group will be added as a member to the **Pre-Windows 2000 Compatible Access** group. This will include both Authenticated and Anonymous users. In Windows 2003, the Everyone group does not include Anonymous users by default; thus, even if the Everyone group is a member of the **Pre-Windows 2000 Compatible Access** group, Anonymous users will still be restricted.

3.3.9 Case Study: Using Null Sessions Authentication to Access Resources

In this case study, a user will establish a Null Session from client XP-CLIENT to Windows 2003 server BILL. On the client computer, the user can use the **NET USE** command to connect to the server using a Null Session. The **NET USE** command can be used to establish an Interprocess Communication (IPC$ share) session using the following syntax:

```
net use \\server\IPC$ "password" /user:domain-name\username
```

When connecting using a Null Session, the username and password are empty. Therefore, the user can connect from client XP-CLIENT to server BILL using the following command:

```
C:\> net use \\bill\ipc$ "" /user:""

The command completed successfully.

C:\>
```

The user can then check the status of the connection using the **NET USE** command again:

```
C:\> net use
New connections will be remembered.
Status        Local     Remote                  Network
-------------------------------------------------------------------
OK                      \\bill\ipc$             Microsoft Windows Network
The command completed successfully.

C:\>
```

On server BILL, an administrator can see the following session information:

```
C:\> net session

Computer             User name       Client Type          Opens Idle time
-------------------------------------------------------------------
\\10.0.1.1                           Windows 2002 Serv    0 00:01:05

The command completed successfully.

C:\>
```

The user has successfully authenticated and established a NULL session to server BILL. The Null Session can be distinguished from authenticated sessions by the empty **User name** field of the **NET SESSION** command.

What resources the user can access on server BILL using a Null Session depends on the server settings. Typically, administrators would be very restrictive in the resources that can be accessed anonymously; but if the server is configured to do so, it can allow access to shared files and other resources (Figure 3.19). For example, if the server allows Anonymous connections to the shared directory **Test** (Figure 3.20) and the permissions for this shared directory allow Anonymous access to it, the user can access this share across the network.

Provided that the user is granted the above permissions, even if anonymous (and unauthenticated), he can still access resources on server BILL:

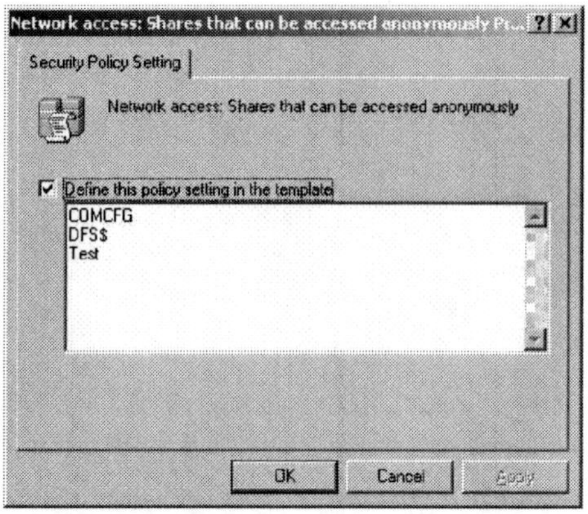

Figure 3.19 A server configured to allow Anonymous access to shares.

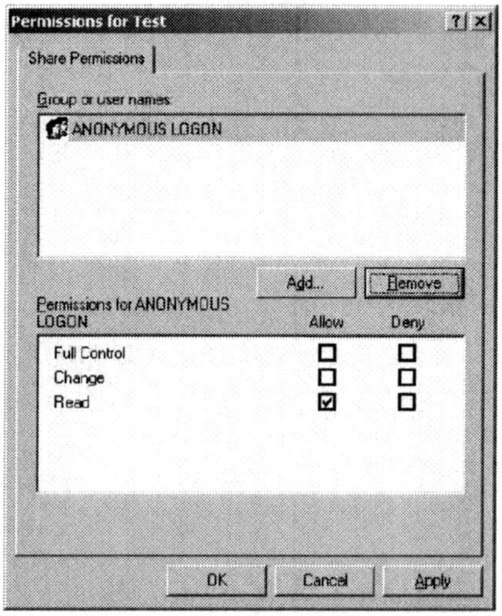

Figure 3.20 Shared Directory Test allows access to Anonymous users.

```
C:\> net use z: \\bill\test
The command completed successfully.

C:\> z:

Z:\> dir
 Volume in drive Z has no label.
 Volume Serial Number is A478-E434
```

```
 Directory of Z:\

10/07/2005  17:35    <DIR>          .
10/07/2005  17:35    <DIR>          ..
10/07/2005  17:35                 9 secret.txt
               1 File(s)              9 bytes
               2 Dir(s)     849,108,992 bytes free

Z:\>
```

3.3.10 Case Study: Domain Member Start-up and Authentication

When a Windows domain member computer starts, it needs to authenticate to the domain of which it is a member. In this case study, member server STEVE boots up and authenticates to domain **ins.com**. Network capture Steve-Startup-And-Logon.Cap (see companion Web site, http://www.iamechanics.com) contains the authentication traffic during start-up.

The following activities related to authentication take place during domain member boot-up:

1. The domain member tries to find a domain controller:
   - Domain members running Windows NT 4.0 or earlier, as well as Windows 2000 and later clients in a Windows NT 4.0 domain:
     - The domain member will try to find a domain controller by means of NetBIOS name resolution (NBNS) requests by either sending directed requests to an NBNS server (WINS), or sending broadcast packets. The domain member will try to find a name that has the a NetBIOS suffix of the domain name in question, and the <1C> type as the sixteenth byte (designates any domain controller).
     - The domain member will broadcast a Mailslot message over connectionless NetBIOS datagrams to the local subnet, and then will send Mailslot messages to the **MAILSLOT\NET\NETLOGON** mailslot on WINS discovered domain controllers. This is done to find the nearest domain controller that is willing to authenticate the client. The client will specify a reply Mailslot.
     - The first domain controller that replies to the client by sending a Netlogon message to the client specified Mailslot is selected to establish a Secure Channel with. It is assumed that the first to reply is the nearest domain controller.
   - Active Directory clients (Windows 2000 and later):

- The client either uses a cached site name (stored in HKLM\SYSTEM\CurrentControlSet\Services\Netlogon\Parameters\DynamicSiteName:REG_SZ or HKLM\SYSTEM\CurrentControlSet\Services\Netlogon\Parameters\SiteName:REG_SZ) to send a DNS request to its DNS server to find SRV records for its own domain in the cached site. The DNS server returns a list of SRV records and corresponding A records (see Frames 16 and 17 in Steve-Startup-And-Logon.Cap).
- Using connectionless (UDP-based) LDAP, the client sends an AD style Netlogon request to the domain controllers returned by the DNS server. In the request, the client includes the domain name, the domain GUID and its own hostname, and performs a search for the LDAP Netlogon attribute. All the domain controllers reply with a connectionless (UDP-based) LDAP reply that includes information about the domain controller, including its DNS and NetBIOS names, the DNS domain name, the domain GUID, the site to which the Domain Controller belongs, as well as the sites of the client, so that if the client belongs to a different site than the one it has stored, the client can now send another query for a Domain Controller in the new site (see Frames 18 and 19 in Steve-Startup-And-Logon.Cap on companion Web site).

2. AD domain members. At this stage, the domain member tries to authenticate using Kerberos and its machine account to a domain controller. The domain member sends a Kerberos AS Request to the domain controller, and the domain controller responds with an AS Reply message (see Frames 28 and 30 in Steve-Startup-And-Logon.Cap).
3. AD domain members. Once it has obtained its Kerberos TGT ticket (AS Reply), the clients request TGS tickets for the SMB/CIFS service on the domain controller, the Kerberos TGT service on the domain controller, and the LDAP service on the domain controller (see Frames 31 through 34 and Frames 54 and 55 in Steve-Startup-And-Logon.Cap); the domain controller supplies the requested tickets.
4. The domain member establishes a Secure Channel with the domain controller (Subsection 4.1.2 provides more information on Secure Channels).

   Note on AD members: Despite the fact that the client has already authenticated using Kerberos (see Frames 28 and 30), the NTLM Secure Channel to the domain controller is built using NTLM to establish the NTLM model of trust.

5. The domain member utilizes the Secure Channel to query the domain controller for a list of trusted domains. The list of domains will be displayed in the GINA logon dialog.
   Note: Windows 2000 and later computers perform this operation by invoking the **NetrLogonGetDomainInfo( )** RPC call of the Netlogon interface (see Frames 158 and 159 in Steve-Startup-And-Logon.Cap on the companion Web site, http://www.identitymechanics.com). Windows NT 4.0 and earlier utilize the **LsarEnumerateTrustedDomains( )** RPC call from the LSA RPC interface.
6. (AD domain members only) The domain member tries to obtain the Group Policies configured for the computer account. This is performed using the following operations:
   - The domain member connects to the domain controller using direct binding RPC calls and binds using the acquired LDAP Kerberos ticket (see Frames 31 through 34 and Frames 54 and 55), utilizes the DRSUAPI interface and invokes the **DsCrack Names( )** RPC procedure to convert its sitename to an LDAP distinguished name (see Frames 56 through 60 in Steve-Startup-And-Logon.Cap on companion Web site).
   - The domain member connects to the domain controller using LDAP and binds using the existing Kerberos ticket. It then queries the domain controller for Group Policy objects that apply to the site to which the domain member belongs by specifying the site Distinguished Name in the BaseDN **LDAP** field (see Frames 243 and 244).
   - The domain member utilizes the existing LDAP session and checks for Group Policy objects applied at the domain level (see Frames 245 and 247 in Steve-Startup-And-Logon.Cap).
   - The domain member connects to the SYSVOL share on the authenticating domain controller using the SMB/CIFS protocol and tries to obtain all the Group Policy settings that are applicable (see Frames 248 through 265 in Steve-Startup-And-Logon.Cap).
7. (Windows NT 4.0 and earlier computers, or Windows 2000 and later in a Windows NT 4.0 domain) The domain member connects to the NETLOGON shared directory on the domain controller using the CIFS/SMB protocol and tries to obtain the **ntconfig.pol** file that contains Windows NT 4.0 and earlier System Policies.
8. The domain member displays the GINA Dialog and prompts the user to login in to the system. Group Policy settings can be still be applied in the background, and computer start-up scripts may still be running.

3.3.11 Case Study: Domain Controller Start-up and Authentication

The trusted domain controller start-up process is similar to the domain member start-up process. Windows NT 4.0 and earlier backup domain controllers (BDCs) establish a Secure Channel to a primary domain controller (PDC) in the same way as a domain member establishes a connection to a domain controller, and they utilize their domain controller machine account to establish the connection. Replication traffic between PDC and BDC may take place during start-up as well, but this is beyond the scope of this book.

Upon start-up, domain controllers of a trusting (resource) domain try to establish a Secure Channel to a domain controller in a trusted (account) domain. The way a trusting domain controller discovers a trusted domain controller is similar to the way a domain member discovers its own domain controller. The Secure Channel between the trusting (resource) domain controller and the trusted (account) domain controller is established using the interdomain trust account that is replicated and known by all trusting (resource) domain controllers.

3.3.12 Case Study: Windows NT 4.0 Domain User Logon Process

Once the Windows workstation has been authenticated as a domain member, it can provide access for domain users who want to access resources on this workstation — either interactively or over the network.

Windows NT 4.0 user authentication utilizes MS RPC. In contrast, the preferred approach to user authentication in Windows 2000 and later operating systems is Kerberos.

The following sequence of events represents interactive user logon from a Windows NT 4.0 computer to a Windows domain:

1. The user submits authentication credentials to GINA (username, password, and NetBIOS domain name for Domain A).
2. GINA on the domain member calls the **LsaLogonUser( )** function (see [46]).
3. The **LsaLogonUser( )** function on the client computer calculates the LM hash and the NTLM hash.
4. The domain member encrypts the LM hash and the NT hash using RC4 and the first 8 bytes of the Secure Channel session key padded to 16 bytes with zeroes as the key.

5. To protect from replay attacks, the client obtains the current time and sums it with the client response to the server challenge. It then uses DES with the first 7 bytes of the session key as the key to encrypt the sum, and then encrypts the result again using DES and the last byte from the session key padded with zero to a 7-byte key as the key.
6. The domain member submits the plaintext username, the encrypted timestamp, the plaintext timestamp, and the encrypted password hashes utilizing the existing Secure Channel and passes the authentication request to the domain controller using the **NetrLogonSamLogon( )** RPC Call to the Netlogon RPC interface.
7. Depending on the configuration, the NTLMSSP provider for SSPI can apply encryption ("sealing") and signing of the Secure Channel to protect Secure Channel data as it traverses the network.
8. The **NetrLogonSamLogon( )** RPC interface on the domain controller decrypts the LM hash and the NT hash using RC4 and the Secure Channel and the first 8 bytes of the session key padded to 16 bytes with zeroes as the key.
9. The **NetrLogonSamLogon( )** RPC interface on the domain controller calculates the timestamp using the same algorithm as the client and ensures that the packet has not been replayed. It then performs another timestamp encryption, using the client provided timestamp, increased by one.
10. The **NetrLogonSamLogon( )** function on the domain controller compares the LM hash and the NT hash with those stored in the directory services database (Registry SAM in Windows NT 4.0 and Active Directory in Windows 2000 and later).
11. If the LM and NT hash values match, the user is authenticated and the domain controller returns an access token structure to the user. The server includes the encrypted sum of the client timestamp with the client response, increased by one, as calculated in Step 9.
12. If NTLMSSP encryption ("sealing") or signing is used, the server reply is encrypted and signed (integrity is authenticated). If the Secure Channel is not encrypted ("sealed") or signed, information is returned in plaintext.
13. The domain member receives either Failure status or the access token of the user as a result.
14. The client authenticates the timestamp provided by the server and ensures that the server reply has not been replayed or tampered with.
15. An access token is created from the user token, and a user shell is created.

3.3.13 Case Study: User Logon to Active Directory Using Kerberos

User logon to Active Directory differs significantly with regard to user authentication due to the extensive use of the Kerberos protocol for user authentication. The case study in subsection 4.2.2.13 provides more information.

3.3.14 Windows NT 4.0 Domain Model

Domain controllers in Windows NT 4.0 and earlier operating systems use the SAM database to store information about domain user, group, and computer accounts. This SAM database has a copy on every Windows NT 4.0 domain controller for the specific domain. The SAM database in Windows NT 4.0 can be modified only on one domain controller, known as the primary domain controller (PDC). All other domain controllers in the domain are known as backup domain controllers (BDCs), and they replicate the modified database from the PDC. Changes cannot be performed on the BDC. When domain administration tools such as User Manager for Domains are used in Windows NT 4.0, these tools always access the PDC.

The shared domain SAM database is the core of user authentication in Windows NT 4.0 domains. The Windows NT 4.0 authentication model is discussed in the following subsections.

3.3.14.1 User Accounts

In Windows NT 4.0 and earlier, user account, group, and computer account information on stand-alone computers, domain members, and domain controllers is stored in the SAM. Accounts created on stand-alone computers and domain members can be used only on the computer where they reside. Accounts created on domain controllers can be used on the domain controllers themselves, as well as on all domain members and any trusting (resource) domain within the organization.

The SAM database on domain controllers is used as the trusted authentication authority for the entire domain, as well as trusting domains. Unlike domain members that have individual and autonomous local SAM databases, all domain controllers use the same SAM database, which is replicated between them. The SAM database itself is almost the same as the one used by individual Windows NT computers and discussed in section 3.2

Windows NT 4.0 provides for two types of domain user accounts: (1) local and (2) global.

Global user accounts are almost exclusively used, so these are "regular" user accounts. They are created in the domain database, and can be members of global and local groups within the domain where they were created, as well as other domains with appropriate trust relationships.

Domain local user accounts are very rarely used, and they typically provide users running non-Windows NT operating systems with limited access to resources only in the domain where they were created. They cannot be used across trusts in trusting domains. An important difference between local user accounts and global user accounts is that, despite the name, local user accounts cannot be used to log on locally (interactively) on a domain member of the domain in which they were created; they can only be used over the network to access resources within this domain.

References to Windows NT user accounts in this book by default mean global user accounts.

3.3.14.2 Group Accounts and Group Strategies

Windows NT 4.0 domains support two types of group accounts: (1) local and (2) global.

Domain local groups in Windows NT can be created on the primary domain controller (PDC) and replicated to backup domain controllers (BDCs). As all local groups in Windows NT 4.0, they can only be used locally on the computers where they exist — in the case of local groups on domain controllers, they are only visible and exist on all domain controllers for the domain, and not on domain members or trusted domains. Domain local groups on Windows NT 4.0 domain controllers are typically used if the domain administrators want to grant permissions to users to access local resources on the domain controllers, such as shared folders and printers.

Both domain local groups and domain member local groups (on member workstations and servers) can contain users and global groups from the domain to which the domain member resides or any trusted domain. They cannot contain other local groups. Visibility of local groups is limited to the database where they exist; domain local groups can be used (and are visible) on domain controllers only, while member local groups can only be used (and are visible) on the domain member where they were created.

Domain global groups can be created on Windows NT 4.0 domain controllers only and cannot be created on domain members or stand-alone computers. These groups can be used to group only users from the same domain where the group is created; they cannot contain users from other domains, nor users from domain members. Global groups — just as domain user accounts — can be used (and are visible) on all domain controllers of the domain where they were created, all domain members, and all the trusting (resource) domains for the domain where they were created.

To provide users with access to resources, the recommended approach is that domain users get assigned to global groups in the same domain where they were created; then these global groups are assigned to local groups in either the same domain or in trusting (resource) domains, and local groups are then assigned access to resources locally, where the local group was created. Thus, by the virtue of being a member of a global group, and then by the virtue of the global group being a member of the local group, which has access to resources, the user also has access to the resources. Apparently, the group nesting specified here results in a set of SIDs being added to the user access token, so that the user is granted access to the resources that he needs to access (see subsection 3.3.15.12).

3.3.14.3 Authentication Protocols: NTLM and LM

The Windows NT 4.0 directory services support the LanManager (LM) authentication protocol and the NT-LanManager (NTLM) authentication protocol. These protocols heavily depend on NetBIOS as a session layer transport for name resolution, session establishment, and sessionless messages across the network.

The NTLM Protocol can be used to authenticate interactive logon sessions to Windows domains. Both the NTLM and LM Protocols can be used to authenticate network access to SMB/CIFS resources, HTTP access to Microsoft IIS, and other applications.

Although the SMB/CIFS Protocol was primarily meant to be used for access to conventional file resources, it provides for access to other network resources, such as named pipes, mailslots, and RPC over SMB/CIFS. A lot of Windows network APIs use the above mechanisms: workstation and user logon, access to the registry of a remote computer, remote computer management using standard Windows Administrative tools, etc. In that respect, many operating system network activities are being authenticated as part of the SMB session that the operating system establishes across the network, and do not use their own authentication protocols.

3.3.14.4 Trust Relationships

Windows NT and earlier only support the NTLM authentication protocol for both user accounts and interdomain trust accounts. Therefore, all trust relationships are non-transitive. This poses some limitations on directory

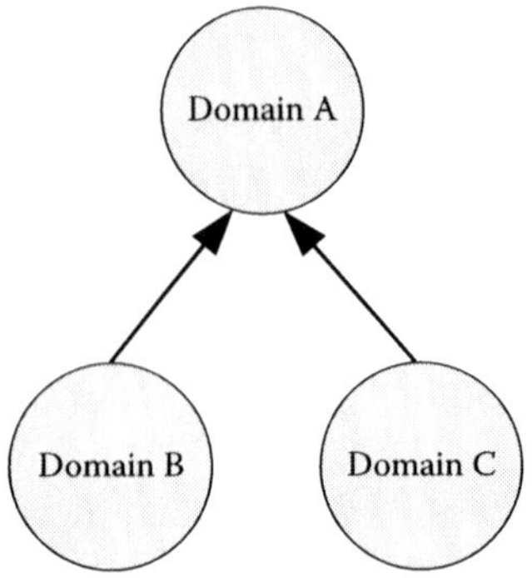

Figure 3.21 Single master domain model.

services and authentication architecture. In essence, every two domains that need to provide each other with access to resources need to have a direct trust relationship between them. This limits hierarchies and domain trees to two levels: (1) an upper trusted (account) level and (2) a lower trusting (resource) level.

A typical design for organizations with more than one domain (administrative boundary) is the Single Master Domain Model (Figure 3.21). In this model, all user accounts are concentrated in a single upper trusted (account) domain: Domain A. Domain B and Domain C have no user accounts (other than the default accounts) and only contain workstations and resources. This allows for decentralized administration: Domain B and Domain C Administrators can have control over their respective workstations, servers, and resources, and they can grant or deny users permissions to access these workstations, servers, and resources. At the same time, the effective user account database can be maintained in a single location — Domain A — and used by all domains in the organization.

Another common scenario in Windows NT 4.0 and earlier domain environments is the complete trust model (Figure 3.22). In this model, every domain in the organization trusts every other domain. In this respect, every domain is both trusted and trusting, connected using two-way trusts to all the other domains. This model decentralizes both administration and the account database; and unlike the single master domain model, there is no single authentication authority used by the organization. A problem with the complete trust model is that the number of trust relationships that must be maintained increases exponentially as the number of domains increases, so that this model is typically avoided for more than three of four domains.

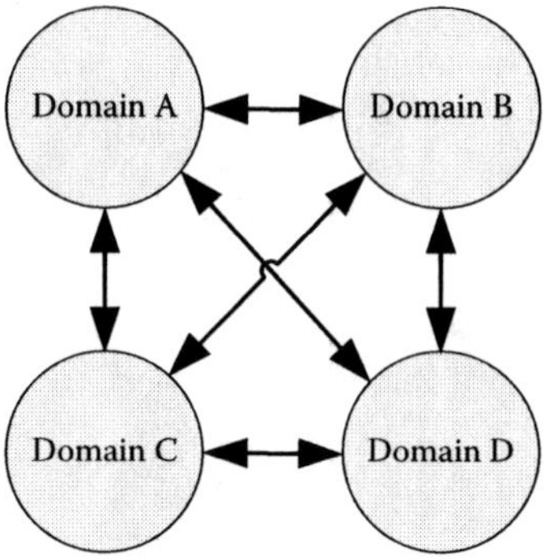

Figure 3.22 Complete trust domain model.

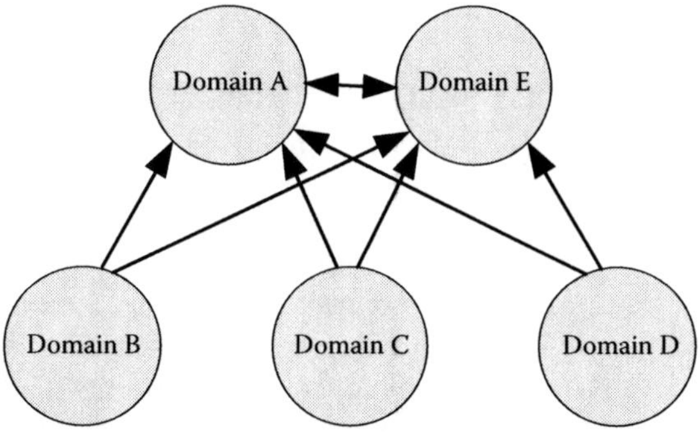

Figure 3.23 Multiple master domain model with two master domains.

An important consideration when designing multiple domain authentication solutions for Windows NT 4.0 and earlier domains is that the domain account database is stored in the SAM, which is essentially part of the registry. The registry file, although well structured, is not a database for large amounts of data. Searches and modifications on large amounts of data within the SAM are inefficient. Therefore, in Windows NT 4.0 and earlier, it is recommended that the SAM file contains no more than 40,000 user accounts. Multiple domains and trust relationships can be used to avoid this limitation, and large organizations typically utilize the multiple master domain model (Figure 3.23), which is a modification of the single master domain model with multiple master (account) domains where user accounts are split using either organizational, functional, or geographical principle. Apparently, each user authenticates to the specific master domain where his account resides but still this account is available throughout the organization.

3.3.15 Active Directory

Windows 2000 introduced the new directory services of the Windows family — Active Directory. This is a revolutionary new concept for the Windows directory services that provides the following features:

- Database storage for directory data (rather than registry based, such as Windows NT 4.0 SAM based directory storage)
- Support for legacy Windows directory services
- Kerberos authentication protocol
- Hierarchical LDAP compliant directory

Furthermore, Active Directory in Windows 2003 has a number of improvements over Windows 2000. The following chapters focus on Windows 2003 and point out the differences from Windows 2000 when they exist.

3.3.15.1 Active Directory Overview

Active Directory is a directory service. Being such, it is responsible for storing information about objects within the organization. Objects include user accounts, group accounts, computer accounts, servers, shares, printers, etc. Administrators and regular users can search for objects in the directory; read, modify, and delete object properties; add and remove objects; etc.

Because Active Directory has information about all the objects in the organization, including users, groups, and computers, and contains information about these users (such as user's telephone number or a computer's service pack level), Active Directory also can store authentication information, including user SIDs, user password hashes (NTLM and LM), user password history, group names and SIDs, group membership information, etc.

3.3.15.2 Logical and Physical Structure

Unlike Windows NT 4.0 directory services that can generally be represented by a flat table with user and group accounts, and a fixed set of properties for these accounts, Active Directory provides for a hierarchical logical structure, and it also provides for a physical structure that helps optimize access to services in enterprise environments that consist of multiple sites connected with slow WAN links.

Logically, Active Directory consists of domains and organizational units (OUs). Domains are still the main security boundary, and the domain administrators have full control over objects in that domain. Domains in Active Directory can form hierarchical structures, called trees. Every tree has a single root domain, under which there may be none, one, or more domains. These domains can be parents to other domains, and so on. Active Directory utilizes DNS, and one of the main purposes DNS serves is that of a domain namespace. All the domains in a tree must belong to a contiguous DNS namespace. The hierarchy of Active Directory domains in a tree must follow an existing DNS hierarchy, and the DNS domain name of an Active Directory domain can be used to determine the place of the domain in an Active Directory tree.

If an organization has more than one DNS namespace — that is, if it has a discontiguous DNS namespace — Active Directory can support more than one tree. All the trees in an Active Directory organization form an Active Directory forest. The first domain installed in the organization is called the Forest Root Domain. It establishes the first domain and the first tree in the forest. It also gives the namespace used by Active Directory for the Configuration and Schema containers, replicated to all the domain controllers in the forest. Each new tree added to the forest establishes a tree-root trust relationship with the Forest Root Domain.

The forest forms a new security boundary in Windows directory services. A global group in the Forest Root Domain by the name of Enterprise Admins can potentially administer any object within the organization, including the organization (forest) configuration and schema. In essence, this is achieved by automatically adding the Enterprise Admins global group to the local Administrators group of every domain that joins the forest. By default, Enterprise Admins is not added to the local Administrators group on domain members, only on domain controllers. However, technically, Enterprise Admins can be added to appropriate groups on forest computers, either manually or by using automation including scripts or GPOs that apply Restricted Groups policies.

Active Directory Organizational Units represent a hierarchical logical grouping structure within the domain, very similar to folders where objects can be placed. OUs in Active Directory are unimportant from an authentication perspective — they are used to apply Group Policies, they allow for delegation of administrative tasks to a group of objects, and they are used by administrators and users to group similar objects for easier searching and navigation within the directory structure; however, users log on to domains, not to organizational units. Regardless of the OU to which a user or computer is a member, authentication will be performed by domain controllers for the domain where the user account resides.

Each object is created within a particular domain in Active Directory, where it can reside in an OU or other container. Information about objects that belong to the same domain is replicated between all the domain controllers for this domain, but not to domain controllers from other domains. To allow users to search for objects that belong to any domain within the forest, Active Directory provides for the so-called Global Catalog. The Global Catalog is a list of all the objects from any domain within the forest, and a selected subset of their attributes. The Global Catalog can have one or more instances, and it is maintained by administratively selected domain controllers within the forest. Virtually every object, regardless of the domain where it is created, has a copy with a limited set of attributes that can be used to perform searches against the Global Catalog.

Physically, Active Directory is built using Windows 2000/2003 server computers that are configured to be domain controllers. Just as in Windows NT 4.0 and earlier domains, domain controllers are responsible for maintaining and physically storing the directory services database, and they can authenticate users. There is typically more than one domain controller per domain, and this provides for high availability and load balancing.

Unlike Windows NT 4.0 and earlier directory services that are unaware of the physical placement of domain controllers, Active Directory introduces the term "site." Sites are locations with good network connectivity (typically a LAN), and can have one or more IP subnets associated with them. Domain controllers form replication relationships to one another and these can be defined either manually by the administrator, or automatically if the administrator provides information to Active Directory on the links that interconnect the sites in the forest. Every domain controller and domain member is a member of a site. Sites are important for Active Directory because they allow clients to easily discover a domain controller in the same site (LAN) that can authenticate them. In addition to that, domain controllers replicate the domain database, schema, configuration, and Global Catalog related information, and they do so on a schedule that is determined by membership to sites and links between sites. Replication between domain controllers that are in the same site happens much more frequently; and based on change notification messages, and replication between domain controllers from different sites happens following a predefined schedule for the link between the sites.

All the domains in the forest share a common Configuration Container (which includes site configuration and membership), a common Global Catalog, a common Schema for objects, and in general comply with common security and infrastructure policies, defined by the Enterprise Admins.

Unlike Windows NT 4.0, all Active Directory domain controllers have a read/write copy of the domain database, so that any domain controller can perform changes on the database. However, some changes should not be performed on two or more domain controllers simultaneously and therefore Active Directory introduces the role of a Flexible Single Master of Operations (FSMO) to designate specific domain controllers as the place to perform specific critical operations. There are three FSMO roles at the domain level and two roles at the forest level. From an authentication perspective, the following two domain FSMO roles are important:

1. *PDC emulator.* This domain-level FSMO role has the following important responsibilities:
   a. *PDC for downlevel clients.* The domain controller that holds the PDC emulator FSMO role is responsible to play the role of a PDC for Windows NT 4.0 and earlier clients. As older operating systems are not aware of the multimaster update mechanism in Active Directory, they always try to find an old style domain controller to use when they need to perform a change, typically to change the workstation or user password. The PDC emulator, as the name reveals, is used to emulate a Windows NT 4.0 Primary Domain Controller for such downlevel clients.
   b. *Time synchronization.* The PDC emulator of the forest root domain will provide master time source for all the computers in the forest. Every PDC emulator of a non-root domain will connect to the forest root domain PDC emulator and synchronize their clocks. Domain controllers for every domain connect to this domain's PDC emulator to synchronize their clocks, and domain members synchronize their clocks with the authenticating domain controller upon start-up. Time synchronization is very important for the Kerberos authentication protocol — the details are discussed in Chapter 4.
   c. *Password tiebreaker.* The multimaster update model of Active Directory poses a problem with information updates. For example, if a user changes his password against a domain controller, it will typically take some time before this password is replicated to all the domain controllers in the domain. Depending on the replication infrastructure, which may vary with the number of domain controllers on the LAN, and the number and type of sites and links between them, the password update process can take from a couple of minutes to a couple of days, or even weeks. If a user changes his password, the change will be propagated using a special urgent update channel from the domain controller performing the change to the PDC emulator, and the password will be immediately replicated to this DC only, so that the PDC emulator always has the latest password. Replication to other domain controllers will follow standard replication paths. If the user that has changed his password then tries to log in, the chances are that the user might encounter

a domain controller that still does not have an up-to-date copy of the user password. When a domain controller fails to authenticate a user, it will assume that the reason for this may be a password change that still has not been propagated and will therefore connect to the domain PDC emulator to check whether the password is correct.

2. *RID Master (RID Pool Master)*. This FSMO role is assigned to a domain controller that will be responsible for distributing domain Relative Identifiers (RIDs) to all the domain controllers in the domain. The reason for a single server to allocate RIDs to users is to avoid duplicate SIDs within the domain.

3.3.15.3 Active Directory Schema

Active Directory objects can have attributes that represent the properties of these objects. Some of the attributes may be mandatory for some objects (such as the SID for user objects), and others may be optional (such as the telephone number for user objects). The types of objects that can be created, as well as these objects' properties, are defined by the Active Directory Schema using object classes. The class within the schema provides the structure used by the object of this class, defines all the attributes and their type, as well as which are mandatory and which are optional. The class is just a formal definition or a template for Active Directory objects. The object is the specific instance of the class, and there can be multiple instances of the class within the directory. For example, the user class defines regular user accounts, and there may be multiple user accounts defined in the directory.

In addition to the standard classes defined in the Active Directory schema, new classes can be defined by the user. For example, if an organization needs to maintain an inventory of its routers, the router class can be defined using the Active Directory schema, and then instances of this object can be created to reflect the existence and the attributes of specific physical objects into the directory.

Active Directory extensibility also provides for new attributes for existing classes and objects. Existing class attributes can be inherited or simply replaced by new attributes. By default, Active Directory does not contain UNIX-specific attributes for users — such as UID or GID. However, in a scenario where Active Directory is expected to coexist with UNIX, the schema can be extended to add new user attributes, including standard UNIX attributes. This is exactly what many Windows NT and UNIX integration tools do, with Microsoft Service for UNIX being a particular example. Information on how to extend the Active Directory schema to coexist with UNIX with regard to user authentication is provided in Chapter 2.7.

Every object in Active Directory has a Globally Unique Identifier (GUID), a 128-bit value used to universally identify the object. GUIDs are different from SIDs; while the SID is only assigned to security principals — such as users, groups, and computers — GUIDs are assigned to any object, including printers, published shared directories, etc. GUIDs are important from a database perspective, and serve purposes such as database replication and object tracking. Unlike SIDs, they have no importance in terms of security.

3.3.15.4 Database Storage for Directory Information

Windows NT 4.0 uses the registry (the SAM file) to store the user directory database, and information exists in the form of flat lists of users and groups. This is a problem in large enterprise environments where the number of users may reach hundreds of thousands, and searches and updates in flat files can be very inefficient.

Active Directory no longer uses the SAM as a directory storage location; it now uses database files. These files were largely influenced by the Microsoft Exchange Jet database engine. As with most databases, a principal information storage file is used (**NTDS.DIT**), as well as one or many transaction log files (**EDB*.LOG** and **RES*.LOG**), checkpoint files (**EBD.CHK**) used for transaction replay and recovery, as well as patch and temporary files.

Domain controllers maintain the Active Directory database. Locally on the domain controller, SAM requests are redirected to Active Directory to allow most legacy applications to run without modification.

Under normal circumstances, domain controllers do not use the SAM database. It is only used in case the Active Directory database is corrupt and requires repair, in which case an administrator can reboot the domain controller in the so-called Directory Services Restore Mode (DRSM) and log in locally to the computer using a local SAM account. The administrator can then repair or restore the database.

Initial synchronization is performed initially when a Windows server is promoted as the first domain controller for the domain and user accounts from the SAM are copied into Active Directory; this mechanism mainly exists to provide for in-place upgrade from Windows NT 4.0 directory services. Once the first domain controller for the domain has been promoted, there is no synchronization between the Active Directory and the SAM database on a domain controller. User accounts exist independently between the two databases.

3.3.15.5 Support for Legacy Windows NT Directory Services

Although a revolutionary concept, Active Directory has not dropped legacy Windows NT 4.0 interoperability. By default, Active Directory domain controllers will coexist with Windows NT 4.0 and earlier domain controllers, as well as with previous operating systems and clients (including MS Network Client for DOS, Windows for Workgroups, Windows 95, Windows 98, and Windows NT). Interoperability is primarily achieved by effectively supporting compatible authentication methods.

From a client perspective, Active Directory domain controllers can behave as Windows NT 4.0 domain controllers. In essence, Active Directory domain controllers may be available using legacy Windows NT APIs, and they can also replicate the directory services database with Windows NT 4.0 domain controllers, if running in the so-called Mixed Mode.

Active Directory objects can and typically will differ from what Windows NT 4.0 directory services support. While Active Directory is a directory for various types of objects, Windows NT directory services are a directory for a fixed set of objects that are security principals. Windows NT 4.0 directory services use a static structure of attributes for each object within the SAM, and this structure is not extensible. Therefore, Windows NT 4.0 and Active Directory domain controllers will be able to replicate some object attributes — such as username, full name, and NT and LM password hashes. Other standard AD attributes, such as object GUID, are not going to be replicated because they do not have an equivalent in the SAM structures.

The discrepancies in attributes for AD and SAM objects are typically not a problem because, by default, legacy clients that only support SAM attributes will be able to obtain all the information they require from both a Windows NT and a Windows 2000 domain controller. Operating systems and applications that may want to use Active Directory will typically invoke new APIs to do so — LDAP and ADSI — and these APIs will try to connect to an Active Directory domain controller, completely ignoring Windows NT 4.0 domain controllers.

The problem with coexistence between domain controllers comes when new Active Directory features must be used for common objects, which are typically security principals. In particular, Active Directory introduces new behavior for group accounts, as well as a new scope of group accounts — Universal Groups — that have no equivalent in Windows NT 4.0 SAM structures, and therefore cannot be replicated. Another difference is represented by Global groups and Domain Local Groups in native Active Directory domains — Global Groups can be nested into other Global Groups, and Local Groups can be nested in other Local Groups. This behavior is not supported by Windows NT 4.0 directory services and, although both Global and Local Groups exist in Windows

NT 4.0 SAM structures, such nesting cannot be replicated to Windows NT 4.0 domain controllers.

To allow for both the coexistence and improved functionality using the new Active Directory features, Windows 2000/2003 domain controllers support different modes of operation for the domain:

- *Windows 2000 Mixed Mode Domain.* By default, Active Directory works in Mixed Mode. In this mode, new Active Directory features such as Universal Security Groups and nesting of groups from the same type are disabled. The domain may have Windows NT 4.0 domain controllers, and they will be able to replicate the relevant portions of the Active Directory database to SAM, and work normally.
- *Windows 2000 Native Mode Domain.* Also known as Windows 2000 Native Mode, in this mode, all domain controllers within the domain must support Active Directory. These domain controllers will not replicate with Windows NT 4.0 domain controllers, and this mode assumes that all Windows NT 4.0 domain controllers have been upgraded or decommissioned. In this mode, all new Active Directory features can be used, including Universal Security Groups and nesting of groups from the same type. Also, groups can be converted from one type to another. Apparently, once the new features have been used and objects that utilize them have been created in the Active Directory database, this database can no longer be considered compatible with the Windows NT 4.0 SAM structures. Therefore, once Native Mode is enabled for a domain, it is not possible to switch back to Mixed Mode and introduce old-style domain controllers.
- *Windows 2003 Native Mode Domain.* This mode was introduced in Windows 2003 to represent some important differences between Windows 2000 and Windows 2003. The following features are important from a user authentication perspective:
  - Ability to rename domain controllers without reinstalling them
  - Logon timestamp attribute replication — used to record the last time a user has logged on and replicates it throughout the domain (surprisingly, this attribute is not replicated in Windows 2000 domains)
  - Constrained Kerberos delegation (see subsection 3.5.2)
  - Selective authentication — the ability to authenticate some users from a trusted domain, and deny authentication for other users from the same trusted domain (see subsection 3.3.15.17)
  - InetOrgPerson (RFC 2798; see [19]) class instead of the standard User class for user accounts that provides compatibility with other LDAP implementations

- *Windows 2000/2003 Interim Mode Domain.* This mode is used in mixed Windows NT and Windows 2000 or Windows 2003 environments to allow some of the Active Directory extensions to be used if they do not cause conflict with existing Windows NT 4.0 domain controllers. This mode is meant for temporary use in the upgrade process.

In addition, Windows 2003 also introduces functional levels for the forest:

- *Windows 2000 Mode Forest.* This is the default mode that provides compatibility with Windows 2000 domain controllers. Windows 2000 and Windows 2003 domain controllers can exist within the forest.
- *Windows 2003 Interim Mode Forest.* This mode is only available during migration from Windows NT 4 to Windows 2003. No Windows 2000 domain controllers can exist in this mode. In this mode, some Windows 2003 forest features are supported because they will not conflict with Windows 2000 domain controllers; this includes features such as Linked Value Replication that allow for more efficient replication of group membership changes across the domain. However, some of the functionality is limited by the presence of Windows NT 4.0 domain controllers, a notable example being the lack of Forest Trusts support in this mode.
- *Windows 2003 Mode Forest.* This provides for new Windows 2003 Active Directory features, including domain rename (which allows both a change in the name and the hierarchy of the forest trees) and inter-forest trusts (which provide for transitive trust relationships with other forests) (see subsection 3.3.15.17). Windows 2003 Mode is supported only when all the domains in the forest are running Windows 2003 Native Mode and all the domain controllers are Windows 2003 or later.

Despite popular belief, the domain mode has nothing to do with the client operating systems in the domain and the authentication protocols used by these operating systems. Active Directory domain controllers support standard NTLM and LM authentication in both mixed and native mode. Legacy clients can communicate with Active Directory domain controllers without additional configuration. The Kerberos authentication protocol is supported in both mixed and native mode, and is the preferred authentication mechanism for clients and servers that support it.

3.3.15.6 Hierarchical LDAP-Compliant Directory

One of the most important features of Active Directory is that it is an LDAP-compliant directory. It has a hierarchical structure that allows for the creation of containers (such as domains (DCs) and organizational units (OUs)), as well as objects (such as users — Common Name (CN)).

There are different methods used to access information in Active Directory. Applications can use the Win32 APIs (including those that reference the SAM), or MAPI; or use the object-oriented Active Directory Services Interface (ADSI), or LDAP.

The main goal of Active Directory is to be a hierarchical information store, and therefore it stores authentication information (such as user logon names and user password hashes) and it supports Kerberos authentication. This puts Active Directory in a role such that Active Directory is both an authentication authority and a resource similar to a database, which also needs to authorize user access to resources. To authorize user access to Active Directory, user authentication must take place first. Apparently, user authentication is provided by Active Directory itself.

In Windows 2003, the behavior of Active Directory with respect to user authentication and authorization for access to the directory can be modified using the **dsHeuristics** attribute of the **CN=Directory Service, CN=Windows NT,CN=Services,CN=Configuration,<Domain>** object for the Forest Root domain. This setting is stored in the Configuration container, replicated to all domain controllers in the forest, and therefore this setting applies to all Windows 2003 domain controllers in the entire forest. The **dsHeuristics** attribute is a string, and each character of this string controls the behavior of Active Directory in a specific way. Characters are counted from left to right. From an authentication perspective, it is important to understand the **dsHeuristics** characters in Table 3.14.

More information on the **dsHeuristics** attribute can be found in [29].

3.3.15.7 Case Study: Exploring Active Directory Using LDP.EXE

Due to the fact that Active Directory stores a vast amount of information about objects within the organization, most of the information that it provides is for authenticated users only. Without being authenticated, a user can see some general information about Active Directory. This information is known as the root context or RootDSE and is required by the LDAP standards. The following is an excerpt from an LDAP connection to domain controller BILL using the **LDP.EXE** generic LDAP client without user authentication:

Table 3.14 dsHeuristics Characters that Influence User Authentication

Character	*Possible Values*	*Description*
7th	2 or other	Setting the 7th character of **dsHeuristics** to 2 allows anonymous (unauthenticated) access to Active Directory, provided that object ACLs permit anonymous access to the specific object or property. A value other than 2 disables unauthenticated access to Active Directory, and only the root context (RootDSE) is available without authentication. In Windows 2003, the default is 0. Windows 2000 **dsHeuristics** does not exist and restricting anonymous access is not supported; Anonymous Access is allowed (same as 2).
9th	1 or 2	Specifies whether the **userPassword** attribute is used to store the user password, and therefore is treated as a special attribute with read and write access to it disabled, or whether **userPassword** is a regular attribute without special restrictions. A value of 1 specifies that **userPassword** should be treated as a special and restricted attribute. A value of 2 specifies that this is a regular attribute. **userPassword** is defined as the place where the password for objects of the Internet standard **inetOrgPerson** class should be stored. By default, Windows 2003 mixed mode domains treat the **userPassword** attribute as regular, and native mode domains treat it as a password attribute for the **inetOrgperson** account.
13th	0 or different	Specifies whether user password attributes such as **unicodePwd** and **userPassword** can be modified over unencrypted (not using SSL) LDAP connection. A value of 0 is the default and specifies that SSL is required to manage user passwords. Both Windows 2000 and Windows 2003 Active Directory require SSL to change the user password through LDAP. Active Directory Application Mode (ADAM) supports this **dsHeuristics** setting and can be configured to allow password change through an unencrypted LDAP session.

```
ld = ldap_open("bill.ins.com", 389);
Established connection to bill.ins.com.
Retrieving base DSA information...
Result <0>: (null)
Matched DNs:
Getting 1 entries:
>> Dn:
   1> currentTime: 12/03/2005 18:01:44 GMT Standard Time GMT Daylight Time;
   1> subschemaSubentry: CN=Aggregate,CN=Schema,CN=Configuration,DC=ins,
    DC=com;
   1> dsServiceName: CN=NTDS Settings,CN=BILL,CN=Servers,CN=Default-First-Site-
    Name,CN=Sites,CN=Configuration,DC=ins,DC=com;
   5> namingContexts: DC=ins,DC=com; CN=Configuration,DC=ins,DC=com;
    CN=Schema,CN=Configuration,DC=ins,DC=com; DC=DomainDnsZones,DC=
    ins,DC=com; DC=ForestDnsZones,DC=ins,DC=com;
   1> defaultNamingContext: DC=ins,DC=com;
   1> schemaNamingContext: CN=Schema,CN=Configuration,DC=ins,DC=com;
   1> configurationNamingContext: CN=Configuration,DC=ins,DC=com;
   1> rootDomainNamingContext: DC=ins,DC=com;
   22> supportedControl: 1.2.840.113556.1.4.319; 1.2.840.113556.1.4.801;
1.2.840.113556.1.4.473; 1.2.840.113556.1.4.528; 1.2.840.113556.1.4.417;
1.2.840.113556.1.4.619; 1.2.840.113556.1.4.841; 1.2.840.113556.1.4.529;
1.2.840.113556.1.4.805; 1.2.840.113556.1.4.521; 1.2.840.113556.1.4.970;
1.2.840.113556.1.4.1338; 1.2.840.113556.1.4.474; 1.2.840.113556.1.4.1339;
1.2.840.113556.1.4.1340; 1.2.840.113556.1.4.1413; 2.16.840.1.113730.3.4.9;
2.16.840.1.113730.3.4.10; 1.2.840.113556.1.4.1504; 1.2.840.113556.1.4.1852;
1.2.840.113556.1.4.802; 1.2.840.113556.1.4.1907;
   2> supportedLDAPVersion: 3; 2;
   12> supportedLDAPPolicies: MaxPoolThreads; MaxDatagramRecv; MaxReceiveBuffer;
    InitRecvTimeout; MaxConnections; MaxConnIdleTime; MaxPageSize;
    MaxQueryDuration; MaxTempTableSize; MaxResultSetSize;
    MaxNotificationPerConn; MaxValRange;
   1> highestCommittedUSN: 45151;
   4> supportedSASLMechanisms: GSSAPI; GSS-SPNEGO; EXTERNAL; DIGEST-MD5;
   1> dnsHostName: BILL.ins.com;
   1> ldapServiceName: ins.com:bill$@INS.COM;
   1> serverName: CN=BILL,CN=Servers,CN=Default-First-Site-Name,CN=Sites,
    CN=Configuration,DC=ins,DC=com;
   3> supportedCapabilities: 1.2.840.113556.1.4.800;
    1.2.840.113556.1.4.1670; 1.2.840.113556.1.4.1791;
   1> isSynchronized: TRUE;
   1> isGlobalCatalogReady: TRUE;
   1> domainFunctionality: 2 = ( DS_BEHAVIOR_WIN2003 );
   1> forestFunctionality: 2 = ( DS_BEHAVIOR_WIN2003 );
   1> domainControllerFunctionality: 2 = ( DS_BEHAVIOR_WIN2003 );
```

Some of the information that Active Directory provides without requiring authentication includes:

- Current time
- Naming contexts supported by the server
- Supported LDAP versions
- Supported LDAP controls
- SASL mechanisms that can be used for authentication to Active Directory via LDAP
- The server DNS and LDAP (DN) names, as well as the Kerberos Service Name (SPN)
- Domain Controller, Domain and Forest versions (Active Directory specific)

3.3.15.8 User Accounts in AD

Information about user accounts, including username, SID, password hashes, group membership, etc., is stored in Active Directory on Windows 2000/2003 domain controllers. User objects in Active Directory are instances of either the **user** class from the Active Directory schema or the **INetOrgPerson** class (Windows 2003 Native Mode domains support a special password attribute for this class).

Table 3.15 represents some of the important attributes of user accounts in Active Directory. Reference [18] provides full information on the **User** class in Active Directory and its attributes.

Users in Windows 2000 and later operating systems can use their User Principal Names (UPNs) instead of their Windows NT 4.0 style logon name (**sAMAccountName**) to log in to the system. User UPNs follow the RFC 822-prescribed format, wherein the name has two parts: an actual username and a domain suffix. The username part is a unique name within the domain that will very often be the same as the Windows NT 4.0 logon name (**sAMAccountName**). By default, the domain part is the same as the name of the domain where the user account is created. However, Active Directory allows the administrator to define the so-called UPN suffixes, and Active Directory can be configured so that UPNs do not have their domain part equal to the name of the domain where they have been created. For example, an organization may have more than one domain but define a common UPN suffix for all the users in the organization, regardless of the domain where their accounts reside. The user must be made aware of the UPN he has been assigned in the same way as he is made aware of his username when his account is created in Active Directory. Both the Windows NT 4.0 username and the UPN will map to the same user account (same SID) but are two different names to refer to it. For most applications, the user can use either name to authenticate.

As an example, user Peter from domain **ins.com** is very likely to use the UPN **Peter@ins.com**. However, if the forest to which the **ins.com** domain belongs defines new UPN suffixes (such as **ad.corp.local**), then Peter may have his UPN defined as **Peter@ad.corp.local** by **ins.com** administrators. Regardless of the new UPN name, it refers to the same account, and user Peter will have the same access token.

Active Directory stores and utilizes the same LAN Manager and Windows NT hash values as Windows NT 4.0; the LM hash is stored in the **dbcsPwd** attribute and the NT hash is stored in the **unicodePwd** attribute. As with SAM, to protect the password hashes from malicious users, the operating system does not allow for easy access to these attributes. As in Windows NT 4.0, by default, the password is not stored in a reversibly encrypted format, and only the password hash is stored in the NTDS file. Similar to Windows NT 4.0, while stored in the NTDS file, the password

Table 3.15 User Attributes in Active Directory

Attribute	*Format*	*Schema Name*	*Description*
Object Class (mandatory)	String — 20 bytes average	objectClass	The classes that the object instantiates. In Windows 2003, user objects inherit the following classes: **user, orgnizationalPerson, top, Person**.
SAM AccountName (mandatory)	String — up to 20 bytes	sAMAccountName	This is the Windows NT 4 username attribute. Users accessing Active Directory from Windows NT 4 and earlier operating systems will log in to the system using this name.
SAM Account Type (optional)	Double Word (4 bytes)	sAMAccountType	Specifies whether the account is a regular user account (SAM_NORMAL_USER_ACCOUNT 0x30000000), a computer account (SAM_MACHINE_ACCOUNT 0x30000001), or an interdomain trust account (SAM_TRUST_ACCOUNT 0x30000002).
User Principal Name — UPN (optional)	String	UserPrincipalName	This is an Internet-style login name, following RFC 822. The format resembles a user e-mail address (example: peter@ins.com). This will typically (but not necessarily) be the user ID, followed by the "@" sign and the domain name where the user account resides.
SID (mandatory)	Typically 16 bytes	objectSid	The Security Identifier (SID) for the user.
Object GUID (optional)	16 bytes	objectGUID	Unique object identifier (this is not the SID of the user account). This is only a unique identifier used internally by the directory services.

Table 3.15 User Attributes in Active Directory (continued)

Attribute	*Format*	*Schema Name*	*Description*
Primary Group (optional)	4 bytes	primaryGroupID	This is the RID portion of the SID of the primary group of which the user is a member. This is only supported for POSIX compliance.
Given Name (optional)	String	givenName	The user's first name.
Surname (optional)	String	sn	The user's surname/last name.
Common Name — CN (mandatory)	String — 64 bytes	cn	This is the name that represents the user to the system, *aka* user ID, username, or account name.
Distinguished Name — DN (mandatory)	String	dn	This is a string that uniquely identifies the object (the user in this instance), as defined by the X.500 standard and RFC1779. The distinguished name in Active Directory will contain the Common Name (CN), followed by the names of the OU of which the user is a member, followed by the domain name that uses the key DC for each subdomain. (example: distinguishedName: CN=Peter Black,OU=Employees,DC=ins,DC=com)
Display Name (optional)	String	displayName	This is typically a combination of the First Name and Surname fields, and represents the user Full name as visualized in Active Directory administrative tools.

User account options (optional)	4 bytes	userAccountControl	Specifies attributes of the user account, such as whether the password is stored using reversible encryption (UF_ENCRYPTED_TEXT_PASSWORD_ALLOWED) or whether the user password will expire (UF_ENCRYPTED_TEXT_PASSWORD_ALLOWED).
Dial-in permission for user (optional)	4 bytes	msNPAllowDialin	This specifies whether the user is allowed to dial in using MS RAS servers, or when RADIUS (IAS) authentication is used by non-Microsoft Network Access Servers (NAS).
NT Hash	16 bytes	unicodePwd	The NT hash of the user password.
LM Hash	16 bytes	dbcsPwd	The LM hash of the user password.
NT Password History (optional)		ntPwdHistory	User password history — NT hash, encrypted using SYSKEY while stored in the NTDS file. Used to enforce password uniqueness.
LM Password History (optional)		lmPwdHistory	User password history — LM hash, encrypted using SYSKEY while stored in the NTDS file. Used to enforce password uniqueness.
Supplemental Credentials (optional)		SupplementalCredentials	This attribute is not documented by Microsoft. It is believed to be used to store the reversibly encrypted password for the user, as well as Kerberos encrypted passwords.
User SID History	Variable	sIDHistory	A list of user and group SIDs for a migrated user.

hashes are protected by means of SYSKEY encryption (see subsection 3.2.8). SYSKEY is enabled by default on Windows 2000/2003 domain controllers.

The **dbcsPwd** and **unicodePwd** attributes can be modified by users with appropriate privileges (object SELF and Administrators) but cannot be read, regardless of the privileges. The attributes can only be modified (written to) over an LDAP/SSL (LDAPS) connection. Modification of the password attributes within plain unencrypted LDAP sessions is not supported. More details on how to programmatically change the user password through LDAP are provided in [20]. More information on the requirements for LDAP over SSL with Windows 2000/2003 Active Directory is provided in [21].

Another attribute that can potentially be used to store the user password is **userPassword**. This same attribute is used by the **inetOrgPerson** class that follows the RFC standard definition found in [19] — RFC 2798. Microsoft supports integration between the **inetOrgPerson** class attribute **userPassword** and the Windows standard **user** class attribute **unicodePwd**. To allow for synchronization between the two, the administrator needs to modify the 9th character of the **dsHeuristics** variable (see subsection 3.3.15.6). In Windows 2003 Native Mode domains, it is possible to use the **inetOrgPerson** class for user objects instead of the standard **user** class. This allows for easier integration with other LDAP implementations.

By default, Windows NT does not store user passwords in encrypted or plain format. Windows NT typically stores password hashes (NT Hash and LM Hash), which are the result of a one-way function (OWF) transformation, and virtually cannot be used to generate the original user password. By definition, one-way functions are irreversible.

However, there are specific authentication protocols that require access to the plaintext user password. Such protocols are the CHAP authentication protocol, typically used by Windows to authenticate remote access users, as well as the SASL Digest Authentication mechanisms used by various applications, including Web/HTTP. Authentication from older MacOS hosts may require reversibly encrypted passwords as well. To meet these requirements, Windows 2000 and later allow the user password to be stored in Active Directory, in addition to the password hash. The password is then stored in the directory services database using reversible encryption. Although this is not documented, it is believed that the **Supplemental-Credentials** attribute in Active Directory is used to store the reversibly encrypted user password. This attribute can neither be read nor written to, and only LSA/SAM functions can access it. The password is encrypted using the SYSKEY encryption algorithm in the same way as password hashes. However, as the algorithm uses symmetric RC4 encryption, provided that the System Key is stored in the registry, the plaintext password

Table 3.16 Digest Authentication Precomputed Hash Values

Username	*Realm*	*Password*
SamAccountName	NetBIOS Domain Name for the domain where the user account resides	password
SamAccountName	DNS Domain Name for the domain where the user account resides	password
User Principlal Name (UPN)	NULL string	password
NetBIOSName	NULL string	password
SamAccountName	"Digest"	password
User Principal Name (UPN)	"Digest"	password
NetBiosName	"Digest"	password

can easily be obtained. The protection of such reversibly encrypted passwords therefore depends on the protection of the System Key. For more information, see subsection 3.2.8.4. As a general recommendation, storing passwords using reversible encryption should be avoided if possible.

Under certain circumstances, in Windows 2003 it is no longer required to store the password using reversible encryption for SASL Digest authentication. Digest authentication needs the MD5 hash of the string, comprised of the following: the username, followed by a colon (":"), followed by the realm name followed by a colon, followed by the plaintext user password (see Chapter 4). Every time the user changes his password, the SASL Digest password hashes in Table 3.16 are automatically calculated and stored as user attributes, supposedly in the **SupplementalCredentials** user attribute.

Active Directory needs to precalculate the above combinations to accommodate different syntax from which the user may choose to identify himself during SASL Digest Authentication. The username and the domain name, however, are not case sensitive. Therefore, if the user has provided his username and realm (domain name) using a different case from that specified in the Active Directory database, Digest Authentication will still fail unless the password is stored using reversible encryption.

More information on how Active Directory stores precomputed Digest Authentication hash values is available in [137].

3.3.15.9 Case Study: User Logon Names in Active Directory

If a user is attempting interactive authentication using his domain account from a workstation in the forest, this workstation can either belong to the

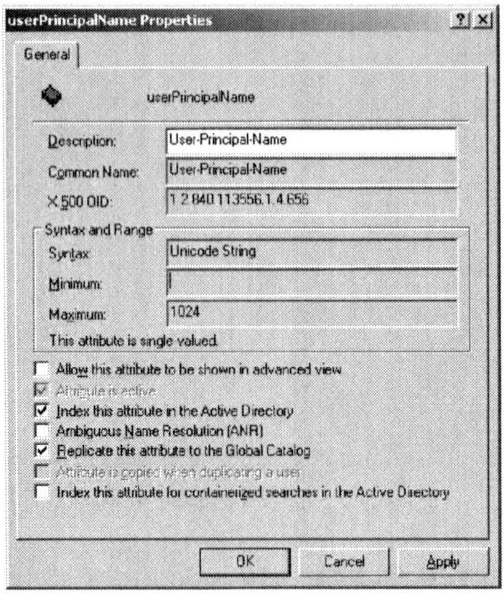

Figure 3.24 userPrincipalName replication to Global Catalog server.

same domain where the user account resides or a workstation in another domain within the forest (or even from an external domain in another forest). If the workstation is in the same domain as the user account, then the authentication information, including the UPN, will be sent to the domain controller, which will then perform a search for the UPN in its local domain database and will find the user account that has this specific UPN and then use the credentials provided to authenticate the user. However, if the workstation from which the user is trying to log in belongs to another domain from the same forest or an external domain from another forest, the authenticating domain controller will need to query the Global Catalog and determine to which domain to forward the authentication request. By default, the **userPrincipalName** attribute of user accounts is configured for replication to the Global Catalog in the Active Directory schema (Figure 3.24).

As a result, if a user tries to log in to Active Directory using his user principal name (UPN), and is doing so interactively from a workstation that is not a member of his own domain, or across the network to a server that is not a member of his own domain, a Global Catalog server must be available to provide the authenticating domain controller with the mapping between the UPN provided by the user and the actual user account in Active Directory.

Unless an application only relies on Windows NT 4.0 style domainname\username identity, users on Windows 2000 and later computers can choose whether they want to use the old format or the UPN format for

Figure 3.25 User login using UPN.

the username. For example, a user interactively logging into a workstation or other domain member may want to use the UPN suffix in Figure 3.25. When the user specifies a UPN in the username field, the "Log on to" part, which normally specifies the domain name, will become dimmed and will not be used by the GINA.

3.3.15.10 Case Study: Using LDAP to Change User Passwords in Active Directory

Active Directory is an LDAP-compliant directory service. It allows users to authenticate to the directory service as a resource and then access information in the directory. Users with appropriate permissions can access object attributes, including the user password attributes.

This subsection demonstrates how a simple LDAP client such as **LDP.EXE** can be used to access resources in Active Directory and, more specifically, how to modify the password attribute for a user. The **LDP.EXE** tool is available from the Windows 2000/2003 Support Tools package on the Windows 2003 Server CD.

The first step is to connect to a domain controller using LDAPS (LDAP over SSL) (Figure 3.26).

Once the connection to the server is established, the user needs to bind to the LDAP server (authenticate) (Figure 3.27). The user employed for the connection in this example is the Administrator that has a broad set of privileges.

Once the user has authenticated to the LDAP server with administrative privileges, he can navigate down the Active Directory tree and find the user object for Peter Black. Below is the output from **LDP.EXE**:

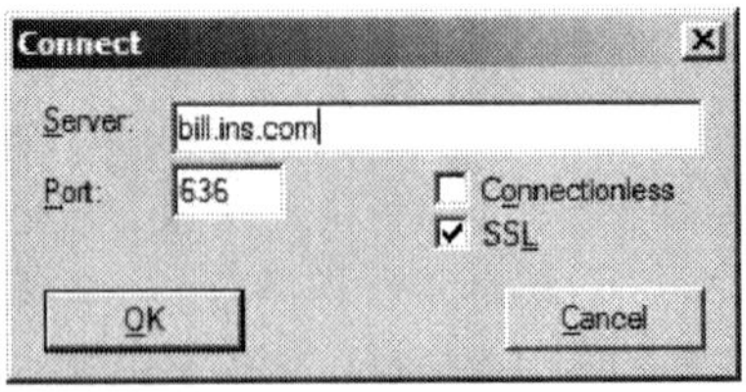

Figure 3.26 LDP.EXE: connect to LDAP server.

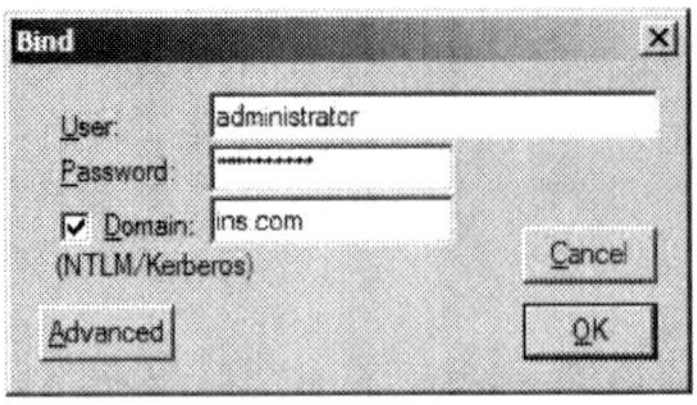

Figure 3.27 LDAP bind.

```
Expanding base 'CN=Peter Black,OU=Employees,DC=ins,DC=com'...
Result <0>: (null)
Matched DNs:
Getting 1 entries:
>> Dn: CN=Peter Black,OU=Employees,DC=ins,DC=com
   4> objectClass: top; person; organizationalPerson; user;
   1> cn: Peter Black;
   1> sn: Black;
   1> givenName: Peter;
   1> distinguishedName: CN=Peter Black,OU=Employees,DC=ins,DC=com;
   1> instanceType: 0x4 = ( IT_WRITE );
   1> whenCreated: 07/23/2005 12:52:16 GMT Standard Time GMT Daylight Time;
   1> whenChanged: 11/09/2005 06:47:48 GMT Standard Time GMT Daylight Time;
   1> displayName: Peter Black;
   1> uSNCreated: 16496;
   1> uSNChanged: 36912;
   1> name: Peter Black;
   1> objectGUID: 4021189a-48a3-4ab3-9814-2a33e595d404;
   1> userAccountControl: 0x10280 = ( UF_ENCRYPTED_TEXT_PASSWORD_ALLOWED |
   UF_NORMAL_ACCOUNT | UF_DONT_EXPIRE_PASSWD );
   1> badPwdCount: 2;
   1> codePage: 0;
   1> countryCode: 0;
   1> badPasswordTime: 11/07/2005 22:41:42 GMT Standard Time GMT Daylight Time;
   1> lastLogoff: 01/01/1601 00:00:00 GMT Standard Time GMT Daylight Time;
   1> lastLogon: 09/11/2005 21:18:29 GMT Standard Time GMT Daylight Time;
   1> pwdLastSet: 11/09/2005 06:30:58 GMT Standard Time GMT Daylight Time;
   1> primaryGroupID: 513;
   1> userParameters: <ldp: Binary blob>;
   1> objectSid: S-1-5-21-676691431-2304381362-2152039065-1113;
   1> accountExpires: 09/14/30828 02:48:05 UNC ;
   1> logonCount: 9;
   1> sAMAccountName: Peter;
   1> sAMAccountType: 805306368;
```

```
  1> userPrincipalName: Peter@ins.com;
  1> objectCategory: CN=Person,CN=Schema,CN=Configuration,DC=ins,DC=com;
  1> msNPAllowDialin: TRUE;
  4> dSCorePropagationData: 07/23/2005 12:56:49 GMT Standard Time GMT
   Daylight Time; 07/23/2005 12:56:49 GMT Standard Time GMT Daylight
   Time; 07/23/2005 12:56:49 GMT Standard Time GMT Daylight Time;
   01/08/1601 15:10:56 GMT Standard Time GMT Daylight Time;
  1> msSFU30Name: Peter;
  1> msSFU30UidNumber: 10007;
  1> msSFU30GidNumber: 20005;
  1> msSFU30LoginShell: /bin/sh;
  1> msSFU30Password: $1$1JEri/..$3.QpnOm2.UaCAA01uEp31/;
  1> msSFU30NisDomain: ins;
  1> msSFU30HomeDirectory: /home/Peter;
msSFU30PosixMemberOf: CN=Marketing,OU=Employees,DC=ins,DC=com;
```

Attributes such as **unicodePwd** and **dbcsPwd** are not shown here — and they cannot be read via LDAP. Nevertheless, a user with appropriate privileges can modify the **unicodePwd** attribute for another user. The password must be provided in Unicode format. **LDP.EXE** requires the \ **UNI:** prefix for Unicode strings (Figure 3.28).

In this example, the existing value for the **unicodePwd** field for the user will be replaced by a new value. The **unicodePwd** user attribute is used to store the user NT hash, and not the plaintext password. Nevertheless, when an LDAP modify operation is invoked, Active Directory will take the Unicode password provided, calculate the NT hash, and then store the hash value in the **unicodePwd** field instead of the plaintext. The output from **LDP.EXE** is:

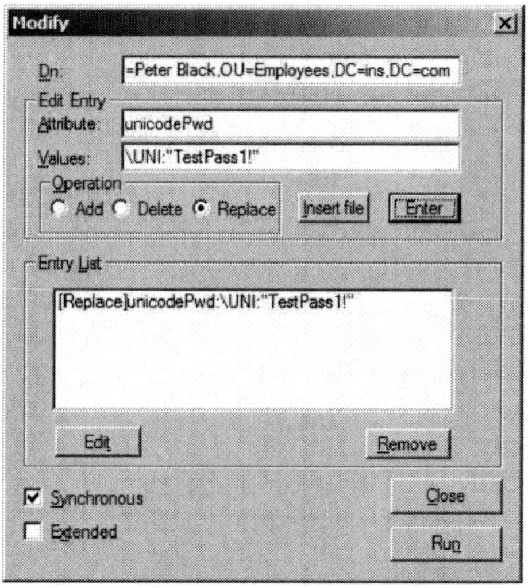

Figure 3.28 Modifying user password in LDP.EXE.

```
-----------
***Call Modify...
ldap_modify_s(ld, 'CN=Peter Black,OU=Employees,DC=ins,DC=com',[1] attrs);
Modified "CN=Peter Black,OU=Employees,DC=ins,DC=com".
-----------
```

The user can now use his new password.

3.3.15.11 Case Study: Obtaining Password Hashes from Active Directory

It is important to understand that utilities such as **pwdump2** and **pwdump3** can still be used by a user with administrative privileges on an Active Directory domain controller to obtain user password hashes. This is due to the fact that these utilities use Windows APIs to obtain password hashes, and these same functions work against SAM as well as against Active Directory.

In a similar way to SAM, tools exist that can perform offline attacks against the Active Directory database. SYSKEY is enabled by default on all Windows 2000 and later computers; but if the System Key is stored in the registry (default location), an attacker who has access to the SYSTEM registry file can obtain the system key, then the password encryption key, which can then be used to decrypt portions of the **NTDS.DIT** file and this will expose both the LM and NT password hashes to the attacker. These hashes are the same as in the SAM, and are subject to the same attacks. For more information, see subsection 3.2.8.6.

If the system key is not stored in the SYSTEM registry file and is instead configured to be provided by an administrator during start-up, or stored on a floppy disk, this can make the task of obtaining user hashes virtually impossible for an unauthorized user, although malicious administrators can still leverage this attack.

3.3.15.12 Group Accounts and Group Strategy in AD

All Active Directory group accounts inherit the **group** class defined in the schema. Table 3.17 gives some of the important attributes defined by this class. Additional information on the **group** class is available in [23].

Active Directory provides for two types of groups: (1) Security and (2) Distribution. Security groups are similar to Windows NT 4.0 groups: they are security principals and can be granted access to resources. Distribution groups are used for purposes other than granting user rights or permissions to resources; for example, they are used by Exchange 2000/2003 as distribution lists (lists of e-mail recipients).

Contrary to the common expectations, Distribution groups that are supposed not to be used for security purposes have SIDs similar to security principals. However, even in Windows 2003, Distribution Group SIDs are not added to the user access token. The user interface does not allow Distribution groups to be granted user rights or permissions to resources.

In addition to global and domain local groups, Active Directory provides for a third type of groups: Universal groups. The three of them — Global, Domain Local, and Universal — can be either Security or Distribution groups. However, Universal Security groups cannot be created in Mixed Mode domains due to the fact that they cannot be replicated to Windows NT 4.0 domain controllers that have no equivalent for this type of group. Universal Security groups can be created once the domain is converted to at least Windows 2000 Native Mode and there are no more Windows NT 4.0 domain controllers.

Universal groups sit in between Global groups and Domain Local groups; they can have user accounts from any domain as their members, and they can have other Global groups and Universal groups as their members. Universal groups are visible in all domains within the forest where they are created, and can be members of other Universal groups, Domain Local groups, or Local groups on member servers and workstations.

To support this functionality for Universal groups, Active Directory stores Universal group membership in Global Catalog servers. Because Universal Security groups have their own SIDs, and users can be members of these groups, it is required in Native Mode Windows 2000 and later domains that either a Global Catalog server be available during user authentication to provide information about group membership of the user who is trying to log in, or there be cached universal group membership information (supported by Windows 2003 domains only). If in a Windows 2000 or later domain, a user tries to log in interactively or across the network, and if no Global Catalog server or cached membership (Windows 2003 only) is available, the user will not be able to log in at all, because the operating system cannot build a security token for this user; members of the Domain Admins group are exempt from this rule to avoid access lockout. For regular users, this behavior may need to be disabled explicitly, if required.

In the case of a single domain forest, all domain controllers have knowledge of all the groups and their membership; and in this scenario, Universal groups do not provide any additional benefits compared to Global and Local groups.

With the advent of Universal groups, group strategies in Windows 2000 Native Mode domains have also changed. The new strategy is as follows:

- User accounts are typically added to Global groups following a functional, geographical, organizational, administrative, or other criteria grouping.

Table 3.17 Group Attributes in Active Directory

Attribute	*Format*	*Schema Name*	*Description*
Object Class (mandatory)	String — 20 bytes average	objectClass	The classes that the object instantiates. In Windows 2003, group objects inherit the following classes: **group**, **top**.
SAM AccountName (mandatory)	String — up to 20 bytes	sAMAccountName	This is the Windows NT 4.0-compatible name of the group. Users accessing Active Directory from Windows NT 4.0 and earlier operating systems will see this name in User Manager and Access Control Lists.
SAM Account Type (optional)	Double Word (4 bytes)	sAMAccountType	This specifies the account type in Windows NT 4.0 terms.
Group Type (mandatory)	Double Word (4 bytes)	groupType	This specifies the type of the group: 0x00000001 – System created 0x00000002 – Global Group 0x00000004 – Domain Local Group 0x00000008 – Universal Group 0x80000000 – specifies a Security Group; if not set, this is a Distribution group.
Member (optional)	String containing Distinguished names	member	Group membership — this attribute is a semicolon-separated list of user and group Distinguished names for objects that are members of this group.

Member Of (optional)	String containing Distinguished names	Is-Member-Of-DL	Inherited from the **top** class — a list of groups of which this group is a member.
SID (mandatory)	Typically 16 bytes	objectSid	The group Security Identifier (SID).
Object GUID (optional)	16 bytes	objectGUID	Unique object identifier — this is not the SID of the group account. This is only a unique identifier used internally by the directory services.
Display Name (optional)	String	displayName	The name of the group as it appears in AD administrative tools.
Name (optional)	String	name	A friendly name for the group (inherited from the **top** class).
Common Name — CN (mandatory)	String — 64 bytes	cn	This is the name that represents the group to the system.
Distinguished Name — DN (mandatory)	String	dn	This is a string that uniquely identifies the object (the group in this instance), as defined by the X.500 standard and RFC 1779. The distinguished name in Active Directory will contain the Common Name (CN), followed by the names of the OU of which the user is a member, followed by the domain name that uses the key DC for each subdomain. (example: distinguishedName: CN=Engineering,OU=Employees,DC=ins,DC=com).

- Global groups from all domains in the forest are added to a single forest-wide Universal group that typically follows the same grouping criteria as the Global groups in it.
- The Universal group is added to all the Local groups that need to be created where the resources in the forest reside: on the file server, on the Web server, on the database server, or on the print server.
- The Local group on the server where the resource resides is granted appropriate permissions to the resource.

Thus, users, by being members of Global groups and by virtue of these Global groups being added to Universal groups that on hand are added to Local groups on resource servers, are provided with the same rights and permissions as the Local groups.

3.3.15.13 Case Study: Exploring the Effects of Group Nesting to User Access Token

This case study assumes that Susan Red is a user who is a member of the Engineering Global Group in the **ins.com** domain, as well as of the Engineering News DL Distribution Group in the same domain (Figure 3.29). The Engineering Global Group is a member of the Enterprise Engineering Universal Group (Figure 3.30). And the Enterprise Engineering Universal group is a member of the Engineering on Steve Local Group,

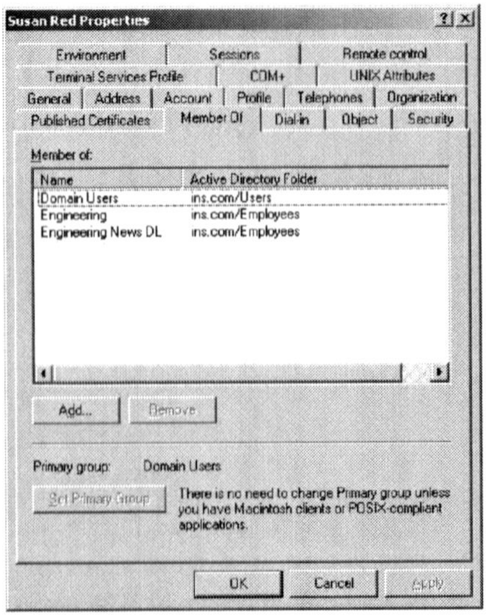

Figure 3.29 Susan Red: group membership.

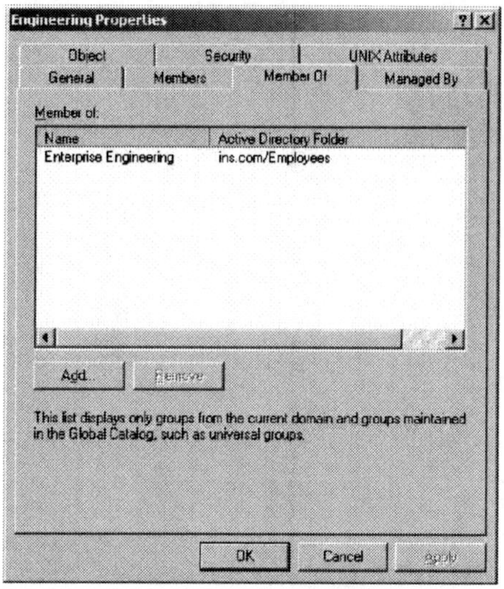

Figure 3.30 Engineering group is a member of the Enterprise Engineering Universal group.

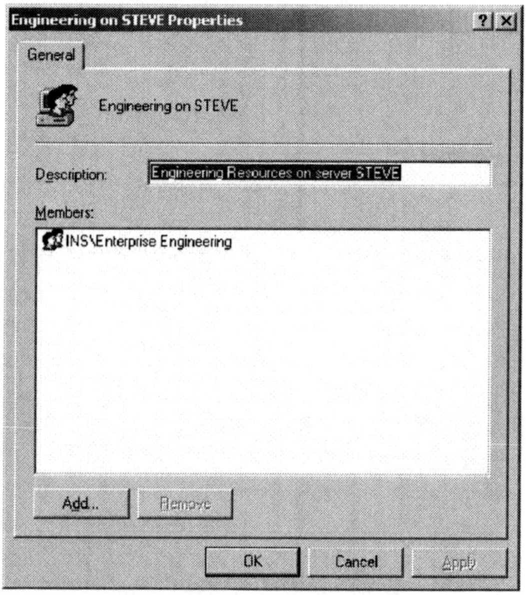

Figure 3.31 Local group Engineering on STEVE.

which resides on server STEVE (Figure 3.31). If Susan Red interactively logs on to server STEVE using her domain account, her access token will be similar to the one on page 268:

```
C:\Documents and Settings\susan> whoami /user /groups

USER INFORMATION
----------------

User Name SID
========= =============================================
ins\susan S-1-5-21-676691431-2304381362-2152039065-1119

GROUP INFORMATION
-----------------

Group Name         Type       SID                   Attributes
================== ========== ===================== ==========================
Everyone           Well-known S-1-1-0               Mandatory group, Enabled
                    group                            by default, Enabled group
STEVE\Engineering  Alias       S-1-5-21-405461271-  Mandatory group, Enabled
 on STEVE           group       1135999247-          by default, Enabled group
                                842743682-1013
BUILTIN\Users      Alias       S-1-5-32-545         Mandatory group, Enabled
                                                     by default, Enabled group
NT AUTHORITY\      Well-known  S-1-5-4              Mandatory group, Enabled
 INTERACTIVE        group                            by default, Enabled group
NT AUTHORITY\      Well-known  S-1-5-11             Mandatory group, Enabled
 Authenticated      group                            by default, Enabled group
 Users
NT AUTHORITY\This  Well-known  S-1-5-15             Mandatory group, Enabled
 Organization       group                            by default, Enabled group
LOCAL              Well-known  S-1-2-0              Mandatory group, Enabled
                    group                            by default, Enabled group
INS\Engineering    Group       S-1-5-21-676691431-  Mandatory group, Enabled
                                2304381362-          by default, Enabled group
                                2152039065-1111
INS\Enterprise     Group       S-1-5-21-676691431-  Mandatory group, Enabled
 Engineering                    2304381362-          by default, Enabled group
                                2152039065-1135

C:\Documents and Settings\susan>
```

It is important to note that although Susan Red is not directly a member of the Enterprise Engineering Universal group or the Engineering on Steve Local group on member server STEVE, her access token has been expanded to include all the group SIDs as if she were a direct member of all the groups. As this information is available in the user's access token at the time of authentication, the resource access authorization process has the effective membership information and does not need to explicitly expand group membership before checking access permissions.

If a domain member is removed from a domain, this does not remove domain accounts and groups from local groups or from access control lists. The local computer administrator needs to clean these assignments manually if there is no intention to rejoin the computer to the domain and retain permissions. When a domain member is removed from the domain, it will not be able to resolve domain user and group names but will show their corresponding SIDs in administrative tools to indicate that the privileges are still there (Figure 3.32).

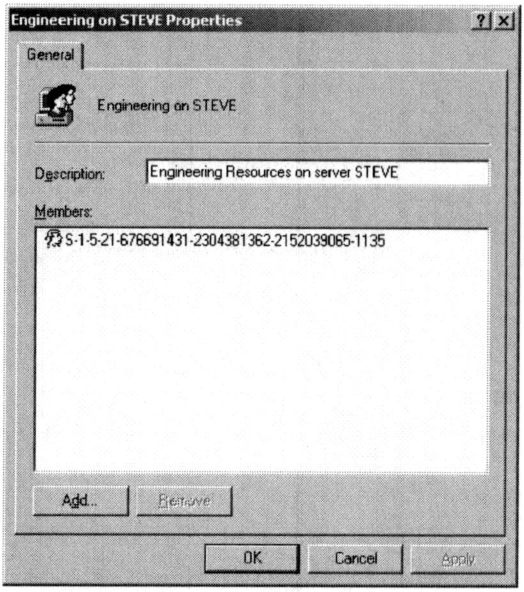

Figure 3.32 Domain Local group when the computer is removed from the domain.

A unique feature of Active Directory Native Mode domains is that group accounts scope or type can be changed (group conversion) as long as the current members or membership do not conflict with the requirements of the target group account type. This feature is not available in Mixed Mode domains because Windows NT 4.0 domain controllers cannot replicate a change in group type — this is not supported by legacy SAM.

In general, a change in group scope or type would be performed by an administrator who wants to leverage existing groups for a different purpose. However, it is interesting to know that in Active Directory forests running Exchange 2000 or later, if users who are not administrators try to assign permissions to Distribution groups using their Outlook clients, the Exchange 2000/2003 Information Store service, which typically has administrative privileges, will silently convert the Distribution group into a security group to perform this operation; see [22] for more details. Although this may present additional convenience for the administrators, it may result in a group that was by now only meant to store information about distribution lists to be eventually added to user access tokens. This behavior can and probably should be disabled by administrators who have high security requirements.

3.3.15.14 Computer Accounts in AD

Computer accounts are instances of the **computer** class of the Active Directory schema. Table 3.18 shows some of the most important attributes of this class. More information on the **computer** class is available in [23].

As already noted, computer accounts are security principals, along with user and group accounts. Table 3.18 shows that computer objects actually inherit the Active Directory user class as well, and therefore have attributes such as **sAMAccountName** (Windows NT 4.0 logon name) and SID.

It is important to note that in both Windows NT 4.0 domains and in Windows 2000/2003 Active Directory domains, each domain member must have a computer account in the domain. When a Windows computer starts up, it authenticates to the domain using its computer account.

In Windows 2000 and later, the computer account in the domain has a SID just like any user account, and is a security principal that can perform tasks on the network. Thus, the System (Local System) account can be used by a domain member to access other computers on the network. The computer account of one computer can be granted permissions (using its domain SID) to access resources on other computers within the same domain, or other domains with appropriate trust relationships. Therefore, with Windows 2000 and later, it is no longer required to create user accounts for services — they will typically use the System (Local System) account on the system where they are running.

3.3.15.15 Trees, Forests, and Intra-forest Trusts

Active Directory was designed for large organizations with a very large number of users. It allows for many domains within the organization as well, although a good infrastructure design will very often require one or only a few domains. The grouping of all domains that belong to the same organization, and typically have common security requirements and administration, is known as a forest. While the domain is the security boundary in Windows NT 4.0 and earlier implementations, and this is almost the case in Active Directory, to a certain extent the forest represents a new security boundary for the organization. The first domain installed in the forest is known as the forest root domain, and this domain contains the global group Enterprise Admins. This group is automatically added to the domain local Administrators group of every new domain created in the forest. However, Enterprise Admins it is not added to the local Administrators group of domain members of that domain.

Only the Enterprise Admins group has privileges to implement settings that affect the entire forest — such as adding new trees to the organization, adding new sites, authorizing DHCP servers, etc. Domain local Administrators groups do not have such privileges. Furthermore, the Enterprise

Table 3.18 Computer Attributes in Active Directory

Attribute	*Format*	*Schema Name*	*Description*
Object Class (mandatory)	String — 20 bytes average	objectClass	The classes that the object instantiates. In Windows 2003, computer objects inherit the following classes: **top, person, organizationalPerson, user, computer.** *Note:* Computer objects inherit all the attributes from user classes, such as **user**, **organizationalPerson**, and **person.**
SAM AccountName (mandatory)	String — up to 20 bytes	sAMAccountName	This is the Windows NT 4.0-compatible name of the computer (NetBIOS name), followed by the "**$**" sign. For example, a computer called BILL (NetBIOS/Hostname) will have its **sAMAccountName** attribute set to "**BILL$**".
SAM Account Type (optional)	Double Word (4 bytes)	sAMAccountType	Specifies the account type in Windows NT terms.
Service Principal Name (SPN — optional)	String	servicePrincipalName	A list of service names in Kerberos service format that are running on this particular computer. SPNs are extensively used for Kerberos authentication; see [33].
Member Of (optional)	String containing Distinguished names	Is-Member-Of-DL	Inherited from the **top** class — a list of groups of which this group is a member.
SID (mandatory)	Typically 16 bytes	objectSid	The group Security Identifier (SID)
Object GUID (optional)	16 bytes	objectGUID	Unique object identifier — this is not the SID of the computer account. This is only a unique identifier used internally by the directory services.

Table 3.18 Computer Attributes in Active Directory (continued)

Attribute	*Format*	*Schema Name*	*Description*
Display Name (optional)	String	displayName	The name of the computer as it appears in AD administrative tools.
Name (optional)	String	name	The NetBIOS/host name of the computer (inherited from the **top** class).
DNS Name (optional)	String	dnsHostName	The FQDN of the computer.
Common Name – CN (mandatory)	String – 64 bytes	cn	This is the name that represents the computer to the system; typically the NetBIOS/Host name.
Distinguished Name – DN (mandatory)	String	dn	This is a string that uniquely identifies the object (the computer in this instance), as defined by the X.500 standard and RFC 1779. The Distinguished name in Active Directory will contain the Common Name (CN), followed by the names of the OU of which the user/computer is a member, followed by the domain name that uses the key DC for each subdomain. (example: distinguishedName: CN=BILL,OU=Domain Controllers,DC=ins,DC=com).
Computer OS (optional)	String	operatingSystem	A string representing the operating system running on this computer (Example: "Windows Server 2003").
OS Version (optional)	String	operatingSystemVersion	A string representing the version and build of the operating system (Example: "5.2 (3790)").
Service Pack (optional)	String	operatingSystemServicePack	A string representing the service pack of the operating system (Example: "Service Pack 1").

Admins group is in a position to apply Group Policies to sites in the organization. Because such policies cross domain boundaries and can potentially apply settings, including security-related settings, to members of every domain in the forest, this group is considered to have very broad privileges. As a result, the forest can be considered an outer security boundary, and the domains can be considered an inner security boundary in the Active Directory model, wherein forest settings can potentially influence domain settings.

In addition, in an interdomain trust account (see subsection 3.3.4) that is essentially a hidden object of types **person**, **organizationalPerson,** and **user** stored in the **Users** container of the domain partition, Active Directory stores additional trust information in objects of type **trusted-Domain**, also known as Trusted Domain Object (TDO). These objects are created in the hidden **System** container of the domain partition. Some of the most important attributes of TDOs are included in Table 3.19. More information on the **trustedDomain** class is available in [34].

Domains in Active Directory form tree structures called domain trees. The root of the tree is the direct or indirect parent of all the domains in the tree. The tree represents a contiguous and hierarchical namespace. If the domains in an organization do not use a contiguous namespace, it is possible to have more than one tree in the forest.

All the domains within a tree are interconnected by implicit two-way transitive trusts known as parent-child trusts. These trust relationships are automatically created when a new domain is added to the forest, and they cannot be modified or deleted.

All the domain trees are connected to the forest root domain by implicit two-way Kerberos transitive trusts, known as tree-root trusts. These trust relationships are also automatically created when a new tree is added to the forest, and they cannot be modified or deleted (Figure 3.33).

As a result of the transitive trust relationships within every tree, as well as the transitive trust relationships between the trees in a forest, every domain directly or indirectly (transitively) trusts and is trusted by every other domain in the forest. This means that any user, regardless of where his account resides in the forest, can log on from any workstation in the forest (as long as he has permission to do so), and can access resources on servers in any domain of the forest (as long as he has permission to do so).

Transitive trusts within the Active Directory forest are built using the Kerberos Protocol, which is discussed in Chapter 4. The Kerberos transitive trust relationships will follow the trust paths across the forest to provide the client with a ticket to access resources on a remote server. If the path between the client and the server is too long, it is also possible to build shortcut trusts. In essence, a shortcut trust is an administrator established (explicit)

Table 3.19 trustedDomain Object Attributes

Attribute	*Format*	*Schema Name*	*Description*
Object Class (mandatory)	String — 20 bytes average	objectClass	The classes that the object instantiates. In Windows 2003, TDO objects inherit the following classes: **top, leaf**, and **trustedDomain.**
Common Name (CN) (optional)	String — 64 bytes average size	cn	The name used to represent the object. For TDO accounts, the Common Name is the same as the DNS name of the domain.
Flat Name (optional)	String — 30 bytes average size	flatName	Contains the NetBIOS name of the domain — if this is a Windows domain, or Null
Trust Partner (optional)	String — 30–60 bytes average	trustPartner	The DNS or NetBIOS name of the domain with which the trust exists.
Trust Direction (optional)	4 bytes	TrustDirection	The direction of the trust.
Trust Type (optional)	4 bytes	TrustType	Specifies whether this is a trust to an external NT domain or a trust to an external Kerberos Realm.

trust between two domains within the same forest. Typically, these two domains do not have a direct trust relationship and it will be established explicitly between them because users from one domain often access resources in the other domain. Unlike parent-child and tree-root trust relationships, shortcut trusts must be established manually in each direction.

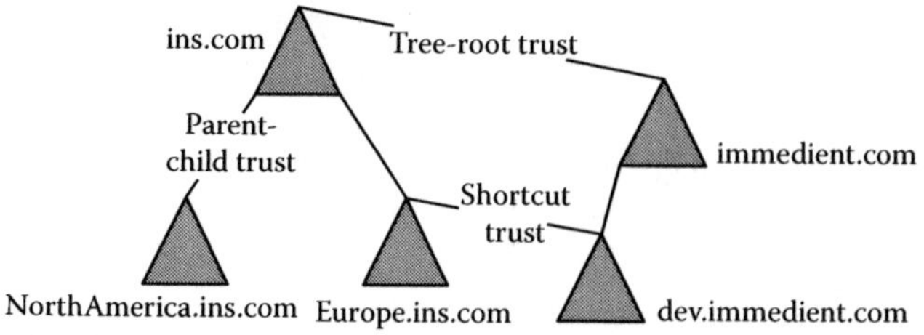

Figure 3.33 Active Directory intra-forest trust relationships.

Once this has been done, the shortcut trust can be used. This trust will always use Kerberos and will be transitive.

When a user in one domain tries to access resources in another domain of the forest, the Kerberos authentication protocol will be responsible for providing the user with a Kerberos Service Granting Ticket (TGS) to access the resource on the destination server.

When a user in an Active Directory forest tries to access resources in another domain, it will send a request for a session ticket to a domain controller in the domain where the client resides. The domain controller will figure out that the server where the resource resides is in another domain (Kerberos realm) and will therefore return a referral ticket (a TGT encrypted with the interdomain trust account password) to a domain controller (KDC) for the next domain in the path. Using this referral, the client goes to the next domain controller in the path and is likely to receive another referral, and this continues until the client finally reaches a domain controller (KDC) in the domain where the resource server resides. This domain controller will finally provide the client with a session ticket for the service. Once the client has the session ticket, it can access the resource server directly until the ticket expires.

3.3.15.16 Case Study: User Accesses Resources in Another Domain in the Same Forest

This case study assumes that user Administrator from domain **immedient.com** needs to access the shared directory TEST on server **bill.ins.com** (see below and Figure 3.33).

```
C:\Documents and Settings\Administrator> whoami /user

USER INFORMATION
----------------

User Name                SID
======================== ==============================================
immedient\administrator  S-1-5-21-1101309658-4153024635-1230627124-500
```

```
C:\Documents and Settings\Administrator> klist tickets

Cached Tickets: (3)

   Server: krbtgt/IMMEDIENT.COM@IMMEDIENT.COM
      KerbTicket Encryption Type: RSADSI RC4-HMAC(NT)
      End Time: 11/20/2005 11:54:52
      Renew Time: 11/27/2005 1:54:52

   Server: ldap/PAUL.immedient.com/immedient.com@IMMEDIENT.COM
      KerbTicket Encryption Type: RSADSI RC4-HMAC(NT)
      End Time: 11/20/2005 11:54:52
      Renew Time: 11/27/2005 1:54:52

   Server: host/paul.immedient.com@IMMEDIENT.COM
      KerbTicket Encryption Type: RSADSI RC4-HMAC(NT)
      End Time: 11/20/2005 11:54:52
      Renew Time: 11/27/2005 1:54:52

C:\Documents and Settings\Administrator> net use * \\bill.ins.com\Test
Drive X: is now connected to \\bill.ins.com\Test.

The command completed successfully.

C:\Documents and Settings\Administrator>x:

X:\> dir
 Volume in drive X has no label.
 Volume Serial Number is A478-E434

 Directory of X:\

07/10/2005  05:35 PM    <DIR>          .
07/10/2005  05:35 PM    <DIR>          ..
07/10/2005  05:35 PM                 9 secret.txt
               1 File(s)             9 bytes
               2 Dir(s)     846,872,576 bytes free

X:\> klist tickets

Cached Tickets: (6)

   Server: krbtgt/IMMEDIENT.COM@IMMEDIENT.COM
      KerbTicket Encryption Type: RSADSI RC4-HMAC(NT)
      End Time: 11/20/2005 11:54:52
      Renew Time: 11/27/2005 1:54:52

   Server: krbtgt/INS.COM@IMMEDIENT.COM
      KerbTicket Encryption Type: RSADSI RC4-HMAC(NT)
      End Time: 11/20/2005 11:54:52
      Renew Time: 11/27/2005 1:54:52

   Server: krbtgt/IMMEDIENT.COM@IMMEDIENT.COM
      KerbTicket Encryption Type: RSADSI RC4-HMAC(NT)
```

```
        End Time: 11/20/2005 11:54:52
        Renew Time: 11/27/2005 1:54:52

     Server: cifs/BILL.ins.com@INS.COM
        KerbTicket Encryption Type: RSADSI RC4-HMAC(NT)
        End Time: 11/20/2005 11:54:52
        Renew Time: 11/27/2005 1:54:52

     Server: ldap/PAUL.immedient.com/immedient.com@IMMEDIENT.COM
        KerbTicket Encryption Type: RSADSI RC4-HMAC(NT)
        End Time: 11/20/2005 11:54:52
        Renew Time: 11/27/2005 1:54:52

     Server: host/paul.immedient.com@IMMEDIENT.COM
        KerbTicket Encryption Type: RSADSI RC4-HMAC(NT)
        End Time: 11/20/2005 11:54:52
        Renew Time: 11/27/2005 1:54:52

X:\>
```

The service principal name (SPN — follows the label **Server:** above) **cifs/BILL.ins.com@INS.COM** is used for SMB/CIFS services on computer BILL at domain **ins.com**, and the ticket is the one that user Administrator from domain **immedient.com** can use to access SMB/CIFS resources on computer **bill.ins.com**.

Figure 3.34 shows the Kerberos authentication process when user **David@NorthAmerica.ins.com** from domain **NorthAmerica.ins.com** (his workstation is a member of the same domain) tries to access the Exchange server computer at domain **Immedient.com** that is in another domain of the same forest. In this example, David is trying to access server **exchange.immedient.com**:

1. David's workstation sends a request for a Ticket Granting Service (TGS) to a **NorthAmerica.ins.com** domain controller (note that the domain members will always connect to their own domain controllers for authentication first).
2. The **NorthAmerica.ins.com** domain controller that receives the request notices that server **exchange.ins.com** is not in the same domain (Kerberos realm); the **NorthAmerica.ins.com** domain controller does not have a shared secret with **exchange.ins.com** and cannot generate a TGS for it. However, it can refer David's computer to another domain controller (KDC) along the trust path that may be able to provide a TGS. Hence, the reply contains a referral TGT that redirects David's computer's request to the **ins.com** tree-top domain. The TGT is encrypted with the interdomain trust account password that **NorthAmerica.ins.com** has for **ins.com**.

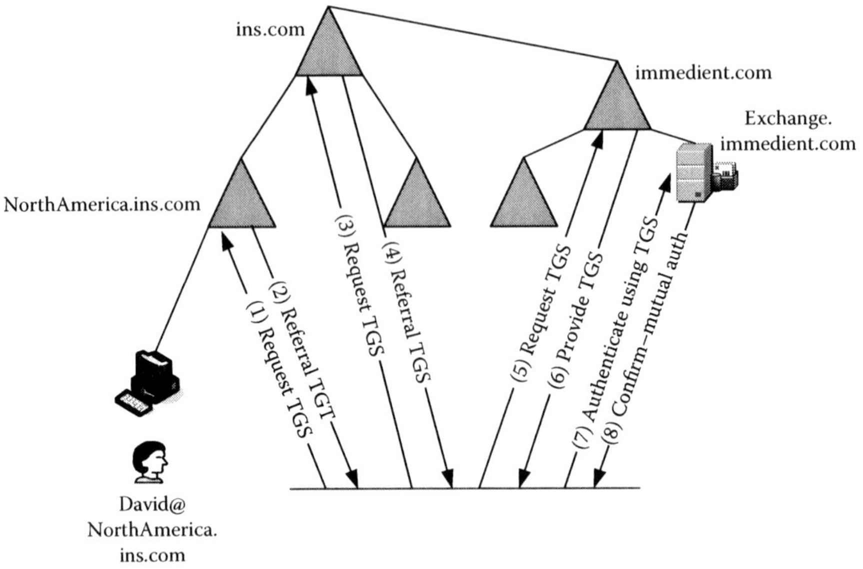

Figure 3.34 Kerberos authentication when accessing resources within the forest.

3. David's computer receives the TGT referral and sends a new TGS request to a domain controller of the **ins.com** domain providing the TGT referral.
4. An **ins.com** domain controller receives the TGS request from David's computer. It decrypts the TGT using the interdomain trust account password that it shares with domain **NorthAmerica.ins.com** and confirms that the TGT is genuine, and that the client can be trusted as it has been authenticated by **NorthAmerica.ins.com** domain controllers. However, the **ins.com** domain controller does not have a shared secret with server **exchange.immedient.com** because this computer belongs to another domain (Kerberos realm). Therefore, it creates another TGT referral, encrypts it with the interdomain trust account password for domain **immedient.com** as a result of the tree-root trust relationship, and returns the referral to David's computer.
5. David's computer now contacts a domain controller of the **immedient.com** domain with a new TGS request for **exchange.ins.com**, and provides the TGT referral that it has from the **ins.com** domain controller to prove that its identity has been verified by a trusted source.
6. A domain controller for the **immedient.com** domain receives the TGS request, and decrypts the TGT referral from **ins.com** to

confirm that it is valid. It then generates a TGS for **exchange.immedient.com** as it shares a secret (account password) with the computer in its own domain, and returns the TGS to David's computer.

7. David's computer sends the TGS to the resource server **exchange.immedient.com**. The resource server receives the request and decrypts it using its shared secret with its domain controller; therefore, it knows the request is genuine. The resource server will find user identification information in the encrypted and signed ticket, and may potentially find the user access token in the ticket.
8. In the reply to the client, the server demonstrates its knowledge of the shared secret and therefore authenticates itself to the user.

Once the authentication has been performed, the two computers are ready to exchange information using the appropriate security context.

3.3.15.17 Trusts with External Domains

Trust relationships can be established between domains that do not belong to the same forest. The trust relationship characteristics will depend on the type of domain with which it is established.

Windows 2000 and Windows 2003 differ in the way they handle trust relationships with parties external to the forest. Oddly enough, Windows 2000 Active Directory domains only support NTLM authentication to external Windows domains, even if these external domains are Windows 2000 or Windows 2003 Active Directory domains, and therefore support Kerberos authentication. Windows 2003 domains support both Kerberos and NTLM authentication for external trusts. The reason for this behavior is that Windows 2003 supports Name Service Routing, while Windows 2000 does not.

In Windows 2000, when a client needs to access a resource with Kerberos authentication, the client needs to obtain a Session Ticket for the resource that needs to be identified by its Service Principal Name (SPN). The SPNs are looked up against the Global Catalog, which is only replicated within the forest (see subsection 3.3.15.2). The Global Catalog partition of the Active Directory database does not contain SPNs for resources from other organizations or external domains in general. In a similar fashion, when a user tries to log in interactively using a User Principal Name (UPN), this will work with Kerberos within the forest. However, a user cannot log on interactively using a UPN across an external trust relationship because the local forest has no means to look up user information in the remote forest Global Catalog or domain database. The Kerberos Protocol depends on the SPN and UPN attributes being available to domain controllers, workstations, and resource servers, and therefore in Windows 2000 if users need to authenticate outside the organization, they can only use NTLM.

Windows 2003 provides for the Name Suffix Routing feature. With name service routing, UPNs and SPNs can be used by users to log on and access resources that might reside in domains external to the forest. When an external or a forest trust (Windows 2003 only) is established between two forests, the domain controllers establishing the trust exchange information about the unique name service suffixes used in each forest. Once this has been done, each forest knows what suffixes the other forest uses, and stores this information in a TDO object in the forest root domain's **System** container. Name Suffix Routing can be configured so that only specific suffixes from the whole set are routed to the remote forest, if desired.

In Windows 2003, if two forests have a forest trust, a user who has an account and uses a workstation in one forest can request access to a resource in the other forest. The service on the resource server will be identified by its Kerberos Service Principal Name (SPN). The client computer's domain controller will send a request to resolve the target SPN to the local forest Global Catalog server, but because the server resides in the other forest, the local Global Catalog server will not be able to resolve it. The request will therefore be redirected to a domain controller of the forest root domain in the external forest that will be able to resolve the SPN using the external Global Catalog server. Then the client will be referred to a domain controller in the external destination domain (Kerberos realm) that will finally provide the client with a TGS for the external resource server.

A requirement when forest trusts are used is proper DNS configuration that allows DNS names to be resolved by clients and servers in both forests. The typical way to accomplish this is by either mixing primary and backup servers in the two forests, or by means of DNS conditional forwarding.

An External Windows Trust relationship is used to communicate with Windows domains external to the forest. The authentication protocols that can be used here are NTLM and Kerberos, depending on whether the forest runs in Windows 2000 or Windows 2003 Native Mode. In both cases, the trust relationship is non-transitive but it can be one-way or two-way. Considering the non-transitiveness of external trusts, every domain from the forest that needs to access resources in the external domain, or needs to be accessed by the users of the external domain, must establish its own trust relationship with the external domain. This closely mimics the behavior of trusts in Windows NT 4.0 with non-transitive NTLM trusts. In case the external trust uses the NTLM Protocol (the only option for Windows 2000 forests), NetBIOS connectivity and name resolution are required.

When an External Windows Trust exists between two domains from different forests, a client from one domain may try to access resources in the other domain over the network. The client will send a TGS request to its own DC. The DC will query the Global Catalog for the SPN of the server in the external domain, and this SPN will not exist there (because the Global Catalog only stores information about local forest resources). In this case, the client will need to fall back to NTLM authentication and contact the resource server directly. The resource server will pass the authentication information to a domain controller in its own domain, and this domain controller will perform pass-through authentication with the directly trusted domain to which the client belongs using the NTLM Protocol.

With external trusts, users who try to access resources across an external trust need to use Windows NT 4.0-style username syntax — domainname\username. User Principal Name (UPN) authentication is not supported across external trusts. The reason for this is that any domain controller for a domain that does not have a copy of the user's account needs to contact a Global Catalog server to resolve the UPN. Because the external domain belongs to another forest that has a different Global Catalog, the UPN cannot be resolved.

A Realm Trust (Kerberos V5 external trust relationship) is used to communicate with external Kerberos V5-compatible domains but not with Windows domains. This type of trust relationship can be transitive or non-transitive, and it can be one-way or two-way. The trust relationship is always established using the Kerberos Protocol.

A Forest Trust can only be established between Windows 2003 Native Mode forests. It is established between the forest root domains of the forests and provides for transitive trust relationships among all the domains of the two participating forests. The trust can be one-way or two-way, and can use Kerberos or NTLM authentication.

The transitiveness of the forest trusts means that any user from any domain (not just the forest root domain) of the participating forests can access resources in any domain in the other forest, provided that he has been granted appropriate permissions. Although forest trusts are transitive among all the domains in both forests, they are not transitive between forests — if Forest A trusts Forest B, and Forest B trusts Forest C, this does not necessarily mean that domains in Forest A trust domains in Forest C.

3.3.15.18 Case Study: Exploring External Trusts

This case study assumes that forest root domain **ins.com** has an external trust relationship with domain **externalorg.com** that belongs to another forest (Figure 3.35). No other domain from the **ins.com** forest has a trust relationship with the **externalorg.com** domain.

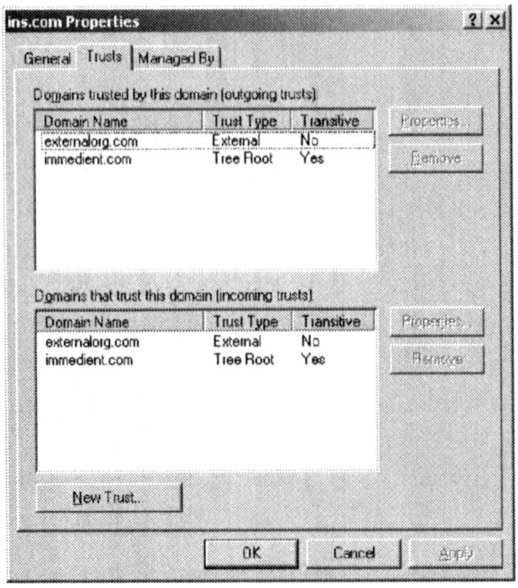

Figure 3.35 External Trust with externalorg.com.

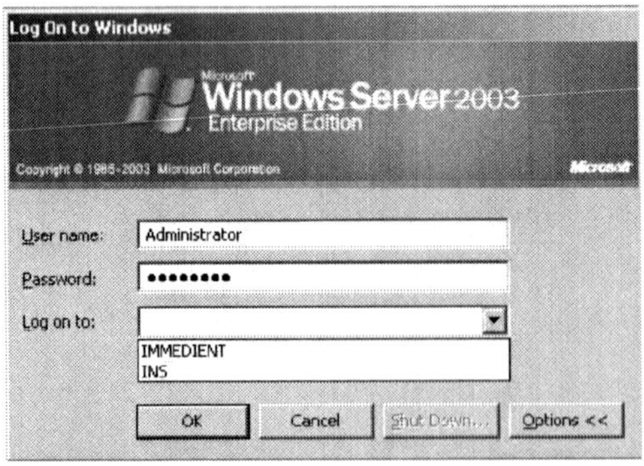

Figure 3.36 Attempt to log on via External Trust.

User Administrator from **externalorg.com** is sitting in front of a computer from the **ins.com** domain and is trying to authenticate. Because the external trust relationship is established directly between the **ins.com** and the **externalorg.com** domains, the user will be able to authenticate.

However, if the same user tries to authenticate interactively from a computer that belongs to the **ins.com** forest but resides in another domain in this forest (one that does not have direct trust relationship), the following will happen.

If the user expands the "Log on to" list on the workstation, the **externalorg.com** domain will not be available there (Figure 3.36).

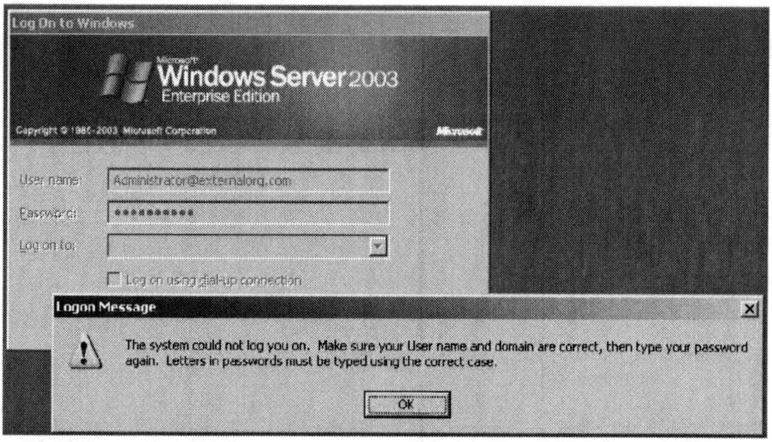

Figure 3.37 Attempt to log on via External Trust using a UPN suffix from immedient.com.

Even if the user tries to authenticate using an UPN, this will not be possible (Figure 3.37). With external trusts, forest root domains do not exchange information about UPN suffixes, and do not know how to route requests for authentication between non-directly connected domains.

3.3.15.19 Case Study: Exploring Forest Trusts

This case study assumes that there is a forest trust between a forest with root domain **ins.com** and a forest with root domain **externalorg.com** (Figure 3.38).

A user sitting in front of a computer who is a member of the **immedient.com** domain, and who has no direct trust relationship with external domain **externalorg.com**, will still see the same list of domains as shown in Figure 3.38. However, if the user uses a UPN suffix, he will be able to authenticate (see Figure 3.39 and below). From the tickets it is clear that the user has authenticated successfully using the Kerberos Protocol.

```
Z:\> klist tickets

Cached Tickets: (9)

   Server: krbtgt/IMMEDIENT.COM@INS.COM
      KerbTicket Encryption Type: RSADSI RC4-HMAC(NT)
      End Time: 12/4/2005 11:24:42
      Renew Time: 12/11/2005 1:24:42

   Server: krbtgt/INS.COM@EXTERNALORG.COM
      KerbTicket Encryption Type: RSADSI RC4-HMAC(NT)
```

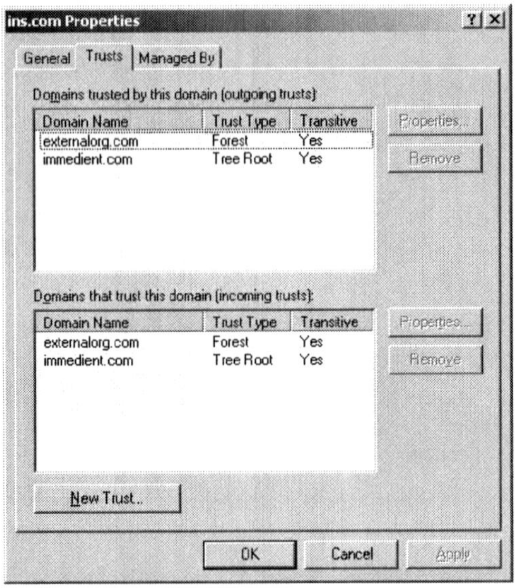

Figure 3.38 Forest Trust with externalorg.com.

Figure 3.39 Forest authentication using a UPN suffix.

```
      End Time: 12/4/2005 11:24:42
      Renew Time: 12/11/2005 1:24:42

   Server: krbtgt/EXTERNALORG.COM@EXTERNALORG.COM
      KerbTicket Encryption Type: RSADSI RC4-HMAC(NT)
      End Time: 12/4/2005 11:24:42
      Renew Time: 12/11/2005 1:24:42

   Server: krbtgt/EXTERNALORG.COM@EXTERNALORG.COM
      KerbTicket Encryption Type: RSADSI RC4-HMAC(NT)
```

```
      End Time: 12/4/2005 11:24:42
      Renew Time: 12/11/2005 1:24:42

   Server: cifs/PAUL.immedient.com@IMMEDIENT.COM
      KerbTicket Encryption Type: RSADSI RC4-HMAC(NT)
      End Time: 12/4/2005 11:24:42
      Renew Time: 12/11/2005 1:24:42

   Server: ldap/PAUL.immedient.com/immedient.com@IMMEDIENT.COM
      KerbTicket Encryption Type: RSADSI RC4-HMAC(NT)
      End Time: 12/4/2005 11:24:42
      Renew Time: 12/11/2005 1:24:42

   Server: LDAP/david.externalorg.com/externalorg.com@EXTERNALORG.COM
      KerbTicket Encryption Type: RSADSI RC4-HMAC(NT)
      End Time: 12/4/2005 11:24:42
      Renew Time: 12/11/2005 1:24:42

   Server: cifs/david.externalorg.com@EXTERNALORG.COM
      KerbTicket Encryption Type: RSADSI RC4-HMAC(NT)
      End Time: 12/4/2005 11:24:42
      Renew Time: 12/11/2005 1:24:42

   Server: host/paul.immedient.com@IMMEDIENT.COM
      KerbTicket Encryption Type: RSADSI RC4-HMAC(NT)
      End Time: 12/4/2005 11:24:42
      Renew Time: 12/11/2005 1:24:42

Z:\>
```

If the user tries to use the NT **domainname\username** syntax to log on from this computer, this will force NTLM authentication from the client computer (Figure 3.40). Because NTLM authentication does not support transitive trust relationships, this is bound to fail.

However, both Kerberos and NTLM authentication will work from the directly connected forest root domain **ins.com**. The user can use either the **domainname\username** syntax, or select the domain name explicitly, or specify a UPN to log on, and all of these will work.

The bottom line is that Kerberos is the only authentication protocol that will work in any domain of both forests when a forest trust exists between them, and user UPN suffixes should be used in such a scenario rather than NT-style **domainname\username** credentials.

3.3.15.20 Selective Authentication

Transitive authentication aims at allowing users to authenticate easily outside domain boundaries. Forest trusts will typically be used when two companies establish a partnership and want to share some specific resources. However, a solution wherein every user and computer from

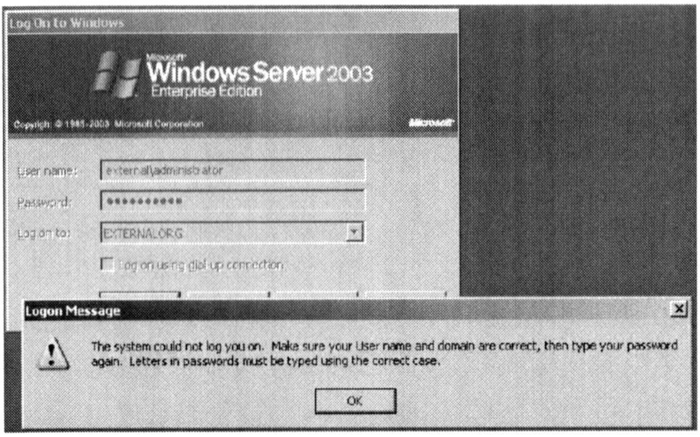

Figure 3.40 Forcing LM authentication from a domain that is not directly trusted.

one organization can authenticate and potentially access resources on every computer in the other organization may be beyond the integration that the companies are trying to achieve. The security of such an open and transparent authentication approach will depend on each and every client computer in both forests setting the correct permissions on resources to allow or deny access to computers in the other forest, which may be a huge challenge — if not impossible — for large organizations.

To allow for transparent authentication, and yet be selective in the specific security principals from one forest that are allowed to access resources in the other forest, Windows 2003 forest trusts provide for the so-called selective authentication.

Selective authentication (or authentication firewall) can be configured on an existing forest trust or external trust (provided that the remote forest runs Windows 2003) in each direction. With selective authentication, a trusting (resource) domain specifies which accounts from trusted (account) domain, or multiple domains, will be allowed to authenticate for each and every computer in the trusting (resource) domain.

When establishing a trust, the administrator can choose between domain-wide authentication (every user from one domain/forest can authenticate to every computer in the other forest) or selective authentication (users from trusted [account] domain can access resources in the trusting [resource] domain only when they are explicitly allowed to authenticate) (Figure 3.41).

If administrators choose to use selective authentication for a trust in the particular direction, then an administrator of the trusting (resource) domain or forest will need to explicitly grant permissions to the users or groups from the trusted (account) domain using the Active Directory Users and Computers console.

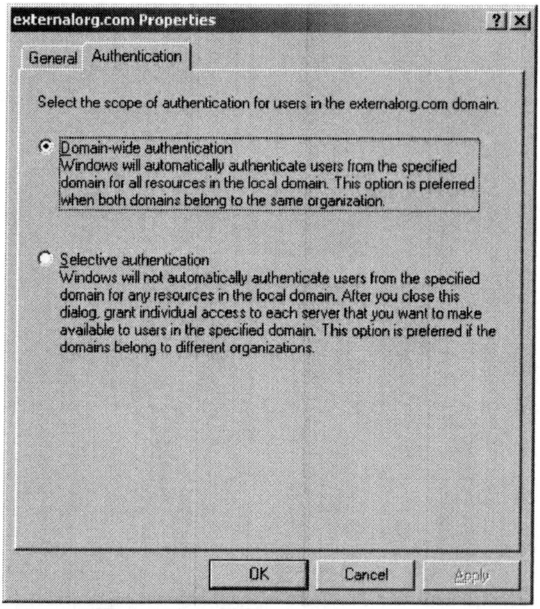

Figure 3.41 Domain-wide and selective authentication.

3.3.15.21 Case Study: Exploring Authentication Firewall and User Access Tokens

This case study assumes that there is a forest trust between Windows 2003 domains **ins.com** and **externalorg.com**, and that selective authentication is allowed for this trust relationship at least one way with **ins.com** being the resource domain. The Domain Admins group from the **externalorg.com** domain and forest need access to resources on server STEVE. Administrators from the **ins.com** domain and forest will need to use Active Directory Users and Computers to explicitly grant the user right **Allowed to authenticate** to Domain Admins from domain **externalorg.com.** By default, if selective authentication is enabled, users from the remote domain **externalorg.com** will not be able to authenticate to any computer in the **ins.com** forest until **ins.com** administrators grant them the right to authenticate (Figure 3.42).

It is interesting to see how the user access token for external users changes, depending on whether domain wide or selective authentication is used for the trust relationship.

Assuming that domain **ins.com** has an external (or forest) trust with domain **externalorg.com**, and Domain Wide authentication is selected for this trust, user Susan from domain **ins.com** logs on interactively on

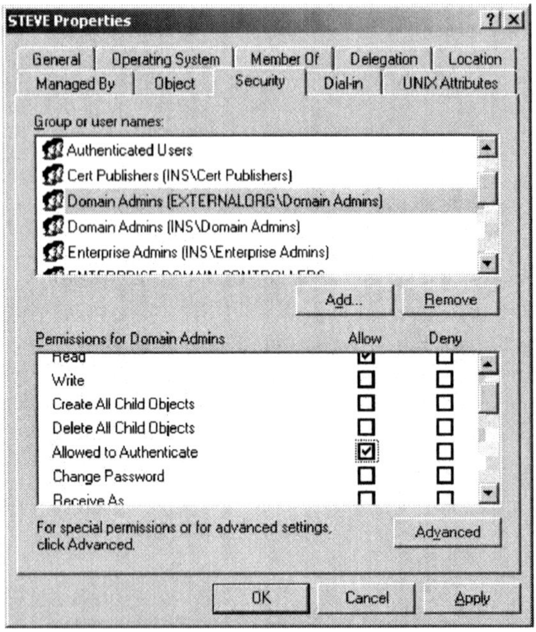

Figure 3.42 Allowing external users to authenticate.

a computer that is a member of the **externalorg.com** domain. Here is what the access token for this user is likely to be:

```
C:\> whoami /user /groups

USER INFORMATION
----------------

User Name SID
========= =============================================
ins\susan S-1-5-21-676691431-2304381362-2152039065-1119

GROUP INFORMATION
-----------------

Group Name             Type       SID                  Attributes
====================== ========== ==================== ==========================
Everyone               Well-known S-1-1-0              Mandatory group, Enabled
                        group                           by default, Enabled group
BUILTIN\Users          Alias      S-1-5-32-545         Mandatory group, Enabled
                                                        by default, Enabled group
BUILTIN\Pre-Windows    Alias      S-1-5-32-554         Mandatory group, Enabled
 2000 Compatible                                        by default, Enabled group
 Access
NT AUTHORITY\          Well-known S-1-5-4              Mandatory group, Enabled
 INTERACTIVE            group                           by default, Enabled group
NT AUTHORITY\          Well-known S-1-5-11             Mandatory group, Enabled
 Authenticated Users    group                           by default, Enabled group
```

```
NT AUTHORITY\         Well-known S-1-5-15             Mandatory group, Enabled
 This Organization     group                            by default, Enabled group
LOCAL                 Well-known S-1-2-0              Mandatory group, Enabled
                       group                            by default, Enabled group
INS\Engineering       Group      S-1-5-21-676691431-  Mandatory group, Enabled
                                  2304381362-           by default, Enabled group
                                  2152039065-1111
INS\Enterprise        Group      S-1-5-21-676691431-  Mandatory group, Enabled
 Engineering                      2304381362-           by default, Enabled group
                                  2152039065-1135

C:\>
```

In the access token above, user Susan has been made a member of the **This Organization group (S-1-5-15)** and this will grant her access to resources in the **externalorg.com** organization, despite the fact that her account resides in another organization (forest).

If in the same scenario, Selective Authentication is configured for the trust relationship between **ins.com** and **externalorg.com**, and Susan has not been explicitly granted the **Allowed to authenticate** permission on the computer that she is trying to log on to, then Figure 3.43 is the message that she is going to get.

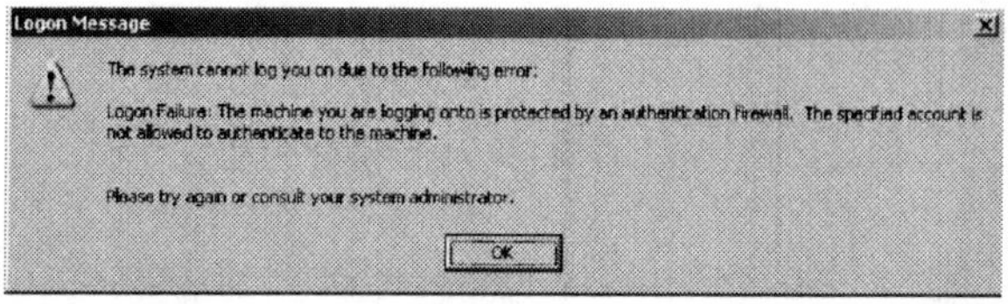

Figure 3.43 Authentication firewall: message to users.

Once Susan has been explicitly granted the right to authenticate on the particular computer and she has logged on through a Selective Authentication trust relationship, here is what Susan's access token would be:

```
C:\> whoami /user /groups

USER INFORMATION
----------------

User Name SID
========= =============================================
ins\susan S-1-5-21-676691431-2304381362-2152039065-1119

GROUP INFORMATION
-----------------

Group Name            Type       SID                  Attributes
===================== ========== ==================== ==========================
Everyone              Well-known S-1-1-0              Mandatory group, Enabled
                       group                            by default, Enabled group
BUILTIN\Users         Alias      S-1-5-32-545         Mandatory group, Enabled
                                                        by default, Enabled group
```

```
BUILTIN\Pre-Windows    Alias       S-1-5-32-554          Mandatory group, Enabled
 2000 Compatible                                          by default, Enabled group
 Access
NT AUTHORITY\          Well-known  S-1-5-4               Mandatory group, Enabled
 INTERACTIVE            group                             by default, Enabled group
NT AUTHORITY\          Well-known  S-1-5-11              Mandatory group, Enabled
 Authenticated Users    group                             by default, Enabled group
NT AUTHORITY\          Well-known  S-1-5-1000            Mandatory group, Enabled
 Other Organization     group                             by default, Enabled group
LOCAL                  Well-known  S-1-2-0               Mandatory group, Enabled
                        group                             by default, Enabled group
INS\Engineering        Group       S-1-5-21-676691431-   Mandatory group, Enabled
                                    2304381362-           by default, Enabled group
                                    2152039065-1111
INS\Enterprise         Group       S-1-5-21-676691431-   Mandatory group, Enabled
 Engineering                        2304381362-           by default, Enabled group
                                    2152039065-1135

C:\>
```

It is important to note Susan's membership to the **Other Organization (S-1-5-1000)** group in this case, which shows that she has logged in from another forest across Selective Authentication.

3.3.15.22 Protocol Transition

Protocol transition allows a service or application that has successfully received a user session authenticated using some other authentication protocol (such as HTTP basic authentication or digest authentication) to request and potentially obtain Kerberos tickets on behalf of the user, and then access other servers. For example, if a Web user authenticates to a Web server using basic authentication, the Web server can use protocol transition to identify or impersonate the basic authentication user, which has already provided valid credentials. Then, the Web server invokes a system call (or instantiates an object) that generates and provides Kerberos keys (based on the assumption that the user has already been authenticated by some other means). The Web server will now have Kerberos tickets for the client application, and will be able to access resources on behalf of the client. Protocol transition grants Kerberos tickets to users, assuming that they have already been successfully authenticated. This is a unique approach, wherein the operating system (more specifically, the KDC) agrees to issue a Kerberos ticket for which the user has not applied, assuming that the user has been authenticated properly by other means.

The Kerberos authentication strength will depend on the initial protocol used to authenticate the user. With protocol transition, the front-end server will be allowed to either identify or impersonate the user. This depends on whether the front-end service user has been granted the **Act as part of the operating system** user right. Impersonation is provided when a user account that has this user right invokes the **LsaLogonUser( )** system call, or when the user tries to access a resource on the network and this resource suggests the use of Kerberos as the authentication protocol. With impersonation, the front-end application, service thread, or process will be issued an access token with privileges and authentication token, equivalent to the authenticating user, and the application or service will be able to act on behalf of the user. Identification is provided in the same way if the front-end service or application user does not have the **Act as part of the operating system** user right. In case of identification, the front-end application or service will be able to obtain information such as the username, user SID, and group membership, but will not be able to obtain an access token equivalent to that of the user, and will need to implement its own authorization logic. More information on the protocol transition feature is provided in [30, 45].

3.4 Federated Trusts

Windows 2003 introduced a new authentication strategy for accessing Web services. It allows for federated access to services between companies, and sets the basis for unified identity management and authorization between companies on the Internet. Federated trusts compliment the existing authentication services that Active Directory services provide and do not change the way they work. Federated trusts are an application-level authentication mechanism and are described later in this book. More information is provided in Chapter 4.

3.5 Impersonation

Typically, users and services log on to a domain or computer using their own credentials, also called primary credentials. However, within their existing session, they may need to perform operations using either lower, or higher, or just different privileges.

For example, it is recommended that domain and computer administrators have two different accounts — one with normal user privileges and one with administrative privileges. For every task, administrators should use the account that provides them with least privileges to perform this particular task.

Services are applications that work independently of user sessions on a computer and have a different set of credentials. When a user connection is established, the service needs to check who the user is, and potentially grant or deny access to specific functions and resources based on its own authorization logic.

This section looks at two different approaches to changing user primary privileges and assuming another user privileges. Credential Manager (discussed in subsection 3.2.12) represents another impersonation approach that manages primary and additional credentials for access to network resources.

3.5.1 Secondary Logon Service

Windows 2000 and later operating systems allow for the so-called Secondary Logon for interactive users. A user can log on to a computer interactively using one set of credentials (primary credentials), and at the same time this user might need access to applications using a different set of credentials without closing his shell and applications using the original set of credentials.

A typical example is when an administrator uses an account with limited privileges for tasks such as accessing his e-mail or the corporate ERP system. However, this administrator has an account with full administrative privileges that he uses whenever he needs to perform administrative tasks, such as creating new domain users. In some cases, this administrator might want to keep his e-mail client and ERP system open with his limited privileges, and without closing his shell he might want to invoke Active Directory Users and Computers to create a user account for a new employee, information for which can be found in the ERP system and an e-mail from the HR department.

Users can utilize the Secondary Logon service and launch one or more applications with a different set of privileges using the **RUNAS.EXE** command from a command line, or by right-clicking an executable file and specifying a set of credentials (Figure 3.44).

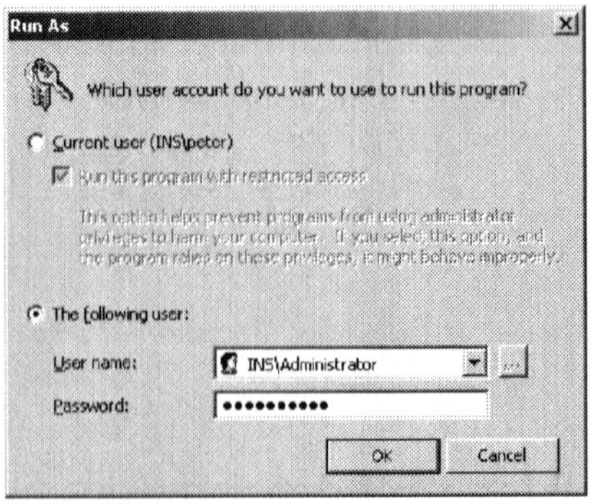

Figure 3.44 Launching applications using a different set of credentials.

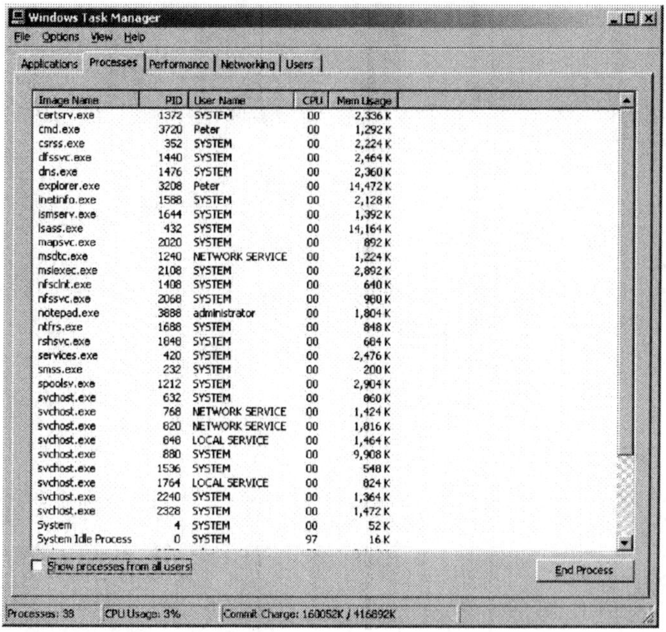

Figure 3.45 Task manager and user processes.

The Secondary Logon Service will then impersonate the interactive user and start an application using the specified user privileges. If an application has started with alternative privileges, any new process that this application launches will use these alternative privileges instead of the original user privileges. Child processes for this process can also create processes. A process running with specific privileges might spawn a tree of processes running with the same privileges unless a user explicitly specifies new privileges for a child process that may then spawn its own tree of child processes.

Information about processes and the user who has started them can be displayed using Windows Task Manager (Figure 3.45). The User Name column in the Processes tab shows what privileges (access token) the specific process is using.

When the user finishes working with alternative credentials, he will typically close all the applications he has opened. Windows processes have a parent-child relationship but, unlike UNIX processes, even if the parent process terminates, child processes may continue to run. The user is responsible for closing all applications running with alternative privileges when he has finished using them; they will not terminate automatically when the process that started them terminates.

To provide for Secondary Logon, Windows 2000 and later must run the Secondary Logon service, which will actually impersonate the user with the specified credentials and start the application. By default, this service is enabled and started. Disabling this service will also disable the secondary logon functionality.

3.5.2 Application-Level Impersonation

Applications running in a specific security context may try to assume the identity of a user in a different security context, and switch their security context to perform operations on behalf of the user. This is known as *impersonation*.

Typically, server applications (such as Windows services) run in a specific user context, which is very often the Local System context in Windows NT 4.0 and Windows 2000, and may be the Local Service or Network Service context in Windows 2003. For example, the Server service in Windows 2003 runs in the context of the Local Service system account. If user Peter connects to the Server service from his workstation, the Server service needs to provide Peter with access to resources for which Peter has permissions. This is essentially resource authorization. To do this, the Server service has two options: (1) check access lists on each file that Peter tries to access, or (2) assume the security context and access token of Peter Black trying to access resources on his behalf and let the operating system decide whether or not Peter has access to each and every specific resource. The first approach with custom security checks is found in many home-grown applications, and typically leads to complex system code, part of the application (rather than the operating system) that companies invest in, and then malicious attackers relatively easily bypass. The second option represents impersonation and basically transfers the responsibility to the operating system, which is assumed to have APIs and security kernels, proven to be secure by the vendor and the operating system users.

An important factor to consider when looking at user authentication is the authentication protocol in use between the client and the server; not all authentication protocols support all forms of impersonation.

Due to the specifics of the NTLM Protocol, it only supports direct authentication between a client and a server, and therefore the server application can impersonate the client on the server computer only (Figure 3.46).

With the NTLM Protocol, the client is the only party in the authentication process that has the cleartext user password. The NTLM Protocol itself relies on the authentication client being able to encrypt a random

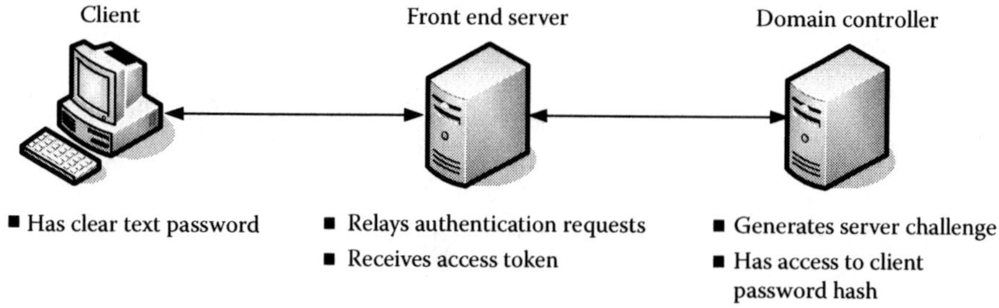

Figure 3.46 NTLM authentication.

server challenge that can only happen if the client has the correct password. When the client authenticates to the front-end server, an access token is created for the client on the front-end server, and the front-end server can assume user privileges on the front-end server, and then access resources on this server on behalf of the client. However, the front-end server does not have the client password, and therefore will not be able to authenticate to another server (back-end server) on behalf of the client. This is a fundamental concept in the security architecture of the NTLM authentication protocol.

When a client authenticates to a front-end server using the NTLM Protocol, the front-end server can only access other servers using predefined privileges. Typically, in this scenario the front-end server will try to either use Null Sessions or a predefined application or service account to access the back-end server. The client identity will be lost as the front-end server accesses back-end servers. Authentication and authorization for resource access on the back-end server can be performed for the front-end servers and services, but not for the clients (Figure 3.47).

To preserve client identity to a certain extent, the front-end server may identify the client (see below) and use specific application or service accounts to connect to back-end servers, depending on some criteria (e.g., group membership). However, this approach is not very popular, may be complex to implement, and is not secure, because the front-end server will need to manage a couple of application or service accounts and their plaintext passwords.

The Kerberos authentication protocol is stateless and relies on tickets issued by a trusted third party to access resources. The ticket is provided by the client and it can potentially be forwarded to or proxied by the front-end server that can then present this ticket to other servers. The Kerberos protocol does not have the limitation of direct authentication between communicating parties and therefore allows for more flexible impersonation with multiple layers of communicating parties.

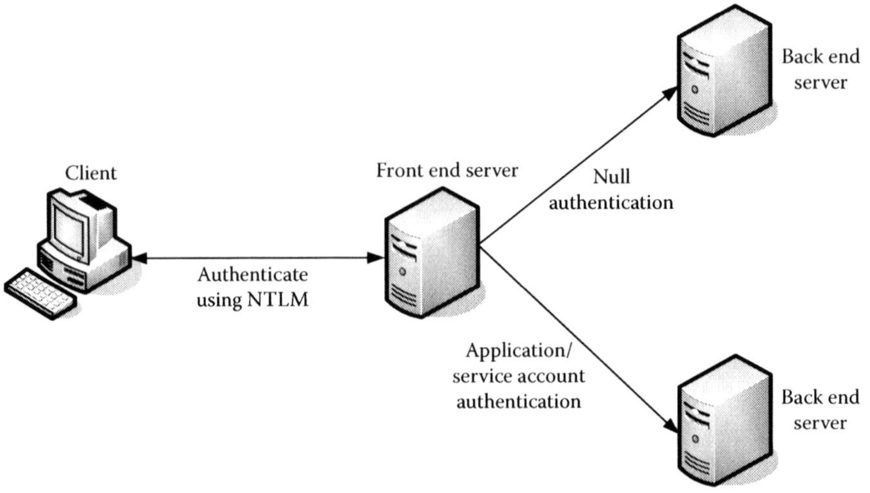

Figure 3.47 NTLM authentication to the front-end server and access to the back-end server.

User impersonation has four main forms in Windows operating systems, and they are discussed in the following sections.

Anonymous Impersonation

This form of user impersonation does not distinguish between users. All users potentially use the same security context. Although an access token is built for the user, all processes utilize this access token and typically undergo access checks as they try to access resources. A typical example for anonymous impersonation are Null Sessions (see subsection 3.3.15.14).

Identify Impersonation

With Identify impersonation, the application is able to distinguish between users, and it can obtain information about these users, which may include their usernames, group membership, or SIDs. However, the application cannot assume the privileges of the user (it cannot obtain an access token for this user), although it knows who the connected user is. Typically, applications using the Identify level of impersonation will have their own mechanisms to allow or deny user access to resources. They will probably have their own Access Control Lists where they record what resources each user can access.

Full Impersonation

With this approach, the server application can impersonate the client, assume the client privileges and security context, and then access local resources on the server on behalf of the user. However, the server application cannot use these privileges to access other network services that require authentication. That is, the server can utilize the user credentials for any action except authenticating on behalf of the user to other servers.

There are many services that use this security model, and the Server service in Windows operating systems is a typical example. When the user connects to the server, he authenticates using some authentication protocol, such as NTLM or Kerberos. The Server service then invokes operating system calls to impersonate the authenticated user, and every file from the server that the user may try to access will be accessed using an access token built using the user authentication credentials. Impersonation in Windows NT can be performed at the thread level. Therefore, the Server service can still run as one process and have a single memory space but a new thread can be invoked for each new user that connects to the Server service; and among the first things the thread would do is to impersonate the client and switch to the privileges of the user. When the user disconnects from the server, the thread that uses his privileges will revert to its original security context and then potentially be destroyed. Some of the things that a server can do to impersonate a user include:

- *Impersonate using known credentials.* The server can invoke the **LogonUser( )** function, provided that the server has the username, the cleartext password, and the domain name for the user who is trying to authenticate. The operating system will take the credentials and try to authenticate the user as if he were standing interactively in front of the console and was trying to log in. The server will then impersonate this user (not all applications will perform this step). It is important to note that the operating system will still require the user to have relevant privileges, such as **Logon Locally**, if the **LogonUser( )** function requests a local logon.
- *Impersonate using IPC authentication.* Provided the client has connected to the server using a protocol that supports interprocess communication authentication, such as NamedPipes over CIFS/SMB, RPC over CIFS/SMB, or direct binding RPC, the IPC Protocol will have authenticated the client before passing the access request to the server application. Therefore, the server application can now invoke an appropriate impersonation function, such as the

ImpersonateNamedPipeClient( ) or **RPCImpersonateClient( )** functions and assume the identity of the authenticated user. Once the client has disconnected, the server can call the **RevertToSelf( )** function to revert to the original server application privileges and stop accessing resources on behalf of the client. As discussed, this might happen for a specific thread only, rather for the entire server process.

Using the Windows IPC approach, the server application does not need to know the user password, and it does not need to know anything about the authentication protocol in use. To a certain extent, the server application does not need to know very much about security and authentication either, as long as this application invokes an impersonation system call every time a new user connects, and reverts to own security context when the user disconnects. Everything that happens between these two calls will be managed by the operating system in terms of authorization and access to resources, and the application can completely concentrate on performing its main task.

Impersonation is supported by many authentication protocols, including the LM, NTLM, and Kerberos.

Delegation

The delegation approach allows a server application to fully or partially assume client identity and then access resources that can reside either locally on the computer where the server application is running, or across the network. The delegation approach allows the server application not only to access the local file system on the server computer, or communicate with local processes on the same computer, but it can also connect to other servers and authenticate on behalf of the user, as if this application were actually directly started by the user. The server applications and services can potentially assume the client identity and act on the client's behalf. In that respect, delegation is a very flexible and scalable approach. Such an authentication approach will require transitive trust relationships from the client to the server, and then potentially to other tiers of servers. To support such authentication, Windows 2000 and later utilize the Kerberos authentication protocol.

Delegation is powerful yet can present security challenges. Providing a service with a ticket may compromise security if the service intentionally or not uses the ticket for purposes other than its intended use. Therefore, two approaches to delegation are typically used:

1. *Authentication delegation.* With authentication delegation, the Kerberos client provides the server with a forwardable ticket that the server can use to access resources on behalf of the client. This is the only delegation method supported by Windows 2000. With this delegation method, the client fully trusts the server that the latter will request only tickets, for which it needs access to fulfill the client request.
2. *Constrained delegation.* This approach was first introduced in Windows 2003 (Windows 2000 only supports unconstrained authentication delegation), and it requires Windows 2003 native mode domains. Constrained delegation is used with forwarded tickets. As discussed above, to use forwarded tickets, the client will typically request a TGT on behalf of the front-end server, and then provide the TGT to the server, which can result in considerable privileges given unrestricted to the front-end server. With constrained delegation, an administrator can restrict the types of services for which the front-end server might request session tickets.

In the example in Figure 3.48, front-end server STEVE is delegated restricted rights to request CIFS/SMB services from back-end server DENNIS, if required. STEVE cannot request tickets for services other than file services for server DENNIS.

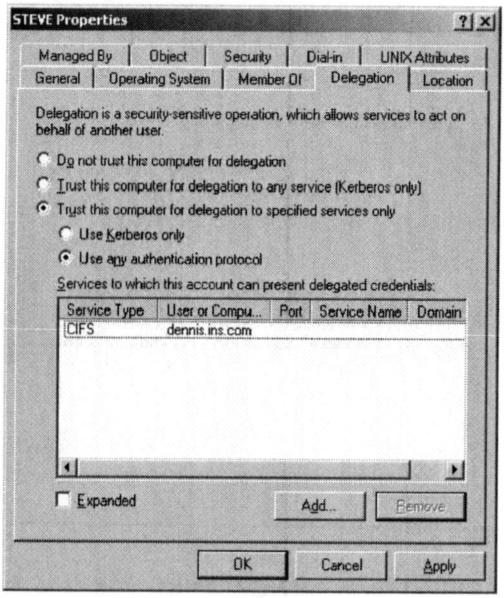

Figure 3.48 Configuring constrained delegation.

Chapter 4

Authenticating Access to Services and Applications

> They who would give up an essential liberty for temporary security, deserve neither liberty or security.
>
> — **Benjamin Franklin**

This chapter provides an overview of user authentication from an application perspective. It introduces some of the most popular security programming interfaces used by open systems today. It then looks into the mechanisms of network user authentication protocols, and finally discusses application impersonation and delegation.

4.1 Security Programming Interfaces

It is important for applications and services to consider security design as part of the application design process. Yet many applications and operating systems have been developed without a sound security design, and some of them have later adopted limited security features. This software development approach very often proves inefficient and palliative. Application architects and software designers often face the challenge of inventing the wheel from a security perspective, which leads to common mistakes and pitfalls. The result is an insecure application or service.

Security programming interfaces exist to standardize the approach to security implementation in application and service architecture. Security programming interfaces implement a set of best practices and specific operational mechanisms that can give applications the security layer of abstraction when communicating over the network. Security programming interfaces have been designed considering the currently known security problems and potential solutions and resolutions; they are widely used and tested. If security weaknesses are found, they are well defined and documented, and typically resolved soon after they have been discovered, by means of new software versions or patches.

This section looks into some common security programming interfaces, their architecture, and the security mechanisms on which they rely. It concentrates on widely used industry security mechanisms. Many other security mechanisms are not discussed in this chapter but they will typically have behavior similar to those discussed below.

4.1.1 Generic Security Services API (GSS-API)

Generic Security Services Application Programming Interface (GSS-API) is an Internet standard application programming interface designed to provide applications with a layer of abstraction for authentication and data protection services. With GSS-API, applications do not need to understand every authentication method, nor do they need to implement their own user authentication mechanisms, or means to sign and encrypt network traffic. Applications can simply use the GSS-API library, available in C, Java, and other languages, to seamlessly integrate industry standard network security services from different vendors.

Although GSS-API is independent of the authentication mechanism in use, it is often distributed with Kerberos implementations on UNIX systems and is therefore considered the primary application-level interface for access to the Kerberos authentication protocol.

GSS-API version 1 was first defined in RFC 1508. Version 2 followed in RFC 2078. The latest release of GSS-API is version 2 update 1 and it is defined in RFC 2743 [50]. The GSS-API standard specifies the following mechanisms in the current version:

- *Credential management.* This series of APIs allows applications to acquire and release authentication credentials. Credentials are acquired using the **GSS_Acquire_cred( )** call and released using the **GSS_Release_cred( )** call.
- *Context level calls.* These calls allow clients and servers to manage the security context of the process or thread using the **GSS_Init_sec_context( )** and **GSS_Accept_sec_context( )**. The server can

use context level calls to assume the identity of the client (impersonation). In addition to that, context level calls allow for delegation of authentication. Furthermore, context levels calls provide for functions that can be used to export the security context using **GSS_Export_sec_context( )** and import by another process using **GSS_Import_sec_context( )**

- *Per message calls.* These calls are meant to provide protection for user data and are not typically used by the authentication process. User data integrity and traffic source and destination can be authenticated by adding a message signature (message integrity code — MIC) to sent messages using the **GSS_GetMIC( )** call. The recipient can verify the signature and therefore the integrity of the packets using the **GSS_VerifyMIC( )** call. In a similar fashion, the **GSS_Wrap( )** function can be used to validate data integrity and potentially encrypt the token passed by the application layer. The recipient then invokes **GSS_Unwrap( )** to decrypt the message.
- *Support calls.* These calls provide functions for user name management, canonization of user names, user name comparison, and management of GSS mechanisms.

It is important to note that GSS-API is not a network protocol and the GSS-API functions by themselves do not communicate over the network. GSS-API calls are typically invoked by an application that needs to utilize GSS-API services. This application is typically able to communicate over the network, and it utilizes its own transport, session, and application layer protocols (and potentially other layers as well), and is able to transfer data over the network (Figure 4.1). The application invoking GSS-API is responsible for encapsulating the GSS-API data structures on both the client and the server into the application network packets, and the application is then responsible to parse the application layer traffic and extract the GSS-API structure on the remote side, then pass it to the GSS-API module there.

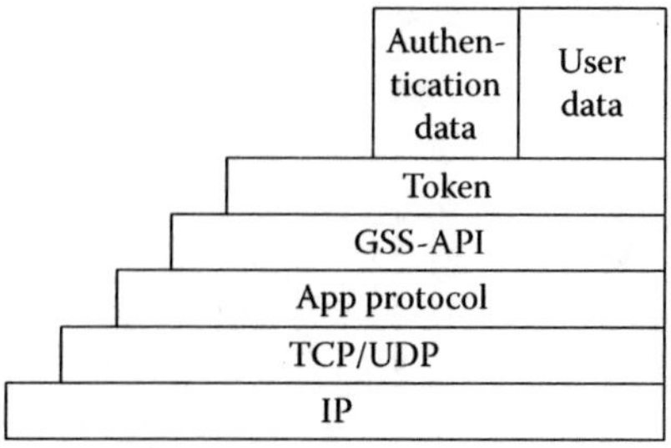

Figure 4.1 GSS-API protocol stack.

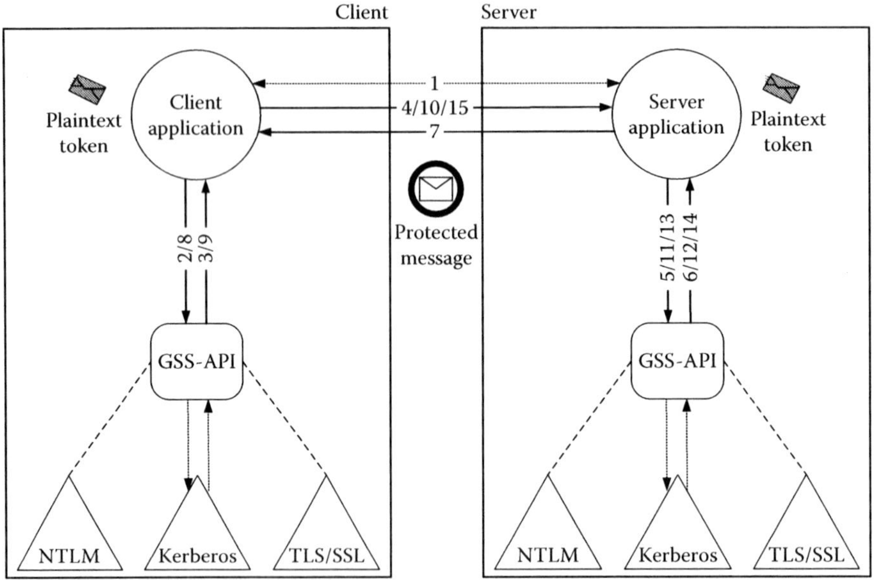

Figure 4.2 The GSS-API interface.

GSS-API is not an authentication protocol but it does support specific authentication mechanisms, such as Kerberos. From a user authentication perspective, GSS-API is a standard interface that applications can use to request services from underlying authentication mechanisms in a uniform way (Figure 4.2). Authentication mechanisms are responsible for generating the specific tokens, used by clients and server to authenticate, and they may also provide key material to protect actual user data.

The client and server applications communicate with their respective local GSS-API layers by exchanging tokens. The tokens can be authentication structures (typically used during the initial stages to perform user authentication); or once authentication has been performed, the tokens may be portions of user data that the client and the server want to protect as information is sent over the network.

The typical network communication process of using GSS-API is as follows (see Figure 4.2):

1. The client establishes a network connection to the server using its own application protocol. This might involve the negotiation of different transport, session, presentation, and application layers.
2. The client is ready to authenticate to the server so it calls the GSS-API standard **GSS_Init_sec_context( )** call on the client computer, specifying the server name as a parameter.

3. The GSS-API library on the client computer parses the provided parameters and generates an authentication token for the target server that it then passes back to the client application.
4. The client application encapsulates the authentication token into its application layer protocol and sends it to the server.
5. The server receives the message from the client, parses it, and extracts the client-generated authentication token. The server invokes the **GSS_Accept_sec_context( )** call and passes the authentication token as a parameter to GSS-API.
6. The GSS-API library on the server analyzes the client-provided information and determines whether or not authentication has been successful. It then generates a reply authentication token that in case of mutual authentication will need to contain the server credentials as well.
7. The client receives the server reply and determines whether authentication was successful. If not, authentication may continue here. At this stage, the client and server can exchange multiple messages, depending on the authentication mechanisms they are trying to use.
8. Once the user has been authenticated, the client can potentially utilize the data protection functions that the GSS-API provides. The client application can use the **GSS_Wrap( )** function and submit an application level data structure to GSS-API with a request to sign the data (protect data against unauthorized modification), protect the origin of the data (protect against spoofing), or encrypt the data (provide confidentiality).
9. GSS-API on the client computer protects ("wraps") the application data and returns the protected token.
10. The client application encapsulates the protected token (wrapped user data) in its application protocol and sends it to the server.
11. The server application uses the **GSS_Unwrap( )** call to pass the protected token to its local GSS-API library.
12. The **GSS_Unwrap( )** call on the server checks the integrity or the origin of the protected token, or decrypts the contents of the token and returns the result to the server application.
13. The server application handles the plaintext data structures following its application logic and potentially prepares a reply structure. The server application passes the reply structure to the GSS-API library by invoking the **GSS_Wrap( )** call on the server side.
14. **GSS_Wrap( )** on the server protects the server data token by signing it or protecting the source, or encrypts the contents and returns it to the server application.
15. The server application encapsulates the reply structure in its application protocol and sends it to the client.

16. The above process continues until the application logic requires that the server and client need to terminate the connection, or bring down the protected layer for some reason. The server uses the **GSS_Delete_sec_context( )** function to do that.

GSS-API can be used with different authentication mechanisms. Some of the authentication mechanisms implement a specific technique for user authentication, while others do not implement an authentication mechanism and only exist to negotiate the actual authentication mechanism that will be used.

Each GSS-API authentication mechanism has a unique object identifier (OID) within the ISO object hierarchy. Even if the client and the server are by different vendors, they should be able to negotiate a common authentication mechanism by specifying its OID. There are currently a limited number of authentication mechanisms defined for GSS-API.

4.1.1.1 Kerberos Version 5 as a GSS-API Mechanism

RFC 1964 (see [51]) defines how Kerberos can be used as a GSS-API mechanism. GSS-API and Kerberos are often seen together, as GSS-API is the preferred UNIX-style approach to using the Kerberos protocol in applications and services. Its compatibility (partial) with the SSPI interface makes it convenient for use in heterogeneous environments with Windows Active Directory and Windows clients. Kerberos version 5 for GSS-API can be identified by the following OID: **iso.org.dod.internet.security.kerberosv5** (1.3.5.1.5.2). The Kerberos authentication protocol is discussed in subsection 4.2.2.4.

The Kerberos version 5 authentication protocol is used in GSS-API calls as part of the application session establishment. Kerberos AP Request and AP Reply messages are typically encapsulated within GSS-API tokens and exchanged between the client and server applications. Kerberos user TGT and TGS tickets must be acquired by the client prior to the session establishment and only AP exchanges will be carried by GSS-API.

The Kerberos authentication process generates a session key that is used to protect Kerberos tickets. Kerberos can provide a session key to the GSS-API layer to be used for data (token) integrity authentication and data encryption. The GSS-API session key is derived from the Kerberos session key in one of the following ways:

- *Actual Kerberos session key* (also known as Context Key): use exactly the same key generated by the Kerberos protocol.
- *Confidentiality key:* the first 8 bytes from the session key and the string f0f0f0f0f0f0f0f0 are XOR-ed together.

- *MD2.5 key:* similar to Kerberos session key, however it uses all the keys in bytewise-reverse order.

GSS-API Message Authentication using Kerberos

Parties communicating using the GSS-API layer can negotiate to sign their own messages before sending them over the network to enable the recipient to authenticate the message contents, the origin of the message, as well as the order of reception of messages. The Kerberos version 5 GSS-API authentication mechanism provides for such capabilities. The **GSS_GetMIC( )** function is called by the sender for each message (token) and the Message Authentication field is calculated. After parsing the received packet, the receiver calls the **GSS_VerifyMIC( )** to check the signature and the order of the received message.

The message integrity check calculation consists of two steps: (1) calculating a checksum (protect message integrity) and (2) calculating message order (anti-replay protection). The checksum calculation is performed by appending the user payload to the first 8 bytes of the packet header. Once this has been done, there are three approaches for generating a signature that contains the above checksum:

1. *DES-MAC-MD5 algorithm.* The Kerberos authentication mechanism for GSS-API calculates the MD5 hash of the concatenated 8-byte packet header and user payload. The resulting 16-byte value is passed to the DES-CBC-MAC algorithm using the Kerberos session key as the key, and an empty initial vector. The result is the 8-byte hash (checksum).
2. *MD2.5 algorithm.* A 16-byte, all-zero block with an initial vector of zero is submitted to the DES algorithm with the 8-byte session key in reverse order as the key. The result from this encryption consists of 16 bytes and it is sent to the MD5 function for another hashing round. The result is an 8-byte checksum (hash).
3. *DES-MAC algorithm.* This algorithm uses DES-CBC MAC on the user data using the 8-byte session key as the key and a zero instant vector. The result is an 8-byte hash (checksum).

The checksum is then stored in the 8-byte SGN_CKSUM of the GSS-API token and submitted to the calling application.

The sender also maintains sequence numbers. The sender calculates its expected send number and stores it in reverse order of bytes (from least significant to most significant byte), then pads it to 8 bytes using the so-called direction indicator (that is, pads it with zeroes if the sender is the party that initiated the session, or with 0xFF if the sender is the one who terminates the GSS-API session). This 8-byte result is then encrypted using DES-CBC and employing the session key as the key, and the checksum (SGN-CKSUM) as the initial vector. The result is the 8-byte sequence hash.

The receiver can calculate the message hash and determine whether the message has been tampered with. Then the receiver can calculate the sequence hash to determine whether the message is genuine or has been replayed. The use of different padding symbols, depending on the session initiator, helps protect against man-in-the-middle attacks — an attacker cannot initiate a session to both a client and a server and simply replay the messages between them, because the session initiator and terminator use different padding.

GSS-API Message Wrapping using Kerberos

Message wrapping (also known as sealing in previous GSS-API versions and in Microsoft Windows SSPI) is used to protect user data from information disclosure and therefore involves encryption and integrity authentication techniques. The only standard (RFC-defined way) to encrypt data is the DES protocol. The sender uses the **GSS_Wrap( )** function to encrypt and sign a token, while the receiver uses **GSS_Unwrap( )** to restore the original token and check its signature. The application token will be padded to a multiple of 8 bytes, with the value of the padding being set to the number of the padded bytes. The DES algorithm uses an empty (zero) initial vector (IV) and the session key as the key.

4.1.1.2 SPNEGO as a GSS-API Mechanism

SPNEGO (Simple and Protected NEGOtiation mechanism) for GSS-API is an interface used by GSS-API to negotiate an authentication mechanism to be used between the client and the server (Figure 4.3). SPNEGO in

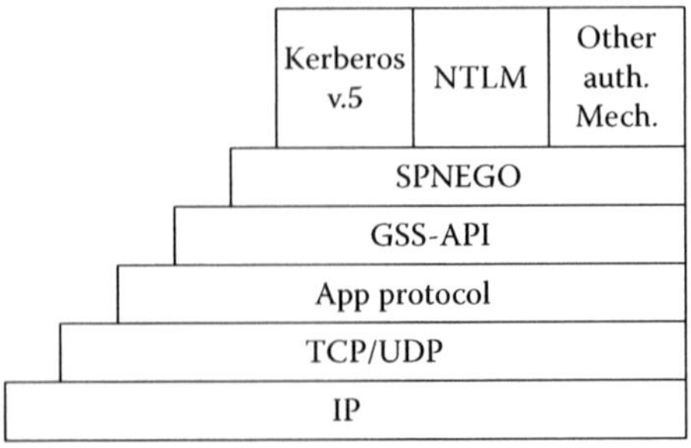

Figure 4.3 SPNEGO protocol stack.

not a stand-alone authentication mechanism. SPNEGO is defined in RFC 2478 (see [52]). It is based on older and obsolete Internet drafts that define this authentication mechanism as SNEGO (Simple GSS-API NEGOtiation mechanism). SPNEGO uses ISO OID **iso.org.dod.internet.security.mechanism.snego** (1.3.6.1.5.5.2).

The SPNEGO mechanism, as the name implies, involves a simple dialogue for negotiating the best authentication mechanism supported by both the client and the server. Once the client and the server have established communication using an application protocol of their own, the GSS-API session using the SPNEGO authentication mechanism will negotiate authentication as follows:

1. The client generates an ordered list of the authentication mechanisms it supports. Each authentication mechanism or a variant thereof is identified with its OID. The client-preferred authentication mechanism is listed first. For each authentication mechanism, the client specifies the options that it supports for this mechanism (this typically includes encryption, replay protection, or delegation).
2. The server receives the SPNEGO token through **GSS_Accept_sec_context( )**. It analyzes the proposed authentication mechanisms and specifies which one is the preferred mechanism, and potentially provides authentication data (e.g., a challenge string in the case of NTLM).
3. The client receives the server reply. If the server and client support at least one common authentication mechanism, they will use it for further authentication.

Once SPNEGO has negotiated a common authentication mechanism, it starts transferring authentication tokens between the client and the server. It is important to note that SPNEGO still exists as a layer in the protocol stack, although the selected authentication protocol can typically be supported as a GSS-API authentication mechanism directly.

The authentication process between the client and the server may take more than one round-trip, depending on the authentication protocol and whether mutual authentication is required. The client and the server may signal to each other whether the authentication has completed (using the GSS_S_COMPLETE flag), or whether authentication needs to continue (using the GSS_S_CONTINUE_NEEDED flag).

In the initial SPNEGO packet, the client may even include its client authentication or preauthentication data, so if the server agrees to use the preferred protocol, proposed by the client, the client authentication can begin immediately from the negotiation packet and a round-trip between the client and the server can be spared.

SPNEGO is supported by Windows 2000 and later operating systems, where it works on top of SSPI, which is compatible with GSS-API to a certain extent. Windows uses SPNEGO to negotiate an authentication mechanism for SMB/CIFS file services, RPC direct binding, or HTTP Windows Integrated Authentication for Internet Information Server. There are SPNEGO modules for the Apache HTTP server. Both Internet Explorer and Mozilla Firefox also support SPNEGO.

4.1.2 Security Support Provider Interface (SSPI)

The Windows Security Support Provider Interface (SSPI) is an operating system component that provides user and system applications and services such as file services and DCE/RPC with an abstraction layer for secure communication in a distributed network environment. Windows SSPI was developed at the same time as GSS-API and is very similar to it. In fact, both implementations can interoperate to a certain extent.

With SSPI, applications and services can authenticate and communicate in a distributed network environment in a standard way without knowing the details of all the authentication protocols, and without implementing key management and cryptographic functions to encrypt and sign network traffic; the SSPI interface can do this all on their behalf. The following are the basic services that SSPI implements:

- *Credential management:* applications can work with usernames, passwords. and tickets.
- *Context management:* allows clients and servers to prepare for and perform authentication, impersonate, and finally revert to the original context.
- *Message support:* provides for message signing and encryption.
- *Packet management:* allows applications to access the SSP packages.

Windows SSPI supports different security packages known as security support providers (SSPs). These include:

- Negotiate SSP: implements the SPNEGO (RFC 2478) protocol (see [43]) and may select and utilize the NTLM SSP or the Kerberos SSP.
- NTLMSSP: handles LM, NTLM, and NTLMv2 authentication.
- Kerberos SSP: handles Kerberos (RFC 1510) authentication.
- Digest SSP: implements the Digest Authentication protocol.
- Secure Channel (also known as SChannel): handles TLS/SSL authentication.

Note: This is different from the NTLM Secure Channel built between trusting NTLM parties using shared secrets, which is discussed later in this book.

Microsoft RPC services can utilize SSPI for authentication and data protection over the network. Many other applications rely on NTLMSSP; Microsoft Messaging API (MAPI) (the interface used between MS Exchange Server and its legacy clients) utilizes DCE/RPC with NTLMSSP, as well as the Distributed COM (DCOM) application architecture.

More information on SSPI can be found in [35, 42, and 44].

4.1.2.1 SSP Message Support

Information about the SSPI data protection mechanisms is not publicly available, although similar mechanisms and constant strings are outlined by Microsoft RFC 2831 (see [39]). In addition, HP/Compaq, along with Microsoft and the OpenGroup, have published semi-official documentation of ActiveX that provides some insight into how NTLMSSP works in its Chapter 11 — see [40].

It is believed that SSPI protection for the Netlogon channel works in the following way.

First, an SSPI session key is calculated using the following algorithm [40]:

1. A 16-byte LM key is created from the user LM password hash or from the NT hash if the LM hash does not exist ([41] provides some vague information on this). The LM key is set equal to the first 8 bytes of the password hash used, and the remainder of the LM key is set equal to a known value — 0xBD.
2. The client and the server challenges (8 bytes each) are summed up to provide the CS Challenge.
3. The CS Challenge is encrypted using DES and the first 8 bytes of the LM key as the key. The result is used as the first 8 bytes of the session key.
4. The CS Challenge is encrypted using DES and the last 8 bytes of the LM key as the key. The result is used as the last 8 bytes of the session key.

In addition to password-derived session keys, SSPI provides for a custom key. In that case, the client generates a new (random) session key and sets the NTLMSSP_NEGOTIATE_KEY_EXCH flag in the SSP message. The client then encrypts the new session key using RC4 encryption with the old (password derived) session key as the key, and transmits it in the **EncryptedSessionKey** field of the SSPI packet. The server decrypts the new session key using the old one that it already has, and then both the client and the server start using the new session key. The advantage of using a random session key that is not derived from the user password is that even if the attacker manages to apply cryptanalysis techniques (such as known plaintext analysis) and obtains the session key, it will not be a function of the user password and is only going to be valid for the duration of the session between the client and the server.

If NTLM version 1 is used for SSPI operations, the session key above is used. However, if NTLM version 2 is used for SSPI, the session key above is used to generate a set of send and receive keys.

The NTLM version 2 SSPI session keys are calculated from the existing session key (see above) by hashing the concatenation of the session key and a constant string using the MD5 hash algorithm. Both the client and the server calculate keys for sending signed messages, sending sealed messages, receiving signed messages, and receiving sealed messages.

The constant strings are believed to be the following:

- Client signing: "session key to client-to-server signing key magic constant"
- Client sealing: "session key to client-to-server sealing key magic constant"
- Server signing: "session key to server-to-client signing key magic constant"
- Server sealing: "session key to server-to-client sealing key magic constant"

Once the keys have been calculated, the client and server perform either signing or sealing, or both.

4.1.2.2 Strong Keys and 128-bit Encryption

At the time of Windows NT 3.51 and Windows NT 4.0, due to export regulations and restrictions in the United States, most software vendors avoided 128-bit encryption to make their code universally exportable to all countries. Furthermore, some countries (e.g., France) had laws and regulations that prohibited the use (and therefore the import) of encryption with keys longer than 40-bits.

Many key generation algorithms (including hash functions, such as MD5) typically generate 128-bit or even longer hashes, and some encryption protocols (including RC4) use 128-bit and even longer keys. To comply with the regulations and still be able to utilize an existing cryptographic base, while at the same time maintaining compatibility with future versions that may use stronger algorithms if regulations change, Microsoft decided to weaken 128-bit keys instead of generating 40-bit or 56-bit keys.

One example where keys have been weakened represents session keys for SMB/CIFS and SSPI. As discussed above, the session key is 16 bytes (128 bits) or more in size. For compatibility as well as for export compliance, Windows NT 4.0 and Windows 2000 computers can be configured to use 56-bit encryption, in which case the 128-bit kit is reduced to effective 56-bit encryption using the following algorithm:

1. Set the last 8 bytes of the calculated session key to 0xBD.
2. Set the seventh byte to 0xA0.

Considering the fact that the last 9 bytes of the session key are set to well-known values, the effective key length for the key that is technically 128 bits in size now becomes only 56 bits (7 bytes).

In a similar fashion, to weaken encryption from 128 bits to effective 40 bits, Windows performs the following operations:

1. Set the last 8 bytes of the calculated session key to 0xBD.
2. Set the fifth byte to 0xE5.
3. Set the sixth byte to 0x38.
4. Set the seventh byte to 0xB0.

Because 11 bytes of the 16-byte (128-bit) session key are now known, the effective key length can be considered equal to the remaining bits — that is, 40 bits (5 bytes).

After U.S. export regulation changes in 1999, it was already possible to export code that utilized 128-bit encryption (see [37]). Therefore, Microsoft added a Group Policy Setting to control the use of 128-bit encryption on many Windows 2000 and later operating systems for network communication protocols, including RPC. The setting is **Domain member: Require strong (Windows 2000 or later) session key** and that corresponds to the following registry value:

HKEY_LOCAL_MACHINE\SYSTEM\CurrentControlSet\Services\Netlogon\Parameters\RequireStrongKey:REG_DWORD

When this value is set, the NTLM SSP protocol uses the NTLMSSP_NEGOTIATE_128 flag in SSPI to negotiate 128-bit encryption between the client and the server.

4.1.2.3 SSPI Signing

Similar to GSS-API, SSPI signing is meant to provide assurance for the authenticity of messages. If an attacker on the network modifies or replays network traffic between the client and the server, SSPI is in a position to detect this and drop messages that have been tampered with.

If NTLM version 1 is used for user authentication, SSPI signing is performed as follows:

1. A checksum is calculated on RPC data using the CRC32 function. The result is a 32-bit CRC checksum.
2. The CRC32 checksum is encrypted using the RC4 algorithm and the SSPI session key as the key.
3. The first 8 bytes of the encrypted CRC4 checksum are added to the SSPI header of the packet for integrity authentication.

If NTLM version 2 is used for user authentication, SSPI signing is performed as follows:

1. Client and server maintain sequence numbers for incoming and outgoing packets.
2. A protection BLOB is calculated by concatenating the message sequence number for the packet and the contents of the entire RPC packet (protects all the RPC data from modification).
3. A keyed hash is calculated using the HMAC-MD5 algorithm on the protection BLOB using the SSPI session key as the key.
4. The keyed hash is added to the packet.

4.1.2.4 SSPI Sealing (Encryption)

In a similar fashion to GSS-API, SSPI can protect the confidentiality of the communication channel between the client and the server by encrypting messages (tokens) exchanged between them. SSPI sealing is relatively straightforward — the RC4 protocol is used using the SSPI session key as the key to encrypt RPC payload. Sealing includes signing, so sealing the signature of the RPC message will also be calculated by following the algorithm above. The signature is calculated on plaintext data, before sealing (encryption).

4.1.2.5 Controlling SSP Behavior Using Group Policies

Group policies provide a setting that can be used on clients and servers to specify the minimum level of security for NTLM SSP connections. These settings are Network security: Minimum session security for NTLM SSP-based (including secure RPC) servers and Network security: Minimum session security for NTLM SSP-based (including secure RPC) clients.

- *Require message integrity:* require message signing.
- *Require message confidentiality:* requires both message signing and encryption.
- *Require NTLMv2 session security:* do not accept SSPI sessions that use protocols earlier than NTLMv2.
- *Require 128-bit encryption:* require the client and server to negotiate 128-bit encryption over NTLM SSP (see below).

4.1.2.6 Microsoft Negotiate SSP

In the same way that the SPNEGO virtual authentication mechanism is used to negotiate an authentication method for GSS-API, Microsoft implements the Negotiate SSP for SSPI that can be used to negotiate an authentication method. In fact, the Negotiate SSP is SPNEGO compatible and RFC 4178 compatible so it can be used to communicate with other SPNEGO-compatible applications from different vendors.

The Negotiate SSP can currently negotiate the use of either Kerberos or NTLM authentication. The security support providers (SSPs) for these two mechanisms are Kerberos SSP and NTLMSSP, respectively.

Some applications are familiar with the NTLM protocol and get involved in the inner workings of the authentication process, while other applications might prefer to have a layer of abstraction and utilize NTLMSSP (or SSPI in general, which would make the authentication process use any available SSP, not only NTLM). The SMB/CIFS protocol and its implementation in Windows provide an example of how a service can use both mechanisms.

The SMB Session Service in Windows uses TCP/139 as its underlying transport protocol. On top of TCP sits the NetBIOS layer, then the SMB layer. NTLM authentication is directly embedded into SMB packets. The SMB protocol has a dialect negotiation mechanism, used to select the semantics and the specific parameters that the client and the server will use during the SMB session. In the end of the SMB dialect negotiation, the server typically provides an NTLM challenge to the client automatically (Figure 4.4).

When NTLM authentication is embedded within SMB, the NTLM authentication process is the following (see Figure 4.5):

1. The client sends the SMB negotiate protocol request (this is SMB protocol-specific negotiation, not SPNEGO) to the server and provides a list of SMB/CIFS dialects that it supports.

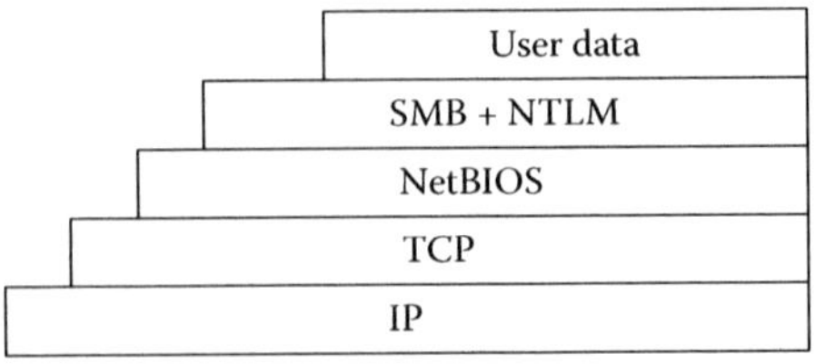

Figure 4.4 SMB over TCP/139 protocol stack.

2. The server replies with the SMB Negotiate protocol reply and selects the SMB dialect to be used by the client and server. In addition to that, the server provides the server challenge (SC) in the **EncryptionKey** field (see Frame 16 in Figure 4.5).
3. The client encrypts the challenge using the LAN Manager and/or NTLM replies (see below) and submits them in the **ANSIPassword** and **UnicodePassword** SMB fields, respectively (see Frame 23 in Figure 4.5).
4. The server performs the same calculation, using the same algorithm as the client and the locally stored LM and NT hash, and returns success or failure code to the client in the SMB **NTStatus** field (see Frame 24 in Figure 4.5).

Windows 2000 and later operating systems implement some extensions to the SMB protocol (Common Internet File System — CIFS). Apart from SMB over NetBIOS on TCP/139, the SMB/CIFS session protocol is now supported on TCP/445 as the transport layer. In general, CIFS over TCP/445 does not implement a full NetBIOS layer (so it is independent of NetBIOS), and utilizes SSPI for authentication and session security, instead of embedding the NTLM authentication into SMB/CIFS messages. SSPI provides a layer of abstraction to SMB/CIFS, and authentication can utilize SMB/CIFS, Kerberos, or other authentication protocol (see Figure 4.6).

Authentication to SMB/CIFS on TCP/445 is performed in the following way (see Figure 4.7):

1. The client and server establish a TCP connection on TCP/445 using the TCP three-way handshake.
2. The client attempts to establish an SMB/CIFS session with the server and sends the SMB Negotiate Protocol Request to the server, providing a list of SMB/CIFS dialects that it supports.
3. The server replies with the SMB Negotiate protocol reply and selects the SMB dialect to be used by the client and server. In addition to that, the server utilizes the SPNEGO layer of the SSPI

```
Frame 15 (191 bytes on wire, 191 bytes captured)
Ethernet II, Src: Vmware_c0:00:01 (00:50:56:c0:00:01), Dst: Vmware_6c:bc:6d (00:0c:29:6c:bc:6d)
Internet Protocol, Src: 192.168.26.1 (192.168.26.1), Dst: 192.168.26.130 (192.168.26.130)
Transmission Control Protocol, Src Port: 2735 (2735), Dst Port: netbios-ssn (139), Seq: 34607721,
Ack: 342754, Len: 137
NetBIOS Session Service
SMB (Server Message Block Protocol)
    SMB Header
        Server Component: SMB
        Response in: 16
        SMB Command: Negotiate Protocol (0x72)
        NT Status: STATUS_SUCCESS (0x00000000)
        Flags: 0x18
        Flags2: 0xc853
        Process ID High: 0
        Signature: 0000000000000000
        Reserved: 0000
        Tree ID: 0
        Process ID: 65279
        User ID: 0
        Multiplex ID: 0
    Negotiate Protocol Request (0x72)
        Word Count (WCT): 0
        Byte Count (BCC): 98
        Requested Dialects
            Dialect: PC NETWORK PROGRAM 1.0
            Dialect: LANMAN1.0
            Dialect: Windows for Workgroups 3.1a
            Dialect: LM1.2X002
            Dialect: LANMAN2.1
            Dialect: NT LM 0.12

Frame 16 (157 bytes on wire, 157 bytes captured)
Ethernet II, Src: Vmware_6c:bc:6d (00:0c:29:6c:bc:6d), Dst: Vmware_c0:00:01 (00:50:56:c0:00:01)
Internet Protocol, Src: 192.168.26.130 (192.168.26.130), Dst: 192.168.26.1 (192.168.26.1)
```

Figure 4.5 NT-NetworkLogon.cap: client uses SMB/CIFS to access a Windows NT 4 domain controller directly.

```
Transmission Control Protocol, Src Port: netbios-ssn (139), Dst Port: 2735 (2735), Seq: 342754,
Ack: 34607858, Len: 103
NetBIOS Session Service
SMB (Server Message Block Protocol)
    SMB Header
        Server Component: SMB
        Response to: 15
        Time from request: 0.000259000 seconds
        SMB Command: Negotiate Protocol (0x72)
        NT Status: STATUS_SUCCESS (0x00000000)
        Flags: 0x98
        Flags2: 0xc853
        Process ID High: 0
        Signature: 0000000000000000
        Reserved: 0000
        Tree ID: 0
        Process ID: 65279
        User ID: 0
        Multiplex ID: 0
    Negotiate Protocol Response (0x72)
        Word Count (WCT): 17
        Dialect Index: 5, greater than LANMAN2.1
        Security Mode: 0x03
        Max Mpx Count: 50
        Max VCs: 1
        Max Buffer Size: 4356
        Max Raw Buffer: 65536
        Session Key: 0x00000000
        Capabilities: 0x000043fd
        System Time: Jan 22, 2006 23:53:48.812500000
        Server Time Zone: 0 min from UTC
        Key Length: 8
        Byte Count (BCC): 30
        Encryption Key: E12A93F52E2038F3
        Primary Domain: DOTNETZONE
```

Figure 4.5 (continued)

```
Frame 23 (372 bytes on wire, 372 bytes captured)
Ethernet II, Src: Vmware_c0:00:01 (00:50:56:c0:00:01), Dst: Vmware_6c:bc:6d (00:0c:29:6c:bc:6d)
Internet Protocol, Src: 192.168.26.1 (192.168.26.1), Dst: 192.168.26.130 (192.168.26.130)
Transmission Control Protocol, Src Port: 2735 (2735), Dst Port: netbios-ssn (139), Seq: 34608078,
Ack: 343009, Len: 318
NetBIOS Session Service
SMB (Server Message Block Protocol)
    SMB Header
        Server Component: SMB
        Response in: 24
        SMB Command: Session Setup AndX (0x73)
        NT Status: STATUS_SUCCESS (0x00000000)
        Flags: 0x18
        Flags2: 0xc807
        Process ID High: 0
        Signature: 0000000000000000
        Reserved: 0000
        Tree ID: 0
        Process ID: 65279
        User ID: 0
        Multiplex ID: 128
    Session Setup AndX Request (0x73)
        Word Count (WCT): 13
        AndXCommand: Tree Connect AndX (0x75)
        Reserved: 00
        AndXOffset: 260
        Max Buffer: 4356
        Max Mpx Count: 50
        VC Number: 1
        Session Key: 0x00000000
        ANSI Password Length: 24
        Unicode Password Length: 24
        Reserved: 00000000
        Capabilities: 0x000000d4
        Byte Count (BCC): 199
        ANSI Password: 8E4929C2D74B672BAF53642936D54B2DDD8A020D759280D2
```

Figure 4.5 (continued)

```
        Unicode Password: 8E4929C2D74B672BAF53642936D54B2DDD8A020D759280D2
        Account: administrator
        Primary Domain: XP-CLIENT
        Native OS: Windows 2002 Service Pack 2 2600
        Native LAN Manager: Windows 2002 5.1
        Extra byte parameters
    Tree Connect AndX Request (0x75)
        Word Count (WCT): 4
        AndXCommand: No further commands (0xff)
        Reserved: 00
        AndXOffset: 314
        Flags: 0x0008
        Password Length: 1
        Byte Count (BCC): 43
        Password: 00
        Path: \\EXCHDC1\ADDRESS
        Service: ?????

Frame 24 (212 bytes on wire, 212 bytes captured)
Ethernet II, Src: Vmware_6c:bc:6d (00:0c:29:6c:bc:6d), Dst: Vmware_c0:00:01 (00:50:56:c0:00:01)
Internet Protocol, Src: 192.168.26.130 (192.168.26.130), Dst: 192.168.26.1 (192.168.26.1)
Transmission Control Protocol, Src Port: netbios-ssn (139), Dst Port: 2735 (2735), Seq: 343009,
Ack: 34608396, Len: 158
NetBIOS Session Service
SMB (Server Message Block Protocol)
    SMB Header
        Server Component: SMB
        Response to: 23
        Time from request: 0.006121000 seconds
        SMB Command: Session Setup AndX (0x73)
        NT Status: STATUS_SUCCESS (0x00000000)
        Flags: 0x98
        Flags2: 0xc807
        Process ID High: 0
        Signature: 0000000000000000
        Reserved: 0000
```

Figure 4.5 (continued)

```
        Tree ID: 2051
        Process ID: 65279
        User ID: 2051
        Multiplex ID: 128
    Session Setup AndX Response (0x73)
        Word Count (WCT): 3
        AndXCommand: Tree Connect AndX (0x75)
        Reserved: 00
        AndXOffset: 132
        Action: 0x0000
        Byte Count (BCC): 91
        Native OS: Windows NT 4.0
        Native LAN Manager: NT LAN Manager 4.0
        Primary Domain: DOTNETZONE
    Tree Connect AndX Response (0x75)
        Word Count (WCT): 3
        AndXCommand: No further commands (0xff)
        Reserved: 00
        AndXOffset: 154
        Optional Support: 0x0001
        Byte Count (BCC): 13
        Service: A:
        Native File System: NTFS
```

Figure 4.5 (continued)

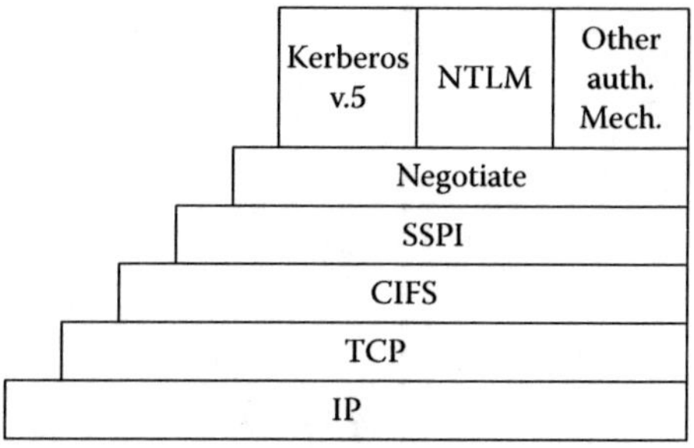

Figure 4.6 Negotiate SSP protocol stack.

```
Frame 9 (229 bytes on wire, 229 bytes captured)
Ethernet II, Src: steve.ins.com (00:03:ff:50:ab:2a), Dst: 02:00:4c:4f:4f:50 (02:00:4c:4f:4f:50)
Internet Protocol, Src: 10.0.2.102 (10.0.2.102), Dst: 10.0.2.1 (10.0.2.1)
Transmission Control Protocol, Src Port: microsoft-ds (445), Dst Port: 2773 (2773), Seq:
3883600201, Ack: 3808981185, Len: 175
NetBIOS Session Service
SMB (Server Message Block Protocol)
    SMB Header
        Server Component: SMB
        Response to: 8
        Time from request: 0.005201000 seconds
        SMB Command: Negotiate Protocol (0x72)
        NT Status: STATUS_SUCCESS (0x00000000)
        Flags: 0x98
        Flags2: 0xc853
        Process ID High: 0
        Signature: 0000000000000000
        Reserved: 0000
        Tree ID: 0
        Process ID: 65279
        User ID: 0
        Multiplex ID: 0
    Negotiate Protocol Response (0x72)
        Word Count (WCT): 17
        Dialect Index: 5, greater than LANMAN2.1
        Security Mode: 0x03
        Max Mpx Count: 50
        Max VCs: 1
        Max Buffer Size: 4356
        Max Raw Buffer: 65536
        Session Key: 0x00000000
        Capabilities: 0x8001f3fd
        System Time: Dec 30, 2005 18:09:51.574823000
        Server Time Zone: 0 min from UTC
        Key Length: 0
        Byte Count (BCC): 102
```

Figure 4.7 XP-Client-Steve-CIFS-Logon.cap: Client connect to server using SMB/CFIS on TCP/445.

```
        Server GUID: BC3690817F2CC6439A716CBBCC53C38D
        Security Blob: 605406062B0601050502A04A3048A030302E06092A864882...
            GSS-API Generic Security Service Application Program Interface
                OID: 1.3.6.1.5.5.2 (SPNEGO - Simple Protected Negotiation)
                SPNEGO
                    negTokenInit
                        mechTypes: 4 items
                            Item: 1.2.840.48018.1.2.2 (MS KRB5 - Microsoft Kerberos 5)
                            Item: 1.2.840.113554.1.2.2 (KRB5 - Kerberos 5)
                            Item: 1.2.840.113554.1.2.2.3 (KRB5 - Kerberos 5 - User to User)
                            Item: 1.3.6.1.4.1.311.2.2.10 (NTLMSSP - Microsoft NTLM Security
Support Provider)
                        mechListMIC: A0101B0E737465766652440494E532E434F4D
                            principal: steve$@INS.COM

Frame 10 (294 bytes on wire, 294 bytes captured)
Ethernet II, Src: 02:00:4c:4f:4f:50 (02:00:4c:4f:4f:50), Dst: steve.ins.com (00:03:ff:50:ab:2a)
Internet Protocol, Src: 10.0.2.1 (10.0.2.1), Dst: 10.0.2.102 (10.0.2.102)
Transmission Control Protocol, Src Port: 2773 (2773), Dst Port: microsoft-ds (445), Seq:
3808981185, Ack: 3883600376, Len: 240
NetBIOS Session Service
SMB (Server Message Block Protocol)
    SMB Header
        Server Component: SMB
        Response in: 11
        SMB Command: Session Setup AndX (0x73)
        NT Status: STATUS_SUCCESS (0x00000000)
        Flags: 0x18
        Flags2: 0xc807
        Process ID High: 0
        Signature: 0000000000000000
        Reserved: 0000
        Tree ID: 0
        Process ID: 65279
        User ID: 0
        Multiplex ID: 64
```

Figure 4.7 (continued)

```
    Session Setup AndX Request (0x73)
        Word Count (WCT): 12
        AndXCommand: No further commands (0xff)
        Reserved: 00
        AndXOffset: 236
        Max Buffer: 4356
        Max Mpx Count: 50
        VC Number: 0
        Session Key: 0x00000000
        Security Blob Length: 74
        Reserved: 00000000
        Capabilities: 0xa00000d4
        Byte Count (BCC): 177
        Security Blob: 604806062B0601050502A03E303CA00E300C060A2B060104...
            GSS-API Generic Security Service Application Program Interface
                OID: 1.3.6.1.5.5.2 (SPNEGO - Simple Protected Negotiation)
                SPNEGO
                    negTokenInit
                        mechTypes: 1 item
                            Item: 1.3.6.1.4.1.311.2.2.10 (NTLMSSP - Microsoft NTLM Security
Support Provider)
                        mechToken: 4E544C4D5353500001000000978208E2000000000000000...
                        NTLMSSP
                            NTLMSSP identifier: NTLMSSP
                            NTLM Message Type: NTLMSSP_NEGOTIATE (0x00000001)
                            Flags: 0xe2088297
                            Calling workstation domain: NULL
                            Calling workstation name: NULL
        Native OS: Windows 2002 Service Pack 2 2600
        Native LAN Manager: Windows 2002 5.1
        Primary Domain:

Frame 11 (416 bytes on wire, 416 bytes captured)
Ethernet II, Src: steve.ins.com (00:03:ff:50:ab:2a), Dst: 02:00:4c:4f:4f:50 (02:00:4c:4f:4f:50)
Internet Protocol, Src: 10.0.2.102 (10.0.2.102), Dst: 10.0.2.1 (10.0.2.1)
```

Figure 4.7 (continued)

```
Transmission Control Protocol, Src Port: microsoft-ds (445), Dst Port: 2773 (2773), Seq:
3883600376, Ack: 3808981425, Len: 362
NetBIOS Session Service
SMB (Server Message Block Protocol)
    SMB Header
        Server Component: SMB
        Response to: 10
        Time from request: 0.010430000 seconds
        SMB Command: Session Setup AndX (0x73)
        NT Status: STATUS_MORE_PROCESSING_REQUIRED (0xc0000016)
        Flags: 0x98
        Flags2: 0xc807
        Process ID High: 0
        Signature: 0000000000000000
        Reserved: 0000
        Tree ID: 0
        Process ID: 65279
        User ID: 2050
        Multiplex ID: 64
    Session Setup AndX Response (0x73)
        Word Count (WCT): 4
        AndXCommand: No further commands (0xff)
        Reserved: 00
        AndXOffset: 358
        Action: 0x0000
            .... .... .... ...0 = Guest: Not logged in as GUEST
        Security Blob Length: 187
        Byte Count (BCC): 315
        Security Blob: A181B83081B5A0030A0101A10C060A2B0601040182370202...
            GSS-API Generic Security Service Application Program Interface
                SPNEGO
                    negTokenTarg
                        negResult: accept-incomplete (1)
                        supportedMech: 1.3.6.1.4.1.311.2.2.10 (NTLMSSP - Microsoft NTLM Security
Support Provider)
                        responseToken: 4E544C4D53535000020000000600060038000000158289E2...
```

Figure 4.7 (continued)

```
NTLMSSP
    NTLMSSP identifier: NTLMSSP
    NTLM Message Type: NTLMSSP_CHALLENGE (0x00000002)
    Domain: INS
        Length: 6
        Maxlen: 6
        Offset: 56
    Flags: 0xe2898215
    NTLM Challenge: 3C0A7B46E37C5E3D
    Reserved: 0000000000000000
    Address List
        Length: 94
        Maxlen: 94
        Offset: 62
        Domain NetBIOS Name: INS
            Target item type: NetBIOS domain name (0x0002)
            Target item Length: 6
            Target item Content: INS
        Server NetBIOS Name: STEVE
            Target item type: NetBIOS host name (0x0001)
            Target item Length: 10
            Target item Content: STEVE
        Domain DNS Name: ins.com
            Target item type: DNS domain name (0x0004)
            Target item Length: 14
            Target item Content: ins.com
        Server DNS Name: Steve.ins.com
            Target item type: DNS host name (0x0003)
            Target item Length: 26
            Target item Content: Steve.ins.com
            Target item type: Unknown (0x0005)
            Target item Length: 14
            Target item Content: ins.com
        List Terminator
            Target item type: End of list (0x0000)
            Target item Length: 0
```

Figure 4.7 (continued)

```
      Native OS: Windows Server 2003 3790 Service Pack 1
      Native LAN Manager: Windows Server 2003 5.2

Frame 12 (428 bytes on wire, 428 bytes captured)
Ethernet II, Src: 02:00:4c:4f:4f:50 (02:00:4c:4f:4f:50), Dst: steve.ins.com (00:03:ff:50:ab:2a)
Internet Protocol, Src: 10.0.2.1 (10.0.2.1), Dst: 10.0.2.102 (10.0.2.102)
Transmission Control Protocol, Src Port: 2773 (2773), Dst Port: microsoft-ds (445), Seq:
3808981425, Ack: 3883600738, Len: 374
NetBIOS Session Service
SMB (Server Message Block Protocol)
   SMB Header
      Server Component: SMB
      Response in: 20
      SMB Command: Session Setup AndX (0x73)
      NT Status: STATUS_SUCCESS (0x00000000)
      Flags: 0x18
      Flags2: 0xc807
      Process ID High: 0
      Signature: 0000000000000000
      Reserved: 0000
      Tree ID: 0
      Process ID: 65279
      User ID: 2050
      Multiplex ID: 128
   Session Setup AndX Request (0x73)
      Word Count (WCT): 12
      AndXCommand: No further commands (0xff)
      Reserved: 00
      AndXOffset: 370
      Max Buffer: 4356
      Max Mpx Count: 50
      VC Number: 0
      Session Key: 0x00000000
      Security Blob Length: 208
      Reserved: 00000000
      Capabilities: 0xa00000d4
```

Figure 4.7 (continued)

```
        Byte Count (BCC): 311
        Security Blob: A181CD3081CAA281C70481C44E544C4D5353500003000000...
            GSS-API Generic Security Service Application Program Interface
                SPNEGO
                    negTokenTarg
                        responseToken: 4E544C4D53535000030000001800180084000000180018 00...
                        NTLMSSP
                            NTLMSSP identifier: NTLMSSP
                            NTLM Message Type: NTLMSSP_AUTH (0x00000003)
                            Lan Manager Response:
86BCD90E2F5A9FD800000000000000000000000000000000
                                Length: 24
                                Maxlen: 24
                                Offset: 132
                            NTLM Response: C1AF3E59D1BAF61FD3E3E70A1A3A90798BAC9C19DF9ADB9F
                                Length: 24
                                Maxlen: 24
                                Offset: 156
                            Domain name: NULL
                            User name: administrator@ins.com
                                Length: 42
                                Maxlen: 42
                                Offset: 72
                            Host name: XP-CLIENT
                                Length: 18
                                Maxlen: 18
                                Offset: 114
                            Session Key: AC4619F74BDBA0B10BB521E70C9EA5EC
                                Length: 16
                                Maxlen: 16
                                Offset: 180
                            Flags: 0xe2888215
         Native OS: Windows 2002 Service Pack 2 2600
        Native LAN Manager: Windows 2002 5.1
        Primary Domain:
```

Figure 4.7 (continued)

```
Frame 20 (238 bytes on wire, 238 bytes captured)
Ethernet II, Src: steve.ins.com (00:03:ff:50:ab:2a), Dst: 02:00:4c:4f:4f:50 (02:00:4c:4f:4f:50)
Internet Protocol, Src: 10.0.2.102 (10.0.2.102), Dst: 10.0.2.1 (10.0.2.1)
Transmission Control Protocol, Src Port: microsoft-ds (445), Dst Port: 2773 (2773), Seq:
3883600738, Ack: 3808981799, Len: 184
NetBIOS Session Service
SMB (Server Message Block Protocol)
    SMB Header
        Server Component: SMB
        Response to: 12
        Time from request: 0.059141000 seconds
        SMB Command: Session Setup AndX (0x73)
        NT Status: STATUS_SUCCESS (0x00000000)
        Flags: 0x98
        Flags2: 0xc807
        Process ID High: 0
        Signature: 0000000000000000
        Reserved: 0000
        Tree ID: 0
        Process ID: 65279
        User ID: 2050
        Multiplex ID: 128
    Session Setup AndX Response (0x73)
        Word Count (WCT): 4
        AndXCommand: No further commands (0xff)
        Reserved: 00
        AndXOffset: 180
        Action: 0x0000
            .... .... .... ...0 = Guest: Not logged in as GUEST
        Security Blob Length: 9
        Byte Count (BCC): 137
        Security Blob: A1073005A0030A0100
            GSS-API Generic Security Service Application Program Interface
                SPNEGO
                    negTokenTarg
```

Figure 4.7 (continued)

```
                    negResult: accept-completed (0)
    Native OS: Windows Server 2003 3790 Service Pack 1
    Native LAN Manager: Windows Server 2003 5.2
```

Figure 4.7 (continued)

protocol and provides a list of supported authentication mechanisms that it is willing to negotiate. In addition to that, the server provides its principal name, which can be used by the client at a later stage in accordance with Kerberos authentication (see Frame 9 in Figure 4.7).

4. The client selects an authentication protocol from the list provided by the server, adds the SSPI (GSS-API), SPNEGO ,and NTLMSSP layers on top of the SMB_Session_Setup_AndX Request message, and replies to the server with the authentication protocol of choice (see Frame 10 in Figure 4.7).
5. The server utilizes the SMB_Session_Setup_AndX Reply message, adding the SSPI (GSS-API), SPNEGO and NTLMSSP layers on top of SMB, setting the SMB **NTStatus** flag to STATUS_MORE_PROCESSING_REQUIRED, and sends the client a Server Challenge (SC) in the **NTLMChallenge** fields of the NTLSSP layer (see Frame 11 in Figure 4.7).
6. The client calculates the LM and NTLM replies and submits them to the server in an SMB_Session_Setup_AndX message, adding again the SSPI layer, the SPNEGO layer, and finally the NTLM layer. Within the NTLM layer the client includes the calculated LM response, the NTLM response, the user name, the client computer name, the session key (typically used by the client to change the password-based session key), and the NTLMSSP authentication flags (see Frame 12 in Figure 4.7).
7. The server calculates the response values using the same algorithm and returns the success or failure result in the **NTStatus** filed of the SMB layer, and potentially indicates the completion of the authentication process using the **negResult** field of the SPNEGO header (see Frame 12 in Figure 4.7).

4.1.2.7 GSS-API and SSPI Compatibility

GSS-API and SSPI were developed in parallel by the IETF and Microsoft, respectively. GSS-API is therefore an open standard while SSPI is proprietary. They serve the same function and despite the fact that the API functions that they implement may be different, they have similar behavior on the network and therefore GSS-API and SSPI clients and servers may be able to interoperate in some specific scenarios, and they will fail in other scenarios.

Mechanisms such as message protection in terms of integrity and encryption implemented by different GSS-API and SSPI mechanisms are often not compatible. The Kerberos protocol is supported as an authentication mechanism/security support provider by both APIs, and generates the same RFC 1510 compliant session keys. However, the integrity and encryption algorithms implemented by GSS-API and SSPI are different and not compatible. In essence, GSS-API and SSPI can be used effectively in user authentication scenarios but not with message protection. More details are available in [53].

4.2 Authentication Protocols

This section delves into the mechanics of the most widely used network authentication protocols. It examines the parameters involved in the authentication process, the steps performed during authentication, and discusses protocol advantages and shortcomings.

4.2.1 NTLM Authentication

The NTLM Authentication Protocol was first introduced as part of the SMB Protocol, primarily used for file sharing between computers in the early LAN Manager and Microsoft Network Client for DOS days. NTLM authentication then evolved and was widely adopted by other vendors as part of LAN Manager third-party licensing, as well as by the open source society that worked to provide a free vendor-independent SMB/CIFS implementation (SAMBA). The NTLM authentication protocol was later used for user authentication in other application protocols (such as HTTP).

4.2.1.1 NTLM Overview

The details of the NTLM authentication protocol have not been published by Microsoft, although Microsoft representatives have contributed to some publications, such as the Open Group ActiveX reference [40] that gives some basic public information. Most of the information about the NTLM authentication protocol is available as a result of the hard work of Internet researchers, such as the SAMBA and SAMBA-TNG teams, as well as the Ethereal development community. In fact, among the best sources describing the NTLM Protocol is Eric Glass's unofficial documentation entitled "The NTLM Authentication Protocol" (see [48]).

As most of this work is based on reverse-engineering of the product, what is currently known may not be entirely correct and there may be more that is not known.

4.2.1.2 The Concept of Trust and Secure Channels

Secure channels are a fundamental concept of the Windows NTLM model of trust. The secure channel is a protected connection between the trusting party and the trusted party. It is used for user logon and authentication, as well as for performing sensitive tasks, such as username and SID translation, group enumeration, and replication between the PDC and the BDCs in Windows NT 4.0 and earlier.

As already discussed, Windows NT relies on a hierarchical trust model; domain members trust the domain (the domain controllers) to provide appropriate security policies. On the other hand, trusting (resource) domains trust trusted (account) domains to provide a list of accounts and global groups. The model of trust is built on the fact that trusting and trusted parties share common secrets.

Upon start-up, trusting Windows NT 4.0 computers (as well as Windows 2000 and later in a Windows NT 4.0 domain) build a secure channel with trusted Windows NT 4.0 Domain Controllers. Following is the model of trust:

- Windows domain members discover a Windows NT 4.0 domain controller for the domain of which they are members, and establish a secure channel with this domain controller using their machine account in the domain. The trust relationship between the workstation and the domain (a specific instance of the domain — a domain controller) is based on the fact that the domain member has a computer account in the domain, and knows the password for this account. This password is stored in the LSA database on the domain member, and in the password field of the computer account in the directory on the domain controller.
- Trusting (resource) domain domain controllers discover trusted (account) domain domain controllers and establish a secure channel using the interdomain trust account. The trust between the trusting and the trusted domain (a specific instance of the trusted domain — a domain controller) is based on the fact that the trusting domain has an interdomain trust account in the trusted domain, and knows the password for this account (a global LSA secret replicated between all domain controllers in the trusting domain).

It is important to understand that the secure channel is always established using computer credentials, and not user credentials. This is because the secure channel is a secure communication channel between computers, and not between users. At the same time, the secure channel can be used to protect user metadata, and potentially data exchanged between a domain member and a domain controller, or between two domain controllers.

The secure channel provides for mutual authentication between the parties establishing this channel. Both the client and the server generate challenges and authenticate the reply from the remote party. Provided that the machine account password is secure, in the end of the secure channel establishment process, both the client and the server have validated the identity of the remote party. From that point on, they can protect traffic through the secure channel by either message integrity authentication or encryption, or both.

DCE/RPC

The secure channel is established as an interprocess communication channel (IPC) between the communicating parties, and it utilizes DCE Remote Procedure Calls (RPCs) as the IPC mechanism. DCE/RPC is a complex protocol that is generally out of the scope of this book. For the purpose of this overview, some basic concepts are introduced here.

DCE/RPC allows one computer to invoke procedures on another computer over the network. As the name implies, this is a mechanism designed for distributed applications in a networked environment. While it can be an essential part of client/server computing, DCE/RPC plays an important role in user authentication in Windows domains.

Some of the core Windows network services available over the network using RPC include:

- Workstation service
- Server service
- Registry service
- Netlogon
- SAM (Security Accounts Manager)
- LSA (Local Security Authority)

A computer on the network can connect to a remote computer on the network and execute code on that remote computer using RPC calls. Procedures available via RPC are known as interfaces, and they have well-known 128-bit identifiers (GUIDs or Interface UIDs) by which remote applications can identify and invoke them. Even when applications from two different vendors communicate with each other, provided that they know the Interface ID of the remote RPC interface, they can connect and communicate with each other across the network.

There are two industry implementations of RPC:

1. *Sun RPC.* This is the original RPC implementation. Sun invented RPC, and many UNIX applications are currently available that use RPC. In the original Sun specification, RPC calls bind directly to TCP or UDP ports.
2. *Microsoft RPC (MSRPC) or DCE/RPC.* Windows NT 4.0 and earlier operating systems use a version of RPC that utilizes the SMB Core protocol (CIFS) as the transport and for purposes such as user authentication. MSRPC typically utilizes transactional mechanisms, such as Named Pipes to provide for communication streams between the parties, and RPC calls are implemented on top of the SMB/CIFS protocol. Microsoft calls this RPC implementation **ncacn_np**. Although it adds an additional communication layer to the RPC protocol stack, this approach has been very successful because it leverages the authentication capabilities of the SMB/CIFS core, and it can run on top of many transport protocols, including TCP, NetBEUI, and SPX. In a similar, although not directly compatible way to Sun's RPC architecture, starting with Windows 2000, Microsoft utilizes direct binding of RPC calls over TCP or UDP transport, and an underlying SMB/CIFS transport is no longer required, so direct binding for RPC can be used. Microsoft has a slightly modified version that utilizes a different portmapper port, and calls this RPC implementation **ncacn_tcp.**

The secure channel in Windows NT 4.0 and earlier utilizes MSRPC calls and Windows 2000, and later Windows operating systems can use MSRPC and direct binding RPCs but may fall back to Windows NT 4.0 style RPC, if required. The secure channel in Windows NT provides for data authentication and encryption. In addition to that, if the secure channel utilizes MSRPC, the underlying SMB/CIFS transport may provide for additional message signing.

4.2.1.3 Domain Member Secure Channel Establishment

Domain members establish a secure channel with a domain controller from their own domain. Windows 2000 and later computers use direct bind RPC for this. Windows NT 4.0 and earlier computers use MSRPC over SMB/CIFS. The secure channel is established in the following way.

First, a session is established between the domain member and the domain controller. Windows 2000 and later AD domain members utilize the RPC portmapper to obtain a dynamic port to connect to (see Frames 145–146 in Steve-Startup-And-Logon.Cap on companion Web site, http://www.iamechanics.com). The client then connects to the dynamic RPC port. Windows NT 4.0 and earlier domain members establish a NetBIOS session and an SMB/CIFS session to IPC$. Using the already-created session, the client binds to the RPC Netlogon interface (see Frames 150 and 151 in Steve-Startup-And-Logon.Cap on companion Web site).

Then the client and server perform secure channel authentication by exchanging and validating challenges and responses. Essentially, the process is the following (see Frames 152 through 155 in Steve-Startup-And-Logon.Cap in Figure 4.8):

1. The client invokes the **NetrServerReqChallenge( )** RPC call to request a challenge from the server (domain controller) (Frame 152 in Figure 4.8). At the same time, to be able to authenticate the server, the client sends an 8-byte client challenge (Cc) to the domain controller. The domain member also specifies its name and the name of the domain controller in the initial request.
2. The server receives the initial request and replies with an 8-byte server challenge (Sc) in the **NetrServerReqChallenge( )** RPC reply (Frame 153 in Figure 4.8).
3. Both the client and server calculate a session key for the secure channel. The algorithm used by both at the same time is the following:
   - The 8-byte sum (S) of the client (Cc) and server (Sc) challenges is calculated.
   - The Sum (S) is encrypted using DES and the first 7 bytes of the machine NT password hash as the key. The result is the encrypted sum (ES).
   - The encrypted sum (ES) is encrypted again using DES and the last 7 bytes of the machine NT password hash as the key. The result is the session key (SK).
4. The domain member invokes the **NetrServerAuthenticate3( )** RPC procedure and provides the encrypted client response (CR) (see Frame 154 in Figure 4.8). The encryption is performed using the following algorithm:
   - Calculate the encrypted server challenge DES-SC by encrypting the server challenge (SC) using DES and the first 7 bytes from the session key as the key.
   - Calculate the client response (CR) by encrypting the encrypted server challenge (DES-SC) using DES and the seventh byte from the session key, padded with zeroes to 56 bits.
5. The server receives the client response and performs the same encryption as above using its own calculated copy of the session key (SK) and its own server challenge (SC). It then either authenticates or rejects the client request for a secure channel.

```
Frame 152 (158 bytes on wire, 158 bytes captured)
Ethernet II, Src: steve.ins.com (00:03:ff:50:ab:2a), Dst: 02:00:4c:4f:4f:50 (02:00:4c:4f:4f:50)
Internet Protocol, Src: 10.0.2.102 (10.0.2.102), Dst: 10.0.1.101 (10.0.1.101)
Transmission Control Protocol, Src Port: 1048 (1048), Dst Port: 1025 (1025), Seq: 2806753336,
Ack: 188656455, Len: 104
DCE RPC Request, Fragment: Single, FragLen: 104, Call: 1 Ctx: 0, [Resp: #153]
Microsoft Network Logon, NetrServerReqChallenge
   Operation: NetrServerReqChallenge (4)
   Server Handle: \\BILL.ins.com
      Referent ID: 0x00020000
      Max Count: 15
      Offset: 0
      Actual Count: 15
      Handle: \\BILL.ins.com
   Computer Name: STEVE
      Max Count: 6
      Offset: 0
      Actual Count: 6
      Computer Name: STEVE
   CREDENTIAL: client challenge
      Credential: 016E99277F3082F6

Frame 153 (90 bytes on wire, 90 bytes captured)
Ethernet II, Src: 02:00:4c:4f:4f:50 (02:00:4c:4f:4f:50), Dst: steve.ins.com (00:03:ff:50:ab:2a)
Internet Protocol, Src: 10.0.1.101 (10.0.1.101), Dst: 10.0.2.102 (10.0.2.102)
Transmission Control Protocol, Src Port: 1025 (1025), Dst Port: 1048 (1048), Seq: 188656455, Ack:
2806753440, Len: 36
DCE RPC Response, Fragment: Single, FragLen: 36, Call: 1 Ctx: 0, [Req: #152]
Microsoft Network Logon, NetrServerReqChallenge
   Operation: NetrServerReqChallenge (4)
   CREDENTIAL: server credential
      Credential: 5E2DAC03B03D15C3
   Return code: STATUS_SUCCESS (0x00000000)

Frame 154 (190 bytes on wire, 190 bytes captured)
Ethernet II, Src: steve.ins.com (00:03:ff:50:ab:2a), Dst: 02:00:4c:4f:4f:50 (02:00:4c:4f:4f:50)
```

Figure 4.8 Steve-Startup-And-Logon.cap.

```
Internet Protocol, Src: 10.0.2.102 (10.0.2.102), Dst: 10.0.1.101 (10.0.1.101)
Transmission Control Protocol, Src Port: 1048 (1048), Dst Port: 1025 (1025), Seq: 2806753440,
Ack: 188656491, Len: 136
DCE RPC Request, Fragment: Single, FragLen: 136, Call: 2 Ctx: 0, [Resp: #155]
Microsoft Network Logon, NetrServerAuthenticate3
    Operation: NetrServerAuthenticate3 (26)
    Server Handle: \\BILL.ins.com
        Referent ID: 0x00020000
        Max Count: 15
        Offset: 0
        Actual Count: 15
        Handle: \\BILL.ins.com
    Acct Name: STEVE$
        Max Count: 7
        Offset: 0
        Actual Count: 7
        Acct Name: STEVE$
    Sec Chan Type: Workstation (2)
    Computer Name: STEVE
        Max Count: 6
        Offset: 0
        Actual Count: 6
        Computer Name: STEVE
    CREDENTIAL: authenticator
        Credential: 5DA89FFD9BA934B7
    Neg Flags: 0x600fffff

Frame 155 (98 bytes on wire, 98 bytes captured)
Ethernet II, Src: 02:00:4c:4f:4f:50 (02:00:4c:4f:4f:50), Dst: steve.ins.com (00:03:ff:50:ab:2a)
Internet Protocol, Src: 10.0.1.101 (10.0.1.101), Dst: 10.0.2.102 (10.0.2.102)
Transmission Control Protocol, Src Port: 1025 (1025), Dst Port: 1048 (1048), Seq: 188656491, Ack:
2806753576, Len: 44
DCE RPC Response, Fragment: Single, FragLen: 44, Call: 2 Ctx: 0, [Req: #154]
Microsoft Network Logon, NetrServerAuthenticate3
    Operation: NetrServerAuthenticate3 (26)
    CREDENTIAL pointer: unknown_NETLOGON_CREDENTIAL
```

Figure 4.8 (continued)

```
        Credential: DCED8EFE1DCC3FBD
    Neg Flags: 0x600fffff
    ULONG: unknown_ULONG
        Unknown long: 0x00000478
    Return code: STATUS_SUCCESS (0x00000000)
```

Figure 4.8 (continued)

6. The server replies to the client with the reply to the **NetrServer Authenticate3( )** RPC and specifies the success or failure of the client authentication request (Frame 155 in Figure 4.8; unfortunately, Ethereal cannot decode properly the contents of this frame). The server also provides its reply (SR) to the client challenge by encrypting the client challenge (CS) with the session key (SK) the same way as the client encrypted the server challenge.
7. The client compares the server reply (SR) with its locally calculated reply based on the client challenge (CS) and the session key (SK). If the server reply and the locally calculated reply match, the client has successfully authenticated the server.

Once the client and the server have been authenticated, they can start utilizing the Secure Channel to communicate with each other. In Windows NT 4.0 SP4 and later, the Secure Channel can be encrypted or signed using NTLMSSP.

4.2.1.4 Domain Controller Secure Channel Establishment across Trusts

Trusted domain controller start-up traffic is similar to domain member start-up traffic. Windows NT 4.0 and earlier backup domain controllers (BDCs) establish a secure channel to a primary domain controller (PDC) in the same way as a domain member, and they utilize their domain controller machine account to establish the connection. Replication traffic between PDC and BDC can also take place during start-up but this is beyond the scope of this book.

All domain controllers in a trusting (resource) domain try to establish a secure channel to a domain controller in a trusted (account) domain. The way a trusting domain controller discovers a trusted domain controller is similar to the way a domain member discovers a domain controller. The secure channel between the trusting (resource) domain controller and the trusted (account) domain controller is established using the interdomain trust account that is replicated and known by all trusting (resource) domain controllers.

4.2.1.5 SMB/CIFS Signing

The SMB/CIFS protocol is beyond the scope of this book. However, it is important to understand that the SMB protocol provides for data integrity authentication (also known as SMB signing).

Regardless of whether it uses SMB/CIFS as the transport layer or TCP/UDP direct binding, the latest implementations of DCE/RPC utilize SSPI data authentication and signing.

Both SMB/CIFS and SSPI (used by DCE/RPC) need a session key to protect network traffic by either encryption (sealing), or data integrity authentication (signing), or both. Session keys used by SMB/CIFS and SSPI provide for session data authentication and potentially encryption.

SMB Session Key Calculation

The algorithm used to calculate the session key for a specific SMB/CIFS signing or SSPI sign/seal connection is not publicly available. However, it is believed that the session key is calculated using the password hash used by the authentication protocol, and potentially session data for version 2 authentication protocols, and it differs depending on which protocol has been used.

The following is a list of algorithms believed to be used for calculating the session key, depending on the authentication protocol used by the client and the server:

- *LM authentication.* The session key is calculated by concatenating the first eight characters of the LM hash with eight zeroes. The resulting 16-byte string is the key.
- *NTLM authentication.* The session key is calculated by generating the MD4 hash of the NTLM hash. Because the NTLM hash is an MD4 function of the Unicode user password, the NTLM session key is the MD4 hash of the MD4 hash of the user password. The resulting 16 bytes are the session key.
- *LM v2 authentication.* The session key is calculated as the MD5-HMAC of the first 16 bytes of the version 2 hash using the first 16 bytes of the LM version 2 HMAC as the key. Note that this key includes session data, exchanged between the client and the server, and does not depend solely on the user password, and thus it prevents replay attacks because it is different for every session. The LM v2 authentication process is discussed later in this chapter.
- *NTLM v2 authentication.* The session key is calculated as the MD5-HMAC of the first 16 bytes of the version 2 hash using the first 16 bytes of the NTLM version 2 HMAC as the key. Note that this key includes session data, exchanged between the client and the server,

and does not depend solely on the user password, and thus it prevents replay attacks because it is different for every session. The NTLM v2 authentication process is discussed later in this chapter.

SMB signing is not an authentication technology but may play a role in user authentication when an authentication protocol — be it either LM/NTLM or SPNEGO — is used over SMB/CIFS. SMB signing is a technology that protects SMB/CIFS session data from improper modification. The primary goal is to prevent SMB traffic integrity attacks in man-in-the-middle scenarios. SMB signing generates a hash of the SMB payload and attaches it to the packet so that if someone modifies the SMB portion of the packet in transit, this will invalidate the signature and the recipient may chose to ignore the packet, due to the fact that it has been tampered with. SMB signing requires Windows NT 4.0 SP3 or later and is available on Windows 9x systems that have the Directory Services client installed.

To be used, SMB signing must be enabled on both the client and the server using the Microsoft Network Server: Digitally Sign Communications (always/if client agrees) and Microsoft Network Client: Digitally Sign Communications (always/if server agrees) Group Policy settings. They correspond to the following registry keys:

HKEY_LOCAL_MACHINE\SYSTEM\CurrentControlSet\Services\LanManServer\Parameters\RequireSecuritySignature:REG_DWORD

and

HKEY_LOCAL_MACHINE\SYSTEM\CurrentControlSet\Services\LanmanWorkstation\Parameters\RequireSecuritySignature:REG_DWORD

SMB Signing Algorithm

The SMB client and server maintain local and remote SMB sequence numbers for the connection. Both the client and the server keep track of the sequence number of the SMB packet they will send, as well as the sequence number they expect to see on incoming packets from the remote peer.

The SMB signing algorithm is not documented but is believed to be the following:

1. A Message Authentication Key is generated by concatenating the SMB Session Key and the LM/NTLM/LMv2/NTLMv2 Client response to the server challenge.

2. An authentication block is created by concatenating the message authentication key, the packet sequence number, and the SMB payload.
3. The MD5 hash of the authentication block is calculated.
4. The first 8 bytes of the MD5 hash of the authentication block are used as the SMB signature and are inserted in the SMB header.

Secure Channel Encryption (Sealing) and Integrity Authentication (Signing) using SSPI

DCE/RPC uses SSP to perform user authentication, as well as to encrypt and authenticate the contents of the Netlogon channel between the client and the server. SSPI relies on the authentication protocol used on the Netlogon channel to provide key material, and on the CryptoAPI to protect Netlogon channel contents.

Network administrators may choose to utilize SSPI to either authenticate the integrity of the secure channel (sign) or encrypt the contents of the secure channel (seal), which also provides for channel integrity authentication. Encryption and integrity authentication can be performed for the entire Netlogon RPC payload (Windows NT 4.0 SP4 and later), or just for the password hash fields. Windows NT 4.0 and earlier operating systems do not support Kerberos and build a secure channel to their domain controllers to provide for NTLM authentication.

The Netlogon channel in Windows NT 4.0 is based on authentication using NTLM and LM challenges, and key material derived from them.

Only user password hashes were encrypted as they traversed the secure channel before Windows NT 4.0 SP4. The remainder of the packet content was not encrypted or authenticated. The lack of encryption is a problem because apart from password hashes, other information, such as user account options, and user logon restrictions, may be considered confidential. The lack of signing might be a problem because anyone that has access to the communications channel between the domain controller and the domain member can modify the packet contents; for example, a malicious user might change the list of SIDs in the packet and therefore modify user privileges. Another problem with pre-Windows NT 4.0 SP4 NTLMSSP and Netlogon protection by encryption is that it is susceptible to known plaintext attacks; the fact that both the moderately strong NTLM password hash and the weak LM hash (which might not even exist, in which case it is set to all zeroes but still encrypted and sent across the network) are encrypted with the same key and algorithm (see below for details) can easily reveal user password hashes to potential attackers that can sniff traffic on the network.

To improve Secure Channel SSP protection, the system administrator can apply the Secure Channel Signing and Sealing settings for both domain controllers and domain members in Windows 2000 and later. The group policy setting **Domain member: Digitally encrypt or sign secure channel data (always/when possible)** controls this behavior. The corresponding registry entries are **HKEY_LOCAL_MACHINE\SYSTEM\CurrentControlSet\Services\Netlogon\Parameters\RequireSignOrSeal:REG_DWORD**, which controls whether SSPI signing/sealing will be used, as well as the **SignSecureChannel: REG_DWORD** and **SealSecureChannel:REG_DWORD** settings, which specify whether only signing (integrity authentication) or both signing and sealing (encryption) will be used.

When secure channel signing is configured on a domain member, SSP performs data signing independently of SMB signing. This is to ensure that both DCE/RPC traffic over SMB/CIFS (also known as MSRPC) and RPC direct binding over plain TCP (without SMB/CIFS) can be protected.

4.2.1.6 Case Study: Pass-through Authentication and Authentication Piggybacking

The secure channel concept is very important for the NTLM trust model. However, it requires that computers taking part in the authentication process be domain members because the secure channel utilizes machine account passwords to build the secure channel.

In some cases, computers might not be domain members but may still require the ability to authenticate users against the domain database. Although there are multiple interfaces for this — such as RADIUS or LDAP — in some cases it might be more useful to utilize the native NTLM authentication rather than other protocols. Some services and applications — such as SAMBA — can utilize unconventional authentication against the domain database. An example of this is the pass-through authentication model that is very similar to a man-in-the middle attack against the domain database. The pass-through authentication model works as follows:

1. The client sends an SMB_SESSION_SETUP message (or equivalent, depending on the protocol in use) to the SAMBA server.
2. The server opens a hollow SMB/CIFS session against a server that belongs to the domain, to which authentication must be performed.
3. As part of the fake SMB session, during the SMB_SESSION_SETUP message to the server from that domain, the SAMBA server receives a challenge string.
4. The SAMBA server relays the challenge string from Step 2 to the original client requiring authentication.

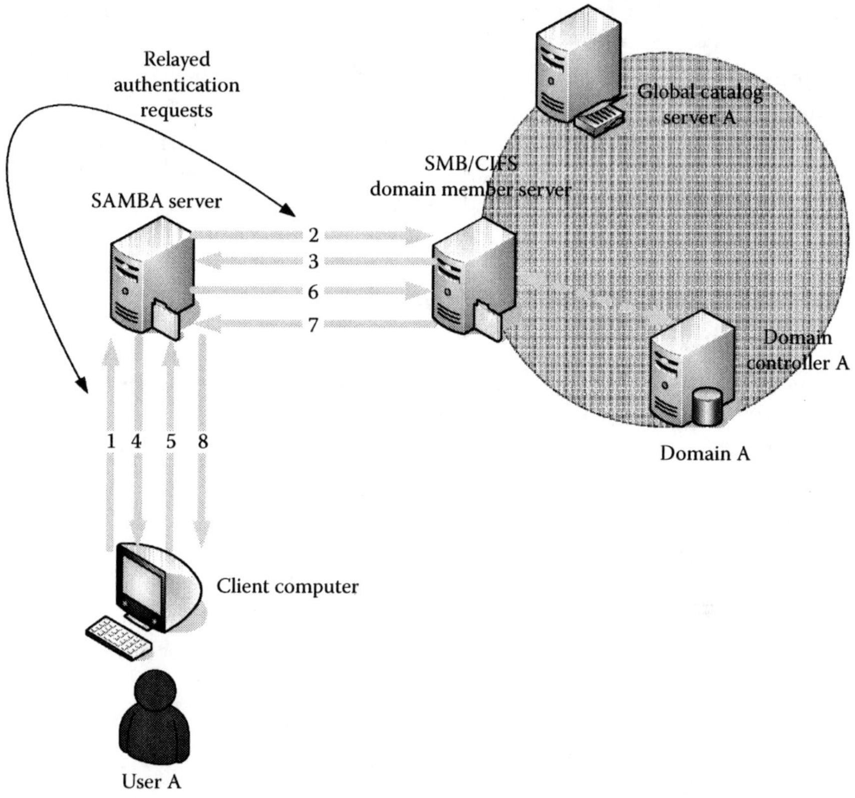

Figure 4.9 NTLM authentication piggybacking.

5. The client follows NTLM, LM, or other authentication methods negotiated with the SAMBA server to encrypt the challenge using a derivative of the user password as the key, and returns the response to the server.
6. Using the already-established hollow session, the server forwards the response to the domain member server for authentication. The domain member server will now query its own domain controller to perform authentication for this user; the reply (successful or unsuccessful authentication) will be sent back to the SAMBA server.
7. The domain member server, the client server, and the client computer receive the NTLM authentication reply, which shows whether or not the user has been authenticated successfully.

With the above authentication piggybacking method (Figure 4.9), the SAMBA server (the man-in-the-middle) only receives a reply of type Success/Failure. An actual access token is not returned to the SAMBA server, as the SMB/CIFS server keeps the token within its internal structures and does not provide it to the client as part of the SMB/CIFS protocol. Therefore, SAMBA (or other potential servers that want to use the man-in-the-middle authentication approach) need to find their own way to generate an access token or equivalent structure (if they need one). Alternatively, after successful user authentication, they can use their own access control lists to allow or deny the user access to resources.

4.2.1.7 NTLM Authentication Mechanics

The NTLM family of authentication mechanisms is primarily used by Microsoft operating systems, but also by other products such as SAMBA. Initially, the LM Protocol (LM version 1) was used for authentication but then NTLM version 1 followed, and later NTLM version 2, LM version 2, and NTLM2 Session Response. This section discusses the operation details behind each of these mechanisms.

To perform authentication, the NTLM family of protocols utilizes the NT hash and LM hash values, stored in the SAM or Active Directory on the server or domain controller, and calculated from the plaintext user password on the client computer. The NTLM family of authentication protocols never sends the user password across the network, not even in an encrypted form. Like most other challenge-response protocols, NTLM uses a derivative of the user password to encrypt a challenge string, provided by the authenticating server.

The following steps represent the general NTLM authentication process:

1. The client requests a challenge from the server, supplying a computer name and a domain name, as well as flags for the authentication. This message is sometimes referred to as an NTLM Type 1 message.
2. The server generates a random challenge (8 bytes, typically time-based) and sends it to the client. Along with the challenge, the server sets the parameters for the connection (flags). The server reply is sometimes referred to as an NTLM Type 2 message.
3. The client encrypts the challenge and sends it to the server (see Frame 28 in Figure 4.10). The client reply can use one or more NTLM algorithms (see below). The client specifies the username for the authenticating user, the domain name for the authenticating user, and the workstation name from where the authentication is taking place. The client can also specify a session key, which may later be used by SSPI for message authentication and encryption (see Chapter 4.1.2).

```
Frame 28 (506 bytes on wire, 506 bytes captured)
Ethernet II, Src: Vmware_c0:00:01 (00:50:56:c0:00:01), Dst: Vmware_6c:bc:6d (00:0c:29:6c:bc:6d)
Internet Protocol, Src: 10.0.2.102 (10.0.2.102), Dst: 192.168.26.130 (192.168.26.130)
Transmission Control Protocol, Src Port: 1026 (1026), Dst Port: netbios-ssn (139), Seq:
3652693367, Ack: 146448, Len: 452
NetBIOS Session Service
SMB (Server Message Block Protocol)
DCE RPC Request, Fragment: Single, FragLen: 384, Call: 3 Ctx: 0, [Resp: #31]
    Version: 5
    Version (minor): 0
    Packet type: Request (0)
    Packet Flags: 0x03
    Data Representation: 10000000
    Frag Length: 384
    Auth Length: 32
    Call ID: 3
    Alloc hint: 312
    Context ID: 0
    Opnum: 2
    Auth type: NETLOGON Secure Channel (68)
    Auth level: Packet integrity (5)
    Auth pad len: 8
    Auth Rsrvd: 0
    Auth Context ID: 0
    Response in frame: 31
    Secure Channel Verifier
        Signature: 7700FFFFFFFF0000
        Packet Digest: F7248233F803487A
        Sequence No: 4CBDE89BF2045727
        Nonce: 0000000000000000
Microsoft Network Logon, NetrLogonSamLogon
    Operation: NetrLogonSamLogon (2)
    Server Handle: \\EXCHDC1
        Referent ID: 0x00020000
        Max Count: 10
        Offset: 0
```

Figure 4.10 Alan-NTDOMAIN-Logon-Simon.cap: Users logs on interactively to a Windows NT domain.

```
            Actual Count: 10
            Handle: \\EXCHDC1
        Computer Name: ALAN
            Referent ID: 0x00020004
            Max Count: 5
            Offset: 0
            Actual Count: 5
            Computer Name: ALAN
        AUTHENTICATOR: credential
            Referent ID: 0x00020008
            Credential: DC2C473C49FB9B7B
            Timestamp: Jan 26, 2006 07:01:39.000000000
        AUTHENTICATOR: return_authenticator
            Referent ID: 0x0002000c
            Credential: B321837C00000800
            Timestamp: Jan  1, 1970 00:00:00.000000000
        Level: 1
        LEVEL: LogonLevel simon
            Level: 1
            INTERACTIVE_INFO: simon
                Referent ID: 0x00020010
                IDENTITY_INFO: simon
                    Domain: DOTNETZONE
                        Length: 20
                        Size: 20
                        Character Array: DOTNETZONE
                            Referent ID: 0x00020014
                            Max Count: 10
                            Offset: 0
                            Actual Count: 10
                            Domain: DOTNETZONE
                    Param Ctrl: 0x00000000
                    Logon ID: 277818
                    Acct Name: simon
                        Length: 10
                        Size: 10
```

Figure 4.10 (continued)

```
                    Character Array: simon
                        Referent ID: 0x00020018
                        Max Count: 5
                        Offset: 0
                        Actual Count: 5
                        Acct Name: simon
                Wkst Name: ALAN
                    Length: 8
                    Size: 10
                    Character Array: ALAN
                        Referent ID: 0x0002001c
                        Max Count: 5
                        Offset: 0
                        Actual Count: 4
                        Wkst Name: ALAN
            LM_OWF_PASSWORD:
                LM Pwd: D4F0BB9D4935F7E2C73A41654EA4D8F0
            NT_OWF_PASSWORD:
                NT Pwd: B99AE010E620DCD72007EC3241B54BF1
    Validation Level: 3
    Auth Padding (8 bytes)

Frame 31 (758 bytes on wire, 758 bytes captured)
Ethernet II, Src: Vmware_6c:bc:6d (00:0c:29:6c:bc:6d), Dst: Vmware_c0:00:01 (00:50:56:c0:00:01)
Internet Protocol, Src: 192.168.26.130 (192.168.26.130), Dst: 10.0.2.102 (10.0.2.102)
Transmission Control Protocol, Src Port: netbios-ssn (139), Dst Port: 1026 (1026), Seq: 146499,
Ack: 3652693882, Len: 704
SMB (Server Message Block Protocol)
DCE RPC Response, Fragment: Single, FragLen: 640, Call: 3 Ctx: 0, [Req: #28]
    Version: 5
    Version (minor): 0
    Packet type: Response (2)
    Packet Flags: 0x03
    Data Representation: 10000000
    Frag Length: 640
    Auth Length: 32
```

Figure 4.10 (continued)

```
    Call ID: 3
    Alloc hint: 572
    Context ID: 0
    Cancel count: 0
    Auth type: NETLOGON Secure Channel (68)
    Auth level: Packet integrity (5)
    Auth pad len: 4
    Auth Rsrvd: 0
    Auth Context ID: 0
    Opnum: 2
    Request in frame: 28
    Time from request: 0.011512000 seconds
    Secure Channel Verifier
        Signature: 7700FFFFFFFF0000
        Packet Digest: F20BF315255028A3
        Sequence No: 652B01B9D13EE5FC
        Nonce: 0000000000000000
Microsoft Network Logon, NetrLogonSamLogon
    Operation: NetrLogonSamLogon (2)
    AUTHENTICATOR: return_authenticator
        Referent ID: 0x0015cf5c
        Credential: CDE8414969A33B7E
        Timestamp: Jan  1, 1970 00:00:00.000000000
    VALIDATION:
        Validation Level: 3
        VALIDATION_SAM_INFO2:
            Referent ID: 0x00159ac8
            Logon Time: No time specified (0)
            Logoff Time: Jan 27, 2006 21:00:00.000250000
            Kickoff Time: Infinity (absolute time)
            PWD Last Set: Jan 26, 2006 07:09:55.796875000
            PWD Can Change: Jan 26, 2006 07:09:55.796875000
            PWD Must Change: Mar 10, 2006 05:57:27.540619000
            Acct Name: Simon
                Length: 10
                Size: 12
```

Figure 4.10 (continued)

```
        Character Array: Simon
            Referent ID: 0x00159bbc
            Max Count: 6
            Offset: 0
            Actual Count: 5
            Acct Name: Simon
    Full Name: Simon Collins
        Length: 26
        Size: 28
        Character Array: Simon Collins
            Referent ID: 0x00159bc8
            Max Count: 14
            Offset: 0
            Actual Count: 13
            Full Name: Simon Collins
    Logon Script: LogonScr.bat
        Length: 24
        Size: 26
        Character Array: LogonScr.bat
            Referent ID: 0x00159be4
            Max Count: 13
            Offset: 0
            Actual Count: 12
            Logon Script: LogonScr.bat
    Profile Path: \\server1\profiles\Simon
        Length: 48
        Size: 50
        Character Array: \\server1\profiles\Simon
            Referent ID: 0x00159bfe
            Max Count: 25
            Offset: 0
            Actual Count: 24
            Profile Path: \\server1\profiles\Simon
    Home Dir: \\server1\home\Simon
        Length: 40
        Size: 42
```

Figure 4.10 (continued)

```
        Character Array: \\server1\home\Simon
            Referent ID: 0x00159c30
            Max Count: 21
            Offset: 0
            Actual Count: 20
            Home Dir: \\server1\home\Simon
    Dir Drive: Z:
        Length: 4
        Size: 6
        Character Array: Z:
            Referent ID: 0x00159c5a
            Max Count: 3
            Offset: 0
            Actual Count: 2
            Dir Drive: Z:
    Logon Count: 0
    Bad PW Count: 0
    User RID: 1008
    Group RID: 513
    Num RIDs: 2
    GROUP_MEMBERSHIP_ARRAY
        Referent ID: 0x00159b94
        Max Count: 2
        GROUP_MEMBERSHIP:
            Group RID: 513
            Attributes: 0x00000007
        GROUP_MEMBERSHIP:
            Group RID: 512
            Attributes: 0x00000007
    User Flags: 0x00000120
    User Session Key: 00000000000000000000000000000000
    Server: EXCHDC1
        Length: 14
        Size: 16
        Character Array: EXCHDC1
            Referent ID: 0x00159c60
```

Figure 4.10 (continued)

```
                Max Count: 8
                Offset: 0
                Actual Count: 7
                Server: EXCHDC1
        Domain: DOTNETZONE
            Length: 20
            Size: 22
            Character Array: DOTNETZONE
                Referent ID: 0x00159c70
                Max Count: 11
                Offset: 0
                Actual Count: 10
                Domain: DOTNETZONE
        SID pointer:
            SID pointer
                Referent ID: 0x00159ba4
                Count: 4
                Domain SID: S-1-5-21-1990600127-808936205-1537874043
                    Revision: 1
                    Num Auth: 4
                    Authority: 5
                    Sub-authorities: 21-1990600127-808936205-1537874043
        Unknown long: 0x00000000
        Unknown long: 0x00000000
        User Account Control: 0x00000000
    = Dont Require PreAuth: This account REQUIRES preauthentication
    = Use DES Key Only: This account does NOT have to use_des_key_only
    = Not Delegated: This might have been delegated
    = Trusted For Delegation: This account is NOT trusted_for_delegation
    = SmartCard Required: This account does NOT require_smartcard to authenticate
    = Encrypted Text Password Allowed: This account does NOT allow encrypted_text_password
    = Account Auto Locked: This account is NOT auto_locked
    = Dont Expire Password: This account might expire_passwords
    = Server Trust Account: This account is NOT a server_trust_account
    = Workstation Trust Account: This account is NOT a workstation_trust_account
    = Interdomain trust Account: This account is NOT an interdomain_trust_account
```

Figure 4.10 (continued)

```
= MNS Logon Account: This account is NOT a mns_logon_account
= Normal Account: This account is NOT a normal_account
= Temp Duplicate Account: This account is NOT a temp_duplicate_account
= Password Not Required: This account REQUIRES a password
= Home Directory Required: This account does NOT require_home_directory
= Account Disabled: This account is NOT disabled
    Unknown long: 0x00000000
    Unknown long: 0x00000000
    Unknown long: 0x00000000
    Unknown long: 0x00000000
    Unknown long: 0x00000000
    Unknown long: 0x00000000
    Unknown long: 0x00000000
    Num Other Groups: 0
    (NULL pointer) SID_AND_ATTRIBUTES_ARRAY:
Authoritative: 1
Return code: STATUS_SUCCESS (0x00000000)
Auth Padding (4 bytes)
```

Figure 4.10 (continued)

4. If the account is a local account on the server, the server encrypts the challenge using the same algorithm as the client, using the LM hash or NT hash values from the local user database SAM. If the account is for a domain user, the server will typically use the **NetrLogonSamLogon( )** RPC and its derivatives to request the challenge encryption to be performed on a domain controller. This is because in the case of domain accounts, the server does not have a copy of the user LM hash or NT hash values. Either the server (for local accounts) or the domain controller (for domain accounts) compares the calculated response values with the client-provided values. If the values match, the user is authenticated. Otherwise, the authentication fails. The server replies to the **NetrLogonSamLogon( )** RPC and specifies user information to be used to used to generate the access token for the client (see Frame 31 in Figure 4.10). Note that the information returned by the server is similar to SAM user structures, as discussed in Chapter 3.

Figure 4.10 shows user Simon logging in to a Windows NT 4.0 domain from Windows 2003 domain member ALAN. Secure channel encryption (sealing) has been disabled so that traffic is not encrypted and authentication structures can be seen in the capture in plaintext.

The NTLM family of authentication protocols requires that the client and server know either the LM hash or the NT hash. The client does not store a copy of the LM hash or the NT hash and typically uses credentials supplied by the user at the time of authentication — such as a username and a plaintext password — to calculate the LM hash or the NT hash. However, it is important to understand that all authentication protocols utilize the password in a hashed form (LM hash or NT hash, or the derivative NTLMv2 hash) as this is what the servers store and use to calculate the expected response from the client. Although there are many tools available on the Internet and in software shops that allow for a plaintext user password to be obtained from the password hash by different methods, a potential attacker only requires a copy of the NT hash or the LM hash to authenticate as the user either interactively or over the network. In essence, this makes the NT and LM hash values virtually equivalent to the plaintext user password in terms of authentication potential and protection requirements.

Some of the protocols from the NTLM family are typically used together during the authentication process. Historically, LAN Manager clients used to generate only an LM response to the server challenge. As Windows NT introduced the NTLM authentication scheme, clients started to generate both the LM and the NT response to maintain compatibility with older LAN Manager clients and still use the stronger NT hash. The problem with this is that security and compatibility typically do not go together; if both a weak and a stronger authentication response exist within the same packet, then an attacker would apparently attack the weak one, rendering the stronger hash useless. Therefore, Microsoft made it possible to disable LM response generation on the client side or on the server side. As the new NTLM v.2 authentication scheme appeared, settings evolved to allow for a selection of responses to be provided by the client and server.

The settings to select a particular NTLM authentication level should be applied on both the client and the server, and they must be compatible (Table 4.1). Client and server authentication behavior can be controlled by modifying **HKEY_LOCAL_MACHINE\System\CurrentControlSet\Control\LMCompatibilityLevel:REG_DWORD**, or using the **Network Security: LAN Manager Authentication Level** group policy setting.

More information on the NTLM Protocol selection settings can be found in [49].

The different mechanisms of the NTLM authentication protocols work in a different way and provide a different level of protection. Table 4.2 provides a comparison of the NTLM authentication mechanisms. The details of operation for the specific authentication mechanisms are discussed on the following pages.

Table 4.1 LMCompatibiltyLevel Settings

Value	*Effect*
0	**Send LM and NTLM responses.** This is the legacy behavior that specifies that the client will generate both an LM hash and an NTLMv1 hash. Domain controllers will accept all possible hash values — LM, NTLM, and NTLMv2.
1	**Send LM & NTLM responses — use NTLM v.2 Session Security if negotiated.** The client generates both an LM hash and an NTLMv1 hash in authentication replies. Clients will try to use SSPI signing. Domain controllers accept LM, NTLM, and NTLM 2 authentication.
2	**Send NTLM response only.** Clients generate an NTLM response, and can use SSPI signing if the server supports it. Domain controllers accept LM, NTLM, and NTLM 2 authentication.
3	**Send NTLM v.2 response only.** The client generates an NTLM v.2 response only, and can support SSPI signing if the server supports it. Domain controllers accept LM, NTLM, and NTLM 2 authentication.
4	**Send NTLMv2 response only-Refuse LM.** The clients generate NTLM v.1 responses, and can use SSPI signing if the server supports it. Domain controllers only consider NTLM and NTLM v.2 responses.
5	**Send NTLMv2 response only-Refuse LM&NTLM.** Clients generate NTLM v.2 responses only, and can use SSPI signing if the server supports it. Domain controllers only consider NTLM v.2 responses.

LM version 1 Authentication Mechanism

The LAN Manager authentication mechanism (LM authentication), as the name implies, was first used in Microsoft's LAN Manager product. It then made its way through Windows 95/98 into the Windows NT product family, and many third-party implementations, such as SAMBA. Many older operating systems — such as Windows 95/98 — only support this authentication protocol out of the box. Today's Windows and SAMBA versions support LM authentication mainly for compatibility reasons.

The LM response is calculated based on the server challenge (SC) in the following way:

1. The client calculates the LM hash from the plaintext user password. The resulting LM hash is 16 bytes in size.
2. The LM hash is padded with nulls to 21 bytes — padded LM Hash.

3. The padded LM hash is split into three thirds: the 7-byte keys LMK1, LMK2, and LMK3.
4. Each of the keys (LMK1, LMK2, and LMK3) is used as an encryption key to encrypt the 8-byte server challenge (SC) using the DES Protocol. The results from the encryption are the RCL1, RCL2, and RCL3 8-byte values.
5. The RCL1, RCL2, and RCL3 values are concatenated to form the LM Response RCL, which is 24 bytes in size. The response is sent to the server.
6. The server calculates the response in the same way as the client and compares the results. If they match, authentication is successful. If they do not match, authentication fails.

Although the encryption algorithm may seem somewhat complex, the LM authentication protocol has some weaknesses and limitations.

First, it is based on the LM hash, which is inherently weak (see Chapter 3 for more details). In addition, the LM authentication protocol is susceptible to man-in-the-middle attacks, used by some implementations as an authentication approach (see Chapter 4.2.1.6). Basically, an attacker can sit in between the client and the server and relay messages between them. An attacker sitting between the client and the server can intercept the authentication and then utilize the authenticated session. In addition to that, as both the server challenge and the client reply are sent over the network, someone with access to the communication channel between the client and the server can obtain the challenge and the response, and it is relatively easy obtain the encryption key, which happens to be based on the LM hash; an attack on the LM hash can then provide the user password. Considering the lack of feedback between the three DES encrypted portions of the server challenge, the client response can be attacked in three separate pieces (the RCL1, RCL2, and RCL3 pieces), which is easy to compute. The inherent weakness of the LM hash makes such attacks feasible, and there are many tools on the Internet that utilize these weaknesses. The LM authentication protocol is susceptible to brute force attacks (attacker may try all or many possible combinations), dictionary attacks (the attacker may use frequently used combinations), and precomputed response (rainbow) attacks (precomputed responses to server challenges and specific passwords). As a result, LM authentication should, in general, be avoided.

NTLM version 1 Authentication Mechanism

The NTLM (NT LAN Manager) authentication mechanism was introduced by Microsoft with the Windows NT family of operating systems. It was

Table 4.2 Comparison of the NTLM Authentication Mechanisms

Parameter	*LM v.1*	*NTLM v.1*	*LM v.2*	*NTLM v.2*	*NTLM2 SR*
Authentication mechanism	Challenge-Response	Challenge-Response	Challenge-Response	Challenge-Response	Challenge-Response
Trust model	Username and password must be known to client; LM hash must be known to server or trusted domain controller	Username and password OR LM hash must be known to client; NT hash must be known to server or trusted domain controller	Username and password OR NTLM hash OR NTLMv2 hash must be known to client; NT hash must be known to server or trusted domain controller	Username and password OR NT hash must be known to client; Username and Domain name must be known to client and server; NT hash must be known to server or trusted domain controller	Username and password OR NTLM hash must be known to client; NT hash must be known to server or trusted domain controller
Applications/services that use this protocol for authentication	SMB/CIFS and MS-RPC, MS-RPC direct binding, HTTP, LDAP	SMB/CIFS and MS-RPC, MS-RPC direct binding, HTTP, LDAP	SMB/CIFS and MS-RPC, MS-RPC direct binding, HTTP, LDAP	SMB/CIFS and MS-RPC, MS-RPC direct binding, HTTP, LDAP	SMB/CIFS and MS-RPC, MS-RPC direct binding, HTTP, LDAP

Mutual authentication	No	No	No	No	No
Protocol security (1–5)	2 (Weak)	3 (Moderate)	4 (Good)	4 (Good)	4 (Good)
Challenge / Seed	Server only: Random/ Time based, 8 bytes	Server only: Random/ Time based, 8 bytes	Server based: Random/ Time based Client: Random	Server based: Random/ Time based Client: Random and Time based	Server based: Random/ Time based Client: Random
Response hash / Encryption approach	DES ECB using a 56+56+16-bit key	DES ECB using a 56+56+16-bit key	HMAC-MD5 using a 128-bit key	HMAC-MD5 using a 128-bit key	DES ECB using a 56+56+16-bit key
Response length	3x64 bits	3x64 bits	3x64 bits	Variable length	Variable length

then adopted by various other products that utilized the SMB/CIFS Protocol, and later other application protocols such as HTTP.

The NTLM v.1 authentication protocol is supported on all Windows NT derivatives, and can be installed on Windows 95/98 clients by installing the Directory Services client software. It is also supported by all SAMBA versions.

The NTLM v.1 Response is calculated based on the server challenge (SC) in the following way:

1. The client calculates the NT hash using the MD4 algorithm on the user's Unicode password. The result is a 16-byte hash.
2. The NT hash is padded with nulls to 21 bytes — padded NT hash.
3. The padded NT hash is split into three thirds: the 7-byte keys NTK1, NTK2, and NTK3.
4. Each of the keys (NTK1, NTK2, and NTK3) is used as an encryption key to encrypt the 8-byte server challenge (SC) using the DES Protocol. The results from the encryption are the RCN1, RCN2, and RCN3 8-byte values.
5. The RCN1, RCN2, and RCN3 values are concatenated to form the NTLM Response, which is 24 bytes in size.

NTLM authentication, although generally stronger than LM authentication, suffers from similar problems. Man-in-the-middle attacks are feasible, and an attacker with access to the communication channel between the client and the server can both intercept the authentication messages and then try to reverse-engineer the encryption key, or hijack the authenticated session. The server challenge and the response are sent in cleartext over the network that makes attacks trying to obtain the password hash feasible. Because the MD4 hash, used by the NT hash calculation, is stronger than the LM hash, the password is not so easily exposed. However, there are numerous attacks on the MD4 algorithm that might be able to compute either the original password or a colliding password (a different password that would generate the same hash). The NTLM authentication protocol is susceptible to brute force attacks (attacker may try all or many possible combinations), dictionary attacks (the attacker may use frequently used combinations), and precomputed response (rainbow) attacks (precomputed responses to server challenges and specific passwords). As a result, the NTLM authentication mechanisms should still be avoided if possible.

NTLM version 2 Authentication Mechanism

The NTLM v.2 authentication protocol was introduced in Windows NT 4.0 SP4. It was meant to provide a stronger authentication mechanism for

Windows-based systems. NTLM v.2 is stronger and more secure than LM v.1 and NTLM v.1. The Directory Services client for Windows 95/98 operating systems adds NTLM v.2 support to downlevel Microsoft operating systems. SAMBA-TNG added support for NTLM v.2 to the SAMBA product.

The NTLM v.2 authentication protocol uses the following algorithm:

1. The client calculates the NT hash using the MD4 algorithm on the user's Unicode password. The result is a 16-byte hash.
2. The uppercase Unicode username and the uppercase Unicode target user database (this is typically the domain name, or can be the server name in the case of local accounts on the server) are concatenated to form the target string (TS).
3. A keyed hash is created from the TS using the HMAC-MD5 algorithm and the NT hash as the key. The result is the 16-byte NTLM v.2 hash.
4. An authentication BLOB is created that is comprised of:
   - 4 bytes — fixed BLOB signature (0x01010000)
   - 4 bytes — reserved (0x00000000)
   - 8 bytes — time stamp — believed to be tens of microseconds since 1 January 1601, 00:00:00.0 UTC
   - 8 bytes — random seed
   - 4 bytes — It is unknown how this field is calculated
   - Variable — NetBIOS and DNS names of the server and domain
     - Domain NetBIOS Name (Type set to 2, followed by length and value)
     - Server NetBIOS Name (Type set to 1, followed by length and value)
     - Domain DNS Name (Type set to 4, followed by length and value)
     - Server DNS Name (Type set to 3, followed by length and value)
   - 4 bytes — padding/unknown (random bytes)
5. The server challenge (SC) and the BLOB are concatenated, and HMAC-MD5 with the 16-byte NTLM v.2 hash as the key is used to generate the first part of the client response (CR1). The second part of the NTLM v.2 client response is the BLOB itself; it has variable length.

Unlike the LM and NTLM responses, which are always 24 bytes in size, the NTLM v.2 response is considerably longer and has variable size. The server sends the server challenge (SC) in cleartext, and the client sends the BLOB itself in a cleartext form. As the client response is based on the

BLOB (which contains a time stamp and a random seed) and the server challenge (random but based on the current time) encrypted with the NTLM v.2 hash, the NTLM v.2 algorithm is relatively well protected from replay and precomputed (rainbow) attacks. On the other hand, because the BLOB is included in cleartext in client responses, and therefore can be considered known to the attacker, it can be computationally feasible to obtain the NTLM v.2 hash used to encrypt the BLOB and the server challenge.

Unlike LM v.1 and NTLM v.1, if the attacker has managed to calculate the key (the NTLM v.2 hash) from the client response, he will still need to calculate the NT hash from the NTLM v.2 hash if he wants to obtain the plaintext password. However, if the attacker does not need the plaintext password, he can use the NTLM v.2 hash to produce responses to server challenges using the NTLM v.2 Protocol. From an NTLM v.2 authentication protocol perspective, the knowledge of the NTLM v.2 hash is equivalent to the knowledge of the NTLM hash, and to the plaintext user password.

NTLM2 Session Response Authentication Mechanism

NTLM2 Session Response was introduced along with NTLM v.2 in Windows NT SP4. As with most other authentication mechanisms, Microsoft does not provide information for the authentication protocol mechanics. In the case of NTLM2 Session Response, Microsoft does not even mention it anywhere, so the name for this mechanism was given by Internet security researchers (see [48]). NTLM2 Session Response is typically used along with NTLM2 SSPI Encryption/Signing — see subsection 4.1.2.1.

The NTLM2 Session Response algorithm is believed to be the following:

1. The client generates a random 8-byte challenge — CC.
2. The client challenge CC is padded to 24 bytes using nulls. This is the LM response (CRL).
3. The client concatenates the server challenge (SC) with the client challenge (CC) — resulting in the challenge string.
4. The challenge string is hashed using the MD5 algorithm. The first 8 bytes of the total 16 bytes of the hash are used to create the NTLM2 session hash (SH).
5. Using the plaintext user password, the client calculates the NT hash using the MD4 hash on the user Unicode plain password. The result is the NT hash.
6. The NT Hash is padded with nulls to 21 bytes, resulting in the padded NT hash.

7. The padded NT hash is split into three parts and generates three 7-byte DES encryption keys (CEK1, CEK2, and CEK3).
8. The 8-byte NTLM2 session hash SH is encrypted using DES and each of the CEK1, CEK2, and CEK3 keys as the key. This results in three 8-byte DES encrypted values CRN1, CRN2, and CRN3.
9. The CRN1, CRN2, and CRN3 8-byte values are concatenated to form a 24-byte NTLM2 response (CRN) that is included in the NTLM Type 3 packet.

The use of random challenges (seeds) from both the client and the server side makes replay and precomputed (rainbow) attacks on the NTLM2 session response authentication protocol difficult to implement. Although some attacks have been reported as capable of reducing the complexity of the encryption, the NTLM2 session response protocol is still considered reasonably secure. As with most challenge-response protocols, dictionary attacks may be effective and brute force attacks may be effective in the long term.

LM version 2 Authentication Mechanism

The LM v.2 authentication protocol was introduced along with NTLM v.2 in Windows NT 4.0 SP 4. It is primarily used for compatibility reasons. It generates a shorter hash with a fixed length of 24 bytes, which makes it suitable for use by pass-through authentication servers that may not have inner knowledge of the authentication protocol, and may just relay the authentication requests to and from a server or domain controller that can use LM v.2 authentication (see subsection 4.2.1.6).

1. Using the plaintext user password, the client calculates the NT hash using the MD4 hash on the user Unicode plain password. The result is the NT hash.
2. The client concatenates the uppercase username and the uppercase authentication database name (servername or domain name) and calculates the HMAC-MD5 for the resultant string using the NT hash as the key. The result is the NTLM v.2 hash.
3. The client creates a random challenge of 8 bytes — the client challenge (CC).
4. The server challenge (SC) is concatenated with the client challenge (CC). The result is the challenge string.
5. The client calculates the HMAC-MD5 value for the challenge string using the NTLM v.2 hash as the key. The 16-byte result is the CRLA value.
6. The CRLA value is concatenated with the client challenge (CC) and used as a client LM v.2 response (CRL).

LM v.2 is similar to NTLM2 session response in terms of the protection that it provides.

4.2.1.8 Case Study: NTLM Authentication Scenarios

The NTLM authentication protocol can be used in a number of scenarios, depending on whether the client is authenticating interactively or across the network, and whether authentication is taking place in a single domain or across a domain trust. This subsection demonstrates some of the most common NTLM authentication scenarios.

Interactive Logon: Windows NT 4.0: User Logs in from Own Domain

Assumptions:

- The domain member has already established a secure channel with its domain controller (see subsection 4.2.1.2).
- Both the user and the computer (domain member) have an account in the same domain — Domain B.

Interactive logon process:

1. The user submits authentication credentials to GINA (username, password, and NetBIOS domain name for Domain A); see phase A in Figure 4.11.
2. GINA on the domain member calls the **LsaLogonUser( )** system call (see [46]).
3. The **LsaLogonUser( )** system call on the client computer (domain member) calculates the LM hash and the NTLM hash.
4. The domain member encrypts the user LM hash and the user NT hash using RC4 and the first 8 bytes of the secure channel session key padded to 16 bytes with zeroes as the key.
5. To protect from replay attacks, the client obtains the current time from the local computer clock and sums it with the client response to the server challenge. It then uses DES with the first 7 bytes of the secure channel session key as the key to encrypt the sum, and then encrypts the result again using DES and the last byte from the session key padded with zero to a 7-byte key as the key.
6. The domain member submits the plaintext username, the encrypted time stamp, the plaintext time stamp, and the encrypted password hashes utilizing the existing secure channel and passes the authentication request to the domain controller using the **NetrLogonSam**

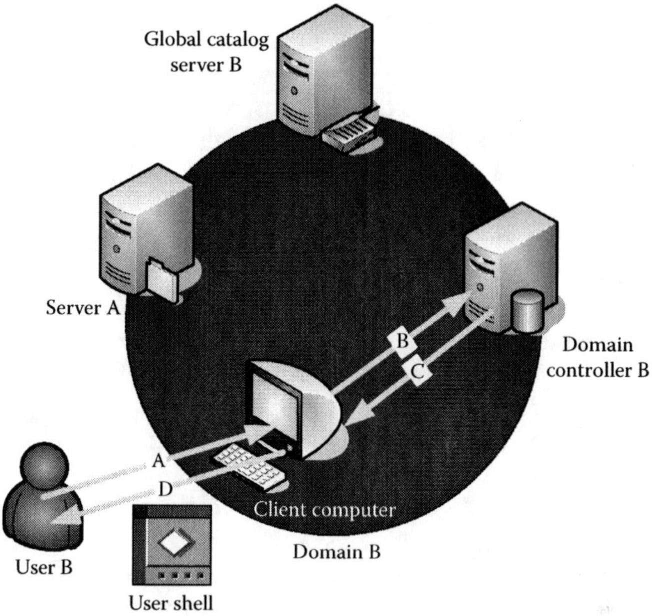

Figure 4.11 Interactive logon in the same domain.

Logon( ) RPC to the Netlogon RPC interface on the domain controller; see phase B in Figure 4.11. It is important to note that although the client uses the current time stamp in the calculation, this value is then sent to the server, and the Secure Channel authentication protocol does not rely on synchronized clocks on the client and the server.

7. Depending on the configuration, NTLMSSP can apply encryption (seal) and signing of the secure channel to protect secure channel data as it traverses the network.
8. The **NetrLogonSamLogon( )** RPC procedure on the domain controller decrypts the LM hash and the NT hash using RC4 and the first 8 bytes of the secure channel session key padded to 16 bytes with zeroes as the key.
9. The **NetrLogonSamLogon( )** RPC interface on the domain controller calculates the time stamp (received in the client logon request) using the same algorithm as the client and ensures that the packet has not been replayed. It then performs another time stamp encryption using the client-provided time stamp, increased by one.

10. The **NetrLogonSamLogon( )** function on the server compares the decrypted LM hash and NT hash values from the client call with those stored in the directory services database (Registry SAM in Windows NT 4.0 or Active Directory in Windows 2000 and later).
11. If the LM and NT hash values match, the user is authenticated and the domain controller returns an access token structure to the user; see phase C in Figure 4.11. The server includes the encrypted sum of the client time stamp with the client response, increased by one, as calculated in Step 9.
12. If NTLMSSP encryption (sealing) or signing is used, the server reply is encrypted and signed (integrity is authenticated). If the secure channel is not encrypted (sealed) or signed, information is returned in plaintext.
13. The domain member receives either failure status or the access token of the user as a result.
14. The client authenticates the time stamp provided by the server and ensures that the server reply is genuine (the server has managed to decrypt the time stamp from the client, increase it by one, and then encrypt it again) and has not been replayed.
15. An access token is created from the user token, and a user shell is created. The access token is used by the user shell to access resources.

It is important to note that the secure channel utilizes the machine account password along with other random parameters to generate a session key for data protection. The **NetrLogonSamLogon( )** function transfers encrypted user credentials over the network but still utilizes the secure channel between the client and server that, in addition to authenticating the communicating parties, may provide for additional channel signing and encryption (sealing). The above interactive authentication sequence is only valid for Windows NT 4.0 domain members, or in Windows NT 4.0 domains. If the client and the server support Kerberos authentication, they will use Kerberos instead. The secure channel is an NTLM technology.

Interactive Logon: Windows NT 4.0: User Logs in from Another Domain across a Direct NTLM Trust Relationship

Assumptions:

- The domain member has already established a secure channel with its domain controller (see subsection 4.2.1.3).
- User account resides in Domain A.

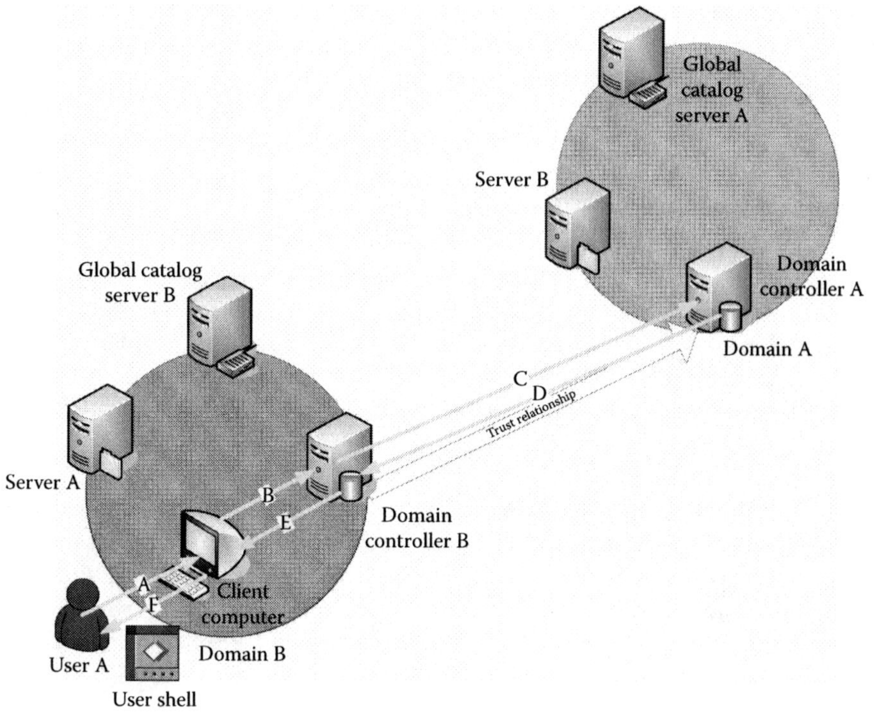

Figure 4.12 Interactive logon across trust relationship.

- Computer account resides in Domain B.
- Domain B (resource) trusts Domain A (account).

Logon process:

1. The user sitting in front of a computer in Domain B submits a username and a password, as well as its own domain name, Domain A; see phase A in Figure 4.12.
2. The client computer sends the request across its secure channel to a domain controller in the same way as it would do for an authentication request in its own domain; see phase B in Figure 4.12.
3. The domain controller of Domain B decrypts the RC4 encrypted password hashes using its session key with the domain member in the same way as it would do for an authentication request in its own domain.
4. Because the domain controller of Domain B does not have information about usernames and password hashes in Domain A, the

domain controller of Domain B performs pass-through authentication. Namely, it behaves like a domain member of Domain A logging into the domain and utilizes the interdomain secure channel that it has to a domain controller in Domain A to encrypt the password hashes using the interdomain secure channel session key as the key, and then passes them using the **NetrLogonSam Logon( )** RPC or one of its derivatives across the secure channel to the domain controller in Domain A as if it were a workstation in Domain A; see phase C in Figure 4.12.

5. The domain controller of Domain A receives the request and handles it the same way as it would handle a request from a domain member in its own domain. It then uses the secure channel to pass a user token (or an authentication failure reply) back to the Domain B domain controller; see phase D in Figure 4.12.
6. The Domain B domain controller receives the authentication request from Domain A domain controllers. If SID filtering is in effect for the trust relationship between Domain B and Domain A, the Domain B domain controller will parse the SIDs in the access token and potentially remove non-complying SIDs (see Chapter 3). It then passes the user token (or authentication failure message) back to the workstation attempting logon; see phase E in Figure 4.12.
7. The user access token on the client workstation is created based on the user token from the server, and an initial shell is created for the user; see phase F in Figure 4.12.

Network Logon: Windows NT 4.0: User Accesses a Server in Own Domain

Assumptions:

- The user, client computer, and server are members of Domain A.
- The client computer and the server have secure channels established with domain controllers of Domain A.

Network logon process:

1. A user who has already been authenticated interactively on the client computer utilizes a client application that requests interaction with the server; see phase A in Figure 4.13.
2. The client application connects to the server and establishes a session using an application protocol, such as SMB/CIFS; see phase B in Figure 4.13.

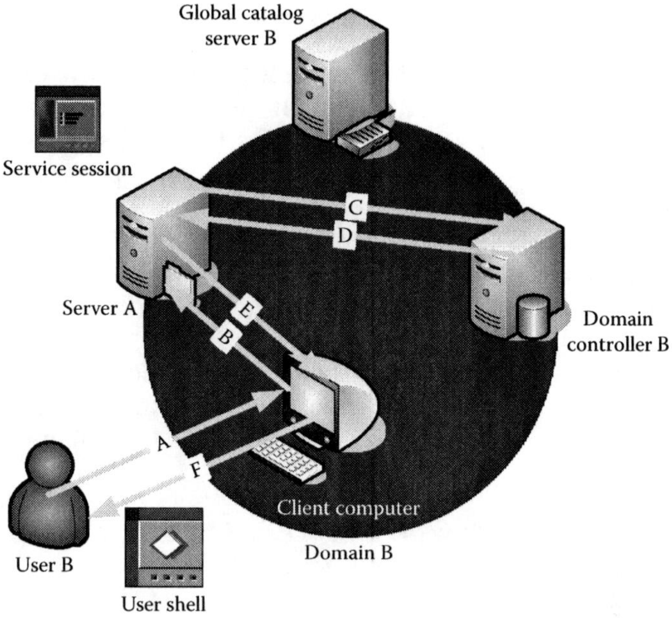

Figure 4.13 Network logon in the same domain.

3. The client computer utilizes the current username and password (or the ones specified by credential manager for this target — see Chapter 3) and tries to authenticate to the server. Depending on the client and server applications, NTLMSSP may be involved here as a security interface, or plain NTLM/LM authentication may take place.
4. The server utilizes the secure channel to its own domain controller by invoking the **NetrLogonSamLogon( )** RPC function. The server submits the LM and NTLM challenges that it generated and sent to the client, as well as the client responses to both challenges; see phase C in Figure 4.13.
5. Using the server-provided challenges, the domain controller calculates the LM response and the NTLM response using the hash values in its own account database for the user trying to authenticate.
6. The domain controller compares the responses it calculated with the responses provided by the client. If the responses match, the client has been authenticated successfully. If the responses differ, the authentication has failed. In any case, the authenticating domain controller replies to the **NetrLogonSamLogon( )** request across the secure channel back to the requesting server. The reply contains

a user token, which is the same as if the client were authenticating interactively; see phase D in Figure 4.13.

7. The server receives the user access token encapsulated within the **NetrLogonSamLogon( )** reply. If the authentication was successful, it uses the user token, provided by the domain controller to build an access token for the user, and then impersonates the user. Many applications will start a separate thread within the server process for the specific user.
8. The server returns a success or failure result to the client as the last phase of the NTLM authentication process; see phase E in Figure 4.13.
9. If the authentication was successful, the client application (the user) is able to access information, based on user authorization for the specific server resource; see phase F in Figure 4.13.

Network Logon: Windows NT 4.0: User Accesses a Server in Another Domain across a Direct NTLM trust Relationship

Assumptions:

- The user and the client computer are members of Domain A.
- The server is a member of Domain B.
- The client computer and the server have secure channels established with their respective domain controllers.
- Domain B (resource) trusts Domain A (account).

Network logon process:

1. A user who has already been authenticated interactively on the client computer utilizes a client application that requests interaction with the server; see phase A in Figure 4.16.
2. The client application connects to the server and establishes a session using an application protocol, such as SMB/CIFS; see phase B in Figure 4.16.
3. The client computer utilizes the current username and password (or the ones specified by credential manager for this target — see Chapter 3) and tries to authenticate to the server. Depending on the client and server applications, NTLMSSP may be involved here as a security interface, or plain NTLM/LM authentication may take place (see Frames 14 through 16 in Figure 4.17).

```
Frame 10 (294 bytes on wire, 294 bytes captured)
Ethernet II, Src: 02:00:4c:4f:4f:50 (02:00:4c:4f:4f:50), Dst: steve.ins.com (00:03:ff:50:ab:2a)
Internet Protocol, Src: 10.0.2.1 (10.0.2.1), Dst: 10.0.2.102 (10.0.2.102)
Transmission Control Protocol, Src Port: 2773 (2773), Dst Port: microsoft-ds (445), Seq:
3808981185, Ack: 3883600376, Len: 240
NetBIOS Session Service
SMB (Server Message Block Protocol)
    SMB Header
        Server Component: SMB
        Response in: 11
        SMB Command: Session Setup AndX (0x73)
        NT Status: STATUS_SUCCESS (0x00000000)
        Flags: 0x18
        Flags2: 0xc807
        Process ID High: 0
        Signature: 0000000000000000
        Reserved: 0000
        Tree ID: 0
        Process ID: 65279
        User ID: 0
        Multiplex ID: 64
    Session Setup AndX Request (0x73)
        Word Count (WCT): 12
        AndXCommand: No further commands (0xff)
        Reserved: 00
        AndXOffset: 236
        Max Buffer: 4356
        Max Mpx Count: 50
        VC Number: 0
        Session Key: 0x00000000
        Security Blob Length: 74
        Reserved: 00000000
        Capabilities: 0xa00000d4
        Byte Count (BCC): 177
        Security Blob: 604806062B0601050502A03E303CA00E300C060A2B060104...
            GSS-API Generic Security Service Application Program Interface
```

Figure 4.14 XP-Client-Steve-CIFS-Logon.cap: User administrator on XP-CLIENT tries to access share test on server STEVE.

```
            OID: 1.3.6.1.5.5.2 (SPNEGO - Simple Protected Negotiation)
            SPNEGO
                negTokenInit
                    mechTypes: 1 item
                        Item: 1.3.6.1.4.1.311.2.2.10 (NTLMSSP - Microsoft NTLM Security
Support Provider)
                    mechToken: 4E544C4D5353500001000000978208E20000000000000000...
                    NTLMSSP
                        NTLMSSP identifier: NTLMSSP
                        NTLM Message Type: NTLMSSP_NEGOTIATE (0x00000001)
                        Flags: 0xe2088297
                        Calling workstation domain: NULL
                        Calling workstation name: NULL
        Native OS: Windows 2002 Service Pack 2 2600
        Native LAN Manager: Windows 2002 5.1
        Primary Domain:

Frame 11 (416 bytes on wire, 416 bytes captured)
Ethernet II, Src: steve.ins.com (00:03:ff:50:ab:2a), Dst: 02:00:4c:4f:4f:50 (02:00:4c:4f:4f:50)
Internet Protocol, Src: 10.0.2.102 (10.0.2.102), Dst: 10.0.2.1 (10.0.2.1)
Transmission Control Protocol, Src Port: microsoft-ds (445), Dst Port: 2773 (2773), Seq:
3883600376, Ack: 3808981425, Len: 362
NetBIOS Session Service
SMB (Server Message Block Protocol)
    SMB Header
        Server Component: SMB
        Response to: 10
        Time from request: 0.010430000 seconds
        SMB Command: Session Setup AndX (0x73)
        NT Status: STATUS_MORE_PROCESSING_REQUIRED (0xc0000016)
        Flags: 0x98
        Process ID High: 0
        Signature: 0000000000000000
        Reserved: 0000
        Tree ID: 0
        Process ID: 65279
```

Figure 4.14 (continued)

```
        User ID: 2050
        Multiplex ID: 64
    Session Setup AndX Response (0x73)
        Word Count (WCT): 4
        AndXCommand: No further commands (0xff)
        Reserved: 00
        AndXOffset: 358
        Action: 0x0000
            .... .... .... ...0 = Guest: Not logged in as GUEST
        Security Blob Length: 187
        Byte Count (BCC): 315
        Security Blob: A181B83081B5A0030A0101A10C060A2B0601040182370202...
            GSS-API Generic Security Service Application Program Interface
                SPNEGO
                    negTokenTarg
                        negResult: accept-incomplete (1)
                        supportedMech: 1.3.6.1.4.1.311.2.2.10 (NTLMSSP - Microsoft NTLM Security
Support Provider)
                        responseToken: 4E544C4D53535000020000000600060038000000158289E2...
                        NTLMSSP
                            NTLMSSP identifier: NTLMSSP
                            NTLM Message Type: NTLMSSP_CHALLENGE (0x00000002)
                            Domain: INS
                                Length: 6
                                Maxlen: 6
                                Offset: 56
                            Flags: 0xe2898215
                            NTLM Challenge: 3C0A7B46E37C5E3D
                            Reserved: 0000000000000000
                            Address List
                                Length: 94
                                Maxlen: 94
                                Offset: 62
                                Domain NetBIOS Name: INS
                                    Target item type: NetBIOS domain name (0x0002)
                                    Target item Length: 6
```

Figure 4.14 (continued)

```
                    Target item Content: INS
                Server NetBIOS Name: STEVE
                    Target item type: NetBIOS host name (0x0001)
                    Target item Length: 10
                    Target item Content: STEVE
                Domain DNS Name: ins.com
                    Target item type: DNS domain name (0x0004)
                    Target item Length: 14
                    Target item Content: ins.com
                Server DNS Name: Steve.ins.com
                    Target item type: DNS host name (0x0003)
                    Target item Length: 26
                    Target item Content: Steve.ins.com
                    Target item type: Unknown (0x0005)
                    Target item Length: 14
                    Target item Content: ins.com
                List Terminator
                    Target item type: End of list (0x0000)
                    Target item Length: 0
        Native OS: Windows Server 2003 3790 Service Pack 1
        Native LAN Manager: Windows Server 2003 5.2

Frame 12 (428 bytes on wire, 428 bytes captured)
Ethernet II, Src: 02:00:4c:4f:4f:50 (02:00:4c:4f:4f:50), Dst: steve.ins.com (00:03:ff:50:ab:2a)
Internet Protocol, Src: 10.0.2.1 (10.0.2.1), Dst: 10.0.2.102 (10.0.2.102)
Transmission Control Protocol, Src Port: 2773 (2773), Dst Port: microsoft-ds (445), Seq:
3808981425, Ack: 3883600738, Len: 374
NetBIOS Session Service
SMB (Server Message Block Protocol)
    SMB Header
        Server Component: SMB
        Response in: 20
        SMB Command: Session Setup AndX (0x73)
        NT Status: STATUS_SUCCESS (0x00000000)
        Flags: 0x18
        Flags2: 0xc807
```

Figure 4.14 (continued)

```
        Process ID High: 0
        Signature: 0000000000000000
        Reserved: 0000
        Tree ID: 0
        Process ID: 65279
        User ID: 2050
        Multiplex ID: 128
    Session Setup AndX Request (0x73)
        Word Count (WCT): 12
        AndXCommand: No further commands (0xff)
        Reserved: 00
        AndXOffset: 370
        Max Buffer: 4356
        Max Mpx Count: 50
        VC Number: 0
        Session Key: 0x00000000
        Security Blob Length: 208
        Reserved: 00000000
        Capabilities: 0xa00000d4
        Byte Count (BCC): 311
        Security Blob: A181CD3081CAA281C70481C44E544C4D5353500003000000...
            GSS-API Generic Security Service Application Program Interface
                SPNEGO
                    negTokenTarg
                        responseToken: 4E544C4D53535000030000001800180084000000180018 00...
                        NTLMSSP
                            NTLMSSP identifier: NTLMSSP
                            NTLM Message Type: NTLMSSP_AUTH (0x00000003)
                            Lan Manager Response:
86BCD90E2F5A9FD80000000000000000000000000000000000
                                Length: 24
                                Maxlen: 24
                                Offset: 132
                            NTLM Response: C1AF3E59D1BAF61FD3E3E70A1A3A90798BAC9C19DF9ADB9F
                                Length: 24
                                Maxlen: 24
```

Figure 4.14 (continued)

```
                        Offset: 156
                    Domain name: NULL
                    User name: administrator@ins.com
                        Length: 42
                        Maxlen: 42
                        Offset: 72
                    Host name: XP-CLIENT
                        Length: 18
                        Maxlen: 18
                        Offset: 114
                    Session Key: AC4619F74BDBA0B10BB521E70C9EA5EC
                        Length: 16
                        Maxlen: 16
                        Offset: 180
                    Flags: 0xe2888215
        Native OS: Windows 2002 Service Pack 2 2600
        Native LAN Manager: Windows 2002 5.1
        Primary Domain:

Frame 20 (238 bytes on wire, 238 bytes captured)
Ethernet II, Src: steve.ins.com (00:03:ff:50:ab:2a), Dst: 02:00:4c:4f:4f:50 (02:00:4c:4f:4f:50)
Internet Protocol, Src: 10.0.2.102 (10.0.2.102), Dst: 10.0.2.1 (10.0.2.1)
Transmission Control Protocol, Src Port: microsoft-ds (445), Dst Port: 2773 (2773), Seq:
3883600738, Ack: 3808981799, Len: 184
NetBIOS Session Service
SMB (Server Message Block Protocol)
    SMB Header
        Server Component: SMB
        Response to: 12
        Time from request: 0.059141000 seconds
        SMB Command: Session Setup AndX (0x73)
        NT Status: STATUS_SUCCESS (0x00000000)
        Flags: 0x98
        Flags2: 0xc807
        Process ID High: 0
        Signature: 0000000000000000
```

Figure 4.14 (continued)

```
    Reserved: 0000
    Tree ID: 0
    Process ID: 65279
    User ID: 2050
    Multiplex ID: 128
Session Setup AndX Response (0x73)
    Word Count (WCT): 4
    AndXCommand: No further commands (0xff)
    Reserved: 00
    AndXOffset: 180
    Action: 0x0000
        .... .... .... ...0 = Guest: Not logged in as GUEST
    Security Blob Length: 9
    Byte Count (BCC): 137
    Security Blob: A1073005A0030A0100
        GSS-API Generic Security Service Application Program Interface
            SPNEGO
                negTokenTarg
                    negResult: accept-completed (0)
    Native OS: Windows Server 2003 3790 Service Pack 1
    Native LAN Manager: Windows Server 2003 5.2
```

Figure 4.14 (continued)

4. The server utilizes the secure channel to its own domain controller by invoking the **NetrLogonSamLogon( )** RPC function across the secure channel to the Domain B domain controller and providing the LM and NTLM challenges that it generated and sent to the client, as well as the client responses to both challenges; see phase C in Figure 4.16.
5. The domain controller for Domain B cannot authenticate the user, so it needs to perform pass-through authentication to domain controllers of Domain A. It does so by using the **NetrLogonSamLogon( )** function (see Frame 42 in Figure 4.18) or some of its derivatives across the secure channel to a Domain A domain controller; see phase D in Figure 4.16.
6. Using the server-provided challenges, the domain controller for Domain A calculates the LM response and the NTLM response using the hash values in its own account database for the user trying to authenticate.

```
Frame 18 (486 bytes on wire, 486 bytes captured)
Ethernet II, Src: steve.ins.com (00:03:ff:50:ab:2a), Dst: 02:00:4c:4f:4f:50 (02:00:4c:4f:4f:50)
Internet Protocol, Src: 10.0.2.102 (10.0.2.102), Dst: 10.0.1.101 (10.0.1.101)
Transmission Control Protocol, Src Port: 1378 (1378), Dst Port: 1025 (1025), Seq: 3989993894,
Ack: 4241083840, Len: 432
DCE RPC Request, Fragment: Single, FragLen: 432, Call: 3 Ctx: 0, [Resp: #19]
    Version: 5
    Version (minor): 0
    Packet type: Request (0)
    Packet Flags: 0x03
    Data Representation: 10000000
        Byte order: Little-endian (1)
        Character: ASCII (0)
        Floating-point: IEEE (0)
    Frag Length: 432
    Auth Length: 32
    Call ID: 3
    Alloc hint: 364
    Context ID: 0
    Opnum: 39
    Auth type: NETLOGON Secure Channel (68)
    Auth level: Packet privacy (6)
    Auth pad len: 4
    Auth Rsrvd: 0
    Auth Context ID: 0
    Response in frame: 19
    Secure Channel Verifier
        Signature: 77007A00FFFF0000
        Packet Digest: 39DC8594DB28C083
        Sequence No: 6F10211460C1A1E6
        Nonce: ADE03B94F073B486
Microsoft Network Logon, NetrLogonSamLogonEx
    Operation: NetrLogonSamLogonEx (39)
    Encrypted stub data (368 bytes)
```

Figure 4.15 XP-Client-Steve-CIFS-Logon.cap: Server STEVE performs network logon on user administrator.

```
Frame 19 (758 bytes on wire, 758 bytes captured)
Ethernet II, Src: 02:00:4c:4f:4f:50 (02:00:4c:4f:4f:50), Dst: steve.ins.com (00:03:ff:50:ab:2a)
Internet Protocol, Src: 10.0.1.101 (10.0.1.101), Dst: 10.0.2.102 (10.0.2.102)
Transmission Control Protocol, Src Port: 1025 (1025), Dst Port: 1378 (1378), Seq: 4241083840,
Ack: 3989994326, Len: 704
DCE RPC Response, Fragment: Single, FragLen: 704, Call: 3 Ctx: 0, [Req: #18]
    Version: 5
    Version (minor): 0
    Packet type: Response (2)
    Packet Flags: 0x03
    Data Representation: 10000000
        Byte order: Little-endian (1)
        Character: ASCII (0)
        Floating-point: IEEE (0)
    Frag Length: 704
    Auth Length: 32
    Call ID: 3
    Alloc hint: 636
    Context ID: 0
    Cancel count: 0
    Auth type: NETLOGON Secure Channel (68)
    Auth level: Packet privacy (6)
    Auth pad len: 4
    Auth Rsrvd: 0
    Auth Context ID: 0
    Opnum: 39
    Request in frame: 18
    Time from request: 0.012427000 seconds
    Secure Channel Verifier
        Signature: 77007A00FFFF0000
        Packet Digest: 638F3E3AF8C1193A
        Sequence No: 54A583A76B0CE408
        Nonce: 64982B6914351437
Microsoft Network Logon, NetrLogonSamLogonEx
    Operation: NetrLogonSamLogonEx (39)
    Encrypted stub data (640 bytes)
```

Figure 4.15 (continued)

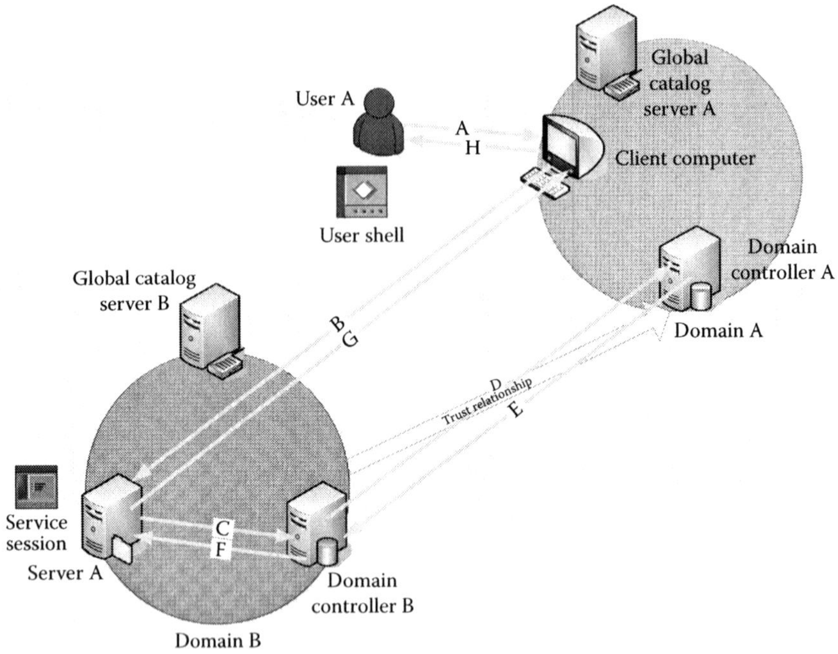

Figure 4.16 Network logon across trust.

7. The domain controller for Domain A compares the responses it calculated with the responses provided by the client. If the responses match, the client has been authenticated successfully. If the responses differ, the authentication has failed. In any case, the authenticating domain controller replies to the **NetrLogonSam Logon( )** request across the secure channel back to the Domain B domain controller (see Frame 44 in Figure 4.18). The reply contains a user token, which is the same as if the client was authenticating interactively; see phase E in Figure 4.16.
8. The domain controller for Domain B receives the reply and decrypts it using the session key for its secure channel to the Domain A domain controller. At this stage, the Domain B domain controller can perform SID filtering and drop some SIDs from the access token received from the Domain B domain controller. It then forwards the reply across its secure channel to the server; see phase F in Figure 4.16.

```
Frame 14 (294 bytes on wire, 294 bytes captured)
Ethernet II, Src: 02:00:4c:4f:4f:50 (02:00:4c:4f:4f:50), Dst: steve.ins.com (00:03:ff:50:ab:2a)
Internet Protocol, Src: 10.0.2.1 (10.0.2.1), Dst: 10.0.2.102 (10.0.2.102)
Transmission Control Protocol, Src Port: 2068 (2068), Dst Port: microsoft-ds (445), Seq:
1035743272, Ack: 1847134790, Len: 240
NetBIOS Session Service
SMB (Server Message Block Protocol)
    SMB Header
        Server Component: SMB
        Response in: 15
        SMB Command: Session Setup AndX (0x73)
        NT Status: STATUS_SUCCESS (0x00000000)
        Flags: 0x18
        Flags2: 0xc807
        Process ID High: 0
        Signature: 0000000000000000
        Reserved: 0000
        Tree ID: 0
        Process ID: 65279
        User ID: 0
        Multiplex ID: 320
    Session Setup AndX Request (0x73)
        Word Count (WCT): 12
        AndXCommand: No further commands (0xff)
        Reserved: 00
        AndXOffset: 236
        Max Buffer: 4356
        Max Mpx Count: 50
        VC Number: 1
        Session Key: 0x00000000
        Security Blob Length: 74
        Reserved: 00000000
        Capabilities: 0xa00000d4
        Byte Count (BCC): 177
        Security Blob: 604806062B0601050502A03E303CA00E300C060A2B060104...
            GSS-API Generic Security Service Application Program Interface
```

Figure 4.17 NTLM-External-AccessByIP-Client-Server-DC.cap: User from trusted domain EXTERNALORG at XP-CLIENT access server STEVE in domain INS.

```
                OID: 1.3.6.1.5.5.2 (SPNEGO - Simple Protected Negotiation)
                SPNEGO
                    negTokenInit
                        mechTypes: 1 item
                            Item: 1.3.6.1.4.1.311.2.2.10 (NTLMSSP - Microsoft NTLM Security
Support Provider)
                        mechToken: 4E544C4D5353500001000000978208E20000000000000000...
                        NTLMSSP
                            NTLMSSP identifier: NTLMSSP
                            NTLM Message Type: NTLMSSP_NEGOTIATE (0x00000001)
                            Flags: 0xe2088297
                            Calling workstation domain: NULL
                            Calling workstation name: NULL
        Native OS: Windows 2002 Service Pack 2 2600
        Native LAN Manager: Windows 2002 5.1
        Primary Domain:

Frame 15 (416 bytes on wire, 416 bytes captured)
Ethernet II, Src: steve.ins.com (00:03:ff:50:ab:2a), Dst: 02:00:4c:4f:4f:50 (02:00:4c:4f:4f:50)
Internet Protocol, Src: 10.0.2.102 (10.0.2.102), Dst: 10.0.2.1 (10.0.2.1)
Transmission Control Protocol, Src Port: microsoft-ds (445), Dst Port: 2068 (2068), Seq:
1847134790, Ack: 1035743512, Len: 362
NetBIOS Session Service
SMB (Server Message Block Protocol)
    SMB Header
        Server Component: SMB
        Response to: 14
        Time from request: 0.001795000 seconds
        SMB Command: Session Setup AndX (0x73)
        NT Status: STATUS_MORE_PROCESSING_REQUIRED (0xc0000016)
        Flags: 0x98
        Flags2: 0xc807
        Process ID High: 0
        Signature: 0000000000000000
        Reserved: 0000
        Tree ID: 0
```

Figure 4.17 (continued)

```
        Process ID: 65279
        User ID: 2050
        Multiplex ID: 320
    Session Setup AndX Response (0x73)
        Word Count (WCT): 4
        AndXCommand: No further commands (0xff)
        Reserved: 00
        AndXOffset: 358
        Action: 0x0000
            .... .... .... ...0 = Guest: Not logged in as GUEST
        Security Blob Length: 187
        Byte Count (BCC): 315
        Security Blob: A181B83081B5A0030A0101A10C060A2B0601040182370202...
            GSS-API Generic Security Service Application Program Interface
                SPNEGO
                    negTokenTarg
                        negResult: accept-incomplete (1)
                        supportedMech: 1.3.6.1.4.1.311.2.2.10 (NTLMSSP - Microsoft NTLM Security
Support Provider)
                        responseToken: 4E544C4D5353500002000000060006003800000158289E2...
                        NTLMSSP
                            NTLMSSP identifier: NTLMSSP
                            NTLM Message Type: NTLMSSP_CHALLENGE (0x00000002)
                            Domain: INS
                                Length: 6
                                Maxlen: 6
                                Offset: 56
                            Flags: 0xe2898215
                            NTLM Challenge: 14EEEBC83C4DC569
                            Reserved: 0000000000000000
                            Address List
                                Length: 94
                                Maxlen: 94
                                Offset: 62
                                Domain NetBIOS Name: INS
                                    Target item type: NetBIOS domain name (0x0002)
```

Figure 4.17 (continued)

```
                Target item Length: 6
                Target item Content: INS
            Server NetBIOS Name: STEVE
                Target item type: NetBIOS host name (0x0001)
                Target item Length: 10
                Target item Content: STEVE
            Domain DNS Name: ins.com
                Target item type: DNS domain name (0x0004)
                Target item Length: 14
                Target item Content: ins.com
            Server DNS Name: Steve.ins.com
                Target item type: DNS host name (0x0003)
                Target item Length: 26
                Target item Content: Steve.ins.com
                Target item type: Unknown (0x0005)
                Target item Length: 14
                Target item Content: ins.com
            List Terminator
                Target item type: End of list (0x0000)
                Target item Length: 0
    Native OS: Windows Server 2003 3790 Service Pack 1
    Native LAN Manager: Windows Server 2003 5.2


Frame 16 (434 bytes on wire, 434 bytes captured)
Ethernet II, Src: 02:00:4c:4f:4f:50 (02:00:4c:4f:4f:50), Dst: steve.ins.com (00:03:ff:50:ab:2a)
Internet Protocol, Src: 10.0.2.1 (10.0.2.1), Dst: 10.0.2.102 (10.0.2.102)
Transmission Control Protocol, Src Port: 2068 (2068), Dst Port: microsoft-ds (445), Seq:
1035743512, Ack: 1847135152, Len: 380
NetBIOS Session Service
SMB (Server Message Block Protocol)
  SMB Header
    Server Component: SMB
    Response in: 31
    SMB Command: Session Setup AndX (0x73)
    NT Status: STATUS_SUCCESS (0x00000000)
```

Figure 4.17 (continued)

```
        Flags: 0x18
        Flags2: 0xc807
        Process ID High: 0
        Signature: 0000000000000000
        Reserved: 0000
        Tree ID: 0
        Process ID: 65279
        User ID: 2050
        Multiplex ID: 384
    Session Setup AndX Request (0x73)
        Word Count (WCT): 12
        AndXCommand: No further commands (0xff)
        Reserved: 00
        AndXOffset: 376
        Max Buffer: 4356
        Max Mpx Count: 50
        VC Number: 1
        Session Key: 0x00000000
        Security Blob Length: 214
        Reserved: 00000000
        Capabilities: 0xa00000d4
        Byte Count (BCC): 317
        Security Blob: A181D33081D0A281CD0481CA4E544C4D5353500003000000...
            GSS-API Generic Security Service Application Program Interface
                SPNEGO
                    negTokenTarg
                        responseToken: 4E544C4D53535000030000001800180008A00000018001800...
                        NTLMSSP
                            NTLMSSP identifier: NTLMSSP
                            NTLM Message Type: NTLMSSP_AUTH (0x00000003)
                            Lan Manager Response:
21387D42471E93F200000000000000000000000000000000
                                Length: 24
                                Maxlen: 24
                                Offset: 138
                            NTLM Response: 3881A085C357F6F8B62A8EAFB313B129C58C4B51D8991BA0
```

Figure 4.17 (continued)

```
                Length: 24
                Maxlen: 24
                Offset: 162
            Domain name: externalorg
                Length: 22
                Maxlen: 22
                Offset: 72
            User name: administrator
                Length: 26
                Maxlen: 26
                Offset: 94
            Host name: XP-CLIENT
                Length: 18
                Maxlen: 18
                Offset: 120
            Session Key: 7DF3B39A969EE6B8BCE4122ABBAB0A82
                Length: 16
                Maxlen: 16
                Offset: 186
            Flags: 0xe2888215
    Native OS: Windows 2002 Service Pack 2 2600
    Native LAN Manager: Windows 2002 5.1
    Primary Domain:
```

Figure 4.17 (continued)

9. The server receives the user access token encapsulated within the **NetrLogonSamLogon( )** reply. If the authentication was successful, it uses the user token provided by the domain controller to build an access token for the user, and then impersonates the user. Many applications will start a separate thread within the server process for the specific user.
10. The server returns a success or failure result to the client as the last phase of the NTLM authentication process; see phase G in Figure 4.16.
11. If the authentication was successful, the client application (the user) is able to access information, based on user authorization for the specific server resource; see phase F in Figure 4.16.

```
Frame 42 (502 bytes on wire, 502 bytes captured)
Ethernet II, Src: 02:00:4c:4f:4f:50 (02:00:4c:4f:4f:50), Dst: Microsof_52:ab:2a
(00:03:ff:52:ab:2a)
Internet Protocol, Src: 10.0.1.101 (10.0.1.101), Dst: 192.168.1.101 (192.168.1.101)
Transmission Control Protocol, Src Port: 1408 (1408), Dst Port: 1025 (1025), Seq: 4108784429,
Ack: 3199283443, Len: 448
DCE RPC Request, Fragment: Single, FragLen: 448, Call: 3 Ctx: 0, [Resp: #44]
    Version: 5
    Version (minor): 0
    Packet type: Request (0)
    Packet Flags: 0x03
    Data Representation: 10000000
        Byte order: Little-endian (1)
        Character: ASCII (0)
        Floating-point: IEEE (0)
    Frag Length: 448
    Auth Length: 32
    Call ID: 3
    Alloc hint: 380
    Context ID: 0
    Opnum: 45
    Auth type: NETLOGON Secure Channel (68)
    Auth level: Packet integrity (5)
    Auth pad len: 4
    Auth Rsrvd: 0
    Auth Context ID: 1
    Response in frame: 44
    Secure Channel Verifier
        Signature: 7700FFFFFFFF0000
        Packet Digest: 0D1D56F4BEF7F1A2
        Sequence No: B33DD17A277ACBAE
        Nonce: 0000000000000000
Microsoft Network Logon, NetrLogonSamLogonWithFlags
    Operation: NetrLogonSamLogonWithFlags (45)
    Stub data (380 bytes)
    Auth Padding (4 bytes)
```

Figure 4.18 NTLM-External-AccessBYIP-DC-to-DC.cap: Pass-through authentication from Domain B to Domain A.

```
Frame 44 (534 bytes on wire, 534 bytes captured)
Ethernet II, Src: Microsof_52:ab:2a (00:03:ff:52:ab:2a), Dst: 02:00:4c:4f:4f:50
(02:00:4c:4f:4f:50)
Internet Protocol, Src: 192.168.1.101 (192.168.1.101), Dst: 10.0.1.101 (10.0.1.101)
Transmission Control Protocol, Src Port: 1025 (1025), Dst Port: 1408 (1408), Seq: 3199283443,
Ack: 4108784877, Len: 480
DCE RPC Response, Fragment: Single, FragLen: 480, Call: 3 Ctx: 0, [Req: #42]
    Version: 5
    Version (minor): 0
    Packet type: Response (2)
    Packet Flags: 0x03
    Data Representation: 10000000
        Byte order: Little-endian (1)
        Character: ASCII (0)
        Floating-point: IEEE (0)
    Frag Length: 480
    Auth Length: 32
    Call ID: 3
    Alloc hint: 412
    Context ID: 0
    Cancel count: 0
    Auth type: NETLOGON Secure Channel (68)
    Auth level: Packet integrity (5)
    Auth pad len: 4
    Auth Rsrvd: 0
    Auth Context ID: 1
    Opnum: 45
    Request in frame: 42
    Time from request: 0.159376000 seconds
    Secure Channel Verifier
        Signature: 7700FFFFFFFF0000
        Packet Digest: 3545192CA869E1A7
        Sequence No: 19F65C1F89C42BBA
        Nonce: 0000000000000000
Microsoft Network Logon, NetrLogonSamLogonWithFlags
```

Figure 4.18 (continued)

```
Operation: NetrLogonSamLogonWithFlags (45)
Stub data (412 bytes)
Auth Padding (4 bytes)
```

Figure 4.18 (continued)

4.2.1.9 NTLM impersonation

Most mechanisms that provide for NTLM authentication are Windows specific. Therefore, Chapter 3 provides more information on how NTLM impersonation works.

4.2.2 Kerberos Authentication

This section presents the MIT Kerberos authentication protocol. It provides brief background information and then presents the naming concepts, the model of trust, the data structures, and the protocol mechanics.

4.2.2.1 Kerberos Overview

The Kerberos authentication protocol was developed by the Massachusetts Institute of Technology (MIT) in the 1980s as part of the Athena project. Sponsored by commercial organizations, the Athena project was expected to define strategies for the use of computers by academic institutions. The Kerberos Protocol was the authentication system for the Athena project. The first three versions of the Kerberos Protocol were internal. Kerberos version 4 was released to the public and immediately became popular. However, due to security flaws in the Kerberos version 4 design, Kerberos version 5 followed shortly and became the *de facto* standard for user authentication in a heterogeneous environment. Also, unlike Kerberos version 4, Kerberos version 5 uses ASN.1 encoding. Other differences include the format of principal names, key salt, the use of forwardable and proxiable tickets, and transitive cross-realm authentication. Virtually all Kerberos implementations in use today are based on Kerberos version 5.

Kerberos version 5 was first defined in RFC 1510 (see [87]). However, many vendors were already developing systems and applications based on Kerberos and the RFC did not cover all the possible implementation flavors and interoperability between them. Therefore, Kerberos version 5 was redefined in RFC 4120 (see [88]), which kept Kerberos version 5 but specified what was already a *de facto* standard and existed in widely used Kerberos implementations.

In addition to the MIT implementation of Kerberos, which is available for UNIX, Windows, and other platforms, other popular implementations are Heimdal and Sun's Kerberos implementation as part of the Java suite.

Microsoft Windows Active Directory also provides an RFC 1510-compatible Kerberos implementation. Although the Windows implementation differs from the MIT and Heimdal implementations in terms of approach and tools, it can still interoperate with them in most scenarios.

4.2.2.2 The Concept of Trust in Kerberos

Unlike NTLM secure channels, which are permanent TCP connections built between trusting parties and used when necessary to transmit sensitive data, the Kerberos Protocol builds trust relationships in a stateless way. The client requests and then caches tickets (service tickets or ticket granting tickets), and these tickets bear the signature of the issuer (a trusted third party — the Kerberos Distribution Center, or KDC). Tickets are requested on an as-needed basis, and are presented to services and applications upon access. Therefore, Kerberos does not need to build and maintain a connection or authentication state.

The Kerberos trust model is primarily password centric — the password is a shared secret between a client and a KDC, or a server and a KDC. Both the client and the server trust the KDC. The Kerberos Protocol heavily utilizes cryptographic technologies and uses the user (principal) and server passwords to derive key material.

All computers that directly trust the same policies and administrative model are members of the same Kerberos realm. The KDC is a party trusted by all the members of the realm. A central role in the Kerberos authentication model is given to the KDC. The KDC defines the security policies of the realm.

There are two services that run within the context of the KDC:

1. Authentication service (AS) is responsible for receiving client pre-authentication and authentication requests
2. Ticket granting service (TGS) is responsible for issuing users with tickets for access to applications and services

In addition to that, the KDC needs to have a directory or a database with all users and their passwords in an appropriate form. This is required because the Kerberos Protocol needs to know the password of every user and service to be able to encrypt their tickets, and decrypt tickets or validate the contents of the tickets.

4.2.2.3 Name Format for Kerberos Principals

The Kerberos Protocol provides for user authentication for access to services. Users and services are Kerberos principals. Both users and services need to have principle names that comply with specific requirements. Names are critical to the Kerberos Protocol because they identify the communicating parties.

The format of Kerberos version 5 principal names is the following:

Component/Component/Component@Realm

The format used by Kerberos version 4 was similar but included dots ('.') instead of slash ('/').

Typically, the following patterns are used:

- For service principal names (SPNs): Name/Instance@Realm
  Examples: host/bill.ins.com@INS.COM
  ftp/dennisom@INS.COM
- For user principal names (UPNs): Name@Realm
  Examples: Susan@INS.COM
  Peter@INS.COM
- Special principals (such as interrealm trust accounts): Service/Realm1@Realm2
  Examples: krbtgt/INS.COM@INS.COM
  krbtgt/IMMEDIENT.COM@IMMEDIENT.COM

Kerberos RFCs recommend that Kerberos utilize DNS for service discovery and other operations and DNS is case insensitive. The Kerberos Protocol is case sensitive. Therefore, RFCs recommend that Kerberos realm names should match DNS names, with all uppercase letters. Kerberos implementations differ in how strictly they follow this requirement. Microsoft's Active Directory uses case-insensitive names.

4.2.2.4 Kerberos Authentication Phases

The Kerberos KDC plays a central role in the Kerberos authentication infrastructure. The KDC is a trusted third party for all clients and servers. It knows all the secrets (or one-way function derivative of the secret) of all clients and all servers, and establishes external trust relationships based on shared secrets with other Kerberos realms.

It is important to understand that unlike most other authentication protocols, Kerberos does not necessarily check whether the user knows the correct password. In the Kerberos authentication model, the KDC may

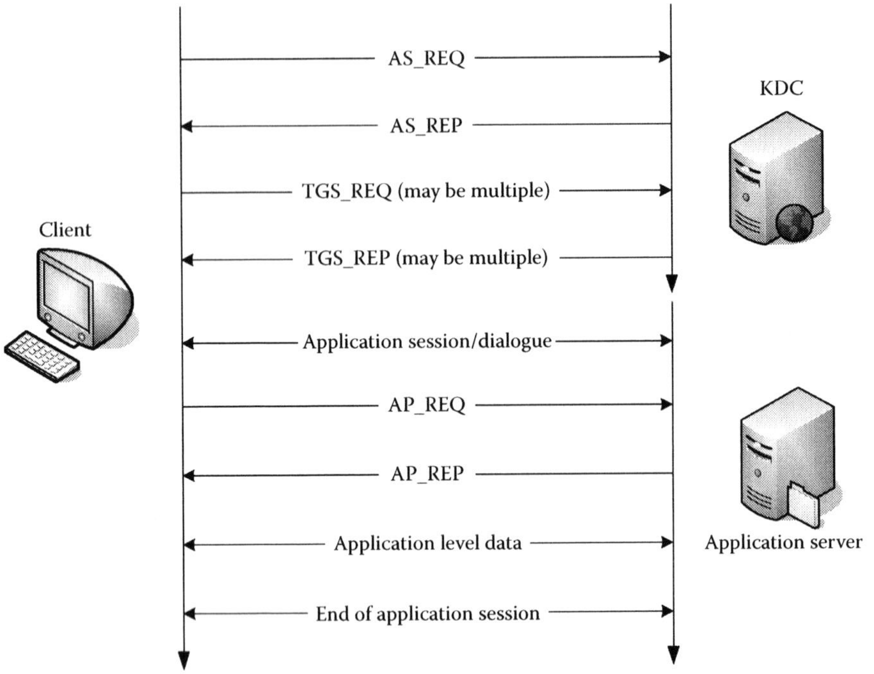

Figure 4.19 Kerberos authentication process.

provide the client with authentication information without checking whether the client has provided a valid password. However, a part of the server response will be encrypted in the client password. Hence, the client needs to know the password in order to decrypt the server reply, and to be able to use the information contained in the reply. If the client does not know the password and receives an encrypted reply that it cannot decrypt, the client cannot effectively use the authentication and authorization information inside (Figure 4.19).

The Kerberos specification defines various messages that can be exchanged between Kerberos clients, servers, and KDCs. A typical Kerberos session, however, is relatively simple and uses three main Kerberos exchange phases.

First, the user authenticates to the KDC and this process is known as the authentication service (AS) exchange. As a result of the authentication, the user receives a ticket granting ticket (TGT). The user can use this ticket for the next key exchange process, known as ticket granting service (TGS) exchange, where the user provides the KDC with its TGT and requests a service ticket for a specific service on a specific server, which the client identifies by the server name. The result is a service ticket (also called session ticket) that the client uses in the application protocol (AP) exchange. The service ticket contains information about the client, signed by the KDC, and therefore the service that trusts the same KDC can use this information as proof that the user is who he says he is, and to authorize him to access resources for which he has been granted access.

The Kerberos Protocol effectively uses the current time on the client or the server to perform user authentication and prevent replay attacks. The problem, however, is that the time on all participating parties should be synchronized — this includes Kerberos clients, the KDC, and Kerberos servers. Kerberos can be configured to tolerate minimal skew (five minutes is the recommended default). However, if the clocks are skewed by more than five minutes, the user may not be able to authenticate and, therefore, access resources.

4.2.2.5 Kerberos Tickets

Kerberos revolves around the concept of tickets (Table 4.3). Upon authentication, the client is issued a ticket that it needs to use to access resources. The client presents the ticket to servers that use it to grant the user access to resources without contacting the KDC. The ticket is protected in such a way that the client cannot modify it, and cannot even read some parts of it. Therefore, servers that receive the ticket can be sure that it was issued by a trusted party — the KDC — and that its content is genuine.

The ticket in its above form is stored by the client in a ticket cache. When the client needs to use a service or request a ticket for a new service, the client selects an appropriate ticket from the ticket cache (one that has a service principal name corresponding to the service that the client wants to access), and uses the Kerberos AP exchange to authenticate to the service by providing the ticket. If the client does not have a ticket for the service, it will request one from the KDC before trying to access the service.

The encrypted part of the ticket uses one of the Kerberos standard encryption mechanisms and the server secret as the key. Thus, the encrypted part of the ticket is not readable (and not modifiable) by the client — it can only be decrypted by the server for which it is intended and the KDC that issued it. The client cannot modify the ticket either.

The concept of tickets in Kerberos is very flexible and efficient: once the ticket has been issued, the client can save it in its cache and then use it when required, without authenticating every time it wants to access resources. The problem with this approach is that everyone who has access to the ticket can potentially present it to the server and have access to resources. If someone is able to sniff on the network and obtain the ticket that the legitimate client is presenting to the server, the intruder can just copy the ticket off the network and use it to access resources on the same server as if it were an authenticated client.

Table 4.3 Kerberos Ticket

*Parameter Name**	*Description**
Pvno	Protocol version number (for Kerberos v.5, this number is 5)
Realm	The realm of the KDC that issued the ticket
Sname	Service principal name (SPN) for which the ticket was issued
Flags	Ticket attributes, including: ■ Reserved (0) — reserved for future use ■ Forwardable (1) — the ticket can be forwarded. This flag is typically set during the AS exchange and is used by the TGS when issuing tickets ■ Forwarded (2) — set by the TGS during the TGS exchange and indicates that the ticket has been forwarded. Only used in a TGS request ■ Proxiable (3) — the ticket can be sent to a proxy and used by a proxy. This flag is typically set during the AS exchange ■ Proxy — indicates that the ticket has been issued to a proxy ■ May postdate(5) — request to issue a ticket that may be postdated ■ postdated (6) — indicates that the ticket is post-dated and will be valid later ■ invalid (7) — the ticket should not be used by servers or KDCs ■ renewable (8) — whether the client can request to have the ticket renewed instead of having a new ticket issued when the current expires ■ initial (9) — ticket was issued by the AS exchange, not by the TGT exchange ■ pre-authent (10) — preauthentication was used ■ hw-authent (11) — hardware authentication was used ■ transited-policy-checked (12) — this ticket comes from a trusted realm and the KDC has validated it ■ ok-as-delegate (13) — allows the KDC to inform the client that the destination service is trusted for delegation
Key	Session key to be used by the client and the server to protect communication between them; the session key is generated by the KDC before issuing the ticket
Crealm	The realm of the client

Table 4.3 Kerberos Ticket (continued)

*Parameter Name**	*Description**
Cname	Client principal name
Transited encoding type	Type of encoding used for the field below
Transited encoding contents	A list of realms/domains that were used as transit before the ticket was issued
Authtime	The time when the original ticket was obtained by the Kerberos principal
Starttime	Specifies the time when the ticket will become valid
Endtime	Specifies the time when the ticket will cease to be valid
Renew-till	The time until the principal can renew its ticket; only used for tickets marked as renewable
Caddr	The IP address of the client; different formats are supported
Authorization-data	Application-specific data that can be used by the server to identify, impersonate, or by other means authorize client access to server resources

* Fields in gray are encrypted.

To prevent malicious third parties from stealing the ticket and presenting it to a server, the Kerberos Protocol defines ticket authenticators (Table 4.4). Every time the client tries to authenticate to a server and access resources, the client needs to provide the server with both the ticket for the server and an authenticator that proves that the client knows the secret in the ticket and is therefore a legitimate requestor.

Every time the client provides a ticket to the server, it also provides an authenticator. The authenticator is encrypted in the session key from the ticket. The client has its copy of the encrypted ticket, and the server can decrypt the server copy using the server secret, so the client can generate the authenticator and the server can verify its content by making sure that it decrypts successfully using the session key from the ticket. Hence, the server will utilize the information in the ticket and will consider the ticket genuine if the authenticator prepared by the client for this ticket is genuine. Because the authenticator also includes a time stamp, it cannot be easily replayed.

The client must not provide the same authenticator twice; the server might consider this a replay attack. To detect such replay attack conditions, servers can store a cache of authenticators they have already seen.

Table 4.4 Kerberos Authenticator

*Parameter Name**	*Description**
Authenticator-vno	Protocol version number (for Kerberos v.5, this number is 5)
Crealm	The realm of the client
Cname	Client principal name
Checksum	A checksum on the application data in the AP_REQ message
Cusek	Current time on the client host (microseconds)
Ctime	Current time on the client host (hour, minutes, and seconds)
Subkey	Optional subkey — the client may request that a key different from the KDC-generated session key be used between to protect client-to-server communication.
seq-number	May be used to prevent replay attacks; typically used by the KRB_PRIV and KRB_SAFE exchange protocols
Authorization-data	Application-specific data that may be used by the server to identify, impersonate, or by other means authorize client access to server resources — same as in the ticket (see subsection 4.2.2.8)

* Fields in gray are encrypted.

4.2.2.6 Kerberos Authentication Mechanics

This subsection discusses the three main Kerberos exchanges: (1) the AS exchange, (2) the TGT exchange, and (3) the AP exchange.

Kerberos AS Exchange

The Kerberos AS exchange is used by the Kerberos client to authenticate to the Kerberos AS and obtain an initial ticket. This ticket can then be used to obtain a TGS ticket, and then tickets to the specific applications and servers. The Kerberos AS exchange often takes place at initial user logon, and can be triggered by computer start-up (for computer authentication) or the GINA (for user logon) on Windows computers, and by the **kinit** application for the MIT and Heimdal implementations.

The AS protocol uses the following messages:

- AS_REQ: the initial client authentication request from the Kerberos client to the Kerberos AS
- AS_REP: the server reply to a client authentication request
- KRB_ERROR: used to indicate an error in the AS authentication protocol or provided data

The Kerberos AS_REQ message has the content shown in Table 4.5.

Sometimes the client may also want (or the server may request) to provide Kerberos preauthentication information in the AS_REQ message. The server may consider preauthentication (if configured and provided) and then generate a reply to the client using the AS_REP message of the AS exchange.

The AS_REP message from the server consists of the fields in Table 4.6.

When the client receives the AP_REP message, it decrypts the client-encrypted part of the message and ensures that the values in it correspond to what it requested initially in the AS_REQ message. The client then decrypts the session key from the client-encrypted part and uses it for further communication with the server.

Once the client has received the AP_REP message, the client has a ticket granting ticket (TGT) and is ready to request a ticket for the actual service that it wants to access. Technically, the designers of Kerberos could have just skipped this step and have users request service tickets for the servers they want to access rather than TGTs. However, the TGT approach has the following advantages:

- The client uses his long-term secret (password) to derive an encryption key only during the TGT request. Later requests and tickets use a random key. This protects the user password from being exposed over the network too often, or from rogue servers.
- The client does not need to reauthenticate multiple times. Just by providing a valid TGT, the client can now request service tickets. Technically, this means that the workstation does not need to ask the user to provide a username and password every time the user needs to access a new service, or cache them, and it can use the ticket directly. Apparently, this means that the ticket needs an equivalent level of protection as the user password or derivative thereof.
- Clients can be authenticated across realms (domains) using referral tickets. To achieve this, clients authenticate and receive a TGT from their own realm and present it to a trusting TGS in another realm.
- Once the user has been authenticated, he possesses a ticket that can be used to access resources. These resources do not need to

Table 4.5 Kerberos AS-REQ & TGS_REQ Messages

*Parameter Name**	*Description**
Pvno	Protocol version number (for Kerberos v.5, this number is 5)
MsgType	Message number. AS_REQ is number 10, and AS-REP is number 11
Padata-type	Type of preauthentication data; most-often based on encrypted time stamps (PA-ENC-TIMESTAMP = type 2)
Padata-value	Actual preauthentication data
KDC Options	This bit-field provides various options that the client may request in the AS_REQ message, and is used by the server in the AP_REP message to provide the actual options that the server has negotiated
Cname	The name of the Kerberos client (the user or computer requesting access — user principal name — UPN)
Realm	Specifies the Kerberos realm to which the client is trying to authenticate; to authenticate successfully, the client must have an account in this realm
Sname	The name of the Kerberos service (service principal name — SPN)
From	Allows the client to specify a start time for a ticket; the ticket may be postdated and start at a later time than the time of the request; the date and time are specified as an ASCII string in the form YYYYMMDDHHMMSS"Z"
Till	Specifies the time when the client would like the ticket to expire, or the time preferred by the server for ticket expiration; the date and time are specified as an ASCII string in the form YYYYMMDDHHMMSS"Z"
Rtime	This parameter is used by the client to specify the time when it would like to renew its ticket (only valid for renewable tickets)
Nonce	This is a randomly generated number; the Kerberos client sends a unique nonce in each request to the server and expects to see the nonce in the encrypted server reply; this proves that messages have not been replayed and that the server has knowledge of the session key

Table 4.5 Kerberos AS-REQ & TGS_REQ Messages

*Parameter Name**	*Description**
Etype	Specifies the encryption algorithm to be used by the client and the server
Addresses	Specifies the IP address of the client that will be using this ticket; can be either the actual Kerberos client or, in the case of proxies, the address of the proxy
Enc-authorization data	TGS Only — includes encrypted authorization data
Additional Tickets	Additional tickets included in the request

* Fields in gray are encrypted.

Table 4.6 Kerberos AS_REP Message

*Parameter Name**	*Description**
Pvno	Protocol version number (for Kerberos v.5, this number is 5)
MsgType	Message number. AS_REP is number 11
Padata-type	Type of preauthentication data
Padata-value	Actual preauthentication data; the server can return information to the client using the Preauthentication field.
Realm	Specifies the Kerberos realm to which the client is trying to authenticate; to authenticate successfully, the client must have an account in this realm
Cname	The name of the Kerberos client (the user or computer requesting access — user principal name — UPN)
Ticket (Server Encrypted Part)	Contains a Kerberos ticket; the first three fields are plaintext but the remainder of the ticket is encrypted in the server secret (the TGT secret); the client cannot decrypt this part — it is meant to be decrypted and used by the server
Client encrypted-part	The same encrypted part that is being sent to the server is provided to the client; it is encrypted using the client chosen protection suite and in the client secret key (password) or a derivative thereof; only the client can decrypt this part

* Fields in gray are encrypted.

know what the authentication method was — such as username and password, certificate, or other approach — as long as the client provides a valid ticket. It is up to the AS servers to determine the authentication policy.

Kerberos Preauthentication

As already discussed, the Kerberos Protocol does not necessarily check that the client knows the correct password for the user account to which it is trying to authenticate. The server may return an AS_REP message to the client, encrypted in the client secret (password), and leave it to the client to decrypt the reply in the information in the reply in the client password (or a derivative thereof). If the client does not know the password, the client cannot use the ticket, which is equivalent to a client that has not been authenticated at all.

The problem with this approach is that a potential attacker can use this to launch a known plaintext attack against the Kerberos Distribution Center (KDC). The attacker can generate a series of requests to the KDC, for which it knows, to a large extent, the structure and some of the fields of the reply that the KDC will generate. The attacker can then analyze the encrypted KDC replies (and they are encrypted in the user password) and deduce the user password.

To avoid such attacks, some Kerberos implementations implement and, by default, require the client to prove its identity before receiving encrypted authentication data in a ticket. This is known as preauthentication. There are different preauthentication methods; the client specifies the specific method that it wants to use by providing its type ID in the AS_REQ message. PA-ENC-TIMESTAMP is a mandatory (for all Kerberos implementations) and popular preauthentication method that encrypts a time stamp (current time) in the client password (or a derivative thereof) using a Kerberos encryption mechanism.

When a KDC receives a request that contains preauthentication data of type PA-ENC-TIMESTAMP, it needs to decrypt the data and compare the time stamp with its current time. If the client has the correct password, the time stamp from the preauthentication structure should decrypt correctly and the time skew on the server time should be minimal. Only when these conditions are met can the server continue with user authentication as normal and generate an AS_REP message to the client.

Servers that require preauthentication will typically return an error message to the client sending the AS_REQ message and advise it to provide preauthentication data in order to continue.

The original design of the preauthentication dialogue to provide proof that the authentication user has knowledge of the password has been extended, and now Kerberos clients and servers use preauthentication to exchange messages that are not necessarily related to the actual authentication process. Table 4.7 lists some of the Kerberos preauthentication messages.

Kerberos TGS Exchange

Once the client has authenticated to Kerberos using the AS exchange, the client has a TGT ticket (returned by the KDC in the AS_REP message) and can provide it to the ticket granting server (TGS) to request a ticket for the specific application or service that it wants to access. The dialogue between the client and the server to obtain tickets for the service is known as TGS exchange.

The TGS exchange consists of a TGS_REQ message from the client to the TGS, and a TGS_REP or a KRB_ERROR message from the server back to the client.

The TGS_REQ message from the client to the server contains user authentication information, and the user request for a service, identified by its service principal name (SPN). The TGS_REQ message has a format very similar to AS_REQ message. Unlike the AS_REQ exchange, however, at the TGS_REQ stage, preauthentication information must be provided and it contains the ticket obtained from the AS_REP message (the TGT), as well as a ticket authenticator.

The TGS server (the KDC) reviews the request and will typically issue a TGS_REP message to the client. In case the target server (identified by its SPN in the client request) resides in a different realm/domain, the TGS server does not have a shared secret (a password) with the destination server and cannot encrypt the server copy of the ticket. Therefore, it will return a referral to another domain rather than a usable ticket for the destination server. This ticket is known as a TGT referral. When the client receives a referral ticket, the client will issue a TGS exchange with the destination server and will provide the TGT referral ticket, obtained by its own TGS in the previous step. This process may take more than one iteration until the client obtains a ticket for the actual target service.

Finally, a TGS server in the domain where the target server resides will issue a TGS ticket to the client and will return it in a TGS_REP message. The format of this message is similar to the format of the AS_REP message.

The TGS_REP message contains the ticket for the destination server, and the server encrypted part of the ticket uses a Kerberos encryption method supported by the target server, and is encrypted in the target server secret key (password) or a derivative thereof.

The client-encrypted part of the TGS_REP message contains the same information as the server-encrypted part but the encryption mechanism

Table 4.7 Kerberos Preauthentication Types

Preauthentication Method	*ID*	*Comment*
PA-TGS-REQ	1	Request for additional tickets
PA-ENC-TIMESTAMP	2	Encrypted time stamp
PA-PW-SALT	3	Information used as salt for the session key
PA-ENC-UNIX-TIME	5	Encrypted UNIX time (deprecated)
PA-ETYPE-INFO	11	Sent by the AS to indicate additional preauthentication requirements
PA-SAM-CHALLENGE	12	Used by Single-use Authentication Mechanisms (SAM)/One-Time Passwords (OTP)
PA-SAM-RESPONSE	13	Used by Single-use Authentication Mechanisms (SAM)/One-Time Passwords (OTP)
PA-PK-AS-REQ_OLD	14	Used by PKINIT
PA-PK-AS-REP_OLD	15	Used by PKINIT
PA-PK-AS-REQ	16	Used by PKINIT
PA-PK-AS-REP	17	Used by PKINIT
PA-ETYPE-INFO2	19	Sent by the AS to indicate additional preauthentication requirements; replaces PA-ETYPE-INFO
PA-USE-SPECIFIED-KVNO	20	Specifies the key version to be used
PA-SAM-REDIRECT	21	Used by Single-use Authentication Mechanisms (SAM)/One-Time Passwords (OTP)
PA-SAM-ETYPE-INFO	23	Used by Single-use Authentication Mechanisms (SAM)/One-Time Passwords (OTP)
PA-ALT-PRINC	24	Used for hardware authentication
PA-EXTRA-TGT	41	Reserved extra TGT
TD-PKINIT-CMS-CERTIFICATES	101	CertificateSet from CMS
TD-KRB-PRINCIPAL	102	The name of the principal
TD-KRB-REALM	103	The realm of the principal

Table 4.7 Kerberos Preauthentication Types (continued)

Preauthentication Method	*ID*	*Comment*
TD-TRUSTED-CERTIFIERS	104	Used by PKINIT
TD-CERTIFICATE-INDEX	105	Used by PKINIT
TD-APP-DEFINED-ERROR	106	Application specific
TD-REQ-NONCE	107	Used to map an error message to a KDC-REQ
TD-REQ-SEQ	108	Used to map an error message to a sequence number
PA-PAC-REQUEST	128	Request for a PAC (see Chapter 4.2.2.8)

is one of those requested by the client in the TGS_REQ message (and may be different from the one used for the server-encrypted part). The session key between the TGS and the client (and contained in the ticket provided by the client in the TGS_REQ message), or the subkey from the authenticator provided by the client is used as a protection key.

Kerberos AP Exchange

Kerberos AP messages are typically carried within the specific application protocol used by the target service. If it supports Kerberos, this protocol provides for the AP_REQ message from the client to the application server and the AP_REP message from the server back to the client.

Many Kerberos v.5 implementations typically provide for a GSS-API layer between Kerberos and the application, so GSS-API or some of its mechanisms (such as SPNEGO) can be used to carry actual Kerberos AP exchange tokens.

The AP_REQ message is sent from the client to the server as part of the application protocol and it provides the target server with client authentication information (Table 4.8).

The AP_REP message contains the server reply. If the client has requested mutual authentication, the server will use the format specified in Table 4.9 to reply to the request. The fact that the server can decrypt the client time parameters from the client request shows that the server has the correct secret key to decrypt the provided ticket, and it can then use the session key to encrypt the reply to the client in this key. As a result, a server that can perform these actions is considered authenticated by the client.

Table 4.8 Kerberos AP_REQ Message

*Parameter Name**	*Description**
Pvno	Protocol version number (for Kerberos v.5, this number is 5)
Msg_type	AP_REQ uses type 14
APOptions	Specifies options for client and server authentication: reserved — reserved for future use use-session-key — specifies that the session key (rather than the server key) is used; this is applicable in user-to-user authentication scenarios mutual-authentication — the client may request to verify the identity of the server as well
Ticket (Server Encrypted Part)	Contains the Kerberos ticket obtained from TGS and encrypted with the server key
Authenticator	Contains the Ticket Authenticator encrypted in the session (or subsession) key

* Fields in gray are encrypted.

Table 4.9 Kerberos AP_REP Message

*Parameter Name**	*Description**
Pvno	Protocol Version Number (for Kerberos v.5, this number is 5)
msg_type	AP_REP uses type 15
Ctime	Client time — should be the same as in the client request
Cusec	Client microseconds – should be the same as in the client request
Subkey	Alternative key to be used for encryption between the client and the server
seq-number	Sequence Number for Replay protection - not used in AP

* Fields in gray are encrypted.

4.2.2.7 Case Study: Kerberos Authentication: CIFS

In this scenario, user Susan on Linux computer LINUS equipped with an MIT Kerberos client and a SAMBA client is trying to access resources on Windows 2003 server BILL; see Figure 4.20. It is important to note that in this particular scenario, both the KDC/AS/TGS and the CIFS server reside on the same computer. This is not necessarily the case in real-life scenarios.

1. The client sends an AS_REQ message to obtain a Kerberos TGT on behalf of user Susan@INS.COM. There is no preauthentication information (see Frame 1 in Figure 4.20).
2. The AS replies with an error message indicating that preauthentication is required for user Susan@INS.COM (see Frame 2 in Figure 4.20).
3. The client retries the AS_REQ this time specifying encrypted time stamp based preauthentication (PA_ENC_TIMESTAMP) (see Frame 3 in Figure 4.20).
4. Authentication is successful and the server returns a ticket and user key encrypted data (see Frame 4 in Figure 4.20).
5. The client establishes a CIFS/SMB session with the CIFS server BILL and negotiates a CIFS dialect to use.
6. The CIFS server replies with the CIFS dialect it wants to use. In the same message, the CIFS server uses GSS-API (in fact, Microsoft SSPI) and SPNEGO (Microsoft Negotiate SSP) to advise the clients of possible authentication methods. Several Kerberos flavors are supported by the server along with NTLM (see Frame 9 in Figure 4.20).
7. The client decides to use Kerberos authentication to access resources on server BILL. It now requests a service granting ticket for this server from the KDC/TGS using a TGS_REQ exchange (see Frame 11 in Figure 4.20). The client provides preauthentication data that includes the TGT ticket and an authenticator for this ticket.
8. The KDC/TGS returns a TGS_REP message with a service ticket for BILL and a client encrypted part (see Frame 12 in Figure 4.20).
9. In a CIFS/SMB message of type SESSION_SETUP_ANDX, the client sends an AS_REP message encapsulated within SPNEGO and GSS-API (SSPI), and apparently transported by the CIFS/SMB session (see Frame 13 in Figure 4.20). The client includes the server ticket (encrypted in the server key and not readable by the client) and an authenticator protected in the session key (same as the key in the server ticket, or a subkey from the authenticator).

```
Frame 1 (185 bytes on wire, 185 bytes captured)
Ethernet II, Src: 02:00:4c:4f:4f:50 (02:00:4c:4f:4f:50), Dst: Microsof_57:ab:2a
(00:03:ff:57:ab:2a)
Internet Protocol, Src: 10.0.2.101 (10.0.2.101), Dst: 10.0.1.101 (10.0.1.101)
User Datagram Protocol, Src Port: 32769 (32769), Dst Port: kerberos (88)
Kerberos AS-REQ
    Pvno: 5
    MSG Type: AS-REQ (10)
    KDC_REQ_BODY
        Padding: 0
        KDCOptions: 40000010 (Forwardable, Renewable OK)
        Client Name (Principal): Susan
            Name-type: Principal (1)
            Name: Susan
        Realm: INS.COM
        Server Name (Unknown): krbtgt/INS.COM
            Name-type: Unknown (0)
            Name: krbtgt
            Name: INS.COM
        from: 2006-03-11 13:20:54 (Z)
        till: 2006-03-12 13:20:54 (Z)
        Nonce: 1142083254
        Encryption Types: des-cbc-md5
            Encryption type: des-cbc-md5 (3)

Frame 2 (194 bytes on wire, 194 bytes captured)
Ethernet II, Src: Microsof_57:ab:2a (00:03:ff:57:ab:2a), Dst: 02:00:4c:4f:4f:50
(02:00:4c:4f:4f:50)
Internet Protocol, Src: 10.0.1.101 (10.0.1.101), Dst: 10.0.2.101 (10.0.2.101)
User Datagram Protocol, Src Port: kerberos (88), Dst Port: 32769 (32769)
Kerberos KRB-ERROR
    Pvno: 5
    MSG Type: KRB-ERROR (30)
    stime: 2006-03-11 13:20:24 (Z)
    susec: 666795
    error_code: KRB5KDC_ERR_PREAUTH_REQUIRED (25)
```

Figure 4.20 Kerberos-CIFS.cap: Samba Client on LINUS is Accessing CIFS Server BILL using Kerberos Authentication

```
    Realm: INS.COM
    Server Name (Unknown): krbtgt/INS.COM
        Name-type: Unknown (0)
        Name: krbtgt
        Name: INS.COM
    e-data
        padata: PA-ENCTYPE-INFO PA-ENC-TIMESTAMP PA-PK-AS-REP
            Type: PA-ENCTYPE-INFO (11)
                Value: 30173015A003020103A10E040C494E532E434F4D53757361... des-cbc-md5
                    Encryption type: des-cbc-md5 (3)
                    Salt: 494E532E434F4D537573616E
            Type: PA-ENC-TIMESTAMP (2)
                Value: <MISSING>
            Type: PA-PK-AS-REP (15)
                Value: <MISSING>

Frame 3 (267 bytes on wire, 267 bytes captured)
Ethernet II, Src: 02:00:4c:4f:4f:50 (02:00:4c:4f:4f:50), Dst: Microsof_57:ab:2a
(00:03:ff:57:ab:2a)
Internet Protocol, Src: 10.0.2.101 (10.0.2.101), Dst: 10.0.1.101 (10.0.1.101)
User Datagram Protocol, Src Port: 32769 (32769), Dst Port: kerberos (88)
Kerberos AS-REQ
    Pvno: 5
    MSG Type: AS-REQ (10)
    padata: PA-ENC-TIMESTAMP
        Type: PA-ENC-TIMESTAMP (2)
            Value: 3041A003020103A23A04383656B06F98E800E62D5EFA3536... des-cbc-md5
                Encryption type: des-cbc-md5 (3)
                enc PA_ENC_TIMESTAMP: 3656B06F98E800E62D5EFA35369CD8175E7EE6BF772DBE92...
    KDC_REQ_BODY
        Padding: 0
        KDCOptions: 40000010 (Forwardable, Renewable OK)
        Client Name (Principal): Susan
            Name-type: Principal (1)
            Name: Susan
        Realm: INS.COM
```

Figure 4.20 (continued)

```
        Server Name (Unknown): krbtgt/INS.COM
            Name-type: Unknown (0)
            Name: krbtgt
            Name: INS.COM
        from: 2006-03-11 13:20:54 (Z)
        till: 2006-03-12 13:20:54 (Z)
        Nonce: 1142083257
        Encryption Types: des-cbc-md5
            Encryption type: des-cbc-md5 (3)

Frame 4 (1279 bytes on wire, 1279 bytes captured)
Ethernet II, Src: Microsof_57:ab:2a (00:03:ff:57:ab:2a), Dst: 02:00:4c:4f:4f:50
(02:00:4c:4f:4f:50)
Internet Protocol, Src: 10.0.1.101 (10.0.1.101), Dst: 10.0.2.101 (10.0.2.101)
User Datagram Protocol, Src Port: kerberos (88), Dst Port: 32769 (32769)
Kerberos AS-REP
    Pvno: 5
    MSG Type: AS-REP (11)
    padata: PA-PW-SALT
        Type: PA-PW-SALT (3)
            Value: 494E532E434F4D537573616E
    Client Realm: INS.COM
    Client Name (Principal): Susan
        Name-type: Principal (1)
        Name: Susan
    Ticket
        Tkt-vno: 5
        Realm: INS.COM
        Server Name (Unknown): krbtgt/INS.COM
            Name-type: Unknown (0)
            Name: krbtgt
            Name: INS.COM
        enc-part rc4-hmac
            Encryption type: rc4-hmac (23)
            Kvno: 2
            enc-part: 6EF9DA4B3380CD1F2ABCCB1B0BCFD515CB37FBCAEA8CFDD1...
```

Figure 4.20 (continued)

```
    enc-part des-cbc-md5
        Encryption type: des-cbc-md5 (3)
        Kvno: 7
        enc-part: F0A2485C403AE0DEFCAED9E673764C1F69E374785B5D6BCF...

Frame 9 (240 bytes on wire, 240 bytes captured)
Ethernet II, Src: Microsof_57:ab:2a (00:03:ff:57:ab:2a), Dst: 02:00:4c:4f:4f:50
(02:00:4c:4f:4f:50)
Internet Protocol, Src: 10.0.1.101 (10.0.1.101), Dst: 10.0.2.101 (10.0.2.101)
Transmission Control Protocol, Src Port: microsoft-ds (445), Dst Port: 58805 (58805), Seq:
849233861, Ack: 1711119073, Len: 174
NetBIOS Session Service
SMB (Server Message Block Protocol)
    SMB Header
        Server Component: SMB
        Response to: 8
        Time from request: 0.001405000 seconds
        SMB Command: Negotiate Protocol (0x72)
        NT Status: STATUS_SUCCESS (0x00000000)
        Flags: 0x88
        Flags2: 0xd801
        Process ID High: 0
        Signature: 0000000000000000
        Reserved: 0000
        Tree ID: 0
        Process ID: 30479
        User ID: 0
        Multiplex ID: 1
    Negotiate Protocol Response (0x72)
        Word Count (WCT): 17
        Dialect Index: 8, greater than LANMAN2.1
        Security Mode: 0x07
        Max Mpx Count: 50
        Max VCs: 1
        Max Buffer Size: 4356
        Max Raw Buffer: 65536
```

Figure 4.20 (continued)

```
        Session Key: 0x00000000
        Capabilities: 0x8001f3fd
        System Time: Mar 11, 2006 13:20:55.511014400
        Server Time Zone: 0 min from UTC
        Key Length: 0
        Byte Count (BCC): 101
        Server GUID: 9A79F2434543AF47AE9373D706786AA0
        Security Blob: 605306062B0601050502A0493047A030302E06092A864882...
            GSS-API Generic Security Service Application Program Interface
                OID: 1.3.6.1.5.5.2 (SPNEGO - Simple Protected Negotiation)
                SPNEGO
                    negTokenInit
                        mechTypes: 4 items
                            Item: 1.2.840.48018.1.2.2 (MS KRB5 - Microsoft Kerberos 5)
                            Item: 1.2.840.113554.1.2.2 (KRB5 - Kerberos 5)
                            Item: 1.2.840.113554.1.2.2.3 (KRB5 - Kerberos 5 - User to User)
                            Item: 1.3.6.1.4.1.311.2.2.10 (NTLMSSP - Microsoft NTLM Security
Support Provider)
                        mechListMIC: A00F1B0D62696C6C2440494E532E434F4D
                            principal: bill$@INS.COM

Frame 11 (1228 bytes on wire, 1228 bytes captured)
Ethernet II, Src: 02:00:4c:4f:4f:50 (02:00:4c:4f:4f:50), Dst: Microsof_57:ab:2a
(00:03:ff:57:ab:2a)
Internet Protocol, Src: 10.0.2.101 (10.0.2.101), Dst: 10.0.1.101 (10.0.1.101)
User Datagram Protocol, Src Port: 32769 (32769), Dst Port: kerberos (88)
Kerberos TGS-REQ
    Pvno: 5
    MSG Type: TGS-REQ (12)
    padata: PA-TGS-REQ
        Type: PA-TGS-REQ (1)
            Value: 6E82041F3082041BA003020105A10302010EA20703050000... AP-REQ
                Pvno: 5
                MSG Type: AP-REQ (14)
                Padding: 0
                APOptions: 00000000
```

Figure 4.20 (continued)

```
            Ticket
                Tkt-vno: 5
                Realm: INS.COM
                Server Name (Unknown): krbtgt/INS.COM
                    Name-type: Unknown (0)
                    Name: krbtgt
                    Name: INS.COM
                enc-part rc4-hmac
                    Encryption type: rc4-hmac (23)
                    Kvno: 2
                    enc-part: 6EF9DA4B3380CD1F2ABCCB1B0BCFD515CB37FBCAEA8CFDD1...
            Authenticator des-cbc-md5
                Encryption type: des-cbc-md5 (3)
                Authenticator data: 386A7E9398D31E3F81894E3C6012A59052EF25BC6357FEB1...
    KDC_REQ_BODY
        Padding: 0
        KDCOptions: 40800000 (Forwardable, Renewable)
        Realm: INS.COM
        Server Name (Principal): bill$
            Name-type: Principal (1)
            Name: bill$
        till: 2006-03-11 23:20:27 (Z)
        Nonce: 1142083258
        Encryption Types: rc4-hmac des-cbc-md5 des-cbc-crc
            Encryption type: rc4-hmac (23)
            Encryption type: des-cbc-md5 (3)
            Encryption type: des-cbc-crc (1)

Frame 12 (1259 bytes on wire, 1259 bytes captured)
Ethernet II, Src: Microsof_57:ab:2a (00:03:ff:57:ab:2a), Dst: 02:00:4c:4f:4f:50
(02:00:4c:4f:4f:50)
Internet Protocol, Src: 10.0.1.101 (10.0.1.101), Dst: 10.0.2.101 (10.0.2.101)
User Datagram Protocol, Src Port: kerberos (88), Dst Port: 32769 (32769)
Kerberos TGS-REP
    Pvno: 5
    MSG Type: TGS-REP (13)
```

Figure 4.20 (continued)

```
  Client Realm: INS.COM
  Client Name (Principal): Susan
    Name-type: Principal (1)
    Name: Susan
  Ticket
    Tkt-vno: 5
    Realm: INS.COM
    Server Name (Principal): bill$
      Name-type: Principal (1)
      Name: bill$
    enc-part rc4-hmac
      Encryption type: rc4-hmac (23)
      Kvno: 8
      enc-part: 212D768A18E8319DA0B163AD2F6971F143C93B03F58F6F29...
  enc-part des-cbc-md5
    Encryption type: des-cbc-md5 (3)
    enc-part: 8B404702F6A9B0629B910E7420E952EA8E233D3427240CD2...

Frame 13 (1350 bytes on wire, 1350 bytes captured)
Ethernet II, Src: 02:00:4c:4f:4f:50 (02:00:4c:4f:4f:50), Dst: Microsof_57:ab:2a
(00:03:ff:57:ab:2a)
Internet Protocol, Src: 10.0.2.101 (10.0.2.101), Dst: 10.0.1.101 (10.0.1.101)
Transmission Control Protocol, Src Port: 58805 (58805), Dst Port: microsoft-ds (445), Seq:
1711119073, Ack: 849234035, Len: 1284
NetBIOS Session Service
  Message Type: Session message
  Length: 1280
SMB (Server Message Block Protocol)
  SMB Header
    Server Component: SMB
    Response in: 14
    SMB Command: Session Setup AndX (0x73)
    NT Status: STATUS_SUCCESS (0x00000000)
    Flags: 0x08
    Flags2: 0xd805
    Process ID High: 0
```

Figure 4.20 (continued)

```
        Signature: EA5779E231411F46
        Reserved: 0000
        Tree ID: 0
        Process ID: 30479
        User ID: 0
        Multiplex ID: 2
    Session Setup AndX Request (0x73)
        Word Count (WCT): 12
        AndXCommand: No further commands (0xff)
        Reserved: 00
        AndXOffset: 0
        Max Buffer: 65535
        Max Mpx Count: 2
        VC Number: 1
        Session Key: 0x00000000
        Security Blob Length: 1199
        Reserved: 00000000
        Capabilities: 0x8000d05c
        Byte Count (BCC): 1221
        Security Blob: 608204AB06062B0601050502A082049F3082049BA0193017...
            GSS-API Generic Security Service Application Program Interface
                OID: 1.3.6.1.5.5.2 (SPNEGO - Simple Protected Negotiation)
                SPNEGO
                    negTokenInit
                        mechTypes: 2 items
                            Item: 1.2.840.48018.1.2.2 (MS KRB5 - Microsoft Kerberos 5)
                            Item: 1.3.6.1.4.1.311.2.2.10 (NTLMSSP - Microsoft NTLM Security
Support Provider)
                        mechToken: 6082047406092A864886F71201020201006E820463308204...
                        krb5_blob: 6082047406092A864886F71201020201006E820463308204...
                            KRB5 OID: 1.2.840.113554.1.2.2 (KRB5 - Kerberos 5)
                            krb5_tok_id: KRB5_AP_REQ (0x0001)
                            Kerberos AP-REQ
                                Pvno: 5
                                MSG Type: AP-REQ (14)
                                Padding: 0
```

Figure 4.20 (continued)

```
                    APOptions: 00000000
                    Ticket
                        Tkt-vno: 5
                        Realm: INS.COM
                        Server Name (Principal): bill$
                            Name-type: Principal (1)
                            Name: bill$
                        enc-part rc4-hmac
                            Encryption type: rc4-hmac (23)
                            Kvno: 8
                            enc-part:
212D768A18E8319DA0B163AD2F6971F143C93B03F58F6F29...
                    Authenticator rc4-hmac
                        Encryption type: rc4-hmac (23)
                        Authenticator data:
BC9418035689C11BF38E4AE93D49BA7F7E27C77C32C778DB...
        Native OS: Unix
        Native LAN Manager: Samba

Frame 14 (267 bytes on wire, 267 bytes captured)
Ethernet II, Src: Microsof_57:ab:2a (00:03:ff:57:ab:2a), Dst: 02:00:4c:4f:4f:50
(02:00:4c:4f:4f:50)
Internet Protocol, Src: 10.0.1.101 (10.0.1.101), Dst: 10.0.2.101 (10.0.2.101)
Transmission Control Protocol, Src Port: microsoft-ds (445), Dst Port: 58805 (58805), Seq:
849234035, Ack: 1711120357, Len: 201
NetBIOS Session Service
SMB (Server Message Block Protocol)
    SMB Header
        Server Component: SMB
        Response to: 13
        Time from request: 0.005451000 seconds
        SMB Command: Session Setup AndX (0x73)
        NT Status: STATUS_SUCCESS (0x00000000)
        Flags: 0x88
        Flags2: 0xd805
        Process ID High: 0
```

Figure 4.20 (continued)

```
        Signature: 85D4C5C4291F5D1E
        Reserved: 0000
        Tree ID: 0
        Process ID: 30479
        User ID: 24577
        Multiplex ID: 2
    Session Setup AndX Response (0x73)
        Word Count (WCT): 4
        AndXCommand: No further commands (0xff)
        Reserved: 00
        AndXOffset: 197
        Action: 0x0000
        Security Blob Length: 26
        Byte Count (BCC): 154
        Security Blob: A1183016A0030A0100A10B06092A864882F712010202A202...
            GSS-API Generic Security Service Application Program Interface
                SPNEGO
                    negTokenTarg
                        negResult: accept-completed (0)
                        supportedMech: 1.2.840.48018.1.2.2 (MS KRB5 - Microsoft Kerberos 5)
                        responseToken: <MISSING>
        Native OS: Windows Server 2003 3790 Service Pack 1
        Native LAN Manager: Windows Server 2003 5.2
```

Figure 4.20 (continued)

10. The server validates the ticket received from the client using its encrypted copy and the authenticator, and then indicates successful authentication to the CIFS/SMB Resource (see Frame 14 in Figure 4.20).

From that point on, the SMB/CIFS server impersonates the user and all further interactions are performed in the user security context.

It is interesting to note that messages to and from the KDC (such as AS_REQ/AS_REP and TGS_REQ/TGS_REP) use the Kerberos transport over UDP (and over TCP in some cases, such as large Protocol Data Units), while the AP_REQ/AP_REP messages, as well as further messages, use the application protocol transport, where they often coexist with GSS-API and SPNEGO.

4.2.2.8 Authorization Information and the Microsoft PAC Attribute

The Kerberos Protocol was designed to provide for user authentication but it can also carry user identification and authorization information in Kerberos tickets (see Table 4.5).

Authorization information is often application and operating system specific. It resides in the **Enc-authorization data** field of Kerberos tickets. Typically, along with other user identification information, it will contain user and group IDs that can be used by the party using the ticket to impersonate or delegate access for authorized users.

Microsoft Active Directory provides a typical approach for utilizing the **Enc-authorization data** field. It stores the NT user access token (see Chapter 3) for the user to whom the ticket was issued. The user access token stored in the **Enc-authorization data** field is referred to as a Privilege Attribute Certificate (PAC). The use and the structure of the Microsoft PAC field are defined in [91]; and Table 4.10 represents the fields of the PAC structure.

There are two signatures (checksums) attached to the PAC. They guarantee that the client has not modified the contents of the PAC and that the server has not generated a fake PAC. The first signature is the one with the server protection key, and the second uses the KDC key.

When the application server receives a ticket containing the above PAC from the client, the server can identify or impersonate the calling user, and thus authorize access to server application resources.

Unlike NTLM, which needs to establish an MS-RPC session over a secure channel with a domain controller to obtain this information, Kerberos carries NT access tokens in user tickets, and all the information is readily available to the application server as part of the access ticket presented by the client. The fact that the ticket is encrypted by the KDC in the application server password guarantees that the ticket and the information within can be trusted.

Table 4.10 Microsoft PAC Structure for Kerberos Authorization Data

PAC Attribute	*Description*
Logon Time	Last time the user logged on
Logoff Time	Logon session expiration time for the current session
Kick Off Time	Time when the user should be forcibly disconnected
Password Last Set	The last time the user changed his password

Table 4.10 Microsoft PAC Structure for Kerberos Authorization Data (continued)

PAC Attribute	*Description*
Password Can Change	Time when the user can change his password
Password Must Change	When does the user password expire?
Effective Name	Downlevel username (SamAccountName attribute)
Full Name	Full name of the user
Logon Script	Path to the user logon script
Profile Path	Directory containing the user profile
Home Directory	User home directory
Home Directory Drive	Drive letter to be mapped to the user home directory
Logon Count	Not used
Bad Password Count	Number of unsuccessful logon attempts with this account since the last successful attempt
User ID	User RID
Primary Group ID	Primary Group RID
GroupIDs	RIDs of groups of which the user is a member
User Flags	Specifies what additional information exists in the PAC
Logon Server	NetBIOS name of the KDC that performed the authentication
Logon Domain Name	NetBIOS name of the domain of which the user is a member
User Account Control	Specifies user account options
SID Count	Number of records in the Extra SIDs field
Extra SIDs	Additional SIDs of groups of which the user is a member
Resource Group Count	Number of resource group SIDs specified in the PAC
Resource Group Domain SID	Domain ID of the Resource Domain
Resource Group IDs	RIDs of Resource Groups

4.2.2.9 Kerberos Credentials Exchange (KRB_CRED)

In some cases, a user or an application working on one computer might want to authorize an application or service on another computer. This is the process of delegation that can have different flavors and is described in Chapter 4.2.2.14.

Because Kerberos authentication, identification, and to a certain extent application authorization processes are based on Kerberos tickets, a service acting on behalf of a user needs to have a ticket granted to this user. However, the service may or may not be able to request a ticket on the user's behalf. The user may need to request the ticket from a KDC and then provide the ticket to the service. The standard KRB_CRED messages provide for a transport that can be used by applications when they need to pass Kerberos tickets over to another party. The Kerberos KRB_CRED message consists of the fields in Table 4.11.

Whether or not Kerberos delegation is appropriate, how tickets will be requested and when they will be transferred is the responsibility of the application. The KRB_CRED message itself is sent on top of the application transport, and not as an autonomous UDP/TCP transport-based message. The KRB_CRED message is encrypted in a session key or a subkey that has already been established between the user and the service or application to which the KRB_CRED message is being sent. The KRB_CRED message typically follows the AP_REQ/AP_REP messages.

4.2.2.10 Kerberos and Smart Card Authentication (PKInit)

Although authentication based on a username and password remains the most popular authentication approach, there are other methods for user authentication. The Kerberos PKINIT specification (see [92]) provides for authentication based on public key cryptography and certificates. At the time of this writing, the PKINIT specification is still an Internet Draft. However, some vendors already provide implementations based on the draft version. In particular, Microsoft Active Directory provides for PKINIT authentication, and similar features exist for the MIT and Heimdal Kerberos implementations.

Considering the fact that certificates and private keys can be stored on smart cards, PKINIT is likely to become a popular, strong, two-factor authentication approach. The private key is stored on the smart card and encrypted in the user PIN. To authenticate, the user needs to provide both the smart card and the PIN code to decrypt the private key.

It is interesting to note that with PKINIT, the user does not need to provide a username in order to authenticate. Instead, the PKINIT dialogue

Table 4.11 KRB_CRED Message Structure

*Field**	*Description**
Pvno	Protocol version number (for Kerberos v.5, this number is 5)
msg_type	KRB_CRED uses type 22
Tickets	Array of Tickets — a sequence of tickets passed from the user to the delegated service or application
Ticket info	Array of Credential Information — information about each of the attached tickets; there is one entry for each attached ticket. This includes: Key — the session key for the ticket Prealm – realm of the principal in the ticket. Pname – principal name Flags – ticket flags Authtime – time of authentication Starttime – time when the ticket will be active Endtime – time when the ticket will expire Renew-till – time until when the ticket can be renewed Srealm – service principal realm Sname – service principal name Caddr – IP Address
Nonce	One-time number that shows that this is not a replayed message; the nonce cannot be reused
Time stamp	Ensure that this is not a replayed message
Usec	Ensure that this is not a replayed message
s-address	Address of the sender of the message
r-address	Address of the recipient of the message

* Fields in gray are encrypted.

with the AS requires that the client provides a valid trusted certificate. The certificate attributes are expected to contain enough identifying information to determine the identity of the authenticating user. Microsoft's Active Directory implementation, for example, utilizes the **Subject Alternative Name** attribute of the certificate to determine the user principal name. Other implementations use other fields, such as the Subject field.

PKINIT authentication only affects the initial TGT request to and from the AS. All other Kerberos messages and mechanisms are unaffected, as they use the TGT and not directly the private key on the smart card.

Kerberos authentication using PKINIT involves the following steps:

1. The client sends an AS_REQ message to the AS. The AS_REQ includes the PA_PK_AS_REQ preauthentication message with the following information: encryption method (PKINIT specific), trusted CAs by the client, Client certificate, and optionally a Diffie-Hellman Nonce.
2. The KDC checks whether the client-provided certificate is valid, whether it has been issued by a trusted (and allowed for PKINIT authentication) certificate authority, whether it's within its validity period, etc.
3. The KDC replies to the user with either a session key, encrypted in the user public key using the specified in the PA_PK_AS_REQ preauthentication message protection mechanisms, and signed with the server private key; or a Diffie-Hellman Nonce signed with the server private key (if the client included a Diffie-Hellman Nonce).
4. The client authenticates the server reply by checking the server signature on the session key or Diffie-Hellman nonce using the server public key.

From that point on, the client has a valid TGT, which it can then use to request service tickets.

4.2.2.11 Kerberos User-to-User Authentication

In a typical Kerberos scenario, authentication takes place between a client computer, a server, and a KDC that is a trusted third party. The client is the active side and authenticates to the KDC, then requests a TGT, and finally requests a service ticket that is encrypted in the server secret. The server has its secret stored locally (LSA Secrets on Windows servers, and keytab or srvtab files for MIT-compatible implementations on all platforms). However, in some cases, the server application does not run with the privileges of the computer (using the computer account in a Windows domain) but with the privileges of another user account. To perform authentication between such user applications that do not have access to long-term secrets on the computer that they are running on, the Kerberos Protocol provides for user-to-user authentication.

With user-to-user authentication, both applications run with the privileges of their respective user accounts and have obtained TGTs from the same or a trusted KDC. One of the applications is considered the client (accessing) and the other is the server (accessed application). The client application is the active one and is responsible for obtaining appropriate tickets to establish communication with the server application. To do so, the client application must obtain the TGT of the server application. How the TGT will be obtained is not defined in the RFC, and is typically a function of the application layer protocol. The client cannot misuse the server TGT because it is encrypted in the secret of the server application, which is not known to the client application. The user-to-user authentication process takes place as follows:

1. The client application obtains the server application TGT by methods specific to the application protocol.
2. The client application submits a TGS_REQ to the KDC and provides its own TGT and the TGT of the server application. The client application sets the ENC-TKT-IN-SKEY flag in the request and indicates that the KDC should use the session key from the server TGT instead of the server secret.
3. From the server application TGT, the KDC determines who the server principal is, and then decrypts the TGT to make sure it is valid. The KDC generates a service ticket for the client with a new random session key, and encrypts it in the session key from the server TGT (which the client requested by raising the ENC-TKT-IN-SKEY flag), then sends it to the client, along with a second copy encrypted in the client session key from the client TGT.
4. The client decrypts its copy of the service ticket and determines the session key it needs to use to communicate with the server application.
5. The client sends to the server an AP_REQ message to try and authenticate to the server application. The client includes the server copy of the ticket encrypted in the server secret.
6. The server application decrypts the ticket and determines the session key, which will match the client session key. The server then replies to the client with an AP_REP message and optionally authenticates itself to the client.
7. In case of successful authentication, from that point on the client and the server communicate as they would normally do.

The user-to-user authentication model very much resembles the client-to-server authentication model. However, with the user-to-user authentication model, the client and server applications need access to the KDC to authenticate and start communicating. This is different from the client-to-server authentication model, where the server application does not need online access to the KDC — a valid ticket is all it needs to grant access.

Another typical example of user-to-user authentication is when Kerberos delegation is used with user accounts to start applications over the network. If an application uses a user key and switches into the user context using an available Kerberos ticket for this user, this application will start working with the privileges of the particular user. However, if another application tries to access the first application over the network, the first application may be in a position where it has a ticket that it can use to impersonate the user but is not able to authenticate to other users over the network, as it does not have the server or user password in which incoming tickets from other users will be encrypted. To resolve this problem, user-to-user authentication is often used in Kerberos delegation scenarios.

4.2.2.12 Kerberos Encryption and Checksum Mechanisms

The Kerberos authentication protocol uses encryption and integrity technologies to provide for user authentication and ticket protection. There are different protection mechanisms available, and the client and the KDC, as well as the client and the server, negotiate the best protection method supported by both parties. The protection mechanisms include data encryption mechanisms and checksum mechanisms; the former encrypt the data and the latter provide for message integrity authentication. Some encryption mechanisms are also capable of protecting message integrity using a checksum or a message digest. To protect data, Kerberos uses the structure in Figure 4.21.

The confounder is a random octet string. It is used as salt for the encryption mechanisms. Different encryption mechanisms use different length confounders. The Checksum field also varies in size — conventional CRC32 checksums only need 4 bytes, while SHA-1 authentication digests require 20 bytes. The Checksum field contains a value used to check the integrity of the message. The Message field is the actual Kerberos piece of information that needs to be protected. The Padding field contains zeroes used to align the Kerberos message at an 8-byte boundary.

The checksum is calculated before the message is encrypted. To calculate the checksum, the client and server generate a random confounder and put the result in the Confounder field, then zero the Checksum bytes, add the actual user message, and pad it to zeroes. Then the checksum algorithm is invoked and the result is stored in the Checksum field. The entire structure from Figure 4.21 is then encrypted using the encryption algorithm negotiated by the client and the server in the protection key.

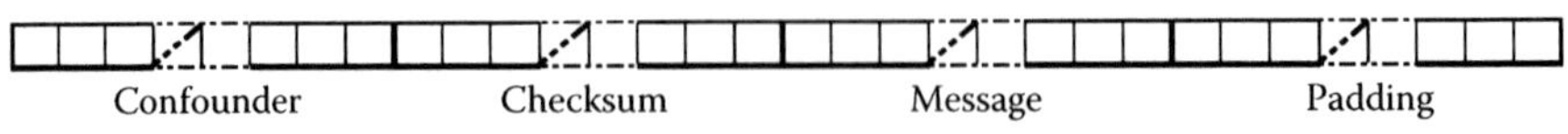

Figure 4.21 Kerberos message format.

Checksum mechanisms are used for data integrity only. They use cryptographic functions to generate a message digest that can later be used to check whether or not the message has been modified. The checksum or digest is a one-way function — the original message cannot be deduced from the checksum.

At the initial phases (such as the Kerberos AS phase), Kerberos protection mechanisms typically utilize the user password (or a derivative thereof) to generate protection keys. In the case of PKINIT, private keys and certificates are used instead. Later (during the AP phase), the client and server typically communicate using an already-established and valid session key, generated by the KDC, or a subkey generated by one of the principals.

Despite the fact that the password is always being used in some form, Kerberos clients, servers, and KDCs have different approaches to generating the protection keys.

The Kerberos client (the GINA and the user shell in Windows, as well as the **kinit** utility in UNIX- and MIT Kerberos-compatible implementations), typically has access to the plaintext password provided by the interactive user. It can therefore use the plaintext password to generate the key material, as well as the protection key.

The Kerberos server (such as Kerberized Telnet or a CIFS server) stores its password in encrypted form in a local file. MIT Kerberos servers use the srvtab or the keytab files; Windows clients and servers store it in the registry as an LSA Secret (see Chapter 3).

The KDC typically has a directory that includes the secrets for all the Kerberos principals — clients and servers. This directory can reside in a dedicated file or in LDAP (Windows servers use the Active Directory password attributes and the **SupplementalCredentials** attribute) to store Kerberos secrets for domain principals. The database used by the KDC is typically encrypted with a master key, so that a compromise of the database file does not automatically reveal all the principals' secrets. At the same time, a compromise of the KDC host can potentially lead to the compromise of the database and its protecting keys. Therefore, the security of the KDC is critical to the security of the Kerberos authentication system as a whole.

Password-derived protection keys are a function of two main variables: (1) the plaintext user password and (2) a random salt. Kerberos IV does not use a salt. Kerberos V defines the user principal name as the salt. The use of a salt during encryption provides for a different ciphertext even when the same plaintext is provided.

There are two types of password derived protection keys currently in use: (1) String-to-Key and (2) Microsoft RC4-HMAC. Both are one-way function (OWF) approaches so that the user password cannot be calculated from the protection key. The protection key is calculated depending on the encryption mechanism, negotiated by the client and the KDC. Some encryption mechanisms use the String-to-Key protection key and others use the Microsoft RC4-HMAC password protection key.

The String-to-Key key generation approach uses the user password and a salt to generate the protection key. This approach is defined in RFC 3961 and is typically used by MIT Kerberos and other compatible implementations.

With the String-to-Key approach, the protection key (called the protocol key) is derived from the user plaintext password, a salt value, and possibly encryption method specific parameters. The Kerberos MIT implementation uses the DES and 3DES encryption protocols to generate the protection keys in the following way: The plaintext user password and salt are passed to the key generation function. The password and the salt are then concatenated and padded with zeroes to an 8-byte boundary. The resultant string is processed in portions of 8 bytes. For each portion, the most significant bit of each byte is removed. Following the original string order, odd portions are reversed from the last bit to the first, while even portions are left in the same order. All portions processed in this way are then XORed together.

The result is a 56-bit string, which is then processed to add parity and expand to 64-bits, and is used later as a 64-bit key with parity in the DES algorithm.

The Microsoft RC4-HMAC approach is defined as an Internet Draft, and not as an RFC. This draft has recently expired so this protection approach may be considered non-standard. The draft is available in [36]. The need to define a new encryption and key derivation approach for Kerberos arose with Windows 2000 when Microsoft first adopted Kerberos as an authentication method. In an effort to have a single password for each user, Microsoft decided to utilize the NT hash to generate Kerberos protection keys. Because the NT hash is readily available as a user attribute (see Chapter 3), the user does not need to maintain a separate password for Kerberos authentication. This contrasts with the MIT approach, where the user may have a login password stored in the **/etc/passwd** or **/etc/shadow** files, and a separate Kerberos password stored in the Kerberos database. The Kerberos protection mechanisms cannot utilize the password in the **/etc/passwd** or **/etc/shadow** files because it is stored in an encrypted form generated by the **crypt( )** function (see Chapter 2). Therefore, the user needs to synchronize his password in both databases, and typically has different commands to change his password. PAM provides a mechanism by which a password change can be propagated to both databases.

Active Directory supports DES-compatible Kerberos secrets configurable on a per-user basis using the **Use DES Encryption types for this account** option. Once this setting has been activated for an Active Directory user, a string-to-key compatible version will be stored for this user next time he changes his password. This is often used for compatibility with MIT Kerberos and other non-Microsoft implementations.

Once the key has been generated, the communicating parties apply a protection scheme for the encrypted portion of tickets and ticket authenticators. Table 4.12 provides some of the Kerberos encryption mechanisms defined in RFC 3961 and RFC 3962 (see [89, 90]). Each algorithm additionally modifies the so-generated key in some way by means of cryptographic functions.

Table 4.13 shows the Kerberos checksum mechanisms.

4.2.2.13 Case Study: Kerberos Authentication Scenarios

With the NTLM authentication protocol, both the client and the server need to access the trusted third party (the domain controller in Windows) for their own domain, and potentially domain controllers may need to communicate with each other. With Kerberos, all the authentication information is stored in the Kerberos ticket, which decreases the number of required communication scenarios. Furthermore, unlike NTLM authentication, which uses a secure channel between the client and the domain controller of the domain to which the client computer belongs, Kerberos authentication does not use a secure channel and has its own methods to protect messages exchanged with the KDC. The Kerberos client does not necessarily send authentication requests (such as TGS requests) to the same realm (Windows domain) to which the client computer belongs. Rather, it might send TGS requests directly to the KDC (domain controller) of the domain where the user is trying to log in.

As a result, there are two main Kerberos authentication scenarios: (1) the client accesses a server in its own realm (or Active Directory domain), or (2) the client accesses a server in a remote realm.

User Authentication and Access to Server in Same Realm (Interactive and Network Authentication)

Assumptions: User and server are Kerberos principals of the same realm (Figure 4.22).

Steps for Kerberos user authentication in the same realm:

1. The user provides his credentials to the Kerberos client interface (GINA in Windows, and **kinit** in MIT-compatible implementations); phase A in Figure 4.22.

Table 4.12 Kerberos Encryption Mechanisms

Encryption Type	*etype*	*Protection/Comment*
des-cbc-crc	1	DES-CBC with four octet CRC, key used as IV
des-cbc-md4	2	DES-CBC encryption, MD4 checksum, zero IV
des-cbc-md5	3	DES-CBC encryption, MD5 checksum, zero IV
des3-cbc-md5	6	3DES encryption and MD5 checksum, 8-byte confounder
des3-cbc-sha1	7	Deprecated
DsaWithSHA1-CmsOID	9	PKINIT
md5WithRSAEncryption-CmsOID	10	PKINIT
sha1WithRSAEncryption-CmsOID	11	PKINIT
rc2CBC-EnvOID	12	PKINIT
RsaEncryption-EnvOID	13	PKINIT
RsaES-OAEP-ENV-OID	14	PKINIT
des-ede3-cbc-Env-OID	15	PKINIT
des3-cbc-sha1-kd	16	3DES encryption and SHA1 checksum, 8-byte confounder
aes128-cts-hmac-sha1-9	17	AES Encryption (RFC 3962; [90])
aes256-cts-hmac-sha1-96	18	AES Encryption (RFC 3962; [90])
rc4-hmac	23	Microsoft implementations using NT hash as the key, RC4 encryption, and MD5 data integrity authentication
rc4-hmac-exp	24	Microsoft implementations using NT hash as the key, U.S. export version, RC4 encryption, and MD5 data integrity authentication

2. The client computer performs an AS exchange with the KDC for the realm where the user account resides and obtains a ticket granting ticket (TGT); phases B and C in Figure 4.22.

Table 4.13 Kerberos Checksum Mechanisms

Checksum Type	*Checksum Type ID*	*Size*	*Protection/Comment*
CRC32	1	4	CRC32
rsa-md4	2	16	MD4 hash
rsa-md4-des	3	24	MD4 hash encrypted with DES, zero initial vector (IV)
des-mac	4	16	Hash based on a number of DES encryption rounds and permutations, zero IV
des-mac-k	5	8	Hash based on a number of DES encryption rounds and permutations, zero IV
rsa-md4-des-k	6	16	MD4 checksum encrypted with DES, the key is used as an IV as well
rsa-md5	7	16	MD5 hash
rsa-md5-des	8	24	MD5 hash encrypted with DES, zero IV
rsa-md5-des3	9	24	MD5 hash encrypted with 3DES
sha1 (unkeyed)	10	20	SHA1
hmac-sha1-des3-kd	11	20	SHA1 and 3DES
hmac-sha1-des3	12	20	SHA1 and 3DES
sha1 (unkeyed)	13	20	SHA1
hmac-sha1-96-aes128	14	20	SHA1 and AES
hmac-sha1-96-aes256	15	20	SHA1 and AES

Note on Active Directory: The AS_REP message that the server sends to the client contains the initial PAC for the user;

3. The client computer performs a TGS exchange requesting access to a specific server and service. The client computer defines which service it wants to access by specifying the service principal name for the service; phase D in Figure 4.22.
4. The client computer receives a service ticket from the KDC; phase E in Figure 4.22.

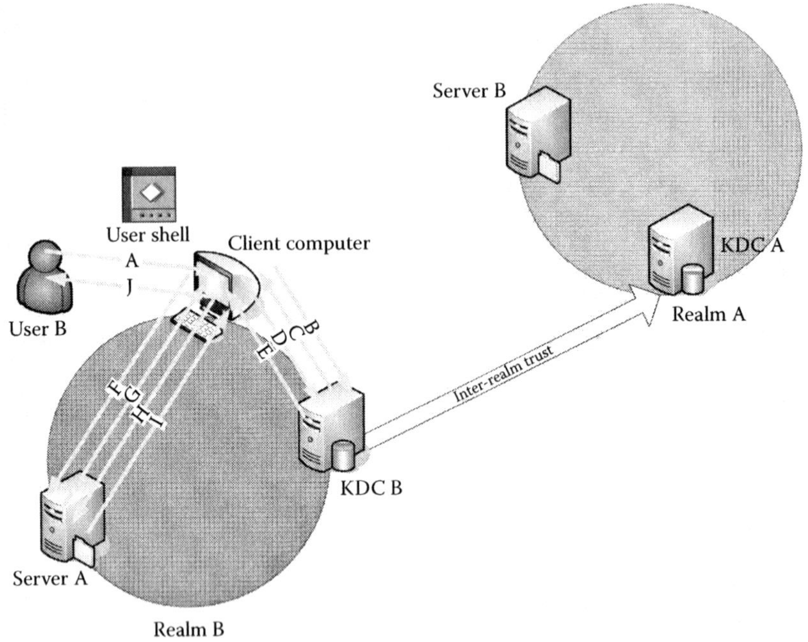

Figure 4.22 Kerberos authentication to resource server in the same realm.

5. The client computer establishes an application protocol session with the server; phases F and G in Figure 4.22.
6. The client computer performs an AP exchange with the server application providing its ticket; phases H and I in Figure 4.22.
7. The client is authenticated and starts accessing resources to which it has access. The server application typically impersonates or identifies the user.

   Note on Active Directory: On Windows platforms, if the service ticket contains a PAC, then the server is able to impersonate the client using the information in the PAC, which is then used to build the user access token for access to resources on the application server.
8. The user can access the application or service; phase J in Figure 4.22.

User Authentication and Access to Server in Remote Realm

Assumptions: User and server are Kerberos principals of different realms that are trusting each other (Figure 4.23).

Steps for Kerberos user authentication to server in a remote trusting realm:

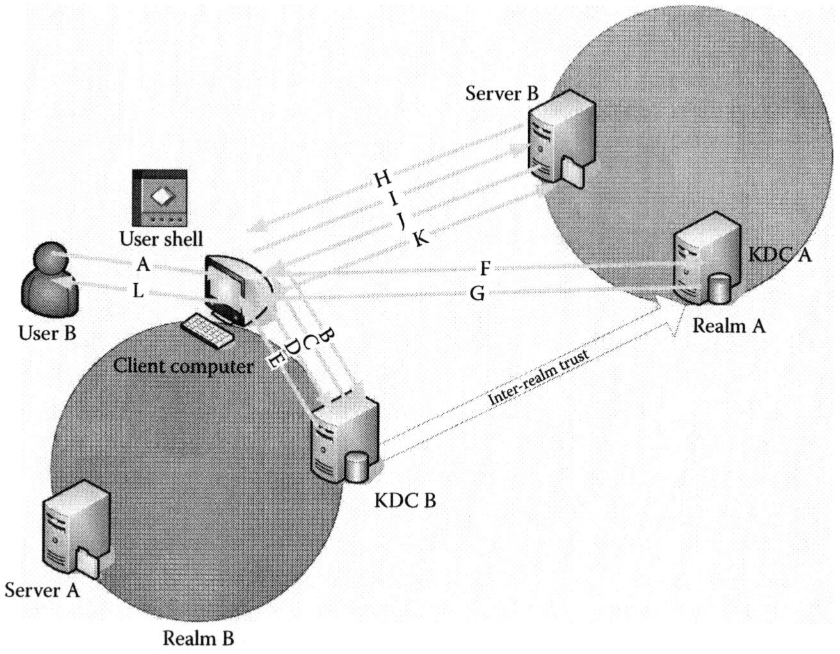

Figure 4.23 Kerberos authentication to server in a remote realm (interactive and network authentication).

1. The user provides his credentials to the Kerberos client interface (GINA in Windows, and **kinit** in MIT-compatible implementations); phase A in Figure 4.23.
2. The client computer performs an AS Exchange with the KDC for the realm where the user account resides and obtains a ticket granting ticket (TGT); phases B and C in Figure 4.23.
   Note on Active Directory: The AS_REP message that the server sends to the client contains the initial PAC for the user if the AS_REQ message is preauthenticated, which by default is required.
3. The client needs to access another realm but does not know how to get to it. It sends a TGS request to its own KDC, providing its TGT; phase D in Figure 4.23.
4. The KDC in the realm of the client determines that the server resides in a remote trusted realm. The client KDC cannot generate a ticket for a server in a remote domain, because it does not have the secret for this remote principal and cannot encrypt the service ticket for it. Therefore, the client KDC replies by providing the client with a referral TGT. This ticket is issued to the name of the

client but is encrypted in the secret shared between the client realm (KDC) and the server realm (KDC); phase E in Figure 4.23.

5. The client uses the referral ticket to access the TGS in the server realm and send another TGS request that specifies that the client needs access to the specific server by identifying it with its service principal name; phase F in Figure 4.23.
6. The TGS in the server realm determines that the server is local to its realm and that it has a secret that it can use to encrypt the service ticket for the server. The TGS in the server realm issues a service ticket and returns it to the client; phase G in Figure 4.23.
   Note on Active Directory: The server realm KDC can decrypt the ticket provided by the client, because it is encrypted in the inter-realm trust secret. For tickets issued by Windows KDCs, and if the initial request was preauthenticated, the ticket contains authorization data (the PAC). At this stage, the server's realm KDC can add SIDs to the PAC as applicable to the realm (domain) where the server resided, or apply policies, such as SID filtering, and remove user and groups SIDs from the PAC of the authenticating user. Then it encrypts the service ticket in the server key and sends it back to the client.
7. The client establishes an application protocol session with the server; phases H and I in Figure 4.23.
8. On top of the application session, the client sends an AP_REQ message to authenticate to the server and optionally requests mutual authentication; phase J in Figure 4.23.
9. The server authenticates the client by looking at the ticket provided in the AP_REQ message.
   Note on Active Directory: On Windows platforms, if the service ticket contains a PAC, then the server is able to impersonate the client using the information in the PAC that is then used to build the user access token for access to resources on the application server.
10. The server sends an AP_REP message back to the client where it announces successful authentication, and potentially authenticates back to the client; phase K in Figure 4.23.
11. The user can access the application; phase L in Figure 4.23.

4.2.2.14 Kerberos Delegation

Kerberos is a distributed authentication protocol and it allows users to delegate to applications and services the right to represent them to other services on the network. Thus, Kerberos can work with distributed and multi-tier applications. Once the user has authenticated to a particular host or layer (front-end server/layer), user credentials in the form of Kerberos tickets are available for applications to use accordingly.

The Kerberos specification allows for delegation, wherein the client provides the front-end server with a ticket to use and access local and network resources on behalf of the client. With regard to the tickets being used, there are two approaches to Kerberos delegation:

1. *Proxy tickets.* With this approach, the client needs to know the particular back-end server to which the front-end server requires access. The client will request a session ticket from the KDC but will raise the PROXIABLE flag in the request and specify the name of the front-end server that will use this proxy ticket. The request also includes the name of the back-end server. The KDC will issue a proxy ticket and will raise the PROXY flag in it to indicate the way it was obtained, and then will send the ticket back to the requesting client. The client will provide the proxy ticket to the front-end server to act on its behalf. The front-end server can use this ticket only for the back-end server and service, as specified in the ticket. If the front-end server needs to access another back-end server on behalf of the client, the client will need to supply another session ticket for this back-end server.
2. *Forwarded tickets.* With this approach, the client does not need to know the name of the back-end server that the front-end server is trying to access, but the client needs to know the name of the front-end server. The client will send a TGT request to a KDC for a forwardable ticket and will specify the name of the front-end server to be issued a TGT. The KDC will issue a TGS for the front-end server, set the FORWARDABLE flag in it, and then send it back to the client. The client can now provide this TGS as well as a session key to the front-end server using Kerberos KERB_CRED messages to the front-end server. Whenever the front-end server needs to access a back-end server on behalf of the client, the front-end server will contact the KDC and provide the client's forwarded TGT, and then obtain a session ticket for the particular back-end server on behalf of the client. This session key will have the FORWARDED flag in it. This can happen for more than one server, should the front-end server need to access many back-end servers. This is possible because, with forwarded tickets, the front-end server now has the ticket granting ticket (TGT), which can be used to request specific session tickets for services on behalf of the user.

Providing a server with a TGT may impose a security risk, especially if the server is trusted to run a limited number of services. Therefore, some Kerberos implementations, such as Active Directory, support the so-called Constrained Delegation, wherein the client can specify the exact services for which it trusts the delegate server.

4.2.3 Simple Authentication and Security Layer (SASL)

The Simple Authentication and Security Layer (SASL) is defined in RFC 2222 (see [55]). SASL is an interface for user authentication mechanisms and an authentication negotiation mechanism, rather than an actual authentication technique. RFC 2222 defines in general terms that the client and server can negotiate authentication using the SASL and, in addition, it defines four of the many SASL authentication mechanisms: (1) Kerberos IV, (2) GSS-API, (3) SKEY, and (4) External. Other SASL mechanisms are also available, and they are defined in other RFCs. Each SASL mechanism has a well-known symbolic name; thus, clients and servers use the authentication mechanism name to negotiate authentication.

SASL authentication negotiation is used for connection-oriented protocols, typically those that involve an interactive session between the client and the server (e.g., POP3, IMAP, and LDAP). SASL does not provide for a transport layer; it is embedded within the transport layer of the client and server applications, requesting authentication.

A typical SASL session works as follows:

1. The client connects to the server using an application protocol.
2. The client and server enter a dialogue to negotiate their capabilities. The server may or may not specify the supported SASL authentication methods by their names.
3. The client uses the AUTH (or other applicable) keyword, followed by the authentication mechanism name to specify the type of authentication it would like to perform. As part of the AUTH request, the client may or may not send an initial authentication token that can spare a round-trip from the authentication mechanism.
4. If the server accepts the selected authentication mechanism, identified by its name, it follows the specific algorithm of the authentication mechanism to authenticate the client.
5. Once the server has authenticated the client, the server will typically impersonate the client and assume the privileges of the user authenticated using the SASL protocol.
6. Depending on the selected authentication mechanism and its parameters, the client can also authenticate the server.
7. From this point on, application commands and data can be exchanged between the client and the server once the client has been authenticated or identified, so the rest of the client/server

session utilizes the appropriate user credentials on the server. The client security context on the server remains valid until the end of the application session because SASL does not permit the client to switch identities.

The importance of SASL is that it can be used by applications as an abstraction layer for user authentication. Essentially, an application that does not support authentication at all can relatively easily be modified to add SASL support by invoking functions from the SASL library, or by directly wrapping the application within SASL code that automatically communicates on the network, authenticates users, impersonates them, and launches the client application within the context of the impersonated user. The application does not need to know about the authentication mechanisms being used. Technically, the SASL library will take care of the authentication dialogue between the client and the server involving the appropriate authentication protocol (typically selected by the client).

There are numerous SASL implementations, some of which are proprietary and an integral part of the application protocol that implements them, while others are modular and can virtually be added as an authentication layer below any application, potentially without rewriting the application. The Cyrus SASL implementation is a popular implementation.

Most SASL mechanisms can be embedded within the TCP or UDP session, used by the application protocol to perform the authentication process between the client and the server, and impersonate the client on the server (Figure 4.24). As a result of the SASL authentication dialogue, a process or a thread on the server will be launched and it will assume user privileges. At this stage, SASL is no longer required and the server can start communicating with the client using the application protocol without worrying about client authentication anymore because the client session from the remote computer is now represented by the process or

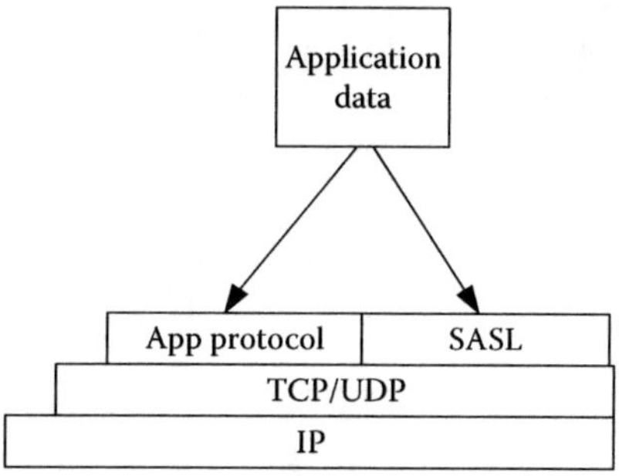

Figure 4.24 SASL protocol stack.

thread that is running on the server with the client privileges. Further interactions between the client and the server will follow the logic of the application protocol, completely ignoring the SASL layer.

On the other hand, some SASL authentication mechanisms provide for data integrity and confidentiality for user data, rather than just for user authentication. In that case, once SASL has performed user authentication at the initial phase, the application protocol can continue to use SASL as an underlying layer for data confidentiality and integrity. In that case, the SASL will persist throughout the entire session between the client and the server, and not only during the initial phase.

Many SASL authentication methods have been used for a long time by various application protocols. The importance of SASL for these authentication methods is that it makes them portable and independent of the application protocol. However, some authentication protocols may prefer their native authentication mechanism or utilize AUTH to perform authentication.

The subsections below discuss some of the popular SASL authentication mechanisms.

4.2.3.1 Kerberos IV

Kerberos IV is an obsolete authentication protocol that is now entirely being replaced by Kerberos V and GSS-API as the security layer (the latter is also an SASL authentication mechanism). The Kerberos IV authentication mechanism is identified by SASL by its name **KERBEROS_V4**.

Authentication using Kerberos IV is typically performed as follows:

1. The client specifies that it will employ Kerberos IV authentication using an SASL authentication command verb such as AUTH KERBEROS_V4.
2. The server sends a random 32-bit challenge to the client.
3. The client returns a Kerberos AP ticket for the specific service being accessed, and a Kerberos authenticator. The authenticator includes the encrypted server challenge. Encryption is performed using the session key between the client and the server (see subsection 4.2.2.2).
4. The server compares the encrypted challenge with its locally calculated copy of the encrypted challenge. If the two match, the client has been authenticated;
5. The server calculates its authentication response to the client by increasing the 32-bit challenge by one, and encrypting it using DES-ECB and the shared session key. The server also adds information about its capabilities, as well as 3 bytes of data specifying the cryptographic buffer size that it supports.

6. The client authenticates the server by decrypting the first 4 octets of the server challenge that contains the incremented server challenge.
7. The client sends the server the DEC-PCBC encrypted original server challenge, as well as client capabilities flag.
8. The server validates the received data and potentially assumes the identity of the authenticating client, or returns an authentication failure message.

4.2.3.2 GSS-API

SASL also allows for GSS-API authentication. This authentication mechanism is identified by SASL by the name **GSSAPI**. The actual mechanics of GSS-API authentication are described in Chapter 4.1.1. By means of using GSS-API, the client and server typically negotiate Kerberos V authentication.

4.2.3.3 S/Key Authentication Mechanism

The S/Key authentication mechanism name used by SASL is **SKEY**. S/Key is a less popular SASL mechanism. The S/Key protocol is described in Chapter 1.

4.2.3.4 External Authentication

The *SASL external* authentication mechanism is identified by the name **EXTERNAL**. This authentication method requires the client to send only the identification information — such as the user ID — to the server. The client and the server then utilize some external mechanism (such as a separate and encrypted [IPSec/SSH/SSL] communication channel) to perform user authentication for this user. Although very useful for applications such as single sign on, this mechanism is not widely used.

4.2.3.5 SASL Anonymous Authentication

The Anonymous authentication mechanism for SASL is defined as an Internet Draft (see [61]). In the past this authentication mechanism was defined in RFC 2245, which is now considered obsolete. The name for this authentication mechanism is **ANONYMOUS**. This mechanism can typically be used by applications that do not need user authentication and that do not need to impersonate the user. Apart from the SASL layer negotiation commands for anonymous authentication (typically AUTH ANONYMOUS), the client might leave a trace of his presence that will only be used to reflect the access in the server logs. The client can submit an arbitrary string, which might be a user ID or an e-mail address. Again, neither of these can be used for impersonation or identification.

4.2.3.6 SASL CRAM-MD5 Authentication

RFC 2195 (see [58]) defines the Challenge-Response Authentication Mechanism MD5 (CRAM-MD5) for IMAP4 and POP3. As the name implies, CRAM-MD5 presents a challenge-response authentication scheme. The authentication process is as follows (see Figure 4.25):

1. The client sends the AUTHENTICATE CRAM-MD5 command to the server, indicating that it wants to start CRAM-MD5 authentication (see Frame 16 in Figure 4.25).
2. The server generates a challenge string and sends it to the client. The authentication process uses Base64 encoded strings. The challenge string consists of the following (see Frame 17 in Figure 4.25):
   - A random string (some implementations use the server process ID, which is pseudo-random)
   - The current time, represented as a time stamp
   - The "@" sign
   - The DNS name of the server (FQDN)
   - A leading and a trailing bracket ("<" and ">," respectively)
3. The client replies with the plaintext username of the authenticating user, followed by a space and an authentication digest that is calculated as the HMAC-MD5 of the server challenge, using the plaintext user password as the key (see Frame 18 in Figure 4.25).
4. The server uses the plaintext user password for the user (username is provided in cleartext by the client as well) and calculates the authentication digest. The server then compares its own authentication digest with the client authentication digest. If the two match, authentication is successful; otherwise, authentication fails.

CRAM-MD5 is a secure method for user authentication but it requires the server to have access to the plaintext user password. As a result, the server or the authentication database needs to either store it in plaintext or use reversible encryption.

CRAM-MD5 does not support mutual authentication. In addition, as with most challenge-response protocols, CRAM-MD5 is susceptible to chosen plaintext attacks, as well as to man-in-the-middle attacks. Considering these disadvantages, the CRAM-MD5 Protocol is not widely used. Support for CRAM-MD5 authentication on Windows platforms is generally not popular.

```
Frame 12 (85 bytes on wire, 85 bytes captured)
Ethernet II, Src: 02:00:4c:4f:4f:50 (02:00:4c:4f:4f:50), Dst: Microsof_56:ab:2a
(00:03:ff:56:ab:2a)
Internet Protocol, Src: 10.0.2.101 (10.0.2.101), Dst: 10.0.1.102 (10.0.1.102)
Transmission Control Protocol, Src Port: 56918 (56918), Dst Port: imap (143), Seq: 1076532457,
Ack: 1798143636, Len: 19
Internet Message Access Protocol
    A00000 CAPABILITY\r\n
        Request Tag: A00000
        Request: CAPABILITY

Frame 14 (249 bytes on wire, 249 bytes captured)
Ethernet II, Src: Microsof_56:ab:2a (00:03:ff:56:ab:2a), Dst: 02:00:4c:4f:4f:50
(02:00:4c:4f:4f:50)
Internet Protocol, Src: 10.0.1.102 (10.0.1.102), Dst: 10.0.2.101 (10.0.2.101)
Transmission Control Protocol, Src Port: imap (143), Dst Port: 56918 (56918), Seq: 1798143636,
Ack: 1076532476, Len: 183
Internet Message Access Protocol
    * CAPABILITY IMAP4rev1 SORT THREAD=REFERENCES MULTIAPPEND UNSELECT IDLE CHILDREN LISTEXT
LIST-SUBSCRIBED NAMESPACE STARTTLS AUTH=PLAIN AUTH=CRAM-MD5\r\n
        Response Tag: *
        Response: CAPABILITY IMAP4rev1 SORT THREAD=REFERENCES MULTIAPPEND UNSELECT IDLE CHILDREN
LISTEXT LIST-SUBSCRIBED NAMESPACE STARTTLS AUTH=PLAIN AUTH=CRAM-MD5

Frame 16 (96 bytes on wire, 96 bytes captured)
Ethernet II, Src: 02:00:4c:4f:4f:50 (02:00:4c:4f:4f:50), Dst: Microsof_56:ab:2a
(00:03:ff:56:ab:2a)
Internet Protocol, Src: 10.0.2.101 (10.0.2.101), Dst: 10.0.1.102 (10.0.1.102)
Transmission Control Protocol, Src Port: 56918 (56918), Dst Port: imap (143), Seq: 1076532476,
Ack: 1798143819, Len: 30
Internet Message Access Protocol
    A00001 AUTHENTICATE CRAM-MD5\r\n
        Request Tag: A00001
        Request: AUTHENTICATE CRAM-MD5

Frame 17 (130 bytes on wire, 130 bytes captured)
```

Figure 4.25 IMAP client Dennis accessing IMAP server Linus using CRAM-MD5 authentication.

```
Ethernet II, Src: Microsof_56:ab:2a (00:03:ff:56:ab:2a), Dst: 02:00:4c:4f:4f:50
(02:00:4c:4f:4f:50)
Internet Protocol, Src: 10.0.1.102 (10.0.1.102), Dst: 10.0.2.101 (10.0.2.101)
Transmission Control Protocol, Src Port: imap (143), Dst Port: 56918 (56918), Seq: 1798143819,
Ack: 1076532506, Len: 64
Internet Message Access Protocol
    + PDY3ODgzMTMwNDUyNDg0MTEuMTEzOTI3NTYyMkBsaW51cy5pbnMuY29tPg==\r\n
        Response Tag: +
        Response: PDY3ODgzMTMwNDUyNDg0MTEuMTEzOTI3NTYyMkBsaW51cy5pbnMuY29tPg== (Base64)
        Response: <6788313045248411.1139275622@linus.ins.com> (Decoded)

Frame 19 (126 bytes on wire, 126 bytes captured)
Ethernet II, Src: 02:00:4c:4f:4f:50 (02:00:4c:4f:4f:50), Dst: Microsof_56:ab:2a
(00:03:ff:56:ab:2a)
Internet Protocol, Src: 10.0.2.101 (10.0.2.101), Dst: 10.0.1.102 (10.0.1.102)
Transmission Control Protocol, Src Port: 56918 (56918), Dst Port: imap (143), Seq: 1076532506,
Ack: 1798143883, Len: 60
Internet Message Access Protocol
    aGVtbWluZ3dheSAyOWYyMGI2NjkzNDdhYTA4MTc0OTA2NWQ5MDNhNDllNA==
        Request Tag: aGVtbWluZ3dheSAyOWYyMGI2NjkzNDdhYTA4MTc0OTA2NWQ5MDNhNDllNA== (Base64)
        Request Tag: hemmingway 29f20b669347aa081749065d903a49e4 (Decoded)

Frame 20 (68 bytes on wire, 68 bytes captured)
Ethernet II, Src: 02:00:4c:4f:4f:50 (02:00:4c:4f:4f:50), Dst: Microsof_56:ab:2a
(00:03:ff:56:ab:2a)
Internet Protocol, Src: 10.0.2.101 (10.0.2.101), Dst: 10.0.1.102 (10.0.1.102)
Transmission Control Protocol, Src Port: 56918 (56918), Dst Port: imap (143), Seq: 1076532566,
Ack: 1798143883, Len: 2
Internet Message Access Protocol
    \r\n

Frame 21 (88 bytes on wire, 88 bytes captured)
Ethernet II, Src: Microsof_56:ab:2a (00:03:ff:56:ab:2a), Dst: 02:00:4c:4f:4f:50
(02:00:4c:4f:4f:50)
Internet Protocol, Src: 10.0.1.102 (10.0.1.102), Dst: 10.0.2.101 (10.0.2.101)
```

Figure 4.25 (continued)

```
Transmission Control Protocol, Src Port: imap (143), Dst Port: 56918 (56918), Seq: 1798143883,
Ack: 1076532568, Len: 22
Internet Message Access Protocol
    A00001 OK Logged in.\r\n
        Response Tag: A00001
        Response: OK Logged in.
```

Figure 4.25 (continued)

4.2.3.7 SASL Digest-MD5 Authentication

RFC 2831 (see [60]) defines the Digest-MD5 authentication mechanism. Digest-MD5 is similar to CRAM-MD5 but has a number of improvements, including:

- *Reauthentication.* The Digest-MD5 Protocol distinguishes between the initial authentication performed by the client that needs to go through all the steps of the authentication process, and subsequent authentication once the client has been authenticated when the process fast-tracked in a safe way.
- *Replay protection.* Digest-MD5 provides for protection against replay attacks.
- *Integrity and confidentiality.* Digest-MD5 provides for message integrity and confidentiality.

Digest authentication can use other cryptographic algorithms to hash and encrypt client and server digests. However, all the RFCs and all the Digest authentication implementations use the MD5 hashing algorithm — hence the name Digest-MD5. The MD5 hash is calculated for the A1 parameter (see below) and the string for which the digest is calculated is comprised of the username, the realm name, and the plaintext password. Because the hash is calculated for a string value, this makes the username, realm name, and password attributes case sensitive when used for digest authentication. One of the authors of RFC 2831 is Paul Leach of Microsoft, and hence the similarity between Digest-MD5 and Microsoft SSPI when it comes to message integrity and confidentiality (see subsection 4.1.2).

Digest-MD5 authentication requires that clients and server exchange authentication parameters. Some of the most common parameters are given in Table 4.14.

Table 4.14 Digest-MD5 Authentication Parameters (continued)

Parameter Name	*Acceptable values*	*Description*
Realm	String	A string specifying the authentication authority that the server belongs to. The client can use this value to make a decision on what authentication credentials to use.
Username	String	Username used for authentication.
Nonce	String	Server nonce — a unique string generated by the server randomly for every client session. This allows for client authentication.
Cnonce	String	Client nonce — same as server nonce but generated by the client. This allows for server authentication.
Nc	Integer	Nonce count — the number of nonces that the client has generated. This value is increased by one for every subsequent authentication attempt.
Qop	"auth", "auth-int," "auth-conf," <token>	Quality of protection — defines the type of protection the client and server will use for authentication and data protection. "auth" specifies that only authentication will be performed, while "auth-int" and "auth-conf" specify that data integrity authentication and data confidentiality will also be protected.
Cipher-opts	"des," "3des," "rc4-40," "rc4-56," or "rc4-128"	Encryption algorithm to be used. DES, 3DES, and RC4 using a 40-bit, a 56-bit, and 128-bit keys are supported.
Algorithm	"md5"	Specifies the hashing algorithm used by Digest-MD5. This is always "md5" for SASL Digest-MD5 authentication.

Table 4.14 Digest-MD5 Authentication Parameters (continued)

Parameter Name	*Acceptable values*	*Description*
Authzid	String	Authorization ID — this parameter is optional. RFC 2222 defines that this parameter can specify the actual username to be used to access the resource, and it may be different from the username used for authentication. For example, a service account can authenticate against IMAP but request to open a user mailbox specifying the authzid parameter. This requires that the service account has permissions for the user mailbox.

The initial Digest-MD5 algorithm works as follows (see Figure 4.26):

1. The client indicates to the server that it wants to use Digest-MD5 authentication, typically by issuing the AUTHENTICATE DIGEST-MD5 command verb (see Frame 44 in Figure 4.26).
2. The server generates a challenge, containing a realm name (**realm**), a random challenge string (**nonce**), Quality of Protection (typically authentication only — **qop**), character set (**charset**), and algorithm for authentication (**algorithm**) (see Frame 45 in Figure 4.26).
3. The client calculates a response that includes the username of the authenticating user (**username**), the realm name for the realm/domain against which the client wants to authenticate (**realm**), the server nonce (the name it received in the previous step — **nonce**), a client-generated nonce (**cnonce**), the number of nonces generated by the client (**nc**), the quality of protection mechanism(s) that the client agrees to (**qop**), the principal name of the service to which the client is authenticating — this is typically the Internet service name followed by a forward slash, followed by the FQDN or the IP address of the server (**digest-uri**), as well as the client response to the server challenge (**response**) (see Frame 47 in Figure 4.26).
4. The server calculates the server response to the client challenge and sends it back to the client using the server response parameter (**rspauth**) (see Frame 49 in Figure 4.26).

```
Frame 40 (85 bytes on wire, 85 bytes captured)
Ethernet II, Src: 02:00:4c:4f:4f:50 (02:00:4c:4f:4f:50), Dst: Microsof_56:ab:2a
(00:03:ff:56:ab:2a)
Internet Protocol, Src: 10.0.2.101 (10.0.2.101), Dst: 10.0.1.102 (10.0.1.102)
Transmission Control Protocol, Src Port: 55032 (55032), Dst Port: imap (143), Seq: 1761393902,
Ack: 2486381598, Len: 19
Internet Message Access Protocol
    A00000 CAPABILITY\r\n
        Request Tag: A00000
        Request: CAPABILITY

Frame 42 (265 bytes on wire, 265 bytes captured)
Ethernet II, Src: Microsof_56:ab:2a (00:03:ff:56:ab:2a), Dst: 02:00:4c:4f:4f:50
(02:00:4c:4f:4f:50)
Internet Protocol, Src: 10.0.1.102 (10.0.1.102), Dst: 10.0.2.101 (10.0.2.101)
Transmission Control Protocol, Src Port: imap (143), Dst Port: 55032 (55032), Seq: 2486381598,
Ack: 1761393921, Len: 199
Internet Message Access Protocol
    * CAPABILITY IMAP4rev1 SORT THREAD=REFERENCES MULTIAPPEND UNSELECT IDLE CHILDREN LISTEXT
LIST-SUBSCRIBED NAMESPACE STARTTLS AUTH=PLAIN AUTH=CRAM-MD5 AUTH=DIGEST-MD5\r\n
        Response Tag: *
        Response: CAPABILITY IMAP4rev1 SORT THREAD=REFERENCES MULTIAPPEND UNSELECT IDLE CHILDREN
LISTEXT LIST-SUBSCRIBED NAMESPACE STARTTLS AUTH=PLAIN AUTH=CRAM-MD5 AUTH=DIGEST-MD5

Frame 44 (98 bytes on wire, 98 bytes captured)
Ethernet II, Src: 02:00:4c:4f:4f:50 (02:00:4c:4f:4f:50), Dst: Microsof_56:ab:2a
(00:03:ff:56:ab:2a)
Internet Protocol, Src: 10.0.2.101 (10.0.2.101), Dst: 10.0.1.102 (10.0.1.102)
Transmission Control Protocol, Src Port: 55032 (55032), Dst Port: imap (143), Seq: 1761393921,
Ack: 2486381797, Len: 32
Internet Message Access Protocol
    A00001 AUTHENTICATE DIGEST-MD5\r\n
        Request Tag: A00001
        Request: AUTHENTICATE DIGEST-MD5

Frame 45 (190 bytes on wire, 190 bytes captured)
```

Figure 4.26 IMAP client Dennis accessing IMAP server Linus using Digest-MD5 authentication.

```
Ethernet II, Src: Microsof_56:ab:2a (00:03:ff:56:ab:2a), Dst: 02:00:4c:4f:4f:50
(02:00:4c:4f:4f:50)
Internet Protocol, Src: 10.0.1.102 (10.0.1.102), Dst: 10.0.2.101 (10.0.2.101)
Transmission Control Protocol, Src Port: imap (143), Dst Port: 55032 (55032), Seq: 2486381797,
Ack: 1761393953, Len: 124
Internet Message Access Protocol
    +
cmVhbG09IiIsbm9uY2U9ImhaYTV6aXVTMEVRT25mWnZBOEM2MGc9PSIscW9wPSJhdXRoIixjaGFyc2V0PSJ1dGYtOCIsYWxnb
3JpdGhtPSJtZDUtc2VzcyI=\r\n
        Response Tag: +
        Response:
cmVhbG09IiIsbm9uY2U9ImhaYTV6aXVTMEVRT25mWnZBOEM2MGc9PSIscW9wPSJhdXRoIixjaGFyc2V0PSJ1dGYtOCIsYWxnb
3JpdGhtPSJtZDUtc2VzcyI=                                 (Base64)
       Response: realm="",nonce="hZa5ziuS0EQOnfZvA8C60g==",qop="auth",charset="utf-
8",algorithm="md5-sess"                                 (Decoded)

Frame 47 (322 bytes on wire, 322 bytes captured)
Ethernet II, Src: 02:00:4c:4f:4f:50 (02:00:4c:4f:4f:50), Dst: Microsof_56:ab:2a
(00:03:ff:56:ab:2a)
Internet Protocol, Src: 10.0.2.101 (10.0.2.101), Dst: 10.0.1.102 (10.0.1.102)
Transmission Control Protocol, Src Port: 55032 (55032), Dst Port: imap (143), Seq: 1761393953,
Ack: 2486381921, Len: 256
Internet Message Access Protocol
dXNlcm5hbWU9ImhlbW1pbmd3YXkiLHJlYWxtPSIiLG5vbmNlPSJoWmE1eml1UzBFUU9uZlp2QThDNjBnPT0iLGNub25jZT0iN
Ghnb0ZpZEk5RHc9IixuYz0wMDAwMDAwMSxxb3A9YXV0aCxkaWdlc3QtdXJpPSJpbWFwLzEwLjAuMS4xMDIiLHJlc3BvbnNlPT
RhMGRhMTYzY2U1NjcyODdmZmE3NzdiYTJlZmJjOTdlLGN
       Request Tag:
dXNlcm5hbWU9ImhlbW1pbmd3YXkiLHJlYWxtPSIiLG5vbmNlPSJoWmE1eml1UzBFUU9uZlp2QThDNjBnPT0iLGNub25jZT0iN
Ghnb0ZpZEk5RHc9IixuYz0wMDAwMDAwMSxxb3A9YXV0aCxkaWdlc3QtdXJpPSJpbWFwLzEwLjAuMS4xMDIiLHJlc3BvbnNlPT
RhMGRhMTYzY2U1NjcyODdmZmE3NzdiYT       (Base64)
      Request Tag:
username="hemmingway",realm="",nonce="hZa5ziuS0EQOnfZvA8C60g==",cnonce="4hgoFidI9Dw=",nc=00000001
,qop=auth,digest-uri="imap/10.0.1.102",response=4a0da163ce567287ffa777ba (Decoded)

Frame 49 (126 bytes on wire, 126 bytes captured)
```

Figure 4.26 (continued)

```
Ethernet II, Src: Microsof_56:ab:2a (00:03:ff:56:ab:2a), Dst: 02:00:4c:4f:4f:50
(02:00:4c:4f:4f:50)
Internet Protocol, Src: 10.0.1.102 (10.0.1.102), Dst: 10.0.2.101 (10.0.2.101)
Transmission Control Protocol, Src Port: imap (143), Dst Port: 55032 (55032), Seq: 2486381921,
Ack: 1761394211, Len: 60
Internet Message Access Protocol
    + cnNwYXV0aD1kMTAzN2RlYTExMDQ1ZTcyMTYyNzNiZGE2YTI5NGJlYg==\r\n
        Response Tag: +
        Response: cnNwYXV0aD1kMTAzN2RlYTExMDQ1ZTcyMTYyNzNiZGE2YTI5NGJlYg== (Base64)
        Response: rspauth=d1037dea11045e7216273bda6a294beb                    (Decoded)

Frame 52 (88 bytes on wire, 88 bytes captured)
Ethernet II, Src: Microsof_56:ab:2a (00:03:ff:56:ab:2a), Dst: 02:00:4c:4f:4f:50
(02:00:4c:4f:4f:50)
Internet Protocol, Src: 10.0.1.102 (10.0.1.102), Dst: 10.0.2.101 (10.0.2.101)
Transmission Control Protocol, Src Port: imap (143), Dst Port: 55032 (55032), Seq: 2486381981,
Ack: 1761394213, Len: 22
Internet Message Access Protocol
    A00001 OK Logged in.\r\n
        Response Tag: A00001
        Response: OK Logged in.
```

Figure 4.26 (continued)

5. The client calculates the server reply and authenticates the server. If server authentication fails, the client can consider that the server identity has been spoofed and disconnect.
6. The server sends "OK Logged in" or similar message to the client, indicating the successful authentication (see Frame 53 in Figure 4.26).

The client and server calculate their responses (**response** and **rspauth,** respectively) using a relatively complex mechanism that utilizes the MD5 hashing algorithm Other hashing algorithms are acceptable but not widely used. The RFC specifies the following formula for the client response:

```
response-string = hex(
                   MD5(
                       hex(MD5(A1)),
                       ":",
                     {nonce,":",nc,":",cnonce,":",qop,":",hex(MD5(A2))}
                   )
                 )
```

where
hex(n) is the hexadecimal representation (string) of the 16-byte value n

MD5(a, b, c..) is the MD5 hash of the string concatenation of the values a, b, and c
{a, b, c} is the concatenation of the strings a, b, and c
passwd — the plaintext user password, encoded as specified by the **charset** parameter

```
A1 = { MD5( { username, ":", realm, ":", passwd } ),
         ":", nonce, ":", cnonce, ":", authzid}
```

The client and server values for A2 are calculated as follows:

- If quality of protection specifies authentication only (auth), then:
  - For the client response: `A2 = { "AUTHENTICATE:", digest-uri}`
  - For the server response: `A2 = { ":", digest-uri}`
- If quality of protection specifies integrity or confidentiality, then:
  - For the client response: `A2 = { "AUTHENTICATE:", digest-uri, ":00000000000000000000000000000000"}`
  - For the server response: `A2 = { ":", digest-uri, ":00000000000000000000000000000000"}`

If a client has already authenticated successfully to a server, the client can fast-track the authentication process later and try to complete subsequent authentication attempts by calculating a response only, rather than requesting a challenge from the server. When it does so, the client increases the client nonce count (**nc**) and calculates the response using the same values as during initial authentication with only **nc** increased accordingly. The client then stores the **nc** value to use it for subsequent authentication attempts.

The server may or may not support subsequent authentication. If it supports subsequent authentication, the server may decide that the time between the previous authentication attempt and the current subsequent authentication attempt is too long and deny subsequent authentication. Whatever the reason for the server to deny subsequent authentication, the server will suggest initial authentication to the client by identifying the authentication session by setting the **stale** parameter to **true**.

The Digest-MD5 specification goes one step beyond authentication and negotiates integrity and confidentiality for user data that bares resemblance to security interfaces, such as GSS-API/SSPI. Whether integrity or confidentiality will be used is negotiated using the **qop** parameter.

Digest-MD5 Message Integrity (Signing)

If the client and server negotiate to use message integrity, this will allow user data to be protected from malicious modification in transit on the network. The client and server calculate integrity session keys that are different for the client and the server.

The client integrity key is calculated as:

```
Kic = MD5({MD5(A1),
  "Digest session key to client-to-server signing key magic constant"})
```

The server integrity key is calculated as:

```
Kis = MD5({MD5(A1),
  "Digest session key to server-to-client signing key magic constant"}).
```

To maintain message integrity, the client and the server calculate sequence numbers for messages that they send. When the client or server submits a message, it concatenates the sequence number as a string to the message (user data) itself, and calculates the HMAC value for the resultant string using the respective Integrity Session Key as the key. A 16-byte message authentication code is then appended to the message, which consists of the first 10 bytes of the message digest, 2 bytes set to 0x1 used as operation code, and 4 bytes set to the message sequence number.

Upon receipt, both the client and the server calculate the message authentication code for the message. If the calculated MAC does not match the MAC in the received message, the message has been tampered with and the client and server may decide to drop the connection, or the message.

Digest-MD5 Message Confidentiality

If negotiated, message confidentiality is provided by calculating a second set of client and server keys. Similar to SSPI, message confidentiality implies message integrity (signing) as well. Message authentication code is calculated for the plaintext message.

Similar to message integrity keys, the client and server calculate a pair of encryption keys. The client integrity key is calculated as:

```
Kcc = MD5({MD5(A1)[0..n],
  "Digest H(A1) to client-to-server sealing key magic constant"})
```

And the server integrity key is calculated as:

```
Kcs = MD5({MD5(A1)[0..n],
  "Digest H(A1) to server-to-client sealing key magic constant"})
```

where MD5(X)[0..**n**] designates the first **n+1** bytes from the MD5 hash for X.

The value **n** is used to specify the key length for encryption operations. The DES Protocol, as well as 56-bit RC4 encryption algorithms, will use the first 7 bytes of MD5(A1) as the key. 3DES, and 128-bit RC4 will use all 16 bytes. 40-bit RC4 only uses the first 5 bytes. Because the DES and 3DES encryption algorithms utilize an initial vector (IV), the last 8 bytes from the respective key are used by the client or server as the DES IV.

With message confidentiality, once the message has been encrypted, a Message Authentication Code is calculated as specified above and added to the encrypted message.

4.2.3.8 SASL and User Password Databases

To allow for CRAM-MD5 or DIGEST-MD5 authentication in UNIX, most SASL implementations require that a separate file be created to store plaintext user passwords. This is required because both CRAM-MD5 and DIGEST-MD5 require access to the plaintext user password, and by default UNIX stores only one-way passwords in the **/etc/passwd** file.

Different implementations use different configuration settings. The Dovecot IMAP/POP3 server, for example, utilizes a plaintext password file, typically called **/etc/cram-md5.pwd**. This file is required to only provide the first two fields — username and plaintext password — to be used by the CRAM-MD5 mechanism. More information on plaintext password files for SASL is provided in Chapter 2.

On Windows platforms, Active Directory provides for reversibly encrypted passwords. Again, this may pose a significant security risk in some environments. CRAM-MD5 and Digest-MD5 authentication mechanisms require that both the client and the server possess the plaintext password for the authenticating user to be able to calculate the MD5 hash. The client typically acquires this password from the interactive user in an authentication dialogue and does not need to store the password at all. In Windows 2000 and later, the server may not be a domain controller, so the reversibly encrypted password may not be locally available; however, due to the decoupled nature of the **LSALogonUser( )** call, the server can perform actual authentication remotely, on a domain controller using Remote Procedure Calls (RPCs). Therefore, despite the fact that the user account and the reversibly encrypted password are stored on a domain controller, an RPC makes the authentication process virtually local to the server. As a result of the **LSALogonUser( )** function, the server also receives a Digest-MD5 session key that it can later use for user reauthentication.

Windows 2003 introduces a new approach. Instead of storing the plaintext or reversibly encrypted user password, Active Directory in Windows 2003 can store a list of precomputed Digest-MD5 hashes in the directory. Basically, every time the user changes his password, Active Directory precomputes a list of Digest-MD5 hashes along with the standard NTLM and LanManager hashes from the plaintext password. Although this may seem a huge leap forward in terms of making Digest-MD5 authentication more secure, this is only partially true. It is generally good that the user password is not stored in plaintext, because this does not readily expose it to attackers — however, it may still be susceptible to dictionary and brute force attacks. The MD5({username, ":", realm, ":", passwd }) digest can be considered equivalent to the user password in terms of sensitivity because anyone who can obtain this digest from Active Directory can utilize it from a client application to calculate Digest-MD5 client responses and authenticate successfully to a server that supports Digest-MD5. Hence, storing precalculated MD5 hashes protects the password itself but does not make the Digest-MD5 authentication mechanism more secure. More information on the Digest MD5 hashes stored by Active Directory is available later in this chapter.

4.3 Transport Layer Security (TLS) and Secure Sockets Layer (SSL)

Transport Layer Security (TLS) is defined in RFC 2246 (see [86]). TLS provides for data confidentiality (encryption), data integrity (data authentication), and compression of application data at the session and presentation layers. TLS works as a security interface between the transport and application layers to provide these services. The client and the server can negotiate protection and compression mechanisms, as well as session keys, independent of the application. TLS may be suitable for applications that are not SSL-aware and may use wrappers for these applications. TLS is a stateful protocol — the client and the server maintain a state for the current connection, both at the transport layer and at the presentation layer where TLS-specific protection information is stored.

TLS is based on the Netscape Secure Sockets Layer (SSL) v.3.0 standard. However, TLS and SSL, although very similar to each other, are not fully compatible. One of the differences between the two protocols relates to the use of dedicated secure channels. SSL implementations typically suggest that applications utilize one TCP port for plaintext traffic and a different port for SSL protected traffic. For example, HTTP utilizes TCP/80, while HTTP-over-SSL (HTTPS) utilizes TCP/443. Both unprotected and SSL protected ports are well known. The port to which a client connects suggests whether or not SSL will be used to protect traffic.

TLS, on the other hand, suggests that only one port should be used for both unprotected and TLS protected communication for a single application. Within the unprotected session, the client and server that support TLS can upgrade to TLS protection using a command verb (such as **STARTTLS**) in interactive protocols (SMTP, IMAP, POP3), or use protocol-specific structures to request the upgrade (RFC 2817 specifies how an upgrade to TLS can be requested using HTTP headers).

Although RFC 2246 does not pose such requirements, in almost all cases the server and potentially the client use X.509 certificates to authenticate each other and negotiate secure channel protection. Alternatively, the server can choose to remain anonymous; in this case, the client and the server typically negotiate dynamic asymmetric keys using the Diffie-Hellman Protocol.

TLS/SSL are important for user authentication in at least two aspects:

1. SSL/TLS can be used to protect the data channel between the client and the server. Hence, if the client and server utilize plaintext authentication mechanisms, such as HTTP Basic authentication, LDAP Simple authentication, or POP3/SMTP Plain authentication, the SSL/TLS layer will be able to protect the actual authentication process within the encrypted and authentication SSL channel. Adding an SSL level of protection to existing application-level protocols and services is considerably easier than rewriting applications and replacing old ones that use the old authentication protocol.
2. The use of X.509 certificates allows for peer authentication and can result in mutual authentication. Typically, the server possesses a certificate and the client does not. In this case, only the server will be authenticated. However, if the server requests a client certificate and the client provides it, the server can then map this certificate to a user account and potentially impersonate the certificate owner on the SSL/TLS server.

The TLS Protocol consists of two main layers: (1) handshake layer and (2) record layer (see Figure 4.27). The handshake layer is used to collect information for the server and the client, and then generate session keys for data protection; this information can later be used for server and user identification, and authentication. In fact, the handshake layer is comprised of three sublayers: (1) the actual handshake protocol, (2) the alert protocol used to convey status information between the client and the server, and (3) the Change Cipher Spec protocol used to confirm protection parameters. The record layer is responsible for actual message protection using the parameters negotiated by the handshake layer, and is used by upper layers (the applications and services) to send and receive information.

According to RFC 2246, the client and the server can negotiate protection by going through four handshake phases (Figure 4.28):

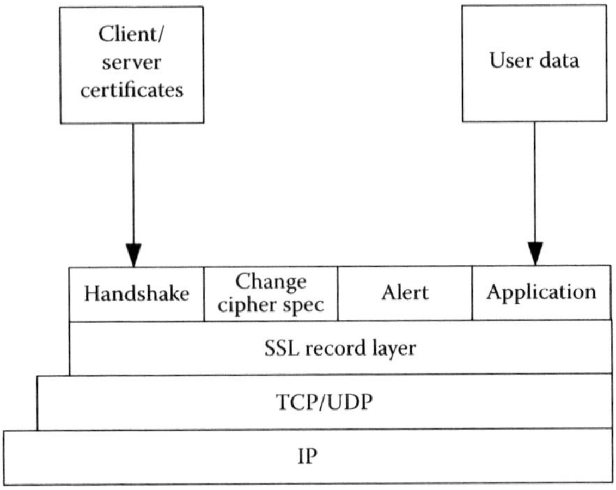

Figure 4.27 SSL protocol stack.

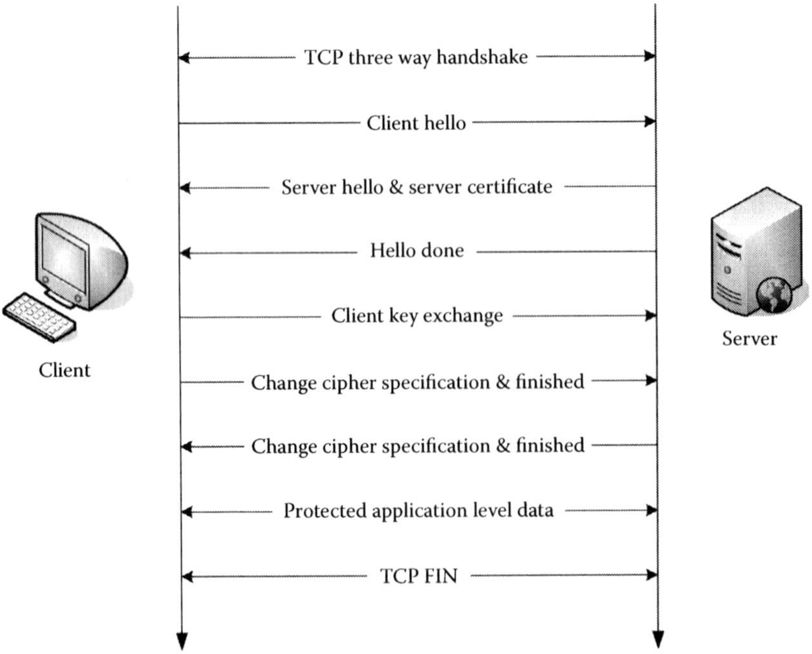

Figure 4.28 Mechanics of generic SSL channel protection.

1. Hello phase
2. Server Authentication phase
3. Client Authentication phase
4. Negotiate Start of Protection phase

The following subsections discuss the phases of the TLS/SSL Protocol.

4.3.1 Hello Phase

The Hello phase is used by the client and the server to negotiate the protocol version, protection and compression capabilities, and random key material. The server defines a session ID at this stage that will be later used by the client and the server to refer to the security agreement between them. The Client Hello and the Server Hello messages are used to exchange information between the client and the server at this stage (Table 4.15).

The Unix Time field and the Random field are referred to as **client_random** and **server_random** for the client and the server in messages from the client and the server, respectively.

Table 4.15 SSL Hello Message Format

Parameter Name	*Size*	*Description*
Version	2 bytes	Contains the highest SSL/TLS Protocol version, supported by the client or server (i.e., 2.0, 3.0, or 3.1 (TLS 1.0))
UnixTime	4 bytes	The current time in UNIX time format
Random	28 bytes	28 random bytes used for key generation
SessionID	Variable	May or may not be present in the client request; the server specifies a unique ID for the session
Cipher Suites	Variable	An ordered list of data protection methods (Public Key Algorithm, Encryption Algorithm, Digest Algorithm) that the client suggests for data protection
Compression Methods	Variable	Specifies whether or not the client and server support data compression

The client is the first to send a Hello message to the server. The server replies with a Hello message that has a similar structure. The server Hello message provides a unique session ID and selects the cipher suite and compression algorithm from those suggested by the client. Apparently, the server will choose a cipher suite and a compression algorithm that are supported and preferred by the server.

4.3.2 Server Authentication Phase

The Server Authentication phase is used to establish the actual protection keys that will be used by the client and the server. This phase includes messages such as Server Certificate, Server Key Exchange (optional), Certificate Request, and Server Hello Done.

A server that has an X.509 certificate typically authenticates to the client by providing this certificate in a Server Certificate message to the client, potentially including other certificates (those in the certificate chain). X.509-compatible certificates contain the server public key among other attributes. If the server does not possess an X.509 certificate (which is uncommon), or the server has a signature-only (no encryption) certificate, the server can suggest that an asymmetric keypair be generated for the session using either Diffie-Hellman or the Fortezza algorithm. The server can use a Server Key Exchange message to suggest that a keypair be generated rather than provided using the Server Certificate message.

If the server possesses a certificate, it can request that the client authenticates using a client certificate. This is accomplished using a Certificate Request message, in which the server specifies the acceptable certificate types that the client can provide, as well as a list of acceptable certificate authorities that must have signed the provided certificates. The latter allows the client to use the appropriate certificate even if it has more than one certificate.

As a final step, the server typically sends a Server Hello Done message, indicating that it has finished submitting identification and authentication information.

The client typically performs the following checks to authenticate the server before continuing with the handshake process:

- Is the server name the same as the one in the certificate that is provided? The DNS name the client is trying to connect to is compared against the common name in the Subject field of the server certificate.
- Is the server certificate valid? Does it have a valid signature, and is it within its validity period?

- Is the server certificate trusted? — checks whether the certificate has been signed by a trusted and valid certificate authority.
- Has the server certificate been revoked? Is the server certificate on the Certificate Revocation List (CRL) of the certificate authority that issued it? To check this, the client may need to download the current CRL for the server's CA.

4.3.3 Client Authentication Phase

The Client Authentication phase is used to provide the server with client identification and authentication information. The client typically replies with a Client Key Exchange message where it generates a pre-master secret between 48 and 128 bits in size, encrypts it using the encryption protocol chosen by the server at the Hello Phase, and the server public key or temporary public key received during the server authentication phase as the key. Upon receipt of the Client Key Exchange message, the server is expected to decrypt the pre-master secret using its private key; this way, the client authenticates the server, as the latter can only obtain the pre-master secret if it has a private key that corresponds to the public key in the certificate.

If the server requests that the client authenticates using certificates, the client will include two more messages in this phase. First, the client includes the Client Certificate message and provides a valid certificate for the authenticating user. Next, the client generates a Certificate Verify message signed with the client private key. For RSA keys, the signature is performed using both MD5-HMAC and SHA-1-HMAC algorithms on the contents of all the handshake messages exchanged to this point using the client private key as the key. For DSS keys, only a SHA-1-HMAC signature is submitted. This message is used as proof that the client possesses the private key for the public key it has provided. The server will check the client signature using the provided public key.

The server typically performs the following checks to authenticate the server before continuing with the handshake process:

- Is the client certificate valid? — Does it have a valid signature, and is it within its validity period?
- Is the client certificate trusted? — checks whether the certificate has been signed by a trusted and valid certificate authority.
- Has the client certificate been revoked? Is the client certificate on the Certificate Revocation List (CRL) of the certificate authority that issued it? To check this, the server may need to download the current CRL for the client's CA.

4.3.3.1 Calculate the Master Secret

The client and the server need to calculate protection keys for the TLS/SSL channel between them. To do so, they first need to calculate a Master Secret for the TLS/SSL session.

The client and server calculate the master secret using a pseudo-random generator key expansion function:

master_secret = PRF(**pre_master, "master secret", client_random, and server_random)**

It is important to note that the master secret depends on random data — such as the client-generated pre-master, and the **client_random** and the **server_random** from the Client Hello and Server Hello messages, respectively. The master secret does not depend on the client or server certificates, which are only used for client and server identity.

The PRF function is used for key expansion. It generates a master key of the negotiated key length:

PRF(secret, label, seed) = P_MD5(**S1, label+seed**) XOR P_SHA-1(**S2, label+seed**)

where S1 and S2 contain the left half and the right half of the **secret** parameter, respectively. If the number of characters is odd, each contains the middle character as well.

S1 = LEFT(**secret**, LEN(**secret**)/2 + mod(LEN(**secret**)/2))

S2 = RIGHT(**secret**, LEN(**secret**)/2 + mod(LEN(**secret**)/2))

The following key expansion functions are repeated **n** times to generate a key of the required length. The MD5 HMAC algorithm generates a hash of length 16 bytes and the SHA-1 HMAC generates a hash of length 20 bytes, so these two functions will be used independently to generate the number of bytes required by the master key.

P_MD5(secret, seed) = B(1) & B(2) & B(3) & … & B(n)

where

B(i>0) = MD5(**secret**, B(i) & B(i–1))
B(0) = **seed**

P_SHA-1(secret, seed) = C(1) & C(2) & C(3) & … & C(n)

where

C(i>0) = SHA-1(**secret**, C(i) & C(i–1))
C(0) = **seed**

4.3.3.2 Calculate Protection Keys

The master secret is not used to encrypt or sign data. A set of keys is generated from the master key that is used by the client and the server.

key_block[i] = PRF(**master_secret, "key expansion", server_random,** and **client_random)**

The above calculation will be repeated as many times as required to generate enough pseudorandom data and feed it into the **key_block** structure. This structure will then be used to allocate contiguous blocks of bytes for the following keys in this order:

- Client MAC Key (**client_mac_key**): used by the client to authenticate data integrity for user data.
- Server MAC Key (**server_mac_key**): used by the server to authenticate data integrity for user data.
- Client Write Key (**client_write_key**): used by the client to encrypt communication.
- Server Write Key (**server_write_key**): used by the server to encrypt communication.
- Client Write IV (**client_write_iv**): used by the client as an IV to the selected encryption algorithm. For algorithms subject to export regulations, see below.
- Server Write IV (**server_write_iv**): used by the server as an IV to the selected encryption algorithm. For algorithms subject to export regulations, see below.

Keys used by algorithms that are subject to U.S. export restrictions undergo additional steps. As export restrictions only regulate data encryption, and not data signing, only the encryption keys are modified.

final_client_write_key = PRF(**client_write_key, "client write key", client_random** and **server_random**)

final_server_write_key = PRF(**server_write_key, "server write key", client_random** and **server_random)**

The IV for algorithms subject to export regulations is shown below:

iv_block = PRF(**"", "IV block", client_random,** and **server_random**)

The **iv_block** is then split into two IV values — **client_write_iv** and **server_write_iv** — for the client and the server side.

4.3.4 Negotiate Start of Protection Phase

Once the server and potentially the client have been authenticated, the client indicates the start of secure communication by sending the Change Cipher Spec and Finished messages. All further messages from the client will be protected. The server replies with the same two messages and all the communication continues using the negotiated protection mechanisms and keys. The Change Cipher Spec message is only an indication to start using the newly negotiated parameters. The Finished message contains a cryptographic hash of the negotiated parameters.

4.3.5 Resuming TLS/SSL Sessions

Even when a session terminates, the client and the server can keep the session ID and session security parameters in their session cache for later use. If later on the client wants to establish a session to the same server using the same parameters, the client can send a Hello message using the previously obtained session ID. If the server still has the session ID in its cache and is willing to resume the session, it replies with a Hello message that includes the same session ID. Both the client and the server then send a Change Cipher Spec message and immediately switch to protected communication.

4.3.6 Using SSL/TLS to Protect Generic User Traffic

Due to the fact that the TLS/SSL protection layer can exist at the session layer of the OSI model between the TCP transport and the application, TLS/SSL can be used to protect any application traffic, including user authentication and user data. The client application may or may not be aware of the TLS/SSL encapsulation, depending on the implementation and the configuration. In this respect, TLS/SSL is often used to protect HTTP Basic authentication, LDAP Simple authentication, and POP3/IMAP authentication, as well as actual user traffic for the above protocols. When SSL/TLS is used for generic session layer protection, it does not provide for actual user identification and authentication, and it is unaware of the messages that are being passed between the applications; it simply applies the encryption and integrity authentication and compression rules negotiated as part of the security association and forwards the messages to other layers accordingly.

A typical SSL handshake that involves client authentication is shown in Figure 4.29.

1. The SSL client sends a Hello message to the SSL server and provides a list of cipher suites that it wants to use (see Frame 4 in Figure 4.29);
2. The SSL server selects to use RSA asymmetric keys, RC4 128-bit encryption, and MD5 message authentication (see Frame 5 in Figure 4.29). In addition to that, the server provides its certificate.
3. The client generates a pre-master secret and encrypts it. It then submits it in a Client Key Exchange message (see Frame 6 in Figure 4.29).
4. The client sends Change Cipher Spec and Finished messages. These indicate effective protection of the channel (see Frame 6 in Figure 4.29).
5. The server replies with Change Cipher Spec and Finished messages.

All packets from that point on are protected and contain protected user data, which may or may not include application-specific user authentication information.

4.3.7 Using SSL/TLS Certificate Mapping as an Authentication Method

In most cases, the server has a certificate (with a public key in it) and presents it to the client. The client authenticates the server by generating the premaster secret and encrypting it with the server public key so that only the server can decrypt it with its private key. Certificate mapping is possible when the client has a certificate and the server requests this certificate from the client. In this case, the client provides a hash of all the messages between the client and the server up to the last one, and generates a keyed hash of these messages using a hashing algorithm (such as MD5 or SHA-1) and the master key as the key. This proves that the client has provided a public key and has a corresponding public key.

Once the server knows that the client owns a private key for a public key (provided by the client as well), the server can now perform a lookup using this public key against a directory to determine the identity of the user. Once the identity has been determined, the server can identify or impersonate the client (see Figure 4.30). A typical SSL handshake that involves client authentication is shown in Figure 4.31.

```
Frame 4 (124 bytes on wire, 124 bytes captured)
Ethernet II, Src: Microsof_50:ab:2a (00:03:ff:50:ab:2a), Dst: 02:00:4c:4f:4f:50
(02:00:4c:4f:4f:50)
Internet Protocol, Src: 10.0.2.102 (10.0.2.102), Dst: 10.0.1.101 (10.0.1.101)
Transmission Control Protocol, Src Port: 2859 (2859), Dst Port: https (443), Seq: 23919220, Ack:
2745640261, Len: 70
Secure Socket Layer
    TLS Record Layer: Handshake Protocol: Client Hello
        Content Type: Handshake (22)
        Version: TLS 1.0 (0x0301)
        Length: 65
        Handshake Protocol: Client Hello
            Handshake Type: Client Hello (1)
            Length: 61
            Version: TLS 1.0 (0x0301)
            Random.gmt_unix_time: Mar 14, 2006 05:18:37.000000000
            Random.bytes
            Session ID Length: 0
            Cipher Suites Length: 22
            Cipher Suites (11 suites)
                Cipher Suite: TLS_RSA_WITH_RC4_128_MD5 (0x0004)
                Cipher Suite: TLS_RSA_WITH_RC4_128_SHA (0x0005)
                Cipher Suite: TLS_RSA_WITH_3DES_EDE_CBC_SHA (0x000a)
                Cipher Suite: TLS_RSA_WITH_DES_CBC_SHA (0x0009)
                Cipher Suite: TLS_RSA_EXPORT1024_WITH_RC4_56_SHA (0x0064)
                Cipher Suite: TLS_RSA_EXPORT1024_WITH_DES_CBC_SHA (0x0062)
                Cipher Suite: TLS_RSA_EXPORT_WITH_RC4_40_MD5 (0x0003)
                Cipher Suite: TLS_RSA_EXPORT_WITH_RC2_CBC_40_MD5 (0x0006)
                Cipher Suite: TLS_DHE_DSS_WITH_3DES_EDE_CBC_SHA (0x0013)
                Cipher Suite: TLS_DHE_DSS_WITH_DES_CBC_SHA (0x0012)
                Cipher Suite: TLS_DHE_DSS_EXPORT1024_WITH_DES_CBC_SHA (0x0063)
            Compression Methods Length: 1
            Compression Methods (1 method)
                Compression Method: null (0)

Frame 5 (1478 bytes on wire, 1478 bytes captured)
```

Figure 4.29 HTTP-SSL.cap: Client access to server without client authentication.

```
Ethernet II, Src: 02:00:4c:4f:4f:50 (02:00:4c:4f:4f:50), Dst: Microsof_50:ab:2a
(00:03:ff:50:ab:2a)
Internet Protocol, Src: 10.0.1.101 (10.0.1.101), Dst: 10.0.2.102 (10.0.2.102)
Transmission Control Protocol, Src Port: https (443), Dst Port: 2859 (2859), Seq: 2745640261,
Ack: 23919290, Len: 1424
Secure Socket Layer
    TLS Record Layer: Handshake Protocol: Multiple Handshake Messages
        Content Type: Handshake (22)
        Version: TLS 1.0 (0x0301)
        Length: 1419
        Handshake Protocol: Server Hello
            Handshake Type: Server Hello (2)
            Length: 70
            Version: TLS 1.0 (0x0301)
            Random.gmt_unix_time: Mar 11, 2006 09:15:11.000000000
            Random.bytes
            Session ID Length: 32
            Session ID (32 bytes)
            Cipher Suite: TLS_RSA_WITH_RC4_128_MD5 (0x0004)
            Compression Method: null (0)
        Handshake Protocol: Certificate
            Handshake Type: Certificate (11)
            Length: 1337
            Certificates Length: 1334
            Certificates (1334 bytes)
                Certificate Length: 1331
        Handshake Protocol: Server Hello Done
            Handshake Type: Server Hello Done (14)
            Length: 0

Frame 6 (236 bytes on wire, 236 bytes captured)
Ethernet II, Src: Microsof_50:ab:2a (00:03:ff:50:ab:2a), Dst: 02:00:4c:4f:4f:50
(02:00:4c:4f:4f:50)
Internet Protocol, Src: 10.0.2.102 (10.0.2.102), Dst: 10.0.1.101 (10.0.1.101)
Transmission Control Protocol, Src Port: 2859 (2859), Dst Port: https (443), Seq: 23919290, Ack:
2745641685, Len: 182
```

Figure 4.29 (continued)

```
Secure Socket Layer
    TLS Record Layer: Handshake Protocol: Client Key Exchange
        Content Type: Handshake (22)
        Version: TLS 1.0 (0x0301)
        Length: 134
        Handshake Protocol: Client Key Exchange
            Handshake Type: Client Key Exchange (16)
            Length: 130
    TLS Record Layer: Change Cipher Spec Protocol: Change Cipher Spec
        Content Type: Change Cipher Spec (20)
        Version: TLS 1.0 (0x0301)
        Length: 1
        Change Cipher Spec Message
    TLS Record Layer: Handshake Protocol: Encrypted Handshake Message
        Content Type: Handshake (22)
        Version: TLS 1.0 (0x0301)
        Length: 32
        Handshake Protocol: Encrypted Handshake Message

Frame 7 (97 bytes on wire, 97 bytes captured)
Ethernet II, Src: 02:00:4c:4f:4f:50 (02:00:4c:4f:4f:50), Dst: Microsof_50:ab:2a
(00:03:ff:50:ab:2a)
Internet Protocol, Src: 10.0.1.101 (10.0.1.101), Dst: 10.0.2.102 (10.0.2.102)
Transmission Control Protocol, Src Port: https (443), Dst Port: 2859 (2859), Seq: 2745641685,
Ack: 23919472, Len: 43
Secure Socket Layer
    TLS Record Layer: Change Cipher Spec Protocol: Change Cipher Spec
        Content Type: Change Cipher Spec (20)
        Version: TLS 1.0 (0x0301)
        Length: 1
        Change Cipher Spec Message
    TLS Record Layer: Handshake Protocol: Encrypted Handshake Message
        Content Type: Handshake (22)
        Version: TLS 1.0 (0x0301)
        Length: 32
        Handshake Protocol: Encrypted Handshake Message
```

Figure 4.29 (continued)

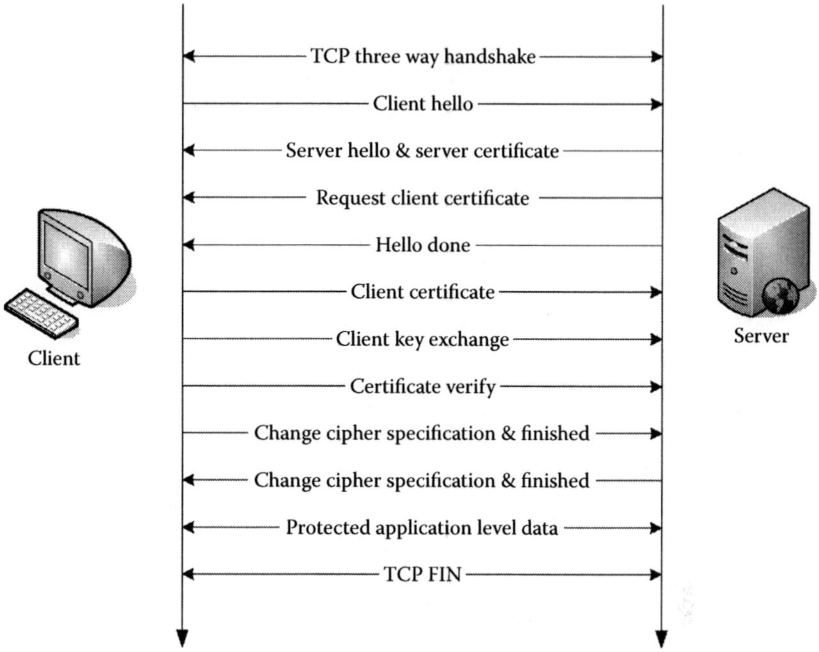

Figure 4.30 SSL communication for channel protection and client authentication.

1. The SSL client sends a Hello message to the SSL server and provides a list of cipher suites that it wants to use (see Frame 4 in Figure 4.31).
2. The SSL server opts to use RSA asymmetric keys, RC4 128-bit encryption, and MD5 message authentication (see Frame 6 in Figure 4.31). In addition, the server provides its certificate and requests that the client do the same.
3. The client generates a pre-master secret and encrypts it. It then submits it in a Client Key Exchange message (see Frame 7 in Figure 4.31).
4. The client provides its certificate, and a Certificate Verify message to confirm the possession of a private key corresponding to the submitted certificate (see Frame 7 in Figure 4.31).
5. Upon receiving the client certificate, the server checks the validity of the signature by decrypting it with the client public key. It then searches for the client certificate in a directory or a flat mapping file and identifies who the user is.
6. The client sends Change Cipher Spec and Finished messages. These indicate effective protection of the channel (see Frame 10 in Figure 4.31).

```
Frame 4 (124 bytes on wire, 124 bytes captured)
Ethernet II, Src: 02:00:4c:4f:4f:50, Dst: 00:03:ff:51:ab:2a
Internet Protocol, Src Addr: 10.0.1.101 (10.0.1.101), Dst Addr: 10.0.2.101 (10.0.2.101)
Transmission Control Protocol, Src Port: 2968 (2968), Dst Port: https (443), Seq: 1, Ack: 1, Len:
70
Secure Socket Layer
    SSLv3 Record Layer: Handshake Protocol: Client Hello
        Content Type: Handshake (22)
        Version: SSL 3.0 (0x0300)
        Length: 65
        Handshake Protocol: Client Hello
            Handshake Type: Client Hello (1)
            Length: 61
            Version: SSL 3.0 (0x0300)
            Random.gmt_unix_time: Mar 11, 2006 11:43:38.000000000
            Random.bytes
            Session ID Length: 0
            Cipher Suites Length: 22
            Cipher Suites (11 suites)
                Cipher Suite: TLS_RSA_WITH_RC4_128_MD5 (0x0004)
                Cipher Suite: TLS_RSA_WITH_RC4_128_SHA (0x0005)
                Cipher Suite: TLS_RSA_WITH_3DES_EDE_CBC_SHA (0x000a)
                Cipher Suite: TLS_RSA_WITH_DES_CBC_SHA (0x0009)
                Cipher Suite: TLS_RSA_EXPORT1024_WITH_RC4_56_SHA (0x0064)
                Cipher Suite: TLS_RSA_EXPORT1024_WITH_DES_CBC_SHA (0x0062)
                Cipher Suite: TLS_RSA_EXPORT_WITH_RC4_40_MD5 (0x0003)
                Cipher Suite: TLS_RSA_EXPORT_WITH_RC2_CBC_40_MD5 (0x0006)
                Cipher Suite: TLS_DHE_DSS_WITH_3DES_EDE_CBC_SHA (0x0013)
                Cipher Suite: TLS_DHE_DSS_WITH_DES_CBC_SHA (0x0012)
                Cipher Suite: TLS_DHE_DSS_EXPORT1024_WITH_DES_CBC_SHA (0x0063)
            Compression Methods Length: 1
            Compression Methods (1 method)
                Compression Method: null (0)

Frame 6 (1485 bytes on wire, 1485 bytes captured)
Ethernet II, Src: 00:03:ff:51:ab:2a, Dst: 02:00:4c:4f:4f:50
```

Figure 4.31 HTTPS-ClientAuthentication.cap: User is authenticated using a client certificate.

```
Internet Protocol, Src Addr: 10.0.2.101 (10.0.2.101), Dst Addr: 10.0.1.101 (10.0.1.101)
Transmission Control Protocol, Src Port: https (443), Dst Port: 2968 (2968), Seq: 1, Ack: 71,
Len: 1431
Secure Socket Layer
    SSLv3 Record Layer: Handshake Protocol: Server Hello
        Content Type: Handshake (22)
        Version: SSL 3.0 (0x0300)
        Length: 74
        Handshake Protocol: Server Hello
            Handshake Type: Server Hello (2)
            Length: 70
            Version: SSL 3.0 (0x0300)
            Random.gmt_unix_time: Mar 11, 2006 11:46:22.000000000
            Random.bytes
            Session ID Length: 32
            Session ID (32 bytes)
            Cipher Suite: TLS_RSA_WITH_RC4_128_MD5 (0x0004)
            Compression Method: null (0)
    SSLv3 Record Layer: Handshake Protocol: Certificate
        Content Type: Handshake (22)
        Version: SSL 3.0 (0x0300)
        Length: 1329
        Handshake Protocol: Certificate
            Handshake Type: Certificate (11)
            Length: 1325
            Certificates Length: 1322
            Certificates (1322 bytes)
                Certificate Length: 1319
    SSLv3 Record Layer: Handshake Protocol: Multiple Handshake Messages
        Content Type: Handshake (22)
        Version: SSL 3.0 (0x0300)
        Length: 13
        Handshake Protocol: Certificate Request
            Handshake Type: Certificate Request (13)
            Length: 5
            Certificate types count: 2
```

Figure 4.31 (continued)

```
        Certificate types (2 types)
            Certificate type: RSA Sign (1)
            Certificate type: DSS Sign (2)
        Distinguished Names Length: 0
    Handshake Protocol: Server Hello Done
        Handshake Type: Server Hello Done (14)
        Length: 0

Frame 7 (1514 bytes on wire, 1514 bytes captured)
Ethernet II, Src: 02:00:4c:4f:4f:50, Dst: 00:03:ff:51:ab:2a
Internet Protocol, Src Addr: 10.0.1.101 (10.0.1.101), Dst Addr: 10.0.2.101 (10.0.2.101)
Transmission Control Protocol, Src Port: 2968 (2968), Dst Port: https (443), Seq: 71, Ack: 1432,
Len: 1460
Secure Socket Layer [Unreassembled Packet: SSL]
    SSLv3 Record Layer: Handshake Protocol: Client Certificate
        Content Type: Handshake (22)
        Version: SSL 3.0 (0x0300)
        Length: 1368
        Handshake Protocol: Client Certificate (11)
        Certificates:
    SSLv3 Record Layer: Handshake Protocol: Client Key Exchange
        Content Type: Handshake (22)
        Version: SSL 3.0 (0x0300)
        Length: 128
        Handshake Protocol: Client Key Exchange (16)
    SSLv3 Record Layer: Handshake Protocol: Certificate Verify
        Content Type: Handshake (22)
        Version: SSL 3.0 (0x0300)
        Length: 1329
        Handshake Protocol: Certificate Verify

Frame 10 (121 bytes on wire, 121 bytes captured)
Ethernet II, Src: 00:03:ff:51:ab:2a, Dst: 02:00:4c:4f:4f:50
Internet Protocol, Src Addr: 10.0.2.101 (10.0.2.101), Dst Addr: 10.0.1.101 (10.0.1.101)
Transmission Control Protocol, Src Port: https (443), Dst Port: 2968 (2968), Seq: 1432, Ack:
1781, Len: 67
```

Figure 4.31 (continued)

7. The server impersonates the user, so the server process will typically assume the privileges of the authenticated user and access resources on the user's behalf.

```
Secure Socket Layer
    SSLv3 Record Layer: Change Cipher Spec Protocol: Change Cipher Spec
        Content Type: Change Cipher Spec (20)
        Version: SSL 3.0 (0x0300)
        Length: 1
        Change Cipher Spec Message
    SSLv3 Record Layer: Handshake Protocol: Encrypted Handshake Message
        Content Type: Handshake (22)
        Version: SSL 3.0 (0x0300)
        Length: 56
        Handshake Protocol: Encrypted Handshake Message
```

Figure 4.31 (continued)

All packets from that point on are protected and contain user data. The user has been authenticated by TLS/SSL and there is no need for application-level authentication and impersonation.

As discussed, once the client has been authenticated, the server can identify or impersonate the client. This is typically done using certificate mapping. There are different approaches to TLS/SSL certificate mapping. Microsoft Schannel, for example, supports the following mapping mechanisms:

- *Identify and Impersonate the user using an Active Directory mapping.* In this case, the server performs a lookup for the client public key against Active Directory. If a user object with a matching public key attribute is found in Active Directory, the server impersonates the user. The model of trust here is the following: if the client has provided a public key and has proved to have a corresponding private key, and if then an administrator has published (mapped) the public key in Active Directory, Schannel can then impersonate the user.
- *IIS one-to-one and many-to-one mappings.* An administrator can provide mapping between users and public keys for the local service (such as IIS). The administrator can provide a list of public keys and the associated user for each public key; the password for the user must be provided as well. When the user authenticates, the server can perform a lookup against the local flat list of certificates and mapped users. Once the correct mapping is found, the server will impersonate the user using the provided username and plaintext password. The difference between one-to-one and many-to-one mappings is that the former uses a separate public

key for each user, while the latter allows the administrator to designate a group of certificates issued by a single CA to be mapped to a single user account (may be convenient when authenticating partners and all the users from the partner organization need the same access in the local organization). It is important to note that in the case of IIS certificate mapping, because the mapping authority is not the NT Directory Service (Active Directory), the user cannot be impersonated by only providing his public key. IIS uses the provided username and password and performs a password logon locally to impersonate the user.

- *S4U mapping*. With this approach, upon successful SSL/TLS session establishment, the server can perform an S4U Kerberos logon against Active Directory. Provided that a certificate mapping is available for the user, the server can impersonate the user and obtain relevant Kerberos tickets on behalf of the user. This is essentially an authentication protocol transition technology, wherein although the client does not use Kerberos authentication to access the server, the Kerberos tickets are eventually issued to the server. The problem with this approach is that the server can now access resources on behalf of the user, which may include the specific resources for which the client authentication request was raised, as well as other resources to which access was not intended. Therefore, S4U may need to be used with constrained delegation settings (see subsection 4.2.2.14).
- *UPN mapping*. Schannel can pick up the user principal name (UPN) from the client certificate and then perform a lookup against Active Directory for users with that same UPN. Schannel can then impersonate the user. This requires that Active Directory administrators add the issuing certificate authority in the Active Directory NTAuth Certificate Store where Enterprise CA Certificates are stored.

Apache provides for similar Certificate Mapping capabilities. Either plaintext files or LDAP can be used to find a user in the directory that has the public key provided by the client during the negotiation process.

4.4 Telnet Authentication

The Telnet Protocol and associated application were created as part of the TCP/IP protocol suite in the early days of the ARPA project (see RFC 137). In the very beginning, Telnet was just a simple way to connect to a host over the network. The Telnet application used to implement a thin layer on top of the TCP/IP protocol suite, wherein it would only send to the server whatever the user typed on the client computer, and then would transfer the server reply, byte by byte (character by character), to the client computer, where information was finally visualized. Technically speaking, the Telnet application provides a terminal emulation environment where the administrators and users connect to the host or device over the network instead of a serial link.

As for most TCP/IP tools, the Telnet application is simple and efficient. However, the Telnet Protocol and application suffer from serious security weaknesses. User authentication using conventional Telnet access is performed using a standard Login dialogue, wherein the server prompts the user for a username and password, and the user provides both in plaintext. The entire communication over the network is a stream of characters in each direction, which can easily be captured, interfered with, etc. Furthermore, in the early Telnet implementations, the entire Telnet session was neither encrypted nor was its integrity being authenticated.

Later on, the Telnet Protocol went through a number of functional changes, and Telnet options were added to the protocol that allow the client and the server to negotiate their behavior in various aspects using in-band special characters that, unlike other characters, are not displayed on the client screen. With the addition of new options, it was realized that user authentication can be added as an option as well and can be protected within an in-band client/server authentication protocol that does not expose the cleartext usernames and passwords. RFC 1409, RFC 1416, and then RFC 2942 (see [72]) defined the Telnet authentication option that can be used for this purpose. Furthermore, under some circumstances, the authentication option allows the client and the server to perform client authentication transparently for the user, without going through the login dialogue and requesting the user to type in his username and password.

For the majority of operating systems and devices, Telnet — where it exists — is becoming obsolete in favor of either SSH or HTTP/HTTS. SSH virtually supports all existing Telnet functionality over protected channels so that many of the shortcomings of the Telnet Protocol from a security perspective are efficiently addressed. HTTP access replaces Telnet more from the perspective of providing users with a graphical user interface to the host or device, and HTTPS adds a layer of protection similar to SSH.

4.4.1 Telnet Login Authentication

The conventional Telnet login authentication method is based on a simple interactive character-based dialogue between the Telnet server and the Telnet client. This mechanism is supported by virtually all Telnet servers and clients.

Telnet login authentication works as follows — see Figure 4.32:

```
Frame 23 (61 bytes on wire, 61 bytes captured)
Ethernet II, Src: Microsof_51:ab:2a (00:03:ff:51:ab:2a), Dst: 02:00:4c:4f:4f:50
(02:00:4c:4f:4f:50)
Internet Protocol, Src: 10.0.2.101 (10.0.2.101), Dst: 10.0.2.1 (10.0.2.1)
Transmission Control Protocol, Src Port: telnet (23), Dst Port: 1778 (1778), Seq: 1219591055,
Ack: 493790861, Len: 7
    Source port: telnet (23)
    Destination port: 1778 (1778)
    Sequence number: 1219591055
    Next sequence number: 1219591062
    Acknowledgement number: 493790861
    Header length: 20 bytes
    Flags: 0x0018 (PSH, ACK)
    Window size: 5840
    Checksum: 0x8f37 [correct]
Telnet
    Data: login:

Frame 26 (55 bytes on wire, 55 bytes captured)
Ethernet II, Src: 02:00:4c:4f:4f:50 (02:00:4c:4f:4f:50), Dst: Microsof_51:ab:2a
(00:03:ff:51:ab:2a)
Internet Protocol, Src: 10.0.2.1 (10.0.2.1), Dst: 10.0.2.101 (10.0.2.101)
Transmission Control Protocol, Src Port: 1778 (1778), Dst Port: telnet (23), Seq: 493790864, Ack:
1219591062, Len: 1
Telnet
    Data: u

Frame 29 (55 bytes on wire, 55 bytes captured)
Ethernet II, Src: 02:00:4c:4f:4f:50 (02:00:4c:4f:4f:50), Dst: Microsof_51:ab:2a
(00:03:ff:51:ab:2a)
Internet Protocol, Src: 10.0.2.1 (10.0.2.1), Dst: 10.0.2.101 (10.0.2.101)
Transmission Control Protocol, Src Port: 1778 (1778), Dst Port: telnet (23), Seq: 493790865, Ack:
1219591063, Len: 1
Telnet
    Data: s
```

Figure 4.32 Telnet-Login.cap: User access to server using Telnet login authentication.

```
Frame 32 (55 bytes on wire, 55 bytes captured)
Ethernet II, Src: 02:00:4c:4f:4f:50 (02:00:4c:4f:4f:50), Dst: Microsof_51:ab:2a
(00:03:ff:51:ab:2a)
Internet Protocol, Src: 10.0.2.1 (10.0.2.1), Dst: 10.0.2.101 (10.0.2.101)
Transmission Control Protocol, Src Port: 1778 (1778), Dst Port: telnet (23), Seq: 493790866, Ack:
1219591064, Len: 1
Telnet
    Data: e

Frame 34 (55 bytes on wire, 55 bytes captured)
Ethernet II, Src: 02:00:4c:4f:4f:50 (02:00:4c:4f:4f:50), Dst: Microsof_51:ab:2a
(00:03:ff:51:ab:2a)
Internet Protocol, Src: 10.0.2.1 (10.0.2.1), Dst: 10.0.2.101 (10.0.2.101)
Transmission Control Protocol, Src Port: 1778 (1778), Dst Port: telnet (23), Seq: 493790867, Ack:
1219591065, Len: 1
Telnet
    Data: r

Frame 37 (55 bytes on wire, 55 bytes captured)
Ethernet II, Src: 02:00:4c:4f:4f:50 (02:00:4c:4f:4f:50), Dst: Microsof_51:ab:2a
(00:03:ff:51:ab:2a)
Internet Protocol, Src: 10.0.2.1 (10.0.2.1), Dst: 10.0.2.101 (10.0.2.101)
Transmission Control Protocol, Src Port: 1778 (1778), Dst Port: telnet (23), Seq: 493790868, Ack:
1219591066, Len: 1
Telnet
    Data: 1

Frame 43 (64 bytes on wire, 64 bytes captured)
Ethernet II, Src: Microsof_51:ab:2a (00:03:ff:51:ab:2a), Dst: 02:00:4c:4f:4f:50
(02:00:4c:4f:4f:50)
Internet Protocol, Src: 10.0.2.101 (10.0.2.101), Dst: 10.0.2.1 (10.0.2.1)
Transmission Control Protocol, Src Port: telnet (23), Dst Port: 1778 (1778), Seq: 1219591069,
Ack: 493790871, Len: 10
    Window size: 5840
    Checksum: 0x0967 [correct]
Telnet
```

Figure 4.32 (continued)

```
    Data: Password:

Frame 45 (55 bytes on wire, 55 bytes captured)
Ethernet II, Src: 02:00:4c:4f:4f:50 (02:00:4c:4f:4f:50), Dst: Microsof_51:ab:2a
(00:03:ff:51:ab:2a)
Internet Protocol, Src: 10.0.2.1 (10.0.2.1), Dst: 10.0.2.101 (10.0.2.101)
Transmission Control Protocol, Src Port: 1778 (1778), Dst Port: telnet (23), Seq: 493790871, Ack:
1219591079, Len: 1
Telnet
    Data: p

Frame 47 (55 bytes on wire, 55 bytes captured)
Ethernet II, Src: 02:00:4c:4f:4f:50 (02:00:4c:4f:4f:50), Dst: Microsof_51:ab:2a
(00:03:ff:51:ab:2a)
Internet Protocol, Src: 10.0.2.1 (10.0.2.1), Dst: 10.0.2.101 (10.0.2.101)
Transmission Control Protocol, Src Port: 1778 (1778), Dst Port: telnet (23), Seq: 493790872, Ack:
1219591079, Len: 1
Telnet
    Data: a

Frame 49 (55 bytes on wire, 55 bytes captured)
Ethernet II, Src: 02:00:4c:4f:4f:50 (02:00:4c:4f:4f:50), Dst: Microsof_51:ab:2a
(00:03:ff:51:ab:2a)
Internet Protocol, Src: 10.0.2.1 (10.0.2.1), Dst: 10.0.2.101 (10.0.2.101)
Transmission Control Protocol, Src Port: 1778 (1778), Dst Port: telnet (23), Seq: 493790873, Ack:
1219591079, Len: 1
Telnet
    Data: s

Frame 51 (55 bytes on wire, 55 bytes captured)
Ethernet II, Src: 02:00:4c:4f:4f:50 (02:00:4c:4f:4f:50), Dst: Microsof_51:ab:2a
(00:03:ff:51:ab:2a)
Internet Protocol, Src: 10.0.2.1 (10.0.2.1), Dst: 10.0.2.101 (10.0.2.101)
Transmission Control Protocol, Src Port: 1778 (1778), Dst Port: telnet (23), Seq: 493790874, Ack:
1219591079, Len: 1
Telnet
```

Figure 4.32 (continued)

```
    Data: s

Frame 53 (55 bytes on wire, 55 bytes captured)
Ethernet II, Src: 02:00:4c:4f:4f:50 (02:00:4c:4f:4f:50), Dst: Microsof_51:ab:2a
(00:03:ff:51:ab:2a)
Internet Protocol, Src: 10.0.2.1 (10.0.2.1), Dst: 10.0.2.101 (10.0.2.101)
Transmission Control Protocol, Src Port: 1778 (1778), Dst Port: telnet (23), Seq: 493790875, Ack:
1219591079, Len: 1
Telnet
    Data: w

Frame 55 (55 bytes on wire, 55 bytes captured)
Ethernet II, Src: 02:00:4c:4f:4f:50 (02:00:4c:4f:4f:50), Dst: Microsof_51:ab:2a
(00:03:ff:51:ab:2a)
Internet Protocol, Src: 10.0.2.1 (10.0.2.1), Dst: 10.0.2.101 (10.0.2.101)
Transmission Control Protocol, Src Port: 1778 (1778), Dst Port: telnet (23), Seq: 493790876, Ack:
1219591079, Len: 1
Telnet
    Data: o

Frame 57 (55 bytes on wire, 55 bytes captured)
Ethernet II, Src: 02:00:4c:4f:4f:50 (02:00:4c:4f:4f:50), Dst: Microsof_51:ab:2a
(00:03:ff:51:ab:2a)
Internet Protocol, Src: 10.0.2.1 (10.0.2.1), Dst: 10.0.2.101 (10.0.2.101)
Transmission Control Protocol, Src Port: 1778 (1778), Dst Port: telnet (23), Seq: 493790877, Ack:
1219591079, Len: 1
Telnet
    Data: r

Frame 59 (55 bytes on wire, 55 bytes captured)
Ethernet II, Src: 02:00:4c:4f:4f:50 (02:00:4c:4f:4f:50), Dst: Microsof_51:ab:2a
(00:03:ff:51:ab:2a)
Internet Protocol, Src: 10.0.2.1 (10.0.2.1), Dst: 10.0.2.101 (10.0.2.101)
Transmission Control Protocol, Src Port: 1778 (1778), Dst Port: telnet (23), Seq: 493790878, Ack:
1219591079, Len: 1
Telnet
```

```
    Data: d
```

Figure 4.32 (continued)

1. Upon successful TCP session establishment (and potentially exchange of Telnet options), the server sends a plaintext string prompting the user for a username (see Frame 23 in Figure 4.32). This is not done using a fixed string; the username prompt only needs to be human readable so that the authenticating user can understand that he is required to provide his username.
2. The user types in his username on the Telnet client computer. The client computer would typically set the TCP PUSH option for packets from the client to the server so that a small number of characters (very often just one — the key that the user has just pressed) are sent to the server immediately. Thus, the username is typically contained in a series of frames, character by character; see Frames 29, 32, 34, 37, and 43 in Figure 4.32.
3. The server then replies with a prompt for the user to provide a password; see Frame 43 in Figure 4.32.
4. The client types in the password. If this is done interactively, each character will appear in a single packet, followed by the end of line sequence (CR+LF) to designate the end of the password; see Frames 45, 47, 49, 51, 53, 55, 57, and 59 in Figure 4.32.
5. The server authenticates the user using his plain username and plain password.

Typically, at this stage the server forks a new process or creates a new thread and impersonates the client. It then typically sets up the user environment and provides the user with a command prompt.

Technically speaking, with Telnet, every character typed locally from the client is sent across to the server (whether it will be just one buffering or many depends on the use of the Nagle algorithm that can potentially buffer remote operations) and then remote characters are sent back to the client. The sending of the characters can be buffered, or one by one as the user presses the key. Anyone with access to the network in between can collect all the characters from the authentication process and obtain the plaintext username and password. In general, this authentication method is insecure and is strongly advised against.

4.4.2 Telnet Authentication Option

The Telnet authentication option was initially defined in RFC 1409 and RFC 1416, and then updated in RFC 2941 (see [72]) as Telnet Protocol Option 0x25. The specifications allow for in-band authentication mechanism negotiation between the client and the server, and then for credential exchange using authentication data protection. The Telnet authentication option is only a generic mechanism for authentication negotiation. The client and server can agree to and use specific authentication mechanisms, such as Kerberos v.4, Kerberos v.5, and others. In addition, the client and server can select to encrypt or provide data integrity for user data within the Telnet session using a session key based on user authentication.

The Telnet authentication option is not widely supported by Telnet clients and servers. The most popular implementation is the Telnet client and server distributed with the MIT Kerberos suite. The authentication methods supported by this suite are Kerberos v.4 and Kerberos v.5. Windows 2000/2003 provide for a Telnet server and a Telnet client that support NTLM authentication using the Telnet authentication option.

To authenticate using the Telnet authentication option, the client and the server first negotiate the authentication option as a regular Telnet option, and then use a sequence of commands to perform the actual authentication. The client and the server use the authentication dialogue to select an authentication mechanism and, in addition to that, specify modifiers for the authentication mechanism (such as whether they want to perform mutual authentication, whether they want to encrypt traffic, and whether the client will forward its delegation credentials to the server).

RFC 2941 defines the authentication commands in Table 4.16.

As part of the Telnet Authentication Dialogue, the client and the server negotiate an authentication mechanism. RFC 2941 defines the authentication types in Table 4.17, some of which are not Internet standards and are proprietary.

The Telnet client and server may decide to negotiate additional session parameters. They do so by setting specific modification type flags in the Telnet Authentication message. Table 4.18 outlines the Telnet Authentication flags.

Table 4.16 Telnet Authentication Option: Commands

Command Number	*Command Name*	*Description*
0	IS	Telnet Client uses this command to select a Telnet Authentication option suggested by the server
1	SEND	Telnet Server uses this command to send authentication options to the client
2	REPLY	Telnet Server replies to a client authentication message submitted using the IS command
3	NAME	Used by the client to provide a name for the user that the client wants to impersonate as part of the Telnet session (authorization identity)

Table 4.17 Telnet Authentication Option: Authentication Types

Authentication Type Number	*Authentication Type Name*	*Description*
0	NULL	No authentication
1	KERBEROS_V4	Keberos v.4 authentication for Telnet, as described in RFC 1411
2	KERBEROS_V5	Kerberos v.5 authentication for Telnet, as described in RFC 2942 It is important to note that Kerberos v.5 for Telnet does not use GSS-API or SPNEGO as the underlying layer and is directly bound to the Telnet Authentication Option commands
3	SPX	SPX authentication, as per RFC 1412
4	MINK	MIT Kerberos related authentication
5	SRP	Authentication using the Secure Remote Password Protocol (SRP), as per RFC 2944
6	RSA	Authentication using RSA keys
7	SSL	Authentication using the Secure Sockets Layer (SSL) Protocol
10	LOKI	Authentication using the LOKI block cipher
11	SSA	Telnet Simple Strong Authentication, as per the X.511 ISO9594-3 standard
12	KEA_SJ	Authentication using the Key Exchange Algorithm (KEA), as defined in RFC 2951
13	KEA_SJ_INTEG	Authentication using the Key Exchange Algorithm (KEA), as defined in RFC 2951
14	DSS	Digital Signature Algorithm (DSA) — FIPS Digital Signature Standard
15	NTLM	Microsoft's Telnet server and client implement the NTLM authentication mechanism

The "kerberized" Telnet server and client from the MIT Kerberos distribution are sometimes used to authenticate Telnet users. The user session that produced Figure 4.33 is similar to the following:

Table 4.18 Telnet Authentication Option Modifiers

Authentication Modifier	*Modification Type*	*Description*
AUTH_WHO_MASK (1)	AUTH_CLIENT_TO_SERVER (0)	The client will authenticate to the server
	AUTH_SERVER_TO_CLIENT (1)	The server will authenticate to the client
AUTH_HOW_MASK (2)	AUTH_HOW_ONE_WAY (0)	Specifies that authentication will be one-way (e.g., either the client will authenticate the server, or the server will authenticate the client)
	AUTH_HOW_MUTUAL (2)	Specifies that both the client and the server will authenticate each other
ENCRYPT_MASK (20)	ENCRYPT_OFF (0)	User data will not be encrypted
	ENCRYPT_USING_TELOPT (4)	Client and server will negotiate encryption using the Telnet TELOPT ENCRYPT option before user authentication takes place
	ENCRYPT_AFTER_EXCHANGE (16)	User authentication using the Telnet Authentication option will take place, and then the client and the server will generate a session key based on the result of user authentication and will encrypt user data within the Telnet session.
	ENCRYPT_RESERVED (20)	Not used
INI_CRED_FWD_MASK (8)	INI_CRED_FWD_OFF (0)	The server should use the client credentials; it should not expect additional credentials to be provided for user impersonation and delegation
	INI_CRED_FWD_ON (8)	Specifies that the client will forward delegation credentials to the server after successful authentication

```
Frame 4 (102 bytes on wire, 102 bytes captured)
Ethernet II, Src: 02:00:4c:4f:4f:50 (02:00:4c:4f:4f:50), Dst: Microsof_51:ab:2a
(00:03:ff:51:ab:2a)
Internet Protocol, Src: 10.0.1.102 (10.0.1.102), Dst: 10.0.2.101 (10.0.2.101)
Transmission Control Protocol, Src Port: 60581 (60581), Dst Port: telnet (23), Seq: 71255988,
Ack: 4166742175, Len: 36
Telnet
    Command: Will Authentication Option
    Command: Do Encryption Option
    Command: Will Encryption Option
    Command: Do Suppress Go Ahead
    Command: Will Terminal Type
    Command: Will Negotiate About Window Size
    Command: Will Terminal Speed
    Command: Will Remote Flow Control
    Command: Will Linemode
    Command: Will New Environment Option
    Command: Do Status
    Command: Will X Display Location


Frame 6 (122 bytes on wire, 122 bytes captured)
Ethernet II, Src: Microsof_51:ab:2a (00:03:ff:51:ab:2a), Dst: 02:00:4c:4f:4f:50
(02:00:4c:4f:4f:50)
Internet Protocol, Src: 10.0.2.101 (10.0.2.101), Dst: 10.0.1.102 (10.0.1.102)
Transmission Control Protocol, Src Port: telnet (23), Dst Port: 60581 (60581), Seq: 4166742175,
Ack: 71256024, Len: 56
Telnet
    Command: Do Authentication Option
    Suboption Begin: Authentication Option
        Auth Cmd: SEND (1)
        Auth Type: Kerberos v5 (2)
        ...0 .1.. = Encrypt: Telnet Options (1)
        .... 0... = Cred Fwd: Client will NOT forward auth creds
        .... ..1. = How: MUTUAL authentication
        .... ...0 = Who: Mask client to server
```

Figure 4.33 Telnet-Krb5.cap: Telnet client using Telnet authentication option and Kerberos v.5 tickets.

```
        Auth Type: Kerberos v5 (2)
        ...0 .0.. = Encrypt: Off (0)
        .... 0... = Cred Fwd: Client will NOT forward auth creds
        .... ..1. = How: MUTUAL authentication
        .... ...0 = Who: Mask client to server
        Auth Type: Kerberos v5 (2)
        ...0 .0.. = Encrypt: Off (0)
        .... 0... = Cred Fwd: Client will NOT forward auth creds
        .... ..0. = How: One Way authentication
        .... ...0 = Who: Mask client to server
    Command: Suboption End
    Command: Will Encryption Option
    Command: Do Encryption Option
    Suboption Begin: Encryption Option
        Option data
    Command: Suboption End
    Command: Will Suppress Go Ahead
    Command: Do Terminal Type
    Command: Do Negotiate About Window Size
    Command: Do Terminal Speed
    Command: Do Remote Flow Control
    Command: Don't Linemode
    Command: Do New Environment Option
    Command: Will Status
    Command: Do X Display Location

Frame 8 (1229 bytes on wire, 1229 bytes captured)
Ethernet II, Src: 02:00:4c:4f:4f:50 (02:00:4c:4f:4f:50), Dst: Microsof_51:ab:2a
(00:03:ff:51:ab:2a)
Internet Protocol, Src: 10.0.1.102 (10.0.1.102), Dst: 10.0.2.101 (10.0.2.101)
Transmission Control Protocol, Src Port: 60581 (60581), Dst Port: telnet (23), Seq: 71256024,
Ack: 4166742231, Len: 1163
Telnet
    Suboption Begin: Authentication Option
        Auth Cmd: NAME (3)
        Name: Susan
```

Figure 4.33 (continued)

```
    Command: Suboption End
    Suboption Begin: Authentication Option
        Auth Cmd: IS (0)
        Auth Type: Kerberos v5 (2)
        ...0 .0.. = Encrypt: Off (0)
        .... 0... = Cred Fwd: Client will NOT forward auth creds
        .... ..1. = How: MUTUAL authentication
        .... ...0 = Who: Mask client to server
        Command: Auth (0)
        Kerberos AP-REQ
            Pvno: 5
            MSG Type: AP-REQ (14)
            Padding: 0
            APOptions: 20000000 (Mutual required)
                .0.. .... .... .... .... .... .... .... = Use Session Key: Do NOT use the session
key to encrypt the ticket
                ..1. .... .... .... .... .... .... .... = Mutual required: MUTUAL authentication
is REQUIRED
            Ticket
                Tkt-vno: 5
                Realm: INS.COM
                Server Name (Service and Host): host/dennis.ins.com
                    Name-type: Service and Host (3)
                    Name: host
                    Name: dennis.ins.com
                enc-part des-cbc-md5
                    Encryption type: des-cbc-md5 (3)
                    Kvno: 3
                    enc-part: 5F552AD0023B9E5A8FCD865B25CE422B7745A11DA9656B1E...
            Authenticator des-cbc-crc
                Encryption type: des-cbc-crc (1)
                Authenticator data: 9D45B86333F48873D18790499E338996DF7B6C33025F13A0...
    Command: Suboption End
    Suboption Begin: Encryption Option
        Option data
    Command: Suboption End
```

Figure 4.33 (continued)

```
    Suboption Begin: Negotiate About Window Size
        Width: 80
        Height: 24
    Command: Suboption End

Frame 10 (205 bytes on wire, 205 bytes captured)
Ethernet II, Src: Microsof_51:ab:2a (00:03:ff:51:ab:2a), Dst: 02:00:4c:4f:4f:50
(02:00:4c:4f:4f:50)
Internet Protocol, Src: 10.0.2.101 (10.0.2.101), Dst: 10.0.1.102 (10.0.1.102)
Transmission Control Protocol, Src Port: telnet (23), Dst Port: 60581 (60581), Seq: 4166742231,
Ack: 71257187, Len: 139
Telnet
    Suboption Begin: Authentication Option
        Auth Cmd: REPLY (2)
        Auth Type: Kerberos v5 (2)
        ...0 .0.. = Encrypt: Off (0)
        .... 0... = Cred Fwd: Client will NOT forward auth creds
        .... ..1. = How: MUTUAL authentication
        .... ...0 = Who: Mask client to server
        Command: Response (3)
        Kerberos AP-REP
            Pvno: 5
            MSG Type: AP-REP (15)
            enc-part des-cbc-crc
                Encryption type: des-cbc-crc (1)
                enc-part: 0B0BF73763DE717FFC595766C03BD90C8B695D063B284790...
    Command: Suboption End
    Suboption Begin: Authentication Option
        Auth Cmd: REPLY (2)
        Auth Type: Kerberos v5 (2)
        ...0 .0.. = Encrypt: Off (0)
        .... 0... = Cred Fwd: Client will NOT forward auth creds
        .... ..1. = How: MUTUAL authentication
        .... ...0 = Who: Mask client to server
        Command: Accept (2)
    Command: Suboption End
```

Figure 4.33 (continued)

```
Suboption Begin: Encryption Option
    Option data
Command: Unknown (0xff)
Data: \215=@\232
Command: Suboption End
```

Figure 4.33 (continued)

```
[root@linus ~]# klist
Ticket cache: FILE:/tmp/krb5cc_0
Default principal: Susan@INS.COM

Valid starting     Expires            Service principal
02/20/06 00:46:29  02/20/06 10:46:48  krbtgt/INS.COM@INS.COM
        renew until 02/21/06 00:46:29
02/20/06 00:46:53  02/20/06 10:46:48  host/dennis.ins.com@INS.COM
        renew until 02/21/06 00:46:29

Kerberos 4 ticket cache: /tmp/tkt0
klist: You have no tickets cached
[root@linus ~]# telnet -l Susan dennis.ins.com
Trying 10.0.2.101...
Connected to dennis.ins.com (10.0.2.101).
Escape character is '^]'.
[ Kerberos V5 accepts you as ``Susan@INS.COM'' ]
Last login: Mon Feb 20 01:16:19 from linus
[Susan@Dennis ~]$
[Susan@Dennis ~]$ id
uid=9114(Susan) gid=9114(Susan) groups=9114(Susan)
[Susan@Dennis ~]$ exit
logout
Connection closed by foreign host.
[root@linus ~]#
```

As can be seen from the output of the **klist** command, the client has a Kerberos ticket for the host/dennis.ins.com@INS.COM service principal name that is used by the Telnet service on host **dennis.ins.com**. Therefore, the client can use the ticket to authenticate to the server using the Telnet Authentication option and providing its Kerberos ticket for **dennis.ins.com** instead of sending her username and password in plaintext. To allow for a mapping between the Kerberos ticket and a local user on the server computer dennis.ins.com, the client uses the **–l** option, which will be passed on to the server as part of the Telnet Authentication Option process in the NAME command to provide an authorization name on the remote host. The user is not provided with the legacy Telnet login dialogue. Instead, the server accepts the Kerberos credentials and maps the Kerberos principal with user principal name Susan@INS.COM to the local account Susan on server **dennis.ins.com** — which is visible from the output of the **id** command.

The Telnet Authentication Option process is as follows (see Figure 4.33):

1. The client connects to the server using the Telnet Protocol.
2. The client provides the server with a list of options that it wants to negotiate. Among them is the Telnet Authentication option (0x25) (see Frame 4 in Figure 4.33).
3. If the server supports the Telnet Authentication option, it replies with a Telnet Authentication SEND command containing a list of authentication methods it supports, as well as modifications for the specific method; these may include mutual authentication, data encryption, etc (see Frame 6 in Figure 4.33).
4. The client submits an authorization name parameter (Telnet Authentication command NAME) (see Frame 8 in Figure 4.33).
5. The client selects an authentication method using the Telnet Authentication IS command, and submits its selection along with client authentication information appropriate for the selected authentication method (see Frame 8 in Figure 4.33).
6. The server follows the authentication mechanism and checks the client response. It then generates a response to the client. It submits the response using the Telnet Authentication Option REPLY command (see Frame 10 in Figure 4.33).
7. If the client requested server or mutual authentication, it follows the authentication protocol mechanism to authenticate the server reply using the Telnet Authentication Option IS command.

4.5 FTP Authentication

FTP (File Transfer Protocol) is the file transfer protocol of the early Internet. It was first defined in RFC 114 where user authentication was mentioned as a potential addition. One year later, this RFC along with several other interim FTP RFCs were made obsolete by RFC 354, where user login authentication was defined. The current version of FTP is defined in RFC 959 (see [74]).

It is important to note that FTP is defined as a protocol, consisting of two channels: (1) a control channel, used to transfer commands and status messages, and (2) a data channel, used for actual user data transfer. The user initially connects to the control channel, authenticates and is potentially impersonated by the server, and performs file operations on the server. If the user initiates a file transfer, this operation can be performed with the privileges of the user, and then the file is transferred using the data session. The data channel is defined to conform to the Telnet specification; however, at the same time, RFC 1123 rejects the use of Telnet Options on the FTP control channel. Hence, user authentication for FTP is different from Telnet authentication.

4.5.1 FTP Simple Authentication

FTP login authentication uses a standard dialogue on the control channel to welcome the user and request authentication credentials. The client needs to use the USER, PASS, and optionally the ACCT verbs to specify the username used for authentication, the password, and the authorization username, respectively. Once authenticated, the user is typically put in his own security context on the server so that he can access files based on the permissions that he was assigned on the server.

A typical FTP session is shown below:

```
[root@linus ~]# ftp dennis.ins.com
Connected to dennis.ins.com (10.0.2.101)
220 Dennis.ins.com FTP server (Version 5.60) ready.
Name(dennis.ins.com:root): DaVinci
331 Password required for DaVinci.
Password: password
230 User DaVinci logged in.
Remote system type is UNIX.
Using binary mode to transfer files.
ftp> pasv
227 Entering Passive Mode (10,0,2,101,128,12)
ftp> ls
150 Opening ASCII mode data connection for /bin/ls.
226 Transfer complete.
ftp> bye
221 Goodbye.
[root@linus ~]#
```

The client FTP interface typically adds to the level of interactivity by inserting username and password prompts. It then passes these as arguments to the USER and PASS commands on to the FTP server.

The ACCT command is implemented by some FTP servers and clients. If the user authenticates using a specific username and password (using the USER and PASS verbs), and has privileges to impersonate as another user and access files on behalf of that user, the ACCT verb can be used to do so. The use of the ACCT verb provides for the so-called user authorization ID.

FTP simple authentication is apparently insecure. Usernames and passwords are transferred in plaintext over the network; there is no protection from data modification attacks, replay, man-in-the-middle, or session hijacking. Thus, FTP simple authentication should be avoided if possible.

4.5.2 Anonymous FTP

Due to the inherent insecurity of the Simple authentication mechanism, many FTP sites implement anonymous FTP authentication. The idea is that if FTP Simple authentication is widely supported but weak, we should not force users to use their real usernames and passwords and thus expose them in cleartext across the network. Instead, anonymous FTP servers implement the special anonymous users **anonymous** and **ftp** that are not used to impersonate the user with own security privileges but with generic, one-for-all privileges. Anonymous FTP servers typically define a special local operating system account with very limited privileges and impersonate all anonymous client connections using this account.

With anonymous authentication, the client agent sends the **USER anonymous** command to the server, and then typically specifies the user e-mail address as the user password. These credentials are used for logging purposes only and not to impersonate the user.

The anonymous FTP authentication approach is appropriate when FTP sites provide public resources, which is the case for many resources on the Internet. However, if the FTP server is to provide resources that require restricted access, then anonymous authentication is not appropriate and other FTP authentication methods should be considered.

4.5.3 FTP Security Extensions with GSS-API

To provide for a secure FTP authentication mechanism, RFC 2228 defines the use of the **AUTH** verb to authenticate users (see [71]). The FTP authentication layer defined by FTP Security Extensions is similar to SASL and plays a similar role: it defines a generic authentication negotiation mechanism. At the same time, RFC 2228 suggests that GSS-API/Kerberos v.5 be the standard protocol for FTP authentication using Security Extensions, and it defines Kerberos v.4 authentication for FTP as well.

RFC 2228 defines eight new verbs that can be used by the FTP to protect both user authentication and user data. The verbs use parameters that are Base64 encoded.

In a similar fashion to SASL authentication, RFC 2228 suggests that the client use the **AUTH** verb to specify a preferred authentication mechanism, such as GSS-API (**AUTH GSSAPI**). The server should reply to the client request to use a specific authentication mechanism by either refusing authentication using the specific mechanism, or requesting that the client proceed with the authentication and enter an authentication dialogue.

Once the client and server have negotiated the authentication mechanism that they will use, they use the **ADAT** verb to send authentication messages in both directions, and messages are Base64 encoded. The number of messages they will exchange depends on the selected authentication mechanism; and in the case of GSS-API authentication, the dialogue can be as simple as a single GSS-API encapsulated Kerberos AP-REQ from the client to the server, and a single GSS-API encapsulated Kerberos AP-REP from the server back to the client.

Upon successful authentication, the client and the server can start to protect both the control channel and the data channel. RFC 2228 only discusses the negotiation mechanism for security protection, and not the actual encryption and data authentication mechanisms — these are provided by the negotiated security mechanism. In the case of GSS-API, native GSS-API encryption and data authentication mechanisms are used.

The control channel can be protected by using confidentiality (encryption), data integrity (data authentication), or a combination of confidentiality and integrity (privacy). The client and server use the **MIC** verb to send messages protected using data integrity, the **CONF** verb for encrypted messages, and the **ENC** verb for privacy protected messages. The client and server may choose to revert to a cleartext control channel using the **CCC** (Clear Command Channel) verb. It is interesting to note that RFC 2228 requires that the CCC command itself be protected. This means that the server and client need to successfully complete the authentication process, start protecting control messages, and only then are they able to downgrade to a cleartext channel. This is an important consideration because it protects against attacks where an attacker might inject **CCC** commands into the control channel that can downgrade the protection level.

Data channel protection is negotiated separately from the control channel. The data channel can be protected using the **PROT** verb and selecting a level of protection from the following: Clear Text (default — **PROT C**), Safe (data integrity only — **PROT S**), Confidential (data encryption without integrity authentication — **PROT E**), or Private (encryption and data integrity authentication — **PROT P**). The client and server need to negotiate protected message size using the **PBSZ** verb.

Encryption without data integrity authentication is not supported by GSS-API, so this is not a valid choice for protecting the control or data channel when GSS-API is selected as the authentication mechanism but may be supported by other security mechanisms.

FTP GSS-API authentication is performed in the following way (see Figure 4.34):

1. The client connects to the server control channel and receives the server banner (see Frame 4 in Figure 4.34).
2. The client uses the **AUTH GSSAPI** command to request GSS-API authentication (see Frame 6 in Figure 4.34).

```
Frame 4 (119 bytes on wire, 119 bytes captured)
Ethernet II, Src: Microsof_51:ab:2a (00:03:ff:51:ab:2a), Dst: 02:00:4c:4f:4f:50
(02:00:4c:4f:4f:50)
Internet Protocol, Src: 10.0.2.101 (10.0.2.101), Dst: 10.0.1.102 (10.0.1.102)
Transmission Control Protocol, Src Port: ftp (21), Dst Port: 54586 (54586), Seq: 3595181175, Ack:
3829956222, Len: 53
File Transfer Protocol (FTP)
    220 Dennis.ins.com FTP server (Version 5.60) ready.\r\n
        Response code: Service ready for new user (220)
        Response arg: Dennis.ins.com FTP server (Version 5.60) ready.

Frame 6 (79 bytes on wire, 79 bytes captured)
Ethernet II, Src: 02:00:4c:4f:4f:50 (02:00:4c:4f:4f:50), Dst: Microsof_51:ab:2a
(00:03:ff:51:ab:2a)
Internet Protocol, Src: 10.0.1.102 (10.0.1.102), Dst: 10.0.2.101 (10.0.2.101)
Transmission Control Protocol, Src Port: 54586 (54586), Dst Port: ftp (21), Seq: 3829956222, Ack:
3595181228, Len: 13
File Transfer Protocol (FTP)
    AUTH GSSAPI\r\n
        Request command: AUTH
        Request arg: GSSAPI

Frame 8 (122 bytes on wire, 122 bytes captured)
Ethernet II, Src: Microsof_51:ab:2a (00:03:ff:51:ab:2a), Dst: 02:00:4c:4f:4f:50
(02:00:4c:4f:4f:50)
Internet Protocol, Src: 10.0.2.101 (10.0.2.101), Dst: 10.0.1.102 (10.0.1.102)
Transmission Control Protocol, Src Port: ftp (21), Dst Port: 54586 (54586), Seq: 3595181228, Ack:
3829956235, Len: 56
File Transfer Protocol (FTP)
    334 Using authentication type GSSAPI. ADAT must follow\r\n
        Response code: Unknown (334)
        Response arg: Using authentication type GSSAPI. ADAT must follow

Frame 10 (1090 bytes on wire, 1090 bytes captured)
Ethernet II, Src: 02:00:4c:4f:4f:50 (02:00:4c:4f:4f:50), Dst: Microsof_51:ab:2a
(00:03:ff:51:ab:2a)
```

Figure 4.34 FTP-GSSAPI.cap: User FTP access using FTP security extensions authentication.

```
Internet Protocol, Src: 10.0.1.102 (10.0.1.102), Dst: 10.0.2.101 (10.0.2.101)
Transmission Control Protocol, Src Port: 54586 (54586), Dst Port: ftp (21), Seq: 3829956235, Ack:
3595181284, Len: 1024
File Transfer Protocol (FTP)
    ADAT
YIIEggYJKoZIhvcSAQICAQBuggRxMIIEbaADAgEFoQMCAQ6iBwMFACAAAACjggOtYYIDqTCCA6WgAwIBBaEJGwdJTlMuQ09No
iEwH6ADAgEDoRgwFhsEaG9zdBsOZGVubmlzLmlucy5jb22jggNuMIIDaqADAgEDoQMCAQOiggNcBIIDWF9VKtACO55aj82GWy
XOQit3RaEdqWVrHvkc/wA6z51whBsieHXAr23BJO
        Request command: ADAT
        Request arg [truncated]:
YIIEggYJKoZIhvcSAQICAQBuggRxMIIEbaADAgEFoQMCAQ6iBwMFACAAAACjggOtYYIDqTCCA6WgAwIBBaEJGwdJTlMuQ09No
iEwH6ADAgEDoRgwFhsEaG9zdBsOZGVubmlzLmlucy5jb22jggNuMIIDaqADAgEDoQMCAQOiggNcBIIDWF9VKtACO55aj82GWy
XOQit3RaEdqWVrHvkc/w

Frame 12 (593 bytes on wire, 593 bytes captured)
Ethernet II, Src: 02:00:4c:4f:4f:50 (02:00:4c:4f:4f:50), Dst: Microsof_51:ab:2a
(00:03:ff:51:ab:2a)
Internet Protocol, Src: 10.0.1.102 (10.0.1.102), Dst: 10.0.2.101 (10.0.2.101)
Transmission Control Protocol, Src Port: 54586 (54586), Dst Port: ftp (21), Seq: 3829957259, Ack:
3595181284, Len: 527
File Transfer Protocol (FTP)

fUJRQVu0NSRCj4hY0SNqHsVxBRp8DS0u5d3zSOtGWpJl25qNBguIvPhlxlywHQi6Kfz0uJxti71IZ5qTD2yH5V/lmfbSfvVY4
6Zl59mHO/UlibjfCJmRUcNUWFAKS2PSY+SnCT92qvEkHDX78uQKgfeGD0Cf/EMSYLg2scQRVVUwOEOGhJ16YkJm0IAoztHOBS
SQRBorDfdfjm0zWFugm/dRiBD6JDTwH+D7W6eK1ly5lRF
        Request command [truncated]:
fUJRQVu0NSRCj4hY0SNqHsVxBRp8DS0u5d3zSOtGWpJl25qNBguIvPhlxlywHQi6Kfz0uJxti71IZ5qTD2yH5V/lmfbSfvVY4
6Zl59mHO/UlibjfCJmRUcNUWFAKS2PSY+SnCT92qvEkHDX78uQKgfeGD0Cf/EMSYLg2scQRVVUwOEOGhJ16YkJm0IAoztHOBS
SQRBorDfdfjm0zWF

Frame 14 (229 bytes on wire, 229 bytes captured)
Ethernet II, Src: Microsof_51:ab:2a (00:03:ff:51:ab:2a), Dst: 02:00:4c:4f:4f:50
(02:00:4c:4f:4f:50)
Internet Protocol, Src: 10.0.2.101 (10.0.2.101), Dst: 10.0.1.102 (10.0.1.102)
Transmission Control Protocol, Src Port: ftp (21), Dst Port: 54586 (54586), Seq: 3595181284, Ack:
3829957786, Len: 163
```

Figure 4.34 (continued)

```
File Transfer Protocol (FTP)

    235

ADAT=YHAGCSqGSIb3EgECAgIAb2EwX6ADAgEFoQMCAQ+iUzBRoAMCAQGiSgRIJaHV/JIchK2EhkjS2SOq332PlChOTWWGN8HZ

EcDhDvHLYqSKUaq+kUbLEiefGMDfpY9frsIk6Vjdw9hrhCSpUhUTeFSBSI74\r\n

        Response code: Unknown (235)

        Response arg:

ADAT=YHAGCSqGSIb3EgECAgIAb2EwX6ADAgEFoQMCAQ+iUzBRoAMCAQGiSgRIJaHV/JIchK2EhkjS2SOq332PlChOTWWGN8HZ

EcDhDvHLYqSKUaq+kUbLEiefGMDfpY9frsIk6Vjdw9hrhCSpUhUTeFSBSI74
```

Figure 4.34 (continued)

3. The server confirms that it supports and will perform GSS-API authentication (see Frame 8 in Figure 4.34).
4. The client uses the **ADAT** verb to send the Base64 encoded GSS-API message that contains a Kerberos **AP-REQ** (see Frames 10 and 12 in Figure 4.34; ADAT request starts in Frame 10 and continues in Frame 12).
5. The server uses the **ADAT** verb to reply with a Base64 encoded GSS-API message that contains a Kerberos **AP-REP** (see Frame 14 in Figure 4.34).
6. The client validates the server identity and can now start protecting both the FTP control channel and the FTP data channel using the **MIC**, **CONF**, and **ENC** commands.

4.5.4 FTP Security Extensions with TLS

Although RFC 2228 endorses the use of GSS-API as the security mechanism, it also defines that other security mechanisms are acceptable. Transport Layer Security (TLS) is one of the acceptable mechanisms and it is described in RFC 4217 (see [75]).

FTP Security extensions with TLS are negotiated when the client issues the **AUTH TLS** command. The server and the client then negotiate a protection layer following TLS/SSL mechanisms (see section 4.3) using ADAT messages with encapsulated TLS negotiation messages on the control channel.

If TLS negotiation utilizes client certificates and authenticates the client, then the latter only needs to use the **USER** FTP command to specify identification information for the user to be impersonated by the server for the current FTP session. If TLS negotiates the transport layer of protection without utilizing client certificates and authenticating the client, then the client needs to issue the **USER** and **PASS** commands to authenticate across the protected control channel.

FTP Security Extensions with TLS supports cleartext and privacy protection on the data channel.

4.6 HTTP Authentication

HTTP is probably the most popular protocol on the Internet today. Users employ HTTP to access Web servers with their browsers. Natively, user access to resources has been open wide; and in the early days of HTTP, user authentication was unimportant and therefore not included in the original HTTP implementations. Historically, most Web browsers try to access resources by simply using the **HTTP GET** verb, which allows them to transfer HTTP resources, including HTML pages, GIF images, Java applets, and other Web components without worrying about authentication. This approach is known as anonymous authentication and is another way of saying that the browser session does not undergo any authentication. As the vast majority of resources on the Internet are public and free to view, using anonymous authentication by default is the most effective way for Web browsers to access public resources.

However, apart from the publicly available resources, such as marketing collateral, contact information, or investor information that a company may want to publish on their Web site, there are resources on the Internet and corporate intranets that must be protected and not available to anyone. Internal corporate procedures, for example, are typically published on intranet Web sites and are available to authenticated users only. Corporate e-mail — if available via a Web interface from the Internet — is another resource that should not be available to anyone who requests access to it, unless they are properly authenticated. Therefore, HTTP needs to provide for appropriate user authentication to certain resources.

Another important aspect of HTTP in terms of user authentication is the HTTP session. HTTP was designed to be stateless from a server perspective; so in HTTP version 1.0 (HTTP/1.0) defined in RFC 1945 (see [68]), the session contains a single HTTP command verb (such as the **HTTP GET** verb) and typically transfers one file, which can be an HTML document, a GIF image, or other object. To visualize all the objects on a single Web page, the client Web browser needs to open numerous sessions to the Web server — one for each object. Because the server does not maintain a client state, and often the requests from a single client can be distributed to a couple of Web servers, each separate HTTP session needs to authenticate separately. This can be processor intensive, especially for a server that has multiple clients connected to it, and may cause performance issues.

HTTP version 1.1 (HTTP/1.1) defined in RFC 2616 (see [69]) specifies that a single HTTP session between the client and the server can be used to transfer multiple objects (files), and defines long-lived HTTP sessions. They can use **Keep Alive** messages to keep the session up for relatively long periods of time so that the client and the server can communicate without reauthenticating. Apparently, this requires the server to maintain session state.

4.6.1 HTTP Anonymous Authentication

Most of the resources on the Internet are public and do not require authentication. Therefore, they are accessed anonymously. Although authentication may be anonymous from a user perspective, the Web server typically utilizes a user account with restricted privileges to access resources on behalf of anonymous Web users. The Web server impersonates this "anonymous" user; and every time a client browser requests access to a resource, the Web server's anonymous process or thread tries to access that resource. As this is an impersonation access model, in most cases the operating system will be responsible for granting or denying access to the specific resource for the anonymous user. The Web server administrators define access for anonymous users by granting or denying access to files and other resources on the Web server for the impersonated anonymous user, as they would do with any other user.

Although anonymous sessions impersonate to a specific anonymous service account on the Web server, Web applications may still be able to extract some identification information from the session and identify the user behind the browser. The HTTP session typically carries session information that may include the IP address of the client (in scenarios such as reverse-proxying or load balancing, this may not be available), the brand and make of the Web browser (the user agent), as well as cookies. The latter are very often used by Web servers to tag the specific client, and recognize or identify it in the future, as it returns to the Web server. Web browsers have mechanisms that can block the server from recognizing the client, including changing the user agent string as well as blocking cookies for some or all Web sites. The client typically cannot easily block the server from recognizing the specific client IP address, because this is part of the network layer of the Web session.

Figure 4.35 shows part of an anonymous session between a client and a server. There is no notion of user authentication. In Frame 4, the client simply uses the **HTTP GET** verb to request the resources it wants to access, and in Frame 5 the server returns the file requested by the client.

```
Frame 4 (358 bytes on wire, 358 bytes captured)
Ethernet II, Src: 02:00:4c:4f:4f:50 (02:00:4c:4f:4f:50), Dst: Microsof_57:ab:2a
(00:03:ff:57:ab:2a)
Internet Protocol, Src: 10.0.2.102 (10.0.2.102), Dst: 10.0.1.101 (10.0.1.101)
Transmission Control Protocol, Src Port: 1091 (1091), Dst Port: http (80), Seq: 155064676, Ack:
1338805079, Len: 304
Hypertext Transfer Protocol
    GET /Security/Anonymous/ HTTP/1.1\r\n
        Request Method: GET
        Request URI: /Security/Anonymous/
        Request Version: HTTP/1.1
    Accept: image/gif, image/x-xbitmap, image/jpeg, image/pjpeg, */*\r\n
    Accept-Language: en-us\r\n
    UA-CPU: x86\r\n
    Accept-Encoding: gzip, deflate\r\n
    User-Agent: Mozilla/4.0 (compatible. MSIE 6.0. Windows NT 5.2. SV1. .NET CLR 1.1.4322)\r\n
    Host: bill.ins.com\r\n
    Connection: Keep-Alive\r\n
    \r\n

Frame 5 (455 bytes on wire, 455 bytes captured)
Ethernet II, Src: Microsof_57:ab:2a (00:03:ff:57:ab:2a), Dst: 02:00:4c:4f:4f:50
(02:00:4c:4f:4f:50)
Internet Protocol, Src: 10.0.1.101 (10.0.1.101), Dst: 10.0.2.102 (10.0.2.102)
Transmission Control Protocol, Src Port: http (80), Dst Port: 1091 (1091), Seq: 1338805079, Ack:
155064980, Len: 401
Hypertext Transfer Protocol
    HTTP/1.1 200 OK\r\n
        Request Version: HTTP/1.1
        Response Code: 200
    Content-Length: 107\r\n
    Content-Type: text/html\r\n
    Content-Location: http://bill.ins.com/Security/Anonymous/index.htm\r\n
    Last-Modified: Sat, 11 Feb 2006 22:48:04 GMT\r\n
    Accept-Ranges: bytes\r\n
    ETag: "8049cf375d2fc61:401"\r\n
```

Figure 4.35 HTTP access using anonymous authentication.

```
    Server: Microsoft-IIS/6.0\r\n
    Date: Sat, 11 Feb 2006 22:55:24 GMT\r\n
    \r\n
Line-based text data: text/html
```

Figure 4.35 (continued)

4.6.2 HTTP Basic Authentication

HTTP Basic authentication is defined in RFC 1945 (see [68]). It presents a simple authentication method that transfers the plain username and password using Base64 encoding across the network. Base64 is an encoding technique and not an encryption mechanism, and therefore user authentication data can be considered transferred in plaintext. The authors of RFC 1945 specify that this authentication method by itself is insecure and should not be used unless the implications of doing so are well understood. However, with the advent of SSL, which can encrypt and authenticate the integrity of the HTTP session between the client and the server, Basic authentication was reinvented and is again widely used. However, it is still arguable whether it is a good idea for the client to provide the server with its plaintext password — which is equivalent to unrestricted delegation of authority.

Basic authentication works in the following way (see Figure 4.36):

1. The client sends a **GET** request (this can be any other HTTP request) to the server attempting the default Anonymous authentication, and specifies the resource that it wants to access as a parameter to the **GET** verb (see Frame 4 in Figure 4.36).
2. The server determines that the resource the client wants to access is protected by Basic authentication. The server replies with the response code "HTTP 401 Unauthorized," which is an indication to the client that anonymous authentication is not allowed for the specific resource. In addition to that, the server specifies the required authentication method for this resource (determined by the server configuration) and the realm (domain) name in the **WWW-Authenticate** HTTP header field. In the case of Basic authentication, WWW-Authenticate is set to "**Basic**" (see Frame 6 in Figure 4.36).

```
Frame 4 (354 bytes on wire, 354 bytes captured)
Ethernet II, Src: 02:00:4c:4f:4f:50 (02:00:4c:4f:4f:50), Dst: BILL.ins.com (00:03:ff:57:ab:2a)
Internet Protocol, Src: 10.0.2.102 (10.0.2.102), Dst: 10.0.1.101 (10.0.1.101)
Transmission Control Protocol, Src Port: 1092 (1092), Dst Port: http (80), Seq: 3498987087, Ack:
753017871, Len: 300
Hypertext Transfer Protocol
    GET /Security/Basic/ HTTP/1.1\r\n
        Request Method: GET
        Request URI: /Security/Basic/
        Request Version: HTTP/1.1
    Accept: image/gif, image/x-xbitmap, image/jpeg, image/pjpeg, */*\r\n
    Accept-Language: en-us\r\n
    UA-CPU: x86\r\n
    Accept-Encoding: gzip, deflate\r\n
    User-Agent: Mozilla/4.0 (compatible; MSIE 6.0; Windows NT 5.2; SV1; .NET CLR 1.1.4322)\r\n
    Host: bill.ins.com\r\n
    Connection: Keep-Alive\r\n
    \r\n


Frame 6 (1514 bytes on wire, 1514 bytes captured)
Ethernet II, Src: BILL.ins.com (00:03:ff:57:ab:2a), Dst: 02:00:4c:4f:4f:50 (02:00:4c:4f:4f:50)
Internet Protocol, Src: 10.0.1.101 (10.0.1.101), Dst: 10.0.2.102 (10.0.2.102)
Transmission Control Protocol, Src Port: http (80), Dst Port: 1092 (1092), Seq: 753017871, Ack:
3498987387, Len: 1460
Hypertext Transfer Protocol
    HTTP/1.1 401 Unauthorized\r\n
        Request Version: HTTP/1.1
        Response Code: 401
    Content-Length: 1656\r\n
    Content-Type: text/html\r\n
    Server: Microsoft-IIS/6.0\r\n
    WWW-Authenticate: Basic realm="INS.COM"\r\n
    Date: Sat, 11 Feb 2006 22:57:39 GMT\r\n
    \r\n
Line-based text data: text/html
```

Figure 4.36 HTTP access using Basic authentication.

```
Frame 9 (401 bytes on wire, 401 bytes captured)
Ethernet II, Src: 02:00:4c:4f:4f:50 (02:00:4c:4f:4f:50), Dst: BILL.ins.com (00:03:ff:57:ab:2a)
Internet Protocol, Src: 10.0.2.102 (10.0.2.102), Dst: 10.0.1.101 (10.0.1.101)
Transmission Control Protocol, Src Port: 1092 (1092), Dst Port: http (80), Seq: 3498987387, Ack:
753019708, Len: 347
Hypertext Transfer Protocol
    GET /Security/Basic/ HTTP/1.1\r\n
        Request Method: GET
        Request URI: /Security/Basic/
        Request Version: HTTP/1.1
    Accept: image/gif, image/x-xbitmap, image/jpeg, image/pjpeg, */*\r\n
    Accept-Language: en-us\r\n
    UA-CPU: x86\r\n
    Accept-Encoding: gzip, deflate\r\n
    User-Agent: Mozilla/4.0 (compatible; MSIE 6.0; Windows NT 5.2; SV1; .NET CLR 1.1.4322)\r\n
    Host: bill.ins.com\r\n
    Connection: Keep-Alive\r\n
    Authorization: Basic U3VzYW46cGFzc3dvcmQxIQ==\r\n
        Credentials: Susan:password1!
    \r\n

Frame 11 (447 bytes on wire, 447 bytes captured)
Ethernet II, Src: BILL.ins.com (00:03:ff:57:ab:2a), Dst: 02:00:4c:4f:4f:50 (02:00:4c:4f:4f:50)
Internet Protocol, Src: 10.0.1.101 (10.0.1.101), Dst: 10.0.2.102 (10.0.2.102)
Transmission Control Protocol, Src Port: http (80), Dst Port: 1092 (1092), Seq: 753019708, Ack:
3498987734, Len: 393
Hypertext Transfer Protocol
    HTTP/1.1 200 OK\r\n
        Request Version: HTTP/1.1
        Response Code: 200
    Content-Length: 103\r\n
    Content-Type: text/html\r\n
    Content-Location: http://bill.ins.com/Security/Basic/index.htm\r\n
    Last-Modified: Sat, 11 Feb 2006 22:49:59 GMT\r\n
    Accept-Ranges: bytes\r\n
```

Figure 4.36 (continued)

```
    ETag: "2014677c5d2fc61:401"\r\n
    Server: Microsoft-IIS/6.0\r\n
    Date: Sat, 11 Feb 2006 22:57:53 GMT\r\n
    \r\n
Line-based text data: text/html
```

Figure 4.36 (continued)

3. Upon receipt of the HTTP 401 response code, the client browser typically prompts the user for authentication credentials. It then constructs a Basic authentication authenticator by concatenating the username with a semicolon (":") character and the user password. The authenticator is then encoded using Base64 encoding and submitted to the server in the **Authorization** field. The client also specifies the authentication method it is attempting (see Frame 9 in Figure 4.36).
4. The Web server tries to authenticate and potentially impersonate the user using the supplied plaintext credentials. It then returns the authentication result using the HTTP standard response 200 OK.

HTTP Basic authentication technically provides the username and password in the clear. User identification information and credentials can therefore be captured, replayed, or modified; the user session can be hijacked, and the authentication approach is generally weak. Unless HTTP Basic authentication is protected with TLS/SSL, it should be avoided.

4.6.3 HTTP Digest Authentication

RFC 2617 defines HTTP Digest authentication (see [63]). HTTP Digest authentication has relatively wide support on the server side (Microsoft IIS, Apache) as well as on the client side (Internet Explorer, Mozilla, Opera). The mechanism is almost the same as SASL Digest-MD5 authentication (see subsection 4.2.3.7) and requires that both the client and the server have access to a plaintext, or reversibly encrypted user password.

The Digest authentication mechanics are shown in Figure 4.37. Similar to the SASL Digest-MD5 authentication mechanism, the server sends a server digest in Frame 6 and the client replies with the client digest in Frame 9. In Frame 10, the server confirms successful authentication.

```
Frame 4 (355 bytes on wire, 355 bytes captured)
Ethernet II, Src: 02:00:4c:4f:4f:50 (02:00:4c:4f:4f:50), Dst: Microsof_57:ab:2a
(00:03:ff:57:ab:2a)
Internet Protocol, Src: 10.0.2.102 (10.0.2.102), Dst: 10.0.1.101 (10.0.1.101)
Transmission Control Protocol, Src Port: 1093 (1093), Dst Port: http (80), Seq: 1889941131, Ack:
2434303757, Len: 301
Hypertext Transfer Protocol
    GET /Security/Digest/ HTTP/1.1\r\n
        Request Method: GET
        Request URI: /Security/Digest/
        Request Version: HTTP/1.1
    Accept: image/gif, image/x-xbitmap, image/jpeg, image/pjpeg, */*\r\n
    Accept-Language: en-us\r\n
    UA-CPU: x86\r\n
    Accept-Encoding: gzip, deflate\r\n
    User-Agent: Mozilla/4.0 (compatible; MSIE 6.0; Windows NT 5.2; SV1; .NET CLR 1.1.4322)\r\n
    Host: bill.ins.com\r\n
    Connection: Keep-Alive\r\n
    \r\n

Frame 6 (1514 bytes on wire, 1514 bytes captured)
Ethernet II, Src: Microsof_57:ab:2a (00:03:ff:57:ab:2a), Dst: 02:00:4c:4f:4f:50
(02:00:4c:4f:4f:50)
Internet Protocol, Src: 10.0.1.101 (10.0.1.101), Dst: 10.0.2.102 (10.0.2.102)
Transmission Control Protocol, Src Port: http (80), Dst Port: 1093 (1093), Seq: 2434303757, Ack:
1889941432, Len: 1460
Hypertext Transfer Protocol
    HTTP/1.1 401 Unauthorized\r\n
        Request Version: HTTP/1.1
        Response Code: 401
    Content-Length: 1656\r\n
    Content-Type: text/html\r\n
    Server: Microsoft-IIS/6.0\r\n
    WWW-Authenticate: Digest qop="auth",algorithm=MD5-
sess,nonce="20d1da125f2fc6013eec4a6f4d1cf34133fffe449de04ce7f6b8e6110c0ee23867e01f774a96c8d5",cha
rset=utf-8,realm="INS.COM"\r\n
```

Figure 4.37 HTTP access using Digest authentication.

```
    Date: Sat, 11 Feb 2006 23:01:21 GMT\r\n
    \r\n
Line-based text data: text/html

Frame 9 (662 bytes on wire, 662 bytes captured)
Ethernet II, Src: 02:00:4c:4f:4f:50 (02:00:4c:4f:4f:50), Dst: Microsof_57:ab:2a
(00:03:ff:57:ab:2a)
Internet Protocol, Src: 10.0.2.102 (10.0.2.102), Dst: 10.0.1.101 (10.0.1.101)
Transmission Control Protocol, Src Port: 1093 (1093), Dst Port: http (80), Seq: 1889941432, Ack:
2434305728, Len: 608
Hypertext Transfer Protocol
    GET /Security/Digest/ HTTP/1.1\r\n
        Request Method: GET
        Request URI: /Security/Digest/
        Request Version: HTTP/1.1
    Accept: image/gif, image/x-xbitmap, image/jpeg, image/pjpeg, */*\r\n
    Accept-Language: en-us\r\n
    UA-CPU: x86\r\n
    Accept-Encoding: gzip, deflate\r\n
    User-Agent: Mozilla/4.0 (compatible; MSIE 6.0; Windows NT 5.2; SV1; .NET CLR 1.1.4322)\r\n
    Host: bill.ins.com\r\n
    Connection: Keep-Alive\r\n
    Authorization: Digest username="Susan", realm="INS.COM", qop="auth", algorithm="MD5-sess",
uri="/Security/Digest/",
nonce="20d1da125f2fc6013eec4a6f4d1cf34133fffe449de04ce7f6b8e6110c0ee23867e01f774a96c8d5",
nc=00000001, cnonce="52447499ed25edfa526e88d3623882ed",
response="6e33ca77c2acbbc5ffc38df51b2f5702" \r\n

Frame 10 (449 bytes on wire, 449 bytes captured)
Ethernet II, Src: Microsof_57:ab:2a (00:03:ff:57:ab:2a), Dst: 02:00:4c:4f:4f:50
(02:00:4c:4f:4f:50)
Internet Protocol, Src: 10.0.1.101 (10.0.1.101), Dst: 10.0.2.102 (10.0.2.102)
Transmission Control Protocol, Src Port: http (80), Dst Port: 1093 (1093), Seq: 2434305728, Ack:
1889942040, Len: 395
Hypertext Transfer Protocol
    HTTP/1.1 200 OK\r\n
```

Figure 4.37 (continued)

```
        Request Version: HTTP/1.1
        Response Code: 200
    Content-Length: 104\r\n
    Content-Type: text/html\r\n
    Content-Location: http://bill.ins.com/Security/Digest/index.htm\r\n
    Last-Modified: Sat, 11 Feb 2006 22:48:36 GMT\r\n
    Accept-Ranges: bytes\r\n
    ETag: "5066494b5d2fc61:401"\r\n
    Server: Microsoft-IIS/6.0\r\n
    Date: Sat, 11 Feb 2006 23:01:30 GMT\r\n
    \r\n
Line-based text data: text/html
```

Figure 4.37 (continued)

4.6.4 HTTP GSS-API/SSPI Authentication Using SPNEGO and Kerberos

Most of today's Web servers and Web browsers support GSS-API/SSPI authentication. Most UNIX-based HTTP clients and servers, including Apache, use GSS-API as a method for Kerberos authentication. Microsoft Internet Information Server uses the SSPI (GSS-API compatible) to negotiate an authentication protocol using SPNEGO negotiation. Microsoft Internet Explorer and Mozilla also support SPNEGO over GSS-API/SSPI and can negotiate Kerberos or NTLM authentication.

The way GSS-API/SSPI authentication for HTTP works is as follows (see Figure 4.38):

1. The client sends a **GET** request (or other HTTP request) to the server attempting the default Anonymous authentication, and specifying the resource that it wants to access as a parameter to the **GET** verb (or other HTTP verb) (see Frame 4 in Figure 4.38).
2. The server determines that the resource that the client wants to access is protected by GSS-API/SSPI authentication. The server replies with response code "HTTP 401 Unauthorized," which is an indication to the client that anonymous authentication is not allowed for the specific resource. In addition, the server specifies

```
Frame 4 (355 bytes on wire, 355 bytes captured)
Ethernet II, Src: 02:00:4c:4f:4f:50 (02:00:4c:4f:4f:50), Dst: BILL.ins.com (00:03:ff:57:ab:2a)
Internet Protocol, Src: 10.0.2.102 (10.0.2.102), Dst: 10.0.1.101 (10.0.1.101)
Transmission Control Protocol, Src Port: 1095 (1095), Dst Port: http (80), Seq: 3274138375, Ack:
4228632977, Len: 301
Hypertext Transfer Protocol
    GET /Security/SPNEGO/ HTTP/1.1\r\n
        Request Method: GET
        Request URI: /Security/SPNEGO/
        Request Version: HTTP/1.1
    Accept: image/gif, image/x-xbitmap, image/jpeg, image/pjpeg, */*\r\n
    Accept-Language: en-us\r\n
    UA-CPU: x86\r\n
    Accept-Encoding: gzip, deflate\r\n
    User-Agent: Mozilla/4.0 (compatible; MSIE 6.0; Windows NT 5.2; SV1; .NET CLR 1.1.4322)\r\n
    Host: bill.ins.com\r\n
    Connection: Keep-Alive\r\n
    \r\n

Frame 5 (1514 bytes on wire, 1514 bytes captured)
Ethernet II, Src: BILL.ins.com (00:03:ff:57:ab:2a), Dst: 02:00:4c:4f:4f:50 (02:00:4c:4f:4f:50)
Internet Protocol, Src: 10.0.1.101 (10.0.1.101), Dst: 10.0.2.102 (10.0.2.102)
Transmission Control Protocol, Src Port: http (80), Dst Port: 1095 (1095), Seq: 4228632977, Ack:
3274138676, Len: 1460
Hypertext Transfer Protocol
    HTTP/1.1 401 Unauthorized\r\n
        Request Version: HTTP/1.1
        Response Code: 401
    Content-Length: 1656\r\n
    Content-Type: text/html\r\n
    Server: Microsoft-IIS/6.0\r\n
    WWW-Authenticate: Negotiate\r\n
    WWW-Authenticate: NTLM\r\n
    Date: Sat, 11 Feb 2006 23:09:16 GMT\r\n
    \r\n
Line-based text data: text/html
```

Figure 4.38 HTTP access using GSS-API/SSPI authentication.

```
Frame 10 (1261 bytes on wire, 1261 bytes captured)
Ethernet II, Src: 02:00:4c:4f:4f:50 (02:00:4c:4f:4f:50), Dst: BILL.ins.com (00:03:ff:57:ab:2a)
Internet Protocol, Src: 10.0.2.102 (10.0.2.102), Dst: 10.0.1.101 (10.0.1.101)
User Datagram Protocol, Src Port: 1097 (1097), Dst Port: kerberos (88)
Kerberos TGS-REQ
    Pvno: 5
    MSG Type: TGS-REQ (12)
    padata: PA-TGS-REQ
        Type: PA-TGS-REQ (1)
            Value: 6E82042C30820428A003020105A10302010EA20703050000... AP-REQ
                Pvno: 5
                MSG Type: AP-REQ (14)
                Padding: 0
                APOptions: 00000000
                Ticket
                    Tkt-vno: 5
                    Realm: INS.COM
                    Server Name (Service and Instance): krbtgt/INS.COM
                        Name-type: Service and Instance (2)
                        Name: krbtgt
                        Name: INS.COM
                    enc-part rc4-hmac
                        Encryption type: rc4-hmac (23)
                        Kvno: 2
                        enc-part: 8842F65FDF7A94FC42B0AD4FD00C8B53A393F7414AF5E0EB...
                Authenticator rc4-hmac
                    Encryption type: rc4-hmac (23)
                    Authenticator data: 746759A2F37B973FBA44B346A483E2796B9DD5AAB8CAA1F4...
    KDC_REQ_BODY
        Padding: 0
        KDCOptions: 40810000 (Forwardable, Renewable, Canonicalize)
        Realm: INS.COM
        Server Name (Service and Instance): HTTP/bill.ins.com
            Name-type: Service and Instance (2)
```

Figure 4.38 (continued)

```
            Name: HTTP
            Name: bill.ins.com
        till: 2037-09-13 02:48:05 (Z)
        Nonce: 741498737
        Encryption Types: rc4-hmac des-cbc-md5 des-cbc-crc rc4-hmac-exp rc4-hmac-old-exp

No.     Time        Source                Destination           Protocol Info
     11 5.269221    10.0.1.101            10.0.2.102            KRB5     TGS-REP

Frame 11 (1282 bytes on wire, 1282 bytes captured)
Ethernet II, Src: BILL.ins.com (00:03:ff:57:ab:2a), Dst: 02:00:4c:4f:4f:50 (02:00:4c:4f:4f:50)
Internet Protocol, Src: 10.0.1.101 (10.0.1.101), Dst: 10.0.2.102 (10.0.2.102)
User Datagram Protocol, Src Port: kerberos (88), Dst Port: 1097 (1097)
Kerberos TGS-REP
    Pvno: 5
    MSG Type: TGS-REP (13)
    Client Realm: INS.COM
    Client Name (Principal): Susan
        Name-type: Principal (1)
        Name: Susan
    Ticket
        Tkt-vno: 5
        Realm: INS.COM
        Server Name (Service and Instance): HTTP/bill.ins.com
            Name-type: Service and Instance (2)
            Name: HTTP
            Name: bill.ins.com
        enc-part rc4-hmac
            Encryption type: rc4-hmac (23)
            Kvno: 8
            enc-part: C0A3EAB69C35B242A1F1D68DE2A87B69D07F47FA9727C5D6...
    enc-part rc4-hmac
        Encryption type: rc4-hmac (23)
        enc-part: AF6CDABA0ECBFA4DC4336F0A4F56AC7042F684E252480033...
```

Figure 4.38 (continued)

```
Frame 12 (1514 bytes on wire, 1514 bytes captured)
Ethernet II, Src: 02:00:4c:4f:4f:50 (02:00:4c:4f:4f:50), Dst: BILL.ins.com (00:03:ff:57:ab:2a)
Internet Protocol, Src: 10.0.2.102 (10.0.2.102), Dst: 10.0.1.101 (10.0.1.101)
Transmission Control Protocol, Src Port: 1095 (1095), Dst Port: http (80), Seq: 3274138676, Ack:
4228634826, Len: 1460
Hypertext Transfer Protocol
    GET /Security/SPNEGO/ HTTP/1.1\r\n
        Request Method: GET
        Request URI: /Security/SPNEGO/
        Request Version: HTTP/1.1
    Accept: image/gif, image/x-xbitmap, image/jpeg, image/pjpeg, */*\r\n
    Accept-Language: en-us\r\n
    UA-CPU: x86\r\n
    Accept-Encoding: gzip, deflate\r\n
    User-Agent: Mozilla/4.0 (compatible; MSIE 6.0; Windows NT 5.2; SV1; .NET CLR 1.1.4322)\r\n
    Host: bill.ins.com\r\n
    Connection: Keep-Alive\r\n
    Authorization: Negotiate
YIIE1QYGKwYBBQUCoIIEyTCCBMWgJDAiBgkqhkiC9xIBAgIGCSqGSIb3EgECAgYKKwYBBAGCNwICCqKCBJsEggSXYIIEkwYJK
oZIhvcSAQICAQBuggSCMIIEfqADAgEFoQMCAQ6iBwMFACAAAACjggOwYYIDrDCCA6igAwIBBaEJGwdJTlMuQ09Noh8wHaADAg
ECoRYwFBsESFRUUBsMYm
        GSS-API Generic Security Service Application Program Interface

Frame 15 (695 bytes on wire, 695 bytes captured)
Ethernet II, Src: BILL.ins.com (00:03:ff:57:ab:2a), Dst: 02:00:4c:4f:4f:50 (02:00:4c:4f:4f:50)
Internet Protocol, Src: 10.0.1.101 (10.0.1.101), Dst: 10.0.2.102 (10.0.2.102)
Transmission Control Protocol, Src Port: http (80), Dst Port: 1095 (1095), Seq: 4228634826, Ack:
3274140660, Len: 641
Hypertext Transfer Protocol
    HTTP/1.1 200 OK\r\n
        Request Version: HTTP/1.1
        Response Code: 200
    Content-Length: 104\r\n
    Content-Type: text/html\r\n
    Content-Location: http://bill.ins.com/Security/SPNEGO/index.htm\r\n
    Last-Modified: Sat, 11 Feb 2006 22:48:52 GMT\r\n
```

Figure 4.38 (continued)

```
    Accept-Ranges: bytes\r\n
    ETag: "f05da2545d2fc61:403"\r\n
    Server: Microsoft-IIS/6.0\r\n
    WWW-Authenticate: Negotiate
oYGfMIGcoAMKAQChCwYJKoZIgvcSAQICooGHBIGEYIGBBgkqhkiG9xIBAgICAG9yMHCgAwIBBaEDAgEPomQwYqADAgEXolsEW
egwm7GkU5CiLGGU2vAoCqKbJBpJvCsMhPYkwteK9firdilLGiiBCveDtzqQRuq+q7yFjfF/tRGbGZOr/bYuoFgJUQfuYLTMdD
1EHwj8S4X8v2AlE8e
        GSS-API Generic Security Service Application Program Interface
            Unknown header (class=2, pc=1, tag=1)
    Date: Sat, 11 Feb 2006 23:09:22 GMT\r\n
    \r\n
Line-based text data: text/html
```

Figure 4.38 (continued)

the required authentication methods (determined by the server configuration) in the **WWW-Authenticate** HTTP header field. In the case of GSS-API/SSPI authentication, **WWW-Authenticate** is set to Negotiate, which is an indication that the Web server wants to negotiate GSS-API authentication using the SPNEGO Protocol. In addition, Microsoft ISS 6.0 suggests NTLM as an alternative authentication method (see below).

3. The client raises a Kerberos TGS request to its KDC for a service ticket to access the Web service. The client specifies **HTTP/bill.ins.com** as the Service Principal Name. It then receives a TGS reply with the ticket for the specified resource (see Frames 10 and 11 in Figure 4.38).
4. The client resubmits the HTTP **GET** request to the server, this time including additional authentication information in the **Authorization** HTTP header. The authentication information includes SPNEGO encapsulated GSS-API/SSPI structures that contain the client Kerberos ticket for the HTTP service — namely the Kerberos AS-REQ message (see Frame 12 in Figure 4.38).
5. The server returns the HTTP 200 OK response, and includes the SPNEGO and GSS-API/SSPI structures that contain the Kerberos AS-REP message in the **WWW-Authenticate** HTTP header field.

Once authenticated, the client is impersonated by the Web server and can access resources to which he has been granted access.

4.6.5 HTTP NTLMSSP Authentication

Apart from GSS-API/SSPI authentication using SPNEGO and potentially encapsulated Kerberos authentication, Microsoft IIS 5.0 and later support GSS-API/SSPI with NTLM authentication without SPNEGO negotiation. This mechanism essentially encapsulates NTLMSSP within HTTP.

The way NTLMSSP within HTTP works is as follows (see Figure 4.39):

1. The client sends a **GET** request (or other HTTP request) to the server attempting the default Anonymous authentication, and specifying the resource that it wants to access as a parameter to the **GET** verb (or other HTTP verb) (see Frame 4 in Figure 4.39).
2. The server determines that the resource that the client wants to access is protected by GSS-API/SSPI authentication. The server replies with response code "HTTP 401 Unauthorized," which is an indication to the client that Anonymous authentication is not allowed for the specific resource. In addition, the server specifies the required authentication methods (determined by the server configuration) in the **WWW-Authenticate HTTP** header field. In the case of NTLMSSP authentication, the **WWW-Authenticate** header is set to NTLM (see Frame 5 in Figure 4.39).
3. The client resubmits the **GET** request and agrees to perform NTLM authentication by encapsulating an NTLM Type 1 message in the HTTP **Authorization** field (see Frame 8 in Figure 4.39).
4. The server provides an NTLM challenge string by returning an NTLM Type 2 message and encapsulating it in the **WWW-Authenticate** HTTP field (see Frame 9 in Figure 4.39).
5. The client calculates an NTLM response and re-submits the **GET** request, including the NTLM Type 3 message in the **Authorization** HTTP field (see Frame 12 in Figure 4.39).
6. The server confirms successful authentication by returning an HTTP 200 OK response (Frame 14 in Figure 4.39).

At this stage, the server impersonates the client and provides access to resources to which the client has been granted access.

4.6.6 HTTP SSL Certificate Mapping as an Authentication Method

Many HTTP servers allow for SSL/TLS protection of the communication channel between the client and the server. More details on how SSL/TLS can be used for user authentication for various protocols, including HTTP, is provided in Chapter 4.3.

```
Frame 4 (457 bytes on wire, 457 bytes captured)
Ethernet II, Src: 02:00:4c:4f:4f:50 (02:00:4c:4f:4f:50), Dst: BILL.ins.com (00:03:ff:57:ab:2a)
Internet Protocol, Src: 10.0.1.1 (10.0.1.1), Dst: 10.0.1.101 (10.0.1.101)
Transmission Control Protocol, Src Port: 3152 (3152), Dst Port: http (80), Seq: 2933641557, Ack:
4276818075, Len: 403
Hypertext Transfer Protocol
    GET /Security/SPNEGO/ HTTP/1.1\r\n
        Request Method: GET
        Request URI: /Security/SPNEGO/
        Request Version: HTTP/1.1
    Accept: image/gif, image/x-xbitmap, image/jpeg, image/pjpeg, application/x-shockwave-flash,
application/vnd.ms-excel, application/vnd.ms-powerpoint, application/msword, */*\r\n
    Accept-Language: en-us,bg;q=0.5\r\n
    Accept-Encoding: gzip, deflate\r\n
    User-Agent: Mozilla/4.0 (compatible; MSIE 6.0; Windows NT 5.1; SV1; .NET CLR 1.1.4322)\r\n
    Host: 10.0.1.101\r\n
    Connection: Keep-Alive\r\n
    \r\n

Frame 5 (1514 bytes on wire, 1514 bytes captured)
Ethernet II, Src: BILL.ins.com (00:03:ff:57:ab:2a), Dst: 02:00:4c:4f:4f:50 (02:00:4c:4f:4f:50)
Internet Protocol, Src: 10.0.1.101 (10.0.1.101), Dst: 10.0.1.1 (10.0.1.1)
Transmission Control Protocol, Src Port: http (80), Dst Port: 3152 (3152), Seq: 4276818075, Ack:
2933641960, Len: 1460
Hypertext Transfer Protocol
    HTTP/1.1 401 Unauthorized\r\n
        Request Version: HTTP/1.1
        Response Code: 401
    Content-Length: 1656\r\n
    Content-Type: text/html\r\n
    Server: Microsoft-IIS/6.0\r\n
    WWW-Authenticate: Negotiate\r\n
    WWW-Authenticate: NTLM\r\n
    Date: Sat, 11 Feb 2006 23:20:24 GMT\r\n
    \r\n
Line-based text data: text/html
```

Figure 4.39 HTTP access using NTLMSSP authentication.

```
Frame 8 (540 bytes on wire, 540 bytes captured)
Ethernet II, Src: 02:00:4c:4f:4f:50 (02:00:4c:4f:4f:50), Dst: BILL.ins.com (00:03:ff:57:ab:2a)
Internet Protocol, Src: 10.0.1.1 (10.0.1.1), Dst: 10.0.1.101 (10.0.1.101)
Transmission Control Protocol, Src Port: 3152 (3152), Dst Port: http (80), Seq: 2933641960, Ack:
4276819924, Len: 486
Hypertext Transfer Protocol
    GET /Security/SPNEGO/ HTTP/1.1\r\n
        Request Method: GET
        Request URI: /Security/SPNEGO/
        Request Version: HTTP/1.1
    Accept: image/gif, image/x-xbitmap, image/jpeg, image/pjpeg, application/x-shockwave-flash,
application/vnd.ms-excel, application/vnd.ms-powerpoint, application/msword, */*\r\n
    Accept-Language: en-us,bg;q=0.5\r\n
    Accept-Encoding: gzip, deflate\r\n
    User-Agent: Mozilla/4.0 (compatible; MSIE 6.0; Windows NT 5.1; SV1; .NET CLR 1.1.4322)\r\n
    Host: 10.0.1.101\r\n
    Connection: Keep-Alive\r\n
    Authorization: Negotiate TlRMTVNTUAABAAAAB4IIogAAAAAAAAAAAAAAAAAAAAAFASgKAAAADw==\r\n
        NTLMSSP
            NTLMSSP identifier: NTLMSSP
            NTLM Message Type: NTLMSSP_NEGOTIATE (0x00000001)
            Flags: 0xa2088207
            Calling workstation domain: NULL
            Calling workstation name: NULL

Frame 9 (1514 bytes on wire, 1514 bytes captured)
Ethernet II, Src: BILL.ins.com (00:03:ff:57:ab:2a), Dst: 02:00:4c:4f:4f:50 (02:00:4c:4f:4f:50)
Internet Protocol, Src: 10.0.1.101 (10.0.1.101), Dst: 10.0.1.1 (10.0.1.1)
Transmission Control Protocol, Src Port: http (80), Dst Port: 3152 (3152), Seq: 4276819924, Ack:
2933642446, Len: 1460
Hypertext Transfer Protocol
    HTTP/1.1 401 Unauthorized\r\n
        Request Version: HTTP/1.1
        Response Code: 401
    Content-Length: 1539\r\n
```

Figure 4.39 (continued)

```
    Content-Type: text/html\r\n
    Server: Microsoft-IIS/6.0\r\n
    WWW-Authenticate: Negotiate
TlRMTVNTUAACAAAABgAGADgAAAAFgomiKip4pcf2dvwAAAAAAAAAAFoAWgA+AAAABQLODgAAAA9JAE4AUwACAAYASQBOAFMAA
QAIAEIASQBMAEwABAAOAGkAbgBzAC4AYwBvAG0AAwAYAEIASQBMAEwALgBpAG4AcwAuAGMAbwBtAAUADgBpAG4AcwAuAGMAbw
BtAAAAAAA=\r\n
        NTLMSSP
            NTLMSSP identifier: NTLMSSP
            NTLM Message Type: NTLMSSP_CHALLENGE (0x00000002)
            Domain: INS
            Flags: 0xa2898205
            NTLM Challenge: 2A2A78A5C7F676FC
            Reserved: 0000000000000000
            Address List
                Length: 90
                Maxlen: 90
                Offset: 62
                Domain NetBIOS Name: INS
                Server NetBIOS Name: BILL
                Domain DNS Name: ins.com
                Server DNS Name: BILL.ins.com
                List Terminator
    Date: Sat, 11 Feb 2006 23:20:24 GMT\r\n
    \r\n
Line-based text data: text/html

Frame 12 (708 bytes on wire, 708 bytes captured)
Ethernet II, Src: 02:00:4c:4f:4f:50 (02:00:4c:4f:4f:50), Dst: BILL.ins.com (00:03:ff:57:ab:2a)
Internet Protocol, Src: 10.0.1.1 (10.0.1.1), Dst: 10.0.1.101 (10.0.1.101)
Transmission Control Protocol, Src Port: 3152 (3152), Dst Port: http (80), Seq: 2933642446, Ack:
4276821837, Len: 654
Hypertext Transfer Protocol
    GET /Security/SPNEGO/ HTTP/1.1\r\n
        Request Method: GET
        Request URI: /Security/SPNEGO/
        Request Version: HTTP/1.1
```

Figure 4.39 (continued)

```
    Accept: image/gif, image/x-xbitmap, image/jpeg, image/pjpeg, application/x-shockwave-flash,
application/vnd.ms-excel, application/vnd.ms-powerpoint, application/msword, */*\r\n
    Accept-Language: en-us,bg;q=0.5\r\n
    Accept-Encoding: gzip, deflate\r\n
    User-Agent: Mozilla/4.0 (compatible; MSIE 6.0; Windows NT 5.1; SV1; .NET CLR 1.1.4322)\r\n
    Host: 10.0.1.101\r\n
    Connection: Keep-Alive\r\n
    Authorization: Negotiate
TlRMTVNTUAADAAAAGAAYAHgAAAAYABgAkAAAABQAFABIAAAACgAKAFwAAAASABIAZgAAAAAAAACoAAAABYKIogUBKAoAAAAPM
QAwAC4AMAAuADEALgAxADAAMQBTAHUAcwBhAG4AWABQAC0AQwBMAEkARQBOAFQA/b4gddkhShUAAAAAAAAAAAAAAAAAAAA9C
knGD9s3ORUM/9oZt0au2
        NTLMSSP
            NTLMSSP identifier: NTLMSSP
            NTLM Message Type: NTLMSSP_AUTH (0x00000003)
            Lan Manager Response: FDBE2075D9214A1500000000000000000000000000000000
            NTLM Response: F42927183F6CDCE45433FF6866DD1ABB6B703EC96B8E4E8C
            Domain name: 10.0.1.101
            User name: Susan
            Host name: XP-CLIENT
            Session Key: Empty
            Flags: 0xa2888205

Frame 14 (447 bytes on wire, 447 bytes captured)
Ethernet II, Src: BILL.ins.com (00:03:ff:57:ab:2a), Dst: 02:00:4c:4f:4f:50 (02:00:4c:4f:4f:50)
Internet Protocol, Src: 10.0.1.101 (10.0.1.101), Dst: 10.0.1.1 (10.0.1.1)
Transmission Control Protocol, Src Port: http (80), Dst Port: 3152 (3152), Seq: 4276821837, Ack:
2933643100, Len: 393
Hypertext Transfer Protocol
    HTTP/1.1 200 OK\r\n
        Request Version: HTTP/1.1
        Response Code: 200
    Content-Length: 104\r\n
    Content-Type: text/html\r\n
    Content-Location: http://10.0.1.101/Security/SPNEGO/index.htm\r\n
    Last-Modified: Sat, 11 Feb 2006 22:48:52 GMT\r\n
    Accept-Ranges: bytes\r\n
```

Figure 4.39 (continued)

```
    ETag: "f05da2545d2fc61:403"\r\n
    Server: Microsoft-IIS/6.0\r\n
    Date: Sat, 11 Feb 2006 23:20:24 GMT\r\n
    \r\n
Line-based text data: text/html
```

Figure 4.39 (continued)

4.6.7 Form-Based Authentication

The Web is a platform for client/server computing. The client browser connected to a server can transfer files from and to that server but it can also use the GET or POST verbs to execute code on the remote Web server by submitting parameters, or can use server-side Java or .Net applications.

Rather than performing authentication prior to exchanging actual user data using HTTP, some Web sites and applications select to perform custom form based authentication. This is an approach where the server application visualizes a login form using standard Web controls, such as text field for a username and password, as well as a login/submit button. The user connects to the Web server using anonymous authentication (e.g., without specifying any authentication parameters), fills in the login form by specifying his username and password, and submits the login button. The server-side application uses functions appropriate for the server platform to authenticate and impersonate the user using the provided plaintext username and password.

The advantage of plaintext authentication is that it has no special requirements for the HTTP authentication method supported by the client and server; the entire HTTP authentication happens over anonymous HTTP, which is supported by any Web browser. The disadvantage is that the username and password are submitted by the Web browser in plaintext — either as part of the URI in the case of the HTTP **GET** verb, or as part of the HTTP fields in the case of the **POST** verb. Therefore, this authentication technique is weak and susceptible to many attacks.

To protect user authentication information, the client and server should utilize a protocol that encrypts the communication channel in between, such as SSL or IPSec.

4.6.8 Microsoft Passport Authentication

Microsoft Passport Authentication (Figure 4.40) is a Microsoft proprietary authentication technology available in Microsoft IIS 5.0 and later. Techni-

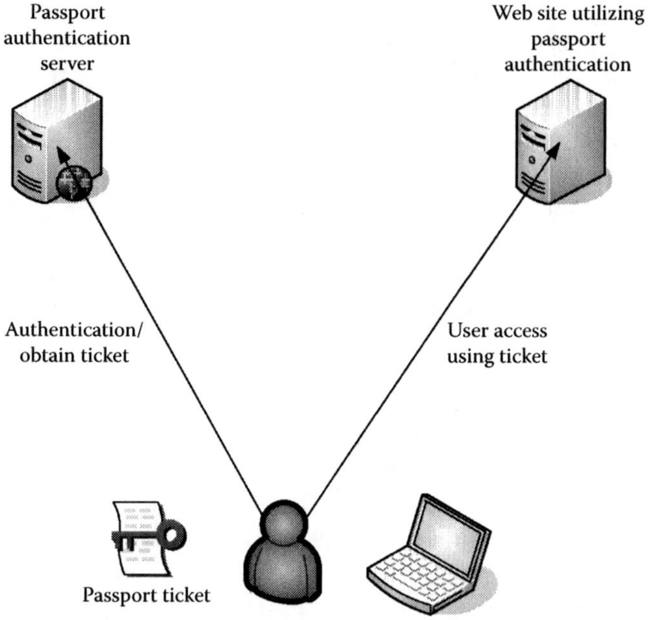

Figure 4.40 Microsoft Passport authentication.

cally, this authentication method can be considered a limited implementation of Federated Authentication (see Chapter 4.18) and Web Single Sign-On (SSO). Microsoft Passport is a hosted Internet authentication service that has its server side implemented by the Passport Authentication servers on the Internet (the **passport.net** name and address space). Its client portion is embedded into IIS 5.0 and later. Microsoft Passport is a paid service.

Many Web sites support a membership directory, and users need to register and provide some identification information that can later be used to log in to the Web site. The problem with this approach is that the user ends up with numerous credentials that conform to the requirements of each Web site and the user needs to remember his username and password, and other information he provided to each Web site.

The idea behind Passport Authentication is simple. Instead of each Web site maintaining its separate membership directory, users provide identification information, such as a username, a password, e-mail address, and potentially other information and register with the Microsoft Passport service (www.passport.com).

Participating Web sites can utilize Microsoft Passport as their Identity and User Authentication Directory and obtain user information and attributes from there. This approach potentially makes every user registered with Microsoft Passport eligible to access resources in Microsoft

Passport member Web sites without further registration. However, participating Web sites still need to maintain a database with information for every user, such as user viewing preferences, subscription information, and other attributes. In that respect, Microsoft Passport only provides the authentication and identification portion, as well as some generic user attributes.

It is important to understand that Microsoft Passport authentication is not meant to impersonate every user and provide them with a unique security context from an operating system point of view. Microsoft Passport authentication provides a user identification approach wherein the Web site utilizing Passport authentication can obtain information such as the username, e-mail address, and other information for the user that the Web site can then use to look up site-specific information for that user. The Passport user authentication process generates a client ticket for the user that the client can then provide to Web sites that it wants to authenticate to. Web sites using Passport authentication are not likely to have specific accounts for every Passport user, and are therefore not likely to impersonate the user and assume a specific security context when the Passport authentication process completes. This is partly because such functionality is not required and user identification is sufficient, and partly because users register with the Passport service without notifying participating Web sites, so that the latter cannot create specific accounts for all Passport registered users. In that respect, Passport authentication is only a user identification mechanism.

To use Passport authentication service, participating Web sites need to contact Microsoft Passport and register for the service. The participating Web site then receives a member key that it stores and protects locally. This key is only known to Microsoft Passport and the participating Web site, and is used to establish the trust relationship between these two parties. The shared key is used by Passport servers to encrypt the client Passport ticket, and by the member Web server to decrypt the client Passport ticket. When the Internet client authenticates to the Passport service, it receives a 3DES encrypted ticket. The client cannot modify or craft the ticket because the shared key is only known to the Passport servers and the Member Web site. The client can only pass the original ticket to the Member Web site. When the Member Web site decrypts the ticket, it can trust the ticket and consider it genuine because only the Passport service could have been the party that encrypted the ticket, as no third party has the encryption key.

When a user tries to access a portion of a Web site that is protected with Passport authentication, the following process takes place:

1. The client Web browser sends a **GET** request for a Passport-protected Web page.

2. The Web server checks client cookies and determines whether the client has already obtained a Passport authentication ticket. If the ticket exists, go to Step 9.
3. If the client does not have a Passport authentication ticket, the server forces the client to authenticate to the Passport service by sending back an HTTP 302 "HTTP Redirect" response and redirecting the user to the Passport service on the Internet. The redirection contains a URL to the Member Web site in the query string.
4. The client Web browser follows the redirection and establishes a Web session with a Passport Web server.
5. The Passport Web server provides the user with a form prompting the user for authentication credentials (see subsection 4.6.7);
6. The user provides a username and a password and is authenticated to the Passport server.
7. The Passport server generates a client ticket, encrypted using 3DES and the key shared with the member Web site, and returns it to the client, along with an HTTP 302 "HTTP Redirect" response to the original Web site so that the user can continue from where he left off the original Web page.
8. The client Web browser connects back to the original URL specified in the redirect message (it matches the one provided by the Member Web server in Step 3).
9. The Member Web server finds the encrypted Passport ticket in the client browser cookies and decrypts it using 3DES and the shared Passport key as the key. It then extracts user identification information and builds the user environment.

4.6.9 HTTP Proxy Authentication

HTTP requests can be either direct from the client to the Web server, or proxied through a Web proxy server. In the latter case, the connection to the proxy server may require user authentication as well. RFC 2616 (see [69]) defines proxy authentication fields and specifies that user authentication to the proxy server can use the same mechanisms as user authentication to a Web server. Still, the client browser is able to distinguish between authentication requested by the proxy server and that requested by the Web server.

When a proxy server requires client authentication, it returns HTTP response code "407 Proxy Authentication Required," unlike HTTP response "401 Unauthorized," which is typically returned by Web servers that request user authentication. Instead of using the **WWW-Authenticate** field of the

HTTP header, proxy servers use the **Proxy-Authenticate** field; and instead of providing the client authentication replies in the **Authorization** HTTP field, the client uses the **Proxy-Authorization** field. Apart from that, user authentication mechanisms to a proxy server are similar to authentication against a Web server.

4.7 POP3/IMAP Authentication

User access to Internet e-mail is typically performed using the IMAP or POP3 Protocols. E-mail is a resource, hence, user authentication should be used to identify and authenticate the user before he is allowed to access e-mail. When a user logs in to an IMAP or POP3 server, the authentication process identifies the user and authenticates his identity. IMAP and POP3 then automatically switch to the user's inbox, and IMAP or POP3 command verbs will be executed on contents of the user mailbox (IMAP4 supports folder structures and may be a bit more complex than this). User authentication is required by both POP3 and IMAP.

POP3 and IMAP4 are similar in terms of user authentication. IMAP authentication is defined in RFC 1731 (see [56]). There are three IMAP4 authentication mechanisms that this document describes: (1) Kerberos v.4, (2) GSS-API, and (3) S/Key. The Login authentication mechanism is implicit. The IMAP4 verb **CAPABILITIES** can be used to enumerate the supported authentication methods. The IMAP4 **AUTHENTICATE** verb can be used by the client to select an authentication protocol other than Login.

The POP3 Authentication verb (**AUTH**) is defined in RFC 1734 (see [57]). POP3 does not provide for a **CAPABILITIES** command verb. The client needs to know what authentication protocols are supported by the server beforehand, and then send the **AUTH** command with the desired authentication protocol as the parameter to request authentication other than basic Login authentication.

4.7.1 POP3/IMAP Password Authentication

Password authentication is defined in RFC 1460 (see [62]) and is part of the POP3 protocol specification. It is not an SASL authentication mechanism.

In a typical POP3 session where password authentication is used, the client connects to the server and uses an authentication dialogue to provide his user credentials (the USER statement to provide a username, and the PASS statement to provide a cleartext password). If the client is successfully authenticated, it can access e-mail messages.

The IMAP4 protocol uses the LOGIN command as defined in RFC 2060 (see [65]) to perform password authentication in a similar way to POP3.

The following example shows POP3 Password authentication:.

```
C:\> telnet exchdc1 110

+OK Microsoft Exchange POP3 server version 5.5.2448.8 ready
user Simon
+OK
pass password
+OK User successfully logged on
stat
+OK 0 0
quit
+OK Microsoft Exchange POP3 server version 5.5.2448.8 signing off
```

Password authentication is a simple authentication mechanism that uses plain usernames and passwords and is susceptible to a wide range of attacks. Unless protected with TLS/SSL, this authentication mechanism should be avoided.

4.7.2 POP3/IMAP Plain Authentication

POP3/IMAP4 Plain authentication is defined in RFC 2595 (see [64]). It is not an SASL mechanism. Plain authentication is supported by some POP3/IMAP servers, including Dovecot and ipop3d. Microsoft Exchange Server does not support Plain authentication.

To authenticate using Plain authentication, the client sends the e-mail alias for the mailbox he is trying to authenticate to, the username that will be used to bind to the mailbox, and the password. These three components of the Plain authentication process are separated by NULL characters ("0") and are Base64 encoded before being sent to the server.

Because the user password is sent by the client to the server in cleartext, the server does not need to store the user password in cleartext or use reversible encryption because it can calculate the one-way hash value stored in its user database by encrypting the plaintext password.

Plain authentication is a weak authentication scheme that is susceptible to various attacks and should generally be avoided unless a secure TLS/SSL channel is used.

4.7.3 POP3 APOP Authentication

APOP is an authentication protocol used by the POP3 Protocol. It is defined as an optional POP3 mechanism in RFC 1460 (see [62]) and is not an SASL mechanism. APOP authentication is primarily used by UNIX-based POP3 servers and is not supported by Microsoft Exchange Server. Client support for APOP is not popular and, as a result, the APOP Protocol is relatively rarely used.

The APOP Protocol is another typical challenge-response authentication mechanism. If a POP3 server supports APOP authentication, it provides a challenge string to the client immediately upon connection. The client needs to provide an encrypted response to the server, based on the user password. The server then compares the locally calculated result with the client-provided response and either authenticates the user successfully or rejects the connection. In fact, the APOP mechanism is very similar to the CRAM-MD5 authentication mechanism but the minor differences between the two authentication protocols make them incompatible.

The steps involved in authenticating a POP3 user using APOP are as follows:

1. The client connects to the server using POP3.
2. The server generates a pseudo-random challenge. Typically, the server generates the challenge by concatenating its process ID (PID), a dot ("."), the current time in UNIX format, an AT sign ("@"), and the server DNS name (FQDN). The challenge is then put in brackets ("<" and ">").
3. The client generates a reply by concatenating the server challenge in brackets with the plaintext user password and calculating the MD5 hash for the resultant string.
4. The client uses the APOP command to perform authentication against the server. It submits the username and the MD5 hashed response as parameters of the APOP command verb.

```
C:\> telnet linus.ins.com 110
+OK POP3 server ready <2721.1139275622@linus.ins.com>
apop hemmingway 294361A935BA67FC29FB7909EC8D821B
+OK Logged in.
quit
+OK Logging out.
```

The server challenge consists of a random number (the server PID), a time stamp, and a known string (the server name). The random number (pseudo-random) and the time stamp provide for anti-replay protection for the APOP authentication method. Unfortunately, the APOP authentication mechanism is susceptible to the same attacks as the CRAM-MD5 authentication mechanism. Similar to CRAM-MD5, APOP requires the server to have access to the plaintext or reversibly encrypted user password, which poses additional security risks.

4.7.4 POP3/IMAP Login Authentication

Login authentication is an SASL mechanism supported by many clients and servers, including Microsoft Exchange Server and Sendmail. For more information on Login authentication, see subsection 4.8.1.

4.7.5 POP3/IMAP SASL CRAM-MD5 and DIGEST-MD5 Authentication

POP3 and IMAP servers are often used with SASL authentication mechanisms, mostly CRAM-MD5 and DIGEST-MD5. More information is available in subsections 4.2.3.6 and 4.2.3.7.

4.7.6 POP3/IMAP and NTLM Authentication (Secure Password Authentication)

Authentication against Microsoft Exchange Server and some other mail servers can be performed using NTLM authentication. Microsoft refers to it as Secure Password Authentication (SPA). In essence, the Exchange client and server use NTLMSSP within the IMAP4 or POP3 Protocol. NTLM authentication is implemented as an SASL mechanism in Microsoft Exchange Server. The POP3 client utilizes the **AUTH NTLM** command to request NTLM authentication, and IMAP4 utilizes the **AUTHENTICATION NTLM** command verb. All data is encoded using Base64, and not encrypted unless TLS/SSL is used to protect the channel.

Once the client has connected to the server, Secure Password Authentication (NTLM over POP3) is performed as follows (see Figure 4.41).

1. The client specifies the authentication method it wants to use, such as NTLM (see Frame 43 in Figure 4.41).
2. The server confirms that this is a valid authentication method (see Frame 44 in Figure 4.41).
3. The client requests NTLM authentication using an NTLM Type 1 message (see Frame 45 in Figure 4.41).
4. The server provides a challenge string in an NTLM Type 2 message (see Frame 46 in Figure 4.41).
5. The client calculates NTLM and LM responses to the challenge and submits them back to the server in an NTLM Type 3 message (see Frame 47 in Figure 4.41).
6. The server confirms successful authentication (see Frame 48 in Figure 4.41).

```
Frame 43 (65 bytes on wire, 65 bytes captured)
Ethernet II, Src: Vmware_c0:00:01 (00:50:56:c0:00:01), Dst: Vmware_6c:bc:6d (00:0c:29:6c:bc:6d)
Internet Protocol, Src: 192.168.26.1 (192.168.26.1), Dst: 192.168.26.130 (192.168.26.130)
Transmission Control Protocol, Src Port: 1580 (1580), Dst Port: pop3 (110), Seq: 1258278311, Ack:
109521, Len: 11
Post Office Protocol
    AUTH NTLM\r\n
        Request: AUTH
        Request Arg: NTLM

Frame 44 (60 bytes on wire, 60 bytes captured)
Ethernet II, Src: Vmware_6c:bc:6d (00:0c:29:6c:bc:6d), Dst: Vmware_c0:00:01 (00:50:56:c0:00:01)
Internet Protocol, Src: 192.168.26.130 (192.168.26.130), Dst: 192.168.26.1 (192.168.26.1)
Transmission Control Protocol, Src Port: pop3 (110), Dst Port: 1580 (1580), Seq: 109521, Ack:
1258278322, Len: 6
    Data (6 bytes)
    Reply: + OK

Frame 45 (112 bytes on wire, 112 bytes captured)
Ethernet II, Src: Vmware_c0:00:01 (00:50:56:c0:00:01), Dst: Vmware_6c:bc:6d (00:0c:29:6c:bc:6d)
Internet Protocol, Src: 192.168.26.1 (192.168.26.1), Dst: 192.168.26.130 (192.168.26.130)
Transmission Control Protocol, Src Port: 1580 (1580), Dst Port: pop3 (110), Seq: 1258278322, Ack:
109527, Len: 58
Post Office Protocol
    TlRMTVNTUAABAAAAB4IIogAAAAAAAAAAAAAAAAAAAAAAFASgKAAAADw==\r\n (Base64)
    NTLMSSP□□,□ÿ□□( □ (Decoded)

Frame 46 (210 bytes on wire, 210 bytes captured)
Ethernet II, Src: Vmware_6c:bc:6d (00:0c:29:6c:bc:6d), Dst: Vmware_c0:00:01 (00:50:56:c0:00:01)
Internet Protocol, Src: 192.168.26.130 (192.168.26.130), Dst: 192.168.26.1 (192.168.26.1)
Transmission Control Protocol, Src Port: pop3 (110), Dst Port: 1580 (1580), Seq: 109527, Ack:
1258278380, Len: 156
Post Office Protocol
    Data (156 bytes)
```

Figure 4.41 POP3-NTLM-Auth.cap: User authentication to a POP3 server using NTLM.

```
    Reply:  + Base64:
TlRMTVNTUAACAAAAFAAUADAAAAAFgokA3WlPctW5dWwAAAAAAAAAAC4ALgBEAAAARABPAFQATgBFAFQAWgBPAE4ARQACABQAR
ABPAFQATgBFAFQAWgBPAE4ARQABAA4ARQBYAEMASABEAEMAMQAAAAAA (Base64)
NTLMSSP□□□0□,‰ЭiOrXNul..DDOTNETZONE□□DOTNETZONE□EXCHDC1 (Decoded)

Frame 47 (280 bytes on wire, 280 bytes captured)
Ethernet II, Src: Vmware_c0:00:01 (00:50:56:c0:00:01), Dst: Vmware_6c:bc:6d (00:0c:29:6c:bc:6d)
Internet Protocol, Src: 192.168.26.1 (192.168.26.1), Dst: 192.168.26.130 (192.168.26.130)
Transmission Control Protocol, Src Port: 1580 (1580), Dst Port: pop3 (110), Seq: 1258278380, Ack:
109683, Len: 226
Post Office Protocol
        Request:
TlRMTVNTUAADAAAAGAAYAHgAAAAYABgAkAAAABQAFABIAAAACgAKAFwAAAASABIAZgAAAAAAAACoAAAABYKIAgUBKAoAAAAPZ
ABvAHQAbgBlAHQAegBvAG4AZQBzAGkAbQBvAG4AWABQAC0AQwBMAEkARQBOAFQAkdh3rd1aCaYAAAAAAAAAAAAAAAAAAAAARY
OmAs8poUoTxzKMoRbKad4deYzoHHZZ (Base 64)
NTLMSSP□□□0□,‰ЭiOrXNul..DDOTNETZONE□□DOTNETZONE□EXCHDC1 (Decoded)

Frame 48 (87 bytes on wire, 87 bytes captured)
Ethernet II, Src: Vmware_6c:bc:6d (00:0c:29:6c:bc:6d), Dst: Vmware_c0:00:01 (00:50:56:c0:00:01)
Internet Protocol, Src: 192.168.26.130 (192.168.26.130), Dst: 192.168.26.1 (192.168.26.1)
Transmission Control Protocol, Src Port: pop3 (110), Dst Port: 1580 (1580), Seq: 109683, Ack:
1258278606, Len: 33
Post Office Protocol
    +OK User successfully logged on\r\n
        Response: +OK
        Response Arg: User successfully logged on
```

Figure 4.41 (continued)

4.8 SMTP Authentication

The Simple Mail Transfer Protocol (SMTP) is the *de facto* standard for sending and relaying e-mail over the Internet. The two primary uses of SMTP are (1) client-to-server communication, which allows clients to submit e-mail to a forwarding host without knowing where exactly the destination resides; and (2) server-to-server communication, wherein servers typically using DNS determine the intended destination for an e-mail message and virtually in a full-mesh topology forward messages to each other.

With the ever-increasing level of spam on the Internet, companies are facing the challenge of restricting client-to-server SMTP communication and only accepting relay messages from trusted clients. Companies will typically completely block requests for relay from the Internet to avoid becoming a transit system for a flooding or spam attack. There are two possible approaches to control relay: (1) user authentication and (2) allowing relaying from a set of source IP addresses. User authentication is the more flexible approach to restrict relaying.

SMTP authentication is rarely used in the server-to-server scenario because of the requirement for a virtually full mesh. In rare cases, such as when companies establish partnerships over the Internet and set up dedicated SMTP hosts to forward messages between the two companies, SMTP authentication can be used in the server-to-server scenario. Yet in such circumstances, companies will typically want to exchange more information than just e-mail messages, so they may look at extranet technologies (very often VPNs), which make SMTP authentication redundant.

To support the above requirements, SMTP supports anonymous connections that are most widely used, and authenticated connections that are used sometimes for client access. The Internet standard for SMTP authentication is RFC 2554 (see [54]). It defines the **AUTH** verb used for SMTP authentication, as well as the requirement for SMTP authentication to support SASL authentication mechanisms.

The authentication methods supported by a particular SMTP server are typically enumerated as part of the server capabilities response to the **HELO** or **EHLO** SMTP verbs. Below is an example of server capabilities for the built-in Windows 2003 SMTP service:

```
telnet bill.ins.com 25

220 BILL.ins.com Microsoft ESMTP MAIL Service, Version: 6.0.3790.1830
 ready at
Sun, 5 Feb 2006 00:05:29 +0000

EHLO
250-BILL.ins.com Hello [10.0.1.1]
250-AUTH GSSAPI NTLM LOGIN
250-AUTH=LOGIN
250-TURN
250-SIZE 2097152
250-ETRN
250-PIPELINING
250-DSN
250-ENHANCEDSTATUSCODES
250-8bitmime
250-BINARYMIME
250-CHUNKING
250-VRFY
250 OK
```

```
quit
221 2.0.0 BILL.ins.com Service closing transmission channel
```

The server supports Login authentication (Microsoft refers to Login authentication as Basic authentication), GSS-API authentication (or SSPI compatible), and NTLM authentication (in Exchange Server and its clients, Microsoft refers to NTLM authentication as Secure Password Authentication, or SPA).

The following subsections review some of the most widely used SMTP authentication mechanisms.

4.8.1 SMTP Login Authentication

SMTP Login authentication is a non-standard SASL authentication mechanism. It has been used for many years and by many products. An attempt was made to define the protocol in the Internet Draft "The LOGIN SASL Mechanism" (see [66]), which expired in March 2004 without becoming an RFC.

The Login authentication method simulates the login dialogue between the client and the server in a Telnet session. The server sends messages prompting the user to enter the username and password. The user responds to server prompts as requested. The Login dialogue is encoded using Base64. This does not make it more secure than plaintext authentication as Base64 is just an encoding technique that allows for a different data representation, and is not an encryption technique. The authentication process can be considered equally protected as plaintext authentication.

Once the client has connected to the server, SMTP Login authentication is performed as follows (see Figure 4.42):

1. The client specifies the authentication method it wants to use — such as Login (see Frame 25 in Figure 4.42).
2. The server replies with the "Username:" prompt using Base64 encoding (see Frame 26 in Figure 4.42).
3. The user provides his username to the server, using Base64 encoding (see Frame 27 in Figure 4.42).
4. The server now sends the "Password:" string (see Frame 28 in Figure 4.42).
5. The client replies using the actual user password here (see Frame 29 in Figure 4.42).
6. The server typically impersonates the client at this stage using the plaintext username and password

As for all other plaintext interactive authentication methods, Login authentication is susceptible to a wide range of attacks and should therefore be avoided unless encapsulated within a TLS/SSL protected channel.

```
Frame 25 (66 bytes on wire, 66 bytes captured)
Ethernet II, Src: Vmware_c0:00:01 (00:50:56:c0:00:01), Dst: Vmware_6c:bc:6d (00:0c:29:6c:bc:6d)
Internet Protocol, Src: 192.168.26.1 (192.168.26.1), Dst: 192.168.26.130 (192.168.26.130)
Transmission Control Protocol, Src Port: 1700 (1700), Dst Port: smtp (25), Seq: 1218090443, Ack:
109912, Len: 12
Simple Mail Transfer Protocol
    Command: AUTH LOGIN\r\n
        Command: AUTH
        Request parameter: LOGIN

Frame 26 (72 bytes on wire, 72 bytes captured)
Ethernet II, Src: Vmware_6c:bc:6d (00:0c:29:6c:bc:6d), Dst: Vmware_c0:00:01 (00:50:56:c0:00:01)
Internet Protocol, Src: 192.168.26.130 (192.168.26.130), Dst: 192.168.26.1 (192.168.26.1)
Transmission Control Protocol, Src Port: smtp (25), Dst Port: 1700 (1700), Seq: 109912, Ack:
1218090455, Len: 18
Simple Mail Transfer Protocol
    Response: 334 VXNlcm5hbWU6\r\n
        Response code: 334
        Response parameter: VXNlcm5hbWU6 (Base64)
        Response parameter: Username: (Decoded)

Frame 27 (64 bytes on wire, 64 bytes captured)
Ethernet II, Src: Vmware_c0:00:01 (00:50:56:c0:00:01), Dst: Vmware_6c:bc:6d (00:0c:29:6c:bc:6d)
Internet Protocol, Src: 192.168.26.1 (192.168.26.1), Dst: 192.168.26.130 (192.168.26.130)
Transmission Control Protocol, Src Port: 1700 (1700), Dst Port: smtp (25), Seq: 1218090455, Ack:
109930, Len: 10
Simple Mail Transfer Protocol
    Message: c2ltb24=\r\n (Base 64)
    Message: simon\r\n (Decoded)


Frame 28 (72 bytes on wire, 72 bytes captured)
Ethernet II, Src: Vmware_6c:bc:6d (00:0c:29:6c:bc:6d), Dst: Vmware_c0:00:01 (00:50:56:c0:00:01)
Internet Protocol, Src: 192.168.26.130 (192.168.26.130), Dst: 192.168.26.1 (192.168.26.1)
Transmission Control Protocol, Src Port: smtp (25), Dst Port: 1700 (1700), Seq: 109930, Ack:
1218090465, Len: 18
```

Figure 4.42 SMTP-Login-Auth.cap: User access to SMTP server using login method.

```
Simple Mail Transfer Protocol
    Response: 334 UGFzc3dvcmQ6\r\n
        Response code: 334
        Response parameter: UGFzc3dvcmQ6 (Base 64)
        Response parameter: Password: (Decoded)

Frame 29 (68 bytes on wire, 68 bytes captured)
Ethernet II, Src: Vmware_c0:00:01 (00:50:56:c0:00:01), Dst: Vmware_6c:bc:6d (00:0c:29:6c:bc:6d)
Internet Protocol, Src: 192.168.26.1 (192.168.26.1), Dst: 192.168.26.130 (192.168.26.130)
Transmission Control Protocol, Src Port: 1700 (1700), Dst Port: smtp (25), Seq: 1218090465, Ack:
109948, Len: 14
Simple Mail Transfer Protocol
    Message: cGFzc3dvcmQ=\r\n (Base 64)
    Message: password\r\n (Decoded)

Frame 30 (91 bytes on wire, 91 bytes captured)
Ethernet II, Src: Vmware_6c:bc:6d (00:0c:29:6c:bc:6d), Dst: Vmware_c0:00:01 (00:50:56:c0:00:01)
Internet Protocol, Src: 192.168.26.130 (192.168.26.130), Dst: 192.168.26.1 (192.168.26.1)
Transmission Control Protocol, Src Port: smtp (25), Dst Port: 1700 (1700), Seq: 109948, Ack:
1218090479, Len: 37
Simple Mail Transfer Protocol
    Response: 235 LOGIN authentication successful\r\n
        Response code: 235
        Response parameter: LOGIN authentication successful
```

Figure 4.42 (continued)

4.8.2 SMTP Plain Authentication

Some SMTP servers (such as Sendmail) support the Plain authentication method. This authentication mechanism is similar to Plain authentication used by POP3 and IMAP4. For more details on Plain authentication, see subsection 4.7.2.

4.8.3 SMTP GSS-API Authentication

Some SMTP servers (such as Sendmail and Microsoft Exchange Server) support GSS-API authentication. In essence, GSS-API provides for Kerberos V authentication. SMTP GSS-API is typically implemented as an SASL authentication mechanism. For an example of GSS-API authentication, see subsection 4.9.4.

4.8.4 SMTP CRAM-MD5 and DIGEST-MD5 Authentication

SMTP CRAM-MD5 and Digest-MD5 authentication methods are SASL compliant and are supported by Sendmail but not by Microsoft Exchange Server. For more information on these authentication methods, see subsections 4.2.3.6 and 4.2.3.7.

4.8.5 SMTP Authentication Using NTLM

NTLM authentication for SMTP is supported by Microsoft Exchange Server, as well as the Windows 2000/2003 built-in SMTP server. SMTP authentication using NTLM can be performed using the **AUTH NTLM** command. The authentication process is similar to the one used by the POP3 and IMAP4 protocols. For more information, see subsection 4.7.6.

4.9 LDAP Authentication

Lightweight Directory Access Protocol (LDAP) is a widely used protocol for access to enterprise directory information. Because an enterprise directory can store a significant amount of information about enterprise objects, appropriate authentication and access control for access to the directory are typically required. In the past couple of years, LDAP has turned into a central point for enterprise identity management and user authentication. Many organizations have chosen to configure their applications and services to use LDAP as the authentication source, and metadirectory applications are available to consolidate directory information and provide different representations of this data as datafeeds to LDAP servers in the enterprise. Microsoft Active Directory and Active Directory Application Mode (ADAM), Sun/Netscape iPlanet Directory Server, and OpenLDAP are examples of popular LDAP servers that can work together in an enterprise environment.

LDAP authentication is specifically addressed in RFC 2829 (see [59]). Essentially, RFC 2829 defines that LDAP authentication should be performed using the native LDAP Simple authentication mechanism, SASL mechanisms, or SSL certificate mapping. The RFC recommends SSL/TLS data protection for the channel between the LDAP client and the LDAP server. Unlike POP3/IMAP, HTTP, and SMTP, LDAP is not a dialogue-based protocol. The client and server send messages to each other using LDAP data structures. The **Bind** messages used for user authentication contain fields that allow for an authentication type and authentication data to be specified, and they are used by LDAP to embed SASL mechanisms into the LDAP data structure.

General information for the LDAP server, including the supported SASL authentication mechanisms, can be obtained by connecting anonymously to the LDAP server's root context, known as RootDSE. Many LDAP clients query the RootDSE in the beginning of every session to an LDAP server. A client connected to the Active Directory LDAP server, for example, is likely to see the following RootDSE information:.

```
ld = ldap_open("bill.ins.com", 389);
Established connection to bill.ins.com.
Retrieving base DSA information...
Result <0>: (null)
Matched DNs:
Getting 1 entries:
>> Dn:
  1> currentTime: 02/14/2006 05:41:20 GMT Standard Time GMT Daylight Time;
  1> subschemaSubentry: CN=Aggregate,CN=Schema,CN=Configuration,DC=ins,DC=com;
  1> dsServiceName: CN=NTDS Settings,CN=BILL,CN=Servers,CN=Default-First-Site-
Name,CN=Sites,CN=Configuration,DC=ins,DC=com;
  5> namingContexts: DC=ins,DC=com; CN=Configuration,DC=ins,DC=com;
CN=Schema,CN=Configuration,DC=ins,DC=com; DC=DomainDnsZones,DC=ins,
DC=com; DC=ForestDnsZones,DC=ins,DC=com;
  1> defaultNamingContext: DC=ins,DC=com;
  1> schemaNamingContext: CN=Schema,CN=Configuration,DC=ins,DC=com;
  1> configurationNamingContext: CN=Configuration,DC=ins,DC=com;
  1> rootDomainNamingContext: DC=ins,DC=com;
  22> supportedControl: 1.2.840.113556.1.4.319; 1.2.840.113556.1.4.801;
1.2.840.113556.1.4.473; 1.2.840.113556.1.4.528;
1.2.840.113556.1.4.417; 1.2.840.113556.1.4.619;
1.2.840.113556.1.4.841; 1.2.840.113556.1.4.529;
1.2.840.113556.1.4.805; 1.2.840.113556.1.4.521;
1.2.840.113556.1.4.970; 1.2.840.113556.1.4.1338;
1.2.840.113556.1.4.474; 1.2.840.113556.1.4.1339;
1.2.840.113556.1.4.1340; 1.2.840.113556.1.4.1413;
2.16.840.1.113730.3.4.9; 2.16.840.1.113730.3.4.10;
1.2.840.113556.1.4.1504; 1.2.840.113556.1.4.1852;
1.2.840.113556.1.4.802; 1.2.840.113556.1.4.1907;
  2> supportedLDAPVersion: 3; 2;
  12> supportedLDAPPolicies: MaxPoolThreads; MaxDatagramRecv; MaxReceiveBuffer;
InitRecvTimeout; MaxConnections; MaxConnIdleTime; MaxPageSize; MaxQueryDuration;
MaxTempTableSize; MaxResultSetSize; MaxNotificationPerConn; MaxValRange;
  1> highestCommittedUSN: 94224;
  4> supportedSASLMechanisms: GSSAPI; GSS-SPNEGO; EXTERNAL; DIGEST-MD5;
  1> dnsHostName: BILL.ins.com;
  1> ldapServiceName: ins.com:bill$@INS.COM;
  1> serverName: CN=BILL,CN=Servers,CN=Default-First-Site-
Name,CN=Sites,CN=Configuration,DC=ins,DC=com;
  3> supportedCapabilities: 1.2.840.113556.1.4.800; 1.2.840.113556.1.4.1670;
1.2.840.113556.1.4.1791;
  1> isSynchronized: TRUE;
  1> isGlobalCatalogReady: TRUE;
  1> domainFunctionality: 2 = ( DS_BEHAVIOR_WIN2003 );
  1> forestFunctionality: 2 = ( DS_BEHAVIOR_WIN2003 );
  1> domainControllerFunctionality: 2 = ( DS_BEHAVIOR_WIN2003 );
```

The **SupportedSASLMechanisms** attribute shows that the LDAP server is willing to use GSS-API with or without SPNEGO authentication negotiation (which in the case of Windows 2003 designates the SSPI interface that can potentially negotiate NTLM or Kerberos), as well as SASL EXTERNAL authentication, or SASL DIGEST-MD5 authentication directly on top of LDAP.

The following subsections discuss some of the most popular LDAP authentication mechanisms.

4.9.1 Simple Authentication

In a common scenario, an LDAP client can authenticate to an LDAP server using the native LDAP Simple authentication mechanism. LDAP authentication is performed using the so-called LDAP Bind operation. The Bind structure used by LDAP contains a DN field (Distinguished Name — the username represented as a user object in X.500-compatible format), and a password field that can be used by the client to provide a plaintext username and password to the server.

Figure 4.43 shows the LDAP authentication process using Simple Bind. In Frame 8, the user supplies the username (Distinguished Name) and password, specifying Simple as the authentication type. The server checks the user password against the password database, potentially also transforming it to the format in which user passwords are stored, and returns successful authentication in Frame 9.

4.9.2 LDAP Anonymous Authentication

LDAP Anonymous authentication support is required by the LDAP specification because the root context of the LDAP Object hierarchy (the RootDSE) must be available to all clients, even to those that have not authenticated yet or cannot authenticate with specific credentials. When a client connects to an LDAP server for the first time, it will typically connect anonymously to the RootDSE context to check the server capabilities. Once this has been done, the client may try to bind to the server using specific user credentials and potentially access protected LDAP resources to which he has access.

LDAP Anonymous authentication is LDAP Simple authentication wherein the client supplies a NULL DN attribute and a NULL password field. The LDAP server is expected to impersonate this client using an anonymous authentication context and provide limited access to resources.

4.9.3 LDAP SASL Authentication Using Digest-MD5

LDAP SASL Digest-MD5 authentication is very similar to SASL Digest-MD5 for POP/IMAP, as well as HTTP Digest-MD5. The difference is that because

```
Frame 8 (125 bytes on wire, 125 bytes captured)
Ethernet II, Src: 02:00:4c:4f:4f:50 (02:00:4c:4f:4f:50), Dst: bill.ins.com (00:03:ff:57:ab:2a)
Internet Protocol, Src: 10.0.2.102 (10.0.2.102), Dst: 10.0.1.101 (10.0.1.101)
Transmission Control Protocol, Src Port: 1085 (1085), Dst Port: ldap (389), Seq: 2438990268, Ack:
3243550055, Len: 71
Lightweight Directory Access Protocol
    LDAP Message, Bind Request
        Message Id: 17
        Message Type: Bind Request (0x00)
        Message Length: 56
        Response In: 9
        Version: 3
        DN: cn=administrator,cn=users,dc=ins,dc=com
        Auth Type: Simple (0x00)
        Password: password1!

Frame 9 (76 bytes on wire, 76 bytes captured)
Ethernet II, Src: bill.ins.com (00:03:ff:57:ab:2a), Dst: 02:00:4c:4f:4f:50 (02:00:4c:4f:4f:50)
Internet Protocol, Src: 10.0.1.101 (10.0.1.101), Dst: 10.0.2.102 (10.0.2.102)
Transmission Control Protocol, Src Port: ldap (389), Dst Port: 1085 (1085), Seq: 3243550055, Ack:
2438990339, Len: 22
Lightweight Directory Access Protocol
    LDAP Message, Bind Result
        Message Id: 17
        Message Type: Bind Result (0x01)
        Message Length: 7
        Response To: 8
        Time: 0.004643000 seconds
        Result Code: success (0x00)
        Matched DN: (null)
        Error Message: (null)
```

Figure 4.43 LDAP-Simple-Bind.cap: User access to LDAP server using Simple Bind.

LDAP is not an interactive protocol, SASL messages are encapsulated within the LDAP Bind structure, rather than exchanged interactively after issuing the **SASL AUTH** verb. Another minor difference is that Digest-MD5 messages are not Base64 encoded and plain ASCII is used instead. For details on the Digest-MD5 mechanics, see subsection 4.2.3.7.

LDAP SASL Digest-MD5 authentication is shown in Figure 4.44. The client sends a request for Digest-MD5 authentication in Frame 8, the server

```
Frame 8 (94 bytes on wire, 94 bytes captured)
Ethernet II, Src: 02:00:4c:4f:4f:50 (02:00:4c:4f:4f:50), Dst: Microsof_57:ab:2a
(00:03:ff:57:ab:2a)
Internet Protocol, Src: 10.0.2.102 (10.0.2.102), Dst: 10.0.1.101 (10.0.1.101)
Transmission Control Protocol, Src Port: kpop (1109), Dst Port: ldap (389), Seq: 2613025041, Ack:
3723539386, Len: 40
Lightweight Directory Access Protocol
    LDAP Message, Bind Request
        Message Id: 35
        Message Type: Bind Request (0x00)
        Message Length: 25
        Response In: 9
        Version: 3
        DN: (null)
        Auth Type: SASL (0x03)
        Mechanism: DIGEST-MD5

Frame 9 (283 bytes on wire, 283 bytes captured)
Ethernet II, Src: Microsof_57:ab:2a (00:03:ff:57:ab:2a), Dst: 02:00:4c:4f:4f:50
(02:00:4c:4f:4f:50)
Internet Protocol, Src: 10.0.1.101 (10.0.1.101), Dst: 10.0.2.102 (10.0.2.102)
Transmission Control Protocol, Src Port: ldap (389), Dst Port: kpop (1109), Seq: 3723539386, Ack:
2613025081, Len: 229
Lightweight Directory Access Protocol
    LDAP Message, Bind Result
        Message Id: 35
        Message Type: Bind Result (0x01)
        Message Length: 214
        Response To: 8
        Time: 0.001978000 seconds
        Result Code: saslBindInProgress (0x0e)
        Matched DN: (null)
        Error Message: (null)
        Server Credentials: qop="auth,auth-int,auth-conf",cipher="3des,des,rc4-40,rc4,rc4-
56",algorithm=md5-sess,
```

Figure 4.44 LDAP-SASL-DIGEST.cap: User access to LDAP server using SASL Digest-MD5.

```
nonce="40b3af573231c601fd9913005e7bbcd8e410e1b1b263873ae35d35759b4c92327a4d4d9b5753e02a",charset=
utf-8,realm="ins.com"

Frame 10 (379 bytes on wire, 379 bytes captured)
Ethernet II, Src: 02:00:4c:4f:4f:50 (02:00:4c:4f:4f:50), Dst: Microsof_57:ab:2a
(00:03:ff:57:ab:2a)
Internet Protocol, Src: 10.0.2.102 (10.0.2.102), Dst: 10.0.1.101 (10.0.1.101)
Transmission Control Protocol, Src Port: kpop (1109), Dst Port: ldap (389), Seq: 2613025081, Ack:
3723539615, Len: 325
Lightweight Directory Access Protocol
    LDAP Message, Bind Request
        Message Id: 36
        Message Type: Bind Request (0x00)
        Message Length: 310
        Response In: 11
        Version: 3
        DN: (null)
        Auth Type: SASL (0x03)
        Mechanism: DIGEST-MD5
        Credentials:
username="administrator",realm="ins.com",nonce="40b3af573231c601fd9913005e7bbcd8e410e1b1b263873ae
35d35759b4c92327a4d4d9b5753e02a",digest-
uri="ldap/bill.ins.com",cnonce="9f8b21bdaa927f7bc1f68e1eb045d7ac",nc=00000001,response=1d2e0c6fdb
e232e52d9e68cda3190cba,qop=auth-int,charset=utf-8

Frame 11 (118 bytes on wire, 118 bytes captured)
Ethernet II, Src: Microsof_57:ab:2a (00:03:ff:57:ab:2a), Dst: 02:00:4c:4f:4f:50
(02:00:4c:4f:4f:50)
Internet Protocol, Src: 10.0.1.101 (10.0.1.101), Dst: 10.0.2.102 (10.0.2.102)
Transmission Control Protocol, Src Port: ldap (389), Dst Port: kpop (1109), Seq: 3723539615, Ack:
2613025406, Len: 64
Lightweight Directory Access Protocol
    LDAP Message, Bind Result
        Message Id: 36
        Message Type: Bind Result (0x01)
        Message Length: 49
```

Figure 4.44 (continued)

```
Response To: 10
Time: 0.005605000 seconds
Result Code: success (0x00)
Matched DN: (null)
Error Message: (null)
Server Credentials: rspauth=291311bf1338bffdfc1c33c9c3d34542
```

Figure 4.44 (continued)

agrees and sends a Digest in Frame 9, the client calculates a reply and submits it to the server along with a client challenge (client nonce) in Frame 10, and finally the server acknowledges successful client authentication and authenticates to the client in Frame 11.

4.9.4 LDAP SASL Authentication Using GSS-API

GSS-API (SSPI) is one of the SASL standard mechanisms and is typically used with the Kerberos v.5 authentication mechanism. It is a secure authentication option supported by most LDAP implementations, including Active Directory, OpenLDAP, and iPlanet Directory Server.

To use GSS-API authentication, the client and server must belong to the same Kerberos realm, or to trusted Kerberos realms. The LDAP protocol uses LDAP Bind messages, setting the **AuthenticationType** field to SASL, and the **Mechanism** field to **GSS-API** or **GSS-SPNEGO**. User authentication is performed in the following way (see Figure 4.45):

1. The client authenticates to a KDC and obtains a Kerberos TGT (see Frames 12 and 13 in Figure 4.45).
2. The client requests and receives a Kerberos TGS from the KDC for the realm where the LDAP server resides (see Frames 14 and 15 in Figure 4.45).
3. The client sends an LDAP Bind request to the server, submitting a Kerberos AS-REQ message encapsulated within GSS-API. There may or may not be a SPNEGO layer as well (see Frame 16 in Figure 4.45).
4. The server replies with an LDAP Bind response message, and eventually acknowledges successful authentication (see Frame 17 in Figure 4.45).

```
Frame 12 (352 bytes on wire, 352 bytes captured)
Ethernet II, Src: 02:00:4c:4f:4f:50 (02:00:4c:4f:4f:50), Dst: Microsof_57:ab:2a
(00:03:ff:57:ab:2a)
Internet Protocol, Src: 10.0.2.102 (10.0.2.102), Dst: 10.0.1.101 (10.0.1.101)
User Datagram Protocol, Src Port: 1174 (1174), Dst Port: kerberos (88)
Kerberos AS-REQ
    Pvno: 5
    MSG Type: AS-REQ (10)
    padata: PA-ENC-TIMESTAMP PA-PAC-REQUEST
        Type: PA-ENC-TIMESTAMP (2)
            Value: 303CA003020117A2350433DDAAD1E726DD18FF638E03EAE1... rc4-hmac
                Encryption type: rc4-hmac (23)
                enc PA_ENC_TIMESTAMP: DDAAD1E726DD18FF638E03EAE15318319C3D362A1E281A2A...
        Type: PA-PAC-REQUEST (128)
            Value: 3005A0030101FF
                PAC Request: 1
    KDC_REQ_BODY
        Padding: 0
        KDCOptions: 40810010 (Forwardable, Renewable, Canonicalize, Renewable OK)
        Client Name (Enterprise Name): administrator@ins.com
            Name-type: Enterprise Name (10)
            Name: administrator@ins.com
        Realm: INS.COM
        Server Name (Service and Instance): krbtgt/INS.COM
            Name-type: Service and Instance (2)
            Name: krbtgt
            Name: INS.COM
        till: 2037-09-13 02:48:05 (Z)
        rtime: 2037-09-13 02:48:05 (Z)
        Nonce: 1527497747
        Encryption Types: rc4-hmac rc4-hmac-old rc4-md4 des-cbc-md5 des-cbc-crc rc4-hmac-exp rc4-
hmac-old-exp
        HostAddresses: STEVE<20>
            HostAddress STEVE<20>
                Addr-type: NETBIOS (20)
                NetBIOS Name: STEVE<20> (Server service)
```

Figure 4.45 LDAP-SASL-GSS-API.cap: User access to LDAP server using SASL GSS-AP.

```
Frame 13 (1335 bytes on wire, 1335 bytes captured)
Ethernet II, Src: Microsof_57:ab:2a (00:03:ff:57:ab:2a), Dst: 02:00:4c:4f:4f:50
(02:00:4c:4f:4f:50)
Internet Protocol, Src: 10.0.1.101 (10.0.1.101), Dst: 10.0.2.102 (10.0.2.102)
User Datagram Protocol, Src Port: kerberos (88), Dst Port: 1174 (1174)
Kerberos AS-REP
    Pvno: 5
    MSG Type: AS-REP (11)
    Client Realm: INS.COM
    Client Name (Principal): Administrator
        Name-type: Principal (1)
        Name: Administrator
    Ticket
        Tkt-vno: 5
        Realm: INS.COM
        Server Name (Service and Instance): krbtgt/INS.COM
            Name-type: Service and Instance (2)
            Name: krbtgt
            Name: INS.COM
        enc-part rc4-hmac
            Encryption type: rc4-hmac (23)
            Kvno: 2
            enc-part: 3F4BC627598C30117D8748820C089CF3BF51182F2680EA97...
    enc-part rc4-hmac
        Encryption type: rc4-hmac (23)
        Kvno: 3
        enc-part: E9BAB7D46771B1D4DCF111C332E056B29F90A5A112639B4D...

Frame 14 (1303 bytes on wire, 1303 bytes captured)
Ethernet II, Src: 02:00:4c:4f:4f:50 (02:00:4c:4f:4f:50), Dst: Microsof_57:ab:2a
(00:03:ff:57:ab:2a)
Internet Protocol, Src: 10.0.2.102 (10.0.2.102), Dst: 10.0.1.101 (10.0.1.101)
User Datagram Protocol, Src Port: 1175 (1175), Dst Port: kerberos (88)
Kerberos TGS-REQ
    Pvno: 5
```

Figure 4.45 (continued)

```
MSG Type: TGS-REQ (12)
padata: PA-TGS-REQ
    Type: PA-TGS-REQ (1)
        Value: 6E82045630820452A003020105A10302010EA20703050000... AP-REQ
            Pvno: 5
            MSG Type: AP-REQ (14)
            Padding: 0
            APOptions: 00000000
                Tkt-vno: 5
                Realm: INS.COM
                Server Name (Service and Instance): krbtgt/INS.COM
                    Name-type: Service and Instance (2)
                    Name: krbtgt
                    Name: INS.COM
                enc-part rc4-hmac
                    Encryption type: rc4-hmac (23)
                    Kvno: 2
                    enc-part: 3F4BC627598C30117D8748820C089CF3BF51182F2680EA97...
            Authenticator rc4-hmac
                Encryption type: rc4-hmac (23)
                Authenticator data: 46C791B82F8F03831DFADFA5E46972488C69C6243F53C28C...
KDC_REQ_BODY
    Padding: 0
    KDCOptions: 40810000 (Forwardable, Renewable, Canonicalize)
    Realm: INS.COM
    Server Name (Service and Instance): ldap/BILL.ins.com
        Name-type: Service and Instance (2)
        Name: ldap
        Name: BILL.ins.com
    till: 2037-09-13 02:48:05 (Z)
    Nonce: 1528483107
    Encryption Types: rc4-hmac des-cbc-md5 des-cbc-crc rc4-hmac-exp rc4-hmac-old-exp
        Encryption type: rc4-hmac (23)
        Encryption type: des-cbc-md5 (3)
        Encryption type: des-cbc-crc (1)
        Encryption type: rc4-hmac-exp (24)
```

Figure 4.45 (continued)

```
            Encryption type: rc4-hmac-old-exp (-135)

Frame 15 (1370 bytes on wire, 1370 bytes captured)
Ethernet II, Src: Microsof_57:ab:2a (00:03:ff:57:ab:2a), Dst: 02:00:4c:4f:4f:50
(02:00:4c:4f:4f:50)
Internet Protocol, Src: 10.0.1.101 (10.0.1.101), Dst: 10.0.2.102 (10.0.2.102)
User Datagram Protocol, Src Port: kerberos (88), Dst Port: 1175 (1175)
Kerberos TGS-REP
    Pvno: 5
    MSG Type: TGS-REP (13)
    Client Realm: INS.COM
    Client Name (Principal): Administrator
        Name-type: Principal (1)
        Name: Administrator
    Ticket
        Tkt-vno: 5
        Realm: INS.COM
        Server Name (Service and Instance): ldap/BILL.ins.com
            Name-type: Service and Instance (2)
            Name: ldap
            Name: BILL.ins.com
        enc-part rc4-hmac
            Encryption type: rc4-hmac (23)
            Kvno: 8
            enc-part: AE4CE05BC2D18F22DAA487BF392170A9DDCA9ADBE890D3C8...
    enc-part rc4-hmac
        Encryption type: rc4-hmac (23)
        enc-part: 5A9B9B35AD22F302AD5AF9B05FF787CD694847D6B3367315...

Frame 16 (1425 bytes on wire, 1425 bytes captured)
Ethernet II, Src: 02:00:4c:4f:4f:50 (02:00:4c:4f:4f:50), Dst: Microsof_57:ab:2a
(00:03:ff:57:ab:2a)
Internet Protocol, Src: 10.0.2.102 (10.0.2.102), Dst: 10.0.1.101 (10.0.1.101)
Transmission Control Protocol, Src Port: 1172 (1172), Dst Port: ldap (389), Seq: 2174236315, Ack:
854555016, Len: 1371
Lightweight Directory Access Protocol
```

Figure 4.45 (continued)

```
LDAP Message, Bind Request
    Message Id: 9
    Message Type: Bind Request (0x00)
    Message Length: 1356
    Response In: 17
    Version: 3
    DN: (null)
    Auth Type: SASL (0x03)
    Mechanism: GSS-SPNEGO
    GSS-API Generic Security Service Application Program Interface
        OID: 1.3.6.1.5.5.2 (SPNEGO - Simple Protected Negotiation)
        SPNEGO
            negTokenInit
                mechTypes: 3 items
                    Item: 1.2.840.48018.1.2.2 (MS KRB5 - Microsoft Kerberos 5)
                    Item: 1.2.840.113554.1.2.2 (KRB5 - Kerberos 5)
                    Item: 1.3.6.1.4.1.311.2.2.10 (NTLMSSP - Microsoft NTLM Security Support
Provider)
                mechToken: 608204EB06092A864886F71201020201006E8204DA308204...
                krb5_blob: 608204EB06092A864886F71201020201006E8204DA308204...
                    KRB5 OID: 1.2.840.113554.1.2.2 (KRB5 - Kerberos 5)
                    krb5_tok_id: KRB5_AP_REQ (0x0001)
                    Kerberos AP-REQ
                        Pvno: 5
                        MSG Type: AP-REQ (14)
                        Padding: 0
                        APOptions: 20000000 (Mutual required)
                        Ticket
                            Tkt-vno: 5
                            Realm: INS.COM
                            Server Name (Service and Instance): ldap/BILL.ins.com
                                Name-type: Service and Instance (2)
                                Name: ldap
                                Name: BILL.ins.com
                            enc-part rc4-hmac
                                Encryption type: rc4-hmac (23)
```

Figure 4.45 (continued)

```
                    Kvno: 8
                    enc-part: AE4CE05BC2D18F22DAA487BF392170A9DDCA9ADBE890D3C8...
                Authenticator rc4-hmac
                    Encryption type: rc4-hmac (23)
                    Authenticator data:
1DCC472815F0EAF7B13EE368E58D197A9A1786AC6B72A54C...

Frame 17 (242 bytes on wire, 242 bytes captured)
Ethernet II, Src: Microsof_57:ab:2a (00:03:ff:57:ab:2a), Dst: 02:00:4c:4f:4f:50
(02:00:4c:4f:4f:50)
Internet Protocol, Src: 10.0.1.101 (10.0.1.101), Dst: 10.0.2.102 (10.0.2.102)
Transmission Control Protocol, Src Port: ldap (389), Dst Port: 1172 (1172), Seq: 854555016, Ack:
2174237686, Len: 188
Lightweight Directory Access Protocol
    LDAP Message, Bind Result
        Message Id: 9
        Message Type: Bind Result (0x01)
        Message Length: 173
        Response To: 16
        Time: 0.003419000 seconds
        Result Code: success (0x00)
        Matched DN: (null)
        Error Message: (null)
        GSS-API Generic Security Service Application Program Interface
            SPNEGO
                negTokenTarg
                    negResult: accept-completed (0)
                    supportedMech: 1.2.840.48018.1.2.2 (MS KRB5 - Microsoft Kerberos 5)
                    responseToken: 60818106092A864886F71201020202006F723070A0030201...
                    krb5_blob: 60818106092A864886F71201020202006F723070A0030201...
                        KRB5 OID: 1.2.840.113554.1.2.2 (KRB5 - Kerberos 5)
                        krb5_tok_id: KRB5_AP_REP (0x0002)
                        Kerberos AP-REP
                            Pvno: 5
                            MSG Type: AP-REP (15)
                            enc-part rc4-hmac
                                Encryption type: rc4-hmac (23)
                                enc-part: D353C342BF9D07E30EF80809F84EB70DEDC95A0744105C1B..
```

Figure 4.45 (continued)

4.10 SSH Authentication

The Secure Shell (SSH) Protocol was developed to overcome the limitations of protocols that utilize unencrypted sessions and authentication (or the lack thereof), including Telnet and Rlogin. Due to the fact that SSH was able to negotiate and apply protection for data traffic, including user authentication, the SSH Protocol was soon widely adopted by the Internet community and numerous software and hardware vendors. In 2006, the SSH protocol was defined in a series of RFCs.

In short, SSH creates a protected (encrypted and authenticated) channel between a client and a server. Typically, the SSH server has a set consisting of a private and a public host key. This pair of keys is used by the client to verify the identity of the server. The SSH session is comprised of a single communication channel between the client and the server, typically on TCP port 22. When the client connects to the server, the two parties immediately negotiate a session key, encryption and integrity authentication algorithms, and start communicating in a secure fashion. Further messages between the client and the server, including user authentication, and user data are protected with the negotiated protection parameters. The SSH Protocol has two versions, and the main difference between the two is the way that the session key is generated.

In SSH v.1, when the server starts, it generates an RSA asymmetric keypair (private and public), known as server keys. These keys are only temporary, and are generated in addition to the host pair of keys, which is permanent. A new RSA server keypair is generated every hour. The server replies to a new client connection with its current server public key and its host public key. The client generates a 256-bit session key, encrypts it using the negotiated algorithm employing the server public key and the server key together as the key. The client submits the thus-encrypted session key to the server. The server must possess the private key for its host key (this proves the identity of the server) and the private key for the session public key in order to decrypt the session key and start communicating with the client. That is how the client verifies the identity of the server in the session key negotiation process. From that point on, the client and server use the session key to protect the data channel.

SSH v.2 only has a host keypair, which is used by clients to authenticate the identity of the SSH server. The client and server negotiate a session key using the Diffie-Hellman algorithm.

The SSH Protocol architecture defined in RFC 4251 provides for three main functional layers (Figure 4.46):

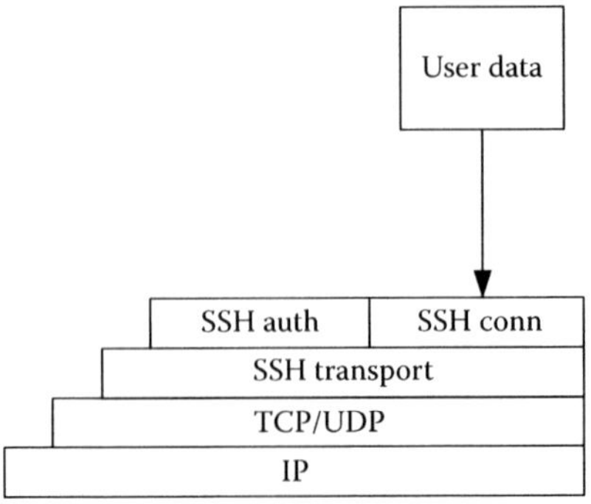

Figure 4.46 SSH Protocol architecture.

1. *Transport layer* (RFC 4253): server authentication uses the host keypair and channel protection with the session key. Other SSH layers depend on this layer. The successful establishment of a transport layer results in the provisioning of a unique identifier for the transport session, known as a session ID.
2. *Authentication layer* (RFC 4252): user authentication mechanisms.
3. *Connection layer* (RFC 4254): provides for protocol tunneling over SSH — port local and remote port forwarding, X.11 tunneling, etc.

The SSH transport layer must be established first so that all further communication is protected. Once transport layer security has been negotiated, the client and server perform authentication. RFC 4252 defines the following authentication methods:

- Public Key authentication.
- Password authentication.
- Host authentication.
- None

User authentication is performed using standard user authentication messages. All RFC 4252-compliant authentication requests use the format depicted in Table 4.19.

In addition to these methods, RFC 4256 (see [78]) defines interactive, dialogue-based authentication similar to Login authentication.

Although SSH allows for traditional **rsh/rlogin** style account mapping between hosts, wherein user authentication is completely bypassed if the client is a known host (known by its hostname or IP address), this behavior is typically disabled and avoided as being insecure. If desired, however, SSH can be configured to map (by username) users from remote trusted

Table 4.19 SSH Authentication Message Format — RFC 4252

Field Name	*Type*	*Description*
SSH Message ID (Type)	Byte/constant	SSH_MSG_USERAUTH_REQUEST (50)
Username	String	The name of the user who is requesting authentication
Service name	String	As the SSH protocol connection layer can multiplex multiple services over SSH, this field needs to specify user authentication for the specific service that will be started immediately after authentication
Authentication method	String	Specifies the RFC 4252 authentication method; standard authentication methods include "publickey" – for SSH public key authentication, "password" – for SSH password authentication, "hostbased" for hostbased authentication and "none" for no authentication. However, different implementations may define new authentication methods.
Authentication message	String	Specific to the authentication method

hosts to local users, and the mapping of remote hosts or users can be performed using the **/etc/hosts.equiv** and **/etc/shosts.equiv** at the server level, and **~/.rhosts** or **~/.shosts** in the local user home directory.

4.10.1 SSH Public Key Authentication

SSH Public Key authentication is the only SSH authentication mechanism that SSH clients and servers are required to support. It is based on asymmetric encryption technologies (signatures) and the requirement that the client possesses a secret private key and the server has a copy of the user's public key defined in a list of authorized keys for the specific user (typically a file containing a list of keys in the user's home directory).

To perform public key authentication, the client submits the authentication request message shown in Table 4.20.

Upon receipt of such an authentication request, the server needs to check the signature, generated by the user to ensure the possession of a

Table 4.20 SSH Public Key Authentication Request

Field	*Value*
SSH Message ID	SSH_MSG_USERAUTH_REQUEST (50)
User Name	The name of the authenticating user
Service Name	The name of the SSH service to which the user is authenticating
Authentication Type	**publickey**
Actual Authentication	**true**
Public Key Algorithm Name	Specifies the public key type (algorithm): this may be **ssh-rsa** for RSA keys and signatures, **ssh-dss** for DSS based keys and signatures, or **pgp-sign-rsa/pgp-sign-dss** for their PGP equivalents
Public Key BLOB	The user public key (or certificate containing the public key)
Signature	A signature following the specified public key algorithm recommendations (see [79] and [80]) on the following structure: ■ Session identifier (String) — the ID of the current SSH Session ■ SSH_MSG_USERAUTH_REQUEST (Byte) = 50 ■ User name (string) — same as above ■ Service name (string) — same as above ■ "**publickey**" — same as above ■ **TRUE** — same as above ■ Public key algorithm name (string) — same as above ■ Public key to be used for authentication (string) — same as above

private key (the public key used to generate the signature is contained in the request), and then check whether the public key provided is a valid key for this particular user. Most OpenSSH implementations check the user public key for validity using the **~/.ssh/authorized_keys** file. Because this file resides in the user home directory of the authenticating user, each user can edit his own file and specify a list of public keys that will map to his particular user account. There may be more than one public key that is a valid user authentication public key for the particular user, which essentially means that there will be more than one private key (one for each public key) that can be used to authenticate as this particular user.

As a result of user public key authentication, the SSH server returns either the SSH_MSG_USERAUTH_PK_OK message to indicate successful authentication, or the SSH_MSG_USERAUTH_FAILURE message to indicate a failed authentication attempt.

The following session shows user root on host **linus.ins.com** that uses SSH public key authentication and a private key stored in file **susan.key** to authenticate to host **dennis.ins.com**. Note that the user is still asked to provide a password to decrypt the private key from the **susan.key** file. Protecting the private key file with a password is an optional requirement, and is recommended.

```
[root@linus ~]# cat susan.key
-----BEGIN RSA PRIVATE KEY-----
Proc-Type: 4,ENCRYPTED
DEK-Info: DES-EDE3-CBC,CBEFD0592A838FB1

Bbk/IxfhcENbcKoMJy9EO1m0IBzdd5DRJpxT5QpqHmUOBG8YwzhAEEN7sNLhkV5p
1GCEU7144AMLAStdsxEQZ908sL4es+yLdDru2PJFxpXxLluuVxAW3rOkRTlU4UUO
Gavoe1Y8Fb28xMLiPuvachpnD68IxBgwOxRTN7WiQctNuy/pHQXuQdN1uGY5ApgY
nGUALBaiRsSJQpjd8mEJMoRvoDKbHrfFSFnQ0MC3i11oILcV1WEUrTC+ghBjoHys
2PZnGmzt4z7wIvYouCrjE4lrxWd48aWnRFr2+7PfoU28FWefXvnv+wIBr/nVjbFO
8gbg+H4FWFP8a+q/RaFF6rbDTyr6SUESDmbyQvusbznnyovwomrEtiWugHKCyy+z
TLjomUQ+8k7sgVNiFRGObGwnHg9RYOop9OU6N+psRr6BCgWaT4pBS9J9Lj+/9iuC
vjjDW0lYek3JahYIy/DubqFR3m7VNHsgLUj/r9bfhNXBHFUSf8/OhUGwjPxGHNnA
g+gvddGujlT2ZbnXsa26zoxRUNqj0wLss1pySCjoqr9xdqs2rc+2XK5eDCxla4gf
0JSW5FxxPMTeKLrGaI/4GWFLB2GQLzOZ3kpCL9A1lPjlUj0OhxK5s0UAOTjK3Kpc
wO/6WT7GxjRf8XI6fm4lBPwD0FbG8wtNVFmCkOKaFQL0PC4TrTs78hXSbOL/QX5r
AqtoIfZ8tHzl0EMIADQ1C/NnskUZ/Av6K3+bMSlx8ysIvhBy8XhfXgjcIC9Qbi5i
n6j3RNkD7cuIdkmrzZTsfa/t+ga1Ct96Tmk1fMMzazE=
-----END RSA PRIVATE KEY-----
[root@linus ~]#
[root@linus ~]# ssh -l Susan -i susan.key dennis.ins.com
Enter passphrase for key 'susan.key': ********
Last login: Mon Feb 20 05:47:35 2006 from linus.ins.com
[Susan@Dennis ~]$
[Susan@Dennis ~]$ id
uid=9114(Susan) gid=9114(Susan) groups=9114(Susan)
[Susan@Dennis ~]$
[Susan@Dennis ~]$ cat .ssh/authorized_keys
ssh-rsa
AAAAB3NzaC1yc2EAAAABIwAAAIEA0KwVxzbZmGndwrBxg/zLXKweiAVl0gSLsVVXjeS14
LEJ//hikuH0nr1wYMPJw08hSwUqO+FfI691JTEM1Gr6mHranhtn6p16j0m4IZgfOVZ40T
BpDoNSkw0NGLgzL1ymuiOUS9fAE3hCEn5DXuTNnNo4N4Bm8OfIGWi4C3naW30= Susan@
Dennis.ins.com
ssh-rsa
AAAAB3NzaC1yc2EAAAABIwAAAIEArGpPxKqSQ2GOpDkhq9C7+e4ISa8wOSvoAfpsCtINe
GRhjfTUJnxKDDETY9kcYUwJrTT0nw9/naMyBipr/icoMs6tefHscDogqm69vy8ias7pPu
kMzWUpQhAUqvTRGsf6xJXPRTci0wX2Yztx1ZAdouyhVlum7e4Rp7Az01ltyj8= Susan@
Dennis.ins.com
[Susan@Dennis ~]$
[Susan@Dennis ~]$ exit
```

4.10.2 SSH Host Authentication

Conventional **rsh** and **rlogin** implementations rely on the **/etc/hosts.equiv** and the **~/.rhosts** files as a model of trust. These two files play the role of allowing users with the same names on trusted remote hosts to execute commands and log in to the local host (using rsh and rlogin) without providing any authentication. The assumption is that if a remote host imposes certain security policies and follows the same naming convention as the local host, then the remote host can be trusted so that users from the remote host can access resources on the local host transparently. The problem with the **/etc/hosts.equiv** and **~/.rhosts** files is that they do not really provide for a secure authentication mechanism to check the identity of the remote host. This trust model is susceptible to various attacks, including remote host IP address and MAC address spoofing, DNS spoofing, man-in-the-middle, etc.

SSH tries to solve the problem of spoofed remote host or remote user identity by providing for SSH Host authentication. With this mechanism, the authentication request from a trusted remote host can be signed using the remote host private key and the identity of the host or the user can no longer be spoofed, or intercepted in a man-in-the-middle attack. The signature on SSH Host authentication requests is checked using the remote host public key stored on the local host. This approach provides better assurance in terms of user privileges within the enterprise, especially if a unique naming convention is chosen for all hosts. SSH v.1 provides for host authentication but it can only be based on RSA keys. SSH v.2 provides for flexibility by incorporating RSA, DSS, and Open-PGP methods.

The authenticating remote host typically stores its private key (host key) in the **/etc/ssh/ssh_host_key** file (SSH version 1), its DSA key (SSH version 2) in **/etc/ssh/ssh_host_dsa_key**, and its RSA key (SSH version 2) in **/etc/ssh/ssh_host_rsa_key**.

```
[root@linus ~]# cd /etc/ssh
[root@linus ssh]# ls -al
total 204
drwxr-xr-x   2 root root   4096 Feb 19 02:09 .
drwxr-xr-x  82 root root  12288 Feb 20 04:03 ..
-rw-------   1 root root 132839 May 16  2005 moduli
-rw-r--r--   1 root root   1543 May 16  2005 ssh_config
-rw-------   1 root root   3051 May 16  2005 sshd_config
-rw-------   1 root root    668 Jul  9  2005 ssh_host_dsa_key
-rw-r--r--   1 root root    590 Jul  9  2005 ssh_host_dsa_key.pub
-rw-------   1 root root    515 Jul  9  2005 ssh_host_key
-rw-r--r--   1 root root    319 Jul  9  2005 ssh_host_key.pub
-rw-------   1 root root    883 Jul  9  2005 ssh_host_rsa_key
-rw-r--r--   1 root root    210 Jul  9  2005 ssh_host_rsa_key.pub
[root@linus ssh]#
```

The key files are protected with permissions that only allow read-write access to root. Authentication requests from the remote host must be signed using the remote host private key. The client SSH application on the remote host that will typically run in the user context does not have (and should not have) access to the secret host authentication key, and this is a fundamental requirement in the SSH model of trust. If the client application had access to the client host private key, it could potentially generate a crafted request to the server, using a different source name for the host, as well as a different username from that with which the user is logged in.

To allow the client application, running with user privileges, to access the host private key, in SSH v.1 the **ssh** client executable used to be **setuid** as root. This is based on the assumption that the **ssh** client application is verified and trusted, and can therefore be **setuid**. SSH v.2 provides a different approach: instead of running **ssh** as root, the section of code generating host signatures has been separated from the main client into the **ssh-keysign** tool, which is **setuid** as well. With that, the **ssh** client application does not need to be setuid as root anymore. The **ssh_config** file can be used to specify whether clients will be able to invoke **ssh-keysign** to sign host authentication requests (the **Enable SSHKeysign** parameter).

The **sshd** server on the local host needs to have a copy of the public key for each private key that remote hosts requesting host authentication may use. These keys are typically stored in **/etc/ssh/ssh_known_hosts**.

SSH host authentication is performed as follows. The client computer submits an SSH host authentication message that uses the format in Table 4.21 to the SSH server.

The SSH server on the local host can check the signature in the Host Authentication request message from the remote host. Because only the remote host has the private key that can be used to sign the authentication structure, if such an authentication request is received by the local host, it can be trusted to be genuine and is not spoofed. The local host can therefore trust that the user mapping is secure, subject to the remote host private key being kept secure.

4.10.3 SSH Password Authentication

The SSH password authentication method provides for user authentication using a plaintext username and password, which are sent by the client in SSH authentication messages (Table 4.22).

When the SSH server receives this authentication request, it can utilize a plaintext or an encrypted password database (by first encrypting/hashing the plaintext password accordingly) to authenticate the user. Depending on

Table 4.21 SSH Host Key Authentication Request

Field	*Value*
SSH Message ID	SSH_MSG_USERAUTH_REQUEST (50)
User Name	The name of the authenticating user
Service Name	The name of the SSH service to which the user is authenticating
Authentication Type	**hostbased**
Public Key Algorithm Name	Specifies the public key type (algorithm) – this may be **ssh-rsa** for RSA keys and signatures, **ssh-dss** for DSS based keys and signatures, or **pgp-sign-rsa/pgp-sign-dss** for their PGP equivalents.
Public Key BLOB	Remote host public key (or certificate containing the public key)
Client Host Name	DNS FQDN of the client host – the authenticating host can be assured that it knows the real name of the remote server
Remote username	The name of the user on the client host – the authenticating host can be assured that the user has not altered the user name
Signature	A signature following the specified Public Key algorithm recommendations (see [79] and [80]) on the following structure: ■ Session identifier (String) — the ID of the current SSH Session ■ SSH_MSG_USERAUTH_REQUEST (Byte) = 50 ■ User name (string) — same as above ■ Service name (string) — same as above ■ "**hostbased**" — same as above ■ Public key algorithm name (string) — same as above ■ Public key or certificate to be used for authentication (string) — same as above ■ Client host name (string) — same as above ■ User name on client (string) — same as above

the server configuration, the server can use external authentication sources as well (such as Kerberos) to complete the user authentication request. The supported replies from the server include SSH_MSG_ USERAUTH_ SUCCESS for successful user authentication, SSH_MSG_USERAUTH_FAILURE for

Table 4.22 SSH Password Authentication Request

Field	*Value*
SSH Message ID	SSH_MSG_USERAUTH_REQUEST (50)
User Name	The name of the authenticating user
Service Name	The name of the SSH service to which the user is authenticating
Authentication Type	**password**
Actual Authentication	**False**
Password	Plaintext password for the user

failed authentication attempts, or SSH_MSG_USERAUTH_PASSWD_CHANGEREQ, which specifies that the authentication is successful but the user is required to change his password.

It is relatively secure to use SSH Password authentication with plaintext passwords because user authentication occurs on top of a secure channel between the client and the server, and attackers cannot eavesdrop on the traffic — nor can they modify data on the protected channel. The disadvantage with plain password authentication is that the SSH server will have a plaintext copy of the password, and therefore can potentially authenticate on behalf of the user and then access resources. As with all plaintext password authentication mechanisms, the server must be trusted to not misuse the plaintext credentials.

4.10.4 SSH Keyboard Interactive Authentication

RFC 4256 (see [78]) defines a generic approach for SSH user authentication that is interactive: the client and server enter an authentication dialogue and can exchange simple messages until the authentication has finished. This SSH authentication mechanism is appropriate for building authentication dialogues, including challenge-response authentication, one-time passwords, etc. All communication occurs on top of the protected SSH transport layer.

4.10.5 SSH GSS-API User Authentication

SSH GSS-API User authentication is currently an Internet Draft, defined in [81]. The specification provides for a simple way to send and receive GSS-API authentication tokens (messages) over the SSH authentication layer, on top of the SSH transport layer.

Table 4.23 SSH GSS-API Authentication Request

Field	*Value*
SSH Message ID	SSH_MSG_USERAUTH_REQUEST (50)
User Name	The name of the authenticating user (this may be empty if not using Kerberos preauthentication, and can be obtained during authentication)
Service Name	The name of the SSH service to which the user is authenticating
Authentication Type	**gssapi-with-mic**
Number of GSSAPI OIDs (n)	Specifies the number of GSS-API mechanisms that the client supports
OIDs (string[n])	Specifies each mechanism that the client supports, from 1 to n

It is interesting to note that the SSH GSS-API specification advises against implementing SPNEGO on top of SSH GSS-API; the assumption here is that the SSH authentication layer provides for authentication protocol negotiation anyway, so nested authentication protocol negotiation should be avoided.

To perform GSS-API authentication, the client and server first initialize GSS-API using SSH_MSG_USERAUTH_REQUEST(50) messages and specifying **gssapi-with-mic** as the authentication method, and then use SSH_MSG_USERAUTH_GSSAPI_TOKEN(61) messages to exchange actual GSSAPI tokens.

The initial GSS-API authentication request is sent by the client, and is shown in Table 4.23. The server replies by either indicating failure (SSH_MSG_USERAUTH_FAILURE), or by selecting a preferred GSS-API authentication method OID (SSH_MSG_USERAUTH_GSSAPI_RESPONSE (60)).

From that point on, the client and the server use SSH_MSG_USERAUTH_GSSAPI_TOKEN messages that contain the result from **GSS_Init_sec_context( )** or **GSS_Accept_sec_context( )**. In the case of Kerberos authentication, these messages will contain a Kerberos AS_REQ and a Kerberos AS_REP message between the client and the server.

GSS-API messages must have their integrity protected (the **integ_req_flag** must be set to True). The client can potentially choose to delegate its identity to the server. The GSS-API authentication process for SSH will typically only authenticate the client, rather than using GSS-API mutual authentication.

Table 4.24 SSH GSS-API Encryption Key Binding Request

Field	*Value*
SSH Message ID	SSH_MSG_USERAUTH_GSSAPI_MIC
MIC/Signature	A signature produced by the GSS_GetMic( ) in the current GSS-API context over the following structure: ■ Session identifier (String) — the ID of the current SSH Session ■ SSH_MSG_USERAUTH_REQUEST (Byte) = 50 ■ User name (string) — the name of the authenticating user from GSS-API ■ Service name (string) — the service name for which authentication is taking place ■ **"gssapi-with-mic"** — this particular string

SSH GSS-API authentication will typically provide for encrypted and integrity protected messages between the client and the server (symmetric encryption and integrity protection within Kerberos AS_REQ and AS_REP messages), depending on the selected authentication mechanism. At the same time, the GSS-API message exchange takes place over an SSH transport channel that will typically be encrypted and integrity protected (depending on the SSH encryption and integrity protection mechanisms). The Kerberos GSS-API specification goes one step further into the integration between SSH and GSS-API by specifying that once GSS-API authentication is complete, the client can decide to perform encryption key binding by sending an SSH_MSG_USERAUTH_GSSAPI_MIC(66) message and binding the SSH transport layer and the SSH authentication layer. This is meant to protect against man-in-the-middle attacks. The server may or may not require that clients perform encryption key binding in the end of GSS-API authentication. Table 4.24 shows the contents of the Encryption Key Binding request message.

4.10.6 SSH GSS-API Key Exchange and Authentication

The SSH GSS-API Draft Specification [81] goes as far as suggesting that GSS-API be used for host authentication, instead of using conventional SSH host public keys. This is convenient for organizations that have an existing Kerberos infrastructure, and provides the ability to authenticate hosts using Kerberos on top of GSS-API. As an addition to the SSH transport layer, the GSS-API Draft Specification defines a Diffie-Hellman key exchange mechanism based on GSS-API for use by the SSH transport layer, which at the same time uses GSS-API mutual authentication for the two hosts.

Table 4.25 SSH GSS-API Key Exchange Authentication Request

Field	*Value*
SSH Message ID	SSH_MSG_USERAUTH_REQUEST (50)
User Name	The name of the authenticating user
Service Name	The name of the SSH service to which the user is authenticating
Authentication Type	**gssapi-keyex**
MIC/Signature	A signature produced by the GSS_GetMic( ) in the current GSS-API context established during the initial key exchange over the following structure: ■ Session identifier (String) — the ID of the current SSH Session ■ SSH_MSG_USERAUTH_REQUEST (Byte) = 50 ■ User name (string) — the name of the authenticating user from GSS-API ■ Service name (string) — the service name for which authentication is taking place ■ "**gssapi-keyex**" – this particular string

Hosts can use the GSS-API key exchange mechanism at the transport layer to authenticate each other and negotiate session keys. The SSH authentication mechanism is defined as **gssapi-keyex**. To use GSS-API key exchange authentication, the client needs to send an SSH_MSG_USERAUTH_REQUEST message to the server, as described in Table 4.25.

Currently, GSS-API key exchange is only supported by a limited number of SSH implementations, but the growing number of Kerberos-based infrastructure solutions is likely to make it more popular in the future.

4.11 Sun RPC Authentication

Sun Remote Procedure Calls (Sun RPC) were invented by Sun Microsystems. The main idea of RPC is to allow for remote execution of code across the network. A client can prepare a set of parameters that can then be provided as procedure arguments at the client computer. The client RPC stub application, however, is responsible for finding an RPC server that will handle the request, and pass on the parameters to the server RPC stub. The server application then executes the requested procedure using the provided parameters, and then returns the result to the client across the network. RPC plays an important role in the world of client/server computing. This role has been increasing ever since 1995, when Sun released the RPC specification to the public (see [82]). Among the

Table 4.26 RPC Authentication: Credentials Structure

Field	*Value*
RPC Authentication type/flavor (byte)	Specifies the type of authentication, used by RPC: ■ AUTH_NULL = 0 ■ AUTH_UNIX = 1 ■ AUTH_SHORT = 2 ■ AUTH_DES (AUTH_DH) = 3 ■ AUTH_KERB4 = 4 ■ RPCSEC_GSS = 6
Authentication body length (word)	Length of authentication parameters body — depends on the authentication flavor
Authentication body	Credentials provided by the party being authenticated — depends on the authentication flavor

most popular applications that use Sun RPC are the Network File System, the Network Information Service (NIS, aka Yellow Pages), and NIS+.

The RPC Protocol provides for mutual authentication. Depending on the specific authentication method chosen, the client can authenticate itself to the RPC server and vice versa. Typically, authentication information is included with every RPC, even if it is part of the same TCP session or UDP conversation. The party being authenticated provides a credentials structure and a verifier structure. The party accepting the authentication request replies with an authentication verifier structure only.

The credentials structure of the RPC message is typically used by the client to provide identification and authentication information to the server. The content of this field depends on the specific authentication method selected. Table 4.26 represents the generic content of the credentials structure:

The verifier structure is used by both the client and the server. Its content depends on the authentication mechanism being used. The client can use this structure to provide for integrity verification of the credentials structure. The server uses the verifier structure to provide replies to client authentication requests, and to authenticate to the client. Table 4.27 shows the generic content of the verifier structure.

The following subsections discuss the RPC authentication mechanisms.

4.11.1 RPC AUTH_NULL (AUTH_NONE) Authentication

In case the server is providing public resources, it may not be required that the server identifies or impersonates the client that is trying to obtain information. In that case, the client and server can use RPC Null authentication. The client will be anonymous to the server, and the client

Table 4.27 RPC Authentication: Verifier Structure

Field	*Value*
RPC Authentication type/flavor (byte)	Specifies the type of authentication used by RPC: ■ AUTH_NULL = 0 ■ AUTH_UNIX = 1 ■ AUTH_SHORT = 2 ■ AUTH_DES (AUTH_DH) = 3 ■ AUTH_KERB4 = 4 ■ RPCSEC_GSS = 6
Verifier body length (word)	Length of verifier body — depends on the authentication flavor
Verifier body	Verifier content — the client can use this field for integrity checking; the server uses this field to provide replies to the client authentication requests and for mutual authentication

application will provide no information to the server as to who the user trying to access the resources is. The server will typically start a new thread or process for the client, and will do so using a generic account for Null (anonymous) access — typically one with very limited privileges. RPC Null authentication is specified in RFC 1831 (see [83]).

A typical example of an application that provides public information is the RPC portmapper. It is used by clients to enumerate the RPC services on a server, and does not per se provide access to the actual applications. For example, a user on computer **linus** can use the **rpcinfo** tool to enumerate RPC services on server **dennis**. This request will use RPC Null authentication, and the capture from the traffic between **linus** and **dennis** as a result of the RPC portmapper service enumeration request is shown in Figure 4.47.

Null authentication is performed as follows (see Figure 4.47):

1. The client either uses UDP or establishes a TCP session with the server. It is common for the RPC port to be dynamically negotiated via the portmapper mechanism.
2. The client submits an RPC request, specifying type AUTH_NULL, and credentials body length of size 0 for both the authenticator and verifier parts (see Frame 4 in Figure 4.47). The remainder of the packet contains the actual RPC request.
3. The server (provided that it supports AUTH_NULL authentication for the selected service) replies with a verifier that has the RPC flavor set to AUTH_NULL and the verifier body length set to 0 (see Frame 6 in Figure 4.47).

```
Frame 4 (110 bytes on wire, 110 bytes captured)
Ethernet II, Src: Microsof_56:ab:2a (00:03:ff:56:ab:2a), Dst: 02:00:4c:4f:4f:50
(02:00:4c:4f:4f:50)
Internet Protocol, Src: 10.0.1.102 (10.0.1.102), Dst: 10.0.2.101 (10.0.2.101)
Transmission Control Protocol, Src Port: 922 (922), Dst Port: sunrpc (111), Seq: 1179008784, Ack:
3502616097, Len: 44
Remote Procedure Call, Type:Call XID:0x7c663030
    Fragment header: Last fragment, 40 bytes
    XID: 0x7c663030 (2087071792)
    Message Type: Call (0)
    RPC Version: 2
    Program: Portmap (100000)
    Program Version: 2
    Procedure: DUMP (4)
    The reply to this request is in frame 6
    Credentials
        Flavor: AUTH_NULL (0)
        Length: 0
    Verifier
        Flavor: AUTH_NULL (0)
        Length: 0

Frame 6 (466 bytes on wire, 466 bytes captured)
Ethernet II, Src: 02:00:4c:4f:4f:50 (02:00:4c:4f:4f:50), Dst: Microsof_56:ab:2a
(00:03:ff:56:ab:2a)
Internet Protocol, Src: 10.0.2.101 (10.0.2.101), Dst: 10.0.1.102 (10.0.1.102)
Transmission Control Protocol, Src Port: sunrpc (111), Dst Port: 922 (922), Seq: 3502616097, Ack:
1179008828, Len: 400
Remote Procedure Call, Type:Reply XID:0x7c663030
    Fragment header: 396 bytes
    XID: 0x7c663030 (2087071792)
    Message Type: Reply (1)
    Program: Portmap (100000)
    Program Version: 2
    Procedure: DUMP (4)
    Reply State: accepted (0)
```

Figure 4.47 Client linus.ins.com accesses the Portmapper on server dennis.ins.com using RPC_NULL authentication.

```
    This is a reply to a request in frame 4
    Time from request: 0.004198000 seconds
    Verifier
        Flavor: AUTH_NULL (0)
        Length: 0
    Accept State: RPC executed successfully (0)
Portmap
    Program Version: 2
    V2 Procedure: DUMP (4)
    Value Follows: Yes
    Map Entry: Portmap (100000) V2
    Value Follows: Yes
    Map Entry: Portmap (100000) V2
    Value Follows: Yes
    Map Entry: STAT (100024) V1
    Value Follows: Yes
    Map Entry: STAT (100024) V1
    Value Follows: Yes
    Map Entry: RQUOTA (100011) V1
    Value Follows: Yes
    Map Entry: RQUOTA (100011) V2
    Value Follows: Yes
    Map Entry: RQUOTA (100011) V1
    Value Follows: Yes
    Map Entry: RQUOTA (100011) V2
    Value Follows: Yes
    Map Entry: NFS (100003) V2
    Value Follows: Yes
    Map Entry: NFS (100003) V3
    Value Follows: Yes
    Map Entry: NFS (100003) V4
    Value Follows: Yes
    Map Entry: NFS (100003) V2
    Value Follows: Yes
    Map Entry: NFS (100003) V3
    Value Follows: Yes
```

Figure 4.47 (continued)

```
    Map Entry: NFS (100003) V4
    Value Follows: Yes
    Map Entry: NLM (100021) V1
    Value Follows: Yes
    Map Entry: NLM (100021) V3
    Value Follows: Yes
    Map Entry: NLM (100021) V4
    Value Follows: Yes
    Map Entry: NLM (100021) V1
    Value Follows: Yes
[Unreassembled Packet: Portmap]
```

Figure 4.47 (continued)

4.11.2 RPC AUTH_UNIX (AUTH_SYS) Authentication

In most cases, a server application will want to authenticate the client and be able to either identify or impersonate the user submitting requests to the application. In the case of impersonation, the RPC server application will typically launch a new thread or process with the privileges of the authenticated user.

RPC AUTH_UNIX (also known as AUTH_SYS) defines an RPC authentication method that allows the client to provide identification information to the server. This information is specific to UNIX and includes the user ID (**uid**), the primary group (**gid**), and auxiliary group IDs for other groups of which the user is a member. The client submits this information using the plaintext structure shown in Table 4.28.

AUTH_SYS authentication is specified in RFC 1831 (see [83]); many UNIX sources refer to it as AUTH_UNIX.

The RPC server returns a verifier field in the RPC reply, and its contents use the structure specified in Table 4.29.

As discussed in Chapter 2, UNIX-style user (**uid**) and group IDs (**gid**) have local significance to the computer where they exist. To use RPC AUTH_SYS, both the client and the server must have exactly the same user and group IDs for all users and groups or they will end up with users being granted higher privileges than they are expected to have, lower privileges, or no privileges at all — just by the virtue of the **uid** or **gid** specified by the client matching a **uid**, or one or more **gid**s on the server. To ensure that all user and group IDs are aligned, the RPC server and all its clients need to use a standard numbering scheme for user and group IDs. The approach to accomplish this can be manual or, alternatively, automatic. User and group information synchronization can

Table 4.28 RPC AUTH_SYS Authentication Structure

Field	*Value*
RPC Authentication type/flavor (byte)	AUTH_SYS = 1 (AUTH_UNIX)
Authentication body length (double word)	<variable — see the parameters below>
Stamp (double word)	This is a unique identifier generated by the client
Machine name (string)	Specifies the client computer name
UID (double word)	This is the UNIX-style user ID (uid) on the client computer for the user making the call
GID (double word)	This is the UNIX-style primary group ID (gid) on the client computer for the user making the call
Auxiliary GIDs (a list of GIDs)	This is a UNIX-style list of group IDs for the groups to which the user belongs
RPC Verifier flavor	AUTH_Null – AUTH_UNIX does not make use of the RPC verifier field in the client request
RPC Verifier length	0 (no verifier parameters)

be used by means of NIS/NIS+ or based on LDAP and other directory access protocols.

AUTH_SYS is performed as follows (see Figure 4.48):

1. The client uses either UDP or establishes a TCP session with the server.
2. The client submits an RPC request, specifying type AUTH_SYS; the client specifies the current **uid**, and **gid** for the interactive user (0 = root in this example) as well as auxiliary groups of which the user root is effectively a member (0, 1, 2, 3, 4, 6, and 10 in this example). The remainder of the packet contains the actual RPC request (see Frame 4 in Figure 4.48).
3. The server replies with a verifier that has the RPC flavor set to either AUTH_NULL or AUTH_SHORT (see Table 4.29 and Frame 6 in Figure 4.48).

Although it provides the server with more information than the AUTH_NULL method, AUTH_SYS is arguably more secure. The RPC client can generate an arbitrary RPC request specifying any set of user IDs (**uid**) and group IDs (**gid**) for the request. If the RPC server wants to respect this information provided by the RPC client, it needs to trust the client

```
Frame 4 (190 bytes on wire, 190 bytes captured)
Ethernet II, Src: Microsof_56:ab:2a (00:03:ff:56:ab:2a), Dst: 02:00:4c:4f:4f:50
(02:00:4c:4f:4f:50)
Internet Protocol, Src: 10.0.1.102 (10.0.1.102), Dst: 10.0.2.101 (10.0.2.101)
Transmission Control Protocol, Src Port: 799 (799), Dst Port: 2049 (2049), Seq: 1480121883, Ack:
3851099761, Len: 124
Remote Procedure Call, Type:Call XID:0x7bbe12e3
    Fragment header: Last fragment, 120 bytes
    XID: 0x7bbe12e3 (2076054243)
    Message Type: Call (0)
    RPC Version: 2
    Program: NFS (100003)
    Program Version: 3
    Procedure: GETATTR (1)
    The reply to this request is in frame 6
    Credentials
        Flavor: AUTH_UNIX (1)
        Length: 64
        Stamp: 0x0000ffae
        Machine Name: linus.ins.com
            length: 13
            contents: linus.ins.com
            fill bytes: opaque data
        UID: 0
        GID: 0
        Auxiliary GIDs
            GID: 0
            GID: 1
            GID: 2
            GID: 3
            GID: 4
            GID: 6
            GID: 10
    Verifier
        Flavor: AUTH_NULL (0)
        Length: 0
```

Figure 4.48 AUTH_SYS: User root from computer linus.ins.com uses NFS to access server dennis.ins.com.

```
Network File System, GETATTR Call FH:0x04046a00

Frame 6 (182 bytes on wire, 182 bytes captured)
Ethernet II, Src: 02:00:4c:4f:4f:50 (02:00:4c:4f:4f:50), Dst: Microsof_56:ab:2a
(00:03:ff:56:ab:2a)
Internet Protocol, Src: 10.0.2.101 (10.0.2.101), Dst: 10.0.1.102 (10.0.1.102)
Transmission Control Protocol, Src Port: 2049 (2049), Dst Port: 799 (799), Seq: 3851099761, Ack:
1480122007, Len: 116
Remote Procedure Call, Type:Reply XID:0x7bbe12e3
    Fragment header: Last fragment, 112 bytes
    XID: 0x7bbe12e3 (2076054243)
    Message Type: Reply (1)
    Program: NFS (100003)
    Program Version: 3
    Procedure: GETATTR (1)
    Reply State: accepted (0)
    This is a reply to a request in frame 4
    Time from request: 0.059021000 seconds
    Verifier
        Flavor: AUTH_NULL (0)
        Length: 0
    Accept State: RPC executed successfully (0)
Network File System, GETATTR Reply
```

Figure 4.48 (continued)

Table 4.29 RPC AUTH_SYS Verifier Returned by Server

Field	*Value*
RPC Verifier type/flavor (byte)	AUTH_NULL or AUTH_SHORT (see Chapter 4.11.3
Authentication Verifier body length (double word)	0 in the case of AUTH_NULL Variable in the case of AUTH_SHORT
Verifier body	Not present in the case of AUTH_NULL Authentication reference structure in the case of AUTH_SHORT

and know that the information in the request is genuine. The server may therefore want to restrict the list of potential clients by using the **/etc/hosts.allow** and **/etc/hosts.deny** files and providing their host-names and IP addresses. However, both the hostnames and the IP addresses can be spoofed, especially considering the fact that RPC historically has been using the UDP transport more extensively. Hence, the server cannot validate that the request is genuine and coming from a trusted source.

Furthermore, even if a legitimate client generates the client request, the plain nature of RPC packets and the fact that there is no message integrity checking by CRC or signatures provide potential attackers with the ability to modify packets in transit so that the request may arrive at the server with a crafted set of identification parameters.

Due to the wide use of the NFS and other RPC-based protocols, many efforts have been made to make the AUTH_SYS method more secure. The most widespread (although not necessarily the best) approach is tunneling RPC within SSH, which can provide for both communicating party authentication (client and server) and user authentication, as well as channel encryption and integrity authentication. Other approaches include IPSec encapsulation for NFS traffic, as well as IP VPN encapsulation for remote users using IPSec, PPTP, and L2TP-over-IPSec.

4.11.3 RPC AUTH_SHORT Authentication

AUTH_SHORT is a variation of AUTH_SYS. If the client and server support RPC AUTH_SYS authentication, upon the first request from the client that contains an AUTH_SYS option, the RPC server replies by setting the verifier type to AUTH_SHORT, and the verifier body contains a server-defined authentication structure (see Table 4.29). The server puts the current client credentials in an internal session and state table, and assigns an index to the table; this index is the value provided to the client in the verifier body.

Next time the client tries to authenticate, it will use AUTH_SYS as the credential flavor and will specify the server-provided authentication structure in the credentials body. The server will perform a lookup on the structure in its internal tables and will find the appropriate credentials and session information for the particular user.

All the shortcomings of AUTH_SYS are also applicable to AUTH_SHORT.

4.11.4 RPC AUTH_DES (AUTH_DH) Authentication

The security that AUTH_NULL and AUTH_SYS RPC authentication methods provide is weak. RPC-based applications, such as NFS, NIS, and NIS+) became widely adopted in the 1990s. To continue using these applications, and at the same time provide for better security and authentication mechanisms, Sun invented Secure RPC based on Diffie-Hellman public keys and DES encryption, which was later defined in RFC 2695 as AUTH_DH.

While AUTH_SYS uses UNIX-style credentials, the AUTH_DH (AUTH_DES) authentication mechanism provides for platform-independent names and potentially easy migration of the RPC platform and applications to other operating systems. In addition, AUTH_DES proposes the use of client and server time stamps as a countermeasure against replay attacks. Finally, AUTH_DES authentication uses public key cryptography mechanisms to provide for client and server authentication. Considering the above characteristics, AUTH_DES has been named Secure RPC mechanism. RFC 2695 (see [84]) specifies this authentication mechanism as AUTH_DH (for Diffie-Hellman); at the same time, many industry implementations refer to the same authentication mechanism as AUTH_DES.

RFC 2695 calls for user identification using unique names rather than user and group IDs. The symbolic name used by a user to authenticate to the RPC server is called the netname. The suggested naming convention is similar to RFC 822 SMTP e-mail addresses (such as Susan@ins.com). RFC 2695 provides a variation and suggests that the username consist of the name of the server or the operating system, followed by the user ID on that server — for example, unix.4356@ins.com can represent user with **uid** 4356 that has an account on a UNIX server at INS.

Another important aspect of AUTH_DES is the requirement for user public and private keys that play an active role in user and server authentication. Before using AUTH_DES, users and RPC servers need to generate a private/public keypair. The public key is stored in a user and host public key directory (the **/etc/publickey** file is used by NIS, and the cred table is used by NIS+). Client public keys can be distributed across all servers and clients in the UNIX domain using NIS/NIS+, or centralized in a directory using LDAP but they must be available for authentication using AUTH_DES. The keys are generated using the Diffie-Hellman Protocol.

The private key is encrypted using the DES-CBC algorithm using a zeroed Initial Vector and the user password as the key, and then is also stored in the **/etc/publickey** file. In order to use the private key, the client needs to decrypt it. Provided that the conventional user password is the same as the password used to encrypt the private key, this will happen automatically. The **keyserver** daemon runs on the client computer and securely caches the decrypted user private key. As the RPC client tries to authenticate to the remote server, authentication requests are actually passed to the **keyserver** daemon on the client computer that generates master and conversation keys, obtains the server public key, and encrypts client credential and verifier data on behalf of the client. In that respect, the **keyserver** facilitates single sign-on for AUTH_DES.

Finally, AUTH_DES requires clock synchronization for RPC clients and servers. Both the client and the server use encrypted time stamps in the

Table 4.30 AUTH_DES Client Authentication Structure: Plaintext

Field	*Value*
Time stamp-seconds (4 bytes)	Current time, expressed as seconds since January 1, 1970
Time stamp-microseconds (4 bytes)	Current time, expressed as microseconds since January 1, 1970
Time to Live — TTL (4 bytes)	Time window for which the user authentication is valid
TTL – 1 (4 bytes)	Same as TTL but decreased by 1

credential and verifier fields to provide for protection from replay attacks, as well as for server authentication.

When an RPC client wants to authenticate to an RPC server using AUTH_DES, the following takes place:

1. The **keyserver** on the client computer generates a random 8-byte conversation key.
2. The **keyserver** uses the public key directory to look up the server public key.
3. The **keyserver** generates a master common key using the Diffie-Hellman algorithm with 192-bit keys. To use it as little as possible, the master common key is not used to encrypt time stamps.; it is only used to encrypt other keys (conversation keys).
4. The client prepares the plaintext authentication structure depicted in Table 4.30.
5. The plaintext structure in Table 4.30 is then encrypted using DES-CBC, the conversation key as the key and a zeroed Initial Vector.
6. Initially, when the client uses AUTH_DES to the server, the client provides a structure known as Full Network Name and Verifier. When the server receives the Full Network Name and Verifier, the server stores the information contained in the structure in its internal tables and assigns an index to it (aka a nickname). The server then returns to the client the internal index (nickname). In subsequent authentication messages, the client specifies the index in the server table (the nickname) rather than the initial authentication structure. This AUTH_DES structure contains the information in Table 4.31.
7. The server performs a lookup in the public key directory and finds the user public key. Using this key, and its own public and private key, the server generates a master common key and uses it to decrypt the conversation key from the Full Network Name structure;

Table 4.31 AUTH_DES Full Network Name and Verifier Structure

Field	*Value*
RPC Authentication type/flavor (byte)	AUTH_DES
Authentication body length (double word)	Variable
Credential Body Initial	Initial Authentication (ADN_FULLNAME = 0) User Name — the name of the authenticating user as a string Encrypted Conversation key — the client generates a random conversation key and encrypts it using 56-bit DES CBC using the common master key as the key Encrypted Window — the DES encrypted TTL field
Credential Verifier Initial	Encrypted Time stamp — the DES encrypted seconds Encrypted Time stamp — the DES encrypted microseconds Encrypted Window-1 — the DES encrypted TTL-1 field

8. The server uses the conversation key to decrypt the Encrypted Time stamp and Window fields, and determines the current time on the client and the time skew. To protect from replay attacks, the server will drop requests that seem to have been generated before other requests already received from the client. The server also drops requests that arrive after the client-specified window has expired — the server uses its own clock to determine whether the packet is within the time window between the client-provided time stamp, and the client provided window (TTL).
9. To authenticate to the client, the server replies with the following AUTH_DES verifier. It is important to note that the server uses the time stamp sent by the client, rather than checking its local time — the server authenticates its identity to the client by proving that it knows the conversation key, and that it can successfully decrypt, manipulate, and encrypt the client-provided time stamp. Once the server has decrypted the client full name from the initial request, the server decreases both the client time stamp and client time stamp — one by one, and then encrypts them using DES CBC with the conversation key (see Table 4.32).

Table 4.32 AUTH_DES Server Verifier and Client Nickname

Field	*Value*
RPC Authentication type/flavor (byte)	AUTH_DES
Authentication body length (double word)	Variable
Server Verifier	Encrypted Time stamp-1 — the DES encrypted seconds Encrypted Time stamp-2 — the DES encrypted microseconds Client Nickname — plaintext index in the server table

Table 4.33 AUTH_DES Nickname Credentials and Verifier Structure

Field	*Value*
RPC Authentication type/flavor (byte)	AUTH_DES
Authentication body length (double word)	Variable
Credential body Subsequent	Subsequent Authentication (ADN_NICKNAME = 1) Nickname — the plaintext nickname, provided by the server during initial authentication
Credential Verifier Initial	Encrypted Time stamp — the DES encrypted seconds Encrypted Time stamp — the DES encrypted microseconds

10. When the client receives the reply from the server, the former is able to authenticate the server, as no other user or computer can know that secret conversation key, calculated independently by the server and the client.
11. In subsequent RPC calls to the server, the client uses the nickname provided by the server at the first authentication request. The client still uses the current time to generate time stamps, which then get encrypted using DES and the conversation key as the key (see Table 4.33).

The AUTH_DH RPC authentication mechanism provides considerable improvements over earlier RPC authentication mechanisms. The use of time stamps provides for effective protection against replay attacks, and the use of public key cryptography mitigates the risks of man-in-the-middle attacks, while at the same time providing a reliable mechanism for key management using public key-based master keys. Unfortunately, the DES encryption algorithm is now considered weak. Another shortcoming of the AUTH_DES authentication mechanism is that its level of protection is equivalent to the strength of the user password and is susceptible to dictionary and, potentially, brute force attacks: anyone with access to the key database can try to guess the user password and potentially decrypt the user private key.

Due to these limitations, as well as to the adoption by the industry of transport and network layer encryption and authentication methods, today the AUTH_DH RPC authentication method is neither widely used nor very popular.

4.11.5 RPC AUTH_KERB4 Authentication

In addition to AUTH_DH, RFC 2695 [84] defines RPC authentication using Kerberos v.4 tickets. The mechanics of this authentication technique is essentially the same as AUTH_DH (see Chapter 4.11.4) with the following considerations:

- Instead of providing a netname, the client provides a Kerberos ticket to the server.
- Users do not need to have keypairs; instead, Kerberos AP tickets are used.
- The Kerberos ticket contains a session key that is used as a conversation key.

The Kerberos v.4 protocol has been widely replaced by Kerberos v.5 so the AUTH_KERB4 RPC authentication method is not in widespread use.

4.11.6 RPCSEC_GSS Authentication

The RPCSEC_GSS authentication mechanism is specified in RFC 2203 (see [85]) and provides for GSS-API-based authentication. Because Kerberos v.5 is the most widespread GSS-API authentication mechanism, RPCSEC_GSS essentially provides for Kerberos v.5 authentication for RPC services.

Table 4.34 RPC RPCSEC_GSS Authentication Initial Negotiation Structure

Field	*Value*
RPC Authentication type/flavor (byte)	RPCSEC_GSS = 6
Authentication body length (double word)	<variable — see the parameters below>
Control procedure	Defines the type of the message — Initial (INIT), continuation of initial request (INIT_CONTINUE), Data (DATA), or termination (DESTROY)
Sequence number	This is undefined during authentication — the server ignores it; once the context has been established, this is used by GSS-API
GSS-API Service	GSS-API data integrity, encryption, or none
Context Handle	This is a unique handle, generated by the server for the current session In the initial message, the client sets this field to NULL In subsequent messages, the client and the server use the server-generated handle
RPC Verifier flavor	AUTH_Null
RPC Verifier length	0 (no verifier parameters)

To use GSS-API, the RPC client and server first negotiate the protection context and authenticate each other. Then they start exchanging RPC requests that are now protected by the GSS-API context.

Essentially, RPCSEC_GSS transports GSS-API tokens as part of RPC authentication structures. The GSS-API authentication and context creation process proceeds as follows:

1. The client connects to the RPC server, setting the RPC authentication flavor to RPCSEC_GSS (6), and provides the structure shown in Table 4.34.
2. The client sets the client-side verifier flavor to AUTH_NULL, and the credentials body length to zero.
3. The client puts the result from the **GSS_Init_sec_context( )** client call into the RPC message body (there is no RPC data in initial packets).
4. The server, upon receipt of the request and initial authentication structures from the client, invokes the **GSS_Accept_sec_context( )** call.

Table 4.35 RPC RPCSEC_GSS Authentication Server Verifier

Field	*Value*
RPC Verifier type/ flavor (byte)	RPCSEC_GSS = 6
Gss-major	Contains GSS Status code
Gss-minor	Contains GSS Status code
Gss-window	Maximum number of outstanding messages to the server — this is set by the server upon successful authentication
GSS-API Token	The token returned from the **GSS_Accept_sec_context( )** call

5. The server submits the following structure to the client (see Table 4.35).
6. The client and server may need to exchange a couple of tokens, depending on the authentication mechanism being used. In the case of Kerberos v5 in GSS-API, the client can submit the GSS-API AP_REQ message, and the server can reply with the AP_REP message, which concludes the authentication process.
7. Subsequent messages between the client and the server can be protected with GSS-API integrity and privacy, depending on the quality of protection (QoP) chosen.

The RPCSEC_GSS RPC authentication method can be used in infrastructures that have deployed Kerberos v.5 authentication. It is currently considered a secure way to authenticate users and transfer data.

4.12 SMB/CIFS Authentication

The Server Message Block/Common Internet File System (SMB/CIFS) Protocol is traditionally used in Windows environments for access to files and printers. In addition to that, the SMB/CIFS Protocol provides for IPC mechanisms, including Mailslots (datagrams/messages) and Named Pipes (streams), as well as Microsoft Remote Procedure Calls (also known as DCE Remote Procedure Calls). In addition to Microsoft's implementation of the SMB/CIFS Protocol, SAMBA represents another popular implementation of the protocol and is typically used on UNIX-compatible operating systems.

The early implementations of the CIFS Protocol utilize NetBIOS services and therefore work on top of the NetBIOS layer over different transports.

In TCP/IP environments, the NetBIOS data stream protocol utilizes TCP/139 and the NetBIOS datagram service utilizes TCP/138. SMB/CIFS over NetBIOS authentication uses specific protocol structures to carry user information such as usernames and passwords, required for user authentication.

Windows 2000 and later implementations introduce NetBIOS-independent SMB/CIFS services that run directly on top of TCP/445. SSPI (GSS-API) is used as a security layer on top of SMB/CIFS to provide for user authentication and communication channel protection. Authentication protocols can be negotiated using the SPNEGO layer.

More information regarding the differences between the two implementations of the SMB/CIFS Protocol relative to user authentication and data security can be found in subsection 4.1.2.6.

4.13 NFS Authentication

The Network File System (NFS) is a popular protocol for accessing network files and directories. It is often used by UNIX-compatible operating systems, although NFS implementations exist for Windows and other operating systems.

The NFS Protocol is closely related to Sun's Remote Procedure Calls (RPC). As the Sun RPC interprocess communication mechanism possesses its own methods for authenticating network users, the NFS Protocol itself does not need to provide for user authentication, and uses the readily available Sun RPC model. More information regarding Sun RPC authentication is available in section 4.11.

4.14 Microsoft Remote Procedure Calls

Microsoft Remote Procedure Calls is a powerful mechanism for client/server computing, derived from the DCE RPC model. Although the idea is the same, the Microsoft RPC model is not compatible with the Sun RPC model.

This book only covers the authentication aspects of MS RPC that are based on underlying security mechanisms, provided by either SMB/CIFS (which may or may not use SSPI) or SSPI directly. The inner workings of MS RPC are discussed in more detail in [II]. The popular mechanisms based on RPC include user logon, domain controller access, remote access to registry and clipboard, remote and local computer and service management, domain controller replication, OLE/COM/DCOM/ActiveX, MAPI, etc.

Microsoft's Remote Procedure Calls can work either within Microsoft's SMB/CIFS Protocol or directly using a portmapper approach.

When embedded within SMB/CIFS — which is typical for older operating systems —the Microsoft RPC mechanism utilizes user authentication provided by the SMB/CIFS protocol, as described in section 4.12.

Microsoft Remote Procedure Calls can also use a direct binding approach without relying on SMB/CIFS. In this case, the client connects to TCP/135 on the server and tries to obtain information about RPC applications on that server. Alternatively, the client can directly connect (bind) to an RPC application by specifying its unique ID. The client and server then choose a free dynamic port (greater than 1023) and the client reconnects to this port, releasing the connection to the portmapper on TCP/135. The rest of the RPC session uses the dynamic port.

The MS RPC Protocol when binding directly on top of TCP utilizes the Microsoft SSPI interface to provide for user authentication and data security. For more information, see subsection 4.1.2.

4.15 MS SQL Authentication

Microsoft SQL Server is one of the most popular database platforms. Once part of Microsoft's BackOffice suite, Microsoft SQL Server tightly integrates with other Microsoft servers, and especially with the underlying operating system, which must be Windows NT compatible.

Microsoft SQL Server provides for two different authentication methods:

1. Windows Integrated Authentication, which uses the underlying operating system authentication features to authenticate users
2. Mixed Mode (SQL Server Native and Windows Integrated) authentication, which uses SQL Server system tables to store information about users and groups and also allows for Windows credentials to be used. SQL Server 6.5 supports native mode only, separately from Mixed Mode.

SQL Server stores SQL user IDs, usernames, and passwords for user authentication in the **sysxlogins** (SQL 6.5 uses **syslogins**) table of the **SYSTEM** database. The usernames are stored in cleartext in this table but the password is stored using a one-way function, based on SHA-1. The password hash is salted. The system user ID (SUID) is analogous to the Windows NT SID and is a unique number identifying the user on the server.

Microsoft does not provide official information on how user information and passwords are stored and protected. The way SQL stores passwords, as well as potential ways to attack them, are provided in [93]. Briefly, it is believed that MS SQL Server stores a hash of the password in the original case, and a version in capital letters only, which due to the reduced keyspace is easier to attack. Before the password hash is calculated, a 4-byte random salt is generated. The salt is stored in cleartext in the database. It is then concatenated to the user-provided password, and the resulting string is processed using SHA-1 to produce the password hash. This hash is calculated in the original password case and in uppercase — this is because, depending on the settings, the SQL database may or may not preserve the case of strings and provide for case-sensitive or case-insensitive sort order. The salt and both hashes are then stored in the **sysxlogins** table. User authentication against the MS SQL local authentication is only performed if the server is configured for mixed mode authentication.

Microsoft SQL Server provides three main transports for network clients:

1. TCP/IP transport
2. Named Pipes — based on Microsoft SMB/CIFS
3. Multiprotocol — based on Microsoft Remote Procedure Calls (RPC)

In each case, application data (typically Transact SQL requests from the client and structured data from the server) are encapsulated within the Tabular Data Stream (TDS) Protocol. The TDS Protocol can work on top of any of the transports above, as well as some additional transports.

In the case of SQL Server (mixed authentication using SQL Server accounts), the TDS layer is also responsible to carry user authentication information. In the case of Windows integrated authentication, this is not required.

4.15.1 MS SQL Authentication over the TCP/IP Transport

The TDS Protocol can bind directly on top of TCP/IP on default port TCP/1433. The TCP layer provides the virtualization of input and output streams that TDS uses to transfer data both ways (Figure 4.49).

In case SQL Server (mixed authentication) is used, the TDS stream is responsible for carrying the login information. Both the username and the user password are transferred across the network. The password undergoes simple obfuscation before being transferred across the network but is easily reversible. User data is not encrypted or authenticated. SQL authentication on top of TCP/IP is therefore easily susceptible to many attacks — from both user authentication and data protection points of view.

The algorithm used to obfuscate user passwords over the network is not officially published by Microsoft but is specified in [94]. To authenticate, the client converts the user password to Unicode, and swaps the left 4 bits

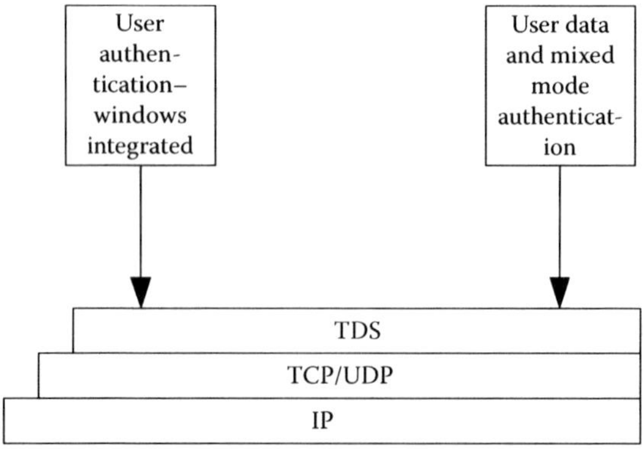

Figure 4.49 User authentication over TCP/IP.

of each byte of the resultant Unicode sequence with the right 4 bits. The result is then XORed with 0xA5 and sent over the network. Apparently, if someone captures SQL login traffic, he can XOR the obfuscated password with 0xA5, and then swap the left 4 bits with the right 4 bits of every byte. The result would be the Unicode user password.

Alternatively, administrators may choose to use TCP/IP access to SQL Server with Windows Integrated authentication. In this case, user authentication is performed using SSPI, which is directly bound on top of TCP/1433, and the user password is not sent across the network using the above obfuscation algorithm. The strength of authentication protection will then depend on the SSPI authentication mechanism, chosen by the client and the server.

Despite the weaknesses that some NTLM authentication mechanisms possess, using SSPI is much more secure than plain SQL Server authentication and should be preferred whenever possible.

4.15.2 MS SQL Server Authentication over Named Pipes

Named Pipes provide for bi-directional communication between the client and server using programming mechanisms that are similar to access to files. A Named Pipe can be considered a virtual file (or stream) on the network (Figure 4.50).

Microsoft provides for Named Pipes IPC mechanisms on top of file services, based on SMB/CIFS. SMB/CIFS, on the other hand, can work on top of the different transports, such as TCP/IP, with or without NetBIOS, NetBEUI, or IPS/SPX. As a result, SQL Named Pipes is a portable mechanism that can potentially work on top of virtually any transport. Apparently, there is communication and processing overhead involved in using Named Pipes.

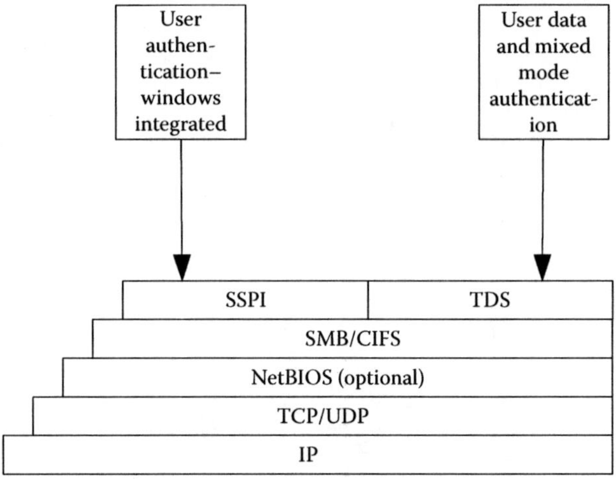

Figure 4.50 User authentication over Named Pipes.

SMB/CIFS authentication is discussed in section 4.12. Unless anonymous access to SMB/CIFS is allowed, the user will be required to authenticate. This will typically happen using a username and password from either the domain of which the MS SQL server is a member, or local accounts on the server itself.

If Windows integrated authentication is used, the fact that the user has been authenticated by the SMB/CIFS layer is sufficient to provide the server with information to identify and impersonate the user. The TDS layer does not need to carry additional user authentication information.

If SQL Server Mixed authentication is used, two layers of authentication will be involved. First, the operating system on the server will authenticate the client SMB/CIFS session using Windows authentication methods (SSPI). Then, once the user has been successfully authenticated by the operating system, TDS will need to carry authentication information as well. It is interesting to note that authentication information at the SMB/CIFS layer and at the TDS layer can differ. The SMB/CIFS layer only provides for authentication at the transport (from an application point of view) layer, and login information contained within TDS will be used to build the effective user security context within MS SQL Server.

4.15.3 MS SQL Server Authentication over Multiprotocol

Similar to the Named Pipes transport, Multiprotocol authentication supports a wide range of transports. Unlike Named Pipes, SQL Multiprotocol communication utilizes Microsoft Remote Procedure Calls (RPC) (Figure 4.51).

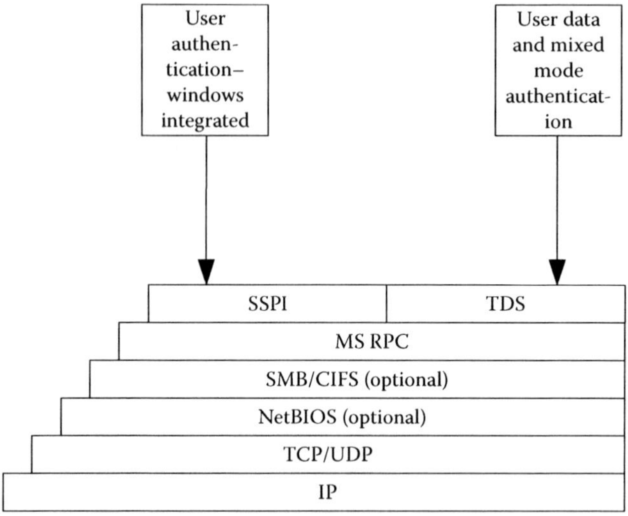

Figure 4.51 SQL user authentication over Multiprotocol.

MS RPC authentication is presented in Chapter 4.14. Similar to Named Pipes, MS RPC requires Windows integrated authentication methods (SSPI) to perform user authentication.

If Windows Integrated authentication is selected by the server and the client, the authentication provided by the RPC layer will suffice and the user can be identified or impersonated by the server. The TDS stream does not need to provide additional login information.

Similar to Named Pipes, if Mixed authentication is performed, authentication needs to take place both at the transport (from SQL server point of view) layer and at the TDS layer. Again, the account may differ but authentication at both layers must be successful to establish a connection.

4.15.4 MS SQL Server and SSL

SQL Server 2000 and later versions provide for SSL protection of the communication channel between the client and the server. The SSL channel can be encrypted (to protect from information disclosure), integrity checked (to ensure that traffic will not be modified in transit), and server identity can be verified. MS SQL Server does not support user authentication (client certificate mapping) using SSL.

In the simplest scenario, only a server certificate is required for the SQL Server. The server and the client can request SSL encryption of the communication channel by setting the "Force protocol encryption" setting. SSL Protection is described in section 4.3. The SSL channel protects the contents of the TDS layer. When Mixed authentication is used, user authentication information is carried by TDS. This authentication information will be encrypted, and its integrity will be authenticated by SSL.

4.16 Oracle Database Server Authentication

Oracle Database server is one of the most popular database servers on the market today. Most major applications and business platfoms support Oracle in some way. Oracle runs on different platforms and operating systems.

Oracle communication over the network takes place over the OracleNet Protocol, which provides a layer of abstraction between Oracle applications and different transport protocols.

4.16.1 Oracle Legacy Authentication Database

On the server side, Oracle supports a number of authentication databases that can be used to authenticate users. The three common authentication databases are:

1. Oracle **SYS.USER$** table (also the DBA_USERS database view)
2. Oracle password file
3. Operating System authentication

With the legacy authentication approach, when the client connects to the Oracle server using the OracleNet Protocol and tries to authenticate, it submits the plaintext username and password to the server. The server can check the provided plaintext credentials against one or more of the above authentication databases.

The **SYS.USERS$** table can be used for user authentication after the Oracle database has been brought up. The **SYS.USER$** table contains separate fields for the username (the Username field) and password hash (Password field) for each user. The password hash algorithm is not published but is documented in a number of information sources on the Internet, such as [95] and [96]. The algorithm is believed as follows:

1. Concatenate the username and the plaintext user password.
2. Convert the resultant string to uppercase.
3. Convert the resultant string to multibyte format.
4. Encrypt the resultant string using DES-CBC in the well-known key "**0x0123456789ABCDEF**".
5. Use the last 64 bits from the encrypted result to produce a new encryption key; ignore parity bits.

6. Encrypt the concatenated plaintext username and password again using DES-CBC in the above key.
7. Convert the result to a printable string and store it as a password hash.

The above algorithm is a one-way function that generates the Oracle password hash. The algorithm provides for a simple salt parameter (the username) that guarantees that even if two users use the same password, the password hash is going to be different. However, the above algorithm also has a number of weaknesses. First, the conversion to uppercase (claimed to be used for compatibility with terminals that only support upper case characters) significantly decreases the keyspace, and makes it possible to use brute force attacks against password hashes. The algorithm is also susceptible to dictionary attacks, as well as to rainbow attacks with precomputed password hashes — at least for users with well-known usernames such as the SYS and SYSTEM administrator accounts, and other users as well. As a result, the Oracle password hashes must be well protected, both as they are stored on the server and as they are being transferred across the network.

The Oracle password file is mainly used to provide administrative access when the database is down and the **SYS.USERS$** table is not available. On UNIX systems, the password file is the **ORACLE_HOME/dbs/orapw$ORACLE_SID** file and on Windows systems — the %**ORACLE_HOME%\database\PWD%ORACLE_SID%.ora** file. Whether this file will be used for user authentication is defined by the REMOTE_LOGIN_PASSWORDFILE parameter in the Initialization parameters of the **init.ora** file.

Operating system authentication is a flexible authentication option that instructs Oracle to pass authentication information onto the underlying OS security mechanisms. Thus, although the user may need to be defined in Oracle, user credentials are stored protected by the operating system authentication database.

4.16.2 Legacy OracleNet Authentication

The OracleNet Protocol (known as SQL*Net in earlier versions of Oracle) provides for simple user authentication. An Oracle client can use this protocol to connect to an Oracle server, and authenticate by sending plain username and password information. This changed in Oracle 7.1 when OracleNet started supporting simple password encryption over the network using modified DES –encryption (Figure 4.52).

Another transport mechanism supported by Oracle is IPC — including local IPC and Windows NT Named Pipes. While local IPC does not require

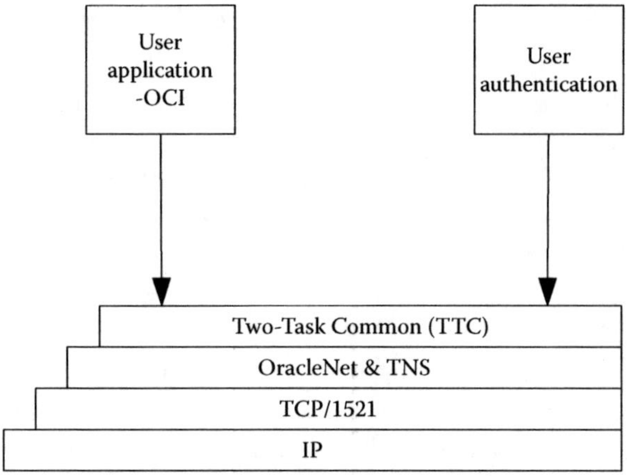

Figure 4.52 Legacy OracleNet protocol stack.

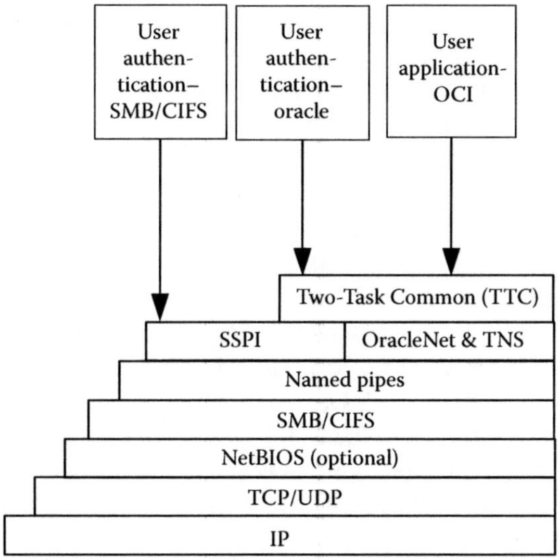

Figure 4.53 OracleNet protocol stack for Windows Named Pipes.

additional authentication because it involves two local processes communicating with each other, the Windows NT Named Pipes mechanism requires user authentication for the SMB/CIFS Protocol. The details for this authentication can be found in section 4.12.

4.16.3 Oracle Advanced Security Mechanisms for User Authentication

The threats posed by plaintext authentication to the Oracle Database Server, as well as the need to encrypt user data, were the driving factors for the Oracle Advanced Security suite of additional security features. It is known as Advanced Networking Option in Oracle Database Server versions 7 and 8

Oracle Advanced Security provides for a number of features important from an authentication perspective:

1. *Oracle Native Encryption*. The OracleNet layer can encrypt the communication channel between the client and the server using DES, 3DES, RC4, or AES. This allows for the protection of user authentication information, along with user data, against disclosure.
2. *Oracle Native Integrity*. The OracleNet layer can authenticate channel integrity using MD5 and SHA-1. This can be used to eliminate some types of man-in-the-middle attacks, as well as authentication mechanism downgrade attacks.
3. *Authentication adapters*. This is a flexible and extendable approach for configuring authentication mechanisms on the server side. Applications do not need to know about the authentication mechanisms used by the server; so even when authentication adapters are added or removed from the authentication model, applications do not need to be redesigned and rewritten.
4. *Certificate-based authentication and the use of smart cards for authentication*. This can work with either SSL protection or RADIUS authentication. User certificates can be stored in LDAP. Users store their private keys in the protected store of the Oracle Wallet application. (See Figure 4.54.)
5. *SSL Protection*. This provides for encryption, integrity checking, and mutual authentication using certificates. SSL is simply embedded as a layer below OracleNet and uses TCP/2484. The Oracle Database Server can be configured to use LDAP to obtain user certificates and effectively provide authentication solely based on user key pairs. SSL Protection and authentication are described in Chapter 4.3.
6. *Kerberos (MIT and CyberSafe) authentication*. This is GSS-API/Kerberos v.5 based authentication. More information on Kerberos is available in subsection 4.2.2.
7. *Security tokens*. RSA SecurID — authentication using security token devices and one-time passwords is supported.
8. *RADIUS-based authentication mechanisms*. Forward authentication requests to a RADIUS server. More information on RADIUS is available in Chapter 5.

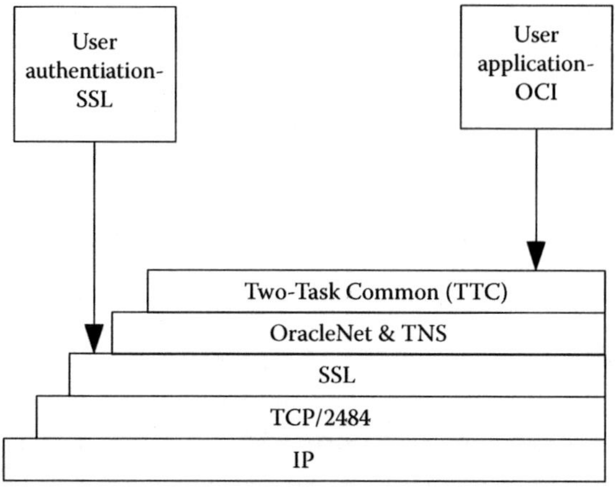

Figure 4.54 User authentication using SSL and certificates.

Oracle Advanced Security provides for a better and more flexible security and authentication mechanism. It is therefore very popular in enterprise environments.

4.17 MS Exchange MAPI Authentication

Microsoft Exchange Server is a popular e-mail platform in many organizations today. It provides access to e-mail by means of legacy Internet protocols but it also has its native approach for accessing the e-mail store — the Exchange Messaging API (or MAPI).

Accessing Microsoft Exchange Server using LDAP (Exchange 2000 and later redirects LDAP requests to Active Directory), POP3, IMAP4, SMTP, and HTTP is standard with regard to user authentication, and information on user authentication for these protocols is provided earlier in this chapter.

The Exchange MAPI Protocol is based on Microsoft Remote Procedure Calls (RPC) and entirely depends on it for user authentication, impersonation, and communication channel protection. MS RPC uses either SMB/CIFS or SSPI directly to provide for user authentication and data security. More information on MS RPC user authentication is available in section 4.14.

4.18 SAML, WS-Security, and Federated Identity

Today's business relies more and more on the Internet. Organizations use the Internet to communicate with their customers; they create virtual shopping centers on the Internet, provide online support to users, and publish documentation, roadmaps, and sales collateral. Organizations also communicate with their partners on the Internet; they exchange business e-mail, check stock availability, place orders, report deliveries, etc.

4.18.1 XML and SOAP

Many organizations share the same vision for the future of business communication on the Internet; the eXtensible Markup Language (XML) is believed to be the universal language that will allow customers to talk to business organizations (customer-to-business, C2B) and businesses to talk to each other (business-to-business, B2B). XML is a World Wide Web Consortium (W3C) specification that provides for a uniform document representation so that C2B and B2B communication can be application and vendor neutral. Each type of document can be described by an XML Schema; and by means of transformations, documents can be converted from virtually any format into universal XML document format, and then, if necessary, into another type of document. XML can therefore be used as the format for simple text documents, pictures, tables, and even for relational databases; and these documents can be exchanged between communicating parties. Most often, XML documents are exchanged over the HTTP transport (Web); but because these documents are simply files, there are no restrictions with regard to the transport they can use. More information on XML is available in [139].

XML not only provides for a universal document format, but also allows network services to communicate with each other over the Internet using a standard communication interface, similar to DCOM, Corba, and RPC. The XML model that is used for communication between applications is called the Simple Object Access Protocol (SOAP). SOAP is the essential transport for Web services and applications. SOAP messages can be represented as XML structures, and as such are typically carried on top of HTTP. This allows Web applications on the Internet to communicate with each other using only HTTP — both to exchange XML documents and to invoke remote processes and functions using SOAP/XML. More information on SOAP is available in [141].

4.18.2 SAML

XML documents provide for a common language between applications and services on the Internet. However, from a security perspective, organizations and individuals are, to a large extent, detached from one another. Organizations maintain their own security and authentication authorities, which are independent from other organizations. Customers may have an account in their own organization or on the local computer. The existing user authentication practices result in a virtually completely decentralized — from an Internet perspective — model where no business entity on the Internet trusts anyone else.

When a user wants to access resources on the Internet, the user may need to authenticate against the Web server of the organization providing these resources. To do that, the user needs to have an account in that organization's account or customer database. If the user needs to access resources in a second organization as well, he needs a second account in the other organization's database, etc.

Business relationships between customers and businesses, as well as between business organizations, sometimes imply a level of trust. For example, two partner organizations that need to share resources with one another are likely to trust one another to a certain extent. However, as each of them has its own authentication authority, users cannot use accounts from their own authentication authority to access resources in the other organization.

The SAML standard allows organizations to establish trust relationships with one another and with their customers. SAML was developed by OASIS (Organization for the Advancement of Structured Information Standards), a non-profit international consortium supported by big international IT organizations such as Hewlett Packard, Oracle, Nokia, and others. More information on SAML is available in [138]. The current version of the SAML standard is 2.0. The previous version (SAML v.1.1) is not compatible with SAML v.2.0, so organizations that want to establish SAML trust relationships need to use the same version of SAML.

Organizations can leverage the existing authentication infrastructure and share resources with one another in a secure, trusted fashion. As a result, customers and users on the Internet whose organization participates in a SAML trust relationship can access resources that reside in trusting organizations to which they have been granted access. Both XML and SAML are platform independent. Documents and information in general that users exchange can be generated by any application and platform capable of supporting XML. In general, user authentication can be performed by any operating system, service, or authentication authority capable of supporting SAML.

To allow users, applications, and services that use the universal document format XML, SAML is also built on top of XML. SAML participants communicate with each other exchanging SAML messages encapsulated within SOAP/XML, typically over HTTP (Figure 4.55).

In the SAML model, when a user authenticates against the authority where his account resides, the user is issued an access token, or Identity

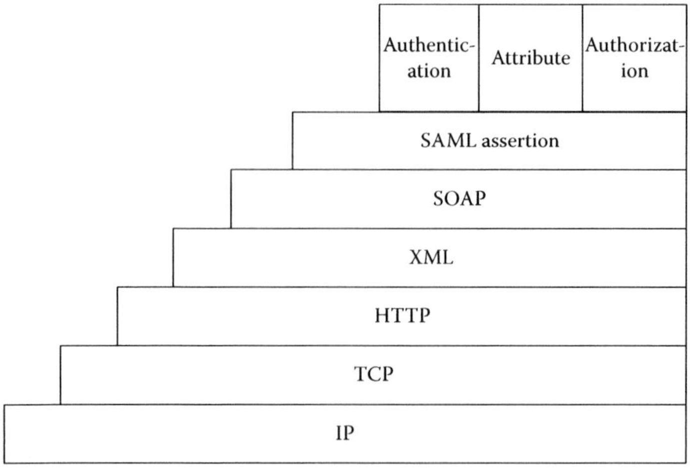

Figure 4.55 SAML protocol stack.

Provider statement (called SAML assertion). The SAML assertion is an XML formatted structure that may contain:

- *User authentication information.* The assertion contains information that shows that the user has authenticated successfully to the authentication authority, and may also indicate when the user authenticated, what type of credentials he used, etc.
- *Authorization information.* The assertion may contain information on what the user is permitted to do or access, user membership to groups, or other information that may be related to authorization to resources.
- *Attributes.* The assertion may contain attributes, such as the user e-mail address, telephone number, etc.

The SAML specification relies on XML encryption and signing mechanisms to protect SAML messages from improper modification, and potentially from disclosure. To provide for encryption and signing, XML can use asymmetric cryptography (often based on X.509 certificates and PKI) or symmetric keys. Certificate-based protection is the preferred approach. More information on XML signatures is available in [140].

SAML assertions are signed by the authentication authority that has issued them, using the XML Signature specification and the private key (or in the rare case when symmetric keys are used — the preshared key) of the authentication authority. In the SAML model of trust, other organizations and trusting authentication authorities will consider the SAML assertion valid and trustworthy because no party other than the trusted organization authentication authority can sign the SAML assertion. To provide further security, SAML communication, which typically happens over HTTP, can be encapsulated within TLS/SSL (HTTPS). HTTPS is widely used in the SAML architecture.

SAML uses the terms "identity provider" (also called SAML authority or asserting party) and "service provider" (also called relying party). The identity provider is the SAML authentication authority where user information is registered. The identity provider authenticates users and provides them with SAML assertions (similar to tickets) that they can use to access resources. Service provider organizations have resources, such as Web servers, media servers, databases, etc. Service providers may have their local user authentication databases but they only contain local accounts that have meaning for the specific service provider, and not dedicated accounts for each Web user. The service provider organization trusts the identity provider organization to authenticate users. The direction of the trust is from the service provider to the identity provider. The identity provider does not necessarily trust the service provider. This is often required as service providers may happen to be competitors, and transitiveness of the trust or a mutual trust with the identity provider is likely to be unacceptable.

There are two main use cases for SAML: (1) Web single sign-on and (2) federated identity.

4.18.2.1 SAML and Web Single Sign-On

The Web single sign-on use case primarily represents a customer-to-business (C2B) model where one organization is designated as an identity provider and one or more other organizations are service providers. The identity provider organization does not provide resources to users; this organization is dedicated to user authentication, as well as generation and management of the SAML trusts. All users who take part in the Web single sign-on model have their accounts in the identity provider organization.

The Web single sign-on use case (Figure 4.56) allows the user to have just one account and password stored in the identity provider database. The user does not need to complete a registration process with each and every service provider that he wants to access, complete registration forms, select a username and password, and provide personal information. All this is done only once when registering with the identity provider, and then all this information can be automatically made available to service providers.

In a Web single sign-on scenario, the user needs to authenticate first by providing a set of acceptable and correct credentials to the identity provider. The credentials depend on the policy imposed by the identity

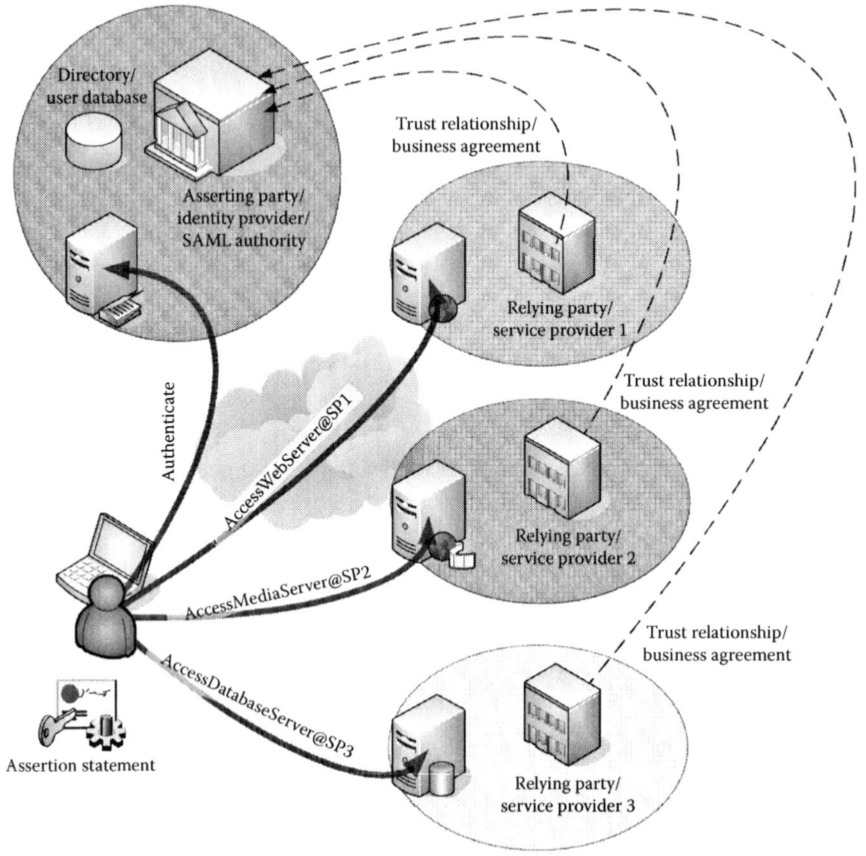

Figure 4.56 SAML Web single sign-on.

provider, and may be a username and a password, a username and a one-time password, a certificate, or other type of credentials. Once the user has been authenticated, the user application (typically a Web browser) will obtain the SAML assertion (similar to an access token or ticket) for this user, which at this stage is similar to a service ticket.

With the SAML assertion signed by the identity provider, the user can connect to a service provider. When the user presents the signed SAML assertion, the service provider checks the signature on the SAML assertion and validates that it was issued by a trusted identity provider. The service provider can then use the information in the security assertion to link the Internet user to a local account (typically generic) and finally provide the user with access to local resources.

In a similar fashion, once the user has obtained the SAML assertion, he can access resources that belong to other service providers, potentially without re-authenticating.

4.18.2.2 Case Study: Web Single Sign-On Mechanics

There are three main scenarios used in the Web single sign-on model. They differ in the sequence of events, as well as the communication paths between SAML participants. The assumption is that all accessed resources are Web resources, and the user uses a Web browser.

Service Provider Redirect/POST Binding

In this scenario, a user has not yet been authenticated by an identity provider. The user tries to access a service provider resource using his Web browser. Because the user has not been authenticated yet, he does not have an SAML assertion (ticket) for the service provider Web server. The Web server sends an HTTP redirect back to the client Web browser and redirects the user to the identity provider authentication Web page. The service provider inserts the referring URL from the service provider Web site in the redirection request. The identity provider asks the user to authenticate, and the user provides his identity and credentials. The identity provider generates an SAML assertion for the user, and redirects the user back to the service provider, using the original URL included in the service provider redirection request. The user Web browser connects again to the service provider URL, and this time presents an SAML assertion, which will probably be mapped to a local user account and the user will be granted access to resources.

It is important to note that although the SAML assertion is provided to the user Web browser, the user cannot modify the SAML assertion because it has been signed by the identity provider, and the user cannot generate a new signature because he does not have the identity provider private key.

Service Provider POST/Artifact Binding

In this scenario, a user has not yet been authenticated by an identity provider. The user tries to access a service provider resource using his Web browser. Because the user has not been authenticated yet, he does not have an SAML assertion (ticket) for the service provider Web server. The service provider SAML service generates an artifact (reference) for the user request, and returns it to the client Web browser, along with a redirect to the identity provider. The client Web browser connects to the identity provider and authenticates, and then provides the artifact to the identity provider. The identity provider uses synchronous SOAP communication to connect directly to the service provider, resolves the artifact, and provides a security assertion to the service provider. In this case, direct communication between the identity provider and the service provider takes place, and the client is not involved into the SAML assertion submission process. The client Web browser is redirected to the service provider, which, now that the artifact has been resolved, provides the client Web browser with access to services.

Identity Provider POST Binding

In this scenario, the user accesses the identity provider first, authenticates and receives a SAML assertion. The user then can use a link on the identity provider's Web site that points to the service provider. The client Web browser connects to the service provider Web site and submits (using the **HTTP POST** verb) the SAML assertion that it already has. The service provider performs account linking and provides the user with access to resources.

4.18.2.3 SAML Federated Identity

The *federated identity* use case is primarily meant for business-to-business (B2B) communication. With this model, two or more partner organizations can federate their authentication authorities and allow users from one organization to access resources in another organization using their own user accounts and credentials. Organizations can potentially establish such trust one way, two way, in a partially or a fully meshed fashion. Depending on the trust relationships, each organization's authentication authority can serve as an identity provider to other organizations in the SAML federation. Each organization's servers can also serve as a service provider to other organizations in the federation.

When a user in a federated identity model (Figure 4.57) authenticates to his authentication authority, he is provided with a SAML assertion. This security assertion can then be used by the user to access resources in another domain in the SAML federation to which the user has been granted access.

4.18.2.4 Account Linking

In both the Web single sign-on and federated identity scenarios, service providers do not need to have a full list of all the user accounts that exist in the identity provider database; very often, this would not even be possible.

The service provider's systems typically have a local user database and impose local security mechanisms that are of importance for the service provider's environment only. External user accounts that are authenticated

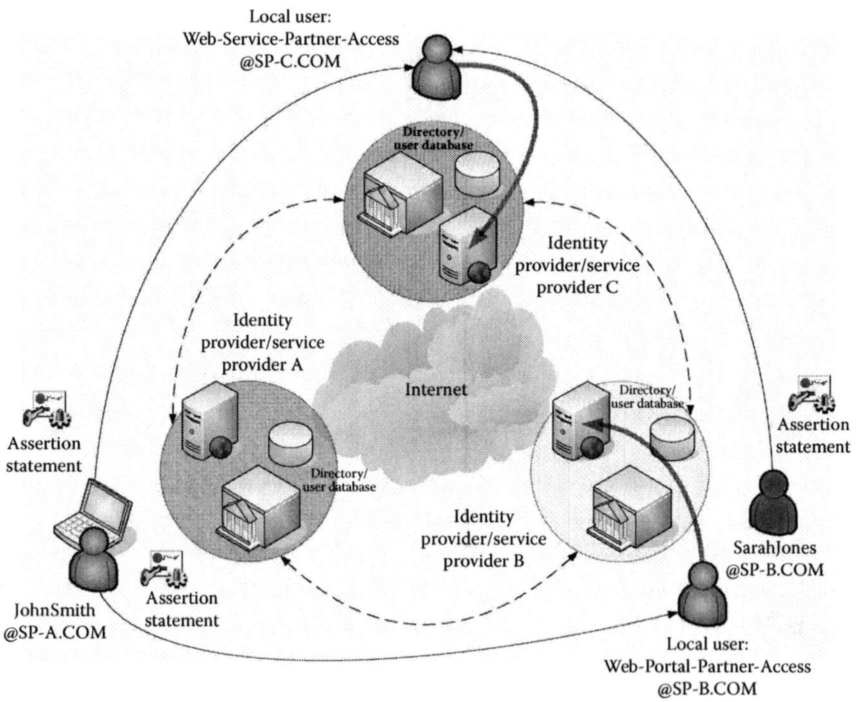

Figure 4.57 SAML federated identity.

by the identity provider need to be mapped to local user accounts so that the local security system is able to impose its access control model.

Depending on the scenario, the mapping of user accounts from the identity provider to the service provider may be in a one-to-one or a many-to-one fashion. The process of mapping SAML user accounts from the SAML identity provider to local user accounts at the service provider is known as account linking.

Most often, external user accounts that are authenticated by the identity provider need to be mapped to generic local user accounts with permissions to access resources. The mapping is performed in a one-to-many fashion; many accounts from the identity provider user database are mapped to a single user account. There may be a separate set of user accounts from the identity provider that maps to another local account at the service provider, etc.

In some situations, such as in a Federated Identity use case, it may be desirable for an account from the identity provider organization to have a specific set of permissions and privileges in the service provider organization. In that case, for this account, one-to-one mapping can be performed so that there is correspondence between the two accounts.

The mechanisms used to link (map) accounts from the Identity Provider to accounts in the Service Provider may be different. SAML supports the following standard account linkage approaches:

- *Out-of-band account linking.* The administrators of both organizations create manual rules for account linking. For example, the accounts from one organization can be statically linked to accounts in another organization based on username mapping.
- *Persistent pseudonym identifiers.* Typically used in federated identity scenarios, pseudonym identifiers allow manual linkage between an account in one organization and an account in a different organization having no common attributes that can be mapped. In this case, a unique identifier (pseudonym) is created for the link, and the accounts from both sides of the trust are linked to the pseudonym. Such pseudonym identifiers can also be generated for Web single sign-on scenarios between two identity providers that federate their identity space. If a user has an account with each of the two identity providers, even if the user ID and attributes are different in both account databases, the user can authorize the creation of a pseudonym ID by logging into each identity provider separately and providing the linkage pseudonym ID. Figure 4.58 shows how account linking with pseudonym identifiers works.
- *Temporary pseudonym identifiers.* These are similar to permanent pseudonym identifiers but are typically short lived and only created for the life of the session.
- *Identity attributes.* Administrators create rules so that linking is performed based on user attributes or other information in the SAML assertion. For example, one-to-one linking can be based on a user Social Security Number attribute in the SAML assertion, and many-to-one linking can be based on a team membership attribute in the SAML assertion. When the user authenticated by the identity provider presents an SAML assertion to the service provider servers, the user is mapped to a relevant service provider local account based on the specified attributes and rules.
- *Termination.* This is used to remove the link between accounts in the identity provider and the service provider.

4.18.3 WS-Security

WS-Security (Web Services Security) is a Federated Identity specification that was developed jointly by Microsoft, IBM, and VeriSign but was then handed over to the Oasis consortium.

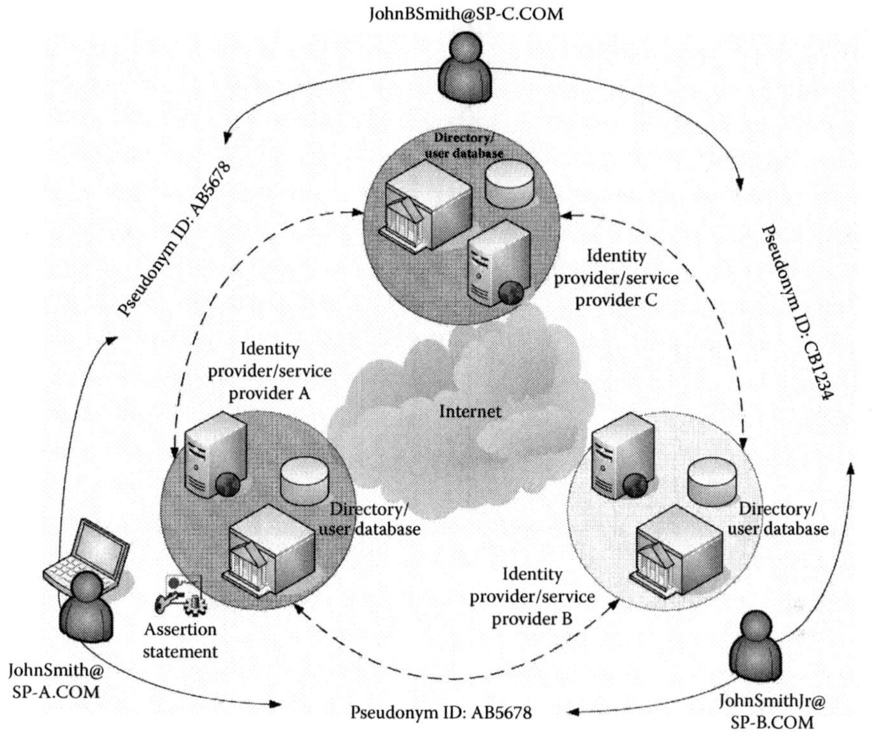

Figure 4.58 SAML account linking using pseudonym identifiers.

The main idea behind WS-Security is the ability to encapsulate security within SOAP messages. More specifically, WS-Security suggests that specific attributes be added to the SOAP message header that can provide for user authentication, confidentiality, and integrity for the SOAP message body. As discussed before, the SOAP specification allows for communication between applications and services on the Internet. Therefore, the encapsulation of user authentication information within the SOAP header provides for user authentication when accessing Web services over the Internet.

User authentication information can be added as an opaque token (BLOB) or directly as XML into the SOAP header. WS-Security supports the following authentication tokens:

- Kerberos Tickets (added as BLOBs in SOAP headers) (for more information, see subsection 4.2.2.1. This section presents the MIT Kerberos authentication protocol. It provides brief background information and then presents the naming concepts, the model of trust, the data structures, and the protocol mechanics.).

- X.509 certificates (added as BLOBs in SOAP headers) (for more information, see subsection 1.4.2).
- SAML assertions (added as XML in SOAP headers) – (for more information, see subsection 4.18.2).

WS-Security is implemented in Microsoft Windows 2003 R2 Active Directory Federation Services, RSA BSAFE, and other products.

Chapter 5

Authenticating Access to the Infrastructure

> Probably the only place where a man can feel really secure is in a maximum-security prison, except for the imminent threat of release.
>
> — **Germaine Greer**

This chapter presents the authentication protocols and mechanisms that provide users with access to the *network infrastructure* — the data-link and network layers. There is typically a separate authentication process for this, wherein the user is identified and allowed to connect to a network device and communicate with other hosts and devices on the network. Authentication for access to the network infrastructure does not necessarily (and typically does not) provide access to applications and services working at the upper layers. Authentication to upper layer applications and services is discussed in Chapter 4.

5.1 User Authentication on Cisco Routers and Switches

The access layer of network infrastructure solutions consists of routers and switches. Routers allow for Layer 3 connectivity and typically terminate LAN (local area network), WAN (wide area network), dial-up, and VPN (virtual private network) connections. Switches provide for Layer 2 access and terminate user connectivity to the wired and wireless LAN. Routers typically require user authentication when used as Network Access Servers for remote user access to the infrastructure. Switches do not necessarily require access for wired LAN connections. Wireless bridges often require authentication for wireless connections.

There are numerous vendors that provide network devices on the market today. Cisco routers and switches are among the most popular. This section focuses on authentication technologies used by Cisco routers and switches.

5.1.1 Authentication to Router Services

Routers and switches are among the main building blocks of today's network infrastructure solutions. There is a wide range of devices available from Cisco. Older high-end switches (5500/6500 series) use a version of the system software known as Cisco Catalyst OS (CatOS). Most Cisco devices use the Cisco Internetwork Operating System (IOS) version, which is also replacing CatOS on 6500 series switches This section concentrates on Cisco IOS.

Switches are Layer 2 devices that, due to their knowledge of MAC addresses within each broadcast entity, can make forwarding decisions based on the destination addresses of incoming frames. Some switches are able to use port-level authentication protocols (such as 802.1x) to authenticate users before providing them with access to the infrastructure at Layer 2.

Routers are Layer 3 devices that have knowledge of IP addresses and subnets, and make forwarding decisions based on the destination IP address (unless policy routing or other advanced techniques are applied). Routers are able to authenticate users at both Layer 2 and Layer 3. Layer 2 authentication is typically performed for dial-up users who use legacy modems and ISDN terminal adapters, as well as for users who connect to the infrastructure using VPNs based on the PPP protocol. Layer 3 authentication is performed for connections based on the IPSec Protocol. Sometimes, higher layer authentication may be involved as well — this includes authentication for access to services on the router or switch (control plane services), or the authentication proxy service that allows a router to interfere with the user Telnet, HTTP of FTP session, request user authentication, and potentially apply temporary access lists.

Apart from user access to the infrastructure, routers and switches also allow for management access to the devices themselves. This allows network administrators to connect to routers and switches by either directly attaching a serial cable to the console port of the device, or by using Telnet or SSH to connect to the device over the network. In each case, management access to the devices can be authenticated.

In addition to the authentication model, Cisco routers and switches utilize a simple user authorization model. Each Cisco IOS command is assigned a privilege level between 0 and 15. When a user logs in, he is automatically assigned a privilege level. Each Cisco IOS command has a default privilege level at which it is available. Depending on this assigned level, the user may or may not be able to run a specific command. Level 15 is known as the Enable level; it provides administrators with full access to all the configuration aspects on the box. Although in general users can be "enabled" at each level between 0 and 15, typically only 0 and 15 are used.

Cisco routers and switches implement user authentication for the cases shown in Table 5.1.

5.1.2 Local User Database and Passwords

The local user database in Cisco IOS is stored as part of the configuration file. The **username** command is used to alter the user database. Table 5.2 represents the information that can be stored in the user database.

Passwords in the Cisco IOS configuration file can be stored in plaintext or encrypted. Encryption can be reversible or one-way. Table 5.3, based on [98], summarizes the available encryption modes for user passwords.

Crypt/MD5 passwords are salted and encrypted using the UNIX Crypt algorithm, which is not easily reversible. It is, however, susceptible to dictionary, brute force, and rainbow attacks, and therefore the configuration file that contains the local user database should be kept secret.

Type 7 reversibly encrypted passwords are based on a relatively simple proprietary encryption algorithm. The first two characters are used as seed for the algorithm. The remaining characters are manipulated using the seed and a feedback function from the previous character. An obfuscation table provides values that are combined with password characters using Exclusive OR (XOR). The details of the algorithm are not published by Cisco but can be found in [99].

By default, only the enable password is stored using MD5 encryption and only if the **enable secret** statement is used. The enable password without the **secret** option and all other passwords are stored in cleartext or reversibly encrypted.

A special configuration option (**service password-encryption**) has been available since Cisco IOS 10.0. it encrypts all plaintext passwords using Type 7 encryption. However, this only obfuscates them and protects them from being readily available to an attacker who is casually looking at the configuration. A determined attacker, however, can use some of the tools on the Internet to convert the Type 7 password back to plaintext because this encryption is reversible.

Table 5.1 Some Cisco Router Services that Require Authentication

Service Name	*Options*	*Examples*	*Typical Authentication Methods*
Exec Access	Exec	User access to router for management purposes	None (use user or line privilege level), or Enable password for the specific level
Line access/ Login access	Console	Access to the router using the serial asynchronous console port	Line password or username and password
	Serial synchronous/ asynchronous, ISDN, AUX	Remote/dial-up access to the router using either Exec or data-link protocols such as SLIP, PPP, and ARAP	Line password or username and password
	Virtual Terminal – vty	Telnet or SSH into the device remotely	Line password or username and password
VPN Access	PPTP/L2TP/L2F	Establish a virtual private (dial-up) network from a client to the router	Username and password

IPSec Access	IPSec between routers or IPSec from client to router	Site-to-site IPSec or IPSec VPDN	Certificates and preshared keys Can also use username and password for VPDN access
HTTP Access	HTTP/HTTPS	Access the router remotely for file management and configuration management	Username and password (or empty username and enable password)
FTP/TFTP Access	FTP/TFTP	Access to the router files using FTP/TFTP	Username and password
SNMP Access	SNMP Access	SNMP poll	Community string or username and password
Routing protocol	RIP/OSPF/EIGRP/ISIS/BGP	Authentication in routing updates	Password
NTP	NTP	Network Time Protocol authentication	Password

Table 5.2 Cisco IOS Local User Database

Field	*Description*
Username	The name of the user
Password/secret	Reversibly or irreversibly encrypted password
Privilege	User default privilege level
Autocommand	EXEC command to be automatically run upon user login
Callback	Callback parameters for the user
User Maxlinks	Maximum number of concurrent connections using this user account
Access-class	Access-list to be applied for outbound connections for this user
Lawful Intercept	Configures the user for lawful intercept of IP traffic that can then be used for investigation and legal purposes
CLI View	Associates a CLI view with the user; this allows the user to see and potentially modify only specific parts of the configuration

Table 5.3 Password Encryption Types in Cisco IOS

Password Encryption Type	*Description*
0 – plaintext	Plaintext user password, visible in the router configuration file
5 – crypt/MD5 based	Irreversibly encrypted password that uses the UNIX crypt/MD5 algorithm (see Chapter 2)
7 – reversibly encrypted	Uses undocumented but publicly available and reversible encryption

As of Cisco IOS 12.0(18)S, Cisco allows for MD5 encryption of user passwords by specifying the **secret** option for selected users. Apparently, this adds some protection for user passwords in the router configuration file but prevents users from using authentication protocols such as CHAP that require the router to have the user cleartext password.

5.1.3 Centralizing Authentication

The use of line passwords and the local user database is often not flexible enough for organizations. Often, the user database already resides on a server and it is better to configure the router to authenticate users against this database rather than creating accounts for them remotely.

The AAA (Authentication/Authorization/Accounting) model on Cisco routers and switches provides for flexible configuration of a centralized security system. For many network services provided by a router or a switch, a network administrator can define a list of AAA techniques that one network service will use, and also define a different set of AAA rules for another service. If the conditions change, the network administrator can change the AAA rules without reconfiguring the service requiring AAA security services. A service can be assigned a named or a default set of AAA rules.

Some of the popular authentication mechanisms supported by AAA include the local user database, the enable password, RADIUS, TACACS+, and Kerberos. The authentication list can be configured as a preference list that includes all the methods required to perform authentication in the preferred order.

5.1.4 New-Model AAA

Cisco routers allow for flexible configuration of user Authentication, Authorization, and Accounting by using the so-called new-model AAA.

With this approach, the system administrator is able to build default and named lists that specify the type and location of services to be used for AAA, as well as the order in which they will be used.

The services that can use AAA on Cisco routers and switches include:

- Login: user login to the device.
- Enable: change of current user privilege level on the device.
- PPP: AAA for PPP (including PPTP, L2TP, L2F, and IPSec XAUTH).
- ARAP: Apple Talk remote access connections.
- 802.1x (Dot1X): IEEE 802.1x port access control.

The authentication resources that can be used include:

- Local: local router or switch user database; case insensitive with regard to usernames.
- Local-case: case-sensitive authentication against the local database.
- RADIUS: authenticate against a RADIUS server.
- TACACS+ authenticate against a TACACS+ server.
- Krb5: authentication against Kerberos
- None: do not authenticate — this is sometimes used to prevent access lockout. At the same time, this may pose security risks.

Each authentication list for a specific server can provide one or more authentication services to use in the order they are provided in the list.

5.2 Authenticating Remote Access to the Infrastructure

Remote access allows users from geographically distant locations to connect to the information services provided by an organization. Flexible working personnel, road warriors (such as sales staff), systems administrators — they are all candidates for remote access.

This section looks at the authentication protocols used to provide users with remote access to the infrastructure. Some of the authentication protocols are used for other purposes as well, such as Wireless User Authentication, which is discussed later in this chapter

5.2.1 SLIP Authentication

The SLIP Protocol was used in the early days of the Internet to provide access between interconnected hosts that used serial links. SLIP was a data-link protocol that only provided transport for IP frames and did not include authentication. When a user connects to a SLIP line, he is usually prompted to enter a username and password. This dialogue typically utilizes a simple interactive conversation between a client and a server, where the server provides username and password prompts, and the client works in terminal mode to enter all the information required. The communication dialogue consists of a plaintext stream of characters in both directions.

Once the user has been authenticated, the SLIP session begins.

5.2.2 PPP Authentication

PPP is a popular data-link protocol used to transfer user traffic across dial-up, serial, and VPN links. Unlike SLIP, PPP was designed with a modular approach in mind, and it supports different network layer protocols, including TCP/IP, IPX/SPX, AppleTalk, NetBEUI, etc. In addition to that, PPP has configuration negotiation mechanisms that, among data-link and network layer settings, can be used for authentication purposes.

The PPP Protocol consists of the following components:

- PPP encapsulation protocol: used to transfer user and system information across WAN links.
- Link Control Protocol: establishing, testing, and tearing down a connection.
- Network Control Protocol: used to configure communication network parameters.
- Authentication protocol: implements different authentication mechanisms on top of PPP.

Table 5.4 PPP Authentication Mechanisms and Their Assigned IDs

LCP Authentication Protocol ID	*Authentication Mechanism Name*
0xC023	Password Authentication Protocol (PAP)
0xC223	Challenge-Handshake Authentication Protocol (CHAP)
0xC227	Extensible Authentication Protocol (EAP)

The PPP Protocol does not require authentication but does support a number of authentication methods. PPP authentication is negotiated by the PPP Link Control Protocol (LCP), and is performed by a specific authentication mechanism that uses a separate PPP protocol encapsulation.

Both the client and the server can request authentication by sending an LCP message containing the Authentication Protocol Configuration option in the LCP negotiation phase. Peers only propose one authentication protocol at a time, in the order of preference configured by the network administrator. As soon as one party suggests an authentication protocol in its order of preference, and this authentication protocol is supported by the remote party as well, the parties can authenticate one way, or mutually.

Authentication negotiation messages are carried within LCP type 3 (Authentication Protocol) packets. The party requesting a specific authentication protocol sends an LCP Configuration-Request packet and specifies the proposed authentication protocol. The remote party replies with either **Configuration-Ack** or **Configuration-Nak** to indicate, respectively, that it agrees or rejects the suggested authentication protocol. If one of the parties proposes a number of authentication protocols and the remote party rejects them, the requesting party may refuse to complete the connection.

The authentication mechanisms used by PPP are implemented as separate PPP negotiation protocols, and include those in Table 5.4.

5.2.3 Password Authentication Protocol (PAP)

PAP authentication is defined in [100] and is considered the simplest authentication method. Virtually all vendors support it. The username and the password are transferred across the network in cleartext, and can be easily captured by someone sniffing on the wire.

A typical PAP authentication session is shown in Figure 5.1. The steps are the following:

```
Frame 11 (68 bytes on wire, 68 bytes captured)
Ethernet II, Src: Cisco_7b:48:f4 (00:0d:ed:7b:48:f4), Dst: GemtekTe_1f:a4:f7 (00:90:4b:1f:a4:f7)
Internet Protocol, Src: 192.168.2.254 (192.168.2.254), Dst: 192.168.2.65 (192.168.2.65)
Generic Routing Encapsulation (PPP)
Point-to-Point Protocol
PPP Link Control Protocol
    Code: Configuration Request (0x01)
    Identifier: 0x01
    Length: 14
    Options: (10 bytes)
        Authentication protocol: 4 bytes
            Authentication protocol: Password Authentication Protocol (0xc023)
        Magic number: 0x0e16503a

Frame 12 (68 bytes on wire, 68 bytes captured)
Ethernet II, Src: GemtekTe_1f:a4:f7 (00:90:4b:1f:a4:f7), Dst: Cisco_7b:48:f4 (00:0d:ed:7b:48:f4)
Internet Protocol, Src: 192.168.2.65 (192.168.2.65), Dst: 192.168.2.254 (192.168.2.254)
Generic Routing Encapsulation (PPP)
Point-to-Point Protocol
PPP Link Control Protocol
    Code: Configuration Ack (0x02)
    Identifier: 0x01
    Length: 14
    Options: (10 bytes)
        Authentication protocol: 4 bytes
            Authentication protocol: Password Authentication Protocol (0xc023)
        Magic number: 0x0e16503a

Frame 23 (73 bytes on wire, 73 bytes captured)
Ethernet II, Src: GemtekTe_1f:a4:f7 (00:90:4b:1f:a4:f7), Dst: Cisco_7b:48:f4 (00:0d:ed:7b:48:f4)
Internet Protocol, Src: 192.168.2.65 (192.168.2.65), Dst: 192.168.2.254 (192.168.2.254)
Generic Routing Encapsulation (PPP)
Point-to-Point Protocol
PPP Password Authentication Protocol
    Code: Authenticate-Request (0x01)
    Identifier: 0x00
```

Figure 5.1 PPTP-PAP.cap: PPP PAP authentication over PPTP.

1. One of the two parties (in this case, the server) suggests that PAP be used as an authentication method (see Frame 11 in Figure 5.1).
2. The remote party acknowledges the suggested authentication method, which in this case is PAP (see Frame 12 in Figure 5.1).

```
    Length: 23
    Data (19 bytes)
        Peer ID length: 9 bytes
            Peer-ID (9 bytes): localuser
        Password length: 8 bytes
            Password (8 bytes): password

Frame 25 (60 bytes on wire, 60 bytes captured)
Ethernet II, Src: Cisco_7b:48:f4 (00:0d:ed:7b:48:f4), Dst: GemtekTe_1f:a4:f7 (00:90:4b:1f:a4:f7)
Internet Protocol, Src: 192.168.2.254 (192.168.2.254), Dst: 192.168.2.65 (192.168.2.65)
Generic Routing Encapsulation (PPP)
Point-to-Point Protocol
PPP Password Authentication Protocol
    Code: Authenticate-Ack (0x02)
    Identifier: 0x00
    Length: 5
    Data (1 byte)
        Message length: 0 bytes
```

Figure 5.1 (continued)

3. The client (or authenticating party in general) submits a PPP PAP authentication message and provides the username and password in cleartext to the authenticating server (see Frame 23 in Figure 5.1).
4. Upon successful authentication, the server acknowledges successful authentication (see Frame 25 in Figure 5.1).

5.2.4 CHAP

The Challenge-Handshake Authentication Protocol (CHAP) is defined in [100] and [101]. As the name implies, CHAP is a challenge-based authentication mechanism. Depending on how the communicating parties are configured, it can authenticate either the client to the server, or vice versa, or even extend the authentication dialogue in both directions and provide for two-way authentication.

To perform user authentication, the server generates a random challenge that must be different every time, assigns it a unique challenge identifier, and then sends both the challenge and the identifier to the client. The server also includes its name in the request so that the client knows to whom it is authenticating. The client concatenates the challenge identifier, the user password, and the random server challenge, and then calculates a hash from the resultant string. This hash, along with the plaintext username, is sent to the remote party (server). The CHAP protocol allows for different hash algorithms to be negotiated and used but the only one supported by all vendors and widely used is MD5. The MD5 hash is 16 bytes in size. Both the client and the server perform the same hash calculation and compare the results to determine whether authentication was successful.

A typical CHAP session is shown in Figure 5.2. The following are the steps in the authentication process:

1. One of the two parties (in this case, the client) requests CHAP authentication (see Frame 15 in Figure 5.2).
2. The other party acknowledges CHAP authentication (see Frame 16 in Figure 5.2).
3. One of the parties (typically the server) submits a CHAP challenge (see Frame 25 in Figure 5.2).
4. The other party (typically the client) calculates and submits a CHAP response (see Frame 27 in Figure 5.2).
5. The party that generated the challenge (typically the server) acknowledges successful authentication (see Frame 28 in Figure 5.2).

The CHAP authentication protocol can be used in the beginning of a connection and during the connection. The RFC specifies that, periodically, parties can request from the remote peer to re-authenticate, challenging them with a new unique string and challenge ID to protect from replay attacks. CHAP also allows for mutual authentication; the client can request authentication from the server and the server may need to show its knowledge of a username and a preshared password for that client.

CHAP is widely supported by many vendors. The CHAP authentication protocol provides better security than PAP but still suffers from some problems. One of the important things to understand is that with CHAP, both parties need access to the cleartext user password, as it is required to generate the hash used for authentication. This is not an issue for the client side because the user will typically provide the plaintext password in an interactive authentication dialogue. However, the problem is that the server needs to store user passwords in cleartext, or using reversible encryption. Because of these limitations, CHAP authentication should be avoided if other, more secure methods are available.

5.2.5 MS-CHAP Version 1 and Version 2

The CHAP authentication protocol is widely supported by many vendors. However, as discussed in the previous section, CHAP requires that the authentication server has access to the plaintext or reversibly encrypted

```
Frame 15 (69 bytes on wire, 69 bytes captured)
Ethernet II, Src: Cisco_7b:48:f4 (00:0d:ed:7b:48:f4), Dst: GemtekTe_1f:a4:f7 (00:90:4b:1f:a4:f7)
Internet Protocol, Src: 192.168.2.254 (192.168.2.254), Dst: 192.168.2.65 (192.168.2.65)
Generic Routing Encapsulation (PPP)
Point-to-Point Protocol
PPP Link Control Protocol
    Code: Configuration Request (0x01)
    Identifier: 0x02
    Length: 15
    Options: (11 bytes)
        Authentication protocol: 5 bytes
            Authentication protocol: Challenge Handshake Authentication Protocol (0xc223)
            Algorithm: CHAP with MD5 (0x05)
        Magic number: 0x0e1da843

Frame 16 (69 bytes on wire, 69 bytes captured)
Ethernet II, Src: GemtekTe_1f:a4:f7 (00:90:4b:1f:a4:f7), Dst: Cisco_7b:48:f4 (00:0d:ed:7b:48:f4)
Internet Protocol, Src: 192.168.2.65 (192.168.2.65), Dst: 192.168.2.254 (192.168.2.254)
Generic Routing Encapsulation (PPP)
Point-to-Point Protocol
PPP Link Control Protocol
    Code: Configuration Ack (0x02)
    Identifier: 0x02
    Length: 15
    Options: (11 bytes)
        Authentication protocol: 5 bytes
            Authentication protocol: Challenge Handshake Authentication Protocol (0xc223)
            Algorithm: CHAP with MD5 (0x05)
        Magic number: 0x0e1da843


Frame 25 (85 bytes on wire, 85 bytes captured)
Ethernet II, Src: Cisco_7b:48:f4 (00:0d:ed:7b:48:f4), Dst: GemtekTe_1f:a4:f7 (00:90:4b:1f:a4:f7)
Internet Protocol, Src: 192.168.2.254 (192.168.2.254), Dst: 192.168.2.65 (192.168.2.65)
Generic Routing Encapsulation (PPP)
Point-to-Point Protocol
```

Figure 5.2 PPTP-CHAP.cap: PPP CHAP Authentication over PPTP.

user password. Microsoft came up with its own versions of CHAP (MS-CHAP v.1 and later MS-CHAP v.2) that use the native password hashes (NT hash, as well as LM hash in early implementations) to authenticate

```
PPP Challenge Handshake Authentication Protocol
    Code: Challenge (1)
    Identifier: 1
    Length: 31
    Data (27 bytes)
        Value Size: 16
        Value: F2D97C8D3F6B62F64BE75FFEE41002D3
        Name: VPN-SERVER

Frame 27 (84 bytes on wire, 84 bytes captured)
Ethernet II, Src: GemtekTe_1f:a4:f7 (00:90:4b:1f:a4:f7), Dst: Cisco_7b:48:f4 (00:0d:ed:7b:48:f4)
Internet Protocol, Src: 192.168.2.65 (192.168.2.65), Dst: 192.168.2.254 (192.168.2.254)
Generic Routing Encapsulation (PPP)
Point-to-Point Protocol
PPP Challenge Handshake Authentication Protocol
    Code: Response (2)
    Identifier: 1
    Length: 30
    Data (26 bytes)
        Value Size: 16
        Value: 60353B3E008E4D3F9D947D950C24F347
        Name: localuser

Frame 28 (60 bytes on wire, 60 bytes captured)
Ethernet II, Src: Cisco_7b:48:f4 (00:0d:ed:7b:48:f4), Dst: GemtekTe_1f:a4:f7 (00:90:4b:1f:a4:f7)
Internet Protocol, Src: 192.168.2.254 (192.168.2.254), Dst: 192.168.2.65 (192.168.2.65)
Generic Routing Encapsulation (PPP)
Point-to-Point Protocol
PPP Challenge Handshake Authentication Protocol
    Code: Success (3)
    Identifier: 1
    Length: 4
```

Figure 5.2 (continued)

the user instead of the plaintext or reversibly encrypted password. As indicated in previous chapters, such a step makes the password hash (NT hash) equivalent to the user password in terms of protection requirements, as anyone who has knowledge of the hash can successfully participate in the authentication process without having the plaintext password.

MS-CHAP v.1 is a Microsoft proprietary authentication method that has been adopted by many vendors. Rather than a separate authentication protocol, it is considered a separate algorithm for the CHAP authentication protocol, identified with ID 0x80.

To perform MS-CHAP v.1 authentication, the server sends the same challenge as with CHAP authentication. However, the algorithm used by the client to calculate the response is different. Initially, when the protocol was first introduced, the client would generate both an LM response and an NTLM response and include them in the reply packet. The LM and NTLM responses are calculated in exactly the same way as the standard NTLM authentication protocol calculates responses in NTLM Type 3 packets, and as described in section 4.2.1.8. However, as a result of the inherent LM protocol insecurity, later implementations of the MS-CHAP v.1 protocol stopped generating the LM response, and the field is now filled with zeroes; that is what RFC 2433 [102] recommends as well. The response packet also contains a field that indicates whether the NT hash is present (when set to 1), or whether the LM hash should be used instead. Considering the fact that an LM hash is not being generated anymore, this flag is always set to use only the NT hash.

In brief, the NTLM response is calculated by generating the NT hash (using MD4) from the plaintext Unicode user password, and padding the hash with five zeroes to 21 bytes. The result is then split into three parts that are used as three DES keys, which in sequence encrypt the 8-byte challenge using the DES algorithm. The three results from DES encryption are then concatenated to form the reply.

Using a copy of the NT hash stored in the local user database or on a domain controller, the server is able to calculate a similar encrypted string and compare it with the client reply. If the two are the same, user authentication is successful.

MS-CHAP v.1 works in pretty much the same way as CHAP. It is considered a different CHAP algorithm. The communication between a client (192.168.2.65) and a server (192.168.2.254) is shown in Figure 5.3.

MS-CHAP v.2 is defined in RFC 2759 [103] and is similar to CHAP and MS-CHAP v.1. The CHAP algorithm ID used by MS-CHAP v.2 is 0x81. The MS-CHAP v.2 authentication request packet is the same as the CHAP and MS-CHAP v.1 packets. However, MS-CHAP v.2 replies from the client to the server are different: the client response to the authenticator challenge is calculated in a slightly different way, and also the client reply contains a challenge (16-byte peer challenge generated by the client) to authenticate the server in turn.

To generate a reply to the server challenge, the client uses the following steps:

1. Concatenate the peer challenge, the authenticator challenge, and the username.
2. Calculate the SHA-1 hash of the string from Step 1.

```
Frame 15 (69 bytes on wire, 69 bytes captured)
Ethernet II, Src: Cisco_7b:48:f4 (00:0d:ed:7b:48:f4), Dst: GemtekTe_1f:a4:f7 (00:90:4b:1f:a4:f7)
Internet Protocol, Src: 192.168.2.254 (192.168.2.254), Dst: 192.168.2.65 (192.168.2.65)
Generic Routing Encapsulation (PPP)
Point-to-Point Protocol
PPP Link Control Protocol
    Code: Configuration Request (0x01)
    Identifier: 0x02
    Length: 15
    Options: (11 bytes)
        Authentication protocol: 5 bytes
            Authentication protocol: Challenge Handshake Authentication Protocol (0xc223)
            Algorithm: MS-CHAP (0x80)
        Magic number: 0x0e1f6c14

Frame 17 (69 bytes on wire, 69 bytes captured)
Ethernet II, Src: GemtekTe_1f:a4:f7 (00:90:4b:1f:a4:f7), Dst: Cisco_7b:48:f4 (00:0d:ed:7b:48:f4)
Internet Protocol, Src: 192.168.2.65 (192.168.2.65), Dst: 192.168.2.254 (192.168.2.254)
Generic Routing Encapsulation (PPP)
Point-to-Point Protocol
PPP Link Control Protocol
    Code: Configuration Ack (0x02)
    Identifier: 0x02
    Length: 15
    Options: (11 bytes)
        Authentication protocol: 5 bytes
            Authentication protocol: Challenge Handshake Authentication Protocol (0xc223)
            Algorithm: MS-CHAP (0x80)
        Magic number: 0x0e1f6c14

Frame 25 (77 bytes on wire, 77 bytes captured)
Ethernet II, Src: Cisco_7b:48:f4 (00:0d:ed:7b:48:f4), Dst: GemtekTe_1f:a4:f7 (00:90:4b:1f:a4:f7)
Internet Protocol, Src: 192.168.2.254 (192.168.2.254), Dst: 192.168.2.65 (192.168.2.65)
Generic Routing Encapsulation (PPP)
Point-to-Point Protocol
PPP Challenge Handshake Authentication Protocol
```

Figure 5.3 PPTP-MS-CHAP-v1.cap: PPP CHAP authentication over PPTP.

3. Expand the NT hash of the user password to 21 byte, padding it with zeroes.
4. Split the 21-byte padded password hash into three 7-byte DES keys.

```
    Code: Challenge (1)
    Identifier: 1
    Length: 23
    Data (19 bytes)
        Value Size: 8
        Value: 2FB0F5024AC454BF
        Name: VPN-SERVER

Frame 26 (117 bytes on wire, 117 bytes captured)
Ethernet II, Src: GemtekTe_1f:a4:f7 (00:90:4b:1f:a4:f7), Dst: Cisco_7b:48:f4 (00:0d:ed:7b:48:f4)
Internet Protocol, Src: 192.168.2.65 (192.168.2.65), Dst: 192.168.2.254 (192.168.2.254)
Generic Routing Encapsulation (PPP)
Point-to-Point Protocol
PPP Challenge Handshake Authentication Protocol
    Code: Response (2)
    Identifier: 1
    Length: 63
    Data (59 bytes)
        Value Size: 49
        Value: 000000000000000000000000000000000000000000000000...
        Name: localuser

Frame 28 (60 bytes on wire, 60 bytes captured)
Ethernet II, Src: Cisco_7b:48:f4 (00:0d:ed:7b:48:f4), Dst: GemtekTe_1f:a4:f7 (00:90:4b:1f:a4:f7)
Internet Protocol, Src: 192.168.2.254 (192.168.2.254), Dst: 192.168.2.65 (192.168.2.65)
Generic Routing Encapsulation (PPP)
Point-to-Point Protocol
PPP Challenge Handshake Authentication Protocol
    Code: Success (3)
    Identifier: 1
    Length: 4
```

Figure 5.3 (continued)

5. Encrypt the first 8 bytes from the challenge digest in Step 2 in each of the three keys from Step 4 using DES encryption.
6. Concatenate the results from the encryption and submit the 24-byte result as the response to the server challenge.

If the user provides the correct response to the server challenge, the client side is considered authenticated but now the server needs to authenticate to the client. The server uses the **Authentication_Success** message to indicate successful authentication to the client, and in the same message the server provides its response to the client challenge and authenticates. To provide a response to the client challenge, the server performs the following calculations:

1. The server hashes the NT password hash using MD4. As a result, the user cleartext Unicode password is hashed twice using MD4.
2. The server concatenates the double password hash, the client response, and a 41-byte well-known string
3. The server calculates the SHA-1 hash for the concatenation from Step 2.
4. The server concatenates the client challenge, the authenticator challenge, and the username.
5. The server calculates the SHA-1 hash for the concatenation from Step 4.
6. The server concatenates the hash from Step 3, the first 8 bytes from the hash from Step 5, and a 41-byte well-known string
7. The server calculates the SHA-1 hash for the concatenated string from Step 6.

Apparently, the client needs to perform the same calculation as the server and compare the results. If they match, the server has been successfully authenticated.

Similar to MS-CHAP v.1, MS-CHAP v.2 is considered just another version of CHAP with a new algorithm ID. The communication between the client and the server is shown in Figure 5.4.

5.2.6 Extensible Authentication Protocol (EAP)

The PPP Extensible Authentication Protocol (EAP) is defined in RFCs 2284 and 3748 [104, 105]. EAP is a general authentication protocol that provides applications with an interface to specific authentication mechanisms. Different authentication mechanisms can be configured for EAP to perform actual user authentication. EAP can also be used on top of other protocols, not just PPP/LCP. In that respect, EAP is just an abstraction layer on top of the data-link layer (PPP Link Control Protocol, 802.3 or 802.2/SNAP).

Following the PPP authentication model, EAP supports four types of messages: Request, Response, Success, and Failure. EAP provides a layer of abstraction from a network access server (NAS) perspective (authenticator), whereby the NAS does not need to understand all the authentication methods and can act as a pass-through device forwarding EAP messages between the client and the back-end security and authentication server, such as RADIUS or TACACS+.

```
Frame 15 (69 bytes on wire, 69 bytes captured)
Ethernet II, Src: Cisco_7b:48:f4 (00:0d:ed:7b:48:f4), Dst: GemtekTe_1f:a4:f7 (00:90:4b:1f:a4:f7)
Internet Protocol, Src: 192.168.2.254 (192.168.2.254), Dst: 192.168.2.65 (192.168.2.65)
Generic Routing Encapsulation (PPP)
Point-to-Point Protocol
PPP Link Control Protocol
    Code: Configuration Request (0x01)
    Identifier: 0x02
    Length: 15
    Options: (11 bytes)
        Authentication protocol: 5 bytes
            Authentication protocol: Challenge Handshake Authentication Protocol (0xc223)
            Algorithm: MS-CHAP-2 (0x81)
        Magic number: 0x0e2174a6

Frame 16 (69 bytes on wire, 69 bytes captured)
Ethernet II, Src: GemtekTe_1f:a4:f7 (00:90:4b:1f:a4:f7), Dst: Cisco_7b:48:f4 (00:0d:ed:7b:48:f4)
Internet Protocol, Src: 192.168.2.65 (192.168.2.65), Dst: 192.168.2.254 (192.168.2.254)
Generic Routing Encapsulation (PPP)
Point-to-Point Protocol
PPP Link Control Protocol
    Code: Configuration Ack (0x02)
    Identifier: 0x02
    Length: 15
    Options: (11 bytes)
        Authentication protocol: 5 bytes
            Authentication protocol: Challenge Handshake Authentication Protocol (0xc223)
            Algorithm: MS-CHAP-2 (0x81)
        Magic number: 0x0e2174a6

Frame 25 (85 bytes on wire, 85 bytes captured)
Ethernet II, Src: Cisco_7b:48:f4 (00:0d:ed:7b:48:f4), Dst: GemtekTe_1f:a4:f7 (00:90:4b:1f:a4:f7)
Internet Protocol, Src: 192.168.2.254 (192.168.2.254), Dst: 192.168.2.65 (192.168.2.65)
Generic Routing Encapsulation (PPP)
Point-to-Point Protocol
PPP Challenge Handshake Authentication Protocol
```

Figure 5.4 PPTP-MS-CHAP-v2.cap: PPP CHAP authentication over PPTP.

It is important to note that unlike most authentication protocols that assume that the client will initiate user authentication, EAP assumes that the authenticating server (typically the NAS) is the first to request authentication by requesting the user's identity. Depending on the authentication

```
    Code: Challenge (1)
    Identifier: 1
    Length: 31
    Data (27 bytes)
        Value Size: 16
        Value: 88ED4ADDFDE8B0CEEBA8D8273500A881
        Name: VPN-SERVER

Frame 27 (117 bytes on wire, 117 bytes captured)
Ethernet II, Src: GemtekTe_1f:a4:f7 (00:90:4b:1f:a4:f7), Dst: Cisco_7b:48:f4 (00:0d:ed:7b:48:f4)
Internet Protocol, Src: 192.168.2.65 (192.168.2.65), Dst: 192.168.2.254 (192.168.2.254)
Generic Routing Encapsulation (PPP)
Point-to-Point Protocol
PPP Challenge Handshake Authentication Protocol
    Code: Response (2)
    Identifier: 1
    Length: 63
    Data (59 bytes)
        Value Size: 49
        Value: 7257324F4F06C115C6327D7A6597304A0000000000000000...
        Name: localuser

Frame 28 (100 bytes on wire, 100 bytes captured)
Ethernet II, Src: Cisco_7b:48:f4 (00:0d:ed:7b:48:f4), Dst: GemtekTe_1f:a4:f7 (00:90:4b:1f:a4:f7)
Internet Protocol, Src: 192.168.2.254 (192.168.2.254), Dst: 192.168.2.65 (192.168.2.65)
Generic Routing Encapsulation (PPP)
Point-to-Point Protocol
PPP Challenge Handshake Authentication Protocol
    Code: Success (3)
    Identifier: 1
    Length: 46
    Message: S=1F48D8010B6D6F666F8623ED08438B53CD8DC4E7
```

Figure 5.4 (continued)

mechanism on top of EAP, this identity information may or may not be taken into consideration. Identity information is transferred at the very beginning of the EAP session. At this stage there is typically no security association between the client and the authenticating server to protect messages between them from unauthorized modification. It must be considered that at this stage that user identity can be forged by someone with access to the communication channel in between.

Table 5.5 EAP Request/Response Message Types

ID	*Type*	*Description*
1	Identity	Used by the authentication server to request the identity of the client Typically used to request the username and the realm name, and is used by the authentication server to determine the specific authentication requirements for this user
2	Notification	Used by the authentication server to send a displayable message to the authenticating user The authentication client should somehow visualize this message for the user to see. (this can be a legal notice message, a message prompting the user to change his password, a sequence number for one-time passwords, etc.)
3	NAK	Used in replies to designate an unacceptable authentication type
4	MD5	PPP CHAP encapsulated within EAP
5	One-Time Password	A displayable message for one-time password authentication
6	Generic Token Card	Requests and responses contain information from the Generic Token Card
13	EAP TLS	EAP Transport Layer Security/Secure Sockets Layer authentication with certificate mapping
17	Cisco LEAP	Cisco Lightweight EAP

The Request/Response messages can be of different types, depending on the parameters being requested. Table 5.5 presents the EAP Request/Response messages.

The following sections present some of the popular EAP authentication methods.

5.2.7 EAP-TLS

EAP Transport Layer Security (EAP-TLS) is defined in RFC 2716 [106]. Essentially, EAP-TLS is a method for encapsulating the TLS/SSL protocol within EAP messages.

EAP-TLS defines a new EAP type for TLS (type 13), and a Flags field. The TLS Start flag is used by the authentication server to indicate that following EAP messages will contain EAP encapsulated TLS messages. When the client sees this flag set in a message from the server, it starts a TLS negotiation process on top of EAP.

The actual TLS/SSL authentication process is described in Chapter 4.3. The security server taking part in the EAP-TLS process must have a certificate and be able to authenticate to the client. In most cases, the server will want to authenticate the client as well, so the client must also have a valid certificate. To perform authentication, the server will try client certificate mapping, wherein attributes from the client certificate, such as the certificate Subject or Alternative Subject fields or the Issuing Certificate Authority for group authentication, will be mapped to the user identity in a security database or a directory. Alternatively, the user-provided certificate can be mapped to a user certificate stored in a directory, or a flat list of users and corresponding certificates. If the user can be successfully mapped, the authenticating server then signals successful authentication and typically moves on to the access authorization phase.

It is important to understand that the use of EAP-TLS and certificates can be a powerful authentication method for access to the infrastructure. Unlike other authentication methods, wherein the client only needs to provide a username and a password (single-factor authentication), in the case of EAP-TLS, the client needs to authenticate by providing a certificate issued by a trusted third party. The client needs to know the private key for this certificate in order to authenticate successfully. This private key can be stored on a smart card, in which case the user can be authenticated using two-factor authentication. This makes the EAP-TLS authentication mechanism very secure, which is very important for remote access to the infrastructure. Technically, the security and network architects can come up with a solution wherein users can only be let in if they possess certificates stored on smart cards. This considerably decreases the exposure to password guessing and other attacks by malicious parties, as EAP-TLS is not a password-based authentication scheme — unless the attacker has a valid certificate, he is not going to be able to authenticate.

[Note: PPTP-EAP-TLS.Cap and PPTP-EAP-TLS-RADIUS.Cap on the companion Web site, http://www.iamechanics.com reveal the actual TLS authentication process.]

5.2.8 EAP-TTLS

EAP-TLS is an authentication mechanism that uses certificate mapping to authenticate the client. EAP Tunneled TLS (EAP-TTLS) is an extension to

EAP-TLS that allows for user authentication using some other authentication mechanism, such as PAP, CHAP, or MS-CHAP. EAP-TTLS is very similar to EAP-TLS in the way it establishes a TLS association between the client and the server, and authenticates the server by means of the server certificate. However, the client does not need to possess a certificate. If PAP is used, PAP authentication messages contain the plaintext username and password for the authenticating user. However, PAP messages will be encapsulated within TLS messages so the information will be encrypted and their integrity will be authenticated as part of the TLS security association.

The EAP-TTLS mechanism is still an Internet draft at the time of this writing. It is not currently able to find sufficient support from vendors, and is likely to fail to become an Internet standard. Still, some vendors provide support for this authentication mechanism.

5.2.9 Protected EAP (PEAP)

Protected EAP (PEAP) is an EAP authentication mechanism proposed by Microsoft, Cisco, and RSA Security. It is currently an Internet draft and is defined in [107]. The current version of PEAP at the time of this writing is 2. PEAP is finding wide support among many vendors.

In essence, PEAP is a way to protect the authentication channel by means of TLS/SSL, and then use other authentication methods within the protected authentication channel. This is sometimes referred to as authentication tunneling.

To authenticate using PEAP, the client and server dialogue consists of two parts:

Part 1: Negotiate TLS/SSL protection. At this stage the server is authenticated using its server certificate (other TLS/SSL mechanisms are possible; see Chapter 4.3). The client does not need to have a certificate.

Part 2: Use other EAP mechanisms to perform authentication within the TLS/SSL channel, established in Part 1.

Part 2 does not start unless Part 1 has completed successfully. The client typically authenticates at this stage. However, if the selected EAP mechanism to be used on top of TLS is a mutual authentication mechanism (such as MS-CHAP v2), the server can be authenticated again at this stage. Most often, MS-CHAP v2 is used at this stage but the client and server can use other EAP mechanisms if they are supported.

Microsoft clients and servers only support MS-CHAP v2 as the inner PEAP authentication protocol. Cisco and other vendors support generic token card (GTC) mechanisms, and may support other mechanisms as well.

PEAP is a very strong authentication mechanism but as with all EAP mechanisms, it is important to understand that the initial authentication negotiation phase is unencrypted and unprotected. An attacker who has access to the communication channel between the client and the server can therefore apply authentication downgrade attacks and make communicating parties use a weaker authentication mechanism. Thus, although the PEAP mechanism itself provides for strong authentication, the process of negotiating PEAP as the authentication mechanism may be compromised.

The use of TLS/SSL as part of the PEAP authentication protocol provides for strong protection of the authentication channel. Typically, the server is authenticated using certificates and unless the server private key is compromised, the client can trust the authenticity of the server. This makes man-in-the-middle attacks very unlikely. The remainder of the communication is protected by means of encryption and data integrity authentication. Unless the encrypted channel is compromised, which is unlikely if current protection algorithms are used, user authentication is protected from eavesdropping, authentication mechanism downgrade, rainbow, and other popular attacks.

Apparently, the lack of client authentication at Part 1 results in any user being able to complete Part 1 and start Part 2. An attacker can therefore still apply dictionary or brute force techniques at Part 2 and try to guess the user password.

A sample PEAP authentication dialogue is provided in Figure 5.11.

5.2.10 Lightweight EAP (LEAP)

Cisco Lightweight EAP (LEAP) is another popular EAP authentication mechanism, primarily used in Cisco wireless products. LEAP is defined as EAP type 17.

Cisco LEAP is a challenge-response authentication mechanism; it implements MS-CHAP v.2 on top of EAP. As a result, the client and the authentication server need to have access to the NT hash of the user password for successful completion of authentication. This is convenient when Windows NT and compatible operating systems are used as the back-end user database, and may require cleartext or reversibly encrypted passwords to be stored by other authentication databases. As MS-CHAP v.2 is a protocol that provides for mutual authentication, and so is LEAP.

When LEAP is used alongside RADIUS, the **cisco-avpair** attribute (**leap:session-key** parameter) is used to provide the client and server with sessions keys, which can later be used to protect network communication. This is important, for example, when LEAP is used to authenticate wireless users.

Cisco LEAP suffers from the same problems as Microsoft MS-CHAP v.2. The authentication process can be attacked using dictionary, rainbow, and brute force attacks, and is generally considered weak. Cisco provides a description of the protocol as well as recommendations for LEAP users in [108].

5.2.11 EAP-FAST

EAP-TLS and PEAP are secure authentication mechanisms supported by various devices but organizations often find them difficult to implement and support due to the requirements for server (both EAP-TLS and PEAP) and client certificates (only required by EAP-TLS). Although very elegant and secure, PKI (public key infrastructure) solutions require resources and effort to design, implement, and support. Both authentication mechanisms require that the server be issued an X.509 certificate by a trusted certificate authority (CA); the server requires that a certificate request be generated and completed, and the client side requires configuration to trust the issuing CA. With EAP-TLS, the clients must be enrolled for a certificate, and a certificate management process must be in place to issue, revoke, recover, and otherwise manage client certificates. Client certificate management is not required by PEAP.

EAP-FAST (Flexible Authentication via Secure Tunneling) was developed by Cisco in an effort to provide a flexible and secure EAP authentication method that can adjust to client environments whether or not the client has an existing PKI implementation. At the time of this writing, EAP-FAST is an Internet draft, defined in [109] and [110].

A key element of the EAP-FAST authentication mechanism is the Protected Access Credential (PAC) file. The PAC consists of the fields shown in Table 5.6.

The PAC must be available to the client and the server before successful authentication can take place. The PAC is generated by the authentication server and can be distributed (provisioned) either manually or automatically.

Table 5.6 EAP-FAST PAC Fields

Field	*Description*
PAC-Key	32-byte random key, shared between the authentication server and the client, that is used as the pre-master secret
PAC-Opaque	Used to identify the client; typically contains a username in a format recognized by the authentication server
PAC-Info	Information about the PAC: issuer, time when it was issued, expiration time, etc.

The idea behind the PAC is to mimic the behavior of PKI for the purposes of EAP-FAST without implementing a full PKI infrastructure. The PAC contains metadata and secret keys, which makes it equivalent to an X.509 certificate and a private key. The authentication server typically has a secret master key, which is then used to generate the client PAC (similar to the private key of an X.509 CA). The difference from X.509 is that with PAC, both the client and the server use the same preshared key, so the encryption approach is symmetric. The server changes the master key at predefined intervals (typically a few weeks or months, similar to PKI key renewal), which requires that clients be provided with new PACs, which can happen either automatically, with the EAP-FAST PAC refreshing protocol, or manually.

5.2.11.1 EAP-FAST Automatic Provisioning (EAP-FAST Phase 0)

Manual provisioning is a more secure process but it also involves more administrative effort. With manual provisioning, network administrators need to generate a PAC for each user who will use EAP-FAST authentication and follow a secure process to transfer the PAC-file to each client's computer. The PAC must be protected on the client's computer as well and, if stolen, may compromise the EAP-FAST security model.

Automatic provisioning (Figure 5.5) is less secure but involves less administrative effort. With this method, the EAP-FAST client first obtains the PAC from the authentication server and then authenticates using the PAC. At the beginning of the automatic provisioning process, the client is anonymous and the authentication server cannot verify its identity. Furthermore, the authentication server can be anonymous to the client. This is a weakness from a security perspective because either the anonymous user or the anonymous authentication server can be an attacker and can compromise the EAP-FAST authentication process by simulating either fake client authentication requests or fake authentication replies and then carry out offline attacks against them.

From a security perspective it is recommended that the authentication server be authenticated. This can be achieved using X.509 certificates for the server. If the certificate used by the server is issued by a CA trusted by the client, then the server can be authenticated. Depending on whether the EAP-FAST authentication server has an X.509 certificate, automatic provisioning can use anonymous or certificate-based peer authentication.

If the authentication server is not configured with an X.509 certificate, the client and the authentication server negotiate TLS using the **TLS_DH_anon_WITH_AES_128_CBC_SHA** cipher suite. A Diffie-Hellman exchange is performed between the two parties to generate key

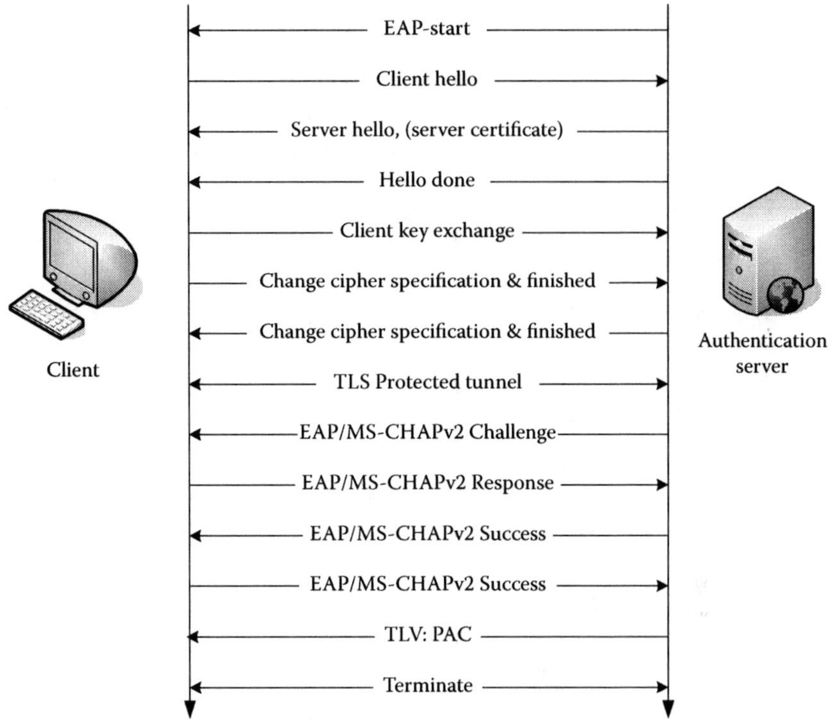

Figure 5.5 EAP-FAST automatic provisioning.

material for session keys, and then traffic between the client and the server is encrypted using AES and its integrity is authenticated using SHA-1.

If the authentication server is configured with an X.509 certificate, then the client and the server can negotiate TLS using the **TLS_DHE_RSA_WITH_AES_128_CBC_SHA** cipher suite. The server provides its certificate to the client using the TLS **ServerCertificate** message, and thus authenticates to the client because it is able to decrypt further messages encrypted by the client in the server public key from the certificate. The client is anonymous at this stage. Once the TLS negotiation is complete, traffic between the client and the server is encrypted using AES and its integrity is authenticated using SHA-1.

Once the client and the server have established a protected TLS channel, they perform mutual authentication over the TLS tunnel using MS-CHAPv2. When this phase completes, the authentication server can provide the client with a PAC.

To automatically obtain the PAC, the client interacts with the authentication server in the following way:

1. The client uses EAP-TLS to establish a secure channel with the server.
2. The client and server perform mutual authentication using MS-CHAPv2 to perform authentication using a username and password within the EAP-TLS protected channel.
3. The authentication server provides the client with the PAC using Type-Length-Value (TLV) parameters.

The client and the authentication server terminate the EAP-TLS session — because it is only meant to provision the PAC and not to perform actual authentication.

Once the client has acquired the PAC, it is ready to start with actual user authentication.

5.2.11.2 Tunnel Establishment (EAP-Phase 1)

At this phase, the client and the server establish a protected TLS tunnel using the PAC to authenticate each other. To establish a tunnel, both the client and the authentication server must posses a valid PAC (Figure 5.6).

The tunnel is established using TLS messages encapsulated within EAP-TLS. The specification recommends that one of the **TLS_RSA_WITH_RC4_128_SHA**, **TLS_RSA_WITH_AES_128_CBC_SHA** or **TLS_DHE_RSA_WITH_ AES_128_CBC_SHA** cipher suites be used. However, instead of using RSA certificates for peer authentication, the client and the server use the PAC. Therefore, unlike the standard **TLS_RSA_WITH_RC4_128_SHA** certificate exchange mechanics, the client and the server automatically use TLS **ChangeCipherSpec** messages to switch to protected communication and skip Certificate exchange with the TLS **ServerCertificate** and **ClientCertificate** messages (see section 4.3 for a detailed overview of TLS). At this stage, a TLS protected channel is established between the client and the server. The channel is encrypted using RC4 or AES and data integrity is authenticated using SHA-1. The communicating peers (client and authentication server) have been authenticated subject to the protection of the PAC. Keys used to protect communication are generated using an algorithm specific to EAP-FAST, and described in [109].

5.2.11.3 User Authentication (EAP-FAST Phase 2)

Once the TLS tunnel has been established at EAP-Fast Phase 2, EAP authentication using any supported authentication mechanism can take place (Figure 5.7). This authentication is known as inner authentication.

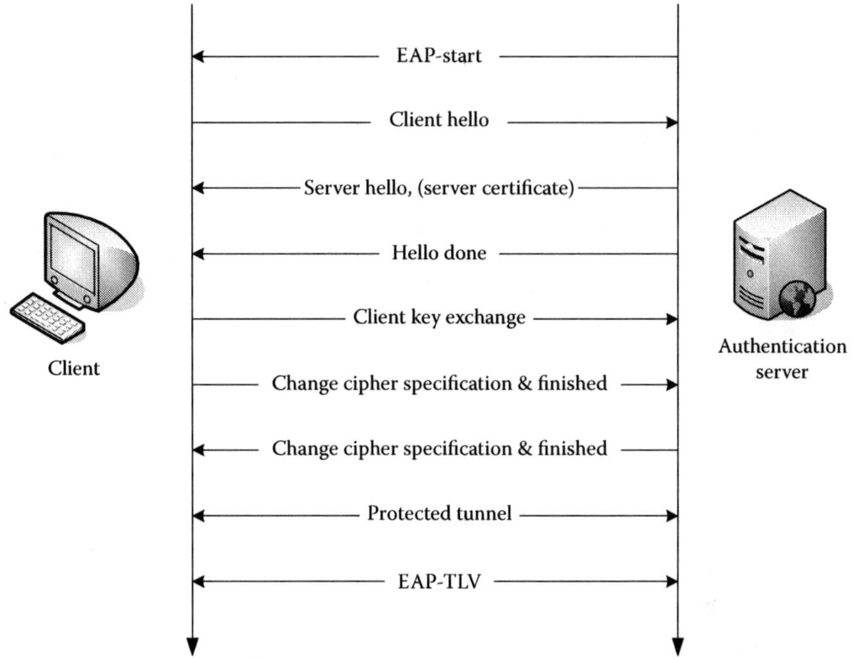

Figure 5.6 EAP-FAST tunnel establishment — Phase 1.

An EAP mechanism is negotiated and authentication is carried out following standard EAP messages, encapsulated within the TLS tunnel.

5.3 Port-Based Access Control

Ethernet (IEEE 802.3) proved to be the winning network access method in the early 1990s, and by the end of the century virtually became the only standard for local area networks. In addition to the investment from some vendors to make Ethernet more popular, one of the main reasons for its success was that Ethernet was relatively simple and cheap to implement. It was also very easy to connect to a wired network; any user can connect to an Ethernet wall jack available near his desk, or in a conference room, DHCP would automatically provide an IP address and other IP configuration information, and the user is immediately provided with access to the network.

In early 2000, Wi-Fi (802.11) emerged and by 2005 became widespread, although primarily for home and small office use. Wi-Fi network access made it even easier for users to connect to the network; wall jacks and cables were no longer required, and anyone within 10 to 50 meters

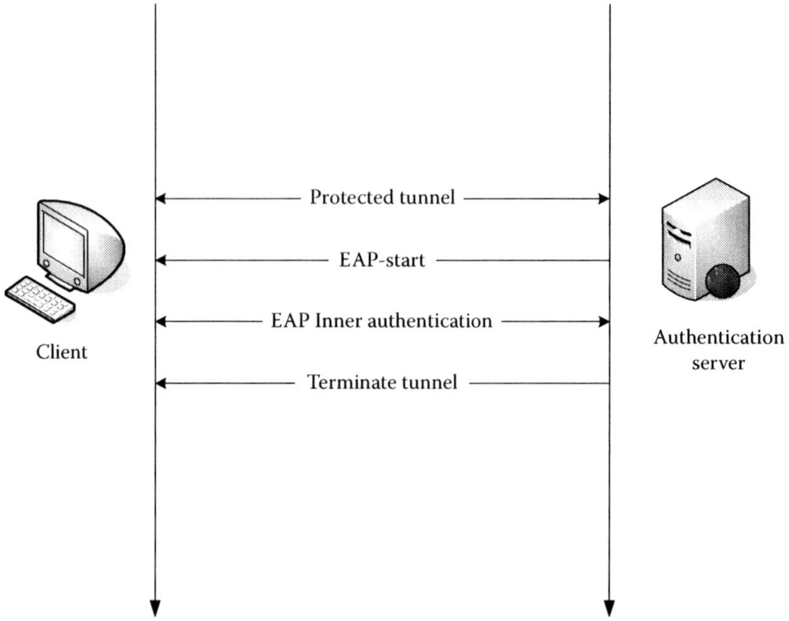

Figure 5.7 EAP-FAST inner authentication — Phase 2.

(depending on Wi-Fi hardware, and may even be more) from the Wi-Fi access point could access the infrastructure, even without having physical access to the building where the network resides. Wi-Fi made it possible to connect to the network from the building's car park or the nearby road. This led to the phenomenon of "wardriving" — network attackers could drive in their cars and detect Wi-Fi access points available for them to connect to.

In most cases, the ease of use and access contradict the principles of information security. While the years between 1970 and 2000 were spent trying to provide easy and seamless access to the network, in 2000 it became necessary to authenticate users before allowing them to access the LAN at the data-link layer.

That is how in 2001, the IEEE introduced the 802.1x standard for port-based access control, which evolved into the 802.1x-2004 standard to address the needs of Wi-Fi access and authentication (see [113]). As WEP authentication was deprecated as an authentication method for wireless networks, 802.1x was endorsed by the 802.11i (WPA/WPA2) standard as the primary authentication method and key management for Wi-Fi networks.

With the advent of port-based access control, many vendors of wired and wireless switching solutions started to offer 802.1x authentication for their products. Cisco even offers 802.1x on routers for both access control to a router interface, and for authentication in order to use a VPN tunnel to transfer traffic.

The following sections discuss port-based access control using the 802.1x standard.

5.3.1 Overview of Port-Based Access Control

Essentially, 802.1x suggests that users be authenticated at the data-link layer before they are allowed to access the LAN infrastructure. This very much resembles WAN access technologies such as dial-up remote access (RAS) and client VPN access, where authentication has virtually always been required. The actual authentication mechanism used by 802.1x is EAP, which was originally invented for PPP authentication, and used for RAS and VPN access.

The 802.1x standard uses the following terms to describe the parties in the authentication process:

- *Supplicant:* the client system that is willing to authenticate and access the network infrastructure. This is typically a client computer, such as a user workstation or a PDA device.
- *Authenticator:* the network device (Network Access Server — NAS, or Access Point — AP) that is taking part in the authentication process and upon successful completion of the authentication process will provide the user with access to the infrastructure.
- *Authentication server:* a network authority that centralizes user authentication services for the organization. In the case of 802.1x, this authentication server typically supports RADIUS for user authentication (see section 5.6)

The 802.1x standard also defines the term "controlled port." This is a port of a LAN switch or a Wi-Fi access point that allows or denies user access to the network based on 802.1x authentication. On the other hand, legacy ports are referred to as uncontrolled ports to indicate the fact that they are not capable of authenticating the user, and will provide unlimited access to the LAN to connected systems.

802.1x-capable network systems (LAN switches and 802.1x access points) can be configured to behave in the following way for each specific port:

- Unconditionally authorize the port: allow the port to communicate without any authentication. This is typically used for legacy systems that are attached to the port and that do not support 802.1x.
- Unconditionally unauthorize the port: disable communication from and to that port.

- Control port access: use 802.1x authentication for this port. The assumption here is that the system connected to that port is capable of authenticating to the network device.

If a port is controlled by 802.1x, it can be either authorized or unauthorized. Authorized ports are allowed to send and receive any traffic on the network. Unauthorized ports are not allowed to send or receive traffic. Ports that are currently authenticating are only allowed to send and receive EAPOL messages (see below).

It is important to note that EAPOL is a data-link layer protocol. 802.1x authentication takes place before network layer configuration and before the supplicant can effectively use its IP protocol (or other network layer protocol) stack. For example, until authorized, the supplicant cannot send or receive ARP messages or use DHCP to configure its TCP/IP protocol stack.

5.3.2 EAPOL

As discussed, 802.1x utilizes EAP (see subsection 5.2.6 Extensible Authentication Protocol (EAP)) for user authentication. The mechanism for encapsulating EAP over LANs is known as EAPOL. EAPOL works at the data-link layer and users Ethernet type 0x888e.

Ethernet encapsulation of EAPOL messages is shown in Figure 5.8.

Wi-Fi (802.11) and Token Ring (802.5) networks use 802.2/SNAP encapsulation for EAPOL messages, as shown in Figure 5.9.

At the MAC layer, the authenticator sends EAPOL messages to either the supplicant-specific MAC address if it is known (as is the case with Wi-Fi 802.11), or to a group MAC address (01-80-C2-00-00-03).

Table 5.7 provides information on the format of EAPOL messages.

Either the supplicant or the authenticator can send the **EAPOL-Start** message to indicate that it wants to start EAPOL authentication. At this

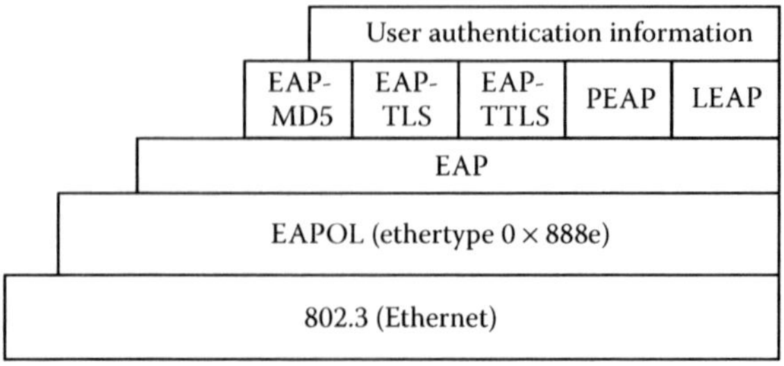

Figure 5.8 EAPOL protocol stack over Ethernet.

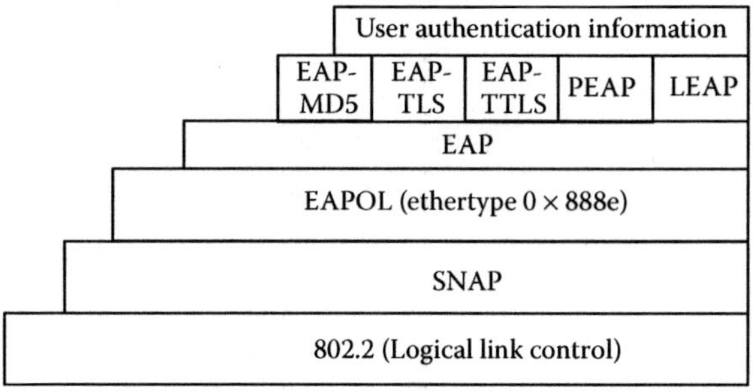

Figure 5.9 EAPOL protocol stack over 802.2.

Table 5.7 EAPOL Message Format

EAPOL Field	*Description*
EAPOL Version	These are always 2 for the current version of EAPOL
Type of Packet	This file is used to specify the content of the EAP encapsulated data; possible values include: 0 — EAPOL encapsulated EAP packet 1 — EAPOL Start 2 — EAPOL Logoff 3 — EAPOL Key – optional key to be used by the supplicant and authenticator 4 — EAPOL encapsulated ASF Alert
Length	The length in bytes of the EAPOL packet body (the following values)
Packet Body	The message carried by the EAPOL protocol; this can be an EAP message, an EAPOL key, or an ASF Alert

stage, the process typically continues with a series of EAPOL encapsulated EAP messages (see subsection 5.2.6), and EAPOL is only used as a transport.

If the supplicant wants to terminate the session to the port, it can issue an **EAPOL-Logoff** message. This message places the port in the unauthorized state.

Figure 5.10 shows typical EAPOL authentication mechanics.

Figure 5.11 shows the user authentication dialogue on an 802.1x-protected network port.

1. The client sends an identity message and preempts the infrastructure edge asking for it (see Frame 1 in Figure 5.11).
2. The server sends an EAPOL Start message (see Frame 2 in Figure 5.11).

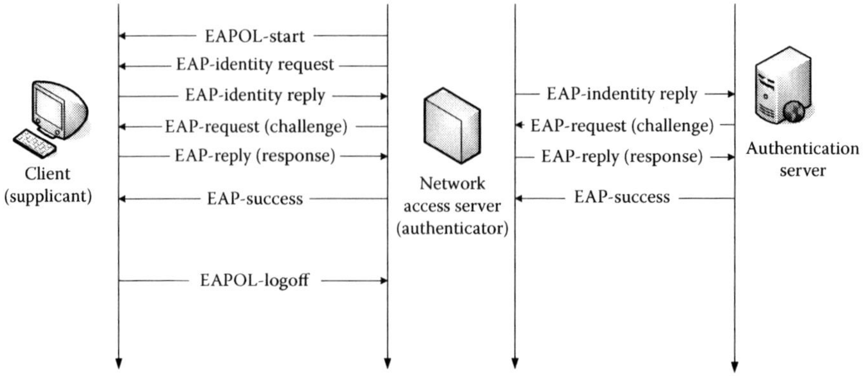

Figure 5.10 EAPOL mechanics.

3. The client replies with an EAPOL Response message and starts TLS/SSL negotiation with the SSL Client Hello, as required by PEAP phase 1 (see Frame 3 in Figure 5.11).
4. The server replies with the SSL Server Hello (see Frame 10 in Figure 5.11).
5. The client and the server switch to a TLS/SSL protected channel (see Frames 11 and 13). The server has been authenticated by its certificate. If the client provided a certificate, the client may have been authenticated as well.
6. Within the protected channel, PEAP performs inner authentication. Microsoft clients will use MS-CHAPv.2 as the inner authentication method (see Frames 15 and 16 in Figure 5.11).
7. The server signals successful user authentication and traffic is allowed on the port (see Frame 23 in Figure 5.11).

5.3.3 EAPOL Key Messages

EAPOL key messages are used by the authenticator and supplicant to exchange link protection keys. Although 802.1x authentication ends up providing protection keys to authenticating parties, they may still decide to exchange new protection keys, and EAPOL key messages are used exactly for this purpose. A typical example for EAPOL key is 802.11i WPA-PSK data protection, where 802.1x authentication is not being used, and only 802.1x key exchange takes place.

The 802.1x standard defines two types of keys that can be used: (1) RC4 and (2) 802.11 compatible. RC4 keys are considered deprecated now, and 802.11 keys and EAPOL format are defined in a separate standard (802.11i).

```
Frame 1 (35 bytes on wire, 35 bytes captured)
Ethernet II, Src: DellPcba_75:86:7c (00:0d:56:75:86:7c), Dst: Spanning-tree-(for-bridges)_03
(01:80:c2:00:00:03)
802.1X Authentication
    Version: 1
    Type: EAP Packet (0)
    Length: 17
    Extensible Authentication Protocol
        Code: Response (2)
        Id: 7
        Length: 17
        Type: Identity [RFC3748] (1)
        Identity (12 bytes): STEVE\chopin


Frame 2 (60 bytes on wire, 60 bytes captured)
Ethernet II, Src: Cisco_7b:48:f4 (00:0d:ed:7b:48:f4), Dst: DellPcba_75:86:7c (00:0d:56:75:86:7c)
802.1X Authentication
    Version: 1
    Type: EAP Packet (0)
    Length: 6
    Extensible Authentication Protocol
        Code: Request (1)
        Id: 8
        Length: 6
        Type: PEAP [Palekar] (25)
        Flags(0x20): Start
        PEAP version 0

Frame 3 (98 bytes on wire, 98 bytes captured)
Ethernet II, Src: DellPcba_75:86:7c (00:0d:56:75:86:7c), Dst: Spanning-tree-(for-bridges)_03
(01:80:c2:00:00:03)
802.1X Authentication
    Version: 1
    Type: EAP Packet (0)
    Length: 80
```

Figure 5.11 8021x-PEAP-MS-CHAPv2.cap: MOBILE-CLIENT connects to an 802.1x protected network port and authenticates using PEAP.

```
Extensible Authentication Protocol
    Code: Response (2)
    Id: 8
    Length: 80
    Type: PEAP [Palekar] (25)
    Flags(0x80): Length
    PEAP version 0
    Length: 70
    Secure Socket Layer
        TLS Record Layer: Handshake Protocol: Client Hello
            Content Type: Handshake (22)
            Version: TLS 1.0 (0x0301)
            Length: 65
            Handshake Protocol: Client Hello
                Handshake Type: Client Hello (1)
                Length: 61
                Version: TLS 1.0 (0x0301)
                Random.gmt_unix_time: Jun 17, 2006 00:19:13.000000000
                Random.bytes
                Session ID Length: 0
                Cipher Suites Length: 22
                Cipher Suites (11 suites)
                    Cipher Suite: TLS_RSA_WITH_RC4_128_MD5 (0x0004)
                    Cipher Suite: TLS_RSA_WITH_RC4_128_SHA (0x0005)
                    Cipher Suite: TLS_RSA_WITH_3DES_EDE_CBC_SHA (0x000a)
                    Cipher Suite: TLS_RSA_WITH_DES_CBC_SHA (0x0009)
                    Cipher Suite: TLS_RSA_EXPORT1024_WITH_RC4_56_SHA (0x0064)
                    Cipher Suite: TLS_RSA_EXPORT1024_WITH_DES_CBC_SHA (0x0062)
                    Cipher Suite: TLS_RSA_EXPORT_WITH_RC4_40_MD5 (0x0003)
                    Cipher Suite: TLS_RSA_EXPORT_WITH_RC2_CBC_40_MD5 (0x0006)
                    Cipher Suite: TLS_DHE_DSS_WITH_3DES_EDE_CBC_SHA (0x0013)
                    Cipher Suite: TLS_DHE_DSS_WITH_DES_CBC_SHA (0x0012)
                    Cipher Suite: TLS_DHE_DSS_EXPORT1024_WITH_DES_CBC_SHA (0x0063)
                Compression Methods Length: 1
                Compression Methods (1 method)
                    Compression Method: null (0)
```

Figure 5.11 (continued)

```
Frame 10 (373 bytes on wire, 373 bytes captured)
Ethernet II, Src: Cisco_7b:48:f4 (00:0d:ed:7b:48:f4), Dst: DellPcba_75:86:7c (00:0d:56:75:86:7c)
802.1X Authentication
    Version: 1
    Type: EAP Packet (0)
    Length: 355
    Extensible Authentication Protocol
        Code: Request (1)
        Id: 12
        Length: 355
        Type: PEAP [Palekar] (25)
        Flags(0x0):
        PEAP version 0
        EAP-TLS Fragments (4515 bytes): #4(1386), #6(1390), #8(1390), #10(349)
            Frame: 4, payload: 0-1385 (1386 bytes)
            Frame: 6, payload: 1386-2775 (1390 bytes)
            Frame: 8, payload: 2776-4165 (1390 bytes)
            Frame: 10, payload: 4166-4514 (349 bytes)
        Secure Socket Layer
            TLS Record Layer: Handshake Protocol: Multiple Handshake Messages
                Content Type: Handshake (22)
                Version: TLS 1.0 (0x0301)
                Length: 4510
                Handshake Protocol: Server Hello
                    Handshake Type: Server Hello (2)
                    Length: 70
                    Version: TLS 1.0 (0x0301)
                    Random.gmt_unix_time: Jun 17, 2006 00:21:09.000000000
                    Random.bytes
                    Session ID Length: 32
                    Session ID (32 bytes)
                    Cipher Suite: TLS_RSA_WITH_RC4_128_MD5 (0x0004)
                    Compression Method: null (0)
                Handshake Protocol: Certificate
                    Handshake Type: Certificate (11)
```

Figure 5.11 (continued)

```
                Length: 1276
                Certificates Length: 1273
                Certificates (1273 bytes)
            Handshake Protocol: Certificate Request
                Handshake Type: Certificate Request (13)
                Length: 3148
                Certificate types count: 2
                Certificate types (2 types)
                    Certificate type: RSA Sign (1)
                    Certificate type: DSS Sign (2)
                Distinguished Names Length: 3143
                Distinguished Names (3143 bytes)
            Handshake Protocol: Server Hello Done
                Handshake Type: Server Hello Done (14)
                Length: 0

Frame 11 (217 bytes on wire, 217 bytes captured)
Ethernet II, Src: DellPcba_75:86:7c (00:0d:56:75:86:7c), Dst: Spanning-tree-(for-bridges)_03
(01:80:c2:00:00:03)
802.1X Authentication
    Version: 1
    Type: EAP Packet (0)
    Length: 199
    Extensible Authentication Protocol
        Code: Response (2)
        Id: 12
        Length: 199
        Type: PEAP [Palekar] (25)
        Flags(0x80): Length
        PEAP version 0
        Length: 189
        Secure Socket Layer
            TLS Record Layer: Handshake Protocol: Multiple Handshake Messages
                Content Type: Handshake (22)
                Version: TLS 1.0 (0x0301)
                Length: 141
```

Figure 5.11 (continued)

```
            Handshake Protocol: Certificate
                Handshake Type: Certificate (11)
                Length: 3
                Certificates Length: 0
            Handshake Protocol: Client Key Exchange
                Handshake Type: Client Key Exchange (16)
                Length: 130
        TLS Record Layer: Change Cipher Spec Protocol: Change Cipher Spec
        TLS Record Layer: Handshake Protocol: Encrypted Handshake Message
            Handshake Protocol: Encrypted Handshake Message


Frame 13 (71 bytes on wire, 71 bytes captured)
Ethernet II, Src: Cisco_7b:48:f4 (00:0d:ed:7b:48:f4), Dst: DellPcba_75:86:7c (00:0d:56:75:86:7c)
802.1X Authentication
    Version: 1
    Type: EAP Packet (0)
    Length: 53
    Extensible Authentication Protocol
        Code: Request (1)
        Id: 13
        Length: 53
        Type: PEAP [Palekar] (25)
        Flags(0x80): Length
        PEAP version 0
        Length: 43
        Secure Socket Layer
            TLS Record Layer: Change Cipher Spec Protocol: Change Cipher Spec
                Content Type: Change Cipher Spec (20)
                Version: TLS 1.0 (0x0301)
                Length: 1
                Change Cipher Spec Message
            TLS Record Layer: Handshake Protocol: Encrypted Handshake Message
                Content Type: Handshake (22)
                Version: TLS 1.0 (0x0301)
                Length: 32
```

Figure 5.11 (continued)

```
                Handshake Protocol: Encrypted Handshake Message

Frame 15 (60 bytes on wire, 60 bytes captured)
Ethernet II, Src: Cisco_7b:48:f4 (00:0d:ed:7b:48:f4), Dst: DellPcba_75:86:7c (00:0d:56:75:86:7c)
802.1X Authentication
    Version: 1
    Type: EAP Packet (0)
    Length: 28
    Extensible Authentication Protocol
        Code: Request (1)
        Id: 14
        Length: 28
        Type: PEAP [Palekar] (25)
        Flags(0x0):
        PEAP version 0
        Secure Socket Layer
            TLS Record Layer: Application Data Protocol: Application Data
                Content Type: Application Data (23)
                Version: TLS 1.0 (0x0301)
                Length: 17
                Application Data

Frame 16 (58 bytes on wire, 58 bytes captured)
Ethernet II, Src: DellPcba_75:86:7c (00:0d:56:75:86:7c), Dst: Spanning-tree-(for-bridges)_03
(01:80:c2:00:00:03)
802.1X Authentication
    Version: 1
    Type: EAP Packet (0)
    Length: 40
    Extensible Authentication Protocol
        Code: Response (2)
        Id: 14
        Length: 40
        Type: PEAP [Palekar] (25)
        Flags(0x0):
        PEAP version 0
```

Figure 5.11 (continued)

```
        Secure Socket Layer
            TLS Record Layer: Application Data Protocol: Application Data
                Content Type: Application Data (23)
                Version: TLS 1.0 (0x0301)
                Length: 29
                Application Data

Frame 23 (60 bytes on wire, 60 bytes captured)
Ethernet II, Src: Cisco_7b:48:f4 (00:0d:ed:7b:48:f4), Dst: DellPcba_75:86:7c (00:0d:56:75:86:7c)
802.1X Authentication
    Version: 1
    Type: EAP Packet (0)
    Length: 4
    Extensible Authentication Protocol
        Code: Success (3)
        Id: 18
        Length: 4
```

Figure 5.11 (continued)

5.4 Authenticating Access to the Wireless Infrastructure

Wireless networks were invented in the 1990s and quickly became popular. The IEEE 802.11 series of standards followed, as well as the establishment of governing and certification bodies for Wi-Fi; so in the early 2000, Wi-Fi technologies became widespread for home applications and consumer Internet access (including wireless spots in cafes, airports, and shopping malls). However, they were somewhat slow to adopt the new technology and there is a good reason for this: security — or the lack thereof.

Wireless technologies such as 802.11, Bluetooth, WiMax, and others are very convenient in allowing easy access to the network infrastructure without the need for cables. To a certain extent, this means that the physical security of the network media has changed in terms of requirements. An attacker who needs access to the corporate infrastructure is much less likely to be able to connect to an unused network cable than to sniff traffic from the wireless network that uses radio waves and complies with standards (e.g., other devices can tune in and listen, or even interfere with the transmission). Depending on the wireless devices being used, physical proximity may be a sufficient factor for an attacker to access the corporate network without having to sneak into the building.

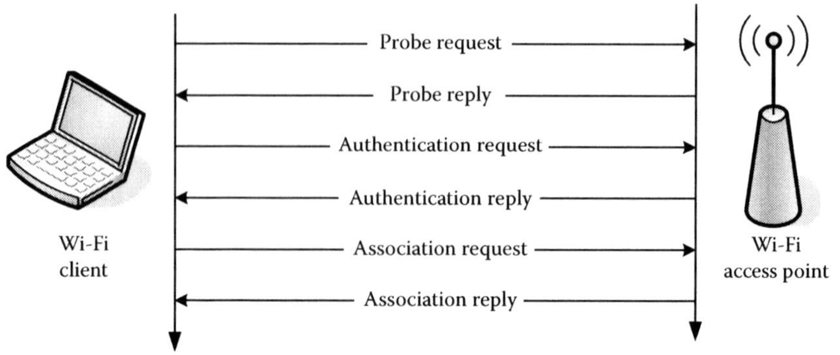

Figure 5.12 802.11 authentication process.

Wi-Fi (802.11) security technologies exist to mitigate these risks. The following sections delve into the authentication technologies that allow network devices and users to access the 802.11 infrastructure.

5.4.1 Wi-Fi Authentication Overview

The 802.11 standard defines two main authentication technologies for access to the Wi-Fi infrastructure: (1) open authentication and (2) shared key authentication. The industry has also developed additional authentication and authorization mechanisms to protect the wireless infrastructure from attackers. The classical 802.11 authentication approach is oriented toward authenticating communicating devices rather than users working on the specific devices (Figure 5.12).

Before a network device connects to the wireless infrastructure, according to the 802.11 standard it must authenticate and associate with an access point. The process is as follows:

1. The Wi-Fi client sends a probe message and tries to find an access point with the specified SSID.
2. All access points (APs) with the request SSID reply to the client and provide their parameters and their current load.
3. Based on the information provided by the access points, the Wi-Fi client selects a specific access point and submits an authentication request.
4. The access point either authenticates the client or rejects the authentication request.
5. If the client has been successfully authenticated, it requests association with the access point.
6. The access point acknowledges that the client has been successfully associated with the access point.

5.4.2 WEP Protection

WEP (Wired Equivalent Privacy) is a data protection technology for 802.11 networks. WEP protects network traffic, including user data, and the authentication process (for shared key authentication only). To protect network traffic, WEP implements technologies for data integrity authentication and data encryption.

WEP is based on secret preshared keys that are known to the access point (AP) and all the devices that communicate on the same wireless LAN (WLAN). To authenticate and associate with an AP, the client needs to know the secret preshared key. The key can be 40 or 104 bits in length. The key that is a fixed string is combined with a random 24-bit initialization vector (IV); thus, some vendors refer to WEP keys as 64-bit or 128-bit, respectively (the latter is sometimes referred to as WEP2). The former was allowed for export worldwide, while the latter was restricted. Because U.S. export restrictions were lifted, both versions can be exported.

Some vendors require that the key be entered as hexadecimal numbers and some require ASCII characters. These two methods are equivalent, as ASCII characters are transformed to numbers anyway. Some vendors also allow for the use of a passphrase. They generate keys from the specified passphrase, and this is believed to be using the entire keyspace, unlike human-readable ASCII keys that users can use.

There may be up to four keys that can be used by the client and the access point. All the keys with the same index are the same on all devices in the WLAN. Clients typically only use one key to send traffic and APs have all the keys so that they can decrypt traffic regardless of the key used by each client. The index of the key used for encryption is included in cleartext in network packets so that the client and the AP (as well as a potential attacker) know which key to use to decrypt the packet they have just received.

The integrity of user payload (802.11 data) is authenticated using a 32-bit CRC32 checksum (called Integrity Check Value — ICV) appended to the user payload.

Network packets (the 802.11 payload and checksum but not the 802.11 header) are encrypted using RC4 in the concatenation of the preshared key and the IV. The data protection algorithm used by WEP is as follows:

1. The sender needs to send a message **M**.
2. The sender generates a random initial vector (**IV**), 24-bits in length.
3. The sender calculates the checksum **ICV** for **M** using a 32-bit CRC checksum (CRC32).
4. The sender needs a keystream to perform streaming encryption. The keystream (**KS**) is calculated using the RC4 key expansion algorithm (Pseudo-Random Number Generation Algorithm). The

expansion is based on the concatenation of the preshared key and the IV as the key. The expansion is performed as many times as required to generate a keystream with the same size as the plaintext message plus the ICV (RC4 stage 1).

The plaintext message is then encrypted by applying bitwise XOR on the message **M** and the keystream **KS** (RC4 stage 2)

The sender then includes the value of the initial vector (**IV**) in the 802.11 header in plaintext, and submits the 802.11 frame for transmission.

The recipient uses the **IV** from the received frame (that should potentially be unique and random) and generates a keystream **KS** using this **IV** and the preshared key that it knows from its configuration. By applying an additional round of XOR with the same keystream, the recipient should be able to decrypt the message and validate the checksum (**ICV**) included in the encrypted part of the message. If checksum validation fails, the recipient will drop the packet.

Soon after the WEP algorithm was announced and vendors started producing the first 802.11-compliant devices, researchers in the academic and commercial communities noticed major security problems with the WEP algorithm. Without delving into all the details, it became clear that:

- Because the ICV is calculated using CRC32, which is a linear algorithm, it is relatively easy to modify the contents of packets and tweak WEP integrity checks. This does not require that the packet be first be decrypted; neither does it require that the checksum be recalculated
- The keyspace for the WEP algorithm was too small – 40 bits, because the 24-bit IV is transmitted in plaintext. This makes WEP encryption susceptible to brute force and dictionary attacks. Later, vendors introduced WEP2, that used 104 bits, which made it somewhat less vulnerable to brute force attacks but dictionary attacks were still possible.
- If an attacker detects two messages with the same IV (and there are only 24 bits, so this can happen after just 16,000,000 packets, or even much less considering the birthday paradox), the attacker can XOR the two encrypted messages and this will result in the keystream used to encrypt the two plaintext messages. If the attacker knows portions of one of the packets (which is not difficult for portions of the IP packet, such as the IP or TCP/UDP header), he can easily recover both packets.
- Although 802.11 recommends that the IV be unique and random for every packet, many vendors have ignored this recommendation. As a result, an attacker can easily recover messages without even waiting for the entire IV keyspace to be depleted, and the IV wraps over.

- Other decryption attack methods include sending encrypted messages to the AP and expecting that it will bounce them back to the sender decrypted. This is based on the fact that both the encryption and the decryption of the packet are performed using the same keystream and the bitwise XOR operation. Tricking the AP into bouncing back traffic was deemed possible by sending ICMP Echo Request messages with the encrypted text as the ICMP payload; ICMP redirection was considered another option for this.
- Preshared key authentication using WEP was a typical example of weak security design. An attacker sniffing on the network would see both the server challenge and the client response — the plaintext and the ciphertext — and therefore would be able to generate the keystream for the particular IV by using bitwise XOR on the plaintext challenge and the encrypted response. The attacker could then potentially authenticate to the server every time by encrypting the server challenge with the so calculated keystream, without even knowing the key.

The operation of WEP, as well as its weaknesses are discussed in [111]. All these security issues with WEP soon caused the IEEE 802.11 committee and the Wi-Fi Association to abandon WEP and propose a new standard, known as 802.11i.

5.4.3 Open Authentication

One of the authentication methods supported by 802.11-compliant devices is the *open authentication* method. As the name implies, this authentication method provides open access for users to the Wi-Fi infrastructure.

To use open authentication, the client submits an authentication request to the AP, specifying open authentication as the authentication method and no authentication credentials (anonymous authentication). If the AP is configured to allow for such authentication, it will report success. The client can then proceed and associate with the AP, then start communicating over the wireless network.

Provided that the user has already requested information about the wireless network (probe request) and has selected an AP, the authentication and association process is the following (see Figure 5.13 and Chapter 5.6):

1. The Wi-Fi client requests authentication specifying Open System as the authentication type (see Frame 4 in Figure 5.13).
2. Without requesting any further information, the Wi-Fi access point replies with a successful authentication response (see Frame 6 in Figure 5.13).

```
Frame 3 (78 bytes on wire, 78 bytes captured)
IEEE 802.11
    Type/Subtype: Beacon frame (8)
    Frame Control: 0x0080 (Normal)
        Version: 0
        Type: Management frame (0)
        Subtype: 8
        Flags: 0x0
    Duration: 0
    Destination address: Broadcast (ff:ff:ff:ff:ff:ff)
    Source address: Cisco-Li_73:b5:56 (00:14:bf:73:b5:56)
    BSS Id: Cisco-Li_73:b5:56 (00:14:bf:73:b5:56)
    Fragment number: 0
    Sequence number: 532
IEEE 802.11 wireless LAN management frame
    Fixed parameters (12 bytes)
        Timestamp: 0x0000000196DAB146
        Beacon Interval: 0.102400 [Seconds]
        Capability Information: 0x0461
    Tagged parameters (42 bytes)
        SSID parameter set: "CorporateAP"
            Tag Number: 0 (SSID parameter set)
            Tag length: 11
            Tag interpretation: CorporateAP
        Supported Rates: 1.0(B) 2.0(B) 5.5(B) 11.0(B) 22.0
            Tag Number: 1 (Supported Rates)
            Tag length: 5
            Tag interpretation: Supported rates: 1.0(B) 2.0(B) 5.5(B) 11.0(B) 22.0  [Mbit/sec]
        DS Parameter set: Current Channel: 11
            Tag Number: 3 (DS Parameter set)
            Tag length: 1
            Tag interpretation: Current Channel: 11
        (TIM) Traffic Indication Map: DTIM 0 of 1 bitmap empty
            Tag Number: 5 ((TIM) Traffic Indication Map)
            TIM length: 4
            DTIM count: 0
```

Figure 5.13 WiFi-Open-Authentication.cap: A Windows XP client associates to an Access Point using Open Authentication.

```
            DTIM period: 1
            Bitmap Control: 0x00 (mcast:0, bitmap offset 0)
        ERP Information: no Non-ERP STAs, do not use protection, long preambles
            Tag Number: 42 (ERP Information)
            Tag length: 1
            Tag interpretation: ERP info: 0x0 (no Non-ERP STAs, do not use protection, long
preambles)
        Extended Supported Rates: 6.0 9.0 12.0 18.0 24.0 36.0 48.0 54.0
            Tag Number: 50 (Extended Supported Rates)
            Tag length: 8
            Tag interpretation: Supported rates: 6.0 9.0 12.0 18.0 24.0 36.0 48.0 54.0
[Mbit/sec]

Frame 4 (37 bytes on wire, 37 bytes captured)
IEEE 802.11
    Type/Subtype: Authentication (11)
    Frame Control: 0x00B0 (Normal)
        Version: 0
        Type: Management frame (0)
        Subtype: 11
        Flags: 0x0
    Duration: 314
    Destination address: Cisco-Li_73:b5:56 (00:14:bf:73:b5:56)
    Source address: GemtekTe_1f:a4:f7 (00:90:4b:1f:a4:f7)
    BSS Id: Cisco-Li_73:b5:56 (00:14:bf:73:b5:56)
    Fragment number: 0
    Sequence number: 79
IEEE 802.11 wireless LAN management frame
    Fixed parameters (6 bytes)
        Authentication Algorithm: Open System (0)
        Authentication SEQ: 0x0001
        Status code: Successful (0x0000)
    Tagged parameters (7 bytes)
        Vendor Specific: Broadcom
            Tag Number: 221 (Vendor Specific)
            Tag length: 5
```

Figure 5.13 (continued)

```
            Vendor: Broadcom
            Tag interpretation: Not interpreted

Frame 6 (30 bytes on wire, 30 bytes captured)
IEEE 802.11
    Type/Subtype: Authentication (11)
    Frame Control: 0x00B0 (Normal)
        Version: 0
        Type: Management frame (0)
        Subtype: 11
        Flags: 0x0
    Duration: 213
    Destination address: GemtekTe_1f:a4:f7 (00:90:4b:1f:a4:f7)
    Source address: Cisco-Li_73:b5:56 (00:14:bf:73:b5:56)
    BSS Id: Cisco-Li_73:b5:56 (00:14:bf:73:b5:56)
    Fragment number: 0
    Sequence number: 533
IEEE 802.11 wireless LAN management frame
    Fixed parameters (6 bytes)
        Authentication Algorithm: Open System (0)
        Authentication SEQ: 0x0002
        Status code: Successful (0x0000)

Frame 8 (64 bytes on wire, 64 bytes captured)
IEEE 802.11
    Arrival Time: May 15, 2006 05:47:40.609783000
    Time delta from previous packet: 0.000840000 seconds
    Time since reference or first frame: 0.363861000 seconds
    Frame Number: 8
    Packet Length: 64 bytes
    Capture Length: 64 bytes
    Protocols in frame: wlan
IEEE 802.11
    Type/Subtype: Association Request (0)
```

Figure 5.13 (continued)

```
    Frame Control: 0x0000 (Normal)
        Version: 0
        Type: Management frame (0)
        Subtype: 0
        Flags: 0x0
    Duration: 314
    Destination address: Cisco-Li_73:b5:56 (00:14:bf:73:b5:56)
    Source address: GemtekTe_1f:a4:f7 (00:90:4b:1f:a4:f7)
    BSS Id: Cisco-Li_73:b5:56 (00:14:bf:73:b5:56)
    Fragment number: 0
    Sequence number: 80
IEEE 802.11 wireless LAN management frame
    Fixed parameters (4 bytes)
        Capability Information: 0x0421
        Listen Interval: 0x000a
    Tagged parameters (36 bytes)
        SSID parameter set: "CorporateAP"
            Tag Number: 0 (SSID parameter set)
            Tag length: 11
            Tag interpretation: CorporateAP
        Supported Rates: 1.0(B) 2.0(B) 5.5(B) 11.0(B) 18.0 24.0 36.0 54.0
            Tag Number: 1 (Supported Rates)
            Tag length: 8
            Tag interpretation: Supported rates: 1.0(B) 2.0(B) 5.5(B) 11.0(B) 18.0 24.0 36.0 54.0
[Mbit/sec]
        Extended Supported Rates: 6.0 9.0 12.0 48.0
            Tag Number: 50 (Extended Supported Rates)
            Tag length: 4
            Tag interpretation: Supported rates: 6.0 9.0 12.0 48.0  [Mbit/sec]
        Vendor Specific: Broadcom
            Tag Number: 221 (Vendor Specific)
            Tag length: 5
            Vendor: Broadcom
            Tag interpretation: Not interpreted

Frame 10 (46 bytes on wire, 46 bytes captured)
```

Figure 5.13 (continued)

```
IEEE 802.11
    Type/Subtype: Association Response (1)
    Frame Control: 0x0010 (Normal)
        Version: 0
        Type: Management frame (0)
        Subtype: 1
        Flags: 0x0
    Duration: 213
    Destination address: GemtekTe_1f:a4:f7 (00:90:4b:1f:a4:f7)
    Source address: Cisco-Li_73:b5:56 (00:14:bf:73:b5:56)
    BSS Id: Cisco-Li_73:b5:56 (00:14:bf:73:b5:56)
    Fragment number: 0
    Sequence number: 534
IEEE 802.11 wireless LAN management frame
    Fixed parameters (6 bytes)
        Capability Information: 0x0461
        Status code: Successful (0x0000)
        Association ID: 0x0001
    Tagged parameters (16 bytes)
        Supported Rates: 1.0(B) 2.0(B) 5.5(B) 11.0(B) 18.0 24.0 36.0 54.0
            Tag Number: 1 (Supported Rates)
            Tag length: 8
            Tag interpretation: Supported rates: 1.0(B) 2.0(B) 5.5(B) 11.0(B) 18.0 24.0 36.0 54.0
[Mbit/sec]
        Extended Supported Rates: 6.0 9.0 12.0 48.0
            Tag Number: 50 (Extended Supported Rates)
            Tag length: 4
            Tag interpretation: Supported rates: 6.0 9.0 12.0 48.0  [Mbit/sec]
```

Figure 5.13 (continued)

3. The client can now attempt to associate with the access point (see Frame 8 in Figure 5.13).
4. The access point associates the client and considers it active on the network (see Frame 10 in Figure 5.13).

Wi-Fi open authentication is as weak as no authentication at all. At the same time, open authentication and successful association with an AP still do not provide the user with access to the wireless infrastructure if WEP encryption for the medium is configured. When WEP is enabled for data traffic, the contents of all 802.11 packets must be encrypted before the packet is sent over the network and must be decrypted using WEP upon reception. If a packet cannot be decrypted using WEP and knowledge of the current encryption key, the packet is useless and is dropped; therefore, even devices that have successfully authenticated are not effectively able to use the infrastructure, unless they know the encryption key for WEP.

Given the weaknesses of WEP, however, open authentication may allow an attacker to authenticate, and then potentially capture traffic, modify packets, or even transmit packets. When open authentication is combined with strong protection mechanisms, such as those defined by WPA/WPA2, user authentication and user data can be much better protected.

5.4.4 Shared Key Authentication

The *shared key authentication algorithm* defined by 802.11 requires peer authentication. The protocol is based on a simple challenge-response scheme. To authenticate the client, the access point sends a unique, 128-bit randomly generated challenge to the Wi-Fi client. The client uses WEP to encrypt the received challenge and returns it to the server.

In detail, shared key authentication works as follows (see Figure 5.14):

1. The Wi-Fi client connects to the access point, specifying shared key as the authentication method (see Frame 4 in Figure 5.14).
2. The Wi-Fi access point generates a random, 128-bit challenge and sends it back to the Wi-Fi client (see Frame 6 in Figure 5.14).
3. The client uses WEP to encrypt the received challenge, and then sends it back to the access point (see Frame 8 in Figure 5.14).
4. The access point compares the received with the locally calculated WEP reply and potentially authenticates the user (see Frame 10 in Figure 5.14).
5. The client sends an association request (see Frame 12 in Figure 5.14).
6. The access point replies with an association reply and provides communication parameters for the Wireless LAN back to the client.

Although shared key authentication for 802.11 may seem a secure authentication mechanism, it is well known that it suffers from many problems. Perhaps the most notable is that if an attacker can sniff on the wireless network and capture the authentication request and the authentication reply for a particular client, the attacker can successfully attach to the network and start sending packets.

The reason for this weakness is because the authentication reply is generated from the plaintext challenge and the WEP keystream by combining them using an XOR operation. Technically, this means that someone

```
Frame 3 (78 bytes on wire, 78 bytes captured)
IEEE 802.11
    Type/Subtype: Beacon frame (8)
    Frame Control: 0x0080 (Normal)
        Version: 0
        Type: Management frame (0)
        Subtype: 8
        Flags: 0x0
            DS status: Not leaving DS or network is operating in AD-HOC mode (To DS: 0 From DS:
0) (0x00)
    Duration: 0
    Destination address: Broadcast (ff:ff:ff:ff:ff:ff)
    Source address: Cisco-Li_73:b5:56 (00:14:bf:73:b5:56)
    BSS Id: Cisco-Li_73:b5:56 (00:14:bf:73:b5:56)
    Fragment number: 0
    Sequence number: 123
IEEE 802.11 wireless LAN management frame
    Fixed parameters (12 bytes)
        Timestamp: 0x0000000019627146
        Beacon Interval: 0.102400 [Seconds]
        Capability Information: 0x0471
    Tagged parameters (42 bytes)
        SSID parameter set: "CorporateAP"
            Tag Number: 0 (SSID parameter set)
            Tag length: 11
            Tag interpretation: CorporateAP
        Supported Rates: 1.0(B) 2.0(B) 5.5(B) 11.0(B) 22.0
            Tag Number: 1 (Supported Rates)
            Tag length: 5
            Tag interpretation: Supported rates: 1.0(B) 2.0(B) 5.5(B) 11.0(B) 22.0  [Mbit/sec]
        DS Parameter set: Current Channel: 11
            Tag Number: 3 (DS Parameter set)
            Tag length: 1
            Tag interpretation: Current Channel: 11
        (TIM) Traffic Indication Map: DTIM 0 of 1 bitmap empty
            Tag Number: 5 ((TIM) Traffic Indication Map)
```

Figure 5.14 WiFi-Shared-Authentication.cap: User authenticates using Shared Authentication.

```
            TIM length: 4
            DTIM count: 0
            DTIM period: 1
            Bitmap Control: 0x00 (mcast:0, bitmap offset 0)
        ERP Information: no Non-ERP STAs, do not use protection, long preambles
            Tag Number: 42 (ERP Information)
            Tag length: 1
            Tag interpretation: ERP info: 0x0 (no Non-ERP STAs, do not use protection, long
preambles)
        Extended Supported Rates: 6.0 9.0 12.0 18.0 24.0 36.0 48.0 54.0
            Tag Number: 50 (Extended Supported Rates)
            Tag length: 8
            Tag interpretation: Supported rates: 6.0 9.0 12.0 18.0 24.0 36.0 48.0 54.0
[Mbit/sec]

Frame 4 (37 bytes on wire, 37 bytes captured)
IEEE 802.11
    Type/Subtype: Authentication (11)
    Frame Control: 0x00B0 (Normal)
        Version: 0
        Type: Management frame (0)
        Subtype: 11
        Flags: 0x0
            DS status: Not leaving DS or network is operating in AD-HOC mode (To DS: 0 From DS:
0) (0x00)
    Duration: 314
    Destination address: Cisco-Li_73:b5:56 (00:14:bf:73:b5:56)
    Source address: GemtekTe_1f:a4:f7 (00:90:4b:1f:a4:f7)
    BSS Id: Cisco-Li_73:b5:56 (00:14:bf:73:b5:56)
    Fragment number: 0
    Sequence number: 2450
IEEE 802.11 wireless LAN management frame
    Fixed parameters (6 bytes)
        Authentication Algorithm: Shared key (1)
        Authentication SEQ: 0x0001
        Status code: Successful (0x0000)
```

Figure 5.14 (continued)

```
    Tagged parameters (7 bytes)
        Vendor Specific: Broadcom
            Tag Number: 221 (Vendor Specific)
            Tag length: 5
            Vendor: Broadcom
            Tag interpretation: Not interpreted

Frame 6 (160 bytes on wire, 160 bytes captured)
IEEE 802.11
    Type/Subtype: Authentication (11)
    Frame Control: 0x00B0 (Normal)
        Version: 0
        Type: Management frame (0)
        Subtype: 11
        Flags: 0x0
            DS status: Not leaving DS or network is operating in AD-HOC mode (To DS: 0 From DS:
0) (0x00)
    Duration: 213
    Destination address: GemtekTe_1f:a4:f7 (00:90:4b:1f:a4:f7)
    Source address: Cisco-Li_73:b5:56 (00:14:bf:73:b5:56)
    BSS Id: Cisco-Li_73:b5:56 (00:14:bf:73:b5:56)
    Fragment number: 0
    Sequence number: 124
IEEE 802.11 wireless LAN management frame
    Fixed parameters (6 bytes)
        Authentication Algorithm: Shared key (1)
        Authentication SEQ: 0x0002
        Status code: Successful (0x0000)
    Tagged parameters (130 bytes)
        Challenge text
            Tag Number: 16 (Challenge text)
            Tag length: 128
            Tag interpretation: Challenge text:
9D30A783E37A9D5A9152EB0C689523AF125592351D25223A...
```

Figure 5.14 (continued)

```
Frame 8 (175 bytes on wire, 175 bytes captured)
IEEE 802.11
    Type/Subtype: Authentication (11)
    Frame Control: 0x40B0 (Normal)
        Version: 0
        Type: Management frame (0)
        Subtype: 11
        Flags: 0x40
            DS status: Not leaving DS or network is operating in AD-HOC mode (To DS: 0 From DS:
0) (0x00)
    Duration: 314
    Destination address: Cisco-Li_73:b5:56 (00:14:bf:73:b5:56)
    Source address: GemtekTe_1f:a4:f7 (00:90:4b:1f:a4:f7)
    BSS Id: Cisco-Li_73:b5:56 (00:14:bf:73:b5:56)
    Fragment number: 0
    Sequence number: 2451
    WEP parameters
        Initialization Vector: 0x8a8400
        Key Index: 0
        WEP ICV: 0xd18b2eeb (not verified)
Data (143 bytes)

Frame 10 (30 bytes on wire, 30 bytes captured)
IEEE 802.11
    Type/Subtype: Authentication (11)
    Frame Control: 0x00B0 (Normal)
        Version: 0
        Type: Management frame (0)
        Subtype: 11
        Flags: 0x0
            DS status: Not leaving DS or network is operating in AD-HOC mode (To DS: 0 From DS:
0) (0x00)
    Duration: 213
    Destination address: GemtekTe_1f:a4:f7 (00:90:4b:1f:a4:f7)
    Source address: Cisco-Li_73:b5:56 (00:14:bf:73:b5:56)
    BSS Id: Cisco-Li_73:b5:56 (00:14:bf:73:b5:56)
```

Figure 5.14 (continued)

```
    Fragment number: 0
    Sequence number: 125
IEEE 802.11 wireless LAN management frame
    Fixed parameters (6 bytes)
        Authentication Algorithm: Shared key (1)
        Authentication SEQ: 0x0004
        Status code: Successful (0x0000)

Frame 12 (64 bytes on wire, 64 bytes captured)
    Arrival Time: May 15, 2006 06:00:52.464752000
    Time delta from previous packet: 0.000780000 seconds
    Time since reference or first frame: 0.218897000 seconds
    Frame Number: 12
    Packet Length: 64 bytes
    Capture Length: 64 bytes
    Protocols in frame: wlan
IEEE 802.11
    Type/Subtype: Association Request (0)
    Frame Control: 0x0000 (Normal)
        Version: 0
        Type: Management frame (0)
        Subtype: 0
        Flags: 0x0
            DS status: Not leaving DS or network is operating in AD-HOC mode (To DS: 0 From DS:
0) (0x00)
    Duration: 314
    Destination address: Cisco-Li_73:b5:56 (00:14:bf:73:b5:56)
    Source address: GemtekTe_1f:a4:f7 (00:90:4b:1f:a4:f7)
    BSS Id: Cisco-Li_73:b5:56 (00:14:bf:73:b5:56)
    Fragment number: 0
    Sequence number: 2452
IEEE 802.11 wireless LAN management frame
    Fixed parameters (4 bytes)
        Capability Information: 0x0431
        Listen Interval: 0x000a
    Tagged parameters (36 bytes)
```

Figure 5.14 (continued)

who has both the plaintext of the challenge and the encrypted response challenge can use the same XOR operation on them and recover the keystream. The initialization vector (IV) is sent in the 802.11 header of

```
        SSID parameter set: "CorporateAP"
            Tag Number: 0 (SSID parameter set)
            Tag length: 11
            Tag interpretation: CorporateAP
        Supported Rates: 1.0(B) 2.0(B) 5.5(B) 11.0(B) 18.0 24.0 36.0 54.0
            Tag Number: 1 (Supported Rates)
            Tag length: 8
            Tag interpretation: Supported rates: 1.0(B) 2.0(B) 5.5(B) 11.0(B) 18.0 24.0 36.0 54.0
[Mbit/sec]
        Extended Supported Rates: 6.0 9.0 12.0 48.0
            Tag Number: 50 (Extended Supported Rates)
            Tag length: 4
            Tag interpretation: Supported rates: 6.0 9.0 12.0 48.0  [Mbit/sec]
        Vendor Specific: Broadcom
            Tag Number: 221 (Vendor Specific)
            Tag length: 5
            Vendor: Broadcom
            Tag interpretation: Not interpreted
```

Figure 5.14 (continued)

all messages, so it is known to the attacker. Without the need to recover the key, the attacker can use the keystream to produce replies to authentication messages and to generate new messages to be sent on the network.

5.4.5 WPA/WPA2 and IEEE 802.11i

The IEEE started working on a new standard to amend and even replace WEP in terms of wireless network protection. In 2004, the IEEE came up with the 802.11i standard known as WPA2 or RSN (Robust Security Network). In the interim, however, vendors had already started implementing some of the pre-standard recommendations that became known as Wi-Fi Protected Access (WPA). As a result, both WPA (the pre-standard method) and WPA2 (the actual standard) are available on most Wi-Fi devices manufactured recently.

Both WPA and WPA2 can use 802.1x for user authentication and key management but differ in the way they protect user traffic. In addition to 802.1x user authentication and key management, WPA introduced the Temporal Key Integrity Protocol (TKIP), which amends the WEP specification by addressing most known issues with WEP keys and integrity authentication. In brief, TKIP suggests the following amendments:

- The key is always 128 bits in size.
- Initialization vectors are 48 bits in size and are generated in a strictly random fashion.
- A unique key (and therefore — keystream) is generated for every packet. This is achieved by hashing the concatenation of the IV and a base key, and the result is then appended to the IV to be used as the key for RC4 or AES encryption (AES is used in WPA2 only).
- The ICV is no longer calculated using CRC32. Instead, the Michael (MIC) Protocol is used in WPA. As a result, the ICV protects both the header and the user payload.
- A counter (sequence number) is added to WiFi packets to protect from replay attacks. The counter is encrypted.
- Broadcast key rotation is introduced; broadcast traffic can be encrypted with a static key, or the key can be distributed automatically to clients, and changed on a periodic basis. Some vendors, such as Cisco, support dynamic keys using 802.1x and EAP.

WPA2 introduces a new protection mechanism for 802.11 — Counter Mode with CBC-MAC Protocol (CCMP). CCMP is an authenticated encryption algorithm and it provides for both data encryption and data integrity authentication. It is based on the FIPS-compliant AES encryption standard. More information on CCMP is given in [112].

TKIP and CCMP use protection keys (pairwise transient keys — PTKs), derived from a common secret that exists between the client and the access point (pairwise master key — PMK). This common secret PMK is either the product of the user authentication process or a static key. In addition to the PMK and PTK, there is also a group transient key (GTK) that is used for broadcast and multicast communication only. The access point is responsible for generating and disseminating such keys to supplicants to allow them to receive broadcast and multicast messages.

The derivation of PTK from the PMK is known as the WPA four-way handshake. This process is considered preparation for user data protection, and not user authentication. At the same time, the client and the access point need to successfully complete the four-way handshake before they are able to communicate in a secure way using the keys derived from this process.

The four-way handshake negotiation needs the PMK and uses EAPOL-key messages between the client and the access point and works in the following way:

1. The authenticator (access point) generates a random nonce (authenticator nonce — ANonce) and sends it to the client (the supplicant).

2. The client generates a random nonce (supplicant nonce — Snonce) and sends it to the access point. Data integrity for this message is protected with a message integrity code (MIC) calculated over the entire body of the EAPOL message.
3. Both the authenticator and the supplicant use the PMK, the client and server nonces, and other information to calculate a PTK.
4. The authenticator generates a new GTK, encrypts in the PTK, and sends it to the supplicant.
5. The supplicant receives the GTK, generates protection keys from it, and returns a message to the access point that the keys have been installed.

WPA and WPA2 (IEEE 802.11i) offer two modes of operation in terms of authentication: (1) enterprise mode and (2) preshared key mode. The following sections review the two methods.

5.4.6 WPA/WPA2 Enterprise Mode

For enterprise-class applications, the 802.11i standard abandoned the idea of authentication using preshared keys and opted for authentication using user credentials based on 802.1x (EAPOL). Instead of authenticating the user as he associates to the wireless network, WAP APs allow for 802.11 open authentication for the client computer or device, and then request from the already associated wireless port to use 802.1x port access control to authenticate the user. Most authentication mechanisms generate session keys during 802.1x authentication, and they are often used in the authentication process itself. They can be derived from the user password, the random strings encrypted using the peer public key or other information. This key could then be used by WPA to protect traffic by deriving dynamic protection keys. These dynamically generated keys, based on user-provided information, present a major advantage over static machine-based WEP keys, which are the same for all the devices that participate in the particular wireless LAN, or at least for the particular AP. Even if an attacker manages to compromise the dynamic key used to protect WPA traffic, the attacker can only decrypt some of the packets, and only for the particular computer or user whose key was compromised. The attacker will not be able to inject traffic on behalf of other users or devices, nor will he be able to authenticate on their behalf.

More information on 802.1x can be found in section 5.3.

Figure 5.15 provides an overview of the process of authentication, association, and establishment of a protected channel between a wireless client and a wireless access point in a WPA/WPA2 environment. The main phases include the following:

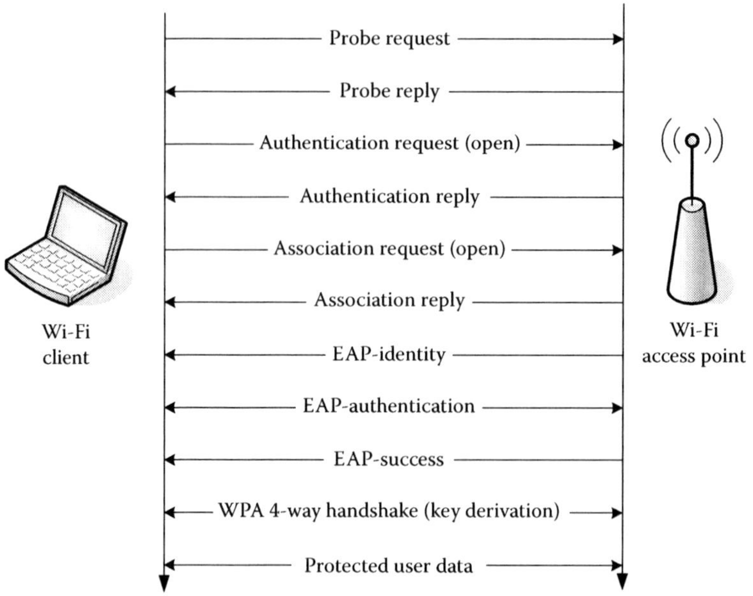

Figure 5.15 WPA/WPA2 enterprise mode authentication and security association.

1. The client actively or passively probes for the wireless access point.
2. The client requests legacy 802.11 Open Authentication and associates with the access point without providing credentials.
3. After client association, the access point commences 802.1x authentication on the port with the wireless client. Authentication takes place using EAPOL-encoded EAP. The actual mechanism that will be used for authentication depends on the preferences and the capabilities of the client and the access point. Upon successful EAP authentication, the client and the access point possess a common session key (in the case of RADIUS, the authentication server will submit this key to the access point, while the client will have it locally).
4. Using the session key from the previous step, the client and the access point execute the WPA four-way handshake protocol and derive actual protection keys from the session key. The 802.1x session key is used as a pairwise master key for the four-way handshake process.
5. The client and the access point start protecting communication using the keys derived in the previous step and WPA (TKIP/Michael) or WPA2 (CCMP-AES) data protection.

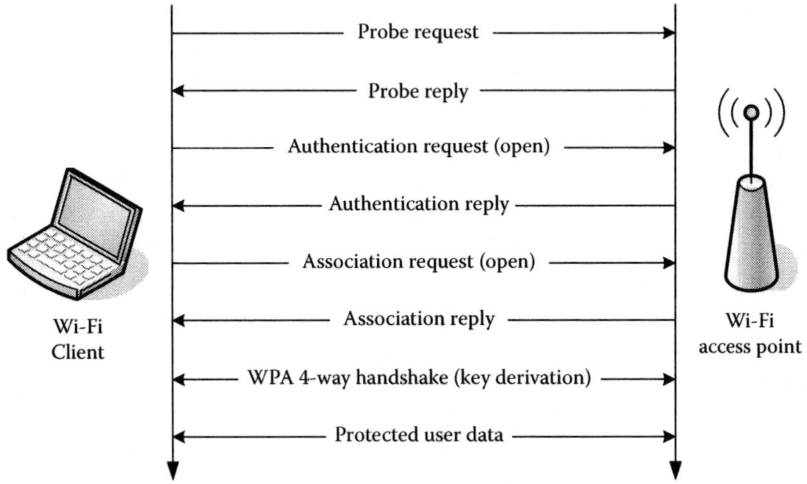

Figure 5.16 WPA-preshared key (WPA-PSK) security association.

5.4.7 WPA/WPA2 Preshared Key Mode (WPA-PSK)

To be able to address the needs of home and small office users who are not likely to invest in complex authentication solutions, the WPA/WPA2 standard retained the WEP concept of using preshared keys. This mode of operation is known as WPA/WPA2 Preshared Key (WPA-PSK). The WPA-PSK mode is not compatible with WEP but is similar in terms of requirements that the client and the access point share a common secret that is used to authenticate client association with the access point, as well as to protect user data by means of traffic encryption and data integrity authentication. The key can be up to 63 bytes in length.

Figure 5.16 shows the security association process when WPA-PSK is used.

WPA-PSK does not provide for actual user authentication; it only ensures that unauthenticated users cannot encrypt and decrypt messages and therefore cannot sniff or communicate on the wireless LAN. The following steps outline the way that a WPA-PSK security association is established.

1. The client actively or passively probes for the access point.
2. The client requests legacy 802.11 open authentication and associates with the access point without providing credentials.
3. Using the preshared key, the client and the access point execute the WPA four-way handshake protocol and derive actual protection keys from the session key. The preshared key is used as a pairwise master key (PMK) for the four-way handshake process.

4. The client and the access point start protecting communication using the keys derived in the previous step, and WPA (TKIP/Michael) or WPA2 (CCMP-AES) data protection.

Due to the fact that the preshared key is used as a pairwise master key in the four-way handshake process, in order to generate protection keys, if the WPA PSK client does not know the correct preshared key, it cannot derive protection keys, and will not be able to decrypt received traffic — neither will it be able to send traffic. This is not a user authentication protocol, yet to a certain extent protects the network from casual attackers.

The problem with WPA-PSK is that unlike WPA Enterprise, where the key is dynamic, WPA-PSK uses a static preshared key. Considering the fact that this key is used to derive keys in the four-way handshake process, the protection that WPA-PSK can provide for user data depends on the strength of user passwords. Dictionary and brute force attacks can easily compromise WPA-PSK protection if the user uses a dictionary word as the preshared key, or if the key is cryptographically weak. Thus, WPA-PSK is generally avoided in enterprise environments.

5.5 IPSec, IKE, and VPN Client Authentication

IPSec is a popular security solution for peer authentication and protection of network traffic from eavesdropping and unauthorized modification while in transit on the network. It allows peers to communicate in a secure fashion, transparently from an application point of view. Most IPSec implementations behave like an extension to the IP layer, and upper layer protocols do not need to understand that there is traffic protection at the network layer.

The IPSec protocol can encrypt network traffic and provide for data integrity authentication. However, IPSec by itself does not provide for peer or user authentication. Other protocols, such as IKE/ISAKMP, provide for peer authentication, and in some non-standard implementations, for user authentication. This section discusses IPSec/IKE peer and user authentication protocols.

5.5.1 IKE Peer Authentication

The Internet Key Exchange (IKE) Protocol provides for peer authentication and key management. IKE v1 is defined in RFC 2409 (see [114]). IKE v2 is defined in RFC 4306 (see [115]) but is not widely implemented at the time of this writing.

IKE is a hybrid protocol that combines a number of other protocols and algorithms. IKE builds upon the foundation of the ISAKMP Protocol and provides for peer authentication and key exchange. The actual key exchange mechanisms used by IKE include portions of the Oakley Protocol and portions of the SKEME Protocol.

IKE can be used for peer authentication; typically, this allows for authentication between two computers or devices but not for authentication between users and applications working on these computers or devices. IPSec is an example of a protocol that uses IKE for peer authentication, and is virtually the only popular protocol that uses IKE at this time.

IKE builds protected channels based on sets of cryptographic transformations that include encryption algorithms (such as 3DES and AES), hash algorithms (such as MD5 and SHA-1), authentication method (such as certificates or preshared keys), Diffie-Hellman group (such as 1 or 2), and key duration (seconds or volume of traffic). VPN clients and servers can negotiate a user authentication protocol to be used by XAUTH authentication (see subsection 5.5.2). Each peer has a local policy that defines combinations of the above IKE cryptographic transformations, assigns priorities (order of preference) to them, and defines which of them will be considered secure and the peer will accept to use them in an IKE security association. Other important parameters are peer identities that define the name by which the parties are known to each other. The identity can be an IP address; a hostname; or in some cases such as VPN user authentication, a group name for a VPN group, defined on the VPN server or the authentication server.

The IKE header contains the Initiator Cookie and the Responder Cookie attributes. These are unique 8-byte values generated by both the party initiating the IKE security association and the party responding to the IKE security association. These values are unique for each security association and are used by both parties to identify the security association on their respective end. The examples in this chapter assume that A is the initiator (client) of the IKE security association, and B is the responder (server).

IKE supports two main types of credentials: (1) certificates and (2) preshared keys. Some implementations (Windows 2000 and later) also allow for Kerberos authentication. Once the communicating parties have been authenticated, IKE builds a security association between them, which is a secure channel where keys for other protocols (such as IPSec) can be exchanged, configuration settings for VPN clients can be provided, and user authentication based on XAUTH can take place.

5.5.1.1 IKE and IPSec Phases

The initial IKE security association takes place using the IKE main mode or aggressive mode, and is known as IKE Phase 1. At this phase, peer

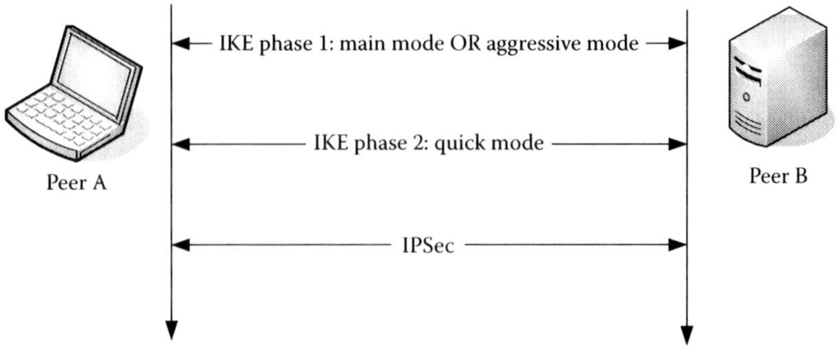

Figure 5.17 Overview of IKE and IPSec.

authentication, and potentially peer configuration as well as user (XAUTH) authentication, take place. Main mode is typically preferred as the more secure approach to performing IKE Phase 1. Main mode requires more steps (three in each direction for peer authentication only), and basically implements one action at a step. Aggressive mode is considered less secure (primarily because some mechanisms disclose the identity of the authenticating peers — see below), and takes fewer steps (three in both directions) to complete because it incorporates more than one message in one step (see Figure 5.17).

IKE Phase 2 is known as Quick Mode and is used to negotiate protection keys for IPSec. Protocols such as IPSec can then use QuickMode to quickly renegotiate keys at predetermined time intervals, or volumes of traffic. IPSec typically follows IKE Phase 2 and protects traffic using the keys provided by IKE Phase 2 (Quick Mode).

To protect the peer authentication process, as well as information within the security association, IKE uses encryption and hash algorithms. It also generates a master key and derives encryption, authentication, and other keys from it.

IKE peer authentication is a powerful and reliable approach to authenticating communicating peers. There are reports of security flaws in particular vendor implementations but, in general, IKE peer authentication is still considered very secure.

Deriving the Master Key

A pseudo-random function (**prf**) can be negotiated by the peers as part of Phase 1 negotiation. If no PRF is negotiated, the HMAC version of the negotiated hashing algorithm is used.

The use of certificates and preshared keys results in four main modes for peer authentication:

1. *Preshared key authentication.* As the name implies, this mechanism uses the preshared key used by the communicating peers to authenticate each peer to the other. A master key for this authentication method is computed using the following formula:
   SKEYID = prf(PreSharedKey, NONCE_A | NONCE_B)
2. *Signature-based authentication.* This mechanism utilizes certificates and signs specific parameters exchanged between peers to authenticate. A master key for this authentication method is computed using the following formula:
   SKEYID = prf(NONCE_A | NONCE_B, DH_SharedSecret)
3. *Public key authentication method 1.* This mechanism is based on certificates and asymmetric encryption of specific parameters exchanged between peers. A master key for this authentication method is calculated using the following formula:
   SKEYID = prf(hash(NONCE_A | NONCE_B), Cookie_A | Cookie_B)
4. *Public Key authentication method 2.* This mechanism is based on certificates, asymmetric and symmetric encryption of parameters exchanged between the peers. A master key for this authentication method is calculated using the following formula:
   SKEYID = prf(hash(NONCE_A | NONCE_B), Cookie_A | Cookie_B)

IKE Message Encryption

Once the master key has been determined, IKE peers generate specific session keys using the following formula:

SKEYID_d = prf(SKEYID, DH_SharedSecret
| Cookie_A | Cookie_B | 0)

SKEYID_a = prf(SKEYID, SKEYID_d | DH_SharedSecret
| Cookie_A | Cookie_B | 1)

SKEYID_e = prf(SKEYID, SKEYID_a | DH_SharedSecret
| Cookie_A | Cookie_B | 2)

SKEYID_e is used during Phases 1 and 2. **SKEYID_a** and **SKEYID_d** are used in Phase 2 only and are therefore not interesting from a user authentication perspective.

If the selected encryption algorithm requires longer keys, key expansion can be used: the **SKEYID_e** value can be fed into the **PRF** algorithm and **SKEYID_e** can be concatenated with the result from **PRF**. This can be repeated as many times as required; then the highest-order bits can be used to form a new **SKEYID_e** value.

If the encryption method leverages an initial vector (IV), it is derived from the concatenation of the Diffie-Hellman public keys:

IV = HASH(DH_Public_A | DH_Public_B)

IKE Message Integrity Authentication and Peer Authentication

The following hash functions are also defined, and they are used to protect IKE message integrity and for peer authentication:

HASH_A = prf(SKEYID, DH_Public_A | DH_Public_B
| Cookie_A | Cookie_B | SAi_b | ID_A)

HASH_B = prf(SKEYID, DH_Public_B | DH_Public_A
| Cookie_B | Cookie_A | SAi_b | ID_B)

IKE Phase 1, as well as Phase 2 (Quick Mode), encrypt messages. Encryption is performed using the negotiated encryption algorithm in the **SKEYID_e** key.

5.5.1.2 Preshared Key Authentication

With preshared key authentication, communicating peers need to share the same key (password), known only to them. No other party should know the secret communications key (XAUTH authentication somewhat changes this idea — see below). Typically, administrators are responsible for generating a secret key and manually configuring communicating parties to use this key to authenticate each other.

To authenticate peers in *main mode* using preshared keys (Figure 5.18), IKE first allows peers to negotiate a transformation for the security association; this includes parameters such as encryption algorithm, hashing algorithm, peer authentication method, and, potentially, user authentication method (XAUTH). Both parties also generate Diffie-Hellman keypairs, then send the key exchange (DH public key) and nonce, and calculate protection keys using Diffie-Hellman. As a final step, both parties authenticate each other by calculating a hash of the nonce provided by the remote peer. The hashes exchanged by authenticating peers are further encrypted in the **SKEYID_e** protection key.

It is important to note that the last two packets of the Main Mode exchange for Pre-shared key authentication are encrypted. That is when communicating parties exchange their identities. This allows for identity

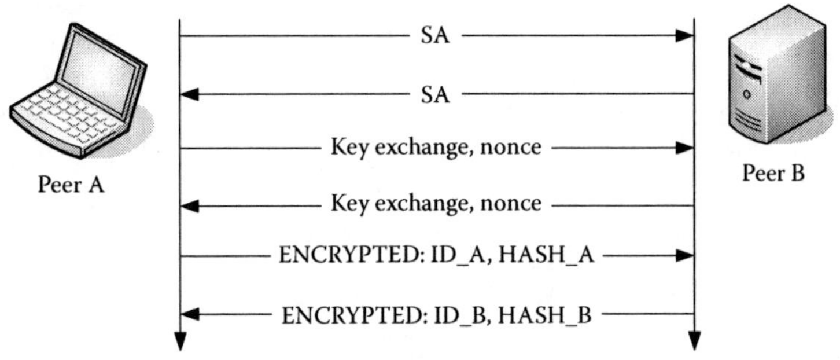

Figure 5.18 IKE preshared key, main mode.

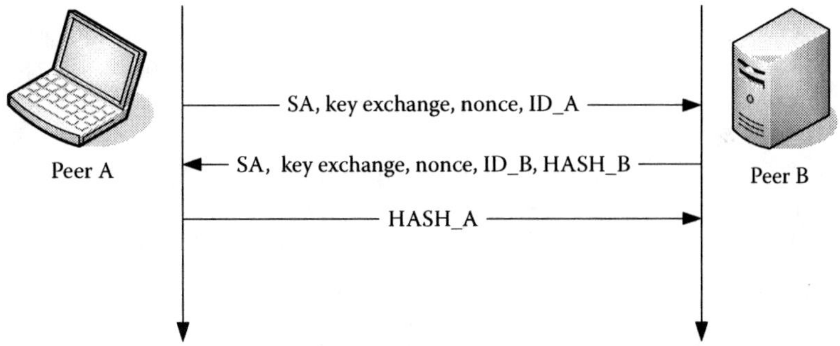

Figure 5.19 IKE preshared key, aggressive mode.

protection — an attacker listening on the wire cannot determine who the authenticating parties are; neither can he spoof their identity easily.

Aggressive mode authentication using preshared keys is shown in Figure 5.19. Authentication is similar to main mode but uses fewer steps. It is important to note that with aggressive mode in this instance, there is no packet encryption at phase 1. Therefore, user identities exchanged in the second and third packets are transferred in cleartext over the network.

5.5.1.3 IKE Signature-Based Authentication

Signature-based authentication is one of the three certificate-based authentication methods. As with other certificate-based methods, this type of authentication requires that the client and the server have private keys and corresponding certificates (public keys).

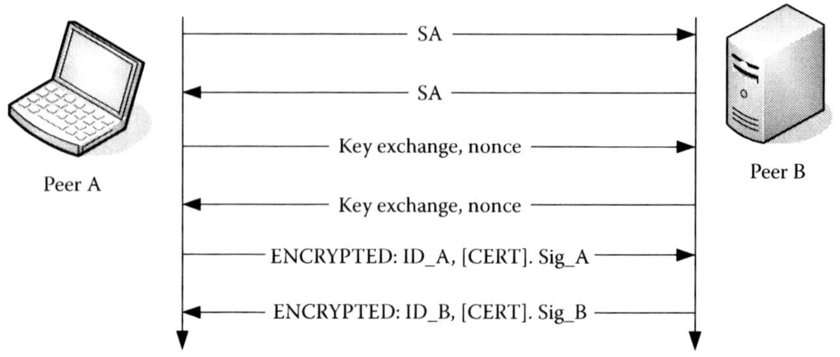

Figure 5.20 IKE signature-based authentication, main mode.

To perform main mode signature-based authentication (Figure 5.20), communicating peers first negotiate a Security Association Transformation. Then they use Diffie-Hellman and exchange DH public keys (key exchange) and nonces. Diffie-Hellman is used on both sides to generate protection keys. Finally, each peer generates a signature on the HASH_A and HASH_B value, respectively, using the negotiated signature or hashing algorithm. The last two packets are sent encrypted in the negotiated encryption algorithm with the **SKEYID_e** key as the key.

The signature keys are calculated using the following formulae:

$$Sig\_A = PRF(SKEYID, HASH\_A)$$

$$Sig\_B = PRF(SKEYID, HASH\_B)$$

The authentication model is based on the fact that the initiator (client) can generate the **Sig_A** octet sequence and the server can calculate the same hash value and compare the results. In a similar fashion, the server can generate **Sig_B** and the client can validate the result, which would prove the identity of the server.

Aggressive mode is similar to main mode but uses fewer packets, and apparently, no encryption is applied to any Phase 1 packets in this mode (Figure 5.21).

5.5.1.4 IKE Public Key Authentication, Option 1

IKE public key authentication, option 1, is one of the supported certificate authentication methods. It is important to note that with this authentication mechanism, peer identity is protected in both main mode (Figure 5.22) and aggressive mode (Figure 5.23). This is because peer authenticity is, by default, encrypted with the recipient's public key.

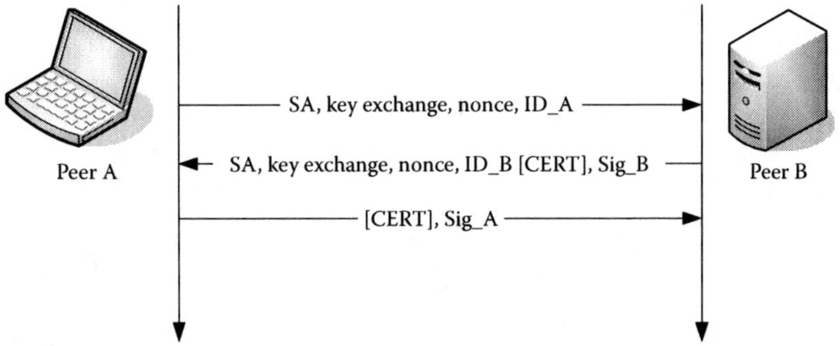

Figure 5.21 IKE signature-based authentication, aggressive mode.

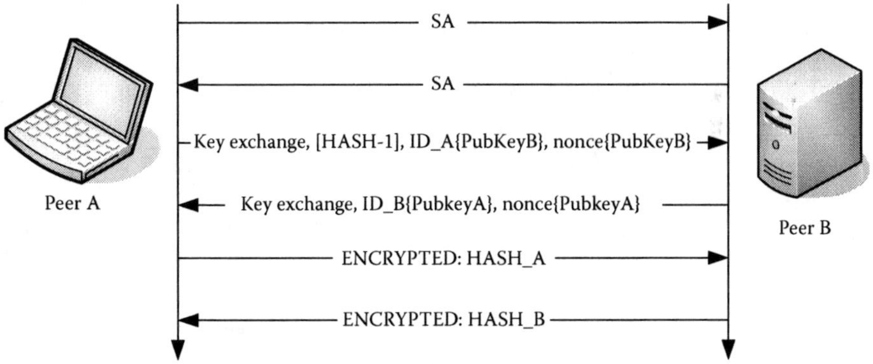

Figure 5.22 IKE public key base, option 1, main mode.

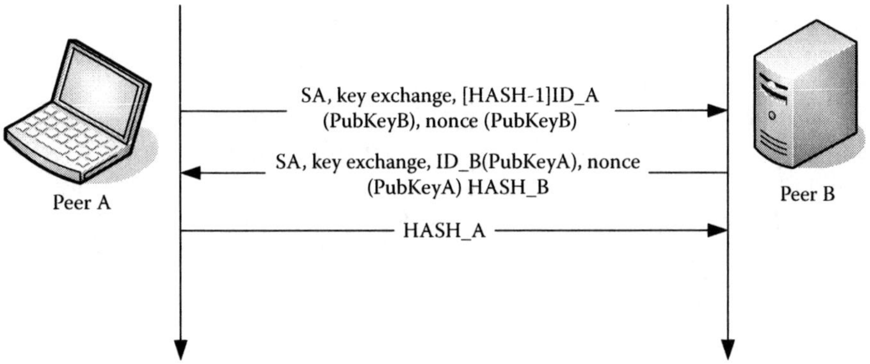

Figure 5.23 IKE public key based, option 1, aggressive mode.

As with other key exchanges, IKE first negotiates an SA between communicating parties. Then peers exchange the usual Diffie-Hellman public keys (key exchange — from both A and B). Included in the payload is also a nonce (from both A and B) that is encrypted in B's public key, and user identity is encrypted in B's public key as well. B needs to decrypt A's identity and other information from the packet received from A, and it uses its private key. Finally, both parties calculate a shared secret using Diffie-Hellman and exchange it encrypted in the current encryption algorithm. Hashes are additionally protected by a separate encryption method.

HASH-1 plays and important role here as well. In some cases, Peers A and B can have more than one certificate. It may then not be predictable as to which certificate the remote peer would choose to use. Therefore, when Peer A decides which certificate it wants to use, it needs to generate a hash for the selected certificate and send it along with the other information. When Peer B receives the hash, it can generate similar hashes for its own certificates and compare the hashes with the request from Peer A. Peer B can then choose a particular certificate that matches the requested hash, and start encrypting and decrypting contents of received packets in the private key corresponding to that certificate.

Aggressive mode (Figure 5.23) is similar to main mode but does not involve symmetric encryption for the last two steps.

It is important to note that this authentication method protects peer identity in both main mode and aggressive mode. The reason for this is that identity information is encrypted in the public key (certificate) of the responder (and the initiator — in the reverse direction), and can only be decrypted using the recipient's private key.

5.5.1.5 IKE Public Key Authentication, Option 2

IKE Public Key Authentication, option 1, is a very secure authentication mechanism but it uses public keys to encrypt IKE traffic, and these keys are typically long (1024 to 2048 bits). This results in more computing resources required to carry out the encryption.

IKE Public Key Authentication, option 2, is a simplified approach, yet similar to option 1, however. With option 2, only two public key encryption operations are required, and a couple of symmetric key encryption operations are performed as well (Figure 5.24).

To generate symmetric keys for encryption, parties perform the following calculation:

NONCE_E_A = prf(NONCE_A, COOKIE_A)

NONCE_E_B = prf(NONCE_B, COOKIE_B)

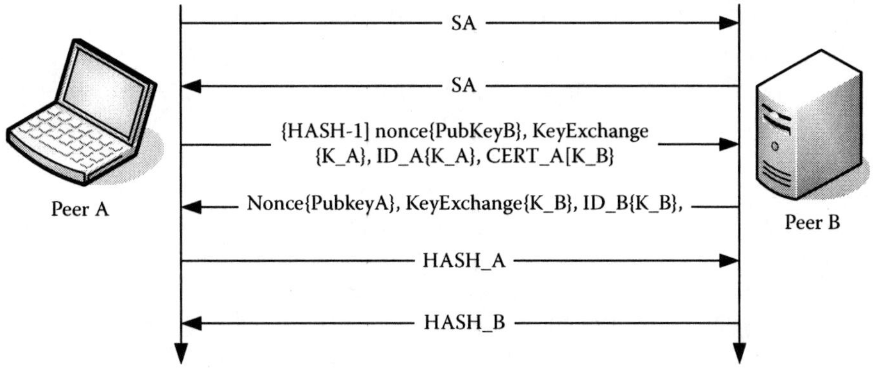

Figure 5.24 Public key authentication, option 2, main mode.

Then, key expansion can be used to generate a symmetric encryption key, K, of appropriate length:

K_A = K1 | K2 | K3, where

K1 = prf(NONCE_E_A, 0)

K2 = prf(NONCE_E_A, K1)

K3 = prf(NONCE_E_A, K2)

The same is performed at Peer B as well:

K_B = K1 | K2 | K3, where

K1 = prf(NONCE_E_B, 0)

K2 = prf(NONCE_E_B, K1)

K3 = prf(NONCE_E_B, K2)

If an initial vector (IV) is used by the encryption algorithm, it is first set to zero and then derived from the encryption process using a feedback function.

With public key authentication, option 2, once the security associations have been established, the peers exchange messages where the nonce generated by Peer A or Peer B is a dynamic value, and is encrypted in B's public key. Other parameters, such as the Diffie-Hellman key exchange, peer identity, and certificates, are encrypted using a symmetric key.

5.5.2 IKE XAUTH Authentication and VPN Clients

The Internet is now widely available and the scope of services that it can be used for is large. Virtual private networks (VPNs) over the Internet allow communicating parties to use the Internet as if it were a direct physical connection between them, and then tunnel all the traffic between them in a secure manner, providing data-link layer connectivity. All the other OSI layers sit on top of the VPN channel and work as if it were a physical connection attached between the VPN client and server.

Vendors of VPN clients and servers take different approaches and use different VPN technologies. Some use protocols such as the Point-to-Point Tunneling Protocol (PPTP) and the Layer 2 Tunneling Protocol (L2TP) with PPP packets for the tunnel between the client and the server. They also utilize PPP authentication on top of the PPP, as discussed in subsection 5.2.2. Microsoft supports user authentication for PPTP and L2TP connectivity only, and peer authentication for IPSec.

Most VPN vendors, however, build their VPN solutions around the concept of IPSec. Traffic between the client and the server is encapsulated within an IPSec tunnel, and is protected using IPSec mechanisms — which happens to be very convenient. Unfortunately, the current IPSec specification is more orientated toward communication between specific devices or servers and only provides for peer authentication using a fixed and closed scope of credentials (passwords and certificates). It lacks the flexibility of PPP in terms of user authentication, wherein, in addition to the legacy PAP, CHAP, and MS-CHAP authentication mechanisms, EAP provides an entirely new scope of authentication methods, including password based, certificate based, one-time passwords, etc. Furthermore, PPP is a very flexible protocol and it provides for mechanisms whereby the server and the client can negotiate the use of specific network layer parameters. For example, using the Network Control Protocol (NCP) of PPP, the server can provide the client with an IP address that the client can use for the duration of the session, as well as with a DNS server, NetBIOS name server and other configuration options that can be dynamically made available to the client as he connects to the network using PPP. By definition, IPSec does not provide for an NCP-like protocol or behavior.

To work around these limitations, VPN vendors decided to extend the IPSec specification. First, they defined an extension to IKE known as IPSec Configuration Mode (MODECFG). Despite the name, MODECFG is actually used during IKE Phase 1 rather than actual IPSec. MODECFG can be used to achieve the same goal as PPP NCP; it can dynamically negotiate network and higher-layer parameters between the VPN client and the VPN server during the IKE negotiation. MODECFG is a rejected Internet draft that can be found in [117]. Despite that fact that it has been rejected, it is still used by many vendors.

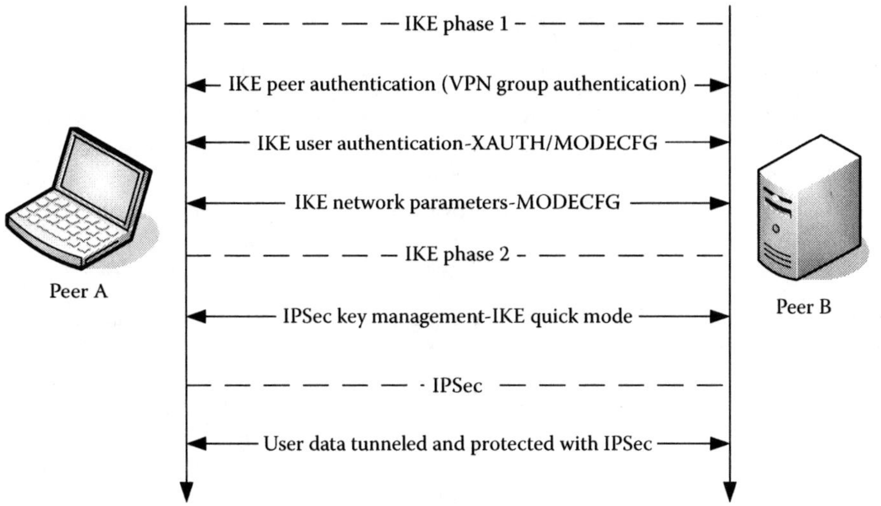

Figure 5.25 IPSec/IKE peer and user authentication.

The second extension to IKE that VPN vendors came up with was the concept of user authentication in addition to peer authentication on the IPSec tunnel (Figure 5.25). The mechanism used to accomplish this is known as IKE Extended Authentication (XAUTH), and it runs on top of MODECFG. For reasons discussed later in this chapter, the draft proposing XAUTH was rejected but the mechanisms described in it are still widely used by many vendors. The draft can be found in [118].

To provide for peer authentication as required by the IPSec standard, VPN vendors implement the so-called group authentication. A group is a set of user accounts defined on the VPN concentrator or external authentication server. VPN users are added to this group. The group is assigned a password, or a certificate, or both. The group is then used as the peer name (peer identity) in IKE peer authentication. Instead of using their IP address as the identity, VPN clients and servers use the group name as a string to identify themselves as peers, and they use the group password or certificate for peer authentication. Apparently with this approach, a group of users (all the users that belong to the VPN group) can authenticate to the VPN concentrator; this happens to be different from the IPSec recommendation wherein peer authentication is used to authenticate two — and only two — communicating parties: the two IPSec peers.

Once the peers have been authenticated using standard IKE and the group password or certificate, a VPN client and a VPN server will typically use XAUTH for user-level authentication. If authentication is successful, the VPN client and VPN server proceed with the negotiation of network layer parameters using MODECFG, then IKE Phase 2 (Quick Mode) and

Table 5.8 MODECFG/XAUTH Messages

Message Type	*MODECFG*	*XAUTH*
ISAKMP_CFG_REQUEST	Used in Pull mode, and typically by the client to request configuration information from the server	The VPN server sends this message to the VPN client to request XAUTH authentication or additional authentication information
ISAKMP_CFG_REPLY	Used in Pull mode with ISAKMP_CFG_REQUEST to reply to a request for configuration with specific configuration parameters	The VPN client uses this message type to submit authentication credentials to the VPN server; this works in conjunction with a ISAKMP_CFG_REQUEST from the server
ISAKMP_CFG_SET	Used in Push mode (typically by the server) to send configuration parameters to the remote party (typically the client)	The VPN server uses this message type to inform the VPN client of the state of the authentication
ISAKMP_CFG_ACK	Used in Push mode along with ISAKMP_CFG_SET (typically by the client) to acknowledge the reception of configuration parameters	The VPN client uses this message to inform the VPN server that it has received the authentication result

the actual IPSec tunnel between them. If XAUTH authentication fails, the client and the server tear down the connection and do not progress through the following phases of IKE and IPSec.

The MODECFG specification defines that IKE Configuration Mode packets should be carried as IKE type 14 attributes. MODECFG further defines the following messages between peers negotiating configuration parameters — see Table 5.8.

In the same way that MODECFG carries attributes such as client or DNS server IP address, it can be used to carry XAUTH messages with authentication attributes. Table 5.9 outlines some of the XAUTH parameters.

Table 5.9 XAUTH Authentication Attributes

Attribute ID	*Attribute Name*	*Description*
16520	XAUTH-TYPE	Type of authentication: can be generic, or one time passwords, or RADIUS-CHAP
16521	XAUTH-USER-NAME	The username or other user identifier
16522	XAUTH-USER-PASSWORD	The user password
16523	XAUTH-PASSCODE	The passcode if a token card is used
16524	XAUTH-MESSAGE	A message that the VPN client will display to the user
16525	XAUTH-CHALLENGE	Challenge string used by the client to calculate a response in a challenge-response authentication method
16526	XAUTH-DOMAIN	The domain of authentication
16527	XAUTH-STATUS	Authentication status: Success (Ok) or Failure
16528	XAUTH-NEXT-PIN	A request to choose a new PIN
16529	XAUTH-ANSWER	User input forwarded to the VPN server

It is important to note that MODECFG and XAUTH take place during IKE phase 1. All the messages are encrypted in a set of keys negotiated in the beginning of IKE Phase 1. The protection strength for MODECFG and XAUTH parameters is therefore the same as the protection for IPSec session keys, negotiated during the Quick Mode phase, which are protected by the same set of IKE Phase 1 keys.

XAUTH can leverage different authentication schemes. Which specific scheme will be used depends on the client and server capabilities, as well as on the SA negotiation process (the first two packets of SA negotiation) where the XAUTH authentication mechanism is negotiated as one of the IKE Security Policy parameters.

For the purposes of SA negotiation, an Internet Draft [118] defines the following authentication mechanisms (Table 5.10).

Figure 5.26 and Figure 5.27 show the simple password authentication and the RADIUS-CHAP authentication mechanisms, respectively.

Figure 5.28 shows the IPSec/XAUTH authentication process.

Table 5.10 XAUTH Authentication Mechanisms

ID	*Authentication Mechanism Name*	*Description*	*Initiated By*
65001	XAUTHInitPreShared	Preshared key authentication	Initiator
65002	XAUTHRespPreShared	Preshared key authentication	Responder
65003	XAUTHInitDSS	Signature-based authentication with DSS	Initiator
65004	XAUTHRespDSS	Signature-based authentication with DSS	Responder
65005	XAUTHInitRSA	Signature-based authentication with RSA	Initiator
65006	XAUTHRespRSA	Signature-based authentication with RSA	Responder
65007	XAUTHInitRSAEncryption	Encryption-based RSA authentication	Initiator
65008	XAUTHRespRSAEncryption	Encryption-based RSA authentication	Responder
65009	XAUTHInitRSARevised Encryption	Revised encryption-based RSA authentication	Initiator

1. The client and server use IPSec aggressive mode (this may differ for different clients) to negotiate an ISAKMP Phase 1 SA (Frames 1 to 3 in Figure 5.28). It is important to note that due to the fact that user authentication is set to work in aggressive mode and uses a preshared key, the identity of the client and the server is exposed in cleartext in Frames 1 and 2, respectively, in Figure 5.28.
2. At the end of ISAKMP Phase 1, the client and server use configuration mode to provide the client with IP-related configuration parameters and to perform XAUTH authentication. Information is encrypted at this stage (see Frames 5 and 6 in Figure 5.28).
3. Once the user has been authenticated, he is connected to the VPN server at the data-link layer and can use network services on the remote network.

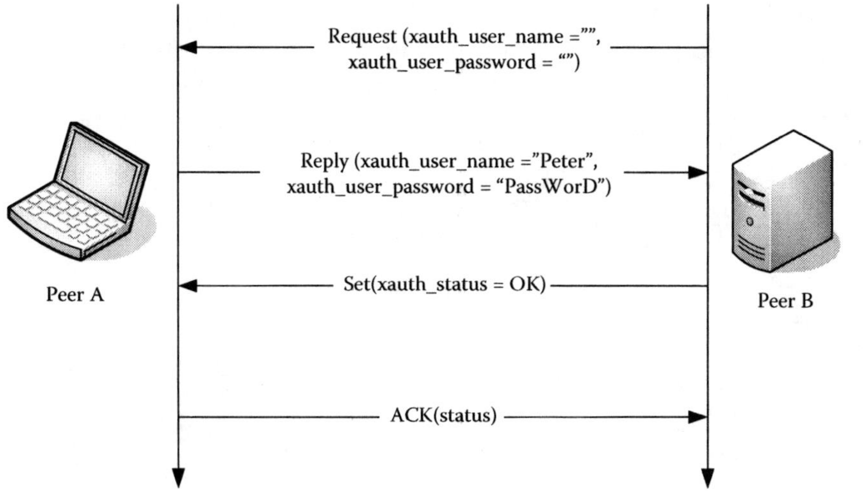

Figure 5.26 XAUTH simple authentication.

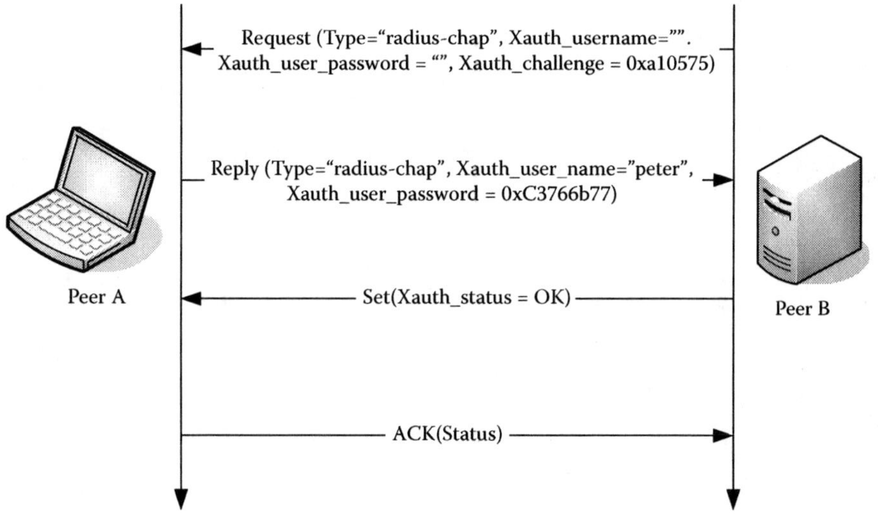

Figure 5.27 XAUTH CHAP authentication.

Despite the level of protection for XAUTH authentication being equivalent to that of IPSec session keys, security researchers on the Internet consider XAUTH authentication weak (see [116]). The IETF also rejected the proposed standard for XAUTH.

```
Frame 1 (913 bytes on wire, 913 bytes captured)
Ethernet II, Src: GemtekTe_1f:a4:f7 (00:90:4b:1f:a4:f7), Dst: Cisco_7b:48:f4 (00:0d:ed:7b:48:f4)
Internet Protocol, Src: 192.168.2.65 (192.168.2.65), Dst: 192.168.2.254 (192.168.2.254)
User Datagram Protocol, Src Port: isakmp (500), Dst Port: isakmp (500)
Internet Security Association and Key Management Protocol
    Initiator cookie: 0xAAE8669D0551E4D3
    Responder cookie: 0x0000000000000000
    Next payload: Security Association (1)
    Version: 1.0
    Exchange type: Aggressive (4)
    Flags
    Message ID: 0x00000000
    Length: 855
    Security Association payload
        Next payload: Key Exchange (4)
        Length: 556
        Domain of interpretation: IPSEC (1)
        Situation: IDENTITY (1)
        Proposal payload # 1
            Next payload: NONE (0)
            Length: 544
            Proposal number: 1
            Protocol ID: ISAKMP (1)
            SPI size: 0
            Number of transforms: 14
            Transform payload # 1
                Next payload: Transform (3)
                Length: 40
                Transform number: 1
                Transform ID: KEY_IKE (1)
                Encryption-Algorithm (1): AES-CBC (7)
                Hash-Algorithm (2): SHA (2)
                Group-Description (4): Alternate 1024-bit MODP group (2)
                Authentication-Method (3): XAUTHInitPreShared (65001)
                Life-Type (11): Seconds (1)
                Life-Duration (12): Duration-Value (2147483)
```

Figure 5.28 IPSec-XAUTH.cap: IPSec VPN user authentication.

```
        Key-Length (14): Key-Length (256)
    Transform payload # 2
        Next payload: Transform (3)
        Length: 40
        Transform number: 2
        Transform ID: KEY_IKE (1)
        Encryption-Algorithm (1): AES-CBC (7)
        Hash-Algorithm (2): MD5 (1)
        Group-Description (4): Alternate 1024-bit MODP group (2)
        Authentication-Method (3): XAUTHInitPreShared (65001)
        Life-Type (11): Seconds (1)
        Life-Duration (12): Duration-Value (2147483)
        Key-Length (14): Key-Length (256)
    Transform payload # 3
        Next payload: Transform (3)
        Length: 40
        Transform number: 3
        Transform ID: KEY_IKE (1)
        Encryption-Algorithm (1): AES-CBC (7)
        Hash-Algorithm (2): SHA (2)
        Group-Description (4): Alternate 1024-bit MODP group (2)
        Authentication-Method (3): PSK (1)
        Life-Type (11): Seconds (1)
        Life-Duration (12): Duration-Value (2147483)
        Key-Length (14): Key-Length (256)
    Transform payload # 4
        Next payload: Transform (3)
        Length: 40
        Transform number: 4
        Transform ID: KEY_IKE (1)
        Encryption-Algorithm (1): AES-CBC (7)
        Hash-Algorithm (2): MD5 (1)
        Group-Description (4): Alternate 1024-bit MODP group (2)
        Authentication-Method (3): PSK (1)
        Life-Type (11): Seconds (1)
        Life-Duration (12): Duration-Value (2147483)
```

Figure 5.28 (continued)

```
            Key-Length (14): Key-Length (256)
        Transform payload # 5
            Next payload: Transform (3)
            Length: 40
            Transform number: 5
            Transform ID: KEY_IKE (1)
            Encryption-Algorithm (1): AES-CBC (7)
            Hash-Algorithm (2): SHA (2)
            Group-Description (4): Alternate 1024-bit MODP group (2)
            Authentication-Method (3): XAUTHInitPreShared (65001)
            Life-Type (11): Seconds (1)
            Life-Duration (12): Duration-Value (2147483)
            Key-Length (14): Key-Length (128)
        Transform payload # 6
            Next payload: Transform (3)
            Length: 40
            Transform number: 6
            Transform ID: KEY_IKE (1)
            Encryption-Algorithm (1): AES-CBC (7)
            Hash-Algorithm (2): MD5 (1)
            Group-Description (4): Alternate 1024-bit MODP group (2)
            Authentication-Method (3): XAUTHInitPreShared (65001)
            Life-Type (11): Seconds (1)
            Life-Duration (12): Duration-Value (2147483)
            Key-Length (14): Key-Length (128)
        Transform payload # 7
            Next payload: Transform (3)
            Length: 40
            Transform number: 7
            Transform ID: KEY_IKE (1)
            Encryption-Algorithm (1): AES-CBC (7)
            Hash-Algorithm (2): SHA (2)
            Group-Description (4): Alternate 1024-bit MODP group (2)
            Authentication-Method (3): PSK (1)
            Life-Type (11): Seconds (1)
            Life-Duration (12): Duration-Value (2147483)
```

Figure 5.28 (continued)

```
        Key-Length (14): Key-Length (128)
    Transform payload # 8
        Next payload: Transform (3)
        Length: 40
        Transform number: 8
        Transform ID: KEY_IKE (1)
        Encryption-Algorithm (1): AES-CBC (7)
        Hash-Algorithm (2): MD5 (1)
        Group-Description (4): Alternate 1024-bit MODP group (2)
        Authentication-Method (3): PSK (1)
        Life-Type (11): Seconds (1)
        Life-Duration (12): Duration-Value (2147483)
        Key-Length (14): Key-Length (128)
    Transform payload # 9
        Next payload: Transform (3)
        Length: 36
        Transform number: 9
        Transform ID: KEY_IKE (1)
        Encryption-Algorithm (1): 3DES-CBC (5)
        Hash-Algorithm (2): SHA (2)
        Group-Description (4): Alternate 1024-bit MODP group (2)
        Authentication-Method (3): XAUTHInitPreShared (65001)
        Life-Type (11): Seconds (1)
        Life-Duration (12): Duration-Value (2147483)
    Transform payload # 10
        Next payload: Transform (3)
        Length: 36
        Transform number: 10
        Transform ID: KEY_IKE (1)
        Encryption-Algorithm (1): 3DES-CBC (5)
        Hash-Algorithm (2): MD5 (1)
        Group-Description (4): Alternate 1024-bit MODP group (2)
        Authentication-Method (3): XAUTHInitPreShared (65001)
        Life-Type (11): Seconds (1)
        Life-Duration (12): Duration-Value (2147483)
    Transform payload # 11
```

Figure 5.28 (continued)

```
        Next payload: Transform (3)
        Length: 36
        Transform number: 11
        Transform ID: KEY_IKE (1)
        Encryption-Algorithm (1): 3DES-CBC (5)
        Hash-Algorithm (2): SHA (2)
        Group-Description (4): Alternate 1024-bit MODP group (2)
        Authentication-Method (3): PSK (1)
        Life-Type (11): Seconds (1)
        Life-Duration (12): Duration-Value (2147483)
    Transform payload # 12
        Next payload: Transform (3)
        Length: 36
        Transform number: 12
        Transform ID: KEY_IKE (1)
        Encryption-Algorithm (1): 3DES-CBC (5)
        Hash-Algorithm (2): MD5 (1)
        Group-Description (4): Alternate 1024-bit MODP group (2)
        Authentication-Method (3): PSK (1)
        Life-Type (11): Seconds (1)
        Life-Duration (12): Duration-Value (2147483)
    Transform payload # 13
        Next payload: Transform (3)
        Length: 36
        Transform number: 13
        Transform ID: KEY_IKE (1)
        Encryption-Algorithm (1): DES-CBC (1)
        Hash-Algorithm (2): MD5 (1)
        Group-Description (4): Alternate 1024-bit MODP group (2)
        Authentication-Method (3): XAUTHInitPreShared (65001)
        Life-Type (11): Seconds (1)
        Life-Duration (12): Duration-Value (2147483)
    Transform payload # 14
        Next payload: NONE (0)
        Length: 36
        Transform number: 14
```

Figure 5.28 (continued)

```
            Transform ID: KEY_IKE (1)
            Encryption-Algorithm (1): DES-CBC (1)
            Hash-Algorithm (2): MD5 (1)
            Group-Description (4): Alternate 1024-bit MODP group (2)
            Authentication-Method (3): PSK (1)
            Life-Type (11): Seconds (1)
            Life-Duration (12): Duration-Value (2147483)
    Key Exchange payload
    Nonce payload
    Identification payload
        Next payload: Vendor ID (13)
        Length: 19
        ID type: KEY_ID (11)
        Protocol ID: UDP (17)
        Port: 500
        Identification Data: vpn-group-1
    Vendor ID payload
        Next payload: Vendor ID (13)
        Length: 12
        Vendor ID: draft-beaulieu-ike-xauth-02.txt
    Vendor ID payload
        Next payload: Vendor ID (13)
        Length: 20
        Vendor ID: RFC 3706 Detecting Dead IKE Peers (DPD)
    Vendor ID payload
        Next payload: Vendor ID (13)
        Length: 20
        Vendor ID: draft-ietf-ipsec-nat-t-ike-02
    Vendor ID payload
        Next payload: Vendor ID (13)
        Length: 24
        Vendor ID: Microsoft L2TP/IPSec VPN Client
    Vendor ID payload
        Next payload: NONE (0)
        Length: 20
        Vendor ID: unknown vendor ID: 0x12F5F28C457168A9702D9FE274CC0100
```

Figure 5.28 (continued)

```
Frame 2 (472 bytes on wire, 472 bytes captured)
Ethernet II, Src: Cisco_7b:48:f4 (00:0d:ed:7b:48:f4), Dst: GemtekTe_1f:a4:f7 (00:90:4b:1f:a4:f7)
Internet Protocol, Src: 192.168.2.254 (192.168.2.254), Dst: 192.168.2.65 (192.168.2.65)
User Datagram Protocol, Src Port: isakmp (500), Dst Port: isakmp (500)
Internet Security Association and Key Management Protocol
    Initiator cookie: 0xAAE8669D0551E4D3
    Responder cookie: 0x1BCA13B86542BDDE
    Next payload: Security Association (1)
    Version: 1.0
    Exchange type: Aggressive (4)
    Flags
    Message ID: 0x00000000
    Length: 430
    Security Association payload
        Next payload: Vendor ID (13)
        Length: 56
        Domain of interpretation: IPSEC (1)
        Situation: IDENTITY (1)
        Proposal payload # 1
            Next payload: NONE (0)
            Length: 44
            Proposal number: 1
            Protocol ID: ISAKMP (1)
            SPI size: 0
            Number of transforms: 1
            Transform payload # 1
                Next payload: NONE (0)
                Length: 36
                Transform number: 1
                Transform ID: KEY_IKE (1)
                Encryption-Algorithm (1): 3DES-CBC (5)
                Hash-Algorithm (2): SHA (2)
                Group-Description (4): Alternate 1024-bit MODP group (2)
                Authentication-Method (3): XAUTHInitPreShared (65001)
                Life-Type (11): Seconds (1)
```

Figure 5.28 (continued)

```
            Life-Duration (12): Duration-Value (2147483)
    Vendor ID payload
        Next payload: Vendor ID (13)
        Length: 20
        Vendor ID: unknown vendor ID: 0x12F5F28C457168A9702D9FE274CC0100
    Vendor ID payload
        Next payload: Vendor ID (13)
        Length: 20
        Vendor ID: RFC 3706 Detecting Dead IKE Peers (DPD)
    Vendor ID payload
        Next payload: Vendor ID (13)
        Length: 20
        Vendor ID: unknown vendor ID: 0xEE0DB4A56543BDDECE88F4EFB664BDED
    Vendor ID payload
        Next payload: Vendor ID (13)
        Length: 12
        Vendor ID: draft-beaulieu-ike-xauth-02.txt
    Vendor ID payload
        Next payload: Key Exchange (4)
        Length: 20
        Vendor ID: draft-ietf-ipsec-nat-t-ike-02
    Key Exchange payload
        Next payload: Identification (5)
        Length: 132
        Key Exchange Data
    Identification payload
        Next payload: Nonce (10)
        Length: 26
        ID type: FQDN (2)
        Protocol ID: UDP (17)
        Port: Unused
        Identification data: VPN-SERVER.ins.com
    Nonce payload
        Next payload: Hash (8)
        Length: 24
        Nonce Data
```

Figure 5.28 (continued)

```
    Hash payload
        Next payload: NAT-D (draft-ietf-ipsec-nat-t-ike-01 to 03) (130)
        Length: 24
        Hash Data
    NAT-D (draft-ietf-ipsec-nat-t-ike-01 to 03) payload
        Next payload: NAT-D (draft-ietf-ipsec-nat-t-ike-01 to 03) (130)
        Length: 24
        Hash of address and port: 02AD92C9A5CDC670CBC3A43E587AE10AE0BC9E61
    NAT-D (draft-ietf-ipsec-nat-t-ike-01 to 03) payload
        Next payload: NONE (0)
        Length: 24
        Hash of address and port: 751B608D3C7E071F1D3B95C72953AE13F529C691

Frame 3 (214 bytes on wire, 214 bytes captured)
Ethernet II, Src: GemtekTe_1f:a4:f7 (00:90:4b:1f:a4:f7), Dst: Cisco_7b:48:f4 (00:0d:ed:7b:48:f4)
Internet Protocol, Src: 192.168.2.65 (192.168.2.65), Dst: 192.168.2.254 (192.168.2.254)
User Datagram Protocol, Src Port: isakmp (500), Dst Port: isakmp (500)
Internet Security Association and Key Management Protocol
    Initiator cookie: 0xAAE8669D0551E4D3
    Responder cookie: 0x1BCA13B86542BDDE
    Next payload: Hash (8)
    Version: 1.0
    Exchange type: Aggressive (4)
    Flags
    Message ID: 0x00000000
    Length: 172
    Encrypted payload (144 bytes)


Frame 5 (118 bytes on wire, 118 bytes captured)
Ethernet II, Src: Cisco_7b:48:f4 (00:0d:ed:7b:48:f4), Dst: GemtekTe_1f:a4:f7 (00:90:4b:1f:a4:f7)
Internet Protocol, Src: 192.168.2.254 (192.168.2.254), Dst: 192.168.2.65 (192.168.2.65)
User Datagram Protocol, Src Port: isakmp (500), Dst Port: isakmp (500)
Internet Security Association and Key Management Protocol
    Initiator cookie: 0xAAE8669D0551E4D3
    Responder cookie: 0x1BCA13B86542BDDE
```

Figure 5.28 (continued)

```
    Next payload: Hash (8)
    Version: 1.0
    Exchange type: Transaction (Config Mode) (6)
    Flags
    Message ID: 0xB47CE10D
    Length: 76
    Encrypted payload (48 bytes)

Frame 6 (126 bytes on wire, 126 bytes captured)
Ethernet II, Src: GemtekTe_1f:a4:f7 (00:90:4b:1f:a4:f7), Dst: Cisco_7b:48:f4 (00:0d:ed:7b:48:f4)
Internet Protocol, Src: 192.168.2.65 (192.168.2.65), Dst: 192.168.2.254 (192.168.2.254)
User Datagram Protocol, Src Port: isakmp (500), Dst Port: isakmp (500)
Internet Security Association and Key Management Protocol
    Initiator cookie: 0xAAE8669D0551E4D3
    Responder cookie: 0x1BCA13B86542BDDE
    Next payload: Hash (8)
    Version: 1.0
    Exchange type: Transaction (Config Mode) (6)
    Flags
        .... ...1 = Encrypted
        .... ..0. = No commit
        .... .0.. = No authentication
    Message ID: 0xB47CE10D
    Length: 84
    Encrypted payload (56 bytes)
```

Figure 5.28 (continued)

The problem with XAUTH is that it relies on group authentication, wherein a group password is used as a preshared secret (or certificate) for IKE peer authentication. Group passwords are known to a group of people, rather than only the two communicating parties, as envisioned by the original IKE specification. As a result of the group preshared key, every member of the group will be able to calculate the **SKEYID** value for the group, and may potentially brute-force or by other means analyze and deduce the **SKEYID_e** value used for encryption. Furthermore, a member of the VPN group who already knows the shared key can pose as the VPN server, or sit between the client and the server in a man-in-the-middle attack and complete the entire Phase 1 dialogue. It can then request the client to provide cleartext username and password, and potentially forward them to a VPN server, if used as a stage of a man-in-the-middle attack.

Despite being considered susceptible to certain attacks and breaking the original IKE intent of user authentication, XAUTH is a very popular authentication method, and widely used by vendors such as Cisco and Nortel. Using certificates with XAUTH provides for much stronger authentication than using preshared keys, so this is the preferred method.

5.6 Centralized User Authentication

The previous sections of this chapter cover authentication mechanisms between a client and an infrastructure edge device such as a remote access server (RAS), a VPN server, or a wireless access point. However, the infrastructure edge device typically requires access to a security server that resides in a central location in order to be able to authenticate and authorize user access. It also requires a protocol to access authentication, authorization, and accounting services that this security server provides. This section discusses the protocols and mechanisms used for communication between an infrastructure edge device and a security server.

As discussed in Chapter 5.1, many devices have a local user database that can technically be used to authenticate users. This may work when a handful of users are going to be provided with access to the infrastructure. However, this approach is not scalable. For example, if an organization with hundreds or thousands of users has three VPN servers that allow users access from the Internet, and users need to use any of the available servers to connect, a security administrator will need to create the same local user database on each of the three VPN servers. As new users are added, or users leave the company, modifications to the user database must be performed on all the VPN servers. Password changes are virtually impossible to handle unless users submit a form with the plaintext password to the security administrator and request that the new password be set on all three VPN servers. And finally, if the company decides to add a wireless access point, a fourth local database will need to be maintained, adding to the administrative efforts.

The problem of decentralized security has existed for a long time, and there are solutions in the marketplace that help provide for a centralized approach where one security server can apply unified access policies across all the infrastructure edge devices. Centralized security results in more than just centralized user authentication. A centralized access control solution typically provides for a set of security servers that are responsible for AAA:

- *Authentication.* Users must be able to authenticate against a centralized user database exposed by the security server. Authentication must be uniform and use the same security database, regardless of whether the user tries to connect to the infrastructure using one edge device or another.

- *Authorization*. Even when the user has authenticated successfully, he should not be provided with unlimited access to the infrastructure. The security server should provide information to the edge device on how to allow the user to access only resources to which this user has been granted access. The authorization information provided by the security server to the edge device very much depends on the type of edge device and its capabilities to restrict user access.
- *Accounting*. The security server should provide for a centralized storage of historical security and other information that edge devices may want to submit. This information can include the time when a user connects to the infrastructure, the time when he disconnects, authorization applied for this user, the access that this user has attempted to obtain, whether the attempt was successful or unsuccessful, general information about configuration changes on the security device, information about use of privileges on the edge device, etc.

When services are centralized and consolidated, the problem that always arises is that all infrastructure components — such as infrastructure end devices — become dependent on the services provided by the centralized security solution. Unlike the distributed security solution, where the user database exists locally and is always available, with a centralized security solution if the security server is not available, users are not able to access the edge device. Therefore, centralized security solutions need to provide for a certain level of availability and typically involve more than one security server.

The security server is responsible for providing AAA services to edge devices. The security server can use a local user and security database, or may be able to access and submit AAA information from and to other servers on the network to carry out the AAA request. The security server can, for example, authenticate users against an external security database (such as Active Directory), or forward the request to another security server. The chaining of AAA requests between security servers can result in such an architecture where not only access to the infrastructure but access to applications and services is also subject to the same security rules and policies. In this case, the framework of security servers may be able to provide for a single sign-on solution.

This section discusses two of the most popular solutions for centralized AAA services (1) RADIUS, which is an Internet standard solution; and (2) TACACS+, which is a Cisco proprietary solution.

5.6.1 RADIUS

RADIUS is the most widely accepted standard for AAA services for access to the infrastructure. Virtually all enterprise network equipment vendors support RADIUS so their devices can be configured to abide by a centralized security policy by using RADIUS.

5.6.1.1 Overview

RADIUS was developed by Livingston Enterprises, which is now part of Lucent Technologies. Livingston developed the RADIUS protocol in an effort to centralize AAA for the edge devices that they were developing at the time. The RADIUS authentication and authorization services standard was later published in RFC 2138, and updated in RFC 2865 (see [119]). Separate RFCs cover accounting services.

The reason authentication and authorization services are discussed in a single document is because RADIUS couples both services together in the actual communication between the edge device and the security server. The edge device requests authentication for a specific user; and if the user authenticates successfully, the reply from the RADIUS server provides authorization information as well. A separate conversation between the edge device and the RADIUS server may provide for accounting services, if required.

Communication between the edge device and the RADIUS server with regard to authentication and authorization takes place using the messages in Table 5.11.

RADIUS does not maintain an open session to the NAS device, and only considers distinct requests from the NAS, without managing the overall client session. Therefore, RADIUS is considered a *stateless* protocol. The architects of RADIUS decided that UDP would be suitable as the transport for RADIUS because of its similarly stateless nature. Older implementations of RADIUS use UDP/1645 (Authentication and Authorization) and UDP/1646 (Accounting), both of which conflicted with other applications. Newer versions use the IANA-allocated UDP/1812 for Authentication and Authorization and port UDP/1813 for Accounting.

The RADIUS packet has a standard format and consists of the fields in Table 5.12.

RADIUS attributes are authentication and authorization parameters passed between the edge device and the RADIUS server, or between the client and the RADIUS server in the case of EAP. The RADIUS standard defines a set of 63 standard attributes but vendors typically define their own non-standard attributes to accommodate the specific features of their products.

Table 5.11 RADIUS Packet Types

RADIUS Code	*Name*	*Description*
1	Access-Request	Used by the edge device to signal to the RADIUS server that a user needs to be authenticated and authorized
2	Access-Accept	Used by the RADIUS server to provide the edge device with authentication status for the user, and potentially provide an access profile (authorization information)
3	Access-Reject	Used by the RADIUS server to inform the edge device that the user has failed to authenticate
11	Access-Challenge	Used by the RADIUS server to provide the edge device with a challenge to be used by the user in a challenge-response authentication scheme

Table 5.12 RADIUS Packet Fields

Field Name	*Description*
Code	Type of the packet; see Table 5.11.
Identifier	Unique identifier for the conversation between the RADIUS client and the RADIUS server. This ID is used to match RADIUS client requests to RADIUS server replies, as there may be a number of conversations between them at any given moment in time.
Length	The length of the RADIUS packet from the Code field to the Attributes field.
Authenticator	16-bytes used by the model of trust in RADIUS. It is used by the RADIUS client (the edge device) to authenticate the RADIUS server in Access-Accept, Access-Reject, and Access-Challenge messages from the RADIUS server to the RADIUS client. In messages from the RADIUS client to the RADIUS server (Access-Request messages), the authenticator is a random 16-byte value, used as a salt to protect the user password.
Attributes	Parameters passed between the edge device and the RADIUS server as part of the authentication and authorization process.

Table 5.13 Popular RADIUS Attributes

Attribute	*Description*
User-name	The name of the user who is trying to authenticate or authorize The name may or may not include the realm-name in the form **domainname\username** or **username@domainname**
User-password	For plaintext password authentication schemes — contains the password of the user encrypted using the algorithm, described above
CHAP-Password	When CHAP is used, contains the CHAP reply to a previous CHAP request from the server
NAS-IP-Address	The IP address of the RADIUS client (infrastructure edge device)
NAS-Port	The physical or logical interface used by the client to connect
Service-Type	The service, request by the client Can be Login for local authentication to the edge device, or it can be Framed for data-link protocols, such as PPP
Calling-Line-ID	The number from which the user is connecting Typically used for dial-up connection

Some of the popular RADIUS attributes are provided in Table 5.13.

The RADIUS server may take into consideration one or more parameters to perform the authentication, or may request additional parameters using the Access-Challenge message to request such information. If configured to do so, the RADIUS server can potentially authenticate a user based on the number from which he has dialed in (Calling-Line-ID) and the username, rather than the username or password.

5.6.1.2 The Model of Trust in RADIUS

The model of trust (Figure 5.29) between the RADIUS client (the infrastructure edge device) and the RADIUS server is based on the use of a shared secret. When the client needs to send confidential information to the RADIUS server, such as the authenticating user's password, the RADIUS client encrypts the password field in the shared secret. To decrypt the password and authenticate the user, the server needs to know the shared secret.

When the RADIUS server sends a reply to a RADIUS client, it needs to provide an authenticator, which is again based on encryption using the

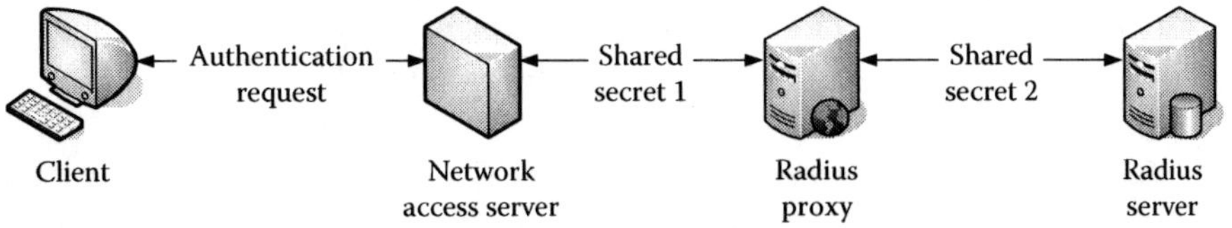

Figure 5.29 RADIUS proxies and the model of trust.

shared secret. This allows the RADIUS client to authenticate the RADIUS server; only a RADIUS server that knows the shared secret can generate the correct authenticator in the server reply.

The domain of administrative authority of a RADIUS server is called a realm. Typically, RADIUS servers can serve one or more realms. To indicate that they belong to a specific realm, users can include the realm name as part of the username that they are providing to RADIUS. Very often, this takes the format of username@domainname. For example, the name John@ins.com indicates that user John has an account in the realm ins.com. Another relatively popular notation for RADIUS realm names in Windows is **domainname\username**, so that user **John** from domain **INS.COM** can use **INS.COM\John** (or just **INS\John**) as his name to authenticate to RADIUS.

The fact that the username may indicate realm membership makes possible the use of RADIUS proxy servers (Figure 5.29). The RADIUS proxy server can accept AAA requests from RADIUS clients (infrastructure edge devices); it can then analyze the realm portion of the provided username and forward these requests to the specific RADIUS servers that are responsible for the specified realm. The RADIUS proxy looks like a RADIUS server for the RADIUS client, and it behaves like a RADIUS client for the RADIUS server for the domain to which it is forwarding the request. The intermediary role of the RADIUS proxy means that it needs to provide for proper RADIUS trust handling also. Because the RADIUS proxy looks like a RADIUS server for the RADIUS client, this means that the client and the proxy need to share a password to communicate and authenticate each other successfully. At the same time, the fact that the RADIUS proxy looks like a RADIUS client from a RADIUS server perspective means that a second shared secret must be used between the proxy and the RADIUS server. To maintain the integrity of the RADIUS trust, the RADIUS proxy needs to decrypt user passwords in Access-Request messages using the shared secret with the RADIUS client, and then reencrypt them with the secret shared with the target RADIUS server. For RADIUS server replies — such as Access-Accept, Access-Reject and Access-Challenge — the RADIUS proxy needs to decrypt the authenticator in the message from the target RADIUS server using the shared secret with the server, then re-encrypt the message with the secret shared with the client and forward the message to the client.

In Access-Request messages, the encryption of the user password field (User-Password) is performed in the following way. The client calculates the MD5 hash of the concatenation of the shared secret and the authenticator field. The result is a 16-byte value. The user password is padded with nulls to 16 characters if it has fewer than 16 characters. The password is then XORed with the MD5 hash and is stored in the User-Password field.

If the password is longer than 16 bytes, a new hash is generated from the MD5 hash of the concatenation of the RADIUS shared password and the previous MD5 hash value. The next 16 bytes of the password are then XORed with this new hash. The process continues until the entire user password has been XORed with values, as calculated in the way described above.

To decrypt the password, the server applies the same algorithm using its own plaintext copy of the RADIUS shared key with this specific RADIUS client. It is important to note that other parts of the RADIUS packet are not encrypted, and neither is their integrity protected by signing or hash algorithms.

The Authenticator field of RADIUS Access-Accept, Access-Reject, and Access-Challenge messages is used by the RADIUS client to authenticate the RADIUS server. The Authenticator value is calculated by the RADIUS server in the following way: the entire RADIUS packet from the Packet Code field to the last attribute in the packet is concatenated with the RADIUS shared secret. The result is then hashed using MD5 and saved as the Authenticator field. Thus, the authenticator provides proof for the client that the server is genuine (because it can calculate the MD5 hash correctly) and also ensures that the packet cannot be easily modified in transit as its content is authenticated by the MD5 hash value.

5.6.1.3 RADIUS Authentication Requests from Edge Devices

Traditionally, the RADIUS Protocol was used by the infrastructure edge devices to request authentication from RADIUS servers on behalf of clients. In this respect, the edge device typically speaks a framed protocol, such as PPP (or some derivative) with the PPP client. The authentication protocol in use depends on what has been negotiated between the client and the edge device. The edge device collects the information from the authentication dialogue and then transforms the PPP-based (such as PAP or CHAP) authentication messages into RADIUS messages, using the appropriate attributes. If the server sends a challenge for additional information,

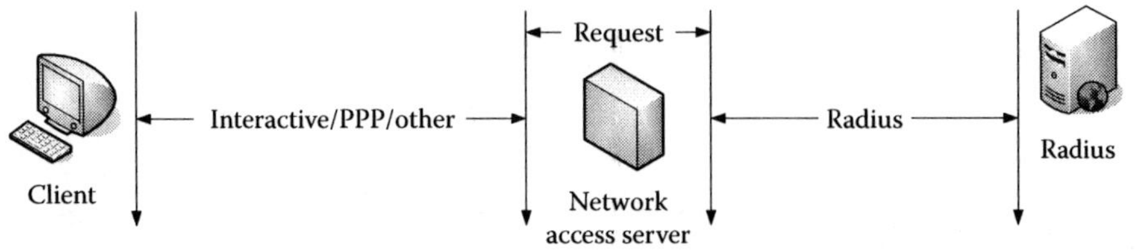

Figure 5.30 RADIUS authentication using legacy authentication protocols.

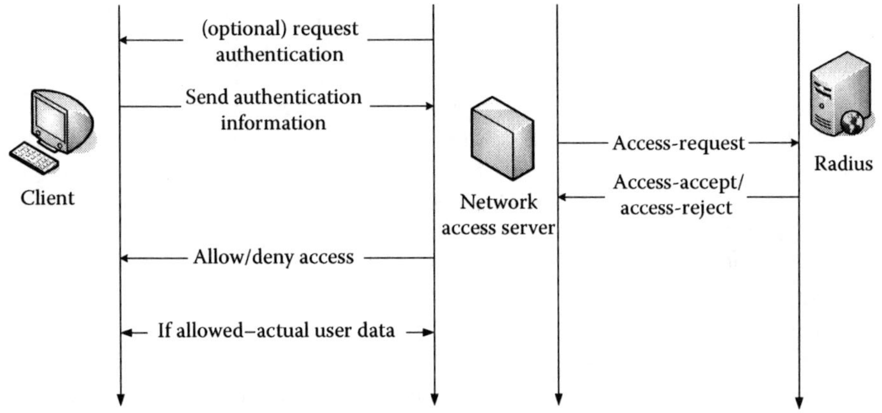

Figure 5.31 Simple user authentication and authorization using RADIUS.

the edge device will need to translate this request to PPP authentication messages and forward the request to the PPP client. When the edge device is generating the RADIUS requests, which is the case for legacy authentication mechanisms, the edge device needs to have the intelligence and support authentication protocols and schemes known to the client (Figure 5.30).

A typical simple user authentication and authorization request against RADIUS is shown in Figure 5.31. If the user is using a simple authentication mechanism (such as PAP) where the access client can provide identification and credential information in a single request, the edge device collects this information and submits it in an Access-Request message to the RADIUS server. The RADIUS server considering the Access-Request message and the attributes supplied by the edge device can authenticate the user, reject access, or request more information to complete the authentication process.

A typical challenge-response user authentication and authorization request against RADIUS is shown in Figure 5.32. Such an authentication

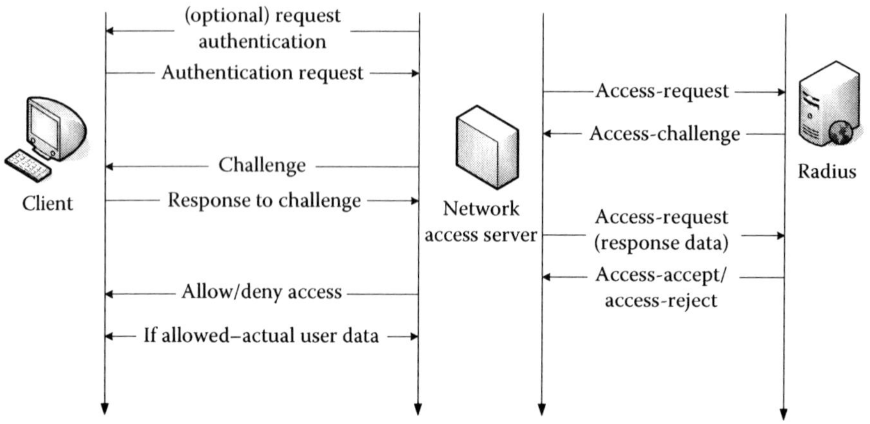

Figure 5.32 Challenge-response authentication & authorization using RADIUS.

dialogue can be used by challenge-response authentication protocols such as CHAP and MS-CHAP. The edge device collects identification information from the client and sends it to the RADIUS server in an Access-Request message. The RADIUS server generates a challenge and sends it back to the edge device that forwards it back to the PPP client. The client then generates a response to the request and sends it back to the edge device, which in turn submits the response in an Access-Request message. The RADIUS server validates the response and, if successful, sends an Access-Accept message back to the edge device. The edge device then informs the PPP client of the successful authentication process and communication continues with actual user data.

5.6.1.4 RADIUS and EAP Pass-through Authentication

Unlike legacy authentication protocols, EAP authentication can be forwarded by the edge device between the client and the RADIUS server without the edge device knowing how to handle each EAP authentication mechanism. For example, if a client tries to connect to an edge device with RADIUS authentication and negotiates the use of the EAP protocol, the edge device will start forwarding EAP messages transparently; it does not need to be able to speak EAP or access the user database — as long as the edge device is forwarding all the EAP messages on top of RADIUS, authentication should take place directly between the PPP client and the RADIUS server. Furthermore, the inherent protection of some EAP authentication methods (such as PEAP and EAP-TLS) allows for a secure channel between the client and the RADIUS server. The edge device can treat all the information as opaque and just forward it between the client and the server.

```
Frame 1 (153 bytes on wire, 153 bytes captured)
Ethernet II, Src: 02:00:4c:4f:4f:50 (02:00:4c:4f:4f:50), Dst: Microsof_50:ab:2a
(00:03:ff:50:ab:2a)
Internet Protocol, Src: 192.168.4.254 (192.168.4.254), Dst: 10.0.2.102 (10.0.2.102)
User Datagram Protocol, Src Port: 1645 (1645), Dst Port: radius (1812)
Radius Protocol
    Code: Access-Request (1)
    Packet identifier: 0xd (13)
    Length: 111
    Authenticator: B638FBDDEB2BFDF17D3C20171C8C5F5C
    Attribute Value Pairs
        AVP: l=12  t=User-Name(1): radiususer
            User-Name: radiususer
        AVP: l=6  t=Framed-MTU(12): 1400
            Framed-MTU: 1400
        AVP: l=16  t=Called-Station-Id(30): 000d.ed7b.48f4
            Called-Station-Id: 000d.ed7b.48f4
        AVP: l=16  t=Calling-Station-Id(31): 000d.5675.867c
            Calling-Station-Id: 000d.5675.867c
        AVP: l=18  t=Message-Authenticator(80): 8590F047A865590B38D0C65E96806FA7
            Message-Authenticator: 8590F047A865590B38D0C65E96806FA7
        AVP: l=17  t=EAP-Message(79) Last Segment[1]
            EAP fragment
            Extensible Authentication Protocol
                Code: Response (2)
                Id: 1
                Length: 15
                Type: Identity [RFC3748] (1)
                Identity (10 bytes): radiususer
        AVP: l=6  t=NAS-IP-Address(4): 192.168.4.254
            NAS-IP-Address: 192.168.4.254 (192.168.4.254)

Frame 2 (141 bytes on wire, 141 bytes captured)
Ethernet II, Src: Microsof_50:ab:2a (00:03:ff:50:ab:2a), Dst: 02:00:4c:4f:4f:50
(02:00:4c:4f:4f:50)
Internet Protocol, Src: 10.0.2.102 (10.0.2.102), Dst: 192.168.4.254 (192.168.4.254)
```

Figure 5.33 8021x-EAP-MD5.cap : Communication between edge device and RADIUS server.

```
User Datagram Protocol, Src Port: radius (1812), Dst Port: 1645 (1645)
Radius Protocol
    Code: Access-challenge (11)
    Packet identifier: 0xd (13)
    Length: 99
    Authenticator: 95628AF5E5F29CBD451BF8730F593D3D
    Attribute Value Pairs
        AVP: l=29  t=EAP-Message(79) Last Segment[1]
            EAP fragment
            Extensible Authentication Protocol
                Code: Request (1)
                Id: 89
                Length: 27
                Type: MD5-Challenge [RFC3748] (4)
                Value-Size: 16
                Value: 59EAA35BC6E55DC3831524CDC2FED644
                Extra data (5 bytes): 5354455645
        AVP: l=32  t=State(24): 434953434F2D4541502D4348414C4C454E47453D302E3166...
            State: 434953434F2D4541502D4348414C4C454E47453D302E3166...
        AVP: l=18  t=Message-Authenticator(80): 931E4C72EA93F1FCA6A965965F5A7D94
            Message-Authenticator: 931E4C72EA93F1FCA6A965965F5A7D94

Frame 3 (202 bytes on wire, 202 bytes captured)
Ethernet II, Src: 02:00:4c:4f:4f:50 (02:00:4c:4f:4f:50), Dst: Microsof_50:ab:2a
(00:03:ff:50:ab:2a)
Internet Protocol, Src: 192.168.4.254 (192.168.4.254), Dst: 10.0.2.102 (10.0.2.102)
User Datagram Protocol, Src Port: 1645 (1645), Dst Port: radius (1812)
Radius Protocol
    Code: Access-Request (1)
    Packet identifier: 0xe (14)
    Length: 160
    Authenticator: CE6737345C9BECDAE419B16BB8880DEB
    Attribute Value Pairs
        AVP: l=12  t=User-Name(1): radiususer
            User-Name: radiususer
        AVP: l=6  t=Framed-MTU(12): 1400
```

Figure 5.33 (continued)

```
            Framed-MTU: 1400
        AVP: l=16  t=Called-Station-Id(30): 000d.ed7b.48f4
            Called-Station-Id: 000d.ed7b.48f4
        AVP: l=16  t=Calling-Station-Id(31): 000d.5675.867c
            Calling-Station-Id: 000d.5675.867c
        AVP: l=18  t=Message-Authenticator(80): 88DC90FE3D3E0371762C65736E67F854
            Message-Authenticator: 88DC90FE3D3E0371762C65736E67F854
        AVP: l=34  t=EAP-Message(79) Last Segment[1]
            EAP fragment
            Extensible Authentication Protocol
                Code: Response (2)
                Id: 89
                Length: 32
                Type: MD5-Challenge [RFC3748] (4)
                Value-Size: 16
                Value: B1D86813A2D9598D59804725D3F3A4E5
                Extra data (10 bytes): 72616469757375736572
        AVP: l=32  t=State(24): 434953434F2D4541502D4348414C4C454E47453D302E3166...
            State: 434953434F2D4541502D4348414C4C454E47453D302E3166...
        AVP: l=6  t=NAS-IP-Address(4): 192.168.4.254
            NAS-IP-Address: 192.168.4.254 (192.168.4.254)

Frame 4 (93 bytes on wire, 93 bytes captured)
Ethernet II, Src: Microsof_50:ab:2a (00:03:ff:50:ab:2a), Dst: 02:00:4c:4f:4f:50
(02:00:4c:4f:4f:50)
Internet Protocol, Src: 10.0.2.102 (10.0.2.102), Dst: 192.168.4.254 (192.168.4.254)
User Datagram Protocol, Src Port: radius (1812), Dst Port: 1645 (1645)
Radius Protocol
    Code: Access-Accept (2)
    Packet identifier: 0xe (14)
    Length: 51
    Authenticator: A53B6C9948CD8FBB12BB79C26859DD10
    Attribute Value Pairs
        AVP: l=6  t=Framed-IP-Address(8): Negotiated
            Framed-IP-Address: Negotiated
        AVP: l=7  t=EAP-Message(79) Last Segment[1]
```

Figure 5.33 (continued)

```
        EAP fragment
        Extensible Authentication Protocol
            Code: Success (3)
            Id: 89
            Length: 5
    AVP: l=18  t=Message-Authenticator(80): 11FABD743AE84860D403BE52E694D280
        Message-Authenticator: 11FABD743AE84860D403BE52E694D280
```

Figure 5.33 (continued)

Figure 5.33 shows RADIUS traffic between the edge device and the RADIUS server:

1. The edge device has received the identity of the user and forwards it to the RADIUS server (see Frame 1 in Figure 5.33) along with additional parameters, such as the source MAC address of the workstation, the MAC address of the edge device port, and other parameters.
2. Because the authentication method is EAP-MD5, which is challenge-response based, the server replies with an access challenge string (see Frame 2 in Figure 5.33). The edge device forwards the EAP message to the client.
3. The client calculates the response and sends it to the infrastructure edge device, which in turn forwards it to the RADIUS server (see Frame 3 in Figure 5.33) along with other RADIUS parameters.
4. The RADIUS server considering the client response and the additional parameters provided by the edge device either authenticate the user or reject the authentication attempt.

5.6.2 TACACS+

TACACS+ (Terminal Access Controller Access Control System Plus) is a Cisco proprietary protocol that provides for user Authentication, Authorization, and Accounting (AAA). TACACS+ is based on the TACACS Protocol used in the early Internet and specified in RFC 1492 [121]. At that time, TACACS did not provide any encryption or data encapsulation of the communication channel between the infrastructure edge and the TACACS host. Later on, the TACACS Protocol evolved into XTACACS and then finally Cisco came up with its proprietary version TACACS+. Cisco even produced an Internet Draft for TACACS+ (see [122]) but it never became a standard.

The TACACS and XTACACS versions are virtually not used today but Cisco's TACACS+ is very popular, especially in Cisco-centric infrastructures; and TACACS+ successfully competes with RADIUS as the primary AAA protocol in many enterprise environments.

5.6.2.1 Overview

TACACS+ is very similar to RADIUS in terms of functionality. At the same time, there are differences in the way the two protocols operate, and there are also differences in the protection of traffic they provide.

The early TACACS Protocol supported both UDP and TCP requests. Cisco's TACACS+ Protocol utilizes TCP for communication between the infrastructure edge device and the TACACS+ server. All TACACS+ data within the TCP channel is encrypted so communication between the infrastructure edge and the TACACS+ server is protected from eavesdropping.

Unlike RADIUS, TACACS+ provides for separate Authentication, Authorization, and Accounting requests. Unlike RADIUS where Authentication and Authorization are coupled, infrastructure edge devices using TACACS+ will first try to authenticate the user and then will send a separate request to obtain information on the user privilege level, and other information that might be used to authorize user access.

TACACS+ messages are exchanged between the infrastructure edge device and the TACACS+ server using TCP/49. Table 5.14 provides insight into the TACACS+ packet contents.

Table 5.14 TACACS+ Fields

Field Name	*Description*
Major Version	Major TACACS+ version — always set to 0xC
Minor Version	Minor versions 0 and 1 are defined
Type	Type of packet — Authentication, Authorization, or Accounting packet
Sequence Number	Packet number ––increased by one for each packet
Flags	Various flags, such as whether the packet is encrypted, etc.
Session ID	A random number that identifies the session This number does not change throughout the session
Length	Total length of the packet body
Body	TACACS+ AAA payload

5.6.2.2 TACACS+ Channel Protection

Similar to RADIUS, TACACS+ uses a model of trust based on a shared secret (password) between the infrastructure edge device and TACACS+ server. The shared password is used to authenticate both the client and the server by encrypting the communication channel between the two; the assumption is that the remote party can be considered authenticated if it can successfully decrypt messages sent to it and encrypt messages that it sends. To guarantee the security of the TACACS+ channel, the password must be complex and only known to the infrastructure edge device and the TACACS+ server.

The body of the TACACS+ packet (but not the header, shown in Table 5.14) is encrypted using a key generated in the following way:

K1 = MD5(**SessionID, SharedSecret, Version, SequenceNumber)**

K2 = MD5(**SessionID, SharedSecret, Version, SequenceNumber, K1)**

...

Kn = MD5(**SessionID, SharedSecret, Version, SequenceNumber,** $\mathbf{K_{n-1}}$**)**

The protection key **K** is the concatenation of the above keys: **K** = **K1** | **K2** | ... | **Kn**

Because the MD5 algorithm will generate a hash of 128 bits at each iteration, the above calculation is repeated as many times as required to obtain a key **K** of length equal to or greater than the length of the message that needs to be encrypted. The body of the TACACS+ packet is then encrypted using XOR and the shared secret **K**. The edge device uses the same key and the XOR operation to decrypt traffic from the client.

It is important to note that this mechanism does not provide for communication integrity. There is a simple anti-replay mechanism by means of packet sequence numbers that are used to calculate the protection key but the specification advises that sequence numbers always start from 1, so they are easily predictable. Furthermore, because of the password nature of the TACACS+ model of trust, the communication channel is susceptible to dictionary, brute force, and rainbow attacks, especially if the password is not strong enough. As a result, the TACACS+ channel between devices and servers should be protected accordingly using other underlying data protection methods, such as IPSec.

5.6.2.3 TACACS+ Authentication Process

The TACACS+ authentication process consists of the messages shown in Table 5.15.

Table 5.15 TACACS+ Authentication Messages

Message	*Description*
START	This is the initial message from the infrastructure edge device to the TACACS+ server, providing basic identification information, such as the username for the user that is trying to authenticate, and the authentication method required (PAP, CHAP, etc.).
REPLY	The reply message is always sent from the TACACS+ server to the client to advise the client of the authentication status. The REPLY message may contain a termination message (PASS for successful authentication or FAIL for failed authentication), or a request for more information (see below).
CONTINUE	This message is used by the infrastructure edge device to provide more information, requested in a REPLY message from the TACACS+ server to the edge device.

The REPLY message sent by the server has a status field, which can take one of the values shown in Table 5.16.

User authentication with TACACS+ is performed as follows (Figure 5.34):

1. The edge device sends a TACACS+ Start message to the TACACS+ server.
2. The server sends a Reply message back to the edge device and specifies other information that may be required, or terminates the authentication process with a PASS or FAIL message.
3. If more information is required by the client, the edge device sends a request to the client by either displaying a dialogue for the user to provide the information (for interactive authentication) or by means of PPP or other data-link authentication mechanism.
4. The client provides additional information requested by the edge device.
5. The edge device provides the additional information to the TACACS+ server in a CONTINUE message.

The server replies with either PASS or FAIL, if the information was sufficient to perform authentication.

The exact steps and the number of iterations depend on the authentication mechanism specified in the START packet. Table 5.17 shows some of the standard authentication methods.

A feature of TACACS+ is that not only can it serve as an authentication server for edge devices, but it can also provide edge devices with authentication information when they connect to remote services as clients. In

Table 5.16 TACACS+ REPLY Message Status

Message	*Description*
PASS (ACCEPT)	The credentials provided are correct and the user is authenticated
FAIL (REJECT)	The credentials provided are incorrect so the user has failed to authenticate
ERROR	An error occurred during the authentication process This implies neither successful nor unsuccessful authentication with regards to the provided credentials
GETUSER	Requests the edge device to send the username back to the TACACS+ server
GETPASSWORD	Requests the user password from the edge device
GETDATA	Provides the edge device with a prompt to be displayed to the user by the edge device The user is then supposed to enter information, and then the edge device sends the user-provided information back to TACACS+ This is useful for one-time password mechanisms.
RESTART	Indicates that, currently, authentication parameters are not acceptable and authentication should start over with a new set of parameters that the client and the server need to negotiate
FOLLOW	Requests the client to continue the authentication with another server The TACACS+ server will provide the name of the server with which the client should continue the authentication process, and may optionally specify an authentication protocol to be used, and a server key (shared secret) to be used for request to that server

this respect, the TACACS+ server can act as a credential store for these outbound connections.

Figure 5.35 shows TACACS+ traffic on the network. Apparently, the communication channel is fully encrypted, so all a potential attacker can see is that traffic contains authentication requests and replies. Unlike RADIUS traffic, the actual content of the requests is encrypted.

Once the session on port TCP/49 has been established, the client sends a TACACS+ START message with all the parameters that it has collected in the authentication dialogue with the client. In this particular example, the dialogue between the client and the infrastructure edge device was using CHAP.

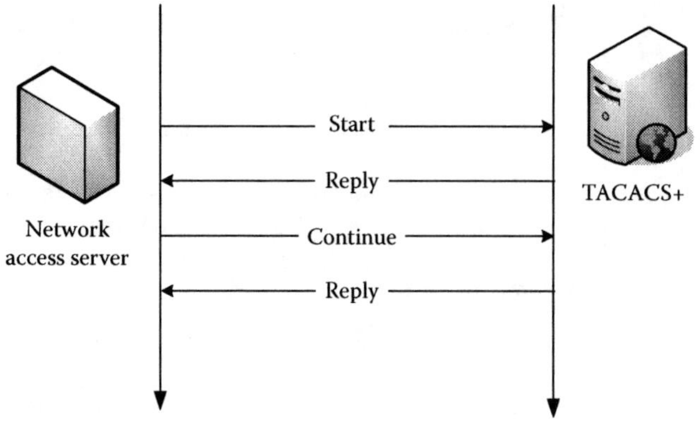

Figure 5.34 TACACS+ authentication process.

Table 5.17 TACACS+ Standard Authentication Mechanisms

Authentication Mechanism	*Steps*
Enable Request	This is a request to change the privilege level for a user on a Cisco device Consists of a single START packet where the username and the clear text password are provided, and a single REPLY message that can be either Pass or Fail.
Inbound ASCII Login	Basic user authentication Consists of a single START packet where the username and the cleartext password may be provided; there may be multiple REPLY messages from the server with requests for more information, followed by CONTINUE messages from the client Finally, the server REPLY message, which can be either Pass or Fail
Inbound PAP login	PAP user authentication Consists of a single START packet where the username and the cleartext password are provided, and a single REPLY message, which can be either Pass or Fail

Table 5.17 TACACS+ Standard Authentication Mechanisms (continued)

Authentication Mechanism	*Steps*
Inbound CHAP Login	CHAP authentication Consists of a single START packet where the username is provided, along with the PPP ID, the CHAP challenge, and the CHAP response fields in the data portion of the START packet The TACACS+ server uses the Challenge and the user password to calculate a response and compare it with the user-provided response A single REPLY message is sent by the server and it can be either Pass or Fail
Inbound MS-CHAP Login	Same as Inbound CHAP Login but uses an MS-CHAP challenge and an MS-CHAP response
Inbound Generic/OTP	The edge device sends a START packet that includes the username for the user who is trying to authenticate The TACACS+ server looks up the user in the user database and potentially generates a challenge for OTP authentication The challenge is added to a textual string that prompts the user to provide his one-time password, and is sent to the edge device The edge device displays the textual prompt, collects user input, and submits it back to the TACACS+ server The server then compares the client OTP reply to its own version of the OTP reply and returns Pass or Fail result
Outbound PAP	Used by the edge device to request from TACACS+ credentials to be used for an outbound connection The edge device specifies the username for which it needs credentials in the START packet The server sends a REPLY message that contains the plaintext password for the requested user
Outbound CHAP	Used by the edge device to request from TACACS+ credentials to be used for an outbound connection The START packet contains the user ID, as well as the PPP ID and the CHAP Challenge The server calculates the CHAP reply and provides it in the REPLY message
Outbound MS-CHAP	Same as outbound CHAP but uses an MS-CHAP challenge and an MS-CHAP response

```
Frame 4 (130 bytes on wire, 130 bytes captured)
Ethernet II, Src: 02:00:4c:4f:4f:50 (02:00:4c:4f:4f:50), Dst: Microsof_50:ab:2a
(00:03:ff:50:ab:2a)
Internet Protocol, Src: 192.168.4.254 (192.168.4.254), Dst: 10.0.2.102 (10.0.2.102)
Transmission Control Protocol, Src Port: 32220 (32220), Dst Port: 49 (49), Seq: 336899499, Ack:
775129710, Len: 76
TACACS+
    Major version: TACACS+
    Minor version: 1
    Type: Authentication (1)
    Sequence number: 1
    Flags: 0x00 (Encrypted payload, Multiple Connections)
    Session ID: 756857821
    Packet length: 64
    Encrypted Request: 4C 8A CB...

Frame 6 (72 bytes on wire, 72 bytes captured)
Ethernet II, Src: Microsof_50:ab:2a (00:03:ff:50:ab:2a), Dst: 02:00:4c:4f:4f:50
(02:00:4c:4f:4f:50)
Internet Protocol, Src: 10.0.2.102 (10.0.2.102), Dst: 192.168.4.254 (192.168.4.254)
Transmission Control Protocol, Src Port: 49 (49), Dst Port: 32220 (32220), Seq: 775129710, Ack:
336899575, Len: 18
TACACS+
    Major version: TACACS+
    Minor version: 1
    Type: Authentication (1)
    Sequence number: 2
    Flags: 0x00 (Encrypted payload, Multiple Connections)
    Session ID: 756857821
    Packet length: 6
    Encrypted Reply: 93 9A 78...
```

Figure 5.35 TACACS.cap: TACACS+ authentication traffic between a NAS and a Cisco ACS server.

The server decrypts the parameters from the START message. These parameters will include edge device challenges and requests, and client replies. The server checks client replies using the locally stored user password or other authentication information, as well as server challenges, and then either signals successful user authentication, or specifies that the authentication request has failed.

Appendix A

References

Printed References

I. *Applied Cryptography, second edition,* Bruce Schneier, ISBN 0-471-11709-9.
II. *DCE/RPC over SMB,* Luke Leighton, ISBN: 1578701503.
III. *The Art of Deception: Controlling the Human Element of Security,* Kevin D. Mitnick, ISBN 0471237124.
IV. *Practical UNIX and Internet Security, second edition,* Simson Garfinkel and Gene Spafford, ISBN: 1-56592-148-8.
V. *Microsoft Windows Server(TM) 2003 Resource Kit,* by Microsoft Windows Server Team, ISBN: 0735622329.
VI. *Microsoft Windows Security Resource Kit, second edition,* by Ben Smith and Brian Komar, ISBN: 0735621748.
VII. *IPSec VPN Design,* by Vijay Bollapragada, Mohamed Khalid, and Scott Wainner, ISBN: 1587051117.
VIII. *Cisco Wireless LAN Security,* by Andrew Balinsky, Darrin Miller, Krishna Sankar, and Sri Sundaralingam, ISBN: 1587051540.
IX. *Official (ISC)² Guide to the CISSP Exam,* by Susan Hansche, John Berti, and Chris Hare, ISBN: 084931707X.
X. *HP-UX 11i Security,* by Chris Wong, ISBN: 0130330620.
XI. *Hacking Exposed, second edition,* by Joel Scambray, Stuart McClure, and George Kurtz, ISBN: 0072127481.
XII. *Building Enterprise Active Directory™ Services: Notes from the Field,* by Microsoft Corporation, ISBN: 0-7356-0860-1.

Online References

Note: The following links were valid at the time of the writing of this book. However, they may have changed over time and may no longer be valid. Provided with a document title, a good search engine on the Internet should be able to show the current location of the document so that the reader can find it online, if needed.

1. MIT Athena Project:
   http://web.mit.edu/ist/topics/athena/index.html
2. DNSSEC How-to, Olaf Kolkman:
   http://www.ripe.net/projects/disi/dnssec_howto/dnssec_howto.pdf
3. PADL Software Pty Ltd.:
   www.padl.com
4. Windows 2000 Active Directory Display Specifiers:
   http://www.microsoft.com/technet/prodtechnol/windows2000serv/technologies/activedirectory/deploy/prodspecs/actvdspl.mspx
5. The MD5 Message-Digest Algorithm:
   http://www.ietf.org/rfc/rfc1321.txt?number=1321
6. The Linux-PAM System Administrators' Guide:
   http://www.kernel.org/pub/linux/libs/pam/Linux-PAM-html/pam.html
7. Making Login Services Independent of Authentication Technologies:
   http://www.sun.com/software/solaris/pam/pam_ste_talk.pdf
8. Open Software Foundation, Request For Comments: 86, V. Samar (SunSoft), R. Schemers (SunSoft):
   http://www.kernel.org/pub/linux/libs/pam/pre/doc/rfc86.0.txt.gz
9. The MD4 Message-Digest Algorithm, R. Rivest, MIT Laboratory for Computer Science and RSA Data Security, Inc., April 1992:
   http://www.ietf.org/rfc/rfc1320.txt?number=1320
10. An Attack on the Last Two Rounds of MD4, den Boer & Bosselaers, 15 Oct. 1991:
    http://citeseer.ist.psu.edu/denboer91attack.html
11. TechNet Webcast: Passwords Demystified - Level 200:
    https://www118.livemeeting.com/cc/mseventsbmo/viewRecordings?id=1032253148&role=attend&pw=webcast
12. BindView Security Advisory: Vulnerability in Windows NT's SYSKEY feature:
    http://archives.neohapsis.com/archives/ntbugtraq/1999-q4/0067.html
13. Windows NT password hash retrieval, Jeremy Allison:
    http://www.insecure.org/sploits/WinNT.passwordhashes.deobfuscation.html
14. Microsoft Windows 2003 TechCenter — Privileges:
    http://www.microsoft.com/technet/prodtechnol/windowsserver2003/library/ServerHelp/589980fb-1a83-490e-a745-357750ced3d9.mspx
15. The Essentials of Replacing the Microsoft Graphical Identification and Authentication Dynamic Link Library:
    http://download.microsoft.com/download/b/7/b/b7b59bf4-f585-4f74-b342-251e9b075115/msgina.doc

16. Microsoft Knowledge Base — PSS ID Number: 289246; MS02-001: Forged SID Could Result in Elevated Privileges in Windows NT 4.0: http://support.microsoft.com/default.aspx?scid=kb;EN-US;q289246
17. Microsoft Knowledge Base — PSS ID Number: 289243; MS02-001: Forged SID Could Result in Elevated Privileges in Windows 2000: http://support.microsoft.com/default.aspx?scid=kb;EN-US;q289243
18. Platform SDK: Active Directory Schema — User Class: http://msdn.microsoft.com/library/en-us/adschema/adschema/c_user.asp?frame=true
19. Definition of the inetOrgPerson LDAP Object Class, M. Smith, April 2000: http://www.ietf.org/rfc/rfc2798.txt?number=2798
20. Microsoft Knowledge Base — PSS ID Number: 269190: How to Change a Windows 2000 User's Password through LDAP: http://support.microsoft.com/default.aspx?scid=kb;EN-US;q269190
21. Microsoft Knowledge Base — PSS ID Number: 321051: How to Enable LDAP over SSL with a Third-Party Certification Authority: http://support.microsoft.com/default.aspx?scid=kb;en-us;321051
22. Microsoft Knowledge Base — PSS ID Number: 843587: How to Stop Automatic Conversion of Universal Distribution Groups to Universal Security Groups in Exchange 2000 and in Exchange 2003: http://support.microsoft.com/default.aspx?scid=kb;en-us;843587
23. Platform SDK: Active Directory Schema — Group Class: http://msdn.microsoft.com/library/en-us/adschema/adschema/c_group.asp?frame=true
24. Platform SDK: Active Directory Schema — Computer Class: http://msdn.microsoft.com/library/en-us/adschema/adschema/c_computer.asp?frame=true
25. Microsoft Knowledge Base — PSS ID Number: 238793: Enhanced Security Joining or Resetting Machine Account in Windows 2000 Domain: http://support.microsoft.com/default.aspx?scid=kb;en-us;238793
26. Microsoft Knowledge Base — PSS ID Number: 154501: How to Disable Automatic Machine Account Password Changes: http://support.microsoft.com/default.aspx?scid=kb;en-us;154501
27. Microsoft Knowledge Base — PSS ID Number: 299656: How to prevent Windows from storing a LAN manager hash of your password in Active Directory and local SAM databases: http://support.microsoft.com/default.aspx?scid=KB;EN-US;q299656
28. CacheDump homepage: http://www.off-by-one.net/misc/cachedump.html
29. Microsoft MSDN: Platform SDK: Active Directory Schema: DS-Heuristics: http://msdn.microsoft.com/library/en-us/adschema/adschema/a_dsheuristics.asp?frame=true
30. Kerberos Protocol Transition and Constrained Delegation: http://www.microsoft.com/technet/prodtechnol/windowsserver2003/technologies/security/constdel.mspx
31. Microsoft Knowledge Base — PSS ID Number: 184017: Administrators can display contents of service account passwords in Windows NT: http://support.microsoft.com/default.aspx?scid=KB;en-us;q184017

32. MSDN Library > Win32 and COM Development > Security > Authentication > Authentication Reference > Authentication Structures > CREDENTIAL: http://msdn.microsoft.com/library/en-us/secauthn/security/credential.asp?frame=true
33. Windows Server 2003 Technical Reference > How Service Publication and Service Principal Names Work: http://www.microsoft.com/technet/prodtechnol/windowsserver2003/library/TechRef/96725ab2-02a8-4c7e-8e0e-d298ec304e3b.mspx
34. Platform SDK: Active Directory Schema — trustedDomain Class: http://msdn.microsoft.com/library/en-us/adschema/adschema/c_trusteddomain.asp?frame=true
35. MSDN Home > MSDN Magazine > August 2000 > Explore the Security Support Provider Interface Using the SSPI Workbench Utility: http://msdn.microsoft.com/msdnmag/issues/0800/security/
36. Kerberos working group — Internet Draft: The Microsoft Windows 2000 RC4-HMAC Kerberos encryption type, M. Swift, J. Brezak: http://ietfreport.isoc.org/idref/draft-brezak-win2k-krb-rc4-hmac/
37. "Read First" Release Notes, Microsoft Windows 2000: High Encryption Pack: http://www.microsoft.com/windows2000/docs/encread-RTM.txt
38. Microsoft Knowledge Base — PSS ID Number: 823659: Client, service, and program incompatibilities that may occur when you modify security settings and user rights assignments: http://support.microsoft.com/kb/823659
39. Request for Comments 2831: Using Digest Authentication as a SASL Mechanism: http://www.ietf.org/rfc/rfc2831.txt
40. The ActiveX Core Technology Reference — Chapter 11: NTLM: http://www.opengroup.org/onlinepubs/009899899/NCH1222X.HTM#ntlm.2.8
41. Microsoft Knowledge Base — PSS ID Number: 828861: Cluster service account password must be set to 15 or more characters if the NoLMHash policy is enabled: http://support.microsoft.com/default.aspx?scid=kb;en-us;828861
42. Microsoft Windows NT Security Support Provider Interface (Downloadable Document): http://www.microsoft.com/ntserver/techresources/security/SecSuppInterface.asp
43. Request for Comments 2478: The Simple and Protected GSS-API Negotiation Mechanism: http://www.ietf.org/rfc/rfc2478.txt?number=2478
44. MSDN Home > MSDN Library > Win32 and COM Development > Security > Authentication > About Authentication > SSPI: http://msdn.microsoft.com/library/en-us/secauthn/security/sspi.asp?frame=true
45. MSDN Home > MSDN Library > Win32 and COM Development > Security > Exploring S4U Kerberos Extensions in Windows Server 2003: http://msdn.microsoft.com/library/default.asp?url=/library/en-us/dnkerb/html/MSDN_PAC.asp

46. Microsoft Windows SDK > Authentication > Authentication Reference > Authentication Functions > LsaLogonUser: http://windowssdk.msdn.microsoft.com/library/en-us/secauthn/security/lsalogonuser.asp?frame=true
47. Microsoft Knowledge Base — PSS ID Number 102716: User Authentication with Windows NT: http://support.microsoft.com/kb/102716/en-us
48. Eric Glass, The NTLM Authentication Protocol: http://davenport.sourceforge.net/ntlm.html
49. Microsoft Knowledge Base — PSS ID Number: 239869: How to enable NTLM 2 authentication: http://support.microsoft.com/default.aspx?scid=KB;en-us;239869
50. Request for Comments: 2743: Generic Security Service Application Program Interface, Version 2, Update 1: http://www.ietf.org/rfc/rfc2743.txt?number=2743
51. Request for Comments: 1964: The Kerberos Version 5 GSS-API Mechanism: http://www.ietf.org/rfc/rfc1964.txt?number=1964
52. Request for Comments: 1998: The Simple and Protected GSS-API Negotiation Mechanism: http://www.ietf.org/rfc/rfc1998.txt?number=1998
53. Microsoft MSDN: Platform SDK: Authentication: SSPI/Kerberos Interoperability with GSSAPI: http://msdn.microsoft.com/library/default.asp?url=/library/en-us/secauthn/security/sspi_kerberos_interoperability_with_gssapi.asp
54. RFC 2554: SMTP Service Extension for Authentication: http://www.ietf.org/rfc/rfc2554.txt?number=2554
55. RFC 2222: Simple Authentication and Security Layer (SASL): http://www.ietf.org/rfc/rfc2222.txt?number=2222
56. RFC 1731: IMAP4 Authentication Mechanisms: http://www.ietf.org/rfc/rfc1731.txt?number=1731
57. RFC 1734: POP3 AUTHentication command: http://www.ietf.org/rfc/rfc1734.txt?number=1734
58. RFC 2195: IMAP/POP AUTHorize Extension for Simple Challenge/Response: http://www.ietf.org/rfc/rfc2195.txt?number=2195
59. RFC 2829: Authentication Methods for LDAP: http://www.ietf.org/rfc/rfc2829.txt
60. RFC 2831: Using Digest Authentication as a SASL Mechanism: http://www.ietf.org/rfc/rfc2831.txt
61. INTERNET-DRAFT: Anonymous SASL Mechanism: http://www.ietf.org/internet-drafts/draft-ietf-sasl-anon-05.txt
62. RFC 1460: Post Office Protocol — Version 3: http://www.ietf.org/rfc/rfc1460.txt?number=1460
63. RFC 2617: HTTP Authentication: Basic and Digest Access Authentication: http://www.ietf.org/rfc/rfc2617.txt
64. RFC 2595: Using TLS with IMAP, POP3 and ACAP: http://www.ietf.org/rfc/rfc2595.txt?number=2595

65. RFC 2060: INTERNET MESSAGE ACCESS PROTOCOL - VERSION 4rev1: http://www.ietf.org/rfc/rfc2060.txt?number=2060
66. INTERNET-DRAFT: The LOGIN SASL Mechanism: http://ietfreport.isoc.org/idref/draft-murchison-sasl-login/
67. Carnegie Mellon University — Computing Services: Cyrus SASL: http://asg.web.cmu.edu/sasl/
68. RFC 1945: Hypertext Transfer Protocol — HTTP/1.0: http://www.ietf.org/rfc/rfc1945.txt?number=1945
69. RFC 2616: Hypertext Transfer Protocol — HTTP/1.1: http://www.ietf.org/rfc/rfc2616.txt?number=2616
70. MSDN Library: NET Framework Developer's Guide: Passport Authentication Provider: http://msdn.microsoft.com/library/default.asp?url=/library/en-us/cpguide/html/cpconThePassportAuthenticationProvider.asp
71. RFC 2228: FTP Security Extensions: http://www.ietf.org/rfc/rfc2228.txt?number=2228
72. RFC 2941: Telnet Authentication Option: http://www.ietf.org/rfc/rfc2941.txt?number=2941
73. RFC 2942: Telnet Authentication: Kerberos Version 5: http://www.ietf.org/rfc/rfc2942.txt?number=2942
74. RFC 959: File Transfer Protocol (FTP): http://www.ietf.org/rfc/rfc959.txt?number=959
75. RFC 4217: Securing FTP with TLS: http://www.ietf.org/rfc/rfc4217.txt?number=4217
76. RFC 4251: The Secure Shell (SSH) Protocol Architecture: http://www.ietf.org/rfc/rfc4251.txt
77. RFC 4252: The Secure Shell (SSH) Authentication Protocol: http://www.ietf.org/rfc/rfc4252.txt
78. RFC 4256: Generic Message Exchange Authentication for the Secure Shell Protocol (SSH): http://www.ietf.org/rfc/rfc4256.txt
79. RFC 3447: Public-Key Cryptography Standards (PKCS) #1: RSA Cryptography Specifications Version 2.1: http://www.ietf.org/rfc/rfc3447.txt
80. U.S. DEPARTMENT OF COMMERCE/National Institute of Standards and Technology: DIGITAL SIGNATURE STANDARD (DSS): http://csrc.nist.gov/publications/fips/fips186-2/fips186-2-change1.pdf
81. Internet-DRAFT: GSSAPI Authentication and Key Exchange for the Secure Shell Protocol draft-ietf-secsh-gsskeyex-10: http://www.ietf.org/internet-drafts/draft-ietf-secsh-gsskeyex-10.txt
82. RFC 1790: An Agreement between the Internet Society and Sun Microsystems, Inc. in the Matter of ONC RPC and XDR Protocols: http://www.ietf.org/rfc/rfc1790.txt?number=1790
83. RFC 1831: RPC: Remote Procedure Call Protocol Specification Version 2: http://www.ietf.org/rfc/rfc1831.txt
84. RFC 2695: Authentication Mechanisms for ONC RPC: http://www.ietf.org/rfc/rfc2695.txt

85. RFC 2203: RPCSEC_GSS Protocol Specification:
http://www.ietf.org/rfc/rfc2203.txt
86. RFC 2246: The TLS Protocol Version 1.0:
http://www.ietf.org/rfc/rfc2246.txt
87. RFC 1510: The Kerberos Network Authentication Service (V5):
http://www.ietf.org/rfc/rfc1510.txt
88. RFC 4120: The Kerberos Network Authentication Service (V5):
http://www.ietf.org/rfc/rfc4120.txt
89. Encryption and Checksum Specifications for Kerberos 5:
http://www.ietf.org/rfc/rfc3961.txt
90. Advanced Encryption Standard (AES) Encryption for Kerberos 5:
http://www.ietf.org/rfc/rfc3962.txt
91. Windows 2000: Kerberos PAC Specification 1.0:
http://www.microsoft.com/Downloads/details.aspx?displaylang=en&FamilyID=BF61D972-5086-49FB-A79C-53A5FD27A092
92. Public Key Cryptography for Initial Authentication in Kerberos draft-ietf-cat-kerberos-pk-init-34:
http://www.ietf.org/internet-drafts/draft-ietf-cat-kerberos-pk-init-34.txt
93. Microsoft SQL Server Passwords, David Litchfield, NGSSoftware Insight Security Research:
http://www.ngssoftware.com/papers/cracking-sql-passwords.pdf
94. Weak Password Encryption Scheme (Modified) in MS SQL Server, K.K. Mookhey, Network Intelligence India Pvt. Ltd.:
http://archives.neohapsis.com/archives/vulnwatch/2002-q4/0056.html
95. An Assessment of the Oracle Password Hashing Algorithm, Joshua Wright, Carlos Cid:
http://www.sans.org/rr/special/index.php?id=oracle_pass
96. Oracle Password Encryption Algorithm?, Newsgroup comp.databases.oracle, Bob Baldwin:
http://groups-beta.google.com/group/comp.databases.oracle/msg/83ae557a977fb6ed?hl=en
97. Cisco IOS Password Encryption Facts:
http://www.cisco.com/warp/public/701/64.html
98. Enhanced Password Security:
http://www.cisco.com/univercd/cc/td/doc/product/software/ios122/122newft/122t/122t8/ft_md5.htm
99. Cisco password decryption:
http://www.insecure.org/sploits/cisco.passwords.html
100. PPP Authentication Protocols:
http://www.ietf.org/rfc/rfc1334.txt
101. PPP Challenge Handshake Authentication Protocol (CHAP):
http://www.ietf.org/rfc/rfc1994.txt
102. RFC 2433: Microsoft PPP CHAP Extensions:
http://www.ietf.org/rfc/rfc2433.txt
103. RFC 2759: Microsoft PPP CHAP Extensions, Version 2:
http://www.ietf.org/rfc/rfc2759.txt
104. RFC 2284: PPP Extensible Authentication Protocol (EAP):
http://www.ietf.org/rfc/rfc2284.txt

105. RFC 3748: Extensible Authentication Protocol (EAP): http://www.ietf.org/rfc/rfc3748.txt
106. RFC 2716: PPP EAP TLS Authentication Protocol: http://www.ietf.org/rfc/rfc2716.txt
107. Internet Draft: Protected EAP Protocol (PEAP) Version 2: http://ietfreport.isoc.org/all-ids/draft-josefsson-pppext-eap-tls-eap-07.txt
108. Cisco Response to Dictionary Attacks on Cisco LEAP: http://www.cisco.com/en/US/products/hw/wireless/ps430/prod_bulletin09186a00801cc901.html
109. Internet Draft: EAP Flexible Authentication via Secure Tunnelling (EAP-FAST): ftp://ftp.isi.edu/internet-drafts/draft-cam-winget-eap-fast-03.txt
110. Internet Draft: Dynamic Provisioning using EAP-FAST draft-cam-winget-eap-fast-provisioning-02.txt: ftp://ftp.isi.edu/internet-drafts/draft-cam-winget-eap-fast-provisioning-02.txt
111. Overview of 802.11 Security: http://grouper.ieee.org/groups/802/15/pub/2001/Mar01/01154r0P802-15_TG3-Overview-of-802-11-Security.ppt
112. RFC 3610: Counter with CBC-MAC (CCM): http://www.ietf.org/rfc/rfc3610.txt
113. IEEE Std. 802.1x-2004 (Revision of IEEE Std. 802.1x-2001): Port Based Network Access Control: http://standards.ieee.org/getieee802/download/802.1X-2004.pdf
114. RFC 2409: The Internet Key Exchange (IKE): http://www.ietf.org/rfc/rfc2409.txt
115. RFC 4306: Internet Key Exchange (IKEv2) Protocol: http://www.ietf.org/rfc/rfc4306.txt
116. Multiple vulnerabilites in vendor IKE implementations, including Cisco, Dec 12 2003: http://www.securityfocus.com/archive/1/347351
117. DRAFT: The ISAKMP Configuration Method: http://www.vpnc.org/ietf-mode-cfg/draft-dukes-ike-mode-cfg-02.txt
118. DRAFT: Extended Authentication within IKE (XAUTH): http://www.vpnc.org/ietf-xauth/draft-beaulieu-ike-xauth-02.txt
119. RFC 2865: Remote Authentication Dial In User Service (RADIUS): http://www.ietf.org/rfc/rfc2865.txt
120. RFC 2866: RADIUS Accounting: http://www.ietf.org/rfc/rfc2866.txt
121. RFC 1492: An Access Control Protocol, Sometimes Called TACACS: http://www.ietf.org/rfc/rfc1492.txt
122. DRAFT: The TACACS+ Protocol, Version 1.78: ftp://ftp-eng.cisco.com/ftp/pub/tacacs/tac-rfc.1.78.txt
123. RSA Laboratories' Frequently Asked Questions about Today's Cryptography, Version 4.1: http://www.rsasecurity.com/rsalabs/node.asp?id=2152

124. Data Encryption Standard (DES) — U.S. Department of Commerce/National Institute of Standards and Technology: http://csrc.nist.gov/publications/fips/fips46-3/fips46-3.pdf
125. Advanced Encryption Standard (AES) — Questions and Answers: http://csrc.nist.gov/CryptoToolkit/aes/aesfact.html
126. RFC 1319: The MD2 Message-Digest Algorithm: http://www.ietf.org/rfc/rfc1319.txt
127. RFC 1320: The MD4 Message-Digest Algorithm: http://www.ietf.org/rfc/rfc1320.txt
128. US Secure Hash Algorithm 1 (SHA1): http://www.ietf.org/rfc/rfc3174.txt
129. SHA1 Collisions can be Found in 2^63 Operations, Michael Szydlo: http://www.rsasecurity.com/rsalabs/node.asp?id=2927
130. The Keyed-Hash Message Authentication Code (HMAC): http://csrc.nist.gov/publications/fips/fips198/fips-198a.pdf
131. Federal Information Processing Standards Publication 186: Digital Signature Standard (DSS): http://www.itl.nist.gov/fipspubs/fip186.htm
132. A public key cryptosystem and a signature scheme based on discrete logarithms, Elgamal, T.: http://ieeexplore.ieee.org/xpl/freeabs_all.jsp?tp=&arnumber=1057074&isnumber=22749
133. The S/KEY One-Time Password System, Neil M. Haller: http://citeseer.ist.psu.edu/cache/papers/cs/5967/ftp:zSzzSzftp.mcc.ac.ukzSzpubzSzsecurityzSzPAPERSzSzPASSWORDzSzSKEY.pdf/haller94skey.pdf
134. RFC 3280: Internet X.509 Public Key Infrastructure Certificate and Certificate Revocation List (CRL) Profile: http://www.ietf.org/rfc/rfc3280.txt
135. RFC 3279: Algorithms and Identifiers for the Internet X.509 Public Key Infrastructure Certificate and Certificate Revocation List (CRL) Profile: http://www.ietf.org/rfc/rfc3279.txt?number=3279
136. Setuid Demystified, Hao Chen, David Wagner, Drew Dean: http://www.csl.sri.com/users/ddean/papers/usenix02.pdf
137. Microsoft TechnNet: How Digest Authentication Works: http://technet2.microsoft.com/WindowsServer/en/Library/717b450c-f4a0-4cc9-86f4-cc0633aae5f91033.mspx
138. Security Assertion Markup Language (SAML) V2.0 Technical Overview, Working Draft 09, 20 July 2006: http://www.oasis-open.org/committees/download.php/19258/sstc-saml-tech-overview-2%200-draft-09.pdf
139. W3C Architecture Domain: Extensible Markup Language (XML): http://www.w3.org/XML/
140. W3C Architecture Domain: XML Signature: http://www.w3.org/Signature/
141. W3C Architecture Domain: SOAP Version 1.2 Part 0: Primer: http://www.w3.org/TR/2003/REC-soap12-part0-20030624/

142. Web Services Security: SOAP Message Security 1.1(WS-Security 2004): http://www.oasis-open.org/committees/download.php/16790/wss-v1.1-spec-os-SOAPMessageSecurity.pdf

Appendix B

Lab Configuration

This appendix provides an overview of the lab setup used in this book to explore authentication technologies and capture traffic.

Table B.1 List of Computers and Devices

Computer/Device	*IP Address*	*Software/Hardware/Firmware*	*Description*
BILL	10.0.1.101	Windows 2003 SP1	Domain Controller, **ins.com** domain Primary DNS server LDAP Server (Active Directory)
STEVE	10.0.2.102	Windows 2003 SP1 Cisco SecureACS Server, 3.0(2) Build 5 MS SQL Server 2000	Member Server, **ins.com** domain
DENNIS	10.0.2.101	Linux/Fedora Core 4	**ins.com** domain member
LINUS	10.0.1.102	Linux/Fedora Core 4	**ins.com** domain member
PAUL	10.0.2.103	Windows 2003 SP1	Domain Controller, **immedient.com** domain
DAVID	192.168.1.101	Windows 2003 SP1	Domain Controller, **externalorg.com** domain
EXCHDC1	192.168.26. 130	Windows NT4 SP6 Exchange Server 5.5 SP4	Domain Controller — Windows NT 4.0 domain, Mail Server

W2K3DC	192.168.26.10	Windows 2003 SP1	External domain controller
XP-CLIENT	10.0.1.1 10.0.2.1 192.168.26.1	Windows XP SP1	Client computer used to attach to different segments, emulate access to services, and capture traffic
MOBILE-CLIENT	192.168.1.65 192.168.2.65	Windows XP SP1	Client computer used to attach to different segments, emulate access to services, and capture traffic
VPN-SERVER	192.168.2.254 192.168.1.254	Cisco 1720 router IOS C1700-ADVSECURITYK9-M (c1700-advsecurityk9-mz.123-14.T7.bin)	VPN server
ACCESS-POINT	192.168.1.1	Linksys WAG354G firmware version: 1.01.03	Wireless Access Point for the CorporateWF zone

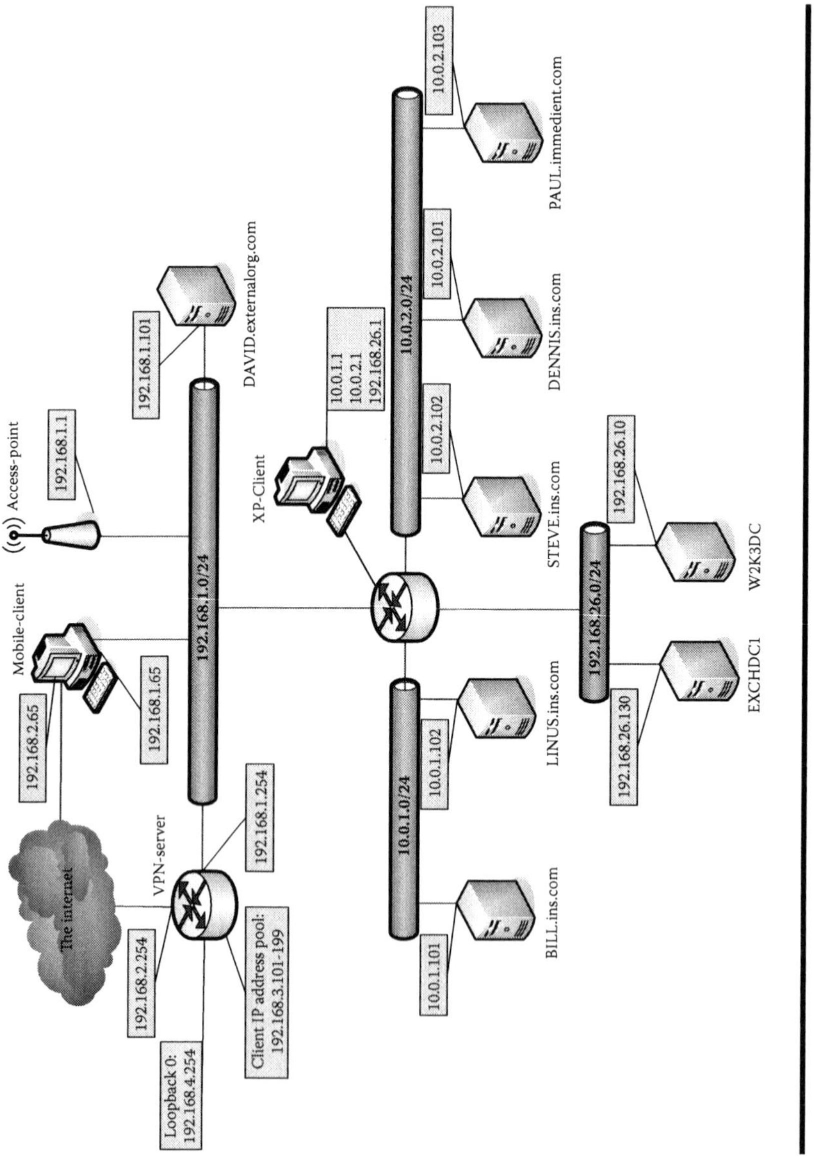

Figure B.1 Lab topology.

Appendix C

Indices of Tables and Figures

Index of Tables

Index of Figures

Index

A

B

C

S

T

V

W

X